THE ROUTLEDGE COMPANION TO CRITICAL ACCOUNTING

The field of critical accounting has expanded rapidly since its inception and has become recognised as offering a wealth of provocative insights in the wake of the global financial crisis. It is now firmly embedded within accounting literature and in how accounting is taught.

Surveying the evolving field of critical accounting, including theory, ethics, history, development and sustainability, this Companion presents key debates in the field, providing a comprehensive overview. Incorporating interdisciplinary perspectives on accounting, the volume concludes by considering new directions in which critical accounting research may travel.

With an international array of established and respected contributors, this Routledge Companion is a vital resource for students and researchers across the world.

Robin Roslender is Professor of Accounting and Finance at the University of Dundee, UK.

ROUTLEDGE COMPANIONS IN BUSINESS, MANAGEMENT AND ACCOUNTING

Routledge Companions in Business, Management and Accounting are prestige reference works providing an overview of a whole subject area or sub-discipline. These books survey the state of the discipline including emerging and cutting-edge areas. Providing a comprehensive, up-to-date, definitive work of reference, Routledge Companions can be cited as an authoritative source on the subject.

A key aspect of these Routledge Companions is their international scope and relevance. Edited by an array of highly regarded scholars, these volumes also benefit from teams of contributors which reflect an international range of perspectives.

Individually, Routledge Companions in Business, Management and Accounting provide an impactful one-stop-shop resource for each theme covered. Collectively, they represent a comprehensive learning and research resource for researchers, postgraduate students and practitioners.

Titles in this series include:

The Routledge Companion to Qualitative Accounting Research
Edited by Zahirul Hoque, Lee D. Parker, Mark A. Covaleski and Kathryn Haynes

The Routledge Companion to Accounting and Risk
Edited by Margaret Woods and Philip Linsley

The Routledge Companion to Wellbeing at Work
Edited by Sir Cary L. Cooper and Michael P. Leiter

The Routledge Companion to Performance Management and Control
Edited by Elaine Harris

The Routledge Companion to Management Information Systems
Edited by Robert D. Galliers and Mari-Klara Stein

The Routledge Companion to Critical Accounting
Edited by Robin Roslender

The Routledge Companion to Trust
Edited by Rosalind Searle, Ann-Marie Nienaber and Sim Sitkin

The Routledge Companion to Tax Avoidance Research
Edited by Nigar Hashimzade and Yuliya Epifantseva

THE ROUTLEDGE
COMPANION TO
CRITICAL ACCOUNTING

Edited by Robin Roslender

Routledge
Taylor & Francis Group

LONDON AND NEW YORK

First published 2018
by Routledge
2 Park Square, Milton Park, Abingdon, Oxon OX14 4RN

and by Routledge
52 Vanderbilt Avenue, New York, NY 10017

First issued in paperback 2020

Routledge is an imprint of the Taylor & Francis Group, an informa business

British Library Cataloguing in Publication Data
A catalogue record for this book is available from the British Library

Library of Congress Cataloging in Publication Data
Names: Roslender, Robin, 1984- editor.
Title: The Routledge companion to critical accounting / [edited by] Robin Roslender.
Other titles: Companion to critical accounting
Description: 1 Edition. | New York : Routledge, 2017. | Includes bibliographical references and index.
Identifiers: LCCN 2017008934 (print) | LCCN 2017014274 (ebook) | ISBN 9781315775203 (eBook) | ISBN 9781138025257 (hardback: alk. paper)
Subjects: LCSH: Accounting.
Classification: LCC HF5636 (ebook) | LCC HF5636 .R68 2017 (print) | DDC 657–dc23
LC record available at https://lccn.loc.gov/2017008934

ISBN 13: 978–0–367–65618–8 (pbk)
ISBN 13: 978–1–138–02525–7 (hbk)

Typeset in Bembo
by Deanta Global Publishing Services, Chennai, India

CONTENTS

Contents

Contents

FIGURES

TABLES

CONTRIBUTORS

Carol Adams is a Professor of Accounting at the University of Durham, UK.

Chandana Alawattage is a Senior Lecturer in Accountancy at the University of Aberdeen, Scotland.

Richard Baker is a Professor of Accounting and Law at Adelphi University, US.

Lisa Baudot is an Assistant Professor in Accounting at the University of Central Florida, US.

Jane Baxter is an Associate Professor of Accounting at the University of New South Wales, Australia.

Peter Bloom is a Senior Lecturer in People and Organisations at the Open University, UK.

Gordon Boyce is an Associate Professor in Social and Environmental Accounting at LaTrobe University, Australia.

Jane Broadbent is an Emeritus Professor of Management at Royal Holloway, University of London, UK.

Judy Brown is a Professor of Accounting at the Victoria University of Wellington, New Zealand.

Chris Carter is a Professor of Strategy and Organisation at the University of Edinburgh, Scotland.

Wai Fong Chua is a Professor of Accounting at the University of Sydney, Australia.

David J. Cooper is a Professor of Accounting at the University of Alberta, Canada.

Jesse Dillard is a Professor of Accounting at Portland State University, US.

Jeff Everett is a Professor of Accounting at York University, Canada.

Richard Fleischman is a Professor of Accounting at the University of South Florida, US.

Sonja Gallhofer is an Emeritus Professor of Accounting, Governance and Accountability at the University of Glasgow, Scotland.

Contributors

Cameron Graham is a Professor of Accounting at York University, Canada.

Rob Gray is an Emeritus Professor of Social and Environmental Accounting at the University of St Andrews, Scotland.

Colin Haslam is a Professor of Accounting and Finance at Queen Mary, University of London, UK.

Jim Haslam is a Professor of Accounting, Governance and Society at the University of Sheffield, UK.

Trevor Hopper is an Emeritus Professor of Business and Management at the University of Sussex, UK.

Ingrid Jeacle is a Professor of Accounting and Popular Culture at the University of Edinburgh, Scotland.

George Katechos is a Lecturer in Finance at the University of Hertfordshire, UK.

David Knights is a Distinguished Scholar in Organisation, Work and Technology at Lancaster University, UK.

Richard Laughlin is an Emeritus Professor of Accounting at Kings College, University of London, UK.

Glen Lehman is a Senior Research Fellow in Accounting at the University of South Australia, Australia.

Skip McGoun is Professor of Finance at Bucknell University, US.

Alan McKinlay is a Professor of Human Resource Management at the University of Newcastle, UK.

Sven Modell is a Professor of Accounting at the University of Manchester, UK.

David Oldroyd is a Professor of Accounting at the University of Newcastle, UK.

David Owen is an Emeritus Professor of Social and Environmental Accounting at the University of Nottingham, UK.

Lee Parker is a Professor of Accounting at RMIT University, Australia.

Alan Richardson is a Professor of Accounting at the University of Windsor, Canada.

John Roberts is a Professor of Accounting at the University of Sydney, Australia.

Keith Robson is a Professor of Accounting and Management Control at HEC Paris, France.

Farzana Tanima is a Lecturer in Accounting at the Victoria University of Wellington, New Zealand.

Nick Tsitsianis is a Senior Lecturer in Accounting at Queen Mary, University of London, UK.

Thomas Tyson is a Professor of Accounting at St John Fisher College, Rochester, US.

Danture Wickramasinghe is a Professor of Management Accounting at the University of Glasgow, Scotland.

Paul Williams is a Professor of Accounting at North Carolina State University, US.

FOREWORD

Onwards: the past and future
of critical accounting

David J. Cooper

A collection of articles outlining developments in a field offers an opportunity to reflect on what we have learned and to consider where critical accounting might go. While there is no doubt that *Accounting, Organizations and Society* was the first accounting journal supportive of critical accounting and published some of the seminal contributions in the field, for example Medawar (1976), Armstrong (1987), Tinker (1980), Tinker, Merino and Neimark (1982) and Cooper and Sherer (1984), it is worth reflecting on how things have changed (or not) since Tony Tinker and I started a journal dedicated to critical accounting in 1990.

Note that the opening to the first editorial of *Critical Perspectives on Accounting* embedded critical accounting in its social, political, cultural and economic context. I believe that, other than the reference to Eastern Europe, our analysis is still highly relevant today, and speaks to the continuing importance of the contributions to the current collection:

> We are launching *Critical Perspectives on Accounting* at a time of massive social changes, changes that focus attention on how we administer - and account for - large societal institutions. While the West reels from environmental calamities, ethical lapses in government and business, and failing financial institutions, Eastern Europe is confronted with replacing undemocratic and repressive bureaucracies with new institutional forms. These changes prompt the same questions: How should we manage large institutions? How should we assess their social productivity and worth? How are they to be made accountable and to whom?
>
> *(Cooper and Tinker, 1990: 1)*

The editorial later argues that

> [A]ccounting inevitably intervenes in human and social conduct, and that the primary choice, therefore, is how to make that intervention progressive and enhancing.
>
> *(1990: 2)*

Robin Roslender, the editor of the current collection, has managed to obtain some excellent reviews of the current state of critical accounting, written by some of the leading researchers in the field. The importance of theorising, not so much for its own sake but for analysing specific empirical situations, is highlighted in the second section of this collection. It is pleasing to see not just a re-reading of some of the main theoretical inspirations, particularly Marx and Foucault, but also thoughtful reviews of some critical theorists that have become more prominent in recent years, notably the critical practice theory of Bourdieu. Section 6 of this collection, further highlights the potential for critical accounting of theories as diverse as actor–network theory, critical realism and agonistic theorising.

It is not surprising that the authors in this collection survey many of the issues that were highlighted in that first editorial in *Critical Perspectives on Accounting*, such as environmental calamities, ethical lapses, failing financial institutions and more democratic, inclusive and accountable institutions (including professional and regulatory organisations). Some of these issues have taken on even more urgency, as the contributions in the third section of this collection attest.

The present collection, particularly in Section 4, also highlights issues that have become more prominent in the last 25 years, such as the increasing financialization of the economy, the increasing globalization of capitalism, the recognition of how accounting connects to popular culture, the effects of colonisation and imperialist exploitation, and the involvement of accounting thought and institutions in enabling particular, capitalist, versions of social and economic development.

In reflecting on the contents of the collection, I am also prompted to think of omissions and neglected themes. No collection can cover the whole field of critical accounting, and I know that not all chapters that were promised for this collection were delivered. So, while critical reflexivity is called for, my observations are not a criticism of the editor nor the design of the collection. That being said, one area that might reasonably have been expected in this collection is the role of critical accounting researchers, for example Sikka and Willmott (1997) or Neu, Everett and Cooper (2001). Shaoul's exemplary work in critical financial analysis, for example Shaoul (1997), deserves to be more widely practised, whether it concerns corporate practices, state privatisations or alternative forms of financing in social and economic development. Our role in informing public policy and influencing the world is essential, lest we are truly "public ineffectuals," as Christine Cooper (2005) complained. Influencing the world includes impacting students through our teaching and here it would be helpful to further consider the increasing commercialisation of universities and the commodification of education, for example Dillard and Tinker (1996). Moreover, it saddens me to note the narrow geographical spread of the authors of this collection; I am sure that colleagues in Continental Europe, Africa, Asia and South America have important challenges and have much to contribute to the critical accounting community. I am also saddened and frustrated that financial economists and dominant academic accounting communities ignore the challenges of critical accounting. The critical accounting community needs to consider ways to be more impactful and inclusive.

Thus, while I heartedly applaud this collection and commend the efforts of the editor and all the contributors, there is much still to be done. A progressive world needs critical accounting more than ever!

References

Armstrong, P. (1987). "The rise of accounting controls in British capitalist enterprises," *Accounting, Organizations and Society*, 12(5): 415–36.

Cooper, C. (2005). "Accounting for the public interest: public ineffectuals or public intellectuals?" *Accounting, Auditing and Accountability Journal*, 18(5): 592–607.

Cooper, D. J. and M. J. Sherer (1984). "The value of corporate accounting reports: arguments for a political economy of accounting", *Accounting, Organizations and Society*, 9(3–4): 207–32.

Cooper, D. J. and T. Tinker (1990). " Editorial," *Critical Perspectives on Accounting*, 1(1): 1–3.

Dillard, J. F. and T. Tinker (1996). "Commodifying business and accounting education: the implications of accreditation," *Critical Perspectives on Accounting*, 7(1): 215–25

Medawar, C. (1976). "The social audit: a political view," *Accounting, Organizations and Society*, 1(4): 389–94.

Neu, D., D. J. Cooper and J. Everett (2001). "Critical accounting intervention," *Critical Perspectives on Accounting*, 12(6): 735–62.

Shaoul, J. (1997). "A critical financial analysis of the performance of privatised industries: The case of the water industry in England and Wales," *Critical Perspectives on Accounting*, 8(5): 479–505.

Sikka, P. and H. Willmott. (1997). "Practising critical accounting", *Critical Perspectives on Accounting*, 8(1–2): 149–65.

Tinker, A. M. (1980). "Towards a political economy of accounting: an empirical illustration of the Cambridge controversies," *Accounting, Organizations and Society*, 5(1): 147–60.

Tinker, A. M., B. D. Merino and M. D. Neimark (1982). "The normative origins of positive theories: ideology and accounting thought," *Accounting, Organizations and Society*, 7(2): 167–200.

SECTION I

1

INTRODUCTION

Robin Roslender

The field designated as critical accounting was virtually unknown as recently as 40 years ago. Since that time it has grown at an exponential rate, resulting in a rich and varied body of insights that have contributed much to the contemporary understanding of the role that accounting, understood as a set of technical practices, and accountancy, understood as a major institution, play within society. As a consequence, critical accounting has powerfully demonstrated the academic discipline of accounting's credentials as a social science, whose myriad intricacies it readily evidences. For a growing number of those who teach accounting in an academic milieu, it is now almost inconceivable that they will not introduce their students to critical accounting in some degree. The collection of contributions included in this volume has been commissioned to further enable this process.

Critical accounting might most easily be identified as being one dimension of accounting studies, understood as the pursuit of non-technical insights about accounting, viewed as a set of technical practices, and about the social institution of accountancy. Accounting studies follows in an established academic tradition that has seen researchers and scholars explore the broader topography of science, technology, law, literature, music, etc., looking beyond their immediate manifestations in order to appreciate how they are impacted by the broader society in which they are embedded and in turn to impact that society. For many years I have felt comfortable to describe this exercise as exploring the conditions and consequences of accounting practices together with the broader social institution of accountancy, being concerned about where these 'come from' and where they are 'going to' or lead. From the outset it is obvious that accounting studies is likely to be strongly informed by sociology, something it shares with many other disciplines. This said, however, it would be misleading to equate accounting studies with a sociology of accounting or accountancy, something that is well demonstrated in the contributions to this collection.

Throughout its evolution to date, the term 'critical accounting' has been hotly contested. The ongoing debate is clearly evident throughout the chapters collected in this book, much as it is in the broader literature of critical accounting research. The crux of the debate is about the meaning of the term 'critical'. For many critical accounting researchers it continues to remain desirable to privilege the radical political connotations of the critical designation, an attribute that strongly characterised the discipline of sociology at the inception of critical accounting. Viewed from this standpoint, critical accounting studies are pursued as part of a broader project to build a better society, through interventions underpinned by rigorous empirical and theoretical enquiries premised on fundamental concerns about the iniquities of the prevailing social arrangements. Critical accounting has as its objective the creation of a better society in much the same way that technical accounting (research) seeks to facilitate better accounting (practice), as this is defined by those whose interests accounting was designed to promote.

Such a characterisation of critical accounting is readily acknowledged to be the accounting equivalent of a 'hard left' or Marxist political position, and thereby to some degree imprisoned in the antiquated thinking that characterised the United Kingdom during the 1970s. It is generally accepted that critical accounting emerged in the later 1970s in the United Kingdom, and most notably at the University of Sheffield, an institution located in one of its most politically radical regions, albeit somewhat ironically in a management school (see Laughlin 2016 for an account of the emergence of the 'Sheffield School'). While this might have been a beneficial point of departure, the world has moved on as a result of which such a stance, and its underlying philosophy of praxis, inevitably manifests some worrying limitations. There is considerable merit in the arguments of those who express such worries, which are of necessity extensively documented in many of the contributions. However, after considerable thought it still seems to me to make sense to identify the field of critical accounting in the 'original' way, thereby providing an intellectual benchmark that will facilitate a better understanding of the critical aspirations of alternative contributions to the broader field. I will return to this position towards the end of these introductory comments.

A very brief history

Although it is possible to identify influential earlier contributions to the accounting studies and critical accounting literatures, for example Scott's *The Cultural Significance of Accounts* or Briloff's *Unaccountable Accounting* respectively, there is a strong case for identifying Lowe and Tinker's 1977 *Journal of Business Finance and Accounting* paper as providing the founding contribution to the field. The paper conveyed a strong critical accounting emphasis, as identified in the preceding paragraphs, on which the authors and many of their associates, including a number with links to the University of Sheffield, quickly built. As a consequence, by the time the first Interdisciplinary Perspectives on Accounting (IPA) conference was held in July 1985, critical accounting's radical political emphases were predominant within the embryonic accounting studies community. Despite a relatively short time frame, an enthusiastic group of researchers had begun to engage with a wide range of insights from the critical sociology canon, including political economy, labour process theory and Critical Theory. This continued to be the case at the two succeeding IPA conferences as well as giving rise to the establishment in 1990 of *Critical Perspectives on Accounting* (CPA), jointly edited by Cooper and Tinker, and the publication in the same year of *Critical Accounts: Reorientating Accounting Research,* edited by Cooper and Hopper, themselves strong advocates of the political economy of accounting and the labour process theory respectively.

As the term 'interdisciplinary' suggests, contributions to the first three IPA conferences emanated from a range of disciplines, an attribute that continues to characterise interdisciplinary accounting research. Nevertheless, sociological contributions were relatively numerous and, more significantly, not confined to critical sociology. In the early 1980s there was a very strong interest in applying interpretive sociologies to the study of accounting, as researchers explored the alternatives to positivistic 'functionalist' sociology and the promise of a more social scientific approach to the study of 'accounting in action'. In 1985 there were also papers that drew upon Giddens' structuration theory perspective as well as elements of institutional theory. Several participants preferred to ground their interdisciplinary accounting studies in the work of Foucault, a French social theorist whose influence had increased within sociology (and beyond) during the previous decade, and had not gone unnoticed within the pages of *Accounting Organizations and Society* (*AOS*), which by the mid-1980s was *the* outlet for interdisciplinary accounting work of any sort.

Arguably more than any other intellectual inspiration in the progress of accounting studies, Foucault's work captures the contested nature of the critical accounting designation. During the 1970s Foucault was embraced by some Marxist writers as offering the basis for a major rejuvenation of the purchase of Marxist theory, offering an alternative to those working within what Burrell and Morgan characterised as the radical structuralist and radical humanist traditions of the sociology of radical change. Not everyone interpreted Foucault in this way, however. Some found his work attractive because it provided an alternative to both the sociology of radical change and the sociology of social systems, a third way so to speak. For others it was Foucault's focus on process, rather than on structure or on action, that was attractive, an attribute his work shared with the generality of postmodern sociology. Whichever formulation of Foucault might be being bought into, in combination with some other axioms of postmodern thinking, it is a short step to asserting that what Foucault has to offer is so different from modernist thinking that it is legitimate to designate his work a critical perspective, while at the same time decoupling it from an explicit commitment to the philosophy of praxis or the pursuit of social betterment that was previously identified as being the hallmark of an 'authentic' critical accounting.

The predominance of work within accounting studies informed by political economy, labour process theory or Critical Theory ended in the early 1990s. Thereafter it became a much more varied oeuvre as further interdisciplinary perspectives, with sociology again to the fore, had their impact. The Marx vs Foucault debate of that time rehearsed the virtues of engaged scholarship and the philosophy of praxis as opposed to equally insightful critical commentaries that undoubtedly enhance the former canon. By this time *CPA* was rapidly establishing itself as the foremost vehicle for those subscribing to a more politicised critique, while *AOS* reflected the broadening of horizons of critical accounting. At this juncture actor–network theory joined structuration theory, institutional theory and a number of Foucauldian sub-perspectives as providing alternative critical ways of seeing. In due course actor–network theory also became more varied in form and content, as did institutional theory, eventually to be complemented by practice theory, which in some formulations appeared to want to share an affinity with interpretivism, the early 'accounting in action' focus arguably resurfacing as 'accounting as practice'. Inevitably, a similar process was also evident within the pages of *CPA*, although such ways of seeing often remained the source of supplementary rather than complementary (or even conflicting) insights.

Critical work, however conceptualised, now appears in a widening variety of journals, although North America continues to lag behind despite the presence of a public interest accounting tradition that emerged in parallel to critical accounting in the UK. The *Accounting, Auditing and Accountability Journal* has published a body of critical contributions over the past two decades, although Marxist contributions remain comparatively less evident within its pages. The *Accounting Forum* has pursued a similar pathway in recent times, while the pages of *Management Accounting Research* contain many fine examples of qualitative case studies of management accounting practice that affirm the value of structuration theory–, institutional theory– and practice theory–informed critical work. Both the *British Accounting Review* and the *European Accounting Review* have also been receptive to submissions from critical accounting scholars, although to date the same cannot be said of the *Accounting Review*, with the notable exception of Chua's seminal 1986 paper that documented the alternatives to a functionalist paradigm for accounting research as these were understood at that time.

Contextualising the present collection

In contrast to the rapid growth of the critical accounting journal literature during the past four decades, the textbook literature has been very limited. This might be readily explained by the observation that, by just about any criterion, critical accounting is an advanced field that is of necessity more oriented towards research inputs and thus best served by the journal literature. A second explanation might be that regardless of critical accounting's status among sections of the accounting research community, as yet it is not an established elective module within degree programmes, even those at the postgraduate level, as a result of which there is unlikely to be much of a need for such textbooks. Conversely, it can be argued that the time has now come to facilitate the growth of critical accounting expertise through the inclusion of such modules within degree programmes, in which process the availability of suitable textbooks has a major role to play. Suitability in this context would seem to pose a pair of challenges to anyone who might be attracted to the idea of producing such a volume: accessibility for readers and reinforcing the research credentials of the field.

In the previous section Cooper and Hopper's 1990 collection of 'critical accounts' was identified as providing a seminal contribution to the establishment of critical accounting. The greatest part of its content was made up of papers that had been presented at the inaugural IPA conference five years previously. To some degree that collection's impact was diluted as a consequence of a number of papers from the conference being published in an issue of *AOS* in 1987, most of which have gone on to be key contributions to the field. Anyone interested in exploring the early promise of critical accounting research is encouraged to get hold of a second collection of papers edited by Chua, Lowe and Puxty, all of whom had strong associations with Sheffield, published in 1989 and entitled *Critical Perspectives on Management Control*. Several years later Puxty published a short introduction to the growing range of framing theories that critical and interdisciplinary researchers might employ in studying management accounting, by now recognised to be the proving ground for such enquiries (Puxty, 1993).

In 1992 Routledge published a volume that I can readily recognise to be a precursor to the present collection, entitled *Sociological Perspectives on Modern Accountancy* (Roslender, 1992). By that time I had become thoroughly immersed within accounting (and to some extent finance), having taken up a lectureship in accounting at the University of Stirling in 1989 and successfully completed the formal examination programme of the (then) Chartered Association of Certified Accountants. Perhaps more significantly, I had come to recognise that what I had learned as a sociology student during the 1970s was of interest to a small but fast-growing group of critical accounting researchers. My own doctoral thesis, on the growth of trade unionism among UK scientific workers between 1960–75, was soundly underpinned by structural Marxist thinking, which seemed particularly applicable within the managerial accounting sub-discipline that promised to be my new home for the foreseeable future. The 1992 text was rather more wide ranging, however, being divided into two parts. Elements of a sociology *of* accounting were sketched out in the first part, complemented by four chapters on sociology *for* accounting that sought to identify how sociological thinking might enhance the contribution that accounting could make to the promotion of a better society. Close to a quarter of a century later I am humbled by the observation that a number of accounting researchers continue to find the text useful.

In 1994 a powerful complement to Cooper and Hopper's 1990 collection was published: *Accounting as Social and Institutional Practice*, edited by Hopwood and Miller. Many of the chapters were further refined versions of papers previously published in *AOS*, the journal that had contributed so much to the progress of critical accounting research during the 1980s, edited by Hopwood since its establishment in 1976. As I have noted earlier, by 1994 the predominance of Marxist critical perspectives was now less assured, critical and interdisciplinary accounting research endeavours fast becoming a more varied whole. Foucault's influence is evident in the pages of Hopwood and Miller's collection, being the first French critical theorist (Laughlin, 1995) to challenge the primacy of the various Marxist perspectives, although other ways of seeing are also present. The only contribution that is explicitly of the Marxist lineage is Armstrong (1994). With the benefit of hindsight it is possible to see this collection as signifying that there is much to be had from the construction of a critical accounting research tradition that decouples insightful critique from an explicit commitment to the philosophy of praxis, a situation that continues to characterise critical accounting research to the present day.

It might be expected that Hopwood and Miller (1994) would have catalysed the publication of more critical accounting textbooks. Although it is possible to identify three that might be designated in this way around that time, by Perks (1993), Macintosh (1994) and Jones (1995), arguably the next landmark occurs a decade later in the form of another collection of papers edited by Macintosh and Hopper (2005). Although abridged versions of papers previously published in *AOS* provide the majority of the content, the genre of critical accounts that Hopper together with Cooper had assembled some 15 years previously were now more in evidence, including Macintosh's "Annual reports in an ideological role: a Critical Theory analysis". A volume of essays in honour of the contribution of Hopwood to the study of accounting, organisations and institutions was published in 2009 a year before Hopwood's untimely death (Chapman, Cooper and Miller, 2009). Many of the contributions come from within the critical accounting community but it would not be difficult to argue that the presence of a significant number of outlying chapters has the consequence of suggesting that this particular volume is more accurately identified as providing a sound introduction to the interdisciplinary perspectives on the accounting field rather than critical accounting.

It was in the autumn of 2010 that I initially received an invitation to submit a proposal for a *Routledge Companion to Critical Accounting*. Although immediately attractive, and without doubt a project that was worthwhile even in the age of the UK Research Excellence Framework, within days I was also invited to take up a new appointment as Chair of Accounting and Finance and Director of Research in the newly established School of Business at the University of Dundee. Like all of the contributors to this volume, I rapidly found myself massively overcommitted, so it was not until the autumn of 2013 that I was actually in a position to draft a proposal. During the intervening period I took every opportunity to sound out colleagues regarding the possibility of a contribution to the *Companion* should this ever become a reality. I am delighted to see that many of those tentative conversations have eventually translated into chapters within the collection.

From the outset I was persuaded that the *Companion* format perfectly suited what I believed was now highly desirable – an accessible introduction to the now mature field of critical accounting that would communicate the richness of its research accomplishments. In this respect the present volume more clearly reflects Cooper and Hopper's collection rather than my own 1992 adventure, so I am delighted that both colleagues have contributed to this volume. In truth I was never attracted by the idea of updating my earlier text, although to be fair no publisher has ever invited me to consider doing so. Having got away with this once, there would be no second opportunity. An introductory collection of this sort had to be an ensemble exercise.

The brief

In late December 2013 I began the process of firming up the contributions to the collection. The basic request was for a chapter of around 9000 words in length, possibly inclusive of references (or maybe not), on a topic area within critical accounting research in which I believed potential contributors had demonstrated an expertise. I indicated that what I had in mind was an essay that might serve as the basis for a masterclass on a particular topic, an exercise that I hoped colleagues would find as interesting and challenging as myself. The belief was that in so doing contributors would make sense of their various areas of expertise in such a way as to make these accessible to students, and possibly junior colleagues, coming new to the main foci that have given rise to the critical accounting literature as it has evolved over the past 40 years. There was no suggestion that what would be provided was a definitive knowledge, as in the textbook tradition, more an authoritative overview, one with which students and their teachers might readily engage.

Contributors were invited to submit a first draft of their chapter by the end of 2014, with the intention that these be forwarded to a third party with a recognised expertise in the field for 'comment'. For the most part it was contributors who provided me with the name(s) of potential (light-touch) reviewers. The only proviso was that these third parties were not themselves contributors to the collection, something that has seemed to work well. There was no suggestion that what was being envisaged was tantamount to a review process, however. Having been appraised of what contributors had been invited to produce for the collection, commentators were invited to offer whatever observations they chose about the draft. These comments were then returned to contributors who were invited to make whatever refinements they might wish to their first draft and thereafter return it to me for editing. On a few occasions in the course of editing contributions I raised further issues with some contributors, usually about clarifying the wording of individual sentences or, more often, correcting reference information. I am delighted to be able to say that the process worked well and, at least as far as I am aware, no friendships became strained.

Unfortunately the proposed two-year timescale was to prove massively overambitious, as a result of which the volume became significantly delayed. In some cases this was the result of the pressure of work, which seems to be a universal feature of academic life in the twenty-first century. From a health and wellbeing perspective, more worrying is the observation that a number of prospective contributors found themselves constrained by health issues. On the other hand, I suspect that a minority of contributors find it difficult to let go of their work in the absence of threats, subtle or otherwise. Inevitably the final list of contributors (and contributions) differed from that of three years ago, although I am delighted to say that I believe this has had no consequence whatsoever on the quality of the volume.

The structure

From the outset the most appropriate structure seemed to me to be self-evident and, as a result, has changed very little over the intervening years. Given the pronounced theoretical underpinnings that critical accounting research has consistently evidenced, the first section had to be devoted to introducing readers to its principal theoretical foundations, those various ways of seeing that Baxter and Chua (2006) neatly designate as 'framing theories', and which Lukka and Vinnari (2014) have subsequently termed its 'method theories'. From the outset, critical accounting researchers were strongly attracted to the need to establish a strong theoretical foundation for the embryonic field. In this project they were greatly assisted by Burrell and Morgan's 1979 text: *Sociological Paradigms and Organisational Analysis*, which set out a range of alternatives to the predominant functionalist paradigm and its positivistic methodological underpinnings. In retrospect it is quite easy to identify powerful expressions of concern about the inherent limitations of this paradigm. Hopwood's founding *AOS* editorial commends the pursuit of case studies of 'accounting in action' that firmly eschew the emphases that characterise functionalism and positivism (Hopwood 1976), while Lowe and Tinker (1977) cautiously explore the promise of research designed to reveal and challenge the ideological underpinnings of the theory and practice of accounting.

The first three chapters in Section 2 introduce readers to the early framing theories of critical accounting. Throughout the 1980s each was extensively explored by the first generation of critical accounting researchers who collectively provided a robust foundation to the literature of critical accounting. In Chapter 2 Wickramasinghe and Alawattage document how researchers have borrowed from the interpretivist tradition to fashion a social scientific paradigm for subsequent accounting research endeavours. Embracing Burrell and Morgan's structural Marxism designation, in Chapter 3 Roslender chronicles the impact that its political economy and labour process variants had on critical accounting research during its first quarter of a century. Gallhofer and Haslam's contribution in Chapter 4 builds on their earlier writing on the accounting resonances evident in the work of Jeremey Bentham to identify the role that Critical Theory has played in shaping critical accounting research from the 1980s through until the present day. The contribution of philosophy rather than sociology in providing a robust foundation for critical accounting research is detailed by Lehman in Chapter 5, in the course of which many of the insights provided in the three previous chapters are reinforced.

These early framing theories have continued to inform the work of critical accounting researchers until the present day. As I observed earlier, the prospectus of potential framing theories has continued to expand since the mid-1980s, with the result that colleagues new to the field now encounter a potentially bewildering array of ways of seeing. Rather than seeking to include a chapter on each of them, two have been privileged in the pursuit of a measure of completeness. In Chapter 6 Knights and Bloom provide a wide-ranging introduction to the substantial impact that the work of Foucault has had on critical accounting research during the past 30 years. The final chapter in the section sets out the many insights that Bourdieu's voluminous output, which predates the emergence of critical accounting, has gifted the field. The theoretical contributions of those 'excluded' from this section are not disregarded in the following pages. Of necessity, significant parts of the remaining chapters are given over by contributors to exploring and advocating a much wider range of framing theories.

Although theoretical contributions have been a major feature of the critical accounting literature from its inception, the greater part of the cumulative stock of knowledge is better understood to be what Lukka and Vinnari designate 'domain theory' (or alternatively substantive theory). The role of Sections 2 and 3 is therefore to provide an introduction to this part of the critical accounting canon. It seemed to make sense to divide this into two parts: one that is focused on topics and issues that were perhaps already beginning to attract the attention of accounting researchers prior to the critical turn in the early 1980s, and the other being concerned with those that have become more visible over time, not least as a consequence of what an enthusiasm for borrowing from the theory literature now made visible.

In the first chapter in Section 3 Richardson provides an overview of the evolution of the accountancy profession to the present day. This is complemented in Chapter 9 by Baker's comparative study of the foundations of auditing practice in three European countries, again evidencing a strong historical emphasis. Both topics had attracted the attention of accounting researchers persuaded of the importance of pursuing what was termed 'accounting studies' at the beginning of this introduction, alongside more technical enquiries. This characterisation also applies to Chapter 10 in which Williams explores a range of ethical issues as these manifest themselves within the context of accounting, as a space within business. It is fair to acknowledge that the other three chapters in the section might be argued to focus on topics and issues of a

more recent origin than the previous three. In Chapter 11 Baudot and Robson develop a critical account of the significance of accounting regulation as this has evolved over recent decades,
while in Chapter 12 Broadbent and Laughlin document some of the negativities that have
resulted from an increasing process of colonisation by accounting thinking, particularly in the
context of public sector organisations. The section concludes with Roberts' scrutiny of the trend
towards a greater extent of accountability within modern society, and in particular its potentially
damaging consequences, unless fully understood by those charged with its implementation or
accomplishment.

Concern for the potential negativities that accounting and finance's increasing importance
in modern society may also be having for the broader environment evidenced a step change in
the mid-1980s. Thereafter social and environmental accounting research became a major focus
for both critical and mainstream scholars, the continuing evolution of which is documented
in Chapter 14 by Gray, Adams and Owen. The many issues associated with the growing presence of accounting within emerging economies are then explored by Hopper and Tanima in
Chapter 15, which directs attention to the role that a number of global institutions including the
International Monetary Fund, the Organisation for Economic Cooperation and the World Bank
have played in this process. In Chapter 16 the topic of corporate governance is viewed from
a more critical standpoint than is usually the case. Parker argues for the pursuit of an engaged,
qualitative research agenda as opposed to the currently predominant emphases evident within
this field. The contemporary financialisation process provides the focus for Haslam, Tsitsianis
and Katechos in Chapter 17, in which the authors draw attention to a number of the dangerous
longer-term consequences of this increasingly subscribed-to financial paradigm within financial
accounting and reporting. Chapter 18 returns attention to the process of globalisation, with
Graham documenting its potentially worrying impact on the activities of the twenty-first-
century accountancy profession and its evolving practices. The section concludes with Jeacle's
chapter on the merits of directing a critical accounting focus on the myriad aspects of popular
culture, a field that to date has attracted much less attention than its importance in our everyday
lives suggests should be the case.

From its inception, critical accounting research, like interdisciplinary accounting research,
has drawn extensively on other disciplines and, as has previously been noted, on sociology in
particular. As it has matured there has been growing evidence that critical accounting research
has also had an impact on a number of disciplines that might be seen as being closely related to
it. It therefore seemed appropriate to invite contributions from researchers engaged in work at
four important interfaces, to provide the content of Section 5. The field of accounting history
has a long and distinguished history as result of which it was already relatively well established at
the advent of critical accounting. Nevertheless, as Fleischman, Tyson and Oldroyd acknowledge
in Chapter 20, its status has been significantly enhanced as a result of a willingness of many
accounting historians to work to incorporate the broad emphases of critical accounting into
their own oeuvre. Accounting education as a specialised field of study is somewhat more recent
in origin but it has grown quickly to become a dynamic site for accounting research activity.
As Boyce's chapter documents, like accounting history the study of the intellectual formation
of accountants has benefited from incorporating critical accounting's emphases in recent times,
particularly in respect of the critical study of accounting pedagogy.

An important catalyst to the emergence of critical accounting was a growing co-location
of accounting academics with their colleagues in business and management during the 1970s.
Many business and management researchers, and particularly those engaged in organisation
studies, had already become familiar with the purchase of a variety of critical perspectives,
resulting in them being able to provide insights for their more inquisitive counterparts in

accounting at a local level. Over time, however, this has evolved into a two-way process, a number of aspects of which, and in particular in relation to the process of 'governing through numbers', are outlined in Chapter 22 by Carter and McKinlay. By contrast, McGoun's final chapter in Section 5 provides an explanation of the relatively limited progress that has been made in respect of the travel of critical perspective–informed research from accounting to its near neighbour finance. At the time that critical accounting emerged, finance research was firmly identifiable as being underpinned by the positivistic methodology that many critical accounting researchers sought to eschew. To a very large extent this remains the case today, despite the emergence of a behavioural finance community that has made some strides during the past two decades, perhaps constrained by a continuing heavy reliance on insights from psychology rather than those disciplines that have informed 40 years of critical accounting research.

The focus for the sixth and final section of the collection was again clearly self-evident: the future of the critical accounting field. Having now established itself as a major presence within accounting research, its continued development is surely likely to prove as fascinating as its evolution to date. As I observed in my opening paragraphs, however, it seems inevitable that this will be a contested process between those who are committed to promoting a project that firmly links the understanding of the conditions and consequences of accounting and the promotion of social betterment, and their counterparts who are seemingly comfortable to pursue a decoupled initiative, despite in some instances having little quibble about the need to work towards the end of social betterment. At the outset I imagined that it would not be too challenging to solicit a number of contributions on the topic. In fact, I was so confident that I invited chapters shorter than the aforementioned 9000 words from colleagues who had individually and collectively made a significant contribution to 40 years of the critical accounting research literature.

In the event this has proved to be a misplaced optimism, as a consequence of which Section 6 incorporates only three such contributions. In Chapter 24 Brown and Dillard identify the necessity to engage the challenge of long-term global sustainability as providing the crucial focus for the next generation of critical accounting research and researchers – other issues are certainly important but this is the big one, not least because society in general has failed to heed at least four decades of warnings of an impending global crisis. In their contribution Baxter and Chua identify the actor–network theory (ANT) of Latour as offering a powerful framing theory that promises much for future critical accounting research enquiries. Already well-established within the literature, as one of several generic post-critical ways of seeing, ANT is argued to be capable of providing a succession of incisive process-focused insights that will reinforce the field's already strong credibility. For Modell the future of critical accounting research would seem to be intimately related to recognising the insights that employing a critical realist research methodology is able to deliver, as an alternative to both the positivistic mainstream and a postmodern constructionist project, while also being more palatably radical than large parts of the canon of Marxist theory. Intriguingly critical realism's credentials as a *methodological* rather than a theoretical position offers critical accounting a means to return to the early debates about how best to replace positivism as the methodology of critical accounting research (see Roslender 2016).

Exercising the editor's prerogative (all too briefly)

In the light of this limited set of thoughts on the future of critical accounting research, it would seem appropriate to offer a few personal observations. Having been fortunate to have studied sociology at a time when the many potential alternatives to the hitherto dominant Parsonian structural–functionalist paradigm were being identified and hotly debated, I was introduced to a discipline in which the presence (and pitfalls) of multiple ways of seeing were to be recognised as highly desirable attributes. Forty years of critical accounting scholarship have certainly evidenced the deployment of a wide array of ways of seeing/not seeing. With the passage of time I have come to understand that every way of seeing potentially offers valuable insights, the perceptiveness of which may be enhanced or diminished as a consequence of the presence of human agency. No way of seeing should be dismissed out of hand therefore. Every way of seeing is, by definition, partial, as a result of which the pursuit of a more complete understanding must avoid the tendency to any form of excessive doctrinal purity. Equally, it is necessary to recognise the need to work hard to integrate insights from different, partial and sometimes contradictory ways of seeing. Shoddy scholarship, sometimes justified by the assertion that 'anything goes', will, in the long term, serve no one's interest and is something the critical accounting research community should actively guard against.

While I have certainly mellowed on the issue of the merits of any and every way of seeing over time, in parallel I have become ever more convinced that as individual researchers, we are clear about *why we are actually seeking knowledge and understanding* in the first place. On those occasions over the past 25 years when I have had the opportunity to teach an introduction to critical accounting module I have emphasised that while mainstream accounting research is concerned with facilitating 'better' accounting, for me the objective of critical accounting research is to contribute to the process of creating a better society, that is, social betterment. Earlier I noted a process of decoupling evident within the evolution of critical accounting over the past 40 years. I understand this, both in terms of a reluctance of many younger colleagues to commit themselves to the sort of radicalism that I experienced during my own intellectual formation, as well as the persuasive lure of alternative ways of seeing the world – something that was also very evident in the later 1960s, at the apogee of countercultural enlightenment. In the end, however, we need to recognise that society remains severely fractured, a process to which accounting continues to contribute extensively. As critical accounting researchers our project is to contribute to rectifying this, for the benefit of the majority. For me the future of critical accounting must entail the recoupling of understanding with the active pursuit of radical social change.

Acknowledgements

A large number of colleagues have contributed to the production of this collection in their many different ways, and it is my great pleasure to acknowledge that support at this point. My initial thanks go to the 39 contributors who accepted my invitation to provide a chapter for the collection. In every case this entailed finding time within increasingly busy research, teaching and management portfolios to organise their thoughts on a particular field and then to write these up in an accessible way. Thereafter came the challenge of assembling the necessary references, accurately, the outcome of which is the provision of an impressive bibliography of critical accounting work to date that will hopefully prove of immense help to the next generation of researchers and teachers. It should also not go unnoted that a number of contributors have also experienced medical issues during the past three years. I hope that their involvement in the project has in some way aided their respective recoveries.

As I noted earlier, contributors were invited to identify colleagues who they felt might usefully offer a 'light touch' commentary on the initial drafts of their chapters. The only constraint on their choice was that, as far as possible, these commentators should not themselves also be contributors to the collection. Thanks therefore go to the following scholars who also found time to fit such a request into their otherwise busy schedules: Pasi Ahonen (Essex); Paul Andon (New South Wales); Patricia Arnold (University of Wisconsin–Milwaukee); Ian Colville (Bath); David Cooper (Alberta); Colin Dey (Stirling); William Forbes (Queen Mary); James Guthrie (Macquarie); Suhkdev Johal (Queen Mary); Bertrand Malsch (Queen's, Kingston); Martin Messner (Innsbruck); Lissa Monk (Dundee); Alistair Mutch (Nottingham Trent); Eric Pezet (Paris 10); Chris Poullaos (Sydney); Abu Rahaman (Calgary); Sue Ravenscroft (Iowa State); Stewart Smythe (Sheffield); Jill Solomon (Sheffield); Stuart Turley (Manchester); Shahzad Uddin (Essex); Eija Vinnari (Tampere); and Stephen Walker (Edinburgh).

In addition to writing the foreword to the collection and providing some characteristically challenging comments on one of the chapters, David Cooper has also been a valuable source of advice, support and insight over the past three years, continuing a friendship that dates back to the inaugural Interdisciplinary Perspectives on Accounting (IPA) conference held in Manchester in July 1985. Trevor Hopper, co-organiser and subsequently co-editor with David of the 1990 collection of 'critical accounts' that has in some part inspired the present volume, has also been a regular correspondent over the past three years, along with Jane Broadbent, Jesse Dillard and Irvine Lapsley.

At Dundee I have been fortunate to have enjoyed the support of a number of colleagues. As my Head of Department since 2012, Bruce Burton has facilitated my requests to 'work at home' on a continuing basis, in tandem with the former Head of College, Chris Whatley. Lissa Monk and our doctoral student Nicola Murray have normally been prepared to listen to my frustrations on the slow progress of the project (among other things…), recently being joined by Graeme Martin in his capacity as Director of Research in the recently reconstituted University of Dundee School of Business.

For a number of years I have been fortunate to have held a visiting professorship in the Department of Business and Management at Aalborg University. Of late this has provided the opportunity to spend time away from the demands of the day job to pursue the detailed editorial tasks that signal the imminent completion of such a project. In Christian Nielsen I have found another generously supportive colleague with whom I have somehow managed of late to publish papers on the intellectual capital topic. In retrospect, I'm not quite sure why we never considered a contribution to this collection. In addition, I have found recent time spent at the Pori campus of the Turku School of Economics similarly calming.

Terry Clague at Routledge has arguably played the most important role in the project. Initially he was willing to wait for what now seems an unreasonable length of time for me to write a proposal for the text. Thereafter he has accommodated to the catalogue of delays to its finalisation, in the shared wish to make sure we produce a credible offering (which I think is my term not his). I hope Terry is as satisfied with the outcome as I am at this time. Thanks also to Sinead Waldron and her successor at Routledge in 2016, Izzie Fitzharris. Both have done their utmost to chivvy me along towards completion, usually with the consequence of me contacting Terry again with an apologetic but always truthful assessment of progress.

Finally, as always, my thanks to my wife Alison, who would readily assert she has never known me to have been as hard worked as over the past four months, which somewhat ironically is the period of time I have been partly retired. A practising management accountant herself, and of many years standing, Alison was perhaps fortunate in pursuing a non-relevant degree in which 'science studies' had a significant role. Whilst in theory she claims a considerable scepticism about the value of the critical accounting project, in her actions throughout her career she has consistently affirmed its many valuable lessons.

Dundee, January 2017.

Robin Roslender

References

Armstrong, P. (1994). "Corporate control in large British companies: the intersection of management accounting and industrial relations in postwar Britain," in A. G. Hopwood and P. Miller (eds): *Accounting as Social and Institutional Practice*, Cambridge: Cambridge University Press.

Baxter, J. and W. F. Chua (2006). "Reframing management accounting practice: a diversity of perspectives," in A. Bhimani (ed.): *Contemporary Issues in Management Accounting*, Oxford: Oxford University Press.

Briloff, A. J. (1972). *Unaccountable Accounting*, New York: Harper Collins.

Burrell, G. and G. Morgan (1979). *Sociological Paradigms and Organisational Analysis*, London: Heinemann Educational Books.

Chapman, C. S., D. J. Cooper and P. Miller (2009). *Accounting, Organizations and Institutions: Essays in Honour of Anthony Hopwood*, Oxford: Oxford University Press.

Chua, W. F. (1986). "Radical developments in accounting thought," *Accounting Review*, 61(4): 601–32.

Chua, W. F., T. Lowe and T. Puxty (eds) (1989). *Critical Perspectives in Management Control*, London: Macmillan.

Cooper, D. J and T. Hopper (eds) (1990). *Critical Accounts: Reorientating Accounting Research*, Basingstoke: Macmillan.

Hopwood, A. G. (1976). "Editorial," *Accounting, Organizations and Society*, 1(1): 1–4.

Hopwood, A. G. and P. Miller (eds) (1994). *Accounting as Social and Institutional Practice*, Cambridge: Cambridge University Press.

Jones, T. C. (1995). *Accounting and the Enterprise: A Social Analysis*, London: Routledge.

Laughlin, R. (1995). "Empirical research in accounting: alternative approaches and a case for middle range thinking," *Accounting, Auditing and Accountability Journal*, 8(1): 63–87.

Laughlin, R. (2016). "Tony Lowe and the interdisciplinary and critical perspectives on accounting project: reflections on the contributions of a unique scholar," in J. Haslam and P. Sikka (eds): *Pioneers of Critical Accounting: A Celebration of the Life of Tony Lowe*, London: Palgrave Macmillan.

Lowe, A. E. and A. Tinker (1977). "Siting the accounting problematic: towards an intellectual emancipation of accounting," *Journal of Business Finance and Accounting*, 4(3): 263–76.

Lukka, K. and E. Vinnari (2014). "Domain theory and method theory in management accounting research," *Accounting, Auditing and Accountability Journal*, 27(8): 1308–37.

Macintosh, N. B. (1990). "Annual reports in an ideological role: a Critical Theory analysis," in D. J. Cooper and T. Hopper (eds): *Critical Accounts: Reorientating Accounting Research*, Basingstoke: Macmillan.

Macintosh, N. B. (1994). *Management Accounting and Control Systems: An Organizational and Behavioral Approach*, Chichester: John Wiley and Sons.

Macintosh, N. B. and T. Hopper (eds) (2005). *Accounting, the Social and the Political: Classics, Contemporary and Beyond*, Amsterdam: Elsevier.

Perks, R. W. (1993). *Accounting and Society*, London: Chapman and Hall.

Puxty, A. G. (1993). *The Social and Organizational Context of Management Accounting*, London: Academic Press.

Roslender, R. (1992). *Sociological Perspectives on Modern Accountancy*, London: Routledge.

Roslender, R. (2016). "Thinking about critical methodology," in J. Haslam and P. Sikka (eds): *Pioneers of Critical Accounting: A Celebration of the Life of Tony Lowe*, London: Palgrave Macmillan.

Scott, D. R. (1931). *The Cultural Significance of Accounts*, New York: Henry Holt and Company.

SECTION II

2

INTERPRETIVISM

Danture Wickramasinghe and Chandana Alawattage

1 Introduction

Exploring the nomenclature and the intellectual traditions that delineate what is meant by 'interpretivism' in the context of accounting research reveals a continuing debate. A common position holds that there is a significant difference between interpretive and critical research, with some commentators arguing that they are different due to their distinct theoretical, methodological and ideological underpinnings. Other commentators take a more equivocal position, however, affirming that they are broadly the same, although while the terms can be used interchangeably there is a need to be consistent in using them in the piece of work at hand. Newcomers to the field may expect a convincing delineation or at least an attempt to minimise any unnecessary ambiguity, however.

Until the 1960s accounting research was rooted in a techno-functional tradition that sought solutions to technical and policy problems in accounting (Baxter and Davidson 1977). This emphasis then gave way to a generic research approach that privileged the use of economic science and statistical tools, often referred to as positive accounting research (Watts and Zimmerman 1978, 1979). At the beginning of the 1980s, the interpretive or naturalistic turn in accounting research emerged as a challenge to the mainstream (Colville 1981; Hopwood 1983; Tomkins and Groves 1983a,b). During the following three decades the interpretive accounting research tradition has become ever broader in nature as it has drawn from the social and sociological theories of Marx, Weber, Habermas, Giddens, Foucault, Latour and Bourdieu, among others (Baxter and Chua 2003). The resulting heterogeneity of interpretivism was clearly evident in the polyphonic debate, which also introduced the novel notion of the 'new' interpretivism (Ahrens *et al.* 2008), and in the other papers in the special issue. The term 'interpretive' has also been (mis)used to mean something other than statistical analysis, juxtaposing interpretation with quantitative analyses. Interpretivism has thus become an elusive, chameleon-like concept that defies the identification of any definitive meaning, a conclusion that is commensurate with interpretivism's own precepts and underpinnings.

This chapter traces the evolution of the interpretive turn in accounting research and outlines the key tenets on which this approach was founded and continues to evolve. At base the interpretive turn implies a greater reliance on the subjective interpretations of the actors involved in social interactions. In this sense, while the researcher's prior theoretical positions and orientations can play a major role in forming the theoretically coherent arguments and/or narratives, the substantive rationalities (Weber 1978; Kalberg 1980) emanating from their opinions, ideas, expressions, beliefs, judgments and so forth also play a central role in making sense of interpretive research in accounting. In the following pages we revisit the different paths that interpretive research in accounting has taken. In order to organise our thinking, we make use of the distinction between seeing interpretation as a politico-ideological act and interpretation as a methodo-philosophical act, as in Sections 3 and 4 of this chapter. Initially, however, we provide an overview of the genesis and evolution of interpretive accounting research. The chapter concludes with the suggestion that now might be an opportune time to revisit the work of Max Weber, arguably the principal intellectual progenitor of the interpretive tradition.

2 Genesis and evolution

The origins of interpretivism in accounting research can be thought of as a social movement – an ideologically structured action mobilising in different social settings to challenge a number of dominant ideologies and established practices, routines and rituals (Davis, McAdam, Scott and Zald 2005; Zald 2000; Zald and McCarthy 1979). Within this movement, accounting academia began to resist (and is still resisting) the dominant mainstream research paradigm that was dominated by a number of root disciplines including psychology, neoclassical economics and systems theory. These frameworks permeated prescriptions and model building with a view to enhancing the effectiveness, efficiency and efficacy of organisational processes. The social movement that emerged challenged these frameworks and identified an alternative – the interpretive tradition.

How did this happen? Before outlining the analytical profile of the social movement's outcome, we will sketch its early contours and subsequent developments. There is no argument among accounting researchers in the interpretive camp that it was *Accounting, Organizations and Society (AOS)* that provided a forum for the genesis, voice and expansion of interpretive research in accounting. Its founding editor, Anthony Hopwood, embarked on this agenda declaring:

> [The] terminology and underlying calculus of 'profits' and 'costs' continue to exert a profound impact on human consciousness and action.
>
> *(Hopwood 1976: 1)*

This was an historical moment in the making of accounting, previously considered to be a technical and professional practice requiring technical advancements in terms of model building and policy making, as a genuine social science. The new agenda called for the emancipation of accounting from the clutches of economics and finance. Hopwood continues:

> The social and behavioral sciences … less familiar to most accountants in terms of both the body of knowledge and the underlying values. And integration of accounting and social perspectives was a very different endeavor from the integration of finance and accounting.
>
> *(Hopwood 1976: 3)*

This beginning, as we now recognise, was persuasive and influential. In due course *AOS* published a number of seminal interpretive papers, including Tomkins, Rosenberg and Colville (1980), Colville (1981) and Rosenberg, Tomkins and Day (1982). Broadly, these works draw on interpretive sociology, which challenged the position of functionalism. Drawing on the ideas of interpretive sociologists such as Weber, Mead, Cooley and Blumer, who emphasised the role of symbols, images and human interaction, these researchers created a space for research to investigate how accounting is implicated in such social phenomena. Interpretive sociology privileged the significance of interpretations of events and things. The governing principle here is that there is a constitutional role for human consciousness to create meanings and value, by reflecting on 'things'. They emphasise that things only exist within the meanings and labels given to them by human beings, through their everyday life experience. Thus, for example, life experience, understanding, giving meanings and using things to reproduce meaning are the interpretive acts of human beings. Organisations, control systems or their budgeting functions are the kinds of things being interpreted by people through these interpretive acts (Wickramasinghe and Alawattage 2007).

Colville (1981) commends a form of action research that integrates Glaser and Strauss's (1967) grounded theory and Berger and Luckmann's (1966) social constructionism. For Colville, accounting is socially constructed so that we need to use a methodology that social scientists employ in understanding social reality. Building on Colville's foundations, as well as Rosenberg *et al.* (1982), Tomkins and Groves (1983a,b) identify "everyday accountants" in their accounting essay written from the perspectives of interpretive sociology. The everyday accountant's reality was discussed in terms of three forms of realities: reality as a symbolic discourse; reality as a social construction; and reality as a projection of human imagination. For this, they draw on three methodological positions, namely symbolic interactionism, ethnomethodology and phenomenology, respectively. These researchers applied their insights in empirical research on contemporary local government accounting practices in the UK, providing a series of interpretations about what they observed. Their studies were the first in the genre of reporting 'sociologically' rather than providing 'statistics' for testing a predetermined theory. The publications were recognised as situational accounting 'stories' that provoked issues and debates.

A sound foundation for a new tradition of interpretive accounting research quickly emerged, being very evident at the first two Interdisciplinary Perspectives on Accounting Conferences in 1985 and 1988. Many subsequent interpretive papers were presented at these conferences, while the researchers who participated began to develop the network of interpretive research. The decade proved to be a golden era for interpretive accounting research with many seminal papers published within the pages of *AOS*. These include Tinker (1980); Tinker, Merino and Neimark (1982); Cooper and Sherer (1984), Berry, Capps, Cooper, Ferguson, Hopper and Lowe (1985); Chua (1986); Neimark and Tinker (1986); Hopper, Storey and Willmott (1987); and Hopper and Armstrong (1991). Not only did these papers promote further sociologically oriented research in accounting, they also encouraged accounting researchers to read social theory seriously. Consequently, a prospectus of social theories became available to accounting researchers with which to theorise accounting practices. These theories were drawn from institutional theory, actor–network theory (ANT), Habermas, Foucault and Bourdieu – all of which and whom are still highly visible in the three main interpretive accounting journals, the *Accounting, Accountability and Auditing Journal* (*AAAJ*), *Critical Perspectives on Accounting* (*CPA*) and *AOS*.

Returning to the notion of a social movement mentioned earlier, in a sense we can see that the development outlined is a social movement constructed within accounting academia. In our view this social movement was charged with developing a set of critiques of the accounting mainstream, which sought to document (a) the lack of attention to the wider sociopolitical implications of organisational practices, and (b) the methodological weaknesses inherent in the prevailing positivistic orientation of accounting research. The term 'interpretive research' is thus used here to denote the alternative approaches that seek to resist and rectify these weaknesses. It is in this way that the genesis of interpretivism might be understood as a resistive social movement. This resistance and rectification has two distinct but interrelated dimensions:

the politico-ideological and the methodo-philosophical, both of which originated from and continue to evolve as a project of understanding accounting beyond its conventional technical/managerial meanings by locating accounting in its wider sociocultural, political, economic and institutional contexts. In the following two sections we document this view.

3 Interpretation as a politico-ideological act

In respect of the politico-ideological dimension, the interpretive project in accounting research initially stemmed from a stream of accounting research that attempted to draw attention to two important aspects of the context of accounting, as it was conceptualised in the 1970s and 1980s: individuals and groups (the micro context); and society (the macro context). While often not always explicit, these were clearly, for our understanding, attempts to advance a political meaning in the theorisation of accounting practices. They were political interpretations because they attempted at understanding and explaining how accounting is implicated in human conditions – the power and role of accounting in determining the situation of human beings within and outside of organisations and their wider social arrangements. These early attempts were also critical of the dominant managerialist and economic overtones of accounting research, initially offering an alternative political and institutional interpretation of how understanding accounting practices had already begun to gain ground during the 1970s.

3.1 Behavioural negligence questioned

First was the project of behavioural accounting, where the purpose was to import industrial psychology and sociology to discuss the social and psychological implications of accounting practices. Proponents of this approach began to ask a range of important questions about the absences in relation to social and behavioural aspects evident in mainstream accounting research. Hopwood poses the following questions:

> How would you design information for control purpose without considering how it would fit in with the other means of influencing behavior in organizational settings? How would you provide information to motivate superior performance without having some understanding of human needs and aspirations? How would you manage the processes of standard setting, budgeting and planning, all of which are essentially social in nature?
>
> *(Hopwood 1974: 2)*

The storytelling project initiated by Colville and his colleagues stemmed from this and evolved into subsequent attempts (Berry *et al.* 1985; Rosenberg *et al.* 1982; Tomkins and Groves 1983a). Reporting on what is going on and revealing underlying sociological meanings shed light on these questions. However, as we see later, this initiative was sidelined by a flood of methodo-philosophical research or, in some interpretations, transformed into this tradition.

Second, the social accounting project brought with it a new vocabulary of social auditing, social performance, social disclosure and accountability, as an extension to, and a critique of, the business and social responsibility discussions of the 1960s and 1970s with their dominantly managerialist overtones and concerns (Gray 2002). Researchers raised their concerns about the ecological impacts of business's and accounting's associated roles in revealing its consequences. Seen from the politico-ideological point of view, both of these projects propelled accounting research beyond its traditional techno-managerial boundaries. In retrospect, however, the power and politics of accounting were conceptualised, especially in their early phases, only in the very limited sense of: (a) the behavioural implications of accounting technologies, especially the cognitive and motivational implications of accounting technologies and procedures on the employees; and (b) the social responsibilities and accountabilities of economic enterprises to report the environmental and social impacts of their economic operations. Despite this limited definition of politics, these early critical excursions signposted the initial path to a much larger and ever-expanding interpretive accounting research project.

3.2 Marxian interpretations

The politico-ideological stream of rather explicit and outspoken politicisation stemmed from a project of importing Marxism as a further interpretive framework on accounting. The origin of this process can be traced back to the introduction of the labour process perspective into the field of management studies (which encompasses accounting) and industrial sociology, where the notions of control and management began to attract contemporary (neo-, anti- and post-) Marxist interpretations. Braverman's (1974) text, *Labor and Monopoly Capital: The Degradation of Work in the Twentieth Century*, resulted in Marx's concepts of the social relations of production, historical materialism and dialectics becoming parts of the key interpretive schemas in management and accounting research, especially in the critical circle. Early contributions informed by Marxist theory include Tinker (1980), Tinker *et al.* (1982), Neimark and Tinker (1986), and Hopper *et al.* (1987). Hopper and Armstrong's (1991) Marxist critique of Johnson and Kaplan's (1987) history of management accounting remains a seminal example of this genre of political interpretation of management accounting. Since then, the Marxist critique of capitalism has served as a theoretical source for politico-ideological interpretations of accounting phenomena (e.g. Bryer 1994, 1999, 2005, 2006, 2015; Cooper 1995; Cooper 2008; Cooper 2015). Prominent within the conceptual framework of this tradition are the labour process, relations *in* and *of* production, surplus value, circuits of capital and historical dialectics, which in due course have evolved into a distinct stream of accounting research providing an insight set of political economic interpretations of accounting practices.

If interpretation is viewed as offering meanings and/or understanding reasons behind social actions and processes (accounting as such), then social theories have become the schemas to frame such interpretations in interpretive accounting research. As a social theory, Marxism offered accounting researchers a distinct political economic logic for looking at the political role of accounting. This logic was fundamentally structural, meaning that it attempts to locate accounting within the wider political structures of capitalism, especially class conflict, capitalist hegemony, state politics and the historical dialectics that they create. Hence, accounting began to receive a different political meaning as a technology *of* and *for* capitalism. Accordingly, in a cumulative sense, capitalism and its history became the contextual parameters within which accounting phenomena were to be located and interpreted. Accounting was interpreted and critiqued as a technology of capitalism, as a calculative practice of exploitation, as a technology through which the real subsumption of labour was materialised, and as a historical force emanating from, and facilitating, the emergence and growth of capitalism, especially in the growth of hierarchies over markets. In this way, Marxism provided a metanarrative of the political role of accounting within the broader metanarratives of capitalist social evolution. Importing Marxism as an interpretive schema furnished a politico-ideological critique on capitalism in general, which identified accounting as a powerful generic technology of capitalism. Theoretical interpretation became a politico-ideological act directed towards explaining the exploitative and hegemonic nature of capitalism through theorising various accounting and management control practices. These critical interpretations, whether explicitly or implicitly, also had the normative intent of emancipating the underdog, especially the ranks of subjugated and exploited employees (Jermier 1998).

The Marxist turn had a double impact on the development of critical interpretive research in accounting. On the one hand, it provided an alternative politico-ideological interpretation and critique to neoclassical economics and systems theory–based managerialism and made various Marxist and neo-Marxist concepts popular among accounting researchers as sensitising devices. In this sense, it provided a broader sociological and political terminology that allowed accounting researchers to view accounting from a politico-ideological perspective. On the other hand, Marxism in accounting research also became a point of departure and a point of critique in itself. Much of the subsequent interpretive research after the later 1980s emanated as a critique of Marxism, especially of its structuralist ontology, economic reductionism and the overemphasis on class politics. As a result, the (critical) interpretation of accounting began to receive political meanings beyond class politics.

3.3 *Foucauldian interpretations*

One of the key theoretical logics for this departure from, and critique of, Marxism was provided by Foucauldian social theory, which initially began to attract support in the mid-1980s. While there was a degree of methodo-philosophical emphasis in the Foucauldian critique and extension of critical interpretations of accounting, it was still predominantly a politico-ideological critique of capitalism and the role of accounting therein. Foucauldian social theory offered an alternative understanding of the historical dynamics of the capitalist system and of modernity, including locating accounting within such historical dynamics. The crucial difference stemmed from Foucault's emphasis on the processes of objectivation and subjectivation rather than exploitation and domination. According to Foucault such processes constitute conditions under which certain relations of subject to object are formed or modified, insofar as these relations constitute a possible knowledge (Foucault 1998: 459). Hence, power relations are relations through which subjects and objects are formed, such power relations being necessarily formed vis-à-vis regimes of knowledge and truth.

In the view of Foucauldian accounting researchers, it is not exploitation and alienation in the sense of class conflicts but rather subjectivation and objectivation that underpin the social processes of domination and control; not within structural parameters of class interests, but within disciplinary apparatuses of the micro- and macrophysics of power and knowledge (Wickramasinghe and Alawattage 2007). The notion of control is now reinterpreted within the terminology of discipline and governmentality. There is a clear difference between the traditional (Marxist) understanding of control and the Foucauldian understanding of the same in terms of disciplining. In a Marxist sense, control is largely concerned with economic and non-economic domination, coercion and exploitation, including hegemony. For Foucauldians, however, especially in the era of modernity, control is exerted through the mechanism of regimes of truth and knowledge, which we commonly call 'disciplines' (such as medicine, psychology, accounting, etc.), and their associated disciplinary institutions (such as hospitals, asylums, schools, universities, factories, offices) that, according to Foucault (2002), all resemble prisons. Within such disciplinary institutions, people are disciplined through the application of a distinct set of disciplinary principles that have been developed and disseminated throughout modernity. Hopper and Macintosh (1993) provide a penetrating case study of how such disciplinary principles operated at the International Telephone & Telegraph Corporation (ITT) under Geneen.

The notion of governmentality refers to the macro-effects of such disciplinary evolutions of society on state apparatuses, evident in the transition of sovereign states from principalities, with the domain of power linked to a sovereign prince or a king/queen, to a modern governmentality, with the domain of power/knowledge invested in the modern government. Modernity and capitalism are now understood as particular regimes of governance, with an emphasis on disciplining by numbers. As a consequence, management accounting becomes invested with a disciplinary meaning: a disciplinary technology whose history is to be understood in the context of the archaeology of knowledge and genealogy of power, and whose political effects can be interpreted in terms of its capacity to ensure a disciplinary gaze – the institutional processes through which governing by numbers became embedded within modern organisational apparatuses (Hopper and Macintosh 1993).

In common with their Marxist counterparts, Foucauldians also embraced the critical intent of emancipation, which was no longer sought through the collective mechanism of class struggle but instead within the individualised agency embedded within the power/knowledge nexus. In this sense, both Marxist and Foucauldian interpretations of accounting exhibit a strong politico-ideological critique of capitalism/modernity and accounting as a key technology therein. Despite their philosophical and methodological differences, both Foucauldians and Marxists embrace an overarching common aim: to explain how capitalism works and how individuals are subjugated, controlled and governed within and beyond the organisational apparatuses of modern (and postmodern) capitalism. While Marxists rely on the proposition of historical dialectics between capital and labour – that is, class conflict – Foucauldians emphasise the micro- and macro-physics of power, especially in the power/knowledge nexus. For Marxists accounting is a political device that needs to be interpreted in terms of capital's attempts to subordinate labour. For Foucauldians accounting operates beyond class conflict, within an institutional setting that was developed to discipline human behaviour according to emerging regimes of knowledge and truth, which provide the basis of disciplinary power – hence the power/knowledge nexus. Within such spaces individuals become the 'governable persons' subject to the institutional apparatuses of (post)modern capitalism, *inter alia* accountancy (Miller and O'Leary 1987; Miller and Rose 1990; Miller 2006).

3.4 Interpretations beyond class and disciplinary apparatuses

The prospectus of theoretical interpretations has subsequently multiplied and diversified to offer politico-ideological critiques from perspectives other than those of class and disciplinarity. Accounting researchers have engaged with a variety of post-Marxist and post-Foucauldian French, German, US and British developments in social, sociological and political theory. In various ways, these new theoretical schemas for interpretation have been drawn upon to provide a range of 'post' interpretations (such as post-structuralist, post-Marxist, post-Foucauldian, postmodern and even postcolonial) of accounting and management control practices.

The German social theorist Habermas has been highly influential for the past three decades, and in particular his (meta-)theory of communicative action that situates human rationality within the structures of interpersonal communication. Habermasian research in accounting locates accounting within the wider communicative parameters of democracy to articulate the politico-ideological role of accounting in human emancipation (Laughlin 1987, 1995; Broadbent and Laughlin 1997). The way in which Habermas conceptualises democracy and democratic processes is important here as the context within which accounting critiques have developed. As Laughlin (1987), one of the leading Habermasian accounting scholars, explains, Habermas' theory of social evolution and communicative action revolves around three main theoretical constructs: the lifeworld; systems; and language decentration. The lifeworld is the cultural space in which individuals seek meaning in their social actions. Baker observes that the lifeworld "encompasses the realm of everyday social reality, which is constituted and reconstituted by the culture, values, habits and myths of a particular social group" (Baker 2008: 92). Systems, on the other hand, are the "self-regulating action contexts which co-ordinate actions around specific mechanisms or media, such as money or power" (Thompson 1983: 285). In a more pragmatic sense,

> [Systems] are the organizing and operating procedures of organizations and institutions which guide and direct human behaviour in social settings (e.g. laws and regulations; religious precepts; values imparted in schools and universities; operating procedures of organizations and institutions).
>
> *(Baker 2008: 92)*

For Habermas, it is the language skill of the individuals – that is, language decentration – to differentiate the lifeworld from systems and, accordingly, to cope with the external world, the social world and the world of inner subjectivity, which provides the social impetus for emancipation and social development. However, there is a tendency, evident throughout the development of capitalism and modernity, towards the inner colonisation of the lifeworld by systems when social actors are unable to differentiate and retain as separate the social and technical spheres of their lives: The technical sphere overpowers the social, far exceeding its boundaries (Laughlin 1987: 486). In this context, social antagonism is understood neither as existing between the classes nor within the power/knowledge nexus but within the dialectics between the systems (world) and the lifeworld. Human emancipation is therefore to be sought through counter-strategies designed to reverse the colonising tendency and to regain the necessary supremacy of the lifeworld over systems. The critical interpretation of accounting stems from understanding the role accounting plays as an element of systems in colonising the lifeworld. In parallel, some Habermasian accounting scholars also see an emancipatory potential in accounting insofar as accounting can be developed into a language through which the lifeworld can be (re)empowered, for example through the mechanism of a radicalised form of social accounting.

Bourdieu's theory of practice, together with his theoretical concepts of field, habitus, forms of capital and symbolic violence, etc., have subsequently been employed to interpret accounting and other calculative practices as particular field-specific schemas of domination and symbolic violence (e.g. Kurunmaki 1999; Alawattage 2011; Cooper and Joyce 2013). In similar fashion, Derrida's deconstructionism (e.g. Arrington and Francis 1989), Giddens' structuration theory (e.g. Scapens and Macintosh 1996), Burawoy's manufacturing consent and politics of production (e.g. Uddin and Hopper 2001), various versions of institutional theory (e.g. Dillard, Rigsby and Goodman 2004; Covaleski, Dirsmith and Michelman, 1993), together with ANT (e.g. Briers and Chua 2001; Alcouffe, Berland and Levant, 2008; Pipan and Czarniawska 2010; Justesen and Mouritsen 2011), have been employed to fashion a rich array of post-Marxist and post-Foucauldian interpretive accounting contributions. Some are explicitly politico-ideological while others are less so. Nevertheless, most of them can be read as political texts that promote radical political aspirations of emancipation and social reform, displaying a generic ideological-political dissatisfaction regarding the way in which prevailing economic and socio-political activities are organised around capitalist enterprises, markets and networks. While documenting the subtler and more mundane practices of domination, subjugation and control rather than class politics, they reaffirm the dominating and subjugating character of (post)modern institutional apparatuses, drawing our attention to the pivotal and damaging roles that accounting plays in their reproduction.

4 Interpretation as a methodo-philosophical act

The second dimension in the evolution of interpretive research in accounting is its methodo-philosophical development, which can be clearly differentiated from the politico–ideological dimension discussed earlier. While interpretive accounting research as a politico–ideological critique concentrates on the political ontology of social systems, organisations and the political role of accounting therein, methodo-philosophical critique concentrates on epistemological issues, especially the dialectic between structure and agency and the ways in which actors, their agency and their practices can be rescued from structural analysis epistemologically. Hence, interpretation as a methodo-philosophical act concentrates on the epistemological possibilities of bringing actors, their agency and their practices (which have been arguably undermined by structures in much of Marxist and post-Marxist structural analyses) to the forefront of the analysis. As both dimensions are interrelated and overlapping, the underlying dichotomy cannot be considered to be between two separate camps akin to two sets of research projects, however. What we do in the following pages is present a different reading of many of the same papers discussed previously, in order to promote a wider understanding of the different threads that count as interpretive accounting research.

Trying to delineate interpretation as a methodo-philosophical act involves, on the one hand, a straightforward methodological critique of mainstream positivistic research, which celebrates hypothetico-deductive approaches, replacing it with post-positivistic research that promotes soft approaches grounded in story-driven inductive methods. On the other hand, this methodo-philosophical act involves a continuous engagement in the reading of alternative sociologically oriented philosophical strands, which allows researchers to use one or several of them to illuminate the data being induced through crafting storylines. In their various ways, all the methodo-philosophical developments in interpretivism, in contrast to the politico–ideological developments discussed earlier, are driven by an underlying philosophical motive of finding a stance on the structure versus agency debate in the social sciences rather than seeking a political ideology.

Within the methodo-philosophical space, methodologically speaking, accounting research can be seen as providing a way of knowing what is going on in three interrelated research sites: accounting in action; accounting in institutions; and accounting in practice. At the same time, philosophically speaking, these methodological sites are to be supplemented by ways of seeing in three respective (broad) theoretical lenses: actor–network theory (ANT); institutional and structuration theory; and practice theory. While alternative lenses exist, including legitimacy theory, stakeholder theory, grounded theory and so forth, we refer to them as we proceed in an effort to define the overall function of methodo-philosophical enquiry. Our aim is not to survey these methods and approaches, however. Rather, we try to outline what constitutes this methodo-philosophical act in interpretive accounting research.

4.1 Accounting in action: the microphysics of accounting

Seeking to promote research that makes sense of accounting in action, rather than simply to document accounting's procedural issues, Hopwood comments:

> Accounting and control departments are variously organized. Planning, budgeting and performance monitoring procedures operate at different organizational levels, are subject to different degrees of participation, have different expectations and practices for their revision, and even can consider very different time periods. Accounting systems

also serve to establish very different patterns of organizational segmentation and relate to the practices for the management of organizational interdependence in a variety of ways.
(Hopwood 1983: 297)

Hopwood did not expect researchers to merely comment on the procedural dimensions of such diversities and fragilities about accounting in action. Instead, researchers, who had begun reading sociological and philosophical material – for example Colville (1981); Tomkins and Groves (1983a,b); Hopper and Powell (1985) – now sought out methodological alternatives and philosophical justifications for studying what is going on and explaining why it is so.

A seminal example of such enquiry firmly rooted in the methodo-philosophical tradition was the pioneering UK National Coal Board (NCB) study by Berry *et al.* (1985). Their focus was to report on how and why managers constructed, interpreted and used accounting information in a different way to what textbooks prescribe (see Scapens 1994). To this end, the researchers conducted extensive conversations with workers in the South Yorkshire coalfield, which allowed them to realise that financial data reported in budgets and performance reports and so on, did not reflect daily practices and managers' discussions at formal and informal meetings. Given the uncertainty about the future of the coal industry and the physical isolation of the workers from ordinary communities, workers' personal interactions, shared sentiments and meanings were what informed meetings and infused managers' behaviour rather than financial measures. During the collection of their data the researchers learned that the form of accounting pursued at the local level, its microphysics, was decoupled from formal control protocols. It was their specific research method that respected a bottom-up approach to data analysis, and their ontology that reality is constructed by actors in action, which gave form to such a realisation of what counts as accounting in actual accounts. In doing so, they intimated that the aura of objectivity and neutrality about accounting in action is mythical (Hopper, Asraf, Uddin and Wickramasinghe, 2015). The NCB researchers quickly recognised that their enquiries and understandings would be enhanced by employing additional theoretical and conceptual insights. Hopper, Cooper, Lowe, Capps and Mouritsen (1986) revisit their insights using Braverman's labour process theory, identified in the previous section as a politico-ideological perspective.

Had they elected to embrace a more methodo-philosophic interpretive perspective at that time, with the benefit of hindsight it is possible to identify ANT as a powerful alternative. Developed by Bruno Latour and his colleagues during the 1980s, ANT provides the means to explore how ideas and technologies develop through networks of heterogeneous relationships that are formed and reformed through time and space. It was embraced by some interpretive accounting researchers, however. An early ANT-informed contribution is provided by Preston, Cooper and Coombs (1992) where the researchers argue that budgets are fabricated rather than just prepared and used as a pre-exiting natural order imposed on lower participants through the mechanism of top-down organisational hierarchy. They found that micropolitics in the organisation were presented as ways in which heterogeneous actors are enrolled into a local network to decide upon budgets as representations of images of these network attempts, and to create a forum for these actors to engage in continuous endorsements until the budgets are accepted, enacted and black boxed. Employing the same ANT theorisation, Robson (1991, 1992) argues that accounting can be viewed as a form of inscription by means of which actors can act at a distance in order to make things visible. These further endeavours in understanding accounting in action provided a solid formation for a research programme within the interpretive accounting space, which in time resulted in many insightful papers (including Briers and Chua 2001; Chua 1995; Chua and Mahama 2012; Jones and Dugdale 2002; Miller 1991; Mouritsen, Larsen and Bukh, 2001; Preston 2006; Qu and Cooper 2011; Quattrone and Hopper 2005).

These developments qualified not only as a philosophical programme of research but also as a methodology for studying accounting in action. As a philosophy, ANT rejects the idea that accounting is a thing that is there, positing instead that accounting is a thing that is being in action, subject to its realisation through negotiations and controversies. This process of this realisation does not occur in a hierarchy, however, as ANT assumes a 'flat' ontology in which every actor may have some power to influence because, as Law observes, "structure is not free-standing like a scaffolding on a building site, but a site of struggle" (Law 1992: 385–6). Hence, at the beginning, it is assumed that nothing is there in a concrete sense but conditions of possibilities are presented for the actors to achieve and realise in action. In this way, accounting is often 'on the move' through action.

As a result, methodologically speaking, the researcher must 'follow the actors' in the form of interviews, conversations, observations and so on, in order to make sense of how accounting is presented in the contours of heterogeneous relationships and their actions. When the researcher explores accounting in action in this way, s/he will experience the processes of translation and fabrication, in addition to making and remaking, and thereby gain an understanding of how issues are problematised, how new actors become 'interested' in developments, how they become involved as a result of the influence of others, and how accounting is kept live in action. All this is methodologically coupled with the assertion of a flat ontology.

At present, the ANT-inspired accounting research programme continues to produce interesting findings in divergent organisational and extra-organisational contexts. For example, along with these formative concepts, and taking a step further, Boedker and Chua (2013) conceptualise accounting as an affective technology given that passion and emotion can act as key drivers of action. In this sense, accounting does not operate as a pure technology but as one that combines numbers with human properties generated through cognitive processes. Such psychologically oriented methodo-philosophical works have also begun to combine accounting with trust where the researchers argue that trust-building processes are often characterised by passions and emotions as well as by fragilities and uncertainties, leaving a space for further investigation (Tomkins 2001).

4.2 Accounting as institution: the macrophysics of accounting

The macrophysics of accounting can be ascribed to those applications of variants of institutional theory in accounting research deployed by researchers who are comfortable to embrace the 'new' interpretivism designation (Ahrens *et al.* 2008). Even though the notion of an institution is difficult to pin down, these accounting researchers quickly concluded that accounting is a social and institutional practice (Chapman, Cooper and Miller, 2009). Drawing on elements of organisational sociology, researchers rely on the ontology that social life is governed by the socially embedded norms, values and shared meanings that lead to homogenous practices, irrespective of their relevance for needs and efficiency (DiMaggio and Powell 1983). Accounting is represented as a homogenous practice across the environment because its adopters must draw on a particular institutional configuration in order to gain legitimacy, success, resources and subsequent survival (Covaleski and Dirsmith 1988; Covaleski, Dirsmith and Rittenberg, 2003; Modell 2001). The construction of accounting cannot be viewed as being local in origin in the manner postulated by ANT researchers, as it entails a process of conformity with the institutional environment in which it is contextualised – the macrophysics of accounting.

This tradition of research examines how local accounting initiatives are informed and shaped by widely accepted, idealised accounting practices such as the balanced scorecard, activity-based costing, International Financial Reporting Standards and so on. Benchmarking these institutions, such research seeks to appreciate the macro–origins of the micro-practices of accounting. An early study by Young (1996) illustrates how US accounting standard setters were blinded by the taken-for-granted assumption that financial markets are inherently efficient and that accounting provides relevant information for decision making in such contexts. As a result, the standard setters inadvertently neglected variations and exotic behaviours in such markets. Similarly, in management accounting research Modell (2002) observes that cost allocation practices continue to be heavily regulated by contestable environmental forces despite the observation that their outcomes create significant ambiguities in practice.

Studies around the creation of ambiguities have subsequently encouraged researchers to expand the scope of institutional research to accommodate more dynamic issues stemming from the role of agency in micro-settings as opposed to the one-way system of institutionalisation (see Greenwood, Raynard, Kodeih, Micelotta and Lounsbury, 2011; Kraatz and Block 2008; Lawrence, Leca and Zilber, 2013; Lawrence Suddaby and Leca, 2009). These latter contributions explore how institutional change is possible, given that heterogeneous actors have the capacity to exert their power, culture and politics in any implementation of established norms and practices of accounting. For example, Oliver (1991) argues that actors often exercise a strategic response rather than passive compliance through compromise, avoidance, defiance and manipulation. Other researchers have endorsed an interactive process of institutionalisation coupled with a greater emphasis on interpretation, sense making, translation and negotiation (Dobbin, Sutton, Meyer and Scott 1993; Weick 1995).

Drawing on the North American philosophy of economic pragmatism, Old Institutional Economics, after Veblen and Commons, Burns and Scapens' (2000) institutional theory approach, also addresses the agency issue. They argue that organisational actors have the capacity to shape taken-for-granted routines before they become institutionalised, with their success being dependent on the extent of power that actors hold. Burns (2000) reports that despite the fact that a particular control system was institutionalised, a buffer was successfully created between the managing director and his staff in his case company, culminating in a failure in the implementation of the new system.

Two further concepts have recently been added to the lexicon of institutional theory: institutional field and institutional work. As part of the institutional change agenda, focusing on the institutional field, that is the terrain of conflicts and struggles where heterogeneous actors compete for their stake (Greenwood *et al.* 2011), researchers have explored the issues of interest, power and resistance and concluded that institutionalisation is an indeterminate possibility rather than a structured structure (Malsch and Gendron 2013). In recent research on institutional work researchers have emphasised the primacy of actors' agencies; for example, Lawrence *et al.* (2009) provide a typology of political, technical and cultural work to illustrate how actors are involved in shaping institutions. More recently, Chiwamit, Modell and Yang use this framework to address the question of how variations would "condition the prevalence and efficacy of different institutional work" (Chiwamit *et al.* 2014: 148). To tackle this, they promote the additional concept of field cohesiveness to examine how consistent and tightly coordinated interests permeate performance management system innovations. They illustrate how different types of institutional work are involved in establishing a performance management system, focusing on the issues entailed in maintaining field cohesiveness.

Over time, where accounting researchers attracted to institutional theory initially celebrated stability, conformity and isomorphism – through which accounting was seen as a macrophysical formation at microsites – researchers have moved on to question the taken-for-grantedness of institutions and come to appreciate the agency of social actors against the isomorphic macro-institutional settings. This journey has created a space for more dynamic research manifesting a clear picture of the methodo-philosophical dimension of interpretive accounting research. Methodologically, this research programme now encourages researchers to undertake multi-level analyses: from the analyses of how established norms are mobilised and how practices are formed and established at the micro-level, to macro-level analyses of how practices come about and are prepared to dis-embed. In addition, meso-level analysis has demonstrated how particular institutional fields become sandwiched between the micro and the macro and the significant roles played by forms of embedded agency (Arnold 2009; Chiwamit *et al.* 2014). Beyond the clutches of positivism, such multi-level analyses require the use of both qualitative and quantitative methods through which researchers can justify a form of a methodological (and theoretical) triangulation (Hopper and Major 2007; Lukka and Modell 2010; Modell 2009).

The evolution of institutional theory-based accounting research has provoked an important ontological and epistemological debate about the sociological position of structure and agency, and especially how actors, their actions and agency, can be afforded the necessary epistemological emphasis in the theoretical analysis of accounting practices. On the one hand, institutions as established orders imply a structural orientation encouraging researchers to neglect the receiving end of these structures at the expense of the flood of provisions of globally diffused accounting institutions on the part of the supply side. On the other hand, agency as a cognitive and dynamic order appraises a psychological orientation pointing to heterogeneous issues such as passion, affection and trust. Despite the obvious merits of the extremities, some argue for one against another depending on their philosophical preferences and methodological choices.

In combining the extremities, another form of theoretical triangulation emerges, as in Dillard *et al.* (2004), Hopper and Major (2007) and Malsch and Gendron (2013). In so doing they gesture in the direction of Giddens' structuration theory, which speaks about a structuration of structure and agency where there is a duality or continual inextricable interaction between these two properties, denoting that, like the two sides of the same coin, all social action involves structure, and all structure involves social action (Giddens 1984; for a review of the accounting literature that has been influenced by this framework, see Englund, Gerdin and Burns, 2011). Accounting is now to be understood as what people actually do in the name of accounting as an institution, but this outcome is a result of this duality, hence it is an ongoing action. In other words, when we do accounting, we draw both on our human consciousness and the extant structures in a dialectic manner, thereby effecting the social construction of reality.

Dillard *et al.* (2004) advance an argument for an institutionalisation which runs through three axes of tension: representation with signification, rationality and legitimation, and power with domination. They argue that these actions take place at the political economy level, organisational field level and organisational level, through the processes of institutionalisation, de-institutionalisation and re-institutionalisation. Hence, accounting is not a thing that is unconsciously practised, since it is institutionalised (or de-institutionalised and re-institutionalised) through these processes of reality construction. Hopper and Major (2007) extend this view by incorporating elements of both ANT and labour process theory to illustrate that practice at the organisational level is more complex than is imagined due to inevitable resistance and reaction, as well as accommodation and consent, on the part of actors who are involved in accounting. In a similar vein, Malsch and Gendron (2013) consider how accounting institutions are reproduced when accounting change initiatives are in process. For them, while agents are involved in introducing new accountings through institutional work, the inescapable prevailing institutions exist as habitus, a concept borrowed from Bourdieu to identify the mental and congnitive structures through which people deal with the social world. Malsch and Gendron continue by arguing that accounting as an institution is always subject to a constant interaction between institutional work and habitus, and that accounting is thus a temporal and a situational practice.

4.3 Accounting as practice: the structuration of accounting

In order to understand a number of the unexplored issues entailed in the structuration process more fully and, in turn, to establish a firm practice theory tradition in accounting (Ahrens and Chapman 2006, 2007), some accounting researchers have subsequently turned to the work of the French philosopher Pierre Bourdieu (Bourdieu 1990, 1977; Bourdieu and Wacquant 1992; Grenfell 2008). Bourdieu was influenced by both Marx and Weber. His engagement with Marx influenced him to comprehend that material interest leads to social inequality while Weber led Bourdieu to realise that agents behave according to their internalised disposition within a particular field.

Accounting researchers have extensively borrowed three interrelated concepts from Bourdieu, those of field, capital and habitus. Each can usefully be understood from a methodo-philosophical standpoint, as well as politico-ideologically. The field is conceptualised as a configuration of relationships in a given social space and of the social positions of the occupants in those relationships. As a contestable terrain a field is thus a place for struggles and manoeuvres over resources, stakes and domination. When studying how accounting is practised in a given context, we can recognise that context from the lenses of the field concept and identify the complexities of the struggles and manoeuvres taking place therein. A field could therefore be an organisation or a collaboration of organisations, or an industry, an association or even a government. In this way Kurunmaki (1999) identified healthcare as a field; Neu, Cooper and Everett (2001) consider accounting academia as a field; Alawattage (2011) views gem mining as a field; and Jayasinghe and Wickramasinghe (2011) focus on a rural village as a field. Bourdieu's assertion that "capital does not exist and function except in relation to a field" (Bourdieu and Wacquant 1992: 101) guides accounting researchers to view the positions of occupants in a field from the lenses of capital, which could be either economic, cultural or social/symbolic. Occupants in the field can ascend over the field based on the capital they possess and accumulate. For Bourdieu, habitus represents the mental and cognitive structures through which people deal with the social world; these structures are developed and internalised through life experiences in the field which stimulate the reproduction of the field. Methodologically, this framework of concepts encourages accounting researchers to adopt ethnographic methods that can appreciate that accounting practices are field-specific practices conditioned by the different forms of capital and reproductive elements of habitus and its associated concepts of doxa, illusio and bodily hexis, further concepts Bourdieu uses to explain the dominating structures and practices of a field.

Malsch, Gendron and Grazzini (2011) observe that Bourdieusian accounting research has now evolved into a mature state, focusing on diverse issues and making important theoretical contributions to the interpretive accounting research programme. Several notable contributions merit mention here. Oakes, Townley and Cooper (1998) study how the language that is implicated in the practices of business planning function towards creating symbolic violence as a form of domination in this particular field. Neu, Friesen and Everett (2003) explore the accounting profession as a field, examining how ethical discourses determine capital formation. In doing so, they conceptualise these ethical discourses as cultural goods traded in symbolic markets, thereby providing a justification for the persistence of professional associations. Beyond such formal research settings, Jayasinghe and Wickramasinghe (2011) examine a traditional village and find how development discourses mobilised by policy makers were implicated in the organisation of resource allocation among the poor in the village.

These and further contributions have impacted upon our realisation of what we mean by accounting as a practice. A clear meaning of what is meant by accounting practice now exists: It provides a discursive platform (of accounting discourses) that the occupants in a given field can draw upon for capital formation purposes, as well as to stay in the game. Be it in the field of professional associations, the healthcare sector or a private limited company, accounting is a calculative practice that the social actors in the field engage in differently according to the way that they have embodied the structure of the field through different forms of capital and other reproductive elements such as habitus.

This understanding provides an epistemological and methodological strategy for producing research. The concepts of field, capital and habitus themselves are a methodological solution to the problems emanating from the question of what is to be focused on, what is studied and how it must be known. Accounting researchers are now in a position to think of field studies infused with a clear philosophical meaning of what these constitute and how fields can be studied and known, rather than the more familiar and ambiguous case study research design. As a result of this epistemological clarity, qualitative researchers can now undertake comprehensive analyses of the relations between structure and agency through mobilising Bourdieu's three relational concepts. In addition, the robust nature of the resulting methodo-philosophical platform enables the generation of further insights as a consequence of theoretical triangulation with both ANT and different variants of institutional theory.

5 Weber revisited

The interpretive turn in accounting research that occurred in the late 1970s was in great part a response to the assuredly scientific and positivistic mainstream evident within the North American research community. It drew heavily on Weberian interpretive sociology, which promoted an epistemological strategy through comparing actual practices with the ideal type. Ideal types can be any concept constructed by a researcher on the basis of either an ontological position or a theoretical orientation, leaving empirical verifications to subsequent research. They are heuristic devices that provide a measuring rod and, perhaps, they can be "one-sided exaggerations" (Ritzer 2010: 120). The belief that accounting is a technical practice independent of the social was itself an ideal type held by positivistic researchers, *inter alia* Watts and Zimmerman (1978, 1979). Weber's most renowned example of an ideal type was bureaucracy, with its attribute of formal rationality, which Weber developed in the course of his research on the nineteenth-century German state. Weber left the concept for further investigation in different situations in order to determine empirical deviations as well as any similarities, including his own insights on substantive rationality. Within Weberian interpretive sociology, actors and their relationships play a vital role in interpreting the social reality by benchmarking the rationality in question. The focus is on how actors' views – their moral points of view (be they material and individualist or radical and collectivistic) – are richly rooted in everyday practices (Dyck and Weber 2006).

Returning to the social movement argument advanced at the beginning of the chapter, as a particular social movement, the interpretive turn in accounting research was originally inspired by interpretive sociology, which became the cornerstone of qualitative case studies in accounting research, evident in early work by Colville (1981), Tomkins and Groves (1983a), and Berry *et al.* (1985). This methodological beginning can be viewed as developing in two complementary directions and grew as a significant movement: the politico-ideological and the methodo-philosophical. Accounting researchers working in the politico-ideological tradition initially pursued case study research by exploring actors' views on what is going on, while being prepared to admit insights emanating from a number of Marxian frameworks. The subsequent deployment of neo-Marxist and post-structural perspectives returned research to an epistemological position where interpretations through actors' views were warranted and justified designating that interpretive sociology, by and large, was the governing epistemology within politico-ideological enquiries.

Within the methodo-philosophical tradition, interpretive sociology is more reflexive than within its politico-ideological counterpart. In ANT-informed accounting research actors and their network of relationships are considered to be the research site where researchers should follow the actors. The findings that accounting practices' emergent nature and the difficulties in enacting them without controversies are thus clear outcomes of the use of interpretive sociology. Institutional theory can also be traced back to Weber: Here researchers endeavoured to explore the question of how and why the concepts of rationality and bureaucratic structures are widespread without necessarily being efficient. When researchers subsequently began to explore the roles of agency and power relations, elements of interpretive sociology again were at the forefront. The practice turn in accounting research, which advanced the researchers' understanding about accounting practices in different fields, has also been significantly influenced by interpretive sociology in that interests defined in relation to social actors' own statuses were regarded as internalised dispositions developed through field logics. The challenge to accounting researchers becomes that of understanding how this is so and how it affects accounting in practice.

Despite the impressive cumulative contribution made by those working within the interpretive tradition of accounting research for close to four decades, it should be acknowledged that its early Weberian resonances are no longer immediately obvious at the present time. For the authors, this is a cause for considerable concern. At the present time, there would seem to be a strong case for the increased direct (re)use of Weberian frameworks, as revisiting Weber is likely to have the result of generating a stream of interesting research, either in terms of triangulating it with the current politico-ideological and methodo-philosophical programmes discussed in this chapter, or in terms of exploring how extant substantive rationalities inform different virtues and moral agencies resulting in different (or radical) accounting practices.

This chapter was submitted by the authors with the following title: "The interpretive turn in accounting research."

References

Ahrens, T. and C. S. Chapman (2006). "Theorizing practice in management accounting research," in C. S. Chapman, A. G. Hopwood and M.D. Shields (eds): *The Handbook of Management Accounting Research*, London: Elsevier.

Ahrens, T. and C. S. Chapman (2007). "Management accounting as practice," *Accounting, Organizations and Society*, 32(1–2): 1–27.

Ahrens, T., A. Becker, J. Burns, C. S. Chapman, M. Granlund, M. Habersam, A. Hansen, R. Khalifa, T. Malmi, A. Mennicken, A. Mikes, F. Panozzo, M. Piber, P. Quattrone and T. Scheytt (2008). "The future of interpretive accounting research – A polyphonic debate," *Critical Perspectives on Accounting*, 19(6): 840–66.

Alawattage, C. (2011). "The calculative reproduction of social structures – the field of gem mining in Sri Lanka," *Critical Perspectives on Accounting*, 22(1): 1–19.

Alcouffe, S., N. Berland and Y. Levant (2008). "Actor-networks and the diffusion of management accounting innovations: a comparative study," *Management Accounting Research*, 19(1): 1–17.

Arnold, P. J. (2009). "Institutional perspectives on the internationalization of accounting," in C. S. Chapman, D. Cooper and P. Miller (eds): *Accounting, Organizations, and Institutions*, Oxford: Oxford University Press.

Arrington, C. E. and J. R. Francis (1989). "Letting the chat out of the bag: deconstruction, privilege and accounting research," *Accounting, Organizations and Society*, 14(1–2): 1–28.

Baker, C. R. (2008). "A Habermasian approach to the analysis of globalisation processes," *International Journal of Social Inquiry*, 1(2): 89–112.

Baxter, W. T. and S. Davidson (1977). *Studies in Accounting*. 3e, London: Institute of Chartered Accountants in England and Wales.

Baxter, J. and W. F. Chua (2003). "Alternative management accounting research – whence and whither," *Accounting, Organizations and Society*, 28(2–3): 97–126.

Berger, P. L. and T. Luckmann (1966). *The Social Construction of Reality: A Treatise in the Sociology of Knowledge*, Harmondsworth: Penguin.

Berry, A. J., T. Capps, D. Cooper, P. Ferguson, T. Hopper and E. A. Lowe (1985). "Management control in an area of the NCB: rationales of accounting practices in a public enterprise," *Accounting, Organizations and Society*, 10(1): 3–28.

Boedker, C. and W. F. Chua (2013). "Accounting as an affective technology: a study of circulation, agency and entrancement," *Accounting, Organizations and Society*, 38(4): 245–67.

Bourdieu, P. (1977). *Outline of a Theory of Practice*, Cambridge: Cambridge University Press.

Bourdieu, P. (1990). *The Logic of Practice*, Stanford, CA: Stanford University Press.

Bourdieu, P. and L. Wacquant (1992). *An Invitation to Reflexive Sociology*. Chicago, IL: University of Chicago Press.

Braverman, H. (1974). *Labor and Monopoly Capital: The Degradation of Work in the Twentieth Century*, New York: Monthly Review Press.

Briers, M. and W. F. Chua (2001). "The role of actor-networks and boundary objects in management accounting change: a field study of an implementation of activity-based costing," *Accounting, Organizations and Society*, 26(3): 237–69.

Broadbent, J. and R. Laughlin (1997). "Developing empirical research: an example informed by a Habermasian approach," *Accounting, Auditing and Accountability Journal*, 10(5): 622–49.

Bryer, R. A. (1994). "Why Marx's labour theory is superior to the marginalist theory of value: the case from modern financial reporting," *Critical Perspectives on Accounting*, 5(4): 313–40.

Bryer, R. A. (1999). "Marx and accounting," *Critical Perspectives on Accounting*, 10(5): 683–709.

Bryer, R. A. (2005). "A Marxist accounting history of the British industrial revolution: a review of evidence and suggestions for research," *Accounting, Organizations and Society*, 30(1): 25–65.

Bryer, R. A. (2006). "The genesis of the capitalist farmer: towards a Marxist accounting history of the origins of the English agricultural revolution," *Critical Perspectives on Accounting*, 17(4): 367–97.

Bryer, R. A. (2015). "For Marx: A critique of Jacques Richard's 'The dangerous dynamics of modern capitalism (From static to IFRS' futuristic accounting)'," *Critical Perspectives on Accounting*, 30: 35–43.

Burns, J. (2000). "The dynamics of accounting change: inter-play between new practices, routines, institutions, power and politics," *Accounting, Auditing and Accountability Journal*, 13(5): 566–96.

Burns, J. and R. W. Scapens (2000). "Conceptualizing management accounting change: institutional framework," *Management Accounting Research*, 11(1): 3–25.

Chapman, C. S., D. Cooper and P. Miller (eds) (2009). *Accounting, Organizations and Institutions: Essays in Honour of Anthony Hopwood*, Oxford: Oxford University Press.

Chiwamit, P., S. Modell and C. L. Yang (2014). "The societal relevance of management accounting innovations: economic value added and institutional work in the fields of and Thai state-owned enterprises," *Accounting and Business Research*, 44(2): 144–80.

Chua, W. F. (1986). "Theoretical constructions of and by the real," *Accounting, Organizations and Society*, 11(6): 583–98.

Chua, W. F. (1995). "Experts, networks and inscriptions in the fabrication of accounting images: a story of the representation of three public hospitals," *Accounting, Organizations and Society*, 20(2–3): 111–45.

Chua, W. F. and H. Mahama (2012). "On theory as a 'deliverable' and its relevance in 'policy' arenas," *Critical Perspectives on Accounting*, 23(1): 78–82.

Colville, I. (1981). "Reconstructing 'behavioural accounting'," *Accounting, Organizations and Society*, 6(2): 119–32.

Cooper, C. (1995). "Ideology, hegemony and accounting discourse: a case study of the National Union of Journalists," *Critical Perspectives on Accounting*, 6(3): 175–209.

Cooper, C. (2015). "Accounting for the fictitious: a Marxist contribution to understanding accounting's roles in the financial crisis," *Critical Perspectives on Accounting*, 30: 63–82.

Cooper, C. and Y. Joyce (2013). "Insolvency practice in the field of football," *Accounting, Organizations and Society*, 28(2): 108–29.

Cooper, D. J. (2008). "Is there a future for interpretive accounting research?" *Critical Perspectives On Accounting*, 19(6): 837–39.

Cooper, D. J. and M. J. Sherer. (1984). "The value of corporate accounting reports: arguments for a political economy of accounting," *Accounting, Organizations and Society*, 9(3–4): 207–32.

Covaleski, M. A. and M. W. Dirsmith (1986). "The budgetary process of power and politics," *Accounting, Organizations and Society*, 11(3): 193–214.

Covaleski, M. A. and M. W. Dirsmith (1988). "The use of budgetary symbols in the political arena: an historically informed field study," *Accounting, Organizations and Society*, 13(1): 1–24.

Covaleski, M. A., M. W. Dirsmith and J. E. Michelman (1993). "An institutional theory perspective on the DRG framework, case-mix accounting systems and health-care organizations," *Accounting, Organizations and Society*, 18(1): 65–80.

Covaleski, M. A., M. W. Dirsmith and L. Rittenberg (2003). "Jurisdictional disputes over professional work: the institutionalization of the global knowledge expert," *Accounting, Organizations and Society*, 28(4): 323–55.

Davis, G. F., D. McAdam, W. R. Scott and M. N. Zald (2005). *Social Movements and Organization Theory*, Cambridge: Cambridge University Press.

Dillard, J. F., J. T. Rigsby and C. Goodman (2004). "The making and remaking of organization context: duality and the institutionalization process," *Accounting, Auditing and Accountability Journal*, 17(4): 506–42.

DiMaggio, P. J. and W. W. Powell (1983). "The iron cage revisited: institutional isomorphism and collective rationality in organizational fields," *American Sociological Review*, 48(2): 147–60.

Dobbin, F., J. R. Sutton, J. W. Meyer and R. Scott (1993). "Equal opportunity law and the construction of internal labor markets," *American Journal of Sociology*, 99(2): 396–427.

Dyck, B. and J. M. Weber (2006). "Conventional versus radical moral agents: an exploratory empirical look at Weber's moral-points-of-view and virtues," *Organization Studies*, 27(3): 429–50.

Englund, H., J. Gerdin and J. Burns (2011). "25 Years of Giddens in accounting research: achievements, limitations and the future," *Accounting, Organizations and Society*, 36(8): 494–513.

Foucault, M. (1998). *Aesthetics, Method and Epistemology: Essential Works of Foucault v2.* Translated by R. Hurley, New York: The New Press.

Foucault, M. (2002). *The Essential Works of Michel Foucault, 1954-1984. v3: Power*, London: Penguin.

Giddens, A. (1984). *The Constitution of Society: Outline of the Theory of Structuration*, Cambridge: Polity Press.

Glaser, B. G. and A. L. Strauss (1967). *The Discovery of Grounded Theory: Strategies for Qualitative Research*, London: Weidenfeld & Nicolson.

Gray, R. (2002). "The social accounting project and *Accounting, Organizations and Society*: privileging engagement, imaginings, new accountings and pragmatism over critique?" *Accounting, Organizations and Society*, 27(7): 687–708.

Greenwood, R., M. Raynard, F. Kodeih, E. R. Micelotta and M. Lounsbury (2011). "Institutional complexity and organizational responses," *The Academy of Management Annals*, 5(1): 317–71.

Grenfell, M. (2008). *Pierre Bourdieu: Key Concepts*, Stocksfield: Acumen.

Hopper, T. and P. Armstrong (1991). "Cost accounting, controlling labour and the rise of conglomerates," *Accounting, Organizations and Society*, 16(5–6): 405–38.

Hopper, T. and N. B. Macintosh (1993). "Management accounting as disciplinary practice: the case of ITT under Harold Geneen," *Management Accounting Research*, 4(3): 181–216.

Hopper, T. and M. Major (2007). "Extending institutional analysis through theoretical triangulation: regulation and activity-based costing in Portuguese telecommunications," *European Accounting Review*, 16(1): 59–97.

Hopper, T. and A. Powell (1985). "Making sense of research into the organizational and social aspects of management accounting: a review of its underlying assumptions," *Journal of Management Studies*, 22(5): 429–65.

Hopper, T., J. Storey and H. Willmott (1987). "Accounting for accounting: towards the development of a dialectical view," *Accounting, Organizations and Society*, 12(5): 437–56.

Hopper, T., J. Ashraf, S. Uddin and D. Wickramasinghe (2015). "Social theorisation of accounting: challenges to positive research," in S. Jones (ed.) *The Routledge Companion to Financial Accounting Theory*, London: Routledge.

Hopper, T., D. Cooper, T. Lowe, T. Capps and J. Mouritsen (1986). "Management control and worker resistance in the National Coal Board: financial controls in the labour process," in D. Knights and H. Willmott (eds) *Managing the Labour Process*, Aldershot: Gower Publishing.

Hopwood, A. G. (1974). *Accounting and Human Behaviour*, Englewood Cliffs, NJ: Prentice-Hall Inc.

Hopwood, A. G. (1976). "Editorial," *Accounting, Organizations and Society*, 1(1): 1–4.

Hopwood, A. G. (1983). "On trying to study accounting in the contexts in which it operates," *Accounting, Organizations and Society*, 8(2–3): 287–305.

Jayasinghe, K. and D. Wickramasinghe (2011). "Power over empowerment: encountering development accounting in a Sri Lankan fishing village," *Critical Perspectives on Accounting*, 22(4): 396–414.

Jermier, J. M. (1998). "Introduction – critical perspectives on organizational control," *Administrative Science Quarterly*, 43(2): 235–57.

Johnson, H. T. and R. S. Kaplan (1987). *Relevance Lost: The Rise and Fall of Management Accounting*, Boston, MA: Harvard Business School Press.

Jones, T. C. and D. Dugdale (2002). "The ABC bandwagon and the juggernaut of modernity," *Accounting, Organizations and Society*, 27(1–2): 121–63.

Justesen, L. and J. Mouritsen (2011). "Effects of actor-network theory in accounting research," *Accounting, Auditing and Accountability Journal*, 24(2): 161–94.

Kalberg, S. (19800. "Max Weber's types of rationality: cornerstones for the analysis of rationalization processes in history," *American Journal of Sociology*, 85(5): 1145–79.

Kraatz, M. S. and E. S. Block. (2008). "Organizational implications of institutional pluralism," in R. Greenwood, C. Oliver, R. Suddaby and K. Sahlin (eds) *The SAGE Handbook of Organizational Institutionalism*, London: Sage Publishing.

Kurunmaki, L. (1999). "Professional vs financial capital in the field of health care: struggles for the redistribution of power and control," *Accounting, Organizations and Society*, 24(2): 95–124.

Laughlin, R. C. (1987). "Accounting systems in organisational contexts: a case for critical theory," *Accounting, Organizations and Society*, 12(5): 479–502.

Laughlin, R. C. (1995). "Empirical research in accounting: alternative approaches and a case for 'middle-range' thinking", *Accounting, Auditing and Accountability Journal*, 8(1): 63–87.

Law, J. (1992). "Notes on the theory of the actor-network: ordering, strategy and heterogeneity," *Systems Practice*, 5: 379–93.

Lawrence, T. B., R. Suddaby and B. Leca (2009). *Institutional Work: Actors and Agency in Institutional Studies of Organizations*, Cambridge: Cambridge University Press.

Lawrence, T. B., B. Leca and T. B. Zilber (2013). "Institutional work: current research, new directions and overlooked issues," *Organization Studies*, 34(8): 1023–33.

Lukka, K. and S. Modell (2010). "Validation in interpretive management accounting research," *Accounting, Organizations and Society*, 35(4): 462–77.

Malsch, B. and Y. Gendron (2013). "Re-theorizing change: institutional experimentation and the struggle for domination in the field of public accounting," *Journal of Management Studies*, 50(5): 870–99.

Malsch, B., Y. Gendron and F. Grazzini (2011). "Investigating interdisciplinary translations: the influence of Pierre Bourdieu on accounting literature," *Accounting Auditing and Accountability Journal*, 24(2): 194–229.

Miller, P. (1991). "Accounting innovation beyond the enterprise: problematizing investment decisions and programming economic growth in the U.K. in the 1960s," *Accounting, Organizations and Society*, 16(8): 733–62.

Miller, P. (2006). "Management accounting and sociology," in A. G. Hopwood, C. S. Chapman and M. D. Shields (eds) *The Handbook of Management Accounting Research*, London: Elsevier.

Miller, P. and T. O'Leary (1987). "Accounting and the construction of the governable person," *Accounting, Organizations and Society*, 12(3): 235–65.

Miller, P. and N. Rose (1990). "Governing economic life," *Economy and Society*, 19(1): 1–31.

Modell, S. (2001). "Performance measurement and institutional processes: a study of managerial responses to public sector reform," *Management Accounting Research*, 12(4): 437–64

Modell, S. (2002). "Institutional perspectives on cost allocations: integration and extension," *European Accounting Review*, 11(4): 653–79.

Modell, S. (2009). "In defence of triangulation: a critical realist approach to mixed methods research in management accounting," *Management Accounting Research*, 20(3): 208–21.

Mouritsen, J., H. T. Larsen and P. N. D. Bukh (2001). "Intellectual capital and the 'capable firm': narrating, visualising and numbering for managing knowledge," *Accounting, Organizations and Society*, 26(7–8): 735–62.

Neimark, M. and T. Tinker (1986). "The social construction of management control systems," *Accounting, Organizations and Society*, 11(4–5): 369–95.

Neu, D., D. J. Cooper and J. Everett (2001). "Critical accounting interventions," *Critical Perspectives on Accounting*, 12(6): 735–62.

Neu, D., C. Friesen and J. Everett (2003). "The changing internal market for ethical discourses in the Canadian CA profession," *Accountiong, Auditing and Accountability Journal*, 16(1): 70–103.

Oakes, L. S., B. Townley and D. J. Cooper (1998). "Business planning as pedagogy: language and control in a changing institutional field, *Administrative Science Quarterly*, 43(2): 257–93.

Oliver, C. (1991). "Strategic responses to institutional processes," *Academy of Management Review*, 16(1): 145–79.

Pipan, T. and B. Czarniawska (2010). "How to construct an actor-network: management accounting from idea to practice," *Critical Perspectives on Accounting*, 21(3): 243–51.

Preston, A. M. (2006). "Enabling, enacting and maintaining action at a distance: an historical case study of the role of accounts in the reduction of the Navajo herds," *Accounting, Organizations and Society*, 31(6): 559–78.

Preston, A. M., D. J. Cooper and R. W. Coombs (1992). "Fabricating budgets: a study of the production of management budgeting in the National Health Service," *Accounting, Organizations and Society*, 17(6): 561–93.

Qu, S. Q. and D. J. Cooper (2011). "The role of inscriptions in producing a balanced scorecard," *Accounting, Organizations and Society,* 36(6): 344–62.

Quattrone, P. and T. Hopper (2005). "A 'time-space odyssey': management control systems in two multinational organisations," *Accounting, Organizations and Society,* 30(7–8): 735–64.

Ritzer, G. (2010). *Sociological Theory,* 8e., New York: McGraw-Hill.

Robson, K. (1991). "On the arenas of accounting change: the process of translation," *Accounting, Organizations and Society,* 16(5–6): 547–70.

Robson, K. (1992). "Accounting numbers as 'inscription': action at a distance and the development of accounting," *Accounting, Organizations and Society,* 17(7): 685–708.

Rosenberg, D., C. Tomkins and P. Day (1982). "A work role perspective of accountants in local government service departments," *Accounting, Organizations and Society,* 7(2): 123–37.

Scapens, R. W. (1994). "Never mind the gap: towards an institutional perspective on management accounting practice," *Management Accounting Research,* 5(3–4): 301–21.

Scapens, R. W. and N. B. Macintosh (1996). "Structure and agency in management accounting research: a response to Boland's interpretive act," *Accounting, Organizations and Society,* 21(7–8): 675–90.

Thompson, J. B. (1983). "Rationality and social rationalization: an assessment of Habermas's theory of communicative action," *Sociology,* 17(2): 278–94.

Tinker, A. M. (1980). "Towards a political economy of accounting: an empirical illustration of the Cambridge controversies," *Accounting, Organizations and Society,* 5(1): 147–60.

Tinker, A. M., B. D. Merino and M. D. Neimark (1982). "The normative origins of positive theories: ideology and accounting thought," *Accounting, Organizations and Society,* 7(2): 167–200.

Tomkins, C. (2001). "Interdependencies, trust and information in relationships, alliances and networks," *Accounting, Organizations and Society,* 26(2): 161–91.

Tomkins, C. and R. Groves (1983a). "The everyday accountant and researching his reality," *Accounting, Organizations and Society,* 8(4): 361–74.

Tomkins, C. and R. Groves (1983b). "The everyday accountant and researching his reality: further thoughts," *Accounting, Organizations and Society,* 8(4): 407–15.

Tomkins, C., D. Rosenberg and I. Colville (1980). "The social process of research: some reflections on developing a multi-disciplinary accounting project," *Accounting, Organizations and Society,* 5(2): 247–62.

Uddin, S. and J. Choudhury (2008). "Rationality, traditionalism and the state of corporate governance mechanisms: illustrations from a less-developed country," *Accounting, Auditing and Accountability Journal,* 21(7): 1026–52.

Uddin, S. and T. Hopper (2001). "A Bangladeshi soap opera: privatisation, accounting, and regimes of control in a less developed country," *Accounting, Organizations and Society,* 26(7–8): 643–72.

Watts, R. L. and J. L. Zimmerman (1978). "Towards a positive theory of the determination of accounting standards," *The Accounting Review,* 53(1): 112–34.

Watts, R. L and J. L. Zimmerman (1979). "The demand for and supply of accounting theories: the market for excuses," *The Accounting Review,* 54(2): 273–305.

Weber, M. (1978). *Economy and Society: An Outline of Interpretive Sociology,* Berkeley, CA: University of California Press.

Weick, K. E. (1995). *Sensemaking in Organizations,* London: Sage Publications.

Wickramasinghe, D. and C. Alawattage (2007). *Management Accounting Change: Approaches and Perspectives,* London: Routledge.

Young, J. J. (1996). "Institutional thinking: the case of financial instruments", *Accounting, Organizations and Society,* 21(5): 487–512.

Zald, M. N. (2000). "Ideologically structured action: an enlarged agenda for social movement research," *Mobilization: An International Quarterly,* 5(1): 1–16.

Zald, M. N. and J. D. McCarthy (1979). *The Dynamics of Social Movements: Resource Mobilization, Social Control and Tactics*m, Cambridge, MA: Winthrop.

3

STRUCTURAL MARXISM

Robin Roslender

1 Introduction

The purpose of this chapter is to provide an introduction to two generic ways of seeing within the broader designation of Marxist perspectives that have been widely subscribed to within critical accounting research: the political economy perspective and the labour process perspective. The scope of the chapter has been restricted to the years between the later 1970s, when critical accounting first began to be fashioned by a relatively small number of scholars, and 2000, by which time much of the legacy of this particular genre of critical accounting research had been firmly established. Subsequent contributions from within this tradition are identified elsewhere in this volume. With the benefit of hindsight it is possible to recognise that during the middle 1980s the political economy and labour process perspectives were arguably at their most fashionable, that is for those in the vanguard of driving critical accounting research forward. In this regard they can be understood to have displaced interpretivist perspectives whose heyday was a couple of years previous to this. Equally, the dominance of the former two ways of seeing was soon to be challenged by Critical Theory, a third generic Marxist perspective that has continued to flourish to the present day, and at least as strongly. It is therefore no coincidence that interpretivism and Critical Theory provide the previous and subsequent chapters within this volume. Taken together they framed the greater part of the critical accounting literature in the 1980s, thereafter sharing this role with a growing range of alternative ways of seeing whose critical credentials continue to be hotly debated.

2 Laying down some markers

The term 'structural Marxism' has been adopted to identify those Marxist perspectives that Burrell and Morgan (1979) designate "radical structuralist." They adopt this terminology in order to differentiate these perspectives from those they designate "radical humanist." The latter provide the focus for the following chapter, where the predominant emphasis is on Critical Theory. The distinction between the two designations, while not being arbitrary, is certainly not uncontestable, although this is not the place to debate it. Within the embryonic interdisciplinary accounting research project, Hopper and Powell (1985) and Chua (1986) quickly elect to collapse the distinction, preferring to employ a single radical designation to encompass a range of Marxist perspectives, along with Hopper, Storey and Willmott (1987).

Burrell and Morgan's designations initially draw attention to a distinction between those Marxisms that have the characteristics of objectivism (radical structuralism) and of subjectivism (radical humanism) respectively. At the extreme, objectivist perspectives combine a realist ontology with a positivistic epistemology, exhibiting a penchant for nomothetic theorisation while embracing a determinist stance on human behaviour. Sociologies (and Marxisms) that might be characterised in this way attract the (often) pejorative designation 'scientific'. By contrast, subjectivist perspectives, the notion of which being equally pejorative, reflect a desire to fashion a genuinely 'social' science, being characteristically nominalist, anti-positivistic, ideographic and voluntaristic. Burrell and Morgan understand each of these oppositions in terms of continua, as a consequence of which it becomes possible to envisage actual Marxist perspectives as being more or less objectivist/subjectivist, something they discuss in the relevant chapters of their text.

An alternative opposition, originating in Marxist theory itself, provides further fundamental insights. Structural Marxism is generally more focused on the 'base' while radical humanism is more concerned with the 'superstructure', an opposition that Marx himself first identified in the Preface to *A Contribution to the Critique of Political Economy* (1859). The base can be understood in terms of the economic and social foundations of society, while the superstructure refers to the ideational, or the political and ideological, realm. Base and superstructure are in a continuing dialectical relationship with each other, meaning that while the base determines or shapes the superstructure, at the same time it is shaped by it. As a result, those who embrace a structural Marxist perspective are often more focused on economic and social forces, in contrast to radical humanists whose primary emphasis is on ideational factors.

A further opposition is between the 'young' Marx and the 'old' Marx. In his formative years, Marx's thinking was heavily influenced by the idealist philosophy of Hegel and the young Hegelians, as a consequence of which his writing assumed a strongly philosophical quality. However, as a critical intellectual he constantly sought to scrutinise both the ideas that attracted him and those on offer from other directions. His *Eleven Theses on Feuerbach* (1845) is often recognised as the beginning of his maturation and the move towards historical materialism, which is regarded as finding its fullest expression in the political economy that characterised Marx's writing in later life, particularly *Theories of Surplus Value* (1863) and his three-volume master work *Capital* (1867/1885/1894). It was these later works of Marx, which also evidenced a strong input from his colleague Engels, that were best known from the time of Marx's death in 1883 until the later 1950s. Thereafter the young Marx's writings became more widely available, read and influential, contributing to a significant revitalisation of the Marxist canon that was beginning to look increasingly tired in the ideologically charged atmosphere of the Cold War.

The broader contribution of Burrell and Morgan's text has been overlooked over time by many accounting researchers, commonly being portrayed as a valuable source of insight on research methodology in business and management (including accounting) studies. As its title indicates, however, what the text actually documents for the most part is a quarter of a century of intense research activity within the sociology of organisations, broadly conceived. During this time the formerly predominant functionalist emphasis, in its many forms, was initially assailed by a younger generation of sociologists who argued for the adoption of an interpretivist approach of some description, an episode that was repeated in the early 1980s within interdisciplinary accounting research, as documented in the previous chapter. In both disciplines, they were quickly followed by colleagues who believed that something more radical was now both desirable and possible. What Burrell and Morgan, like Clegg and Dunkerley (1980), provided was a comprehensive sourcebook for anyone within business and management research to draw upon. In the case of those attracted to what Burrell and Morgan designated the sociology of radical change, as opposed to the sociology of regulation, radical humanists argued for embracing a

Marxism that challenged the continuing shortcomings of an evolving capitalist social order, while their structuralist colleagues were persuaded that there was still much to be documented in respect of the continuing persistence of the capitalist social formation. Within accounting research, the discovery of a range of radical change-oriented ways of seeing provided a powerful catalyst to the critical accounting research project that had emerged as one dimension of interdisciplinary accounting research. By the end of the decade the critical accounting project, and structural Marxism and radical humanist perspectives, had both established themselves as the dominant emphases within interdisciplinary accounting research.

3 So what is being critical?

Perhaps the easiest way to begin to answer this question is to recall Marx's famous dictum known as the Eleventh Thesis on Feuerbach:

> The philosophers have only interpreted the world in various ways; the point, however, is to change it.

(Marx, 1845: 286)

In Marx's view it was imperative that those whose studies of society had uncovered or documented the persistence of a disturbing, largely concealed social order embraced the necessity to go beyond simply reporting their insights. Their task was to challenge what existed, the *is*, while simultaneously reformulating their knowledge to identify an alternative social order, the *ought*. There is no pretence here that as students of the social order, researchers must profess a commitment to objectivity or value-freeness. Engaged enquiry, which Marx unequivocally commended, albeit not by name, meant that if what your research revealed was unpalatable to you, it was incumbent on you to make this clear. Equally, it was necessary that you acknowledge that how you framed and organised your enquiries was recognised to be value-laden, as a result of which it was more than likely that you would find what you expected to find. In this respect all knowledge is contestable and must be acknowledged as such. At the same time, however, what provides any insights with credibility is the rigour with which they have been obtained. In this regard, rigour is a more powerful attribute than objectivity, and surely less contestable.

Contestability is a fundamental part of the lexicon of all Marxist theory, arguably no more clearly evident than in the axiom that the capitalist social formation is shaped by the persistence of class struggle. At its simplest this struggle is between the greater part of the population, referred to as the 'working class' or 'proletariat', and the minority ruling class, referred to as the 'capitalist class' or 'bourgeoisie'. Even during his own lifetime Marx recognised that in practice the class structure was more nuanced than this, as a result of which the class struggle was unlikely to resolve itself with any ease. During the 1960s and 1970s the changing nature of the class structure and resultant struggle was extensively documented and debated, not least as an aspect of the turn to a critical sociology. This debate continues to the present, albeit now recognised to be something of a low-return intellectual investment. A range of related, contemporary debates, as they impact on accounting, are explored throughout this volume.

The principal consequence of the existence of the basic division between the working class and the ruling class is that, for the most part, the ways in which the working class both lives and understands or makes sense of their lives is determined by the minority. As Marx observes in *The German Ideology* (1846) "The ideas of the ruling class in every epoch are the ruling ideas." The continued existence of class divisions, and thus the class struggle, is justified by the ruling class. The veracity of this proposition is evident well over a century and a half later in the widespread acceptance of many clearly contestable assertions, such as the views that prevail within accounting and finance that those who are prepared to take financial risks merit any resultant rewards or that labour as a resource should be used efficiently and replaced by machines as necessary. Equally, the argument that the continued increased affluence for the mass of the working classes of Western societies, combined with extensive social mobility, is invoked to demonstrate the naivety of Marxist class analysis. The success with which successive generations of the ruling class, readily assisted by its lieutenants from within the upper echelons of the middle class, some of whom were born into very modest circumstances, have retained control of social formations reflects the strength of that class's hegemonic dominance as Gramsci (1971) designated the prevailing ideational arrangements of capitalism.

Marxist scholarship can be characterised as the systematic unpicking of capitalist hegemony with the objective of demonstration of its myriad failings, misrepresentations and inequities, as a prelude to the formulation of a progressive hegemony that best serves the interests of the mass. This was never envisaged to be an easy nor an automatic process. Unfortunately, it has turned out to be much more difficult than anyone had ever imagined, which is certainly a major reason why the fundamentals of a Marxist critique continue to hold. How deeply embedded capitalist hegemony would become among the masses was clearly underestimated. Beyond this are the practical difficulties entailed in communicating critique to the masses coupled with the vulnerability of those individuals who are prepared to challenge the ruling ideas of any epoch. While it has long been possible to act as critical social commentator and hold down influential positions within society, there is a constant threat of being exposed as a danger to society 'as we know it', while being prepared to accept the rewards that such positions attract, or both. There have always been those individuals of independent means – Marx's own close associate Engels was one such person as were several early figures within the Frankfurt School – but their situation brings with it its own contradictions that are readily exploited by the ruling class as necessary.

In the context of accounting, the foregoing interpretation of what being critical entails, has translated into exploring and exposing how accounting theory and practice has become implicated within the contemporary capitalist hegemony. While there had always been a small group of accounting academics who had sought to promote such an agenda, among whom Abe Briloff is probably the most famous, it was in the later 1970s that a step change in the critical scrutiny of accountancy occurred. At the time, an embryonic critical agenda was bundled together with concerns about the applicability of a positivist methodology for the study of the non-technical aspects of accounting. As a consequence, what subsequently became designated 'critical accounting' was initially progressed as a constituent element of interdisciplinary accounting research, which in the early 1980s exhibited a preference for a generic interpretivist methodology (Roslender and Dillard, 2003). As noted at the outset, Burrell and Morgan's 1979 text was to prove of immense value here, not least by allowing interested researchers to quickly understand the options, including those designated radical structuralist; that is, structural Marxism.

4 An initial road map

In their discussion of radical structuralism, Burrell and Morgan identify "three distinct lines of development" (Burrell and Morgan, 1979: 329). Bearing in mind the corpus of extant literature they sought to review, their categorisation is inevitably somewhat arbitrary. On balance, however, it was, and remains, useful for those encountering Marxist theories for the first time. The first line of development is identified with scholarly formulations of scientific Marxism, sometimes attributed more to Engels than Marx himself, and in large part the philosophy that underpinned the Soviet Union and similar social formations. Within this formulation both historical and dialectical materialism play a central role. An alternative designation is that of political economy, or more precisely the radical reinterpretation of that science in the hands of Marx. It is from this stream of literature that many of the fundamental elements of the lexicon of Marxism in general originate, which is hardly surprising as it was fashioned to demonstrate the pivotal role played within capitalist social formations by the class struggle.

The second line of development was much more contemporary and something of a challenge to the former orthodox Marxism. Burrell and Morgan designate this "Mediterranean Marxism", identifying its key proponents as Althusser and Coletti, both of whom produced nuanced theories of the capitalist social formation that remained true to a commitment to contribute to its demise but sought to address the inherent shortcomings of earlier predominantly economistic analyses. In so doing a younger generation of Marxist academics were also attempting to incorporate a number of insights from the increasingly popular Critical Theory tradition, with its more idealist emphases, into their thinking. Althusser's work, like that of many of his associates and followers, was marked by a high degree of abstractness deployed to provide detailed analyses of the dynamics of the capitalist social formation and its various constituent structures. Largely absent from such work was a reference to people (or subjects) who were instead portrayed as agents populating the structures which provided the principal focus for analysis. In this regard Mediterranean Marxism can be understood in part as a reaction to the subjectivist emphases that could be identified with the humanism of Critical Theory, together with its inherent historicism and idealism.

Conflict theory, the third subset of radical structuralism identified, predates the rise of Critical Theory and Mediterranean Marxism by a few years. One way to understand its place is as a first response by a younger generation of sociologists worried by the hitherto disguised conservatism of the dominant structural functional paradigm of the 1950s. No longer prepared to accept the explanations of their older colleagues, many younger sociologists found interesting ideas within the Marxist literature that allowed them to develop more challenging accounts of their societies. C. W. Mills was probably atypical in the sense of being a highly politicised commentator who systematically exposed the failings of his native United States. At the same time, in common with many of his contemporaries, he also derived many insights from the writings of Weber, which had the result of moderating the tone of their critiques and commentaries. Ultimately conflict sociology came to be regarded as an exemplar of an *un*critical sociology, which needed to be rejected in favour of a tradition more informed by the newly encountered Marxist writings identified as 'radical structuralism' and 'radical humanism'.

In chapter 11 of their text Burrell and Morgan identify Braverman's seminal 1974 study, entitled *Labor and Monopoly Capital*, as an influential example of a radical structuralist contribution to the study of organisations. Few would disagree that Braverman significantly changed the way in which sociologists viewed work, almost overnight. Braverman sought to address an absence within Baran and Sweezy's 1966 political economy of monopoly capitalism, viewing work as a critical element of the capitalist mode of production that he designated the 'labour process'. Braverman argued that throughout the twentieth century it is possible to recognise the progressive deskilling of work, as a result of which the majority of employees are unable to derive much satisfaction from their employments. As well as providing a rationale for reducing the wages of employees, this process is designed to ensure that control of the workers largely resides with those in managerial positions, via the systematic divorce of conception from execution. This is asserted to be the principal objective of the degradation of work in the twentieth century, the subtitle of Braverman's text. In his view the spread of the labour process to white-collar jobs is already well underway, while the passage of time necessitates its continued extension to more and more providers of mental as opposed to manual labour. In this way, Braverman's thesis complements the writings on the new working class that had emanated from French Marxist industrial sociologists during the 1960s (e.g. Mallet, 1963; Gorz, 1964), as well as the subsequent theoretical analyses of the contemporary class structure advanced by Poulantzas (1973) and Carchedi (1977).

Irrespective of its many, inevitable, shortcomings, to some extent mitigated by the ambition that underpinned the production of the text itself, Burrell and Morgan offered those interested in employing radical or Marxist perspectives in their studies of accounting theory and practice a highly valuable foundation on which to build. Without it, it is difficult to imagine that a generic critical accounting project, as this has been hitherto characterised in this chapter, would have become so dominant among the interdisciplinary accounting research community by the later 1980s. The following pages seek to document this rise to dominance.

5 Encountering political economy

The origins of critical accounting research, as it was to evolve during the 1980s, lie with an initially small group of UK accounting academics, who viewed the University of Sheffield as their intellectual home. In retrospect, an early contribution from Lowe and Tinker published in 1977 can be identified as heralding the arrival of a putative Marxist perspective on the theory and practice of accounting. After several years of exploration of the interface between accounting and organisations and society, which inevitably resulted in an increasing encounter with (critical) sociology, Lowe and Tinker's paper identifies the urgent need to begin to explore and expose the ideological nature of much accounting and those who practice it. For them the prevailing methodology of accounting is characterised by an "ideological "blindness" based on an acceptance of the philosophy of pluralism. What is now required is a process of intellectual emancipation, the objective of which will be the construction of a more socially progressive accounting praxis.

A little over two years later Tinker published a paper in which political economy is argued to promise the means to the latter praxis. Although Tinker talks of "classical" political economy, while omitting any reference to Marx, at various points in the paper the alternative analysis that political economy fashions is readily recognisable as being extensively infused with the terminology of Marxist theory. The power of a political economy perspective is demonstrated in the Delco case study that provides the centrepiece of the paper, as an empirical illustration of the Cambridge Controversies alluded to in the paper's title (Tinker, 1980). In the accompanying commentary, Cooper (1980) initially invites Tinker to be more expansive in his critique of marginalist economics and to provide further evidence in relation to the Delco case study. Having done so, he returns the focus to the 'accounting as ideology' theme asserted by Lowe and Tinker (1977). In Cooper's view:

> Accounting may be viewed as a means of sustaining and legitimizing the current social, economic and political arrangements. This view treats accounting as a form of ideology [false consciousness]; although accounting prescriptions may suggest the need for changes at the margin, the basic structure of the status quo is regarded as desirable.
>
> *(Cooper, 1980: 164)*

The remainder of Cooper's commentary is a plea for more of his (and Tinker's) accounting academic colleagues to focus their research endeavours towards questioning what has traditionally been taken for granted, including the neoclassical marginalist economic foundations of accounting, as a crucial prerequisite of any broader critical accounting project. In the absence of such an endeavour, accounting is destined to remain an ideologically informed practice and those who pursue it ideologists, to the detriment of the mass of society.

The next contribution to the case for embracing a political economy of accounting perspective comes in a third paper published by Tinker, co-authored with Merino and Neimark, which explores the disguised normative origins of value-free positive theories (Tinker, Merino and Neimark, 1982). Although it was possible to identify growing support for a more social-scientifically informed accounting research tradition in the guise of inter-disciplinary accounting (Roslender and Dillard, 2003; Roslender, 2015), by the early 1980s positive accounting theory was rapidly emerging as the dominant paradigm, particularly in North America (Watts and Zimmerman, 1986). What better target to choose to demonstrate the need to pursue a more critical perspective? In a closely argued contribution that reprises elements of Tinker's earlier critique of marginalism, Tinker *et al.* identify the conservative underpinnings of positive accounting theory, its resultant ideological attributes and (ironic) normative inclinations (see also Christenson's [1983] mainstream critique of positive account-ing). By contrast, Cooper (1983) elects to broaden out the scope of any critical accounting perspective, by drawing attention to insights provided in Burrell and Morgan's (1979) study of the contribution of contemporary sociological analysis to progressing organisational analysis. In doing so he demonstrates the limitations of the well-intentioned importation of sociologi-cal and related insights into recent research, essentially the interpretivist turn, and particularly their inability to break free from the constraints of the sociology of regulation as identified by Burrell and Morgan.

Together with Sherer, in 1984 Cooper documents the superior merits of a political economy approach, over private-value and social-value approaches, for the study of accounting within the economic, social and political environment in which it is practised, initially identifying it with Tinker (1980) along with Burchell, Clubb, Hopwood, Hughes and Nahapiet (1980). After identifying the principal characteristics of a political economy approach, Cooper and Sherer discuss the three "imperatives" of such an approach. The first of these is to be "explicitly norma-tive," which they identify as entailing the rejection of traditional pretensions of value neutral-ity. Having embraced the precepts of Marxist political economy it is simply inappropriate to then proclaim objectivity – instead as an engaged researcher it is necessary to make your values (political position) evident. The second imperative is to be "descriptive." A seemingly unfortu-nate choice of terminology is reinforced as Cooper and Sherer admit some sympathy for calls to develop a "positive" approach to accounting research, as in the case of Watts and Zimmerman (1978). However, they quickly provide the necessary corrective by means of a reference to the study of accounting in action:

> Such studies would attempt to describe and interpret the behaviour of accounting and accountants in the context of the institutions, social and political structures and cultural values of the society in which they are historically located.
>
> *(Cooper and Sherer, 1984: 221)*

The third imperative is to be "critical," which for Cooper and Sherer entails actively seek-ing to demonstrate the unsavoury, inequitable, contestable form that accounting theory and practice currently assumes. Coupled with this is the challenge to fashion not only alternative understandings of accounting but to strive to develop alternative accounting practices that are more aligned with a differently structured society. Or put simply, being critical when pursuing accounting research seeks to promote the construction of a better society rather than simply a better accounting practice.

It is possible to identify three contributions from 1985 that capture the progress the criti-cal accounting project had made during the previous five years. Tinker's *Paper Prophets: A Social*

Critique of Accounting is the first critical accounting monograph, combining a more refined statement of the precepts of the political economy perspective on accounting with a range of empirical materials that communicate the reasons why it is necessary to embrace a radical critical perspective on accounting in action. In parallel, Berry, Capps, Cooper, Ferguson, Hopper and Lowe's 1985 seminal case study of the changing nature of the management control system within the UK coal industry, instigated at the behest of a right-wing Conservative government committed to dismantling the power of the working class and its trade unions, affirms the promise of a critical perspective previously identified by two of its co-authors, Lowe and Cooper (see also Hopper, Cooper, Lowe, Capps and Mouritsen, 1986; Berry 1988; Capps, Hopper, Mouritsen, Cooper and Lowe, 1989). A third paper, by Ogden and Bougen (1985), provides a radical perspective on the continuing debate surrounding the disclosure of accounting information to trade unions. The authors frame their paper in terms of the continuing conflict between capital and labour, deploying Braverman's 1974 thesis on the progressive deskilling of labour as a means of securing control of the workplace. These structural processes ensure that any accounting information that management elects to disclose to trade unions is, by definition, ideologically biased against labour and thereby designed to reproduce the prevailing social organisation of work that characterises the capitalist social formation.

6 Exploring the labour process perspective (and beyond)

Many of the still embryonic critical accounting research fraternity came together at the first Interdisciplinary Perspectives on Accounting (IPA) conference, held in Manchester in July 1985. A paper presented at this conference by Hopper, Storey and Willmott, and subsequently published in 1987 in *Accounting, Organizations and Society* (*AOS*), commends the adoption of a labour process perspective in the study of accounting practice (Hopper *et al.*, 1987). The labour process perspective is identified as an alternative to both conventional (functionalist) and naturalistic perspectives. Its relationship with a political economy perspective is not discussed, although it is clear that the two perspectives are recognised to share similar origins and emphases. The labour process perspective, after Braverman, places a significant focus on work and the organisation as the context for work, as a consequence of which Hopper *et al.* are readily able to establish the link between the labour process perspective and management accounting research (as in the table in Hopper *et al.*, 1987: 446). In this regard, and in retrospect, it becomes possible to view the labour process perspective, within its organisational focus, as complementing the more society-oriented political economy perspective.

A second paper presented at the conference reinforces the case for embracing labour process thinking. Armstrong, an industrial sociologist, utilises a number of elements of the labour process literature to underpin an exploration of the rise (and persistence) of accounting controls within British companies (Armstrong, 1987). The increasing credibility accorded to the audit profession from the mid-nineteenth century resulted in the broader accounting profession being in a position to install its own preferred modes of internal control within enterprises following the First World War. Although these largely originated in the management accounting sub-discipline, they were successfully mastered and implemented by those traditionally more familiar with financial accounting and reporting. Thereafter the profession was well positioned to persuade shareholders of the superiority of its prospectus of control technologies, and thereby ensuring a continuing pre-eminence within British management hierarchies (see also Armstrong, 1984, 1985, 1986). Armstrong (1989) documents the ways in which the operation of a direct labour reporting system in a small footwear factory, with a predominantly female workforce, is made to serve the interests of senior management at the expense of both shop-floor workers and their own supervisors. Consistent with the precepts of labour process theory, as previously rehearsed in the work of Hopper *et al.* (1987), Armstrong highlights how senior management successfully delegate blame for excessive expenditure on labour costs to their subordinates as a result of the manner in which they have to elected construct the local accounting control system.

Knights and Collinson's IPA paper, published in 1987 alongside those of Hopper *et al.* and Armstrong, reinforces the case for exploring what a labour process perspective has to offer critical accounting researchers. It differs significantly from the other two contributions, however, commending a variant of "post-Braverman labour process literature" that seeks to extend its fundamental theoretical framework by incorporating elements of Foucault's power-knowledge perspective, providing a way of seeing that is particularly valuable in understanding how accounting can readily be deployed in disciplining the shop floor. Knights and Collinson were not alone in representing Foucault as sharing the radical inclinations associated with both political economy and labour process theory, as well as Critical Theory. Chua (1986) famously affirms this position in her highly influential paper in *The Accounting Review*. Conversely, early Foucault-informed papers including those by Burchell, Clubb and Hopwood (1985), Loft (1986) and Miller and O'Leary (1987) were recognisable as being less radically oriented, and in retrospect provided a perceptive understanding of Foucault's broader contribution to the interdisciplinary perspectives on the accounting research tradition, as opposed to critical accounting research (Roslender and Dillard, 2003).

A further cluster of papers published in the mid-1980s introduced prospective critical accounting researchers to a broader Marxist literature. Neimark and Tinker (1986) drew on key contributions from a range of Marxist writers, including Baran and Sweezy, Habermas, Mandel and Ollman, to develop a dialectical approach to management control. The following year they published a political economy–based study of female exploitation in the context of General Motors' annual reporting practices in the six decades up until 1976 (Tinker and Neimark, 1987). In parallel Lehman and Tinker (1987) advance a provocative thesis on the ideological underpinnings, and thus conditions and consequences, of a range of accounting and kindred outputs. A further literature is embraced, including contributions from influential Marxist writers such as Adorno, Althusser, Gramsci and Stuart Hall, alongside post-Marxists such as Barthes, Derrida and Laclau. Several of Gramsci's insights are also explored in Richardson's (1987) paper, which provides a concise comparison of the different ways in which the structural-functionalist, social constructionist and hegemonic perspectives view legitimation. For Richardson, the identification of accounting as a legitimating institution constitutes one of the key insights to be found in the extant critical accounting literature.

Confirmation of the breadth and robustness of the theoretical underpinnings of the rapidly evolving critical accounting literature was evident in the collection of papers, published in 1990 as *Critical Accounts: Reorientating Accounting Research,* most of which were presented at the IPA in 1985, and edited by Cooper and Hopper. Contributions informed by structural Marxist writing are much in evidence, alongside others that draw on the work of Foucault, Giddens and Habermas. In the final section of the collection, several papers explore the place of the accounting profession within the class structure as it manifests itself within capitalist corporations, an issue that had been left largely implicit during much of the previous decade despite falling within the ambit of both political economy and labour process theory. Roslender (1990), drawing on a number of structural Marxist accounts of the evolving class structure of late capitalism, offers a further range of insights on the subject, which in turn are scrutinised in Hopper's accompanying reply (Hopper, 1990).

7 The end of an era

Throughout the 1980s *AOS* had been by far the principal outlet for critical accounting work. With the benefit of hindsight, however, it is possible to see that as the decade drew to a close critical accounting contributions, as these have been identified in the previous pages, became much less evident in the journal. During 1988 only Tinker's review of Panglossian accounting theories sought to continue in the critical genre, with Richardson (1989) performing the same service the following year. In 1990 there was to be no return to prior practice, although in 1991 there were indications that normal service might be being resumed. In the first issue, Armstrong (1991) develops a provocative reinterpretation of the agency problematic beloved of functional-ist (positivist) accounting researchers. Using a conceptual framework that draws extensively on previous contributions from both political economy and labour process perspectives, Armstrong presents a detailed analysis that demonstrates that the generic problem of agency is the result of the contradictions embedded within the capitalist agency relationship itself, which in turn ensure that such problems cannot ever be resolved within capitalist society. In an earlier paper Armstrong (1989) had argued that it is these contradictions that result in both the installation of monitoring within the ranks of managerial employees and the pursuit of deskilling wherever feasible, telling insights that cannot be had from simply conceptualising managerial work as a(nother) labour process.

The 1991 double issue five/six was devoted to a collection of papers initially presented at the IPA in 1988, now badged as "The new accounting history" (Miller *et al.*, 1991). Included is a paper jointly written by the two principal stalwarts of the labour process perspective, Hopper and Armstrong (1991), who take as their subject matter the continued reconstruction of cost accounting as a means to retain control of labour within organisations. The paper provides an alternative analysis of the history of management accounting to that presented in Johnson and Kaplan's seminal 1987 study of that discipline's fortunes. In so doing, Hopper and Armstrong consistently emphasise the need to develop accounting technologies that promise to deliver the continued control of labour within the corporation, suggesting that the new management accounting technologies that commentators like Johnson and Kaplan urge the profession to develop will inevitably be shaped by similar imperatives. Central to Hopper and Armstrong's thesis is the way in which the pursuit of increased efficiencies within the labour process disguises the resultant increased effort levels on the part of labour within the evolving control process. Wardell and Weisenfeld (1991) provide a range of historical details pertinent to Hopper and Armstrong's arguments from a broadly labour process perspective after Buroway *et al.*, as well as Braverman. By contrast, a second paper in the new accounting history collection (Bryer, 1991) employs Cooper and Sherer's political economy of accounting approach to frame a study of the questionable role of accounting within the UK "railway mania" episode of 1845.

In the year's final issue, Moore (1991) presents a powerful challenge to critical and radical accounting researchers. A student of neither discipline, rather a literary theorist, Moore reviews and critiques a decade of critical accounting scholarship invoking the progress identified with critical legal studies, which for Moore only predates critical accounting by several years, as a benchmark. In the course of the paper Moore offers a range of interesting observations, each of which clearly merits detailed scrutiny. He is unimpressed by critical accounting's lack of a radical presence within both the discipline and its complementary practices, something that he believes threatens to undermine its future prospects, suggesting that it promises to become "an interest-ing sidelight, but never a rich alternative, to the state of affairs in accounting today" (Moore, 1991: 770). What is particularly noticeable in Moore's review of the extant literature of critical accounting is that it appears skewed towards contributions that do not fit the structural Marxist designation but instead privilege postmodern and post-structuralist thinking. Moore himself is at home with such work but nevertheless seems to appreciate that this may also have the consequence of compromising the fashioning of a genuinely radical critical accounting project.

The latter genre of contributions was by now increasingly more visible within the pages of *AOS*, a trend that has continued to the present. At the same time, contributions underpinned by structural Marxism become less evident within the journal, although never disappearing completely even to the present day. Between 1992 and 1995 arguably only a single paper extended the portfolio of structural Marxist thinking within accounting: Arnold and Hammond's study of the ideological role that accounting and social disclosure played in the debates about South African divestment activities in the United States during the previous two decades (Arnold and Hammond, 1994). Unsurprisingly, the specific focus on ideology is more consistent with a political economy perspective than labour process thinking. At the same time the emphases evident throughout the paper readily distinguish this appropriation of the concept of ideology from those associated with its use by critical accounting researchers working within the Critical Theory tradition, which by this time had begun to significantly outstrip structural Marxist contributions.

8 The emergence of *Critical Perspectives on Accounting*

The establishment of a new journal, *Critical Perspectives on Accounting* (*CPA*), in 1990 meant that critical accountants now had a further highly credible vehicle for publishing their work. *CPA* provided a space in which there would be significantly less competition for visibility with contributions underpinned by the increasingly ascendant postmodern and post-structural perspectives, although such work was never to be proscribed within its pages. *Advances in Public Interest Accounting* had previously published two collections of critical work in 1986 and 1987, in the more liberal US tradition of 'public interest accounting'. From the outset, the *Accounting, Auditing and Accountability Journal*, founded in 1988, indicated a willingness to contribute to the spread of critical perspectives, albeit as one constituent of a broad-range accounting studies portfolio.

Jointly edited by Cooper and Tinker, *CPA* immediately became *the* critical accounting journal, the place where 'new' critical/radical thinking underpinned by the philosophy of praxis, be it theoretical or empirical in emphasis, was to be made accessible to the accounting research community. At the same time, *CPA* was something of an anachronism, committed to pursuing a pathway that was arguably more fashionable 15 years earlier. In this respect, *AOS* was much more à la mode with its growing emphasis on postcritical contributions. For these reasons, the pages of *CPA* were the place where structural Marxist writing was more likely to flourish, which they did alongside many other different ways of seeing, including Critical Theory together with some that had previously been embraced by contributors to *Advances in Public Interest Accounting*.

The inaugural issue includes Neimark's 1990 provocative assault on the critical credentials of the growing corpus of contributions to the critical accounting canon informed by postmodern philosophy. Those reliant on the work of Foucault are subjected to particular attention, although it is evident that several further 'popular' postmodern thinkers are viewed by Neimark as offering a similar contestable genre of 'critical' insights. It is not that postmodern philosophy lacks any capacity to provide incisive commentaries on the theory and practice of accounting and much beyond. Neimark recognises that they have played their part in demystifying the social world alongside Marxist thinking during the previous quarter of a century. The issue is whether postmodern philosophy (and by extension post-structuralism) seeks to realise the intentions of the philosophy of praxis as that is understood within Marxist thought, and which had come increasingly to the fore in the previous decade of critical accounting work, whether informed by structural Marxism or by Critical Theory. Neimark concludes her paper with the powerful reminder:

> But as Marx noted long ago, the role of philosophy is not to describe the world but to change it. And the aspirations of critical accountants should be no less.
>
> *(Neimark, 1990: 110)*

Inevitably, several years later *CPA* devoted a special issue to "Accounting and Praxis: Marx after Foucault," in which Grey (1994) and Hoskin (1994) offer highly nuanced responses to Neimark's critique. These are designed to promote a healthy rapprochement between the two now dominant standpoints within critical accounting, something also evident in Armstrong's 1994 paper. Given Armstrong's labour process theory credentials, it is no surprise that, on balance, he reasserts the primacy of Marxist over Foucauldian thinking for the critical accounting project. Neimark (1994) is accorded the final say, at least for the moment. In essence she elaborates on her previous conclusion, that irrespective of the considerable merits of Foucauldian and kindred accounting research oeuvres, the purposeful decoupling of theory from practice that is widely evident therein is not consistent with critical accounting praxis as Neimark understands and commends it. The ironic acknowledgement about being "a Material Girl," is a further reaffirmation that it is Marxist theory, and within it structural Marxism, that promises the most purchase on the challenge of understanding the topography of late twentieth-century capitalism (and within it accounting) with the expressed intent to seek to change in an effort to make it serve the interests of the majority rather than those of the minority.

In retrospect, it is possible to see that during the 1980s most of the key elements of structural Marxism were set out by its principal accounting advocates in the papers reviewed in the previous pages. As a consequence, the pages of *CPA* were largely taken up by contributions that sought to employ these ideas in fashioning critical accounts rather than rehearsing the details of relatively obscure Marxist theoreticians. Such an observation might feasibly be levelled at some of those more attracted to postmodern and post-structural thinking at this time, however. Occasionally a paper would appear that, intentionally or otherwise, served to remind readers of the legacy provided by structural Marxism. Neu (1992) sets out the case for using a political economy approach to provide a further set of insights on the functionality or otherwise of the regulatory process underpinning new stock issues. By framing his case study of PETCO in this manner, Neu is able to document the manner in which the prevailing arrangements for new stock issues may privilege the interests of owner-managers at the expense of the broader pool of potential investors, thereby posing questions about the taken-for-granted notion of market efficiency. Hooks and Moon (1993) also embrace a political economy perspective in their study of the evolution of the Management Discussion and Analysis extension to the corporate reporting approach. In so doing they document the continuing conflicts and tensions that exist between the various participants within this particular regulatory space, concluding that the interests of the corporations seem to prevail both directly and as a consequence of the regulatory agencies themselves representing the public interest in ways that reinforce the power of the corporations.

A new pathway within the generic political economy of accounting perspective is evident in the *CPA* paper by Williams *et al.* (1994a). Their approach is characterised by the derivation of an alternative set of accounting information emphasising the crucial contribution that labour continues to make to the global capital accumulation process (see also Williams *et al.*, 1994b, 1995). Williams *et al.* take issue with Johnson's view that the key to restoring US competitiveness lies with the widespread adoption of Total Quality Management rather than a reformed managerial accounting discipline, as commended in his seminal 1987 critique co-authored with

Kaplan, subsequently the leading figure in the fashioning of the new management accounting (Johnson, 1992, 1994). For Williams *et al.* narratives of this sort serve to disguise an increasingly global economic reality in which competitiveness continues to be accomplished by means of the payment of low wages and the successful exploitation of labour, using recent comparative data from the car industry to document their argument. Three years later Shaoul (1997) employs a variation of Williams *et al.*'s approach to provide a compelling alternative, critical financial analysis of the economic performance of the recently privatised water industry in England and Wales (see also Shaoul, 1998).

Yuthas and Tinker (1994) also take issue with Johnson's "relevance regained" arguments, identifying a range of crucial silences within it: the growth of cheap imported labour within the United States; ever cheaper sources of labour in the Pacific Rim and former communist countries; the rapidly evolving global capital market; and the fashioning of readily portable production technologies. They conclude by suggesting that Johnson (and Kaplan) provide the Clinton administration with the same means to disguise the fundamental contradictions that characterise late capitalism that Jensen and Meckling gifted the earlier Reagan, Bush and Thatcher administrations. The challenge to critical accounting research is to ensure that the systematic demystification of these economic contradictions continues to expand.

Despite being introduced to critical accounting researchers in the later 1980s, the value of Gramsci's work to developing a critical perspective on accounting was explored in only a relatively limited way in the following years. This lacuna was partially addressed in Cooper's 1995 case study of the power struggle that had occurred in the UK National Union of Journalists. Gramsci's concept of hegemony (or hegemonic control) is commended for its capacity to transcend the base/superstructure distinction within Marxist theory, drawing attention to the existence of a dialectical relationship between them. This relationship results in accounting as an ideology impacting on the base or economic foundations of society that simultaneously impact upon accounting, thereby contributing to the reproduction of the status quo, *inter alia* the persistence of a state that seeks to perpetuate the interests of the ruling capitalist class.

The following year, Roslender (1996) returns to the conditions of contemporary accounting labour that he had previously identified as meriting close enquiry by critical accounting researchers (Roslender, 1990). Combining elements from political economy and labour process theory he draws attention to the increasingly hierarchical nature of much accounting work within large organisations and the concomitant deskilling of such labour, resulting in a progressive proletarianisation within the accounting profession, a process that had previously been evident within comparable occupational groups. This view is recognised to be at odds with the way in which many critical accounting researchers implicitly think about practitioners. In the course of pursuing research on accounting labour Roslender believes that critical accountants may find a means of connecting with their colleagues, which in turn might catalyse the promotion of the broader critical accounting project.

It was probably inevitable that as the 1990s drew to a close it was not too difficult to recognise that *AOS* was largely populated with contributions that had very little concern with promoting the philosophy of praxis while publication within *CPA* implied such a commitment to be *sine qua non*. Undoubtedly a damaging state of affairs, not a great deal has changed in the intervening years. It is therefore something of a contradiction that three of the most insightful papers published at the end of the period under scrutiny in this chapter, which might be identified as being underpinned by structural Marxist thinking, are to be found within the pages of *AOS*.

After several years of relative quiet, the Marx versus Foucault debate reignited in 1998 with the publication of a pair of critiques of Miller and O'Leary's 1994 study of the role that managerial accounting technologies, among others, had played in the development of Caterpillar's Plant

With a Future (PWAF) programme at its Decatur plant in Illinois. Arnold (1998) acknowledges the many insights provided by contributions to the literature of critical accounting informed by postmodern and post-structuralist thinking in the previous decade but expresses a concern that these invariably downplay the relevance of the broader context in which accounting and kindred practices occur. In the case of Miller and O'Leary's Caterpillar study, Arnold observes that they left the research site at just about the same time as an eight-year period of harmonious industrial relations came to an abrupt end, following the introduction of "a surprisingly aggressive anti-union stance" (Arnold, 1998: 667). It was during this eight-year period that the PWAF initiative was fashioned, delivering a set of workplace experiences, encapsulated in the term 'economic citizenship', which even those committed to the deployment of a historical materialist (Marxist) framework might, albeit with some caution, commend to be implemented more broadly. However, the return to a more familiar mode of labour–capital conflict in 1991, and a lengthy strike that was broken in April 1992 when Caterpillar threatened the permanent replacement of employees, serves to remind critical accounting researchers of the 'limits' of postmodern and post-structuralist ways of seeing. The promise of a structural Marxist perspective is concisely articulated in the following terms:

> Absent from [Miller and O'Leary's] account of the role of accounting and other managerial expertise in the construction of subjectivity is any problematization of those concerns that constitute the core of historical materialism: class, ideology, material interests, political economy, social structure, relations of production. Even capitalism is taken for granted as the history of industrial production is rewritten in the vocabulary and theories of postmodernism.
>
> *(Arnold, 1998: 682)*

In a subsequent *CPA* paper, Arnold (1999) provides a complementary critique of the underpinnings of the array of new manufacturing regimes evident in post-Japan US industry, focusing on the various new management accounting techniques that have been pressed into service by capital, rather than how these might (not) be scrutinised by critical accounting researchers.

Froud, Williams, Haslam, Johal and Williams (1998) take Miller and O' Leary to task in two ways. Initially they scrutinise the manner in which Miller and O'Leary engage with the narrative advanced by Decatur's management in respect of the PWAF initiative, an approach significantly at odds with that embraced in the work of Arnold (1998, 1999). Froud *et al.* identify that while Miller and O'Leary clearly succeed in distancing and dissociating themselves from this narrative, at the same time they avoid constructing a counter-narrative that would see them actually abandoning a managerialist standpoint in favour of something more politically engaged. This is implied to constitute the appeal of postmodern enquiry for many who commend it. In the second half of their paper, Froud et *al.* explore four decades of economic activity at Decatur using the alternative framework of accounting analysis identified earlier. They are able to provide a further story to complement those of both Miller and O'Leary, and Arnold, to the effect that in developing the PWAF Caterpillar significantly overcommitted itself, albeit to some extent for reasons that might be adjudged either beyond their control and/or arguably well intentioned, the upshot of which was that by 1991 it was recognised that the only way in which the company might continue to exist, let alone generate significant profits, was to attack the financial settlement that it had previously gifted to its workforce, with all its attendant rhetoric. In no sense are Froud *et al.* to be regarded as apologists for Caterpillar's senior management – in their view, it is always labour that must bear the cost of capital's mistakes.

Finally, a powerful reminder of the insights that might be gained by adopting a labour process perspective in accounting research is evident in Cooper and Taylor's 2000 paper documenting the changing working practices of accounting clerks from the mid-nineteenth century through to the end of the twentieth century. They observe that hitherto this largely unresearched section of accounting labour can be shown to have been subjected to systematic and progressive deskilling in accordance with Braverman's thesis on the degradation of labour. As a consequence, the great majority of those who now occupy the previously prestigious role of "bookkeeper" find themselves engaged in work that is highly repetitive and unskilled, relatively poorly paid and lacking in much of a prospect of promotion. Such roles are increasingly likely to be filled by young women, the "Ms Taylor" referred to in the paper's title. The paper concludes with the suggestion that the experiences of accounting clerks may soon become a feature of the lives of a growing proportion of professionally qualified accountants (see Roslender 1990, 1996). There are already indications that some large organisations are enthusiastic about outsourcing the activities of their accounting and finance functions, while elsewhere in the industry a distinction is evolving between those who are attracted to the development of entrepreneurial skills rather than simply contenting themselves with the utilisation of hard-earned technical competences. The prospect of a two-tier accounting profession, with its attendant negativities, is possibly rather closer than many aspiring accounting professionals might imagine or indeed wish (see also Cooper, 1997).

9 Never forget where we are coming from

In a recent paper Lukka and Vinnari (2014) explore the distinction between what they term "method" theories and "domain" theories (see also Lukka, 2005). The former are those theoretical frameworks that accounting researchers have embraced in order to frame their research, particularly their empirical research. Such theoretical frameworks have previously been termed "framing" theories by Baxter and Chua (2003, 2005). By contrast, domain theories are those explanations and understandings that have accrued as a result of research activity. Every method or framing theory informs what researchers 'see', as a consequence of which the resultant stock of understandings does not assume a neat, well-organised compendium that is readily accessible to the accounting research community. All knowledge is therefore partial in the sense that its various constituent elements reflect both the method and domain theories that inform and underpin them. The challenge for the individual researcher is to be able to make sense of the resultant stock of disorganised knowledges as a prerequisite to engaging in further enquiries that will have the inevitable consequence of further complicating what is known.

The partiality attribute is doubly significant in the context of structural and critical Marxist perspectives. Embracing such a way of seeing also entails making a commitment to the philosophy of praxis understood as the project of bringing about a fundamental change in the nature of the present social order, one that is designed to promote the interests of the mass over those of the minority. Such knowledges and understandings have been advanced for a specific purpose, one that remains as necessary today as it was when a number of the founders of critical accounting, following in the footsteps of several generations of Marxist scholars, embarked upon establishing their programme.

References

Armstrong, P. (1984). "Competition between the organisational professions and the evolution of management control strategies," in K. Thompson (ed.): *Work, Employment and Unemployment*, Milton Keynes, UK: Open University Press.

Armstrong, P. (1985). "Changing management control strategies: the role of competition between accountancy and other organizational professions," *Accounting, Organizations and Society*, 10(2): 129–48.

Armstrong, P. (1986). "Management control strategies and inter-professional competition: the case of accountancy and personnel management," in D. Knights and H. Willmott (eds): *Managing the Labour Process*, London: Macmillan.

Armstrong, P. (1987). "The rise of accounting controls in British capitalist enterprises," *Accounting, Organizations and Society*, 12(5): 415–36.

Armstrong, P. (1989). "Management, labour process and agency," *Work, Employment and Society*, 3(3): 307–22.

Armstrong, P. (1991). "Contradictions and social dynamics in the capitalist agency relationship," *Accounting, Organizations and Society*, 16(1): 1–25.

Armstrong, P. (1994). "The influence of Michel Foucault on accounting research," *Critical Perspectives on Accounting*, 5(1): 25–55.

Arnold, P. J. (1998). "The limits of postmodernism in accounting history: the Decatur experience," *Accounting, Organizations and Society*, 23(7): 665–84.

Arnold, P. J. (1999). "From the union hall: a labor critique of the new manufacturing and accounting regimes," *Critical Perspectives on Accounting*, 10(4): 399–23.

Arnold, P. and T. Hammond (1994). "The role of accounting in ideological conflict: lessons from the South African divestment movement," *Accounting, Organizations and Society*, 19(2): 111–26.

Baran, P. and P. A. Sweezy (1966). *Monopoly Capital: An Essay on the American Economic and Social Order*, New York: Monthly Review Press.

Baxter, J. and W. F. Chua (2003). "Alternative management accounting research – whence and whither?" *Accounting, Organizations and Society*, 29(2–3): 97–126.

Baxter, J. and W. F. Chua (2006). "Reframing management accounting practice: a diversity of perspectives," in A. Bhimani (ed.): Oxford: Oxford University Press.

Berry, A. J., T. Capps, D. Cooper, P. Ferguson, T. Hopper and E. A. Lowe (1985). "Management control in an area of the NCB: rationales of accounting practices in a public enterprise," *Accounting, Organizations and Society*, 10(1): 245–67.

Berry, A. J., T. Capps, D. J. Cooper, T. M. Hopper and E. A. Lowe (1988). "NCB accounts: a mine of misinformation?" in D. J. Cooper and T. M. Hopper (eds): *Debating Coal Closures: Economic Calculation in the Coal Dispute 1984-85*, Cambridge: Cambridge University Press.

Braverman, H. (1974). *Labor and Monopoly Capital: The Degradation of Work in the Twentieth Century*, New York: Monthly Review Press.

Bryer, R. (1991). "Accounting for the 'railway mania' of 1845 – a great railway swindle?" *Accounting, Organizations and Society*, 16(5–6): 439–86.

Burchell, S., C. Clubb, A. G. Hopwood, J. Hughes and J. Nahapiet (1980). "The roles of accounting in organisations and society," *Accounting, Organizations and Society*, 5(1): 5–27.

Burchell, S., C. Clubb, and A. G. Hopwood (1985). "Accounting in its social context: towards a history of value added in the United Kingdom," *Accounting, Organizations and Society*, 10(4): 381–413.

Burrell, G. and G. Morgan (1979). *Sociological Paradigms and Organisational Analysis*, London: Heinemann Educational Books.

Capps, T., T. Hooper, J. Mouritsen, D. Cooper and T. Lowe (1989). "Accounting in the production and reproduction of culture," in W. F. Chua, T. Lowe and T. Puxty (eds): *Critical Perspectives in Management Control*, London: Palgrave Macmillan.

Carchedi, G. (1977). *On the Economic Identification of Social Classes*, London: Routledge and Kegan Paul.

Christensen, C. (1983). "The methodology of positive accounting," *The Accounting Review*, 58(1): 1–22.

Chua, W. F. (1986). "Radical developments in accounting thought," *The Accounting Review*, 61(4): 601–32.

Clegg, S. and D. Dunkerley (1980). *Organisation, Class and Control*, London: Routledge and Kegan Paul.

Cooper, C. (1995). "Ideology, hegemony and accounting discourse: a case study of the National Union of Journalists," *Critical Perspectives on Accounting*, 6(3): 175–209.

Cooper, C. (1997). "Against postmodernism: class oriented questions for critical accounting," *Critical Perspectives on Accounting*, 8(1–2): 15–41.

Cooper, C. and P. Taylor (2000). "From Taylorism to Ms Taylor: the transformation of the accounting craft," *Accounting, Organizations and Society*, 25(6): 555–78.

Cooper, D. (1980). "Discussion of towards a political economy of accounting," *Accounting, Organizations and Society*, 5(1): 161–6.

Cooper, D. (1983). "Tidiness, muddle and things: commonalities and divergencies in two approaches in management accounting research," *Accounting, Organizations and Society*, 8(2–3): 269–86.

Cooper, D. J. and T. M. (eds) (1990). *Critical Accounts: Reorientating Accounting Research*, London: Palgrave Macmillan

Cooper, D. J. and M. J. Sherer (1984). "The value of corporate accounting reports: arguments for a political economy of accounting," *Accounting, Organizations and Society*, 9(3–4): 207–32.

Froud, J., K. Williams, C. Haslam, S. Johal and J. Williams (1998). "Two stories and an argument," *Accounting, Organizations and Society*, 23(7): 685–708.

Gorz, A. (1964). *Strategie Ouvriere et Neocapitalisme*, Paris: Seule.

Gramsci, A. (1971). *Selections from the Prison Notebooks*, translated by Q. Hoare and G. Nowell Smith, London: Lawrence and Wishart.

Grey, C. (1994). "Debating Foucault: a critical reply to Neimark," *Critical Perspectives on Accounting*, 5(1): 5–24.

Hooks, K. L. and J. E. Moon (1993). "Management Discussion and Analysis: an examination of the tensions, *Critical Perspectives on Accounting*, 4(3): 225–46.

Hopper, T. (1990). "The relevance of Weberianism to class analysis of accounting: a reply to Roslender," *Advances in Public Interest Accounting*, 3: 213–25.

Hopper, T. and P. Armstrong (1991). "Cost accounting, controlling labour and the rise of conglomerates," *Accounting, Organizations and Society*, 16(5–6): 405–38.

Hopper, T. and A. Powell (1985). "Making sense of research into the organizational and social aspects of management accounting: a review of its underlying assumptions," *Journal of Management Studies*, 22(5): 429–65.

Hopper, T., J. Storey and H. Willmott (1987). "Accounting for accounting: towards the development of a dialectical view," *Accounting, Organizations and Society*, 12(5): 437–56.

Hopper, T., D. Cooper, T. Lowe, T. Capps and J. Mouritsen (1986). "Management control and worker resistance in the National Coal Board: financial controls in the labour process," in D. Knights and H. Willmott (eds): *Managing the Labour Process*, London: Macmillan.

Hoskin, K. (1994). "Boxing clever: For, against and beyond Foucault in the battle for accounting theory," *Critical Perspectives on Accounting*, 5(1): 57–85.

Johnson, H. T. (1992). *Relevance Regained: From Top-Down Control to Bottom-Up Empowerment*, New York: The Free Press.

Johnson, H. T. (1994). "Relevance regained: total quality management and the role of management accounting," *Critical Perspectives on Accounting*, 5(3): 259–67.

Johnson, H. S. and R. S. Kaplan (1987). *Relevance Lost and Found: The Rise and Fall of Management Accounting*, Boston, MA: Harvard Business School Press.

Knights, D. and D. Collinson (1987). "Disciplining the shopfloor: a comparison of the disciplinary effects of managerial psychology and financial accounting," *Accounting, Organizations and Society*, 12(5): 457–77.

Lehman, C. and T. Tinker (1987). "The 'real' cultural significance of accounts," *Accounting, Organizations and Society*, 12(5): 503–22.

Loft, A. (1986). "Towards a critical understanding of accounting: the case of cost accounting in the UK 1914-1925," *Accounting, Organizations and Society*, 11(2): 137–70.

Lowe, E. A. and A. M. Tinker (1977). "Siting the accounting problematic: towards an intellectual emancipation of accounting," *Journal of Business Finance and Accounting*, 4(3): 263–76.

Lukka, K. (2005). "Approaches to case research in management accounting: the nature of empirical intervention and theory linkage," in S. Jonsson and J. Mouritsen (eds): *Accounting in Scandinavia – The Northern Lights*, Copenhagen: Liber and Copenhagen Business School Press.

Lukka, K. and E. Vinnari (2014). "Domain theory and method theory in management accounting research," *Accounting, Auditing and Accountability Journal*, 27(8): 1308–38.

Mallet, S. (1963). *La Nouvelle Classe Ouvriere*, Paris: Seuil.

Marx, K. (1845). *Marx and Engels: Basic Writings on Politics and Philosophy*, edited by L. S. Feuer, Glasgow: William Collins and Sons.

Marx, K. (1846). *The German Ideology*, translated by C. J. Arthur, London: Lawrence and Wishart.

Marx, K. (1859). *A Contribution to the Critique of Political Economy*, translated by S. W. Ryazanskaya, London: Lawrence and Wishart.

Marx, K. (1863). *Theories of Surplus Value*, Moscow: Progress Publishers.

Marx, K. (1867). *Capital: Vol 1*, Moscow: Progress Publishers.

Marx, K. (1885). *Capital: Vol 2*, Moscow, Progress Publishers.

Marx, K. (1894). *Capital: Vol 3*, Moscow: Progress Publishers.

Miller, P. and T. O'Leary (1987). "Accounting and the construction of the governable person," *Accounting, Organizations and Society*, 12(3): 235–65.

Miller, P. and T. O'Leary (1994). "Accounting, 'Economic Citizenship' and the spatial reordering of manufacture," *Accounting, Organizations and Society*, 19(1): 15–43.

Miller, P., T. Hopper and R. Laughlin (1991). "The new accounting history: an introduction," *Accounting, Organizations and Society*, 16(5–6): 395–403.

Moore, D. C. (1991). "Accounting on trial: the critical legal studies movement and its lessons for radical accounting," *Accounting, Organizations and Society*, 16(8): 763–91.

Neimark, M. (1990). "The king is dead: long live the king," *Critical Perspectives on Accounting*, 1(1): 103–14.

Neimark, M. (1994). "Regicide revisited: Marx, Foucault and accounting," *Critical Perspectives on Accounting*, 5(1): 87–108.

Neimark, M. and T. Tinker (1986). "The social construction of management control systems," *Accounting, Organizations and Society*, 11(4–5): 369–95.

Neu, D. (1992). "Reading the regulatory text: regulation and the new stock issue process," *Critical Perspectives on Accounting*, 3(4): 359–88.

Ogden, S. and P. Bougen (1985). "A radical perspective on the disclosure of accounting information to trade unions," *Accounting, Organizations and Society*, 10(2): 211–24.

Poulantzas, N. (1973). *Political Power and Social Classes*, London: New Left Books.

Richardson, A. J. (1987). "Accounting as a legitimating institution," *Accounting, Organizations and Society*, 12(4): 341–55.

Roslender, R. (1990). "The accountant in the class structure," *Advances in Public Interest Accounting*, 3: 195–212.

Roslender, R. (1996). "Critical accounting and the labour of accountants," *Critical Perspectives on Accounting*, 7(4): 461–84.

Roslender, R. (2015). "Accountancy" in M. Bevir and R. A. W. Rhodes (eds): *The Routledge Handbook of Interpretive Political Science*, London: Routledge.

Roslender, R. and Dillard, J. F. (2003). "Reflections on the interdisciplinary perspectives on accounting project," *Critical Perspectives on Accounting*, 14(3): 325–51.

Shaoul, J. (1997). "A critical financial analysis of the performance of privatised industries: the case of the water industry in England and Wales," *Critical Perspectives on Accounting*, 8(5): 479–505.

Shaoul, J. (1998). "Critical financial analysis and accounting for stakeholders," *Critical Perspectives on Accounting*, 9(2): 235–49.

Tinker, A. M. (1980). "Towards a political economy of accounting: an empirical illustration of the Cambridge controversies," *Accounting, Organizations and Society*, 5(1): 1147–60.

Tinker, T. (1985). *Paper Prophets: A Social Critique of Accounting*, New York: Praeger.

Tinker, T. (1988). "Panglossian accounting theories: the science of apologising in style," *Accounting, Organizations and Society*, 13(2): 165–89.

Tinker, T. and M. Neimark (1987). "The role of annual reports in gender and class contradictions at General Motors 1917-1976," *Accounting, Organizations and Society*, 12(1): 71–88.

Tinker, A. M., B. D. Merino and M. D. Neimark (1982). "The normative origins of positive theories: ideology and accounting thought," *Accounting, Organizations and Society*, 7(2): 167–200.

Wardell, M. and L. W. Weisenfeld (1991). "Management accounting and the workplace in the United states and Great Britain," *Accounting, Organizations and Society*, 16(7): 655–70.

Watts, R. L. and J. L. Zimmerman (1978). "Towards a positive theory of the determination of accounting standards," *The Accounting Review*, 53(1):112–34.

Watts, R. L. and J. L. Zimmerman (1986). *Positive Accounting Theory*, Englewood Cliffs, NJ: Prentice Hall

Williams, K., C. Haslam, T. Cutler, S. Johal and R. Willis (1994a). "Johnson 2: knowledge goes to Hollywood," *Critical Perspectives on Accounting*, 5(3): 281–93.

Williams, K., C. Haslam, S. Johal and J. Williams (1994b). *Cars: Analysis, History, Cases*, New York: Berghahn Books.

Williams, K., C. Haslam, J. Williams, S. Johal, A. Adcroft and R. Willis (1995). "The crisis of cost recovery and the waste of industrial nations," *Competition and Change*, 1(1): 67–93.

Yuthas, K. and T. Tinker (1994). "Paradise regained? Myth, Milton and management accounting," *Critical Perspectives on Accounting*, 5(3): 295–310.

4

CRITICAL THEORY

Sonja Gallhofer and Jim Haslam

1 Introduction

We elaborate here upon our critical theoretical perspective for the historical analysis of accounting. Our perspective is that of a Critical Theory approach informed by insights from post-structuralist and postmodern theory. We are concerned to discuss here a research project, informed by this theoretical perspective, which we have been involved in for over two decades. We articulate key aspects of our project and the insights gained from it to date – adding some further insights (thus, articulating a summary and extension) – in order to illustrate and promote our particular critical theoretical approach to accounting history. The project is our reading of the writings on accounting of the English philosopher and reformer Jeremy Bentham (1748–1832).

Within the confines of this text, we are only able to give a flavour of our argumentation and its evidential support. Those motivated to pursue a fuller picture would benefit from a reading of the key texts on Critical Theory, post-structuralist and postmodern theory identified throughout this volume, together with our earlier published work on Bentham (see, notably, Gallhofer and Haslam, 1993, 1994a,b, 1995, 1996, 2003).[1] The structure of the chapter is as follows. Initially we offer a brief elaboration upon the theoretical framing embraced here. We then introduce and offer some justification for our focus upon Bentham's writings on accounting. In the fourth section of the chapter we examine some key insights from our reading, elaborating on our findings through an appreciation of key quotes from texts of Bentham. The paper concludes with a number of comments intended to re-affirm the relationship that exists between Bentham's writings on accounting and the pursuit of the philosophy of praxis in the present epoch.

2 A brief elaboration on theoretical framing

Those developments in social theory and the humanities that have been given the labels 'post-structuralism' and 'postmodernism', and which have had so much influence in analyses of the social in general, have hugely impacted on the domain of history (Attridge, Bennington and Young, 1987; Young, 1990; Best, 1995; Best and Kellner, 1997). The more positivistic historians, with their facticity and antiquarian tendencies, have long been challenged by those of a more interpretivist epistemological orientation as well as by those whose history is shaped by an explicitly critical perspective. Such challenging has been added to or refined by those influenced by post-structuralist and postmodern lenses. As a consequence, historians who view the past in terms of a linear and universal progress towards the present have been challenged by those questioning this perspectival assumption. In the 'new' history, detailed particularities of the past are afforded greater attention. And anachronistic, or chronocentric (Cousins, 1987), tendencies in history research have also been problematised by the view that we should be taking the past more seriously as difference.

Critical historians have in this regard not been exempted from the transformative challenges. Thus 'conventional' Marxist history is challenged for its overly confident and absolutist eschatology as well as epistemology (see Laclau and Mouffe, 1987; Gallhofer and Haslam, 2003; Gallhofer, Haslam and Yonekura, 2015; see also Grossberg, 1986; Kolb, 1986; Caplan, 1989; Patterson, 1989; Schöttler, 1989; Agger, 1992; Mouffe, 1993; Veron, 1994; Best, 1995; Calhoun, 1995; Derrida, 1996; Landry, 2000; Howarth, Norval and Stravrakis, 2002; Critchley and Marchart, 2004; Lechte, 2006; Liu, 2009; Breckman, 2013). Marxist history has also seen criticism for its Western-centricity or Eurocentricity, its presumption of a single World History in which the other is an excess that alludes the Eurocentric narrative (see Young, 1990; Calhoun, 1995; Barker, 2003; Lechte, 2006; Liu, 2009; Beck, 2015).

These theoretical concerns have been noted and are influential vis-à-vis the history of accounting and the critical history of accounting (Gallhofer and Haslam, 2003). In our own critical historical studies of accounting, we have sought to pursue a critical theoretical approach informed by the developments in social theory and the humanities hitherto referred to. We have particularly been influenced by the post-Marxism of Laclau and Mouffe (see Laclau, 1990; Laclau and Mouffe, 1987, 2001), which in turn is influenced by currents of post-structuralism and postmodern theory (modifying Laclau and Mouffe's earlier Gramscian critical theoretical position). We see our critical accounting history as a critical theoretical history refined by an interaction with post-structuralist, postmodern and post-Marxist theory (Gallhofer and Haslam, 2003). In this regard, we follow the path of appreciating the post-structuralist and postmodern insights not as a kind of pessimistic negation of critical praxis but as offering *more* possibilities for extending and deepening a (more pragmatist) critical praxis, not less, consistent with Laclau and Mouffe (1987, 2001) and Laclau (1990, 1996). These possibilities include re-interpreting particularities of the past to gain a myriad of insights for today – including, in this regard, reinterpretation of the modern practices and texts that are problematised by new perspectives (see Radin and Michelman, 1991; Pieterse, 1992; Crump, 1995; Gallhofer and Haslam, 2003; Parashar, 2008)!

Going beyond the view that the past is a simple immature or underdeveloped version of the present, or the view that the present represents in simple terms progress on the past, is not so easy in practice. It cuts against what may be understood as a deeply ingrained myth and taken for granted way of seeing (Attridge *et al.*, 1987; Young, 1990). Bracketing the present (and our current cultural location) and seeking to go beyond current understandings (including our local ones) is not possible in a pure or absolute sense. Retaining an openness to what may be found in the past may be difficult when general or overly strong prior theorising is adopted (for instance, a critical theorising reflecting a particular interest). It may constrain ways of seeing at least in terms of particular aspects or dimensions. A concern ought to be to unearth and locate things that are today covered over by what may be metaphorically appreciated as layers of deposits that have formed upon them. Yet having and developing awareness of these issues may enhance sensitivity and openness in pursuing a critical theoretical perspective refined by post-structuralist, postmodern and post-Marxist thinking. Struggling to overcome or to counter the difficulties is a worthy exercise. It enhances opportunities to gain a variety of insights from history (beyond more general insights from history, such as helping us to better understand the present). In this regard, accountings envisaged or operational in past contexts may inspire, stimulate and suggest ways of bettering the present – in terms of at least some particular aspects of their manifestation. New visions of accounting and its functioning may be appreciated in and for the present. Understanding past manifestations of accounting contextually may problematise aspects of accounting today. Historical appreciation may enhance an understanding of emancipatory as well as repressive dimensions of accounting and its possibilities (Gallhofer and Haslam, 1993, 1995, 2003).

The tenets of critical thought apply to critical history and encompass three dimensions (to be appreciated through a reflexive lens): the concern to understand things in practice; the concern to envision a better world; and the concern to work out how to approach the better place (see Benhabib, 1986; Held and McGrew, 2000; Gallhofer and Haslam, 2008). Our theoretical perspective reflects these dimensions, including in history research. But in seeking to find problematic dimensions in the past, or insights in terms of positive potentialities from the past for today, we are concerned to avoid tendencies towards dogmatic thinking. The concern is to be open, in seeking to develop and refine theoretical argumentation, to the field and to appreciating the past, including in this case Bentham's text, as difference and in its particularities. The same concern is expressed in Laughlin (1995). A critical theoretical historical perspective, in its concern to understand things in the past, seeks to develop an appreciation of context – in the project that will be discussed the context of Bentham's writings – through a mix of interpreting original material around a focus and a critical reading of the secondary literature (see Gallhofer and Haslam, 2003: chapter 2). In seeking to understand the past, an iterative or circular approach is adopted to refine theoretical argumentation.[2]

3 Jeremy Bentham's accounting writings: justifying the focus

So much was Bentham in advance of his age, that Sir Samuel Romilly recommended him not to publish several of his works, as he felt assured that printing them would lead to prosecution and imprisonment. Many...I have not deemed it safe to give to the world...they remain in the archives.

(Bowring, 1877: 339)

As Anne Loft would also testify, the late Anthony Hopwood was keen to promote the study of Jeremy Bentham's writings on accounting and related phenomena. Hopwood was aware of earlier narrowly descriptive studies of some of Bentham's texts that had focused on accounting, including Goldberg (1957) and Hume (1970), the latter focusing on the writings of Jeremy and his brother Samuel (see also the more expansive Hume, 1981). Hopwood's interest in Bentham arose from his interest in social analysis and the twentieth-century theorising of Michel Foucault. Foucault's articulation of 'panoptisme' mobilises Bentham's Panopticon as a metaphor of modern society (Foucault, 1977a,b). This articulation fits well with a branch of the social critique of Bentham's thought (e.g. Himmelfarb, 1968), as a result of which it has come to be widely received along with Foucault's enormous influence on social theory (Foucault helping to shift social theory in that direction that came to be labelled 'post-structuralist' and 'postmodern'). Hopwood introduced both Loft and ourselves to a text by Bahmueller (1981), a text that is influenced by social-theoretical developments and begins to indicate (beyond Goldberg, 1957, and Hume, 1970) the different way in which Bentham saw accounting, beyond what became the conventions of today.

Bentham is a controversial figure, not least because of the aforementioned intervention of Foucault. On the negative side he is seen as the exponent of a crude and narrow materialistic utilitarianism, for example by Williams (1987), and as a promoter of bourgeois interests (see, e.g. the review in Mack, 1962). In Foucault, Bentham's Panopticon is illustrative of a mode of disciplinary control that is at the very least ambivalent, with its problematic dimensions emphasised (an emphasis influential in the work of Loft, 1988). On the other hand, Bentham is seen as a radical progressive whose work was dedicated to the emancipation of the oppressed (e.g. in Boralevi, 1984). Here we should note that Habermas has viewed Bentham in positive terms as an advocate of the construction of the public sphere with its radical social potential (Habermas, 1992; see also Calhoun, 1992; Bronner, 1994; Best, 1995). Russell (1962) views Bentham as progressive and pragmatic in a number of respects. Interpretations of Bentham have shifted as he has come to be seen through different theoretical lenses but also as more of his writing, much of which has remained unpublished until relatively recently in the archives at University College London, has been published. The diverse views on and interpretations of Bentham's writing include Mack (1962); Russell (1962); Letwin (1965); Himmelfarb (1968); Foucault (1977a,b); Bahmueller (1981); Hart (1982); Rosen (1982); Harrison (1983); Boralevi (1984); Long (1987); Postema (1988); Akinkummi and Murray (1997); Williams (1987); Dinwiddy (1989); Twining (1989); Pitkin (1990); Lyons (1991); Parekh (1993); Semple (1993); Crimmins (1994, 1996); Blake (1997); Boyne (2000); and also Žižek (2001).

Given that many have come to see Bentham, through a reading of Foucault, in negative terms (see Semple, 1993), it may be seen as unusual for a critical perspective to explore Bentham's writings on accounting with an agenda including openness to appreciating more emancipatory possibilities in these writings.[3] But this sense of the unusual or of irony would in our view underappreciate the character of Foucault's writings on Bentham. Foucault wrote immediately on 'panoptisme' and the Panopticon as a metaphor for modern society. Foucault does not offer a critique of Bentham's texts but focuses in on an articulation of the Panopticon to elaborate upon disciplinary society. We should also add that a close reading of Foucault, even *Discipline and Punish*, reflects an appreciation of ambivalence that is characteristic of post-structuralist and postmodern theory (see Connolly, 1988). The emphasis in his articulation of panoptisme is on the negative of a disciplinary mode of control but this is part of an attempt to counter what he sees as problematic simplifications and myths of history, including critical history. There is an appreciation of ambivalence even in this context and even in the articulation of the Panopticon (Gallhofer and Haslam, 2003: chapter 2). For us, such an interpretation is consistent with the reading that sees characteristics of a critical and open history, which is reflective of the developments in theory in the social sciences and the humanities, as including a concern to be open to possibilities in the past beyond a one-sided appreciation (*supra*). And we have already noted that there are various differing interpretations of Bentham.

There are other reasons why a focus on Bentham's writings on accounting are of interest to us. Bentham wrote on accounting prior to the formal professionalisation of accountancy. Accountancy's formal professionalisation impacted on the discourse of accounting and it is of interest to explore ways of seeing accounting prior to the formal professionalisation. If, amongst writers prior to the mid-nineteenth century, Bentham was not alone in writing about how accounting might aid administration for better 'modern' governance, and if he was not the only philosopher or universal scholar who gave attention to accounting in this respect or in relation to advocating and promoting the public sphere (see Habermas, 1992; Gallhofer and Haslam, 2003: chapter 2), the significant place of accounting in his thought stands out (e.g. Bentham, 1797: 100–1; University College London Bentham Archives, cliiia: 33–4; Gallhofer and Haslam, 2003: 47). In this last respect, Bentham's writings do stand out as especially worthy of analysis. The significance Bentham gives to accounting is scarcely appreciated in much of the Bentham literature. When Cumming (1961) mocks Bentham's chrestomathic education programme, emphasising that the programme ends with bookkeeping, he overlooks the particular meaning and sense of 'bookkeeping' in Bentham. The context in which Bentham wrote is also a significant one – in terms of the crystallisation of modern forms of governance that continue to be influential (Anonymous, 1832; Polanyi, 1945; Cullen, 1975; Evans, 1983; Gallhofer and Haslam, 1995, 2003: chapter 2).

4 Some key insights

Pursuing a critical theoretical history refined by interaction with post-structuralist, postmodern and post-Marxist thought, we find that reading Bentham's texts on accounting offers a variety of interesting insights (see Gallhofer and Haslam, 1993, 1994a,b, 1995, 1996, 2003).

4.1 Reading Bentham in terms of accounting as negation or accounting as a problematic control

One can recognise and develop the substance in various critical analyses of Bentham that emphasise the negative in Bentham. These critical analyses are also relevant in respect of Bentham's governance and accounting visions. They are given emphasis in Loft (1988) (see also Gallhofer and Haslam, 1994a).

Bentham reflects tensions that are present in any radical progressive project (and Bentham is quite aware of these tensions and aims to be sensitive in relation to them, as Letwin, 1965, acknowledges), although sometimes they are writ large in Bentham and suggest more immediate problematics. He seeks that the people be in control but wants to direct them first. In intervening he may encourage distrust, which may have a problematic impact on behaviour. He wants to respect the differences of people but wants a cost-efficient way to do this and is enthusiastic about applying universal principles. This is very evident in his letter to the Right Honourable John Parnell, 2 September, 1790, British Museum Manuscript, MS 33541, f. 160 (extracts from which are published in Gallhofer and Haslam, 2003: 60; see also Boyne, 2000: 288–9). The strong impact of control may very easily come to be not substantially progressive but more the opposite (Gallhofer and Haslam, 1994a).

Further, perhaps a more important point here is that one can envisage how projects that at least ostensibly follow Bentham's principles can subsequently accrue (additional) problematic dimensions in their mobilisation. For instance, Bentham saw publicity serving a radical and expansive democracy and he especially wanted to shine a light on the activities of the relatively powerful (Gallhofer and Haslam, 2003). However, clearly in practice Bentham's ideas could be used, for instance, to control for example factory workers and in an especially repressive way (see Hartley, 1988). Indeed, as we have already indicated, Bentham's own projects, if articulated as being in the interest of the governed and the oppressed (including the poor and prisoners), are already suggestive of problematic dimensions (Gallhofer and Haslam, 1994a).

One can appreciate that the usage in prior research of particular lenses (often shaped in the twentieth century) to study Bentham has often encouraged an emphasis on the negative in Bentham, who is portrayed as a kind of control freak. Some studies are problematic in only seeing or settling on the negative, in what amounts to a one-sided rhetoric, as in the case of Letwin (1965) where she refers to Bentham's production of "devices of a monstrous efficiency that left no room for humanity." Our concern in studying Bentham has been influenced by critical theoretical sensitivity to seeking to understand the character of the past context in which Bentham wrote. We have tried to go beyond chronocentric views and adopt a more balanced perspective. This has allowed us to also see more of the positive potential in Bentham's writings, including in terms of its particularities. None of the points made thus far suggest that one should not be concerned to intervene for social progress. And Bentham is concerned to try to intervene to make the world a better place.

4.2 Accountability and governance in the service of humanity, including an appreciation of the longevity of progressive accounting ideas

In being concerned to try to intervene to make the world a better place, Bentham sees accounting as central to this project. From a critical theoretical perspective, it is worth reflecting on and trying to see the relevance of the ideas that Bentham has articulated in this respect. Our analyses have uncovered and illuminated a number of prescriptive suggestions in Bentham that at least remain of relevance today. These suggestions may be illustrated in quotations from Bentham's texts. We summarise insights in the following paragraphs (see Gallhofer and Haslam, 1993, 1994a,b, 1995, 1996, 2003).

Bentham saw accounting and transparency as aiding good governance (Bentham in this regard using the word 'management' in a text published in 1797) for well-being. Better information is here understood as making for better decisions and better governance. Greater openness and transparency controlled behaviour so that all would move forward in terms of well-being. In seeking to promote openness and transparency he referred to publicity (making things visible to the public) and accounting publicity – the construct 'accounting publicity' came to be commonly used in his context (Gallhofer and Haslam, 1995). Publicity implied 'bookkeeping' since records had to be kept to furnish a system of disclosure. The terms 'accounting', 'publicity' and 'bookkeeping' substantively become equivalent terms in Bentham's works. Publicity or openness was a very radical idea in Bentham's time. In the early nineteenth century the British state would be properly regarded as authoritarian and anti-democratic (Foot, 1984). Accounting publicity was linked to revolution in the discourse of the British state (Gallhofer and Haslam, 1995). The following quotation indicates something of the significance Bentham saw in accounting for governance:

> With the instruction, and under the check, of an adequate system of book-keeping, the management may be better conducted by the most ordinary hand, than by the ablest hand without that advantage.
>
> *(Bentham, 1797: 100–1)*

Bentham's 'local-consideration' principle for his system of governance encompassing publicity reflects a quite pragmatic, context-aware, cautious and sensitive stance. He acknowledges that it was problematic to literally disclose everything – or, to put it in less abstract terms, there are legitimately private spaces of confidentiality (Gallhofer and Haslam, 1993). And he refers here to not wanting to push uniformity too far – different types of governance might better fit particular purposes in particular contexts (Gallhofer and Haslam, 1993, 2003). The following quotation is from Bentham in respect of his local-consideration principle: "[and in respect of book-keeping a] local-consideration observing principle – not to push the principle of uniformity too far" (Bentham, 1797: 50, see also p. 53).

His recognition of two duties for the manager of a micro-organisation (it was a principle applicable beyond the context of the 'industry house', see Gallhofer and Haslam, 1993) indicates a strong emphatic prescription of something like what is now termed 'corporate social responsibility' in the present argot (see in this regard Gambling, 1974; Zadek, Pruzan and Evans, 1997; Adams and Harte, 2000; Lehman, 2001; Cooper, Taylor, Smith and Catchpole, 2005). Bentham suggests that publicity – of matters of a moral character – is more especially important for trying to ensure that managers fulfil their 'duty to humanity'. It is deemed even more important than publicity in respect of the 'duty to economy'. If we should acknowledge an overlap between these duties, this appears to be, in substance, the reverse of where we are today. Bentham elaborates on his position as follows:

> The duty of the manager of an industry house has two main branches: duty towards those under his care, resolvable into *humanity* – and duty to his principals (the company) resolvable into *economy*. *Publicity*, the most effectual means of applying the forces of moral motives, in a direction tending to strengthen the union between his interest and the humane branch of his duty.
>
> *(Bentham, 1797: 51–2)*

Moreover, Bentham's concern that publicity meet the 'several obligations' (also something he intended as generally applicable, see Gallhofer and Haslam, 1993) indicates that Bentham sought that publicity serve a range of constituencies, similar to the stakeholder approach that is often referred to today (and often in relation to corporate social responsibility disclosures):

> [Bookkeeping ...] an indispensable security for the due discharge of the several obligations, which the direction of the company will have ... to the various parties interested – viz. the paupers ... the rateable parishioners ... the stock-holders ... government – and the public at large.
>
> *(Bentham, 1797: 99–100)*

Bentham also wanted the publicity to communicate and he sought to go beyond a (suspiciously) mystifying expertise. Publicity had to be shaped by its purpose. The following pair of observations are indicative and suggest Bentham can be regarded as having a critical perspective on accounting:

> *Correct, complete, clear, concise, easy to consult* – in case of *error*, so framed as not to cover it, but to *afford indication* of it – *appropriate*, i.e. adapted to the particular practical purpose it has in view – the purpose, for the sake of which the labour thus bestowed is expended – in these epithets may be seen the *qualities* desirable in a system of this kind.
>
> *(Bentham, 1816: 61–2)*

> [The Italian mode of accounting, that is based on double-entry bookkeeping, is a] language composed entirely of fictions, and understood by nobody but the higher clan of merchants and their clerks...The real use...might be a subject well worthy of investigation.
>
> *(Bentham, 1797: 106n)*

These quotations indicate that Bentham's progressive radicalism is reflected in how he envisaged accounting, that is, critically and as an artefact for social progress, and thereby reflecting a holistic view of well-being that was not simply restricted to the crudely materialistic. And that he wrote these ideas over 200 years ago indicates their longevity, arguably adding a weight of history to their contemporary relevance.

One can at least outline how the insights may inform a critical perspective for today. There is an indication here of how communicative practices, albeit imperfectly, can serve a range of interests, identities and projects that are progressive and how they might be part of aligning differing interests in a way that would advance well-being. There is an indication of how accounting publicity can enhance accountability for social well-being. The more problematic or negative dimensions discussed earlier might be seen in terms of potential pitfalls suggestive of the need for a cautious and pragmatist approach.

4.3 Delineation of accounting in Bentham's efforts to design accounting for social progress

One can read Bentham's writings on accounting as contributing to an expansive account-ing delineation that is of great relevance today. It very much challenges conventional views of accounting that are now especially influential in the profession, general discourse and academia. The insight in Bentham's texts is here appreciated to some extent by Hoskin and Macve (1986) as well as in our own work. The openness maintained in our critical history process thus allows us to gain key insights from our journey into these past texts. Here we add to this prior work by indicating that Bentham's contribution to accounting delineation (see Gallhofer *et al.*, 2015) provides for a way of summarising his writings on accounting, and can be appreciated here as extending and adding to our prior commentaries.

Bentham refers to bookkeeping and publicity in terms of an extensive practice of govern-ance, with a great variety of applications for a variety of purposes:

> In the Chrestomathic school, the principle thereby indicated will of course be pursued; but, proportioned to the superior extent of the *field* assumed by it, will necessarily be the extent and variety of the *application* made of it. In the practice of this most univer-sally useful art [book-keeping].
>
> *(Bentham, 1816: 62)*

Accounting is not restricted to a 'pecuniary economy' but serves all the 'points' of management or governance:

> Pecuniary economy, usually regarded as the sole object of book-keeping, will here be but as one out of a number; for the system of book-keeping will be neither more nor less than the history of the system of management in all its points.
>
> *(Bentham, 1797: 101; see University College London Bentham Archives, clii: 360)*

Accounting is an instrument of radical democracy. It should serve not only the wealthy and powerful but might be pressed into the service of the oppressed and the poor:

> [B]ook-keeping was one of the arts which I should have to learn … the cries of the poor called aloud and accelerated the demand for it.
>
> *(University College of London Bentham Archives, cliiia: 33–4, draft of a letter to the scientific agriculturist Arthur Young)*

Commercial bookkeeping and commercial accounting publicity is but one branch of a more generic delineation of bookkeeping and accounting publicity at large:

> The *commercial* process or operation, on the subject of which, under the name of Book-keeping, works in such multitude have been published, is but a branch – a particular application – of an art, of the most extensive range, and proportion-able importance viz. the art of *Book-keeping at large*.
>
> *(Bentham, 1816: 61)*

Accountings in general are to be mobilised in relation to dimensions of social progress. These ideas may illuminate the perspective articulated by Gallhofer *et al.* (2015), who elaborate on accounting delineation in relation to a post-Marxist critical new pragmatist perspective. Bentham's envisioning of accounting publicity is consistent with a concern to intervene to try to make the world a better place. Analysis of Bentham's writings suggests caution and care about how this might be done. There is a lot that is problematic and so much that can go wrong. But with the concern to steer a way through these negatives, a concern to intervene and change things – rather than an opposite concern – remains integral to a critical praxis. Bentham's message from centuries ago is to indicate the importance of 'accounting' in this.

5 Concluding comments

Bentham's notion that accounting publicity or transparency can promote social progress and well-being is a very worthy focus of study. Accounting publicity is of great significance for Bentham. Turning his attention to the governance of the social, Bentham proposes that publicity, openness or transparency (expansively understood) is the handmaiden to, and arguably second only to, his Panopticon principle. Since the rationale for the Panopticon is that it enhances the possibility of openness and transparency, Bentham might have more properly labelled publicity itself his most important principle of governance.

By careful analysis of Bentham's writings on publicity, employing a critical theoretical perspective on history that is refined by post-structuralist and postmodern thought, we have been able to gain some general insights into the potential of publicity to do social good. At the same time, insights are given into the potential problematic issues associated with such publicity. Some of these insights come from Bentham's own writings, which may be understood as reflecting a critical perspective on accounting. Bentham's writings indicate the longevity of many proposed accountings, including an expansive form of micro-organisational social accounting to stakeholder constituencies in the name of making the micro-organisational practice more ethical (as well as more economically efficient). In certain contexts, an appreciation of such longevity may be helpful in promoting a proposed practice in policy and general discourse. It can be argued that Bentham offers a great contribution in re-formulating the delineation of accounting, and we have seen this as an extension of our prior work here that adds to points we have previously made. His notion of 'bookkeeping at large' points to an equating of accounting with publicity in general. It includes what he acknowledges to be bookkeeping in its more everyday usage (that is, 'commercial bookkeeping'). It is consistent with his radical commitment to link a variety of forms of accounting publicity to progressive ends for well-being. As a result, the work by Gallhofer *et al.* (2015) might be read as translating this expansive but functional notion of accounting delineation into a post-Marxist new pragmatist critical perspective for praxis.

Of course, we are not here promoting a Benthamite position in a return to a pristine modernism, nor suggesting that Bentham is the high point of a theory for praxis. We are reading Bentham through our critical theoretical lens, which has also much to note, as we have indicated, about the *downsides* of Bentham's texts. We are, however, emphasising that from a critical perspective, an appreciation of Bentham's *texts* does not stop with an appreciation of the negative.

Today the global context suffers from a deficit of democratic governance for well-being, including a deficit of transparency, rather than the opposite. Individual nation state governments (or their talking heads) stress what they *cannot* do (e.g. spend resources to maintain or enhance a system supporting social welfare) and *must* do (e.g. reduce corporate taxes and reduce taxes on those financial income streams that are deemed to be more mobile away from host nations) in proclaiming the need to maintain or enhance competitiveness, fuelling a race to the bottom in global standards and threatening to make a mockery of nation state democracy (Held and McGrew, 2000). This race to the bottom – which currently favours those currently wealthy in the world but which has an uncertain trajectory that is actually generally threatening – is a particularly poor response to the problems of the world. Our critical theoretical reading indicates the sense in which Bentham, who used the word 'international' and saw himself as a citizen of the world (Mack, 1962), pointed over two centuries ago to the need for a better global infrastructure – including accounting publicity – for better global well-being. He also began to trace and express sensitivity to the problematics of mobilising and operationalising this infrastructure. From a critical perspective, refined by post-structuralist and postmodern insights, reading Bentham on accounting reminds us of important dimensions of and provides insights for praxis today.

This chapter was submitted by the authors with the following title: "Critical accounting history: reading Bentham on accounting (a summary and an extension)."

Notes

1   Those interested in reading our critical histories of accounting that are focused on subjects other than Bentham's work are referred to Gallhofer and Haslam (1991, 2003: chapter 3, 2006).
2   Regarding the location of Bentham's writings for our study, the publication of Bahmueller (1981) (*subter* in the main text) especially provided some pointers to where Bentham's writings on accounting might be found in the archives at University College London. We were given permission to consult these archives and came to appreciate the handwriting of both Bentham and those to whom in later life he dictated. If we were unable to read any particular texts we were able to consult those engaged in the Bentham project (charged with bringing Bentham's notes through to publication) and they were more often than not able to decipher it. We assessed the archive extensively, using relevant findings to indicate where other relevant texts might be located. We recorded all the relevant quotations we could find. We already read Bahmueller (1981) as effectively conceiving accounting in broad terms in the writings of Bentham and we were very open to any understanding of accounting in broad terms in the Bentham texts we explored, a strategy which we saw as being consistent with a concern to be open to finding things out from the field. At the same time, we followed up on pointers to Bentham texts that have been published. For instance, Bentham (1797) and Bentham (1816) were sources of several illuminating quotations. In our research we also consulted documents and letters at the British Library and the Public Records Office.
3   Indeed, it may be seen as ironic to mobilise a perspective that is refined by post-structuralist and postmodern thinking influenced by Foucault to focus on Bentham in a way that appreciates these positive potentialities.

References

Adams, C. A. and G. Harte (2000). "Making discrimination visible: the potential of social accounting," *Accounting Forum*, 24(1): 56–79.
Agger, B. (1992). *The Discourse of Domination: From the Frankfurt School to Postmodernism*, Evanston, IL: Northwestern University Press.
Akinkummi, A. and K. Murray (1997). "Inadequacies in the Mental Health Act, 1983 in relation to mentally disordered remand prisoners," *Medicine, Science and the Law*, 37(1): 53–7.
Anonymous (1832). *An Address to the British Public by the Saint Simonian Missionaries*, London: Rolandi, Bossange, Barthes and Lowell, MA: Effingham and Wilson.
Attridge, D., G. Bennington and R. Young (1987) (eds). *Post-structuralism and the Question of History*, Cambridge: Cambridge University Press.
Bahmueller, C. (1981). *The National Charity Company: Jeremy Bentham's Silent Revolution*, Berkeley, CA: University of California Press.
Barker, C. (2003). *Cultural Studies: Theory and Practice*, London: Sage Publications.
Beck, U. (2015). *The Reinvention of Politics: Rethinking Modernity and the Global Social Order*, Oxford: John Wiley and Sons.

Benhabib, S. (1986). *Critique, Norm and Utopia: A Study of the Foundations of Critical Theory*, New York: Columbia University Press.

Bentham, J. (1797). *Pauper Management Improved: Particularly by Means of an Application of the Panopticon Principle of Construction*, London (first published 1797 in Arthur Young's Annals of Agriculture, first published separately, 1812, London, from which the quotations are taken).

Bentham, J. (1816). *Chrestomathia*, London.

Best, S. (1995). *The Politics of Historical Vision: Marx, Foucault, Habermas*, New York: Guilford Press.

Best, S. and D. Kellner (1997). *The Postmodern Turn*, New York: Guilford Press.

Blake, K. (1997). "Bleak House, political economy, Victorian studies," *Victorian Literature and Culture*, 25(1): 1–21.

Boralevi, C. L. (1984). *Bentham and the Oppressed*, Berlin and New York: de Gruyter.

Bowring, J. (1877). *Autobiographical Recollections of Sir John Bowring with a brief memoir by Lewin B. Bowring*, London: Henry S. King.

Boyne, R. (2000). "Post-Panopticism," *Economy and Society*, 29(2): 285–307.

Breckman, W. (2013). *Adventures of the Symbolic: PostMarxism and Radical Democracy*, New York: Columbia University Press.

Bronner, S. E. (1994). *Of Critical Theory and Its Theorists*, Oxford: Blackwell.

Calhoun, C. (1992) (ed.). *Habermas and the Public Sphere*, Cambridge, MA: MIT Press.

Calhoun, C. (1995). *Critical Social Theory: Culture, History and the Challenge of Theory*, Oxford: Blackwell.

Caplan, J. (1989). "Postmodernism, poststructuralism and deconstruction: notes for historians," *Central European History*, 22 (3–4): 260–78.

Connolly, W. (1988). *Political Theory and Modernity*, Oxford: Blackwell.

Cooper, C., P. Taylor, N. Smith and L. Catchpowle (2005). "A discussion of the political potential of social accounting," *Critical Perspectives on Accounting*, 16(7): 952–74.

Cousins, M. (1987). "The practice of historical investigation," in D. Attridge, G. Bennington and R. Young (eds): *Post-structuralism and the Question of History*, Cambridge: Cambridge University Press.

Crimmins, J. E. (1994). "Bentham's political radicalism re-examined," *Journal of the History of Ideas*, 55(2): 259–81.

Crimmins, J. E. (1996). "Contending interpretations of Bentham's utilitarianism," *Canadian Journal of Political Science – Revue Canadienne de Science Politique*, 29(4): 751–77.

Critchley, S. and O. Marchart (2004). *Laclau: A Critical Reader*, London: Psychology Press.

Crump, S. (1995). "Towards action and power: post-enlightenment pragmatism?" *Discourse: Studies in the Cultural Politics of Education*, 16(2): 203–17.

Cullen, M. J. (1975). *The Statistical Movement in Early Victorian Britain: The Foundation of Empirical Social Research*, Hassocks: Harvester Press.

Cumming, I. (1961). *Useful Learning: Bentham's Chrestomathia with Particular Reference to the Influence of James Mill on Bentham*, University of Auckland, Bulletin No. 56, Ed. Series No. 3.

Derrida, J. (1996). "Remarks on deconstruction and pragmatism," in C. Mouffe (ed.): *Deconstruction and Pragmatism*, London and New York: Routledge.

Dinwiddy, J. (1989). *Bentham*, Oxford: Oxford University Press.

Evans, E. J. (1983). *The Forging of the Modern State: Early Industrial Britain, 1783-1870*, 2e, London: Longman.

Foot, P. (1984). *Red Shelley*, London: Bookmarks.

Foucault, M. (1977a). "L'oeil de pouvoir, preface to Bentham, J. *Le Panoptique*," Paris: Belfond.

Foucault, M. (1977b). *Discipline and Punish: The Birth of the Prison*, translated by A. Sheridan, Harmondsworth, UK: Penguin Books.

Gallhofer, S. and J. Haslam (1991). "The aura of accounting in the context of a crisis: Germany and the First World War," *Accounting, Organizations and Society*, 16(5–6): 487–520.

Gallhofer, S. and J. Haslam (1993). "Approaching corporate accountability: fragments from the past," *Accounting and Business Research*, 23(s1): 32–30.

Gallhofer, S. and J. Haslam (1994a). "Accounting and the Benthams: accounting as negation," *Accounting Business and Financial History*, 4(2): 293–73.

Gallhofer, S. and J. Haslam (1994b). "Accounting and the Benthams: or, accounting's potentialities," *Accounting, Business and Financial History*, 4(3): 431–60.

Gallhofer, S. and J. Haslam (1995). "Accounting and modernity," *Advances in Public Interest Accounting*, 6: 203–32.

Gallhofer, S. and J. Haslam (1996). "Analysis of Bentham's chrestomathia: or, towards a critique of accounting education," *Critical Perspectives on Accounting*, 7(1–2): 13–31.

Gallhofer, S. and J. Haslam (2003). *Accounting and Emancipation: Some Critical Interventions*, London and New York: Routledge.

Gallhofer, S. and J. Haslam (2006). "Mobilising accounting in the radical media during the First World War and its aftermath: the Case of Forward in the context of red Clydeside," *Critical Perspectives on Accounting*, 17(2): 224–52.

Gallhofer, S. and J. Haslam (2008). "The possibilities of accounting in the global context: critical reflections on the internet as a new technology of communication," in M. Lada and A. Kozarkiewicz (eds): *Rachunkowosc: w otoczeniu nowych technologii*, Warsaw: Beck.

Gallhofer, S., J. Haslam and A. Yonekura (2015). "Accounting as differentiated universal for emancipatory praxis: accounting delineation and mobilization for emancipation(s) recognising democracy and difference," *Accounting, Auditing and Accountability Journal*, 28(5): 846–74.

Gambling, T. (1974). *Societal Accounting*, London: George Allen and Unwin.

Goldberg, L. (1957). "Jeremy Bentham: critic of accounting method," *Accounting Research*, 8: 218–45.

Grossberg, L. (1986). "History, politics and postmodernism: Stuart Hall and cultural studies," *Journal of Communication Inquiry*, 10(2): 61–77.

Habermas, J. (1992). *The Structural Transformation of the Public Sphere: An Inquiry into a Category of Bourgeois Society*, translated by T. Burger with the assistance of F. Lawrence, Cambridge, MA: MIT Press.

Harrison, R. (1983). *Bentham*, London: Routledge and Kegan Paul.

Hart, H. L. A. (1982). *Essays on Bentham's Jurisprudence and Political Theory*, Oxford: Oxford University Press.

Hartley, D. (1998). "In search of structure: theory and practice in the management of education," *Journal of Education Policy*, 13(1): 153–62.

Held, D. and A. McGrew (2000) (eds). *The Global Transformation Reader: An Introduction to the Globalization Debate*, Cambridge: Polity Press in association with Blackwell.

Himmelfarb, G. (1968). "The Haunted House of Jeremy Bentham," in G. Himmelfarb (ed.): *Victorian Minds*, New York: Knopf.

Hoskin, K. and R. Macve (1986). "Accounting and the examination: a genealogy of disciplinary power," *Accounting, Organizations and Society*, 11(2): 105–36.

Howarth, D., A. Norval and Y. Stravrakis (2002) (eds). *Discourse Theory and Political Analysis*, Manchester: Manchester University Press.

Hume, L. (1970). "The development of industrial accounting: the Benthams' contribution," *Journal of Accounting Research*, 8(1): 21–33.

Hume, L. (1981). *Bentham and Bureaucracy*, Cambridge: Cambridge University Press.

Kolb, D. (1986). *The Critique of Pure Modernity: Hegel, Heidegger and After*, Chicago IL: University of Chicago Press.

Laclau, E. (1990). *New Reflections on the Revolution of Our Times*, London: Verso.

Laclau, E. (1996). *Emancipation(s)*, London: Verso.

Laclau, E. and C. Mouffe (1987). "Post-Marxism without apologies," *New Left Review*, 166: 79–106.

Laclau, E. and C. Mouffe (2001). *Hegemony and Socialist Strategy: Towards a Radical Democratic Politics*, 2e, London: Verso.

Landry, L. Y. (2000). *Marx and the Postmodern Debates: An Agenda for Critical Theory*, Santa Barbara, CA: Praeger Publishing.

Laughlin, R. C. (1995). "Empirical research in accounting: alternative approaches and a case for 'middle-range' thinking," *Accounting, Auditing and Accountability Journal*, 8(1): 63–87.

Lechte, J. (2006). *Fifty Key Contemporary Thinkers: From Structuralism to Postmodernity*, London and New York: Routledge.

Lehman, G. (2001). "Reclaiming the public sphere: problems and prospects for corporate social and environmental accounting," *Critical Perspectives on Accounting*, 12(6): 713–33.

Letwin, S. R. (1965). *The Pursuit of Certainty: David Hume, Jeremy Bentham, John Stuart Mill, Beatrice Webb*, Cambridge: Cambridge University Press.

Liu, A. (2009). *Local Transcendence: Essays on Postmodern Historicism and the Database*, Chicago, IL: University of Chicago Press.

Loft, A. (1988). *Understanding Accounting in its Historical and Social Context: The Case of Cost Accounting in Britain, 1914-1925*, New York: Garland.

Long, D. (1987). "Bentham as revolutionary social scientist," *Man Nature*, 6: 115–45.

Lyons, D. (1991). *In the Interest of the Governed: A Study of Bentham's Principle of Utility and Law*, revised edition, New York: Oxford University Press.

Mack, M. P. (1962). *Jeremy Bentham: An Odyssey of Ideas, 1748-1792*, London: Heinemann

Mouffe, C. (1993). *The Return of the Political*, London: Verso.

Parashar, A. (2008). "Re-conceptualizing regulation, responsibility and law," *Macquarie Law Journal*, 8: 59–77.

Parekh, B. (1993) (ed.). *Jeremy Bentham: Critical Assessments*, London: Routledge.

Patterson, T. (1989). "Post-structuralism, post-modernism: implications for historians," *Social History*, 14(1): 83–8.

Pieterse, J. N. (1992). "Emancipations, modern and postmodern," *Development and Change*, 23(3): 5–41.

Pitkin, H. F. (1990). "Slippery Bentham: some neglected cracks in the foundations of utilitarianism," *Political Theory*, 18(1): 104–31.

Polanyi, K. (1945). *Origins of Our Time: The Great Transformation*, London: Victor Gollancz.

Postema, G. J. (1988). "Bentham's equality-sensitive utilitarianism," *Utilitas*, 1(1): 41–61

Radin, M. J. and F. Michelman (1991). "Pragmatist and poststructuralist critical legal practice," *University of Pennsylvania Law Review*, 139(4): 1019–38.

Rosen, F. (1982). "Jeremy Bentham: recent interpretations," *Political Studies*, 30(4): 575–81.

Russell, B. (1962). *History of Western Philosophy and its Connection with Political and Social Circumstances from the Earliest Times to the Present Day*, London: Allen and Unwin.

Schöttler, P. (1989). "Historians and discourse analysis," *History Workshop Journal*, 27(1): 37–65.

Semple, J. (1993). *Bentham's Prison: A Study of the Panopticon Penitentiary*, New York: Oxford.

Twining, W. (1989). *Reading Bentham*, London: British Academy.

Veron, J. (1994). "Who is afraid of the linguistic turn – the politics of social history and its discontents," *Social History*, 19(1): 81–97.

Williams, R. (1987). *Culture and Society: Coleridge to Orwell*, London: The Hogarth Press.

Young, R. (1990). *White Mythologies: Writing History and the West*, London and New York: Routledge.

Zadek, S., P. Pruzan and R. Evans (1997) (eds). *Building Corporate Accountability: Emerging Practices in Social and Ethical Accounting, Auditing and Reporting*, London: Earthscan Publications.

Žižek, S. (2001). *Did Somebody Say Totalitarianism? Five Interventions in the (Misuse) of a Notion*, London: Verso.

5

PHILOSOPHICAL TRADITIONS

Glen Lehman

1 Introduction

This chapter introduces and briefly summarises four dominant generic philosophical traditions that have played a prominent role in both accounting and philosophical research (see Table 5.1).[1] These four traditions share a common concern, in that each challenges the dominance of economic and positivist approaches to accounting research. Each tradition is used to examine key social and environmental dilemmas that confront accounting systems in the context of the communities to whom they report. The social and environmental issues that confront accounting may include but are not limited to how accounting implements moral codes in business and how accounting influences interactions with the world.

Within each philosophical tradition it is possible to identify key accounting writers who work within its accounting variant (see Burrell and Morgan, 1979). The first tradition encompasses procedural approaches to ethics such as modern liberalism and utilitarianism; the focus of these approaches is to develop rules of conduct for business. The second tradition informs critical approaches to accounting that challenge the prevailing capitalist social system and its propensity to generate social inequalities and environmental problems. The third tradition encompasses a number of more recent 'subversive' approaches including both postmodern and post-structural perspectives, amongst others. The final tradition is concerned with those interpretivist approaches that are used to examine the assumptions that influence institutions such as accounting, business and governance. The following sections examine each of the four dominant traditions in detail and explore how they have influenced accounting thought.[2]

2 Procedural ethics

2.1 Utilitarian and Kantian philosophies as applied to accounting

The utilitarian approach as developed by Jeremy Bentham (1789) posits that rather than an act being right or wrong, the strongest and most prominent issue is that it maximises the greatest happiness of the greatest number of people. Utilitarianism can take two forms known as act utilitarianism and rule utilitarianism; in the former case, the consequences of an action are examined, in the latter case the consequences of choosing a rule to follow are assessed. The rule form of utilitarianism is what leads to it being considered a procedural approach along with act

Table 5.1 Philosophical traditions and critical accounting

Procedural Ethics	Critical Theory	Postmodernism	Interpretivism
Kant, Bentham, Mill Accounting theorists: Gallhofer and Haslam, Gaa, Williams.	Marx, early Habermas Accounting theorists: Laughlin, Broadbent, Power, Tinker.	Foucault, Derrida, Lacan Accounting theorists: Arrington, Francis, Messner.	Gadamer, Heidegger Accounting theorists: Cooper, Willmott, Roslender.

utilitarianism, which takes a teleological approach to ethics where the focus is on how good or bad an action is as opposed to developing procedures and rules to adjudicate the rightness or wrongness of those actions.

Utilitarian theorists in the context of accounting, such as Gallhofer and Haslam (1997a,b, 2003; see also Gallhofer, Haslam, Monk and Roberts, 2006), have often been inspired by Bentham's work. In the context of accounting they point out that Bentham's utilitarianism "advocated openness [transparency] to as many people as possible so that governance would come to operate in the general interest" (Gallhofer and Haslam, 2003: 43). Utilitarianism is often criticised because it has the potential to ignore the plight of the least advantaged, however, since the greatest happiness principle has the potential to glide over structural and social inequalities in the social system.

The consequentialist or utilitarian approach stands in contrast to the deontological approach proposed by Immanuel Kant. Kant's formal term for his approach to determining the rightness of an action is referred to as a 'categorical imperative' (Kant, 1789). A categorical imperative can be defined as a procedural decision-making device to determine the ethical validity of an action. Actions that are consistent with the procedure would be universal and therefore morally permissible. For Kant an action is moral when it can be universalised against the procedural test. Kant sets out the action in the form of a maxim where a maxim then constructs a general principle that captures the action under consideration. The ethical content of the maxim is then judged according to whether it can be universalised. If the maxim is not universal it contains contrary actions that would be considered to be unethical. The categorical imperative serves as a formal decision-making model which can be applied to accounting to determine the ethical content of accounting reports, conceptual frameworks and standards. Kant states:

> And could I say to myself that everyone may make a false promise when he is in a difficulty from which he cannot escape? Immediately I see that I could will the lie but not a universal law to lie. For with such a law there would be no promises at all, inasmuch as it would be futile to make pretense of my intention in regard to future actions to those who would not believe this pretense or – if they over hastily did so – would pay me back in my own coin. This maxim would necessarily destroy itself as soon as it was made a universal law.
>
> *(Kant, 1789: 19)*

In this quotation the teleological application within Kant's approach becomes evident. For Kant, teleology is about determining the rightness of an action. He endeavours to determine whether an action can be universalised. The example he presents is that of lying. Obviously, a lie could not be universalised because if everyone lied, no one could be believed.

Kant's work has been widely applied in business ethics. An example often used is that of a contractual situation as it involves the formality of making a promise. If everyone were to break a promise or contract, there would be no contracts made. This maxim would not be permissible because it cannot be universalised; that is if everyone broke their promise or contract the economic system could not operate effectively. Kant's focus on universal rules gives rise to the action-guiding-decision model that is often adapted to accounting research. Kant is appealing to accounting researchers because his categorical imperative can easily be adapted and this is because he offers a procedural device that may be used to guide justice in liberal-democratic systems. The ideas developed by Kant have been used by accounting theorists to examine notions of fairness and justice within financial reporting. In the following section, these ideas are developed in an accounting context.

2.2 Liberalism and decision usefulness – applying Kant and Rawls

This section examines how Kant's approach to determining the rightness of an action has been applied in accounting. Kant's work is developed for modern times in John Rawls's text: *A Theory of Justice* (1971). Accounting theorists such as Paul Williams have used John Rawls's procedural decision-making model because it extends the categorical imperative to human rights issues (Rawls, 1971, 1980, 1982, 1985). With its origins firmly in Kantian philosophy, the procedural decision-making model has been used to determine the justice of accounting decisions in terms of the rights of people.

Accounting theory, in its utilisation of Kantian and Rawlsian decision-making models, is firmly focused on the impacts of corporations on the rights of people. Often Rawls's work is introduced by explaining how it develops Kant's categorical imperative, previously referred to as the 'principles of justice' intended to govern and guide a well-ordered society. The Kantian and Rawlsian focus on rights and justice is particularly appealing to accounting which claims to be about satisfying the rights of citizens, communities and relevant publics. Accounting researchers use Rawls's decision-making model, which is called the 'original position', to determine the fairness and justice of particular actions. The original position is based on 12 crucial elements,[3] with the veil of ignorance being the most prominent element (Rawls, 1971). The original position operates behind a veil of ignorance and can be thought of as an ethical device to determine the ethical content of an action (Gaa, 1986). Behind this veil, representative individuals who are motivated by the economic assumptions of rationality and self-interest choose principles of justice. Rawls developed the original position using this economic approach where representative individuals would choose and develop the principles of justice. The principles of justice are concerned with the rights of individuals and the plight of the least advantaged. These are that (i) each person is to have equal liberty to the most extensive total system of equal basic liberties compatible with a similar system of liberty for all; and (ii) social and economic inequalities are to be arranged so that they are both (a) to the greatest benefit of the least advantaged, consistent with the just saving principle, and (b) attached to offices and positions open to all under conditions of fair equality of opportunity.

Williams (1987), a prominent accounting theorist, uses the Rawlsian original position to extend the accounting focus. The focus is on those user groups who are expected to give a just and fair account of their actions. This may involve providing information concerning the environmental and social impacts of corporations to these groups or parties as part of an accountability relationship (Williams, 1987: 170). The focus turns to the fairness of general-purpose financial reporting where information is assumed to be relevant to making and evaluating decisions about the allocation of scarce resources. In developing the moral dimension in critical accounting, Williams and Ravenscroft (2015) focus on the obligatory implications of the moral dimension,[4] while also proposing an inclusive democratic structure in which accounting plays a pivotal role in reporting corporate impacts.

From the perspective developed in the work of Williams (1987) and Williams and Ravenscroft (2015) it is argued that decision-useful information is inadequate as an ethical decision-making device for organising accounting practice and research. They challenge the claim made by the accounting profession that if the information is decision useful it satisfies its accountability criteria. Williams (1987) points out that in subsuming accountability within the definition of decision useful-ness, accounting has avoided its moral obligations by not developing its accountability relationships.

2.3 The early liberal social accounting model

Gray, Owen and Maunders (1987) develop these liberal themes in the context of social account-ing, exploring the rights of stakeholders and other user groups, again using Rawls's work. Their focus on the rights of stakeholders challenges the economic and instrumental focus that dominates modern accounting theory and practice. Their social accounting focus is on the public and social sphere, which to function effectively requires that citizens must be informed about the impact of accounting data and business decisions on society. This may not be the case when accounting simply reports economic outcomes that submerge societal demands for improved accountability. Social accountants such as Gray *et al.* (1987), argue that stakeholders must be provided with more detailed information concerning how accounting data, decisions and reports impact on the natural environment and the social sphere (see also Gray, 1983, 1990a,b,c; Gray, Owen and Adams, 1996).

In particular, Gray *et al.* (1987) emphasise the need for accounts that have a broader focus to address the legitimate interests of stakeholders in the accountability relationship. This then gives rise to a broader focus on pluralism which is a central feature of their approach to accounting and accountability research. This broader focus involves acknowledging the pluralism that is implicit in accountability relationships. They argue that pluralism in its modern form is about acknowledging that there are many different viewpoints and value systems which impact on accountability relationships. Their commitment to accountability reflects their (liberal) view that the seeds of justice are to be found in existing accounting and accountability structures of governance. Gray, Owen and Maunders (1991) comment that

> [w]e see little fruitful development in merely standardizing social accounting tech-niques in the absence of a more fundamental political challenge being mounted to the privileges of existing corporate power in capitalist society. However, our analysis parts from that of Puxty [who is a major critic of conventional and social accounting as discussed in the following section] in seeing the necessary seeds of change already implanted in such society and therefore a role for social accounting in developing a far wider form of accountability.
>
> *(p. 14)*

In sum, it is important to remember that social accounting approaches such as the early work of Gray *et al.* (1987) re-conceptualise not only accountability research but how concepts such as decision usefulness might be developed to create a deeper moral appreciation of the role of information (see also Merkl-Davies and Brennan, 2011; Williams and Ravenscroft, 2015).

2.4 Subsequent developments in liberal accountability thought

To this point, the critical focus in liberal accountability thought has been about how human interests have been eroded when accounting focuses primarily on the criterion of decision usefulness, the maximisation of profit over people. As observed earlier, Gray *et al.* (1987) argue that accounting concepts such as decision usefulness and its reliance on utilitarian maximising strategies share a common goal to maximise the greatest happiness of the greatest number. Social accountants argue that these strategies give undue emphasis to profit-maximising goals. This, of course, is the traditional concern with utilitarianism that in maximising the greatest happiness of the greatest number, the rights of the least advantaged are not given full consideration. It is, therefore, a contention of social accounting scholarship that utilitarian principles can glide over serious ethical and moral issues.

Furthermore, inspired by Rawls's work on justice the social accounting project argued that the focus on decision usefulness neglects to recognise the fact that accounting is highly situated in the context of human interests, that is, accounting fails in its quest to create a just and transparent system (Arrington and Puxty, 1991: 31; see also Baynes, 1992; Pallot, 1991; Lehman, 2015). According to social accounting researchers, this leads to a focus on decision usefulness and an emphasis on economic variables at the expense of an appreciation of the moral relationships between corporations and society (Williams and Ravenscroft, 2015). In this regard, critical and social accounting aims to move beyond economic self-interest to emphasise moral relationships between citizens, stakeholders and corporations.

This liberal social accounting perspective, as developed by Gray *et al.* (1987) and Williams (1987), concerns the specification of moral obligations and duties between corporations and society. These strands of liberal thought in Gray *et al.* (1987) challenge the facilitating economic features associated with decision-useful financial information.[5] Moreover, in the spirit of decision usefulness technical accountants argue that the numbers reported "passively and objectively record and represent the results of organisational reality" (Roberts, 1991: 355). That is, the numbers in the financial statements are assumed to accurately reflect the impact of corporations on the natural environment and society.

Therefore, the early work of Gray *et al.* (1995) and Owen, Gray and Bebbington (1997) is about defining points of intersection between the critical, environmental and social accounting models. In their early work they offer a 'middle ground' approach where different philosophical perspectives coalesce and enable a consensus to emerge. However, critics of social accounting argue that the middle ground itself has become contested as a consequence of the competing demands from stakeholders. These arguments are developed by Gray, Kouhy and Lavers (1995), who consider where accountability demands between alternative moral perspectives can be achieved. They argue that their social accounting model did not rely on comprehensive philosophical doctrines. For example, they claim that their position is not necessarily in conflict with more radical philosophical perspectives. They explain:

> These two points of view are essentially different ways of looking at the issues (Held, 1980) and are, fundamentally, irreconcilable in that the bourgeois perception treats as important issues which the Marxian analysis will see as relatively trivial.
>
> *(Gray et al., 1995: 53)*

They acknowledge that bourgeois and Marxian political economies are essentially irreconcilable, because Marxism aims to overthrow capitalism while bourgeois frameworks aim to create change within current social structures. Gray *et al.* (1995) continue in their search for an overlapping consensus or middle ground without drawing on Marx's political economy. Thus, this middle ground reflects their liberal sources through the provision of additional information. The early arguments made by Gray and his co-authors remain committed to the belief that environmental and social change can be achieved within the current capitalist system, a position that is also fully consistent with the promotion of an evolutionary approach to the reform of accounting. The key question remains, however, concerning whether corporate environmental and social reporting can lead to meaningful change without fundamentally reconstructing capitalism and its corporate structures.

2.5 The promise of interstitial accounts

In his recent work Gray has embraced a more philosophically robust perspective that involves the creation of interstitial[6] social transformations that emanate from the work of Erik Olin Wright, as in Gray, Malpas and Brennan (2014). Citing Wright (2010) they describe interstitial accounting in the following way:

> "Interstitial" is a term used by Wright to refer to new institutions that are built "in the niches of capitalism". This notion derives from the obvious recognition that hegemony is never complete and that, equally, a capitalist society is never completely capitalist. There always exists within capitalism many non-capitalist forms whether these be part of the public sector, part of civil society or in family, religious or grass roots initiatives. His personal agenda for change relies upon the building of non-capitalist forms within the niches of capitalism and he illustrates what he means by reference to four examples: participatory city budgeting, Wikipedia, the Mondragon worker cooperatives and unconditional basic income.
>
> (Gray et al., 2014: 259)

The issue that follows from interstitial accounting is whether corporations can create and develop opportunities for 'counter-hegemony' to reflect on humanity's unsustainable practices.[7] Optimism regarding the development of counter-hegemonic strategies has been eroded over the years by various critics, hence the enthusiasm evident in Gray *et al.* (2014). Thomson (2014: : 275) argues that the merit of developing interstitial environmental and social accounting "is to confront organisations with the truth of their unsustainability whilst facilitating cooperation with institutions engaged in sustainable transformation are compelling." Nevertheless, there is still value in developing symbiotic social accounts that can be easily and quickly embedded in organisational practices.

According to Thomson (2014), commenting on Gray *et al.* (2014), while there are clear limits to the benefits of symbiotic social accounting, new accounts can still produce social and ecological benefits even if they are constrained by the current capitalist system. Also, for the purposes of understanding the trajectory of social accounting, Thomson (2014) expresses concern with social and environmental accounting research (SEAR) which has been commodified by corporate propaganda and green washing. For their part, Gray *et al.* (2014) argue that accounting research should search to create synergistic impacts of carefully planned and targeted symbiotic social accounting research. This new direction for environmental and social accounting is to create new niches in capitalism from which future interstitial transformations could emerge (Thomson, Grubnic and Georgakopoulos, 2014). The new direction involves creating and complementing interstitial structures that will rupture oriented social accounting research and practices.

3 Critical Theory

3.1 Critical approaches to accounting and language

Jurgen Habermas has had a major influence on the development of critical accounting. Habermas's ethical and procedural model – the Ideal Speech Community (ISC) – can be used to determine the rightness of the various actions that citizens make.[8] Habermas began as a critical and radical theorist, subsequently moving in a more procedural direction like Kant and Rawls. His theory of communicative action focuses on language as a decision-making device, within which context the concept of the ISC plays a pivotal role.[9] Arrington and Puxty (1991) observe that

> Habermas provides an ethical-political model — what he calls the 'Ideal Speech Community' — as a regulative ideal to guide public argument oriented toward the formation of a rational consensus with respect to the shape and rationality of interested social actions. That model binds public argument to the following procedural conditions of justice-in-argument, and it is the ethic that provides the foundation for his social theory.
>
> *(p. 45)*

The ISC is a procedural decision-making device which Habermas (1987) has constructed to determine ethical outcomes in the public sphere. The device has been applied to accounting issues such as the viability of conceptual frameworks, the public private partnership phenomenon as well as the role of accounting in society. The key insight is that as a decision-making device, the ISC determines the rightness of social actions through rational discourse. This discourse is said to be free from forms of economic, political and social domination. Arrington and Puxty (1991) explain that the ISC is used to determine the rightness of social actions in the public sphere. They emphasise the concept of justice-in-argument as ascribed to Habermas as being in line with Kant's categorical imperative, which was discussed in the previous section.

The ISC therefore acts as a decision device to determine the rightness of social actions and claims presented by citizens. For Habermas, justice-in-argument involves the following procedural tests: (i) the comprehensibility of the utterance; (ii) the truth of its propositional component; (iii) the correctness and appropriateness of its performatory component; and (iv) the authenticity of the speaking subject (Habermas, 1973: 18). These four procedures provide the components of the ISC to regulate discourse in the public sphere. More fundamentally, the claims adjudicated in the ISC move in the theoretical space between the actual and what is possible (Power and Laughlin, 1992: 448).

In the context of accounting research, such research activities must generate (i) unrestricted participation in the accounting arena; (ii) the equality of opportunities in the accounting discourse; (iii) correctness and cooperative motives in constructing conceptual frameworks; and (iv) the mechanism to determine the communicative claims concerning the 'good' society. Again, the key issue is about determining the rightness of various claims reported by accountants in annual, environmental and financial reports. When using Habermas's work it is important to remember that critical accountants argue that the ISC leads to fair and neutral decisions and outcomes. From this perspective, it is claimed that the ISC can replace or supplement the current accounting conceptual framework.

A key objective of Habermas's philosophy is to reclaim the public sphere from the high tide of modernity. The term 'technological modernity' is meant to convey the idea that there exists a danger to the everyday world of human affairs when bureaucrats and procedural administrators colonise it. These important issues impact on the philosophy of accounting research and reflect the concern that procedures can ensnare workers in unfair practices.

Habermas employs the concepts of system, lifeworld and steering to deliberate about the development of society towards a more just and free system. His argument is that the lifeworld is a cultural space that gives meaning to societal life, itself a reservoir of human social developments that contrasts with the more tangible systems. It is the lifeworld that "gives these systems meaning and attempts to guide their behaviour through steering media" (Laughlin, 1987: 486). Systems, on the other hand, are the self-regulating actions around which specific mechanisms or media, such as money or power (Broadbent *et al.*, 1991: 3) are developed. Lifeworlds are the communicatively formed (over time) life experiences and beliefs that guide attitudes, behaviours and actions. Systems are expressions of lifeworld concerns and can be represented at the micro-level as functionally tangible organisations. In Habermas's view,

> [w]e speak of social integration in relation to the systems of institutions in which speaking and acting subjects are socially related (*vergellschaften*). Systems are seen here as lifeworlds that are symbolically structured. We speak of system integration with a view to the specific steering performance of a self-regulated system. Social systems are considered here from the point of view of the capacity to maintain their boundaries and their continued existence by mastering the complexity of an inconstant environment. Both paradigms, lifeworlds and system, are important.
>
> *(Habermas, 1974: 4)*

What remains important to any critical theorisation of accounting that follows Habermas's later work is not simply providing a clear criterion for distinguishing between legitimate and illegitimate roles for accounting and the law but also making an explicit commitment to these structures as a regulative ideal. The work of Habermas, therefore, is particularly appealing to critical accounting researchers because of its commitment to reforming procedure as a regulative ideal. The communicative structure of an actually carried out discourse *must* involve all those people affected by a proposed norm. In this way each person is given political space for their views to be expressed and their actions evaluated. This is necessary so that there is an exchange of roles which provides all participants with equal opportunities. In this Habermasian-inspired process, roles are reversed so that various claims and propositions are given fair and equal consideration. In effect, this role-reversal process occurs where each participant asserts their proposition or action, which is then subjected to the ISC. The procedural tests therefore determine the rightness of the claims advanced by participants in the ISC. The procedural focus of the ISC is on whether the proposition passes the procedural tests in the idealised arena.

According to Habermas, the aim of this regulative process is to create awareness of the dangers that lie within a technological society. For Habermas,

> [a]s far as philosophy is concerned, it might do well to refurbish its link with the totality by taking on the role of interpreter on behalf of the lifeworld.
>
> *(Habermas, 1987: 313)*

Habermas's claim is that the task of philosophy is to create a process where cognitive self-reflection offers the hope of emancipation for all humanity. He creates a framework to sustain the traditional philosophical claim for truth (Habermas, 1987: 313). This Habermasian regulative process ranges across the whole spectrum of human knowledge, not just the fruits of science and technology.

3.2 Adapting Habermas: searching for a middle-range accounting research approach

Accounting scholars attracted to Habermas's regulative model and the ISC are also implicitly committed to his theory of language (see Laughlin, 2008, 2010, 2011, 2012). Habermas's approach to language guides the way critical accounting scholars use his work to examine connections between accounting and democratic theory. It is often argued that accounting is complicit in colonising the social world (Laughlin, 1987), a process which must be challenged by developing new systems towards a normative model of rational argumentation (Shapiro, 1998). Broadbent and Laughlin (2004) explore the effects of accounting on healthcare systems and the implications of modern bureaucratic accounting, offering some political recommendations. For example, Broadbent and Laughlin (2004) intimate that the healthcare sector has been colonised by free market forms of reason and rationality, at the expense of a caring health system. Free market reforms put money and rationality first and people second.

For Habermas, modern society must be restructured in such a way that each individual is aware of the distortions of modernity and its culture of money, power and procedural rationality. This is to be achieved through the development of undistorted communication which moderates the often unanalysed and distorting variable, that is, power, in the public sphere. Laughlin (2011) takes the Habermasian framework in a new direction when he applies the model to particular accounting issues and impacts on society. He introduces the concept of a skeletal ontology to illustrate the various ways in which it is possible to interpret empirical observations and bureaucratic structures. The minimal ontology offered by Laughlin (1995) involves the factors people consider to be primary for their existence. Laughlin (1995) uses Merton's concept of the 'middle range' to chart his skeletal ontology through an empirical contextualisation of accounting issues which take place at the policy level (Merton, 1968). Laughlin essentially moves in a pragmatic direction acknowledging the important role that Merton's analysis plays in the explanation of social behaviour. At the same time, he also moves away from Merton's analysis in his search to locate theories of accounting "with a pervasive concern with consolidating special theories into more generalisable theories" (Laughlin, 1995: 79). Later, Laughlin adds that

> [t]he 'middle-range' … has no faith in the development of such a general theory. Put simply the 'middle range' … maintains that there can only ever be 'skeletal' theories in social phenomena – the hope for a grand theory, similar to Parsonian thought, is wistful and incorrect quasi-scientific thinking of a highly questionable nature. But this is only one of the areas of difference – the 'middle-range' thinking in this essay also differs to Merton's emphasis on methodology (with its desire finally, although maybe immediately, to adopt highly theoretical methods for investigation) and change (with its purposeful distance from getting involved in any value judgements about what is being investigated).

The argument of this passage is that accounting is a practice that moves within a space of reason. The critical accounting issue, therefore, involves answering the question concerning whether Habermas's regulative model will achieve its aim. In answering this question, it will be recalled that the primary aim is to assess communication that is incompatible with the good or better life. That is, the Habermasian process is really about reversing roles so that justice is achieved (as discussed earlier in this section). This framework then connects with the formal procedures in the ISC community to adjudicate people's actions and claims (Habermas, 1993: 56–7). Can such a focus on procedure accommodate the substantive claims that shape the identity of many people? The next section examines the limits of procedural accounting ethics.

3.3 Radical accounting: Marxist-inspired critical accounting

Tinker, Neimark and Lehman (1991) commend a philosophical and radical analysis of account-ing. Their key contribution is to explain how accounting is implicated in the generation of inequalities in capitalist society through aspects of Marx's *Capital*. They explain that accounting is a compliant participant in the capitalist exploitative system that perpetuates the class divisions responsible for wealth inequalities. It is then argued that capitalism is an apology for the exist-ing social structure which critical philosophy attempts to change. Accounting is assumed to be a compliant participant in the creation of false realities which are built on the exploitative processes of capitalism. Tinker *et al.* (1991) argue that emancipatory accounting must be used to unlock systemic inequalities that perpetuate injustice and inequality. The challenge for critical accountants is to reveal the various negative features of capitalism in the belief that equality and justice should be shared by all social beings (see Cooper, 2015).

The philosophy underpinning a radical, emancipatory critical accounting seeks to document the distortions between what is reported and the actual relationships which they report. Critical accounting theorists emphasise how accounting is a mechanism that perpetuates the generation of surplus value that in turn creates the inequalities in capitalism, as outlined earlier. Thus, the focus of this strand of critical accounting is on the means by which surplus value is appropri-ated by the owners of production (capitalists) in the form of surplus economic rents. The critical accounting project therefore also seeks to design and restructure the basic institutions of modern communities, such as accounting. This would be part of an administrative solution inspired by the Marxist telos of an unalienated society.

This strand of critical accounting aims to not only reveal the inequalities in capitalism but offer an agenda which involves a telos of an emancipatory politics. Before the emancipatory goals are specified, however, Tinker *et al.* (1991) reveal how accounting is implicated in the inter-connections and interrelationships which make accounting culpable in major financial scandals, and environmental and social disasters (see also Spence, 2009). They argue that

> [i]n assuming that accounting disclosure could help humanise capitalism, they [advo-cates of a reformist social accounting] seemed to forget that the market imperative often impels corporations to dump chemicals haphazardly rather than employ expen-sive reprocessing methods, 'cheat n billings' to government agencies, bribe govern-ment officials, condone shoddy workmanship, etc. These same client interests are also likely to underlie the accounting profession's technical objections to impounding social costs and benefits in financial statements. These underlying antagonisms, inter-ests and loyalties are inherent in capitalism and were left unanalysed by social respon-sibility theories. In consequence, their palliatives only dealt with symptoms not causes.
>
> *(Tinker et al., 1991: 33)*

In an earlier monograph entitled *Paper Prophets*, Tinker (1985) outlines a number of the more bizarre financial scandals that had occurred in recent years in both the UK and US, including the Love Canal in the US as well as the Slater Walker scandal in the UK. In the former episode Hooker Chemical was found to be responsible for releasing toxic chemicals into the Love Canal near Niagara Falls. Hooker Chemical was eventually found to be negligent in their disposal of waste, though not reckless in the sale of the land, in what became a test case for liability clauses (se also Laughlin and Puxty, 1986).[10]

The critical perspective developed by Tinker (1985) and Tinker *et al.* (1991) documents the complex of underlying social relationships that exist between business and corporate reporting.

Issues such as site contamination, banking collapses and financial scandals are not given full consideration in the accounting conceptual framework. The critical perspective on accounting, therefore, aims to provide an alternative view of organisational reality coupled with a critical interventionist stance. The emphasis is clearly on how accounting can assist in changing these destructive realities through introducing Marx's theory of value within accounting research, thereby explaining how accounting is built on principles of utility that support the assumptions of capitalism and wealth inequality, to the disbenefit of the mass of society.

For Tinker *et al.* (1991), the utility-maximising assumptions that shape modern capitalism are based on neo-classical economic assumptions. They argue that this focus on the maximisation of utility damages social relations and perpetuates an unjust and unfair capitalist social system. These issues are reflected in how processes of economic and utility maximisation guide the construction of modern neo-classical economics. In challenging neoclassical economic assumptions, they explain how accounting contributes to a social reality which benefits the owners of capital at the expense of workers. They draw on Marx's concept that capitalism acts as a reifying process that exploits people and alienates them in the production process. Marx used the term 'reification' to explain how social relationships are transformed into subjects and then into objects of production.[11] The end result of this process is that people's identity and values are rendered passive or determined, while the objects of production are rendered as the active and determining factors of social relationships. The social structure is determined by economic factors underlining capitalism which in turn shape social relationships. People are objectified and commodified such that economic relationships determine social relationships, rendering people passive and indeterminate.

According to this analysis, people are turned into mere things in the search of greater profits. The end result is that the interplay between social relationships and the social structure is the determining factor. Tinker *et al.* (1991) explain how a reformist social accounting project is unable to create change because it assumes that people's position in society is fixed and stable. They explain that social accounting reforms glide over the structures of capitalism without providing viable social alternatives. In their continuation of this critique, it is argued that accounting reports are constructed based on neo-classical utility assumptions. The task for critical accounting is to reveal the underlying relationships that exist among accounting, capitalism and organisations.

3.4 Critical perspectives on accounting reform proposals

In the remaining paragraphs in this section we outline how a number of accounting theorists, including Broadbent, Laughlin, Puxty and Sikka, move between the various critical and procedural perspectives. In this context, the work of Puxty (1986, 1991) is especially instructive through its commitment to a critical perspective that uses Habermas's earlier work on language and social change. The power in language is explored to examine connections between accounting, capitalism and the dynamics in language.

Puxty was highly critical of the social accounting project of Gray *et al.* (1987) because it relied on change coming about through existing institutions. From Puxty's perspective, critical accountants must enquire why powerful corporations would give up their privileges to enter a 'middle-ground' consensus (see also Bryer 2012, 2013a, 2013b, 2015). The central issue for critical accounting, then, involves determining whether corporations are able to create social change. More fundamentally, this strand of critical accounting explains how early liberal and middle-of-the-road social accounting reforms fail to argue why social accountants accept pluralism, the status quo and capitalism. Puxty argued that this belief seemed optimistic. This is because the evolutionary gradualism in procedural and social accounting fails to explore the laws and structural strengths of capitalism. Puxty explains his approach in the following passage:

> The two levels are related, but independent. Thus although we acknowledge the Marxian insight that labour is fundamental in the economic process, and hence that the employment relation is necessarily one of exploitation, we do not thereby suppose that a political and social superstructure is a result derivative of and dependent on that process. The level of human interaction has its own laws of development.
>
> *(Puxty, 1991: 42)*

Puxty's work involves exploring connections between Habermas's work on language and Marx's critique of capitalism. Puxty analyses the historical dynamics of capitalism and its impact on communication in the public sphere. Underlying these observations is the supposition that 'true knowledge' of the dynamics of capitalism allows us to create unalienated societies. The novelty of Puxty's developments in accounting theory involves his extensions of Habermas's argument that human communities and their language are entwined. Communicative structures are integral to Puxty's philosophy; through language and communication it is assumed that understanding and reconciliation can be achieved. On this view the power of communication and language frees accounting and its governance structures from the colonising potential within economic interests.

Highly critical of capitalism, Puxty searches to remove the barriers which impede accounting from contributing to a fair and just society. His work is about challenging and freeing the public sphere from instrumental and procedural barriers. Puxty explains how the public sphere has been captured by technical approaches such as accounting. He uses Habermas's early work to explain and expose the barriers that impede the development of improved relationships. As an example, Puxty enquired whether bankers and other corporate managers would directly assist some of the poorest countries to retrench workers to maximise profits. How are these decisions made? What are the connections between profit and identity?

Puxty's work also explores whether the distribution of income and wealth is becoming progressively more unequal. From his communicative and critical perspective the challenge is not only to develop social accounting or interstitial accounts, or to extend accounting beyond its initial focus. The challenge is to tackle the entrenched interests of capitalism in the public sphere. More recently Sikka has taken up this challenge, developing accounting research employing Gramsci's critical work on the public sphere. Sikka (2011, 2015) is concerned with the inequalities and structural problems of contemporary capitalism and also focuses on the voluntarism within the liberal and procedural philosophies of reform social accounting. That is, corporations have 'structural strengths' in contrast to other sectors of society.

From these radical perspectives it is argued that procedural, social and technical accounting is just one part of that structural strength which maintains capitalism's dominant and hegemonic position. Mainstream accounting theory and practice, in neglecting the totality in favour of a conceptual framework approach, severs its links with the lifeworld. This effectively immunises accounting from other social science approaches that endeavour to understand the impact of accounting in society. As a consequence, the exploitative process and instrumental virus that plagues accounting, as identified by Tinker, Puxty, Sikka and others, leads to a blindness and immunity in accounting to social and ecological issues that concern many citizens and communities.

4 The postmodern turn

4.1 Derrida and deconstruction

Over the past 30 years, postmodern perspectives have become increasingly influential in criticising both Western accounting and Western political thought. Notably, Arrington and Francis (1989) introduce Derrida's work to accounting, using his approach to deconstruct positive and technical accounting frameworks. The focus of postmodern perspectives in accounting is on revealing the repressive presence within modernity, while their aim is to give space to ideas and voices that have been submerged by procedural approaches such as those outlined in Section 2.1. The deconstructive strategy is to reveal how earlier Western political thought has been bedded down in procedural and universal frameworks, as exemplified in the previous two sections. In their seminal 1989 paper "Letting the chat out of the bag," Arrington and Francis (1989: 3) demonstrate through Derrida's deconstruction that "positive theory and the empirical tradition are not entitled to the kind of epistemic privilege and authority that they have enjoyed in silencing other kinds of writings about accounting." They continue, offering the following explanation:

> Deconstruction shares with Foucauldian scholarship a desire to question Enlightenment models of rationality, theory, facticity and history as progress. This critical stance is perhaps best described by the intellectual movement termed postmodernism (see Lyotard, 1984), an attempt to arrive at a new beginning for understanding the nature of human inquiry.

Arrington and Francis then proceed to reveal the structures of power that privilege certain ways of doing accounting. For example, they deconstruct Jensen's highly influential assertion that positive accounting theory must be privileged over other ways of knowing and writing.

Their argument is built on Derrida's perplexing view that we never fully know what we are doing, a phrase that is really about revealing the unforeseen impacts of Western thought and its systems on others. This explanation of deconstruction summarises their concern with Western concepts, ideas and values that glide over difference and diversity. Arrington and Francis's particular concern is with how accounting and accountability frameworks rely on an ethical framework that in turn relies too heavily on procedural ways of thinking that erode moral responsibility. They adapt Derrida's work to deconstruct accounting codes and practices to reveal how ethical and responsibility frameworks "incite us to irresponsibility" (Derrida, 1992: 61; see also McKernan, 2012; Miller and O'Leary, 1987; Morgan and Willmott, 1993).

The aim of postmodern accounting deconstruction is not only to break open accounting but to escape current procedural constraints and disclose new worlds. The professed aim of this new world view is to provide space for alternate possibilities and viewpoints to be given expression. Postmodern accounting philosophy is committed to freeing accounting research from procedural and universal approaches that guide and shape much modern accounting research. Here the work of Nelson (1993) is particularly relevant, including the way he discloses the goods revealed through deconstruction. Nelson (1993: 207) argues:

> [T]here is reason to worry that these post-modern goods defined within accounting as a practice remain inadequately acknowledged by the daily conduct of accounting and even by its academic theory.

Nelson's postmodernism focuses on the social goods that exist within practices such as accounting – honesty, magnanimity and openness, to name a few. In a way similar to Arrington and Francis (1989), Nelson (re)discovers new concepts of ethics to open accounting research to different ideas and values.

Accounting theorists who utilise Derrida's work also draw attention to the limitations of accountability, which they believe are not addressed in modern accounting conceptual frameworks. They utilise Derrida's work on deconstruction to operate on what is often referred to as 'Western foundational thinking'. This is undertaken through two steps – the first step reverses dichotomies and then second works to corrupt the dichotomies themselves. The deconstructive strategy reveals that ethics and philosophy are concepts that are undecidable in their nature. They cannot be expressed through procedure or universal approaches to ethical thinking. That is, an undecidable concept cannot conform to either side of a dichotomy or opposition because there are no absolutes or universals. For example, 'undecidability' returns in later periods of Derrida's work to reveal paradoxes involving concepts such as forgiveness, gift giving or hospitality. Apparently, and paradoxically, this occurs when the conditions which permit the possibility of concepts at the same time set the conditions for their impossibility. This complex idea means that a concept can never be treated as an absolute because there are no reference points in time and space which operate indubitably. The concept embodies both its possibility and impossibility. Because of this, it is undecidable whether authentic accounting frameworks are either possible or impossible.

In sum, political philosophers argue that the utility of Derrida's perspective resides in the supposition that "there is nothing outside the text, no object, transcendental or empirical, outside of language to provide solid ground and referent for language" (Derrida, 1976: 158). Applied to accounting, this means that there are no absolutes nor is there an ideal of accountability to strive towards. The implication is that public space must be provided to free people from colonialism, imperialism and universal proceduralism. Postmodern thinking implies that this space does not currently exist and employs a 'come hither' approach which aims to disclose accounting and society to what is foreign and unknown.

4.2 Recent developments: Messner, accountability and postmodernism

Messner (2009) argues that it is well known that demands for higher accountability standards have been criticised from postmodern quarters. He points out that it is very difficult or even impossible to provide justifications to impose high ethical standards on accounting. He argues that these standards end up doing 'violence' to the accountable self – the concern is that individual selves are imprisoned in procedure. Additionally, more procedure and accountability end up in a bureaucratic structure that limits autonomy and imposes administrative costs on organisations. There are, in other words, certain limits to accountability that need to be acknowledged in order to prevent accountability from turning into what Judith Butler (2005) terms 'ethical violence'.

Messner continues that accountability can place unreasonable demands on accounting systems and accountability structures. Responding to these demands involves understanding the role of deconstruction and interpretation in accounting and organisational settings. It is important to remember that ethical systems focus on decision-making structures that are instrumental and end up creating more procedures. Moreover, postmodern accounting and accountability research aims to subvert the dominant structures of control and power of which accounting is a complaint partner. The subversive accounting position within postmodernism provides the language of accounting and accountability with a focus on plural constituencies. The aim is to move accounting from an 'accounting for-the-self' to an 'accounting for-the-other'. Citing the work of Schweiker (1993), Messner observes that

> [Shearer] adopts Levinas' (1998) claim that our relationship to others, and thus our moral obligation to others, comes before any ontological sense of having a distinct identity as an autonomous self. Put another way, ethics must always precede ontology, if we are to take seriously the fact that we are always already exposed to others and their demands before we can actively manage this relationship on the basis of our own interests and demands. As a consequence, any conception of accountability needs to acknowledge this priority of the other, because the 'motive for being accountable is never simple, unadorned self-interest. It entails a constitutive relation to others beyond simple contractual relations'.
>
> *(Messner, 2009: 921)*

Messner is rehearsing the pre-ontological status of these relationships when he argues that accountability decisions must go through the ordeal of the undecidable. He argues that to do otherwise would mean that these decisions "would not be free decision[s] and [would] only be the programmable application or unfolding of a calculable process" (Derrida, 1992: 24). Derrida's massive philosophical work on language is important for accountability (Messner, 2009; Campbell, McPhail and Slack, 2009; McKernan, 2012). The postmodern approach to language can be used to examine accountability, responsibility and transparency as a means to accommodate various ideas, issues and values associated with the 'ubiquitous Other'.[12]

One of the strengths of Derrida's approach to understanding accountability and social reality involves his invitation to face up to the remarkable nature of the Other. The aim is to be open to the unknown which is different and foreign. The implication for accountability is that there is an ideal – perhaps unattainable – yet we must make this effort to come in contact with it (McKernan, 2012). For accountability and critical accounting purposes, these Derridean-inspired arguments are that we can only achieve what is possible by doing the impossible. In other words, accountability must pass through the abyss created by our language to accommodate and recognise the Other. Derrida's perspective reflects a view that language does not constitute and does not reflect moral concepts. On this postmodern view, accountability must engage with the Other to disclose new forms of accounting and organisational structures.

In the next section, the interpretivist tradition is briefly discussed. The aim is to explore the philosophical implications of interpretivism and determine whether knowledge is socially constructed. How might accounting open communities to other values? What is the unknown and by what means can we engage with and account for these activities?

5 Interpretivism and accounting research

The final philosophical tradition considered here is that of interpretivism. Perhaps the most important feature of interpretivist accounting thought is its commitment to understanding the intersubjective relationships on which accounting is based (Chua, 1988; Ahrens *et al.*, 2008). One means to define interpretivism is through Hopwood's observation that accounting tends to confine "the user to a rhetorical representation by others usually the audit industry or capital market regulators" (Hopwood, 1994: 249). Hopwood's point is that accounting, in reducing itself to audit or capital market issues, becomes a reductionist enterprise. Interpretivists challenge this view of accounting and explain that it is part of a complex and dialogic process that situates humanity in various realities. No one reality holds sway.

Interpretivist accounting researchers engage the world to further challenge and explain the impacts of accounting on communities, peoples and nation states. Moreover, within interpretivism lies an expressive approach to language that is built on a view that language mirrors the external and natural world. Accounting is a language with a life of its own – it cannot be reduced to any of its constituent dimensions and elements. We are accordingly challenged to recognise the fallibility and risks we take in our accounting decisions and judgments. There is no escape from judgment. If we are to overcome the arbitrary nature of defining interpretivism it is useful to refer to the sociological work of Gadamer (1975) and Taylor (1993). Interpretivism can also be expressed in the way it involves narratives, stories and other discursive means to enchant the public sphere (Francis, 1990). This leads to the view that interpretivism would include exploring the role of institutions such as accounting. The aim is to demystify the contradictory concepts, dilemmas and trajectories which confront our communities and their public spheres.[13] In Taylor's view,

> [a] successful interpretation is one which makes clear the meaning originally present in a confused, fragmentary, cloudy form. But how does one know that this interpretation is correct? Presumably because it makes sense of the original text: what is strange, mystifying, puzzling, contradictory is no longer so, is accounted for. The interpretation appeals throughout to our understanding of the 'language' of expression, which understanding allows us to see that this expression is puzzling, that it is in contradiction to that other, etc., and that these difficulties are cleared up when the meaning is expressed in a new way.
>
> *(Taylor, 1971: 5)*

Interpretivism therefore involves an account of the person focusing on self-interpretations that are not something that can be understood with absolute certainty (see Baynes, 2010: 442). Taylor has stated that interpretivism is about complexity – that is, for Taylor the only way to handle complex situations is with an approach that attempts to build up richer narratives, pictures and stories about these situations. In accounting this would involve understanding how it involves cultural, environmental and social factors. It is impossible to arrive at a full appreciation of any complex situation – that would be impossible. The interpretivist viewpoint is that to understand complexity itself requires a complex approach. Interpretation is an ongoing iterative approach that continues unabated. The language of accounting is a conversation that only stops periodically when decisions need to be made at that moment in time (synchronic). Therefore, it is important to remember that accounting is a complex narrative which does not end with a profit and loss statement or a balance sheet record (Roslender and Dillard, 2003; Roslender, 2015; Roberts and Ng, 2012).

Accounting and business research emphasises interdisciplinary research but has not fully analysed the connections between accounting and social action (Roslender, 2015). These connections are however explored by Broadbent and Unerman (2011) and Roslender (2015), who commend the interdisciplinary exploration of the connections between accounting and social action by means of research strategies that utilise interpretivism to recognise the many different methods that can be employed to understand accounting. They concur with the Hegelian and Taylorian observation that social phenomena must be considered "either individually or in combination with each other" (Broadbent and Unerman, 2011: 12), adding that within qualitative research,

> [a] common attribute of these methods is that they analyse the data within its economic, social and political context – the social and political factors that lead to and constrain

the development of a regulatory framework for example, or the reward structures that are employed in an organisation. It is important in interpretive research to understand and make visible the taken-for-granted assumptions of those involved and surrounding the issues being researched so that we can understand the nature of their own interpretations and do not impose our own frameworks of understanding on others.

(Broadbent and Unerman, 2011: 12)

Thus the first step for interpretivist researchers is to gather evidence from a range of different sources, such as interactions with people (e.g. interviews with a range of different stakeholders); non-participant observations (e.g. attending meetings and observing activity); environmental observations; analyses of organisations and their behaviours; analyses of techniques adopted by other nations and research from archives and wider sources such as the press or associated organisations (e.g. trade associations or trade unions).

The approach of Broadbent and Unerman (2011), as well as the sociological approach of Taylor, shares affinities with the interpretivism discussed in the work of Willmott (2008). For Willmott interpretivism is about building richer narratives and stories such as the impact of accounting on society. He provides a lengthy list of interpretivist approaches and the accounting researchers who advocate them, which demonstrates the maze-like complexity of the interpretivist approach to understanding the world. Willmott (2008: 921) indicates that interpretivism can be useful for:

- understanding the everyday practice of accounting – such as target setting, performance evaluation and so on (Granlund);
- contributing to conventional and mainstream problems of accounting by providing its distinctive insights (Hansen);
- illuminating the fundamental, systematic mismatches between espoused theories and theories-in-use (Mikes);
- developing answers on how to do things and carry on (Quattrone);
- advancing interventionist and activist research (Khalifa);
- offering a different way of reporting whose cornerstone is showing the impossibility of giving an objective account of financial transactions (Quattrone);
- providing materials for building accounting theories (Granlund);
- considering the implications of accounting practices in relations of ruling and in the (re) production of social, economic and cultural differences and inequalities (Mennicken).

In Willmott's view, interpretivism emphasises understanding the human factor in its environmental and social contexts and thereby entails critically analysing instrumental means–end approaches. By contrast, instrumental methodologies fail to fill the 'silence' surrounding what we report to relevant user groups.

Willmott advances the following incisive characterisation of interpretivism:

Let me state my take on the identity of IAR (Interpretivist Accounting Research). I start from the assumption that IAR lacks an essential identity; and, relatedly, that (*necessary*) efforts to provide it with such an identity are problematical and ultimately elusive (*impossible*). What does this lack mean or imply? I do not mean that when one examines what passes for IAR, it is found to lack some of the characteristics which have been authoritatively associated with, or attributed to, it (e.g. by Baxter and Chua, 2003; Chua, 1986, 1988; Morgan and Willmott, 1993).

(Willmott, 2008: 921)

Willmott is emphatic that he is not arguing that the criteria used to identify interpretivist accounting research clearly differentiate it from mainstream research. Rather, he argues that any boundary drawn between mainstream and interpretive research is arbitrary, shifting and, as a consequence, dogged by the paradoxes of othering. In his view, interdisciplinary accounting research does not have an essential identity and he likens it to an empty signifier that is open and drained of particularity. He continues that the empty signifier aspects of this tradition may render it having numerous, and to a degree competing, meanings (hence the different variants identified earlier), none of which are able to grasp or fix what accounting research aspires to define, represent or fill.

Roslender (2015) takes a slightly different approach, arguing that IAR is about making clear the various assumptions on which different accounting approaches are constructed. He recalls Colville's (1981) *Accounting, Organizations and Society* paper that critiques behavioural accounting, and advocating an 'action approach' in its place. Colville (1981) rejects the natural science model in favour of his action approach, which involves a sensitive analysis of a particular accounting issue. The researcher is assumed to be expert in respect of the ability to choose the appropriate sociological approach which will shed light on the problematic scenario under consideration.

Roslender identifies how accounting researchers might utilise the broad church concept of interpretivism to incorporate social science approaches that are non-reductive in their attempts to understand reality. From the broader social sciences, these evaluative approaches may include symbolic interactionism, grounded theory and social constructionism. In a manner similar to Taylor, Roslender makes the argument that to understand the complex world we must utilise a myriad range of approaches without these necessarily being compatible. It is the task of the interpretivist researcher to provide a rich account of the reality that they are examining; for example, symbolic interactionism is often used to explore the language and symbols that people use in their everyday lives. It is by interpreting the meaning of particular social interactions, Roslender argues, that we are able to begin to understand the intricate relationships that exist in particular, accounting, organisational and social contexts. He aligns symbolic interactionism with grounded theory which is an approach that begins with the researcher entering a field of action with no preconceived theory or strategy to understand the problematic situation. The researcher begins with a question and then builds up a picture through observation, discussion and the collection of various qualitative data. As more data are collected and as data are reviewed, codes can then be grouped into concepts and then into categories. These categories may become the basis for new theory, which Roslender suggests necessarily entails a form of evaluative interpretation.

This brief overview of interpretivism and the views of some of the key accounting researchers who advocate its deployment demonstrate its inherent heterogeneity. While Willmott suggests that interpretivism is an empty signifier, Taylor and Roslender can be seen to be offering approaches to interpretivism that focus on the provision of best accounts that attempt to reflect the complexities of the problematic scenarios under consideration. In particular, Roslender provides a useful evaluative approach which incorporates symbolic interactionism, grounded theory and social constructivism – all sharing a concern with the provision of better and improved accounts of the reality that confronts accounting and business researchers.

6 Conclusion

This chapter encourages critical accounting researchers to consider the ethical and moral debates concerning the public interest role of accounting. It introduces and briefly summarises four dominant philosophical traditions, designated the procedural, critical, subversive and interpretivist traditions, demonstrating the connections between accounting and philosophical research. This classification uses ideas central to Derrida, Habermas, Kant and Rawls to provide a framework in which to situate critical accounting approaches. It also offers some ideas to overcome the procedural limitations that may be seen to have thwarted critical reforms to some degree.

Each tradition challenges the dominance of (mainstream) economic and positivist approaches to accounting research through a process of evaluation and interpretation. Procedural approaches were considered in the light of liberal and utilitarian theories that have gained prominence in the broader social sciences. The role of procedure in social science research was then examined using critical approaches from the language-based perspectives of Habermas.

The third tradition is identified as that of postmodernism, which also challenges the universalising aspirations of both procedural and critical theory. Postmodern accounting thought was used to deconstruct the dominant assumptions within positivist accounting theory to expose the hidden assumptions and values that reflect the ideas and values of those citizens excluded from the fruits of modernity. The final tradition, that of interpretivism, endeavours to provide a robust account of a problematic situation, text or scenario that makes clear the meaning implicit in the problematic situation that many citizens might find to be confusing or fragmentary. Interpretivism was also seen to be an evaluative approach which combines the elements of previously mentioned traditions in interpreting reality.

Notes

1 My structure offered here is influenced by the work of Burrell and Morgan (1979) who provide an analysis of social science paradigms to think about accounting in its social contexts. See also Merkl-Davies and Brennan (2011).
2 Merkl-Davies (2013); Merkl-Davies, Brennan and McLeay (2011); Merkl-Davies, Brennan and Vourvachis (2013).
3 Rawls (1971) lists the 12 elements on pp. 146–7. They are the following: (1) the nature of the parties; (2) the subject of justice; (3) the presentation of alternatives; (4) the time of entry; (5) the circumstances of justice; (6) the formal conditions on principles; (7) knowledge and beliefs; (8) the motivation of parties; (9) rationality; (10) the agreement condition; (11) the compliance condition; and (12) no agreement point.
4 Williams focuses on the obligatory relationships created through transactions drawing attention to the moral dimensions of accounting and accountability.
5 cf. Gray (1983); Roberts and Scapens (1985); Gray *et al.* (1987, 1988, 1991); Williams (1987); Laughlin (2011); Laughlin and Lowe (1990); Roberts (1991, 2009).
6 Interstitial accounts derive from Wright (2010) who searches for niches within capitalism to bring about the desired awareness of environmental and social issues.
7 The use of the term 'counter-hegemony' is based on Gray *et al.* (2014) who search to locate social space to challenge the instrumental and exploitative dimensions of capitalism.
8 In a similar manner to Rawls's original position, the deliberations made in language concern the determination of whether accounting outcomes are fair and just.
9 In terms of the table the regulative and post-Kantian theme can be found in Broadbent, Laughlin and Read (1991). They argue that the evaluatory model should concentrate on judging the constitutive or regulative characteristics from the *organisational systems viewpoint* (Broadbent *et al.*, 1991: 9–10). The issue that presents itself is whether accountability structures must be regulated in this way. A further question concerns whether the organisational form can ever be considered as an agent capable of delivering social change. These particularly important questions must be given consideration if modern social and accountability theory is to build a richly textured, multidisciplinary conceptual foundation for analysis and research on corporate social change activities.

10 They then sold the site to the Niagara Falls School Board in 1953 for $1, with a deed explicitly detailing the presence of the waste and including a liability limitation clause about the contamination. The construction efforts of housing development, combined with particularly heavy rainstorms, released the chemical waste, leading to a public health emergency and an urban planning scandal.

11 The theory's basic claim is simple: the value of a commodity can be objectively measured by the average number of labour hours required to produce that commodity. Modern economics has rendered the labour theory largely redundant because profits include other factors such as forgone consumption or entrepreneurial endeavour. Marxists contend that notwithstanding problems with the labour theory of value, it is the social relationships that must be considered. These social relationships are both changing and changeable. The ability to alter and change the social structure is the determining factor under capitalism. The ability to change social relations is in contrast with those utility-maximising approaches which reify the existing social structure. Reification is defined as the process where labour is commodified and then traded in markets.

12 See also Arendt (1958); Shearer (2002); Shotter (2005); Messner (2009); Lo and Brennan (2012).

13 A special issue of *Critical Perspectives on Accounting* concerning this topic appeared in 2008 but the focus was on the theory of interpretation as opposed to the evaluative dimensions within the hermeneutic approach as it aims to disclose new visions for human communities. In this sense, interpretivism contains a teleological dimension concerning what is a good society. For present purposes, this involves the type of information and thinking that challenges the problematics within contemporary managerialism and positivism (see Ahrens *et al.*, 2008).

References

Ahrens, T., A. Becker, J. Burns, C. S. Chapman, M. Granlund, M. Habersam, A. Hansen, R. Khalifa, T. Malmi, A. Mennicken, A. Mikes, F. Panozzo, M. Piber, P. Quattrone, T. Scheytt (2008). "The future of interpretive accounting research – a polyphonic debate," *Critical Perspectives on Accounting*, 19(6): 840–66.

Arendt, H. (1958). "What is authority?" in H. Arendt: *Between Past and Future* (published 1961), New York: Penguin Books.

Arrington, C. E. and J. R. Francis (1989). "Letting the chat out of the bag: deconstruction, privilege and accounting research," *Accounting, Organizations and Society*, 14(1): 1–28.

Arrington, C. E. and A. G. Puxty (1991). "Accounting, interests and rationality," *Critical Perspectives in Accounting*, 2(1): 31–59.

Baxter, J. A. and W. F. Chua (2003). "Alternative management accounting research: whence and whither," *Accounting, Organizations and Society*, 28 (2–3): 97–126.

Baynes, K. (1992): *The Normative Grounds of Social Criticism: Kant, Rawls and Habermas*, Albany, NY: SUNY Press.

Baynes, K. (2010). "Self, narrative and self-constitution: revisiting Taylor's 'Self-Interpreting Animals,'" *The Philosophical Forum*, 41(4): 441–57.

Bentham, J. (1789). *An Introduction to the Principles of Morals and Legislation* (republished 1907), Oxford: Clarendon Press.

Brennan, A. and Y. S. Lo (2014). *Understanding Environmental Philosophy*, London: Routledge.

Broadbent., J. and R. C. Laughlin (2004). "Management of a research team," in C. Humphrey and B. Lee (eds): *The Real Life Guide to Accounting Research: A Behind the Scenes View of Using Qualitative Research Methods*, Oxford: Elsevier.

Broadbent, J. and J. Unerman (2011). "Developing the relevance of the accounting academy: the importance drawing from the diversity of research approaches," *Meditari Accountancy Research*, 19(1–2): 7–21.

Broadbent, J., R. Laughlin and S. Read (1991). "Recent financial and administrative changes in the NHS: a Critical Theory analysis," *Critical Perspectives on Accounting*, 2(1): 1–31.

Bryer, R. A. (2012). "Americanism and financial accounting theory. Part 1: was America born capitalist?" *Critical Perspectives on Accounting*, 23(7–8): 511–55.

Bryer, R. A. (2013a). "Americanism and financial accounting theory. Part 2: the rise of the 'modern business enterprise', America's transition to capitalism and the genesis of management accounting," *Critical Perspectives on Accounting*, 24(4–5): 273–318.

Bryer, R. A. (2013b). "Americanism and financial accounting theory. Part 3: Adam Smith, the rise and fall of socialism and Irving Fishers' theory of accounting," *Critical Perspectives on Accounting*, 24(7–8): 572–615.

Bryer, R. (2015). "For Marx: A critique of Jacques Richard's 'The dangerous dynamics of modern capitalism (From static to IFRS' futuristic accounting)'," *Critical Perspectives on Accounting*, 30: 35–43.

Burrell, G. and G. Morgan (1979). *Sociological Paradigms and Organisational Analysis*, London: Heinemann Books.

Butler, J. (2005). *Giving an Account of Oneself*, New York: Fordham University Press.

Campbell, D., K. McPhail and R. Slack (2009). "Face work in annual reports a study of the management of encounter through annual reports, informed by Levinas and Bauman," *Accounting, Auditing and Accountability Journal*, 22(6): 907–32

Chua, W. F. (1986). "Radical developments in accounting thought," *Accounting Review*, 61(4): 601–34.

Chua, W. F. (1988). "Interpretive sociology and management accounting research," *Accounting, Auditing and Accountability Journal*, 1(2): 59–79.

Colville, I. (1981). "Reconstructing 'behavioural accounting'," *Accounting, Organizations and Society*, 6(2): 119–32.

Cooper, C. (2015). "Accounting for the fictitious: a Marxist contribution to understanding accounting's roles in the financial crisis," *Critical Perspectives on Accounting*, 30: 63–82.

Derrida, J. (1976). *Of Grammatology*, translated by F. P. Spivak, Baltimore, MD: Johns Hopkins University Press.

Derrida, J. (1992). *Given Time: 1 Counterfeit Money*, Chicago, IL: University of Chicago Press.

Francis, J. R. (1990). "After virtue? accounting as a moral and discursive practice," *Accounting, Auditing and Accountability Journal*, 3(3): 5–17.

Gaa, J. C. (1986). "User privacy in corporate financial reporting: a social contract approach," *Accounting Review*, 61(3): 435–45.

Gadamer, H. G. (1975). *Truth and Method*, New York: Sheed and Ward.

Gallhofer, S. and J. Haslam (1997a). "The direction of green accounting policy: critical reflections," *Accounting, Auditing and Accountability Journal*, 10(2): 148–96.

Gallhofer, S. and J. Haslam (1997b). "Beyond accounting: the possibilities of accounting and critical accounting research," *Critical Perspectives on Accounting*, 8(1–2): 71–96.

Gallhofer, S. and J. Haslam (2003). *Accounting and Emancipation: Some Critical Interventions*, London: Routledge.

Gallhofer, S., J. Haslam, E. Monk and C. Roberts (2006). "The emancipatory potential of online reporting: the case of counter accounting," *Accounting, Auditing and Accountability Journal*, 19(5): 681–718.

Gray, R. H. (1983). "Accountability, financial reporting and the not-for-profit sector," *British Accounting Review*, 15(1): 3–23.

Gray, R. H. (1990a). "Accounting and economics: the psychopathic siblings – a review essay," *British Accounting Review*, 22(4): 373–88.

Gray, R. H. (1990b). *The Greening of Accounting: The Profession After Pearce*, Certified Research Report Number 17, London: Chartered Association of Certified Accountants

Gray, R. H. (1990c). "Business ethics and organisational change," *Managerial Auditing*, 5(2): 12–22.

Gray, R. H. and R. Laughlin (1991). "Editorial: the coming of the green and the challenge of environmentalism," *Accounting, Auditing and Accountability*, 4(1): 5–8.

Gray, R.H., A. Brennan and J. Malpas (2014). "New accounts: towards a reframing of social accounting," *Accounting Forum*, 38(4): 258–73.

Gray, R.H., R. Kouhy and S. Lavers (1995). "Corporate social and environmental reporting: a review of the literature and a longitudinal study of UK disclosure," *Accounting, Auditing and Accountability Journal*, 8(2): 47–77.

Gray, R. H., D. L. Owen and K. T. Maunders (1987). *Corporate Social Reporting: Accounting and Accountability*, Hemel Hempstead: Prentice Hall.

Gray, R. H., D. L. Owen and K. T. Maunders (1988). "Corporate social reporting: emerging trends in accountability and the social contract," *Accounting, Auditing and Accountability Journal*, 1(1): 6–20.

Gray, R. H., D. L. Owen and K. Maunders (1991). "Accountability, corporate social reporting and external social audits," *Advances in Public Interest Accounting*. 4:1–21.

Gray, R. H., D. L. Owen and C. Adams (1996). *Accounting and Accountability: Changes and Challenges in Corporate Social and Environmental Reporting*, Hemel Hemsptead: Prentice Hall.

Gray, R. H., C. Dey, D. Owen, R. Evans and S. Zadek (1997). "Struggling with the praxis of social accounting: stakeholders, accountability, audits and procedures," *Accounting, Auditing and Accountability Journal*, 10(3): 325–64.

Habermas, J. (1974). *Theory and Practice*, translated by J. Viertel, Boston, MA: Beacon Press.

Habermas, J. (1987). *Theory of Communicative Action Volume 2: Lifeworld and System: A Critique of Functionalist Reason*, Oxford: Beacon Press and Cambridge: Polity Press in association with Basil Blackwell.

Habermas, J. (1993). *Justification and Application: Remarks on Discourse Ethics*, translated by C. C. Cronin, Cambridge: Polity.

Hopwood, A. G. (1994). "Some reflections on 'The harmonization of accounting within the EU'," *European Accounting Review*, 3(2): 241–54.

Kant, I. (1789). *Foundations of the Metaphysics of Morals* (republished 1980), New York: Macmillan.

Laughlin, R. C. (1987). "Accounting in organisational contexts: a case for critical theory," *Accounting, Organizations and Society*, 12(5): 479–502.

Laughlin, R. (1995). "Empirical research in accounting: alternative approaches and a case for 'middle range' thinking," *Accounting, Auditing and Accountability Journal*, 8(1): 63–87.

Laughlin, R. C. (2008). "A conceptual framework for accounting for public-benefit entities", *Public Money and Management*, 24(4): 247–54.

Laughlin, R. C. (2010). "A Comment on 'Towards a paradigmatic foundation for accounting practice'," *Accounting, Auditing and Accountability Journal*, 23(5): 759–63.

Laughlin, R. C. (2011). "Accounting research, policy and practice: worlds together or worlds apart?" in E. Evans, R. Burritt and J. Guthrie (eds): *Bridging the Gap Between Academic Research and Professional Practice*, Sydney: The Institute of Chartered Accountants in Australia.

Laughlin, R. C., and A. G. Puxty (1986). "The socially conditioning and socially conditioned nature of accounting: a review and analysis through Tinker's 'Paper Prophets'," *British Accounting Review*, 18(1): 77–90.

Laughlin, R. C., and E. A. Lowe (1990). "A critical analysis of accounting thought: prognosis and prospects for understanding and changing accounting systems design," in D. J. Cooper and T. Hopper (eds): *Critical Accounts: Reorientating Accounting Research*, Basingstoke, Hampshire: Macmillan Press.

Lehman, G. (2015). *Charles Taylor's Ecological Conversations*, London: Palgrave.

McKernan, J. F. (2012). "Accountability as aporia, testimony and accounterability," *Critical Perspectives on Accounting*, 23(3): 258–78.

Merkl-Davies, D. M. (2013). "Accounting narratives and impression management," in L. Jackson, J. Davison and R. Craig (eds): *Routledge Companion to Communication in Accounting*. London: Routledge

Merkl-Davies, D. M. and N. M. Brennan (2011). "A conceptual framework of impression management: new insights from psychology, sociology, and critical perspectives," *Accounting and Business Research*, 41(5): 415–37.

Merkl-Davies, D. M., Brennan, N. M. and S. J. McLeay (2011). "Impression management and retrospective sense-making in corporate narratives: a social psychology perspective," *Accounting, Auditing and Accountability Journal*, 24(3): 315–44.

Merkl-Davies, D. M., N. M. Brennan and P. Vourvachis (2013). "A taxonomy of text analysis approaches in corporate narrative reporting research," working paper, Centre for Impression Management in Accounting Communication, Bangor Business School.

Merton, R. K. (1968). *Social Theory and Social Structure*, revised edition, New York: The Free Press.

Messner, M. (2009). "The limits of accountability," *Accounting, Organisations and Society*, 34(8): 918–38.

Miller, P. and T. O'Leary (1987). "Accounting and the construction of the governable person," *Accounting, Organizations and Society*, 12(3): 235–65.

Morgan G. and H. C. Willmott (1993). "Critical sociology and accounting research," *Accounting, Auditing and Accountability Journal*, 6(4): 3–36.

Nelson, J. S. (1993). "Account and acknowledge, or represent and control. On postmodern politics and economics of collective responsibility," *Accounting, Organizations and Society*, 18(2–3): 207–31.

Owen, D., R. Gray and J. Bebbington (1997). "Green accounting: cosmetic irrelevance or radical agenda for change?" *Asia-Pacific Journal of Accounting*, 4(2): 175–99

Pallot, J. (1991). "Legitimate concern with fairness: a comment," *Accounting, Organisations and Society*, 16(2): 201–08.

Power, M. and R. Laughlin (1992). "Critical theory and accounting," in M. Alvesson and H. Willmott (eds): *Critical Management Studies*, London: Sage Publications.

Puxty, A. G. (1986). "Social accounting as immanent legitimation: a critique of a technicist ideology," *Advances in Public Accounting*, 1: 95–111.

Puxty, A. G. (1991). "Social accountability and universal pragmatics," *Advances in Public Interest Accounting*, 4: 35–45.

Rawls, J. (1971). *A Theory of Justice*, Oxford: Oxford University Press.

Rawls, J. (1980). "Kantian constructivism in moral theory," *The Journal of Philosophy*, 77(9): 515–72.

Rawls, J. (1982). "The basic liberties and their priority," in Sterling M. McMurrin (ed.): *The Tanner Lectures on Human Values*, Salt Lake City, UT: University of Utah Press.

Rawls, J. (1985). "Justice as fairness: political not metaphysical," *Philosophy and Public Affairs*, 14(3): 223–51.

Rawls, J. (1988). "The Priority of Right and Ideas of the Good," *Philosophy and Public Affairs*, 17(4): 251–74.

Roberts, J (1991). "The possibilities of accountability," *Accounting, Organizations and Society*, 16(4): 355–68.

Roberts, J. (2009). "No one is perfect: the limits of transparency and an ethic for 'intelligent' accountability," *Accounting, Organizations and Society*, 34(8): 957–70.

Roberts J. and W. Ng (2012). "Against economic (mis)conceptions of the individual: constructing financial agency in the credit crisis," *Culture and Organization*, 18(2): 91–105.

Roberts, J. and R. W. Scapens (1985). "Accounting systems and systems of accountability – understanding accounting practices in their organisational contexts," *Accounting, Organizations and Society*, 10(4): 443–56.

Roslender, R. (2015). 'Accountancy," in M. Bevir and R. A. W. Rhodes (eds): *The Routledge Handbook of Interpretive Political Studies*, London: Routledge.

Roslender, R. and J. F. Dillard (2003). "Reflections on the interdisciplinary perspectives on accounting project," *Critical Perspectives on Accounting*, 14(3): 325–51.

Schweiker, W. (1993). "Accounting for ourselves: accounting practice and the discourse of ethics," *Accounting, Organizations and Society*, 18(2–3): 231–52.

Shapiro, B. (1998). "Towards a normative model of rational argumentation for critical accounting discussions," *Accounting, Organizations and Society*, 23(7): 641–63.

Shearer, T. (2002). "Ethics and accountability: from the for-itself to the for-the-other," *Accounting, Organizations and Society*, 27(6): 541–73.

Shotter, J. (2005). "Inside the moment of managing': Wittgenstein and the everyday dynamics of our expressive-responsive activities," *Organization Studies*, 26(1): 113–35.

Sikka, P. (2011). "Accounting for human rights: the challenge of globalization and foreign investment agreements," *Critical Perspectives on Accounting*, 22(8): 811–27.

Sikka, P. (2015). "The corrosive effects of neoliberalism on the UK financial crises and auditing practices: a dead-end for reforms?" *Accounting Forum*, 39(1): 1–18.

Spence, C. (2009). "Social accounting's emancipatory potential: a Gramscian critique," *Critical Perspectives on Accounting*, 20(2): 205–27.

Taylor, C. (1971). "Interpretivism and the science of man," *Review of Metaphysics*, 25(1): 3–51.

Taylor, C. (1993). "Engaged agency and background to Heidegger," in C. Guignon (ed.): *The Cambridge Companion to Heidegger*, Cambridge: Cambridge University Press.

Thomson, I. (2014): "Responsible social accounting communities, symbolic activism and the reframing of social accounting: a commentary on 'New accounts: towards a reframing of social accounting'," *Accounting Forum*, 38(4): 274–77.

Thomson, I., S. Grubnic and G. Georgakopoulos (2014). "Exploring accounting-sustainability hybridisation in the UK public sector," *Accounting, Organizations and Society*, 39(6): 453–76.

Tinker, T. (1985). *Paper Prophets: A Social Critique of Accounting*, New York: Holt, Reinhart and Winston.

Tinker, T., M. Neimark and C. Lehman (1991). "Falling down the hole in the middle-of-the-road: political quietism in corporate social reporting," *Accounting, Auditing and Accountability*, 4(2): 28–54.

Williams, P. F. (1987). "The legitimate concern with fairness," *Accounting, Organisations and Society*, 12(2):169–89.

Williams, P. F. and S. Ravenscroft (2015). "Rethinking decision-usefulness," *Contemporary Accounting Research*, 32(2): 763–88.

Willmott, H. (2008). "Listening, interpreting, commending: a commentary on the future of interpretive accounting research," *Critical Perspectives on Accounting*, 19(6): 920–25.

Wright, E. O. (2010). *Envisioning Real Utopias,* London: Verso.

6

FOUCAULT

David Knights and Peter Bloom

1 Introduction

Ever since the global financial crisis, even those with a great faith in the propriety of the accountancy profession to act as custodians of moral fiduciary standards in corporate business have begun to show some skepticism regarding its independence. Yet critical accounting research had long before emerged to express dissatisfaction with the lack of independence of conventional accounting as a discipline that was clearly steeped in a status quo conservatism that assumed technical and subsidiary subordination to its corporate clients. As a clear servant of capitalism, accounting became the target for a group of social scientists, some of whom were trained accountants but many not, who sought to politicise the discipline. Drawing on a wide range of critical theories, critical accounting research challenged the way that conventional accounting not only facilitated the smooth functioning of capitalist organisation but also legitimised it politically and ethically. In effect, critical accounting sought to shed new light on the function of accounting technologies and practices for creating and reinforcing contemporary power and control (see for instance Broadbent, 2002; Laughlin, 1999; Mitchell, Sikka and Willmott, 2001) within organisations but also in capitalist society more generally.

Because of their opposition to the form of social life within which we live, the theoretical frameworks of social theorists/philosophers were inspirational to the development of critical accounting, with Marx and Foucault being particularly and enduringly important. Although less pre-eminent, other thinkers – notably Hegel, Heidegger, Marcuse and Habermas – as well as more recent social scientists studying workplace industrial relations (Hyman, 1989; Kaufman, 1993) and the labour process (Braverman, 1974; Edwards, 1980; Knights and Willmott, 1990) also contributed to the development of a critical accounting research agenda. Acknowledging this broad range of theoretical grounding, and providing a brief summary of the Marxist and neo-Marxist inspired literature on critical accounting, however, this chapter focuses on the work of Foucault (1975, 1980, 1982) and his understanding of how power–knowledge relations constitute us as accounting, or more precisely "accountable", subjects. As will be shown, this occurs not only in terms of our consenting to the norms implicit in given practices but also in invoking in us a sense of feeling accountable to both our organisations and ourselves as "responsible" subjects.

Some of the earliest critical accounting research drew on the archeological and genealogical analyses of Foucault (1973, 1980, 1982) in tracing historically specific discourses and practices of accounting that were produced by, yet also productive of, modern rationality and subjectivity (Hopwood, 1987; Hoskin, 1994; McPhail, 1999; Neimark, 1994; Stewart, 1992). Accounting, in this sense, is analysed as part of an evolving contemporary form of "governmentality" that is associated with present-day disciplining technologies of power and the self (Foucault, 1997a, b; Miller and O'Leary, 1987; McKinlay and Pezet, 2010). This work departed from conventional treatments of accounting as a set of politically neutral techniques designed to facilitate business practice and was more sophisticated than Marxist critiques that simply dismiss it as the legitimising arm of capitalism. While never neutral and far more than just a source of legitimacy, these interpretations of accounting are not invalid but are complemented by the governmental and disciplinary focus of Foucault. The argument we set out to make here, however, is that a further complement to this focus is to be found in the later Foucault (1997a, 2004, 2005, 2011), where the focus is on how individuals are transformed into subjects who turn accounting in on themselves through processes of 'subjectivation'. Here rather than accounting and accountability remaining a specialist financial technology for governing organisations and institutions, it becomes appropriated by us all as we seek to hold ourselves to account in everyday life. Subjectivity is then colonised through idealised images of what it is to be human that require continual confirmation through both self-monitoring and accountability to significant others. Our concern then, is to explore accounting not just as a financial technology of corporate governance but also as a global social discourse and practice that positively transforms individuals into "accountable subjects," who feel compelled to engage in the practices invoked by power in order to secure (our) "their identities, sense of meaning and reality" (Knights, 2002: 581).

The argument proceeds as follows. While providing a brief summary of the Marxian or neo-Marxian character of some critical accounting research in the first section, the chapter moves quickly to focus on those accounting theorists who have grounded their work in some aspect of Foucault's thinking. Our aim is not to provide a comprehensive literature review but to extend the analysis beyond the dominant focus on accounting as governmentality. Drawing on the later theories of Foucault, in the third section we suggest that a key experience of contemporary neo-liberal discourse and practice is the production of the accountable subject both as a target of external power or governmentality and of subjective self-development. This type of subjectivation is examined further in the fourth section to show how it reflects and reinforces prevailing power/knowledge relations, norms and values that sustain principles of capitalist and market systems of inequality in the production and distribution of material and symbolic goods. The chapter concludes with a broader discussion highlighting the potential contribution of the later Foucault for critical accounting research and organisation studies more generally.

2 Accounting and capitalism – Marx and critical accounting research

The concept of accounting has long been the subject of critical study. While mainstream accounts view it largely as a naturalised financial process essential to organisations, critical perspectives highlight its role for reproducing power relations and dominant values. Common to these analyses is an attempt to illuminate the social, rather than mere economic, character of accounting. They have therefore combined to expand the scope of how accounting is understood and researched as a socially constructed and historically situated practice.

Marxism stands as a traditional lens for critically viewing accounting. This perspective primarily studies accounting as part of the general reproduction of an exploitative capitalist system (Burchell, Clubb and Hopwood, 1985; Hopper, Storey and Willmott, 1987; Tinker, 1984). To this end, accounting necessarily reflects existing elite interests and contributes to maintaining social and political power (Hopwood, 1985; Loft, 1986). In this respect, Lehman and Tinker (1987: 503) argue that the "accounting literature as disinterested inquiry or rigorous scholarship understates the social origins of research," as it masks the historical relations of power giving rise and being legitimated by these discourses and practices. For this reason, they contend that "discursive accounting practices are more productively regarded as ideological weapons for participating in conflicts over the distribution of social wealth." Crucial to this analysis is how accounting regimes entrench the power of the capitalist class over labour (Armstrong, 1987; Bryer, 1999). From this vantage point, a diverse array of accounting programmes can be understood as sustaining class relations and reproducing the capitalist mode of production.

Critical theory, by contrast, highlights the significance of accounting in the formation and reproduction of specific social values and identities (Power, Laughlin and Cooper, 2003) that are instrumental to efficient performance, productivity and profitability within contemporary capitalist economies (Brown, Dillard and Hopper, 2015). Many critical theorists in accounting have drawn on the theory of structuration (Giddens, 1984), which identifies society as constituted by agents and structures, neither of which should be given priority as is the case when either the voluntary actions of individuals or the determining forces of social systems are privileged. Structuration theory has been applied in a wide range of contexts including, for example, the analysis of "how accounting systems are implicated in the construction, maintenance, and changes of the social order of an organization" (Macintosh and Scapens, 1990: 455), the way accounting practices shape organisational and social life (Laughlin, 1987; Burchell, Clubb, Hopwood, Hughes and Nahapiet, 1980), or more broadly their effect on twenty-first-century English life in general (Broadbent, 2002). These critical approaches speak to sociologically oriented research on accounting within and outside of the confines of the workplace. In this kind of research, accounting is identified as a "technology" for the social construction of reality and its relation to hegemonic power relations (Dillard, 1991; Miller, 2006). Applying a more interpretive approach, Chua (1988) explores the interrelation of accounting and management practices more generally whereas Meyer (1986) examines the constitutive effect of social environments on organisational accounting. Here, accounting is linked to institutions that attempt to deal with changing and uncertain external forces, giving a precarious stability to processes and settings marked by uncertainty and ambiguous rules. Extending research of accounting as a social and institutional practice (Hopwood and Miller, 1994) to incorporate a historical dimension (Fleischman, Mills and Tyson, 1996) the part that accountancy played in the general formation or genesis of capitalism as a political and economic system was examined (Bryer, 2004; Hoskin and Macve, 1986).[1]

It may be clear from this brief review of the literature that it is important to distinguish accounting from accountancy. The former can be seen as the generic condition and consequence of the historically specific professional technology and practice of accountancy. Bryer, in this regard, places accountancy within a broader history of economic change from feudalism to capitalism, arguing that:

> Modern accounting emerged over a much longer period of transition through intermediate forms. Their roots lie in the obsession of their parents – feudal lords and merchants. Their history embraces the social upheavals in agriculture from the end of the fourteenth century; the commercial revolution of the sixteenth century; the civil wars of the mid-seventeenth century; and the agrarian revolution that followed. The modern obsessions with profitability and accountability did not suddenly appear in the nineteenth century.
> *(Bryer, 2000: 134)*

More recently, Chiapello (2007) argues that accountancy was fundamental to the creation of the very notions of capitalism. This has led to broader discussions of the effect of accountancy ideologies on the development of the state within capitalism (Miller, 1990). Analogously, it was examined how accountancy as a normative ideal provided some legitimacy for the precedence given to positivist theories historically in the academic study of organisations and accountancy (Tinker, Merino and Neimark, 1982).

A crucial, but to some extent relatively unexplored, aspect of these studies is the function of accounting for producing historically specific subjectivities. Smith (2002), notably, maintains the importance of explicitly 'accounting for subjectivity'. Specifically, at stake is how accountancy as a historical knowledge and connected set of practices conditions the actions and accepted practices of management (Fay, Introna and Puyou, 2010). In this vein, Flamholtz, Bullen and Hua (2002) highlight the evolution of contemporary organisational subjectivities combining human resource and accounting values. Returning to the work of Chiapello (2007), accountancy stands as fundamental to the very development of a capitalist subjectivity.

Following a more explicitly egalitarian position, Gallhofer and Haslam (1997) draw on critical perspectives to theorise how accounting can be transformed into a positive catalyst for radical social change. To this end, they envision what is termed an 'enabling accounting' centred on "its ability to act as a force for radical emancipatory social change through making things visible and comprehensible and helping engender dialogue and action towards emancipatory change" (Gallhofer and Haslam, 1992: 82). However, much of the critical research on accounting implicitly, if not explicitly, subscribes to an emancipatory politics (see also Neu, Cooper and Everett, 2001) for which we have some misgivings due to its tendency to resort to some essentialist view of what it is to be human and to be somewhat patronising in legislating for what is considered to be in the best interests of those subjects it claims to want to emancipate. Still a key advantage of critical accounting studies is that it deconstructs the political neutrality of a technology that claims, and is often taken for granted as merely oiling the wheels rather than planning, the route of capitalist development.

Such critical research gestures to the significance of accountancy as a formative historical knowledge. More precisely, it sheds critical light on the effect of accounting knowledge in regulating capitalist identities, both inside and outside of the workplace. Yet, it also highlights a certain gap within the critical accounting literature. Namely, how accountancy as a social knowledge has the effect of not simply regulating, but also actually constituting or producing, the capitalist subject? However, we don't see this as a one-way process so perhaps it is more important to consider how the constitutive power of accountancy is both a condition and consequence of the contemporary development of the capitalist subject. The theories of Foucault are particularly prescient for exploring these questions, as we show in more detail in the next section.

3 The early impact of Foucault on critical accounting research

A crucial task for critical accounting studies is to understand the status of accounting as a historically specific discourse for constituting the contemporary subject. Accounting can be traced back to the 'birth of the sciences of man (sic)', which have been attributed not to major philosophical breakthroughs in the great academies but to such lowly events as the development of files and records constituting "the individual as a describable, analysable object" (Foucault, 1979: 190, quoted in Knights, 2002). Foucault provides a potentially useful analytical framework for illuminating exactly this concern (Foucault, 1980, 1982). Notably, his work helps to situate accounting as a force that constitutes, reflects and reproduces present-day discourses and practices (Armstrong, 1994; Hoskin, 1994; McPhail, 1999; Stewart, 1992). In this respect, a Foucauldian analysis enables us to account for accounting not only critically but also historically.

Foucault has taken on an increasing importance within the field of accounting research over the past several decades. Initial Foucauldian-inspired interventions in this area focused on the role of accounting for disciplining individuals within organisations. Highlighted was the significance of accounting for the broader development of a shift away from what Foucault (1975) terms the 'classical sovereign' who embodied absolute power to the extent that any transgression was perceived as a direct assault on his/her reign or authority and must therefore be punished through extreme physical violence as a public spectacle. Modernity, by contrast, results in a distribution and economy of power that is both more orderly and robust, for since it is no longer the property of a single person or institution it is not so easily targeted and readily overthrown. The basis for this power is surveillance and discipline such that subjects are prevented from transgression, for just as we are never more than a few feet from a rat, so power is forever encroaching on our space. This approach, however, has been criticised for over-generalisation and its failure to account fully for the diversity of and changes within accounting as a modern empirical phenomenon. Armstrong exemplifies such critiques, stating that

> The use of such a high level concept in accounting research naturally tends to suppress detail. In consequence, the approach offers little purchase on such everyday phenomena as change in accounting systems, the relationship between accounting and other means of managerial control and the difference between accounting systems in different contexts.
>
> *(1994: 25)*

Partially in response to such criticisms, a new wave of critical accounting research developed drawing on the Foucauldian concept of governmentality. This notion directed attention to accounting's contextually specific kinds of power, knowledge and reasoning that condition the self-formation processes of the modern subject. Despite his antipathy towards Foucault, Armstrong (1994) provides a good discussion of this emerging trend while more supportive accounts are provided by MacKinnon (2000) or Rose, O' Malley and Valverde (2006). In particular, governmentality reflects significant aspects of the conditions that make it possible for individuals to be transformed into subjects that are readily self-monitoring and accountable to themselves and others. While conceptually ambiguous enough to allow for the study of accounting within a wide array of settings and heterogeneous manifestations, this analysis drew our attention particularly to self-governance. Central to such a project, thus, was to understand how accounting contributed to understandings of the 'governance of the present' in all its complexities and incompleteness (McKinlay and Pezet, 2010). More precisely, it established how accounting was important for establishing contemporary social relations and the configuration of the modern self.

Connected, but in some ways predating, this move towards governmentality were attempts to distinguish and bring together Foucauldian notions of discourse and practice. In place of previous idealist considerations of accounting that were built on abstract assumptions bearing little relation to empirical events, Foucault enabled us to "trace more precisely how certain practices (e.g. those of writing, pedagogy and valuing) have a primary role in establishing any given dominant form of rationality" (Hoskin, 1994: 57). In other words, we can see how practices that are informed by accounting discourse reflect and reproduce a set of norms, values and ways of thinking that turn us all into subjects that calculate the price of everything whilst failing to understand the value of anything.[2] This calculability is simply a medium and outcome of the broader principles of market-based capitalism but accounting discourse lends it technical legitimacy thus instantiating a generalisable shift in the operation of power/knowledge around self-monitoring and self-disciplinary modes of accountability and control.

Accounting, in this view, complements what Foucault theorises as a self-disciplined present-day subject and as part of a contemporary governmentality associated with technologies of power and of the self (Foucault, 1991, 1994; Miller and O'Leary, 1987; McKinlay and Pezet, 2010). The purpose of historising accounting, therefore, is to illuminate its ongoing sense of constituting individuals as self-disciplinary subjects within larger regimes of power. These efforts resonated with earlier attempts to infuse historical perspectives on accounting with Foucauldian genealogical approaches (Hoskin and Macve, 1986; Miller and O'Leary, 1987). Specifically relevant to themes of power and social ordering, Hopwood (1987) seeks to understand accounting through an archaeological lens that understood its conditions of possibility in the 'ordering of things'. The shift towards governmentality, then, represents a contemporary continuation of these critical historiographies on the evolving relation between accountancy and power.

In an attempt to summarise the value of Foucault's archaeology and genealogy for understanding accounting, we present in Table 6.1 a model that seeks to show how representational knowledge has truth effects in its transformation of subjectivity.

The early attempts to use Foucault, therefore, helped scholars to reconsider the status of the accounting subject. They reveal accounting as an evolving and historically specific discourse that organised both rationality and practices. They highlight how accounting links to a particular economic knowledge that prioritises instrumental rationality for maximizing productivity and therefore profit. Economics then reifies individualistic, instrumental rational action and accounting turns this into a technique of calculability. This provides one of the conditions that make it possible for individuals to be transformed into subjects that engage in routine calculations of their performance in accounting for themselves through processes of self-monitoring and self-disciplining.

Nevertheless, this raises renewed questions regarding how deeply accounting discourse(s) affect the thinking of individuals (Armstrong, 1994). There remains a critical tension around how much these discourses actually impact the behaviour of individuals as opposed to just how they account for their actions (Miller and O'Leary, 1987). Much evidence is available, however, to show how accounting knowledge has been instrumental in reflecting and reproducing managerial control and values within contemporary neo-liberal capitalist economies (Brown *et al.*, 2015). Moreover, it is also seen how accounting operates as a truth that is produced by the way that individuals "govern themselves and others" (Foucault, 1981: 8–9, quoted in Grey, 1994: 21). This takes us to the later Foucault and his concept of subjectivation.

Table 6.1 Truth effects of the power of positive knowledge (adapted from Knights, 2006)

Representations of	Hidden assumptions of subjectivity	Through	Objectification of	Exercises of power based on this knowledge have truth effects in norms of
1. Life	Organic being	biology	the body and its functions	health
2. Language	Speaking being	linguistics	speech and writing	communication
3. Labour and Capital	Economic maximizing being	economics	production and exchange	wealth
4. Business activity	Calculating being	accounting	procedures of financial calculation	accountability

4 Reflecting on the impact of the later Foucault for accounting research

Thus far this chapter has presented the contribution of Foucault to critical accounting studies. While such Foucauldian analysis has produced significant insights, a fuller engagement with Foucault's work can go even further in shedding critical light on accounting, especially its participation in the social construction of the contemporary subject. In particular, we now turn its attention to relatively under-explored Foucauldian themes – the difference between subjection and subjectivation, on the one hand, and the critical reconsideration of ethics and selfhood within the later Foucault, on the other.

As mentioned in the previous section, a crucial point of departure for accounting research is the relation of accounting as a historically and socially situated set of regulative practices. Although not perfectly, this division mirrors the shift by critical Foucauldian scholars from their earlier writing on discipline towards governmentality; which, in turn, reflects the simultaneous desires to understand how accounting discourses constitute an individual's thoughts and actions, respectively. In his later works, Foucault does much to address this exact issue. Notably, he observes that power is always both 'non-subjective' and 'intentional' (Foucault, 1990) in so far as its target is to discipline both individual behaviour and self-knowledge.

Recent critical scholarship has drawn on these insights to suggest the need for developing the subjective aspect of subjection. Foucault, himself, introduces the concept of subjectivation, denoting a form of identification that, in the words of Butler, "consists precisely in this fundamental dependence on a discourse we never chose but that, paradoxically, initiates and sustains our agency" (Butler, 1997: 2). Taking this idea further, Butler argues that more attention must be paid to the affective dimension of subjection. Butler, in this vein, asks:

> To what extent has the disciplinary apparatus that attempts to produce and totalize identity become an abiding object of passionate attachment? We cannot simply throw off the identities we become, and Foucault's call to refuse those 'identities' will certainly be met with resistance…In particular, how are we to understand not merely the disciplinary production of the subject but the disciplinary cultivation of an attachment to subjection?
>
> *(1997: 102)*

We would contest that this is a direct attachment to subjection but rather can end up indirectly being so, largely through the attachment to accomplishing a stable and secure identity (Knights and Willmott, 1990). It is possible to reflect on this to recognise its illusory grounding given the impossibility of anticipating, let alone controlling the image, others have of us.

Within organisational studies, Roberts (2005) points to how disciplinary regimes inexorably depend for their reproduction on the subjectivities they produce. Such scholarship helps bridge the gap in understandings on the relation of the non-subjective and intentional aspects of power. According to Knights:

> Foucault removes all trace of the human subject from the centre of his analysis; he argued that social practices and their discursive formations are independent of those who speak for them (Foucault, 1973, 1979a). By this, Foucault did not mean to imply that the intentions of subjects are non-existent but merely that their outcomes in aggregated sets of social practices are wholly independent of what was intended.
>
> *(2002: 23)*

97

As Tie (2004) notes, notions of subjection suffer from a form of 'agent-less agency'. This critique is not meant to imply that there is ever a non-socially constructed manifestation of agency. Rather, it presupposes that processes of subjection create a subject that does not require any intentional agency for its existence. Supplemental to this agent-less agency of subjection, is the reintroduction of that agent through subjectivation. Here, the subject becomes an individual, not simply acting in accordance with the governing agency provided to them but also reflecting on it as a foundation for their knowledge of self. Consequently, as Stozier (2002: 78) observes "the disappearance of the subject in one place [of the framework] simply marks its appearance in another."

It is precisely in this original distinction between subjection and subjectivation that it becomes possible to begin constructively combining the mutually constituting social construction of the acting and thinking accounting subject. Here the governmentality of accountancy encompasses the non-subjective rationality unconsciously disciplining practices alongside the process of subjectivation guiding the intentional self that discursively emerges from this governance. Governmentality, in terms of accountancy, thus encompasses the ways that the rationality of accountancy regulates the very instantiation of an acting subject as well as sets the stage for an 'accounting rationality' of the socially inscribed thinking individual. To this end, it is necessary to study both separately and combined the 'subject of accounting' and the 'accounting subject', a relationship gestured to in the model presented in Table 6.1.

Foucault's later writings on ethics, subjection and freedom provide an interesting theoretical lens for such critical investigation. He highlights ethics as a process of "self-cultivation" that is representative of engaging the body and self in different ways (Foucault, 1984). At play in this description is the dual nature of power. In the first place, any ethics is a historically inscriptive ethos for producing the subject and disciplining their actions. Nevertheless, it is precisely in the conscious cultivation of this ethos as an active ethics that individuals can encounter differing experiences of freedom. Foucault's account of the twentieth-century 'training of the body' exemplifies this complex phenomenon of ethical cultivation:

> The 'mastery and awareness of one's body' originally shaped for purposes of military training and education produced in its wake 'responding claims and affirmations, those of one's own body against power, of health against the economic system, of pleasure against the moral norms of sexuality, marriage, decency.
>
> *(Foucault, 1980: 56)*

This relationship, of course, is necessarily infused with issues of domination and resistance. Returning again to Foucault's previous example, suddenly, "what had made power strong becomes used to attack it ... But the impression that power weakens and vacillates here is in fact mistaken; power can retreat here, re-organise its forces, invest itself elsewhere ... and so the battle continues" (Foucault, 1980: 56). Accordingly, power and domination have an often cyclical relation, in which discourses breed resistances which are then available to being reconfigured into new forms of subjection.

Importantly, for Foucault power is connected to, but nonetheless distinguishable from, domination. The former reflects the agency one has in their historical construction as a social subject. The latter, is the attempt to stagnate social relationships to the advantage of a particular group or set of values (Foucault, 1984). Resistance, therefore, is found in both the direct ways individuals respond against such dominating power and in the ability to do otherwise than as prescribed by its agency. It is important again to stress that there is no pure freedom or resistance for Foucault. Rather, it is the differing manifestations of power, counter-power and agency that emerge from historical processes of subjection and subjectivation. As Ortner (1995: 186) describes:

[E]very culture, every subculture, every historic moment, constructs its own forms of agency, its own modes of enacting the process of reflecting on the self and the world and of acting simultaneously within and upon what one finds there.

This theoretical intervention inspired by the later Foucault, reframes then questions the relationship between accountancy and the subject. Rather than understand it as a rationality which is purely regulative (either of actions or thought), it is perhaps more fruitful to ask how an accountancy discourse is providing individuals with common and diverse forms of agency and what types of selves and ethics are produced from such a positive historical inscription? Along these lines, it must be studied what intentional identifications have resulted from the self-disciplining neo-liberal subject associated with accounting discourses. Furthermore, what types of dominations and resistances has this, in turn, created? The next section will explore these issues through an examination of the "accountable self."

5 Approaching the "accountable self"

Accountancy both conditions and is conditioned by prevailing social discourses and practices. Within the contemporary period, it has evolved alongside the transition from chiefly sovereign to disciplinary forms of power. Rather than centering on the figure of a ruler, power is instead composed of an

ensemble formed by the institutions, procedures, analyses and reflections, the calculations and tactics that allow the exercise of this very specific albeit complex form of power, which has as its target population, as its principal form of knowledge political economy, and as its essential technical means apparatuses of security.

(Foucault, 1991: 102–3)

Significantly, this increasingly disciplinary society has produced novel forms of subjection and subjectivation but the latter transforms us into subjects who secure our sense of meaning and identity from the very accountability that power invokes. In this sense accounting is the discipline of the age in socially constructing an active, thinking and embodied subject that is accountable for itself.

Disciplinary power is commonly associated with the self-disciplining subject. In this respect, the subjection to disciplinary technologies translates into a 'governance of the present' premised on the agency of the subject to embrace such disciplining. It is worthwhile then considering self-discipline as a type of entrenched social mentality for conceiving and acting out agency as a subject. It is, in this respect, an "often invisible rationality which is behind an assemblage of actions and mechanisms that are in place to govern certain actions" (Gouldson and Bebbington, 2007: 12). The exercise of such agency is, thus, largely non-subjective insomuch that it represents a naturalised almost unthinking rationality for seeing and acting in one's surrounding environments.

Accountancy discourses are complementary to and constitutive of such a mentality. The capacity to chronicle actions as a means to judge their overall efficacy reflects this type of neo-liberal agency. Quoting Rose (1999: 61):

As our twenty-first century begins, the ethics of freedom have to underpin our conceptions of how we should be ruled, how our practices of everyday life should be organized, how we should understand our life and predicament.

Fundamental to this self-disciplining form of social freedom is a rationality of accounting. Filling in the time sheet, taking only an hour for lunch, organising time to effectively meet deadlines, even explicitly budgeting for the firm's bottom line represent the subjection to this contemporary type of 'self-disciplining agency. Required then, according to Thomas and Hewitt (2011: 1378), "is a fuller exploration of the articulation process involved in trying to fix the meanings attached to professionalism, autonomy and management." To this end, it is imperative to understand how socialised agency, as a guide for both action and thought, is being articulated in terms of a 'self-accounting' subject.

To reiterate, this self-disciplining through accounting is distinguishable from individual thinking and identification. Fleming and Sturdy's discussion of 'neo-normative control' exemplifies the non-subjective aspect of this phenomenon. The ability to be oneself, often counter to officially approved values of the firm, did not take away from, and in fact could critically reinforce, that ability and willingness of individuals to be self-disciplining accounting subjects. The acting out of these 'monotonous and repetitive' tasks demanded an array of capabilities all involving the ability to account for one's actions to monitor and improve their performance – processes that were not fundamentally representative of these actor's broader thoughts or beliefs.

Yet self-discipline also impacts upon subjectivation. It is not only that individuals are made into self-disciplining subjects but also that they can identify with this subjection. To clarify, self-disciplining creates the foundations for a range of selves to emerge, one of which may be an explicit investment in becoming a more successful 'self-disciplined' person. This intentional identification and desire for action had been acknowledged, for example, in ideas of responsible autonomy (Friedman, 1977; McGregor, 1960; Peters and Waterman, 1982), long before we were aware of a Foucauldian framework to analyse it. More recently, it is echoed in calls for individuals to be 'self-directed' and 'self-leading'. As Pink (2009: 90) suggests, "Perhaps it is time to throw the word 'management' onto the linguistic ash heap … This era doesn't call for better management. It calls for a renaissance of self-direction."

These identities can be supplementary forces for strengthening this underlying governmentality. Picking up on the more affective dimension of this process, Tie (2004) draws upon a Lacanian psychoanalytic perspective to speak of how disciplinary power can rely upon an appealing cultural fantasy of 'self-help'. Here fantasy is construed as an extension of a governing discourse, an attractive conscious identification to revolve selfhood around that which reinforces underlying social knowledges. This subjection to 'self-discipline' is attached to a fantasy of 'self-help' and a belief in infinite human potential (Costea, Crump and Amiridis, 2007) whereby individuals can continually improve themselves. Tie contends that "the field of self help can thereby return to the subject surmounted beliefs about the possibility of being secure and able, beliefs that are now experienced as strangely familiar, as troublingly powerful" (2004: 172).

Critically, this subjectivation is a direct response to the subjection of such agent-less agency. In other language, it is precisely the experience of being produced as a self-disciplining subject, outside one's control and largely unidentifiable to everyone else that catalyses the desire to forge an autonomous unique self. This desire stands as one of the many conditions of possibility related to an individual's pursuit of autonomy. Selfhood here is a coping mechanism to deal with the reality of being subjected to power. While disciplinary regimes render us 'self-accounting', they do not meet with much opposition since we all desire agency and to be seen as agents rather than mere subjects of the power to make us accountable. Importantly, such subjectivation is driven by more than just compensation – they can also be strategic parts of such subjection – nevertheless this can be a powerful yet typical affective factor.

Significantly, such subjectivation is necessarily wide ranging and not so easily manageable or predictable. Rather, it is crucial to understand how the subjection to self-disciplining is providing the foundations for a subjectivation linked to being accountable. To this end, the subjection to a disciplinary accounting regime creates the social conditions for an accountable self. More precisely, it forges a sense of uniqueness and autonomy within a social order that has been inclined to treat humans as mere numbers on a spreadsheet to be processed and computed. A governmentality premised on the accounting discourses, then, must also confront and adapt to this rise of an accountable self.

6 Controlling the "accountable self"

The accountable self is not only a product of the contemporary disciplining of the subject to accounting discourse, it can also help to reinforce such processes. More specifically, the accountable self reflects and reproduces contemporary forms of managerial control since the imperative to account for oneself, routinely becomes a demand to fulfill the prerogatives of the firm. Specifically, it strengthens the regulative power of managers at the same time as interpolating subjects into managerialist values of efficiency and productivity. In this respect, the construction of selfhood around the ability to personally chronicle, monitor and modify one's actions is transformed into a crucial modality for disciplining the present-day employee subject.

Within the literature, accounting discourses and practices have long been critically associated with control strategies (see for instance Ezzamel and Willmott, 1998; Flamholtz, 1983; Mitchell *et al.*, 2001). Expanding on these readings, this analysis highlights the embeddedness of these control strategies with the subjectivation of individuals through processes of self-accounting. Importantly, for self-discipline the gaze of the sovereign is made ubiquitous, apparent in all and every facet of one's social existence. The relative freedom associated with being self-directing creates its own sense of anxiety for although creating "a need and ultimately a space for the practices of freedom," individuals are left to their own devices to "resolve the indeterminacies in the message from the Other that assail them from all sides" (Kripp, 2010: 97). Consequently, all experiences are shaped by and offer an opportunity to appropriately discipline one's own conduct. Similarly, accountable selves must constantly note and justify their behaviour in line with societal expectations. These expectations are inseparable from evolving but nonetheless comparatively stable configurations of power–knowledge relations. The managerial demand to be accountable is transferred into a universal call to be able to personally justify all one's intentional present actions and future plans.

This controlling subjectivity of self-accounting is witnessed in present-day discourses extolling both the autonomy of the subject and the continued power of the employer or manager. Cremin (2010), for instance, points to the deep contradiction in discourses of employability whereby the freedom to chronicle one's behaviour is directly related to conforming with the demands of the employer. This mirrors, again, past ideals of responsible autonomy (Friedman, 1977), whereby freedom is conditional on the ability of the individual to account adequately and regularly for their standing as a responsible worker.

The increasing popularity of flexible work exemplifies how the self-accounting subject facilitates contemporary strategies of managerial control. On the surface, such policies allow individuals to work where and when they desire. For this reason, it is touted as a form of empowerment in which individuals are trusted to be 'responsible' for their own self-management (Du Gay, Salaman and Rees, 1996) and the proper balancing of their work and home life (Brocklehurst, 2001). To this end, it would seem to be the antithesis of traditional governance based on accountability. Rather, it emphasises 'results-only' ethics whereby people at all levels stop doing any activity that is a waste of their time, the customer's time or their company's time (Ressler and Thompson, 2011). Nevertheless, this empowerment myth (Harley, 1999) creates a fresh impetus for self-accounting. As long as it generates productive results, there is space to organise one's own affairs but individuals are compelled to maximise their time, to justify how and where they spent it not only to their superiors but also just as significantly to themselves.

This subjectivation to becoming an accountable self reflects and contributes, moreover, to contemporary processes of ethical cultivation. In this capacity, accounting explicitly conditions how individuals conceive of themselves as ethical. The ethos of accountancy (premised on a continuous monitoring and assessment of one's actions) sets the co-ordinates for ethical action and judgment. To give one example, there is an imperative to be constantly improving oneself by 'learning from experience', and this stands as a present-day ethical injunction to be continually subjected to processes of self-accounting. In this spirit, the more 'self-accounting' one is, the more ethical one becomes. The desire to be 'healthy' or 'happy' is translated into an ethical demand to properly account for our daily behavior for the sake of our own self-improvement. Present is an ethic in which "people need to be proactive when faced with ill-defined circumstances" (Sennett, 2000: 51; see also Cremin, 2010: 133).

This intentional ethical framework for action is found for instance, in contemporary discourses of employability, highlighting the need to be accountable for one's success or failure to secure employment. In effect, this accountability for oneself is perceived as a form of empowerment that enhances one's employability (Bloom, 2013). In this respect,

> the burdensome nature of the employability discourse, as students struggle with aspirations, expectations and comparisons. Most importantly, employability appears to be bound up with transition from student to adult, and the associated tension between the potential for freedom and acceptance of personal responsibility.
>
> *(Hurlow and Parselle, 2012: 3)*

To this end, selfhood is transformed into a question of being accountable. Implicit in such subjectivation is the question of not only what is one accountable for but also to whom we are accountable. In this regard, the accountable self is associated with the responsibility people have to themselves and their existing and future employers to be a productive and disciplined employee.

This phenomenon of accountability extends well beyond conventional issues of work into all facets of life. Corporations and governments progressively call on their employees and subjects not only to be professionally competent but personally healthy. Underlying these 'progressive' policies is an often rather insidious form of managerial power. The organisation is invested with the task of assuring the well-being of its workforce, in and out of the workplace, therefore legitimising its right to monitor their personal conduct and a demand that they be healthy and this can catalyse additional anxieties on the part of employees in relation to their employers. Expanding on this insight, it can be said that the need to account for our personal conduct is transferred into a subjectivity of regularly self-accounting for our behaviour outside of work, as a means for both meeting organisational expectations and chronicling our own self-worth. For Cederstrom (2011) this also gestures towards a deeper subjective interpolation to such boundaryless managerial control.

There are then disintegrating boundaries between one's professional and personal selves. Fleming and Spicer (2004: 90), for instance, speak of a "boundaryless subject" in which one is simultaneously always a producer, always a family member and always a consumer. Crucially, they serve as an important way for the continual 'reboundarying' of work and life, a means of grounding and accounting for oneself in a seemingly unbounded 24/7 world. In a similar vein, Pedersen (2011) notes the shifting focus of many contemporary employers and employees away from purely organisational or professional goals, respectively, and towards the ability of a firm to provide personal fulfillment to its members. More strategically oriented, Cederstrom (2011) depicts new managerial control strategies revolving around themes of personal healthiness – in which organisations foster a culture of supposed employee well-being, similar to the earlier function of personnel, linked to their physical and mental health that at once deepens an individual's attachment to their company while also reinforcing managerial ideologies of productivity and self-discipline. Critically, it is not that the need for well-being in and of itself should be demonised but rather its use for exploitive purposes. To this end, it reflects how the understandable and even potentially positive desire to account for oneself and life choices are transformed into managerial techniques for encouraging work intensification and professional anxiety.

Going even further arguably, critical organisational scholars chronicle the recent incorporation of one's personal experiences into a broader organisationally friendly career narrative. Cremin (2007), for example, observes the framing of gap years by students intentionally seeking to temporarily avoid employment as part of a long-term employment biography to enhance one's curriculum vitae and therefore employability. Similarly, Bloom (2013) theorises how discourses of employability are transformed from a demand to conform to managerial desires to one that represents personal freedom and the potential to control one's own employment fate.

Importantly, such self-accounting is just one part of the broader dynamic of power in operation within these control strategies. Returning to the Foucauldian framework, individuals remain disciplined subjects, conforming to a wide array of organisational technologies conditioning their practices. In this regard, their status as subjects is one of subjection to organisational processes of disciplining in line with managerial values of efficiency and productivity. The practices associated with such governmentality reflect and reproduce established accounting protocols – such as chronicling their daily work using new digital technologies or effectively budgeting their time and resources – though now taken on and monitored often primarily by oneself. Self-accounting, however, also represents the subjectivation complementary to this subjection.

7 Conclusion

This chapter highlights the importance of the accountable self for understanding contemporary power and control as it relates to modern day accounting discourses and, in doing so, it has sought to demonstrate the importance of the later theories of Foucault for critical accounting studies. Specifically, it sought to shed light on the dynamic, though relatively underexplored, relationship between Foucault's concepts of subjection and subjectivation, both of which in different ways are the target of power–knowledge regimes. Drawing on these Foucauldian traditions, it can be argued that crucial to the subjection of individuals to accounting regimes is the production of the accountable self – a process of subjectivation. This subjectivation arises out of and can reinforce the disciplining of subjects to contemporary capitalist demands for efficiency and productivity in line with current accounting knowledges.

The chapter has sought to contribute to the broader critical accounting literature in a number of ways. Theoretically, its aim has been to illuminate the importance of the later Foucault for this field of study. A key conceptual challenge, in this regard, is one of connecting historical, disciplinary and governmental analyses of the accounting subject. Put differently, it has attempted to bridge a range of research foci: those that attended to the historical construction of the subject linked to accounting discourses and practices; those that emphasised the disciplinary function of accounting for this subject; and finally, those that pointed to accounting discourses as a 'governing rationality'. How could a Foucault perspective account for, if you will, the historically situated acting and thinking accounting subject?

By drawing on Foucault's analysis, we can address these concerns. The socio-historical production of the subject is not a singular phenomenon for it is composed of many different processes – but most notably, in our view, the relation of subjection to subjectivation. The former represents the inscribing of a subject within a historically evolving set of power configurations. The latter, conversely, denotes the cultivating of selfhood attached to, but necessarily always easily compatible with, this subjection. In the case of accounting, the subjection to disciplinary power based on accounting discourses and practices serves as the grounding for the creation of a 'self' extolling exactly such values. Here the agent-less conscription as an evolving historical 'subject of accounting' is translated into a viable and dynamic intentionally acting accounting subject. Using different Foucauldian terminology, an underlying historical ethos of accounting is channeled into a conscious cultivation of an ethically accountable self.

This theoretical relationship is witnessed in the present-day rise of the accountable self. The current subjection to accounting discourses and technologies is manifested in a selfhood premised on the ability to continually account for oneself as an active self. Here self-disciplining power is attached to a socially constructed knowledge of self in which an individual experiences a sense of agency through recording and monitoring their actions and behavior over time. Consequently, the ethos of accounting becomes a critical ethical imperative to be self-accounting in order to maximise one's personal well-being and professional success. The domination and control associated with an 'accounting society' is made manifest and strengthened by the simultaneous and diverse production of an accountable self.

Clearly when processes of subjectivation involve individuals identifying with and securing a sense of themselves precisely through engaging in the practices to which they are *subjected*, power–knowledge relations and their accounting regimes of accountability are comparatively stable. However, we endorse Foucault's encouragement of the kind of self-reflexivity that facilitates a refusal of the subjectivity that we find ourselves identifying with through so many historical and contemporary practices within power–knowledge regimes. After recent political events around BREXIT and the US presidential elections, we cannot but be aware that resistance to power–knowledge regimes does not always take the progressive form of promoting difference and diversity, and equality and egalitarianism across myopic, politically constructed boundaries. Still we should retain some optimism to recognise that subjection and subjectivation can be resisted and hopefully at some future point in history, it will be in a direction that is as far as possible from the quasi-fascist nationalism and racism of our contemporary times. It is the socialised understanding of freedom that allows subjects to experience themselves as intentional agents, providing them the very foundation upon which to continually reproduce themselves as accountable self-disciplining subjects.

This chapter was submitted by the authors with the following title: "Accounting for the 'accountable self' with the later Foucault."

Notes

1 Hoskin recognises that as Foucault argues, there are no such things as origins in a genealogical analysis. He therefore uses the term 'genesis' but this maybe does not overcome the problem, a concern that while interesting falls outside of the scope of this chapter.
2 This is, of course, a paraphrasing of Oscar Wilde's famous definition of a cynic (Wilde, 1893/2007).

References

Armstrong, P. (1987). "The rise of accounting controls in British capitalist enterprises," *Accounting, Organizations and Society*, 12(5): 415–36.

Armstrong, P. (1994). "The influence of Michel Foucault on accounting research," *Critical Perspectives on Accounting*, 5(1): 25–55.

Bloom, P. (2013). "Fight for your alienation: the fantasy of employability and the ironic struggle for self-exploitation," *ephemera*, 13(4): 785–807.

Braverman, H. (1974). *Labor and Monopoly Capital: The Degradation of Work in the Twentieth Century*, New York: Monthly Review Press.

Broadbent, J. (2002). "Critical accounting research: a view from England," *Critical Perspectives on Accounting*, 13(4): 433–49.

Brocklehurst, M. (2001). "Power, identity and new technology homework: implications for 'new forms' of organization," *Organization Studies* 22(3): 445–66.

Brown, J., J. Dillard and T. Hopper (2015). "Accounting, accountants and accountability regimes in pluralistic societies: taking multiple perspectives seriously," *Accounting, Auditing and Accountability Journal*, 28(5): 626–50.

Bryer, R. A. (1999). "A Marxist critique of the FASB's conceptual framework," *Critical Perspectives on Accounting*, 10(5): 551–89.

Bryer, R. A. (2000). "The history of accounting and the transition to capitalism in England. Part 1: theory," *Accounting, Organizations and Society*, 25(2): 131–62.

Bryer, R. (2004). "The roots of modern capitalism: a Marxist accounting history of the origins and consequences of capitalist landlords in England," *The Accounting Historians Journal*, 31(1): 1–56.

Burchell, S., C. Clubb and A. G. Hopwood (1985). "Accounting in its social context: towards a history of value added in the United Kingdom," *Accounting, Organizations and Society*, 10(4): 381–413.

Burchell, S., C. Clubb, A. G. Hopwood, J. Hughes and J. Nahapiet (1980). "The roles of accounting in organizations and society," *Accounting, Organizations and Society*, 5(1): 5–27.

Butler, J. (1997). *The Psychic Life of Power: Theories in Subjection*. Stanford, CA: Stanford University Press.

Cederström, C. (2011). "Fit for everything: health and the ideology of authenticity," *ephemera*, 11(1): 27–45.

Chiapello, E. (2007). "Accounting and the birth of the notion of capitalism," *Critical Perspectives on Accounting*, 18(3): 263–96.

Chua, W. F. (1988). "Interpretive sociology and management accounting research – a critical review," *Accounting, Auditing and Accountability Journal*, 1(2): 59–79.

Costea, B., N. Crump and K. Amiridis (2007). "Managerialism and 'infinite human resourcefulness': a commentary upon the 'therapeutic habitus', 'derecognition of finitude' and the modern sense of self," *Journal of Cultural Research*, 11(3): 245–64.

Cremin, C. (2007). "Living and really living: the gap year and the commodification of the contingent," *ephemera*, 7(4): 526–42.

Cremin, C. (2010). "Never employable enough: the (im)possibility of satisfying the boss's desire," *Organization*, 17(2): 131–49

Dillard, J. F. (1991). "Accounting as a critical social science," *Accounting, Auditing and Accountability Journal*, 4(1): 8–28.

Du Gay P., G. Salaman and B. Rees (1996). "The conduct of management and the management of conduct: contemporary managerial discourse and the of the 'competent manager'," *Journal of Management Studies*, 33(3): 263–83.

Edwards, R. C. (1980). *Contested Terrain*, London: Heinemann Educational Books.

Ezzamel, M. and H. Willmott (1998). Accounting for teamwork: a critical study of group-based systems of organizational control," *Administrative Science Quarterly*, 43(2): 358–96.

Faÿ, E., L. Introna and F. R. Puyou (2010). "Living with numbers: accounting for subjectivity in/with management accounting systems," *Information and Organization*, 20(1): 21–43.

Flamholtz, E. G. (1983). "Accounting, budgeting and control systems in their organizational context: theoretical and empirical perspectives," *Accounting, Organizations and Society*, 8(2–3): 35–50.

Flamholtz, E. G., M. L. Bullen and W. Hua (2002). Human resource accounting: a historical perspective and future implications," *Management Decision*, 40(10): 947–54.

Fleischman, R. K., P. A. Mills and T. N. Tyson (1996). "A theoretical primer for evaluating and conducting historical research in accounting," *Accounting History*, 1(1): 55–75.

Fleming, P. and A. Spicer (2004). "'You can checkout anytime, but you can never leave': spatial boundaries in a high commitment organization," *Human Relations*, 57(1): 75–94.

Foucault, M. (1973). *The Archaeology of Knowledge*, London: Tavistock.

Foucault, M. (1975). *Discipline and Punish: The Birth of the Prison*, New York: Random House.

Foucault, M. (1980). *Power/Knowledge: Selected Interviews and Other Writings 1972-1977*, edited by C. Gordon, Brighton, UK: Harvester Press.

Foucault, M. (1981). "Questions of method," *Ideology and Consciousness*, 8: 1–14.

Foucault, M. (1982). "'The subject and power," *Critical Inquiry*, 8(4): 777–95.

Foucault, M. (1984.) "The ethics of care of the self as a practice of freedom," in J. Bernaeur and D. Ramussen (eds): *The Final Foucault*, Cambridge, MA: M.I.T. Press.

Foucault, M. (1990). *The History of Sexuality. Volume II*, New York: Vintage Books.

Foucault, M. (1991). "Governmentality" in G. Burchell, C. Gordon and P. Miller (eds) *The Foucault Effect: Studies in Governmentality*, Chicago, IL: University of Chicago Press.

Foucault, M. (1994). *Power: The Essential Works 1954 – 1984*, edited by J. D. Fabuion, London: Penguin Books.

Foucault, M. (1997a). *Ethics: Subjectivity and Truth*, London: Allen Lane.

Foucault, M. (1997b). *Ethics: Essential Works of Foucault 1954–1984 volume 1*, edited by P. Rabinow, Harmondsworth: Penguin Books.

Foucault, M. (2001). *Power: Essential Writings*, translated by R. Hurley, London: Allen Lane.

Foucault, M. (2004). *Society Must Be Defended: Lectures at the Collège de France, 1975–1976*, London and New York: Allen Lane.

Foucault, M. (2005). *The Hermeneutics of the Subject: Lectures at the College de France 1981–1982*, New York: Palgrave Macmillan.

Foucault, M. (2011). *The Courage of Truth: Lectures at the College de France 1983–4*, Basingstoke: Palgrave Macmillan.

Friedman, A. L. (1977). *Industry and Labour*, London: Macmillan.

Gallhofer, S. and Haslam, J. (1997). "Beyond accounting: the possibilities of accounting and "critical" accounting research," *Critical Perspectives on Accounting*, 8(1): 71–95.

Giddens, A. (1984). *The Constitution of Society: Outline of the Theory of Structuration*, Cambridge: Polity Press

Gouldson, A. and J. Bebbington (2007). "Corporations and the governance of environmental risk," *Environment and Planning C: Government and Policy*, 25(1), 4–20.

Grey, C. (1994). "Debating Foucault: a critical reply to Neimark," *Critical Perspectives on Accounting*, 4(1): 5–24.

Harley, B. (1999). "The myth of empowerment: work organization, hierarchy and employee autonomy in contemporary Australian workplaces," *Work, Employment and Society* 13(1): 41–66.

Hopper, T., J. Storey and H. Willmott (1987). "Accounting for accounting: towards the development of a dialectical view," *Accounting, Organizations and Society*, 12(5): 437–56.

Hopwood, A. G. (1985). "The tale of a committee that never reported: disagreements on intertwining accounting with the social," *Accounting, Organizations and Society*, 10(3): 361–77.

Hopwood, A. G. (1987). "The archaeology of accounting systems," *Accounting, Organizations and Society*, 12(3): 207–34.

Hopwood, A. G. and P. Miller (eds) (1994). *Accounting as Social and Institutional Practice*, Cambridge: Cambridge University Press.

Hoskin, K. (1994). "Boxing clever: For, against and beyond Foucault in the battle for accounting theory," *Critical Perspectives on Accounting*, 5(1): 57–85.

Hoskin, K. W. and R. H. Macve (1986). "Accounting and the examination: a genealogy of disciplinary power," *Accounting, Organizations and Society*, 11(2): 105–36.

Hurlow, S. and G. Parselle (2012). "Negotiating the employability discourse," paper presented at *Society for Research into Higher Education Annual Research Conference*, Newport, Wales.

Hyman, R. (1989). *The Political Economy of Industrial Relations: Theory and Practice in a Cold Climate*, London: Palgrave Macmillan.

Kaufman, B. E. (1993). *The Origins and Evolution of the Field of Industrial Relations in the United States*, Ithaca, NY and London: Cornell University Press.

Knights, D. (2006). "Passing the time in pasttimes, professionalism and politics: reflecting on the ethics and epistemology of time studies," *Time and Society*, 15(2–3): 251–74.

Knights, D. (2002). "Writing organization analysis into Foucault," *Organization*, 9(4): 575–93.

Knights, D. and H. Willmott (eds) (1990). *Labour Process Theory*, London: Macmillan

Kripp, H. (2010). "The politics of the gaze: Foucault, Lacan and Žižek," Culture Unbound: *Journal of Current Cultural Research*, 2: 91–102.

Laughlin, R. C. (1987). "Accounting systems in organizational contexts: a case for critical theory," *Accounting, Organizations and Society*, 12(5): 479–502.

Laughlin, R. (1999). "Critical accounting: nature, progress and prognosis," *Accounting, Auditing and Accountability Journal*, 12(1): 73–8.

Lehman, C. and T. Tinker (1987). "The 'real' cultural significance of accounts," *Accounting, Organizations and Society*, 12(5): 503–22.

Loft, A. (1986). "Towards a critical understanding of accounting: the case of cost accounting in the UK, 1914–1925," *Accounting, Organizations and Society*, 11(2): 137–69.

McGregor, D. (1960). *The Human Side of Enterprise*, New York: McGraw-Hill.

Macintosh, N. B. and R. W. Scapens (1990). "Structuration theory in management accounting," *Accounting, Organizations and Society*, 15(5): 455–77.

McKinlay, A. and E. Pezet (2010). "Accounting for Foucault," *Critical Perspectives on Accounting*, 21(6): 486–95.

MacKinnon, D. (2000). "Managerialism, governmentality and the state: a neo-Foucauldian approach to local economic governance. *Political Geography*, 19(3): 293–14.

McPhail, K. (1999). "The threat of ethical accountants: an application of Foucault's concept of ethics to accounting education and some thoughts on ethically educating for the other," *Critical Perspectives on Accounting*, 10(6): 833–66.

Meyer, J. W. (1986). "Social environments and organizational accounting," *Accounting, Organizations and Society*, 11(4): 345–56.

Mitchell, A., P. Sikka and H. Willmott (2001). "Policing knowledge by invoking the law: critical accounting and the politics of dissemination," *Critical Perspectives on Accounting*, 12(5): 527–55.

Miller, P. (1990). "On the interrelations between accounting and the state," *Accounting, Organizations and Society*, 15(4): 315–38.

Miller, P. (2006). "Management accounting and sociology," *Handbooks of Management Accounting Research*, 1: 285–95.

Miller, P. and T. O'Leary (1987). "Accounting and the construction of the governable person," *Accounting, Organizations and Society*, 12(3): 235–65.

Neimark, M. K. (1994). "Regicide revisited: Marx, Foucault and accounting," *Critical Perspectives on Accounting*, 5(1):87–108.

Neu, D., D. J. Cooper and J. Everett (2001). "Critical accounting interventions," *Critical Perspectives on Accounting*, 12(6): 735–62.

Ortner, S. B. (1995). "Resistance and the problem of ethnographic refusal," *Comparative Studies in Society and History*, 37(1): 173–93.

Pedersen, M. (2011). "'A career is nothing without a personal life': on the social machine in the call for authentic employees," *ephemera*, 11(1): 63–77.

Peters, T. and R. H. Waterman (1982). *In Search of Excellence: Lessons from America's Best-Run Companies*, New York: Harper and Row.

Pink, D. (2011). *Drive: The Surprising Truth about What Motivates Us*, New York: Penguin Books.

Power, M., R. Laughlin and D. J. Cooper (2003). "Accounting and Critical Theory," in M. Alvesson and H. Willmott (eds): *Studying Management Critically*, London: Sage Publications.

Ressler, C. and J. Thompson (2011). *Why Work Sucks and How to Fix It: The Results Only Revolution*, New York: Wiley.

Roberts, J. (2005). "The power of the 'imaginary' in disciplinary processes," *Organization*, 12(5): 619–42.

Rose, N. (1999). *Powers of Freedom: Reframing Political Thought*. Cambridge: Cambridge University Press.

Rose, N., P. O'Malley and M. Valverde (2006). "Governmentality," *Annual Review of Law and Social Science*, 2: 83–104.

Sennett, R. (2000). *The Corrosion of Character: The Personal Consequences of Work in the New Capitalism*, New York: Norton.

Smith, C. S. (2002). "Perspective and point of view: accounting for subjectivity," *Language and Computers*, 39(1): 63–79.

Stewart, R. E. (1992). "Pluralizing our past: Foucault in accounting history," *Accounting, Auditing and Accountability Journal*, 5(2): 57–74.

Strozier, R. M. (2002). *Foucault, Subjectivity, and Identity: Historical Constructions of Subject and Self*, Detroit, MI: Wayne State University Press.

Thomas, P. and J. Hewitt (2011). "Managerial organization and professional autonomy: a discourse-based conceptualization," *Organization Studies*, 32(10): 1373–93.

Tie, W. (2004). "The psychic life of governmentality," *Culture, Theory and Critique*, 45(2): 161–76.

Tinker, A. (1984). "Theories of the state and the state of accounting: economic reductionism and political voluntarism in accounting regulation theory," *Journal of Accounting and Public Policy*, 3(1): 55–74.

Tinker, A. M., B. D. Merino and M. D. Neimark (1982). "The normative origins of positive theories: ideology and accounting thought," *Accounting, Organizations and Society*, 7(2): 167–200.

Wilde, O. (1893/2007). *Lady Windermere's Fan*, London: FQ Classics.

7

BOURDIEU

Jeff Everett

1 Introduction

While not without his detractors (see, for example, Nash, 1999), Pierre Bourdieu is considered by many to be one of the most eminent sociologists of the late twentieth century (Silva and Warde, 2010: 1). It is not surprising then that his work has been embraced by accounting researchers and used in a variety of ways. Extending a recent review of this use by Malsch, Gendron and Grazzini (2011), this chapter examines how Bourdieu's ideas and work enhance the critical accounting project. I specifically focus on Bourdieu's general methodological approach and his 'scholarship with commitment', arguing that critical accountants have only just begun to tap into the rich framework that he provides. I also discuss how he positions his academic work relative to his political activism and his need to "intervene in the affairs of the city" (Bourdieu, 2000: 41).

The first section of the chapter provides a brief outline of what the term 'critical' means to academic accountants who have commented on the idea[1] and how these meanings align with Bourdieu's own commitments. The chapter then examines Bourdieu's methodological and conceptual approach and his political activism. The third section supplements Malsch *et al.* (2011) by providing an updated assessment of the accounting literature that draws on Bourdieu and by drawing attention to concepts that have to date received relatively little attention from accounting researchers.

2 Critique in critical accounting

As Mouritsen, Larsen and Hansen (2002: 511) observe, "critique is very many different things." It depends on the critic's mindset, intended purpose (and, by extension, object of concern), the methodology and conceptual tools employed, and the degree to which the critique is made public. It is not surprising then that the term has a variety of meanings in critical accounting, although on the whole I would argue that those meanings tend to align with Bourdieu's own sense of the term.

Regarding the critical mindset, one can adopt a pessimistic or cynical viewpoint, or, as a number of critical accountants have advocated (e.g. Cooper, 2002; Cooper and Sherer, 1984), a more optimistic or idealistic one. Optimism need not be devoid of skepticism, as one can be hopeful without abandoning a sense of doubt (Gray, Dillard and Spence, 2009). Some critical accountants further believe that critique is obligatory, arguing that as a privileged member of society one has a moral responsibility to advocate and seek change. Critique may also be all consuming – one critical accountant, the late Tony Lowe, is said to have been constantly engaged in critique (Carter and Tinker, 2006). A number of critical accountants further see critique as being about resistance (Gaffikin, 2009), envisioned as being either reformist or revolutionary, with the predominant interest being in the former (Gray *et al.*, 2009; Mouritsen *et al.*, 2002).

Bourdieu was not explicit about whether his critique was underpinned by a moral obligation – he was largely silent on ethics (for an exception, see Bourdieu, 1996: 56) – although implicitly this seems to be the case. Critical of 'ivory-tower intellectuals' and 'paper revolutionaries' alike, he clearly saw an urgent need to speak out publicly against the spin and mystifications of think-tanks and economic journalists. Their conservative *doxa*, although presented as progressive, was clearly a problem, one that could be countered only with truth and reason (Bourdieu, 2004). Bourdieu's critique was also unrelenting, both in regard to actors in the wider socio-economic field and those in the more restricted academic field (a field wherein he created many enemies) (Bourdieu, 1998, 2003, 2008). Moreover, like many critical accountants, Bourdieu espoused the need for 'radical doubt', and he advocated resistance, as the titles of two of his works (1998, 2003) suggest. As far as his position on the pessimism–optimism scale goes, Bourdieu was also far from cynical, as his deep commitment to change motivated him to speak in favour of a 'realistic utopia' (2003). Firmly believing that research could effect change in the political field, Bourdieu was perhaps even "extraordinarily idealistic" (Swartz, 2010: 50). "The time has come," he said, "when scholars need to intervene in politics with their competence in order to impose utopias based in truth and rationality" (Swartz, 2010: 53).

In respect of the purpose or objective of research, critical accountants have adopted a variety of positions. Some see the point of critical research as providing a voice (Gallhofer, Haslam and Yonekura, 2013) for African-Americans, women and/or the working class (Cooper and Hopper, 1987), while others wish to intervene in policy debates (Neu, Cooper and Everett, 2001). Yet others take as their goal a more general enabling of accountability (over decision-usefulness) (Williams and Ravenscroft, 2015), the development of a theory of interests (Cooper and Hopper, 1987), or the unification of theory and practice (Cooper, 2002). Others, focusing on the academic field of production and calling for more 'self-critique', even 'radical self-critique' (Gallhofer *et al.*, 2013; Macintosh and Shearer, 2000; Reiter and Williams, 2002), raise questions regarding the field's 'ivory-tower' isolation and naïveté (Mouritsen *et al.*, 2002), a much-needed call in a time when university researchers are being asked to make their work more relevant to the needs of the public. Some seek to expose the reputation-building agendas of academics working in dominant accounting schools (Wilkinson and Durden, 2015), while yet others, reflecting the overwhelmingly societal orientation that characterises the subfield, call for a "critical understanding of the role of accounting processes and practices and the accounting profession in the functioning of society and organisation" (Laughlin, 1999: 78).

Bourdieu's project was certainly aligned with one of these goals, the unification of practice and theory, though it also aimed to expose the status-seeking behavior of (especially élite) academics. More specifically, however, Bourdieu's academic work was concerned with the various manifestations of privilege and power, and how institutional groups engaged in legitimation struggles in order to accumulate or, in some cases, redefine the valued forms of capital in a field (Swartz, 2010: 46). His political work, in a not unrelated manner, was concerned with "the excesses of neo-liberal economic management" and the increasing role of the media and think-tanks in helping powerful actors disseminate what he termed 'the neo-liberal vulgate' (Silva and Warde, 2010: 2). These are decidedly more political aims than simply building theory, unifying theory and practice, or studying accounting processes, actors and practices (to the extent that such study is normatively aimed only at satisfying one's curiosity, which for some is probably the case). As some critical accountants would have it, for example Tinker (1991), the point of such study is to effect *praxis*, which is to say, not simply understand the world, but understand the academic's active role in it and the way that it, in turn, shapes their ways of thinking and acting (Tinker and Gray, 2003: 737).

Regarding the methodology employed, critical accountants are largely guided by method-ologies which admit of the always-normative character of research (Gallhofer *et al.*, 2013); the need for close, empirical proximity to socio-economic actors; the study of power and wealth distribution; and an understanding of the macro-social, historical and institutional environ-ment in which that distribution takes place (Cooper and Sherer, 1984; Laughlin, 1999; Poullaos, 2004). The preferred methodologies also tend to enable a break with the larger research field's theoretical and methodological homogeneity (Wilkinson and Durden, 2015) and a critical approach in accounting is said to also demand theoretical imagination and innovation (Cooper and Sherer, 1984; Gallhofer *et al.*, 2013; Laughlin, 1999; Macintosh and Shearer, 2000). While critical accounting research has tended to rely on qualitative methods for these reasons, it is difficult to justify an exclusive focus on such methods (Everett, Neu, Rahaman and Maharaj, 2015). Indeed, Bourdieu would applaud the use of quantitative methods to the extent that they furthered these objectives.

Conceptually, critical accountants have employed or advocated the use of a host of conceptual tools, many of which Bourdieu also relies on. Gray *et al.* (2009), for example, invoke notions of injustice, hegemony and misery. Misery is also mentioned in Cooper (2002), as are the concepts of inequality, 'the neo-liberal economic agenda', structure, agency, class and ideology. Cooper and Sherer (1984) also refer to the notion of ideology, adding to this the concepts of power, conflict, interest, emancipation, social welfare, the public interest and 'the social'. Gallhofer *et al.* (2013) see the ideas of contradiction, repression, disempowerment and praxis as important, while Carter and Tinker (2006) highlight the notion of class. In the context of critical accounting, mention is also made of reflexivity, economic rationalism, the status quo, surveillance, globalisation and, again, resistance (cf. Kaidonis, 2009; Poullaos, 2004).

Many of these ideas were highly important to Bourdieu, especially the ideas of power, domina-tion, inequality, structure, agency, class, praxis and resistance. That said, there are a host of concepts used by Bourdieu that have yet to become a part of the critical accounting lexicon, including *doxa*, misrecognition, *hexis*, *conatus*, *metanoia*, *hysteresis* and *illusio*. Some of Bourdieu's more well-known concepts, particularly those of capital, field, *habitus* and symbolic violence, have been taken up in the accounting literature, but these are not always used in combination, which potentially limits the efficacy of the analysis (Malsch *et al.*, 2011). That Bourdieu has worked to develop new concepts or revise and reintroduce others is not a function of some need to be original; rather, it is to step outside of the language games that characterise the political and orthodox scientific fields. Orthodox understandings of the world are problematic because they obscure arbitrarily imposed labels and classifications that themselves have material and symbolic effects. Bourdieu was for this reason always quick to challenge common sense and the taken for granted. Conceptual categori-zations and divisions – and accounting relies on many of these – act as a means by which symboli-cally powerful actors are able to impose their visions on less dominant groups.[2]

Finally, regarding the dissemination of research, there is a debate within critical accounting about whether or not research should be made available and useful to those engaged in political action (Cooper, 2002; Gallhofer *et al.*, 2013). Commenting on this, Laughlin (1999: 77–8) states:

> Some academics would maintain that our 'job' is to critically expose and leave it to others to engage, evaluate and change what we are observing. Others argue strongly

for real involvement in this change process seeing this as a vitally important part of the academic project.

Neu *et al.* (2001) advocate a more interventionist role, though they suggest that critical research need not be produced explicitly for consumers, including non-governmental organisations or grass-roots organisations. Drawing on Bourdieu's ideas, they similarly advocate that research be useful, as long as it is rooted in reason and presents a challenge to the common sense.

Bourdieu (2004) is clear that social science must be conducted according to the established standards set within the (relevant subfield of the) scientific community. It was his respect for these standards (and the virtue of truth) that caused him to distance himself from post-structuralism and postmodernism, despite the fact that some have located him within these intellectual movements (see e.g. Robbins, 2007). This meant that he was also unwilling to countenance the idea that non-academics should be setting the agenda for researchers, or even less, allowing non-researchers to evaluate the quality of that research. He always believed in producing strictly for other producers, not consumers, which is to say, other members of the scientific field, since it is there that the evaluative standards of reason and critique are the highest. Firmly committed to the ideas of disinterestedness and scientific autonomy – which, he reminds us, was never a given and remains the product of conquest (Bourdieu, 2004: 47) – he was highly suspicious of getting too close to groups outside of the academy, especially political parties. Yet at the same time he repudiated the idea of the privileged ivory-tower intellectual living the leisured life of contemplation and, equally, the production of knowledge useful only to dominant élites. Rather, his vision was one of rigorous science being carried out according to its own rules, but which, at the same time, addressed questions of importance to those for whom "the distance from necessity was not great" (Bourdieu, 1984, *passim*). While his work upheld the highest standards of social science, it *simultaneously* focused on public issues, such as colonisation, class inequality, education, and housing (Swartz, 2010). Bourdieu's scholarship with commitment, then, necessarily separates two key sets of actors, the scientific collective and the 'outside world', which are then linked through "sustained and vigorous exchange" (Bourdieu, 2000: 44).

In sum, while there are a variety of views among accounting researchers as to what exactly constitutes 'the critical', there are numerous 'family resemblances' among the mindsets, purposes, concepts, methodologies and interventions that they espouse. Many if not most of these, I would argue, are aligned with the work and ideas of Bourdieu. In the following section, I look at Bourdieu's methodology.

3 Bourdieu's social praxeology

A variety of resources are available for those interested in Bourdieu's concepts, including texts by Swartz (1997), Grenfell (2012) and Webb, Schirato and Danaher (2002). Everett (2002) demonstrates the applicability of Bourdieu's work to the study of organisations, while Malsch *et al* (2011) documents the use of his work in accounting. For this reason, I will only briefly comment on his concepts. I would, however, like to focus on Bourdieu's general methodological approach or *praxeology* (Bourdieu and Wacquant, 1992). In part this is because it is rather unusual as viewed from either a purely positivist or interpretivist perspective,[3] but also because few accounting researchers devote much attention to what Bourdieu sees as the necessary front- and back ends of a research project. While my goal is not to dictate how Bourdieu must be used – he would have bridled at the idea of someone attempting to establish a canon – I do feel that it is hard to achieve the potential of Bourdieu's approach if only his concepts are used and his methodology is ignored.

To properly understand Bourdieu's methodological approach one needs to understand the context within which it was developed. Important in this regard are a number of key debates that occurred in the philosophical, sociological and anthropological literatures. These specifically regard a number of important dualisms: namely, structure versus agency; realism versus idealism; and subject versus object. The need to transcend these dualisms very much shaped Bourdieu's ontology and epistemology – the starting points or assumptions that undergird his work. Regarding structure versus agency, he believed that individual social actors have free will, but that they are also seriously constrained at times by the material and, equally important, symbolic structures within which they exist. Neglecting these structures and the way they shape cognition and behavior renders any investigation incomplete. Bourdieu was also not an epistemological realist, somehow believing that things like *capital* and *habitus* exist prior to the observations of the social scientist. Yet, at the same time, he was not of the mind that all is a social construction, at least in the sense that all knowledge can be reduced to its social and historical conditions. Domination, inequality and suffering are 'real', the problem is that the social scientist is unable to see these things 'in themselves' because s/he always brings in a set of presuppositions that shape the act of observation. Bourdieu's understanding here was influenced by Gaston Bachelard (see Chimisso, 2001), and it is this understanding that makes the construction of the research object an important front end, and reflexivity an important 'back end', research activity. Finally, regarding the subject versus object dualism, Bourdieu saw limitations in viewing the world exclusively through either a (Durkheimian) positivist/objectivist or a (Schützian) phenomenological/subjectivist lens – he felt that both had important strengths and both were needed to adequately grasp social practice. Bourdieu (1990) provides a highly instructive discussion of the respective weaknesses or blind spots of the two perspectives (especially 1990: 30–51; see also Bourdieu and Wacquant, 1992: 7–11).

With these dualisms in mind, we now consider his methodology. Grenfell (2010) discusses this in terms of three key stages: (i) the construction of the research object; (ii) a three-level approach to field study; and (iii) participant objectivation. The first essentially asks the researcher to reflect seriously upon the research objects that they study, the approaches that are typically used to study them and the reasons for studying them. This is because social science is *shaped* by historical and social conditions (which is not to say *determined* by them), and consequently one is forced to confront a variety of 'epistemological obstacles' that are the products of these conditions. Racism is one such obstacle: In a racist society social science can become stuck measuring 'race-related attributes', such as health, wealth, intelligence and education, unaware that racial groups are not even genetically distinct, reliably measured, or scientifically meaningful (Smedley and Smedley, 2005). Thus, the category 'race' becomes taken for granted, and science proceeds as if it were, like the racism upon which it is based, real.

As a first stage in any research project, then, it is necessary to deconstruct accepted practices, forms and concepts, asking, "what do terms include and exclude" (Grenfell, 2010: 20). In relation to accounting, for example, it is accepted practice that doctoral students learn (using strictly quantitative methods) how to study the effects that accounting disclosures have on a variety of dependent variables, such as stock prices, as if this was somehow critically important to the public or even important to practicing accountants. In accounting research it is also easy to treat a number of very familiar categories as if they were 'real' things, such as the 'profession', 'regulation', and 'business'. These categories are really just vague labels, or floating signifiers that have no fixed meaning (Gray *et al.*, 2009), and in blindly adopting them one runs the risk of being forced in the direction of a specific theory, method or audience that is interested in the result. Accepted practices, forms and concepts all demand careful consideration *prior* to undertaking the research.

Related to Bourdieu's own work, and relevant to critical accounting research, to accept the notion of class typically implies a concern with material resources – wealth and income – and it also tends to invoke a theoretical framing that takes class to be important, such as Marxism. Seeing the need to supplement Marx's ideas and incorporate Weber's powerful insights on social status, Bourdieu endeavored to avoid relying on the notion of class, developing in its place the notion of *capital*, which enabled him to maintain a focus on a wider array of dominated groups, such as women and racialised minorities, and not simply those lacking financial resources. He was able to show how these groups' embodied cultural capitals – their skin colour, dress, linguistic skills, cultural preferences, and so on – have an important effect on their life chances (which is not to say that income and wealth are not also important). For Bourdieu, there are dangers in blindly adopting pre-constructed research objects – they come with embedded meanings, impositions and silent confusions – and there are opportunities in unpacking and examining the seemingly normal, mundane and banal. Indeed, Bourdieu recommends starting with a phenomenon, or at least a research question, rather than a theory, in order to avoid being captured by that theory and the (scholastic) presuppositions that come with it (Grenfell, 2010: 23). This requirement would seem to satisfy appeals in critical accounting for more theoretical imagination and innovation (Cooper and Sherer, 1984; Gallhofer *et al.,* 2013; Laughlin, 1999; Macintosh and Shearer, 2000).

Having thought about and carefully constructed the research object, the second stage in Bourdieu's research process is field analysis. This involves three sub-stages: (i) analysing the position of the field vis–à–vis the field of power; (ii) mapping the structure of objective relations; and (iii) analysing the habitus of agents (Grenfell, 2010). All three of these sub-stages require empirical investigation, all three are necessary, and, ideally, they are followed in this order (Grenfell, 2010: 22). It is worth noting that each of these stages corresponds to what Malsch *et al.* (2011), following Dobbins (2008), see as a separate element in Bourdieu's integrated theory: a theory of social structure; a theory of power relations; and a theory of the individual.

Concerning the first, a 'field' is, quite simply, any arena of symbolic and material struggle, in which some actors have more power than others. A field is not necessarily an organisation or an institution, and it is quite unlikely to be one of those things. The study of tax avoidance and tax evasion, for example, requires much more than the study of accounting; it also requires the study of tax law and the actions of tax lawyers, state authorities and others (Oats, 2012). The study of accounting standards would also be incomplete without incorporating an analysis of the role of securities legislation, securities regulators and others. An analysis of pension accounting similarly requires an understanding of the actions of actuaries and others, and so on. As a relational method, the key is to start with the phenomenon and work outward, which will bring the researcher into contact with other actors in a larger network of fields. It should also allow the researcher to better understand how the field in question is positioned vis-à-vis the field of power.

By 'power', Bourdieu is referring to *capital*, which comes in a variety of forms, depending on the field. Money is a form of economic capital; a credential is a form of cultural capital, as is knowledge; and participation in a network of relations provides social capital (insofar as that participation provides benefits). Where a form of capital is deemed legitimate, its possessor accumulates the most enduring form, symbolic capital. Those with symbolic capital in turn are able to name or consecrate that which is seen as legitimate, further enhancing the value of that form. Note that the function of power is field specific; one does not derive symbolic power from being wealthy in the field of avant-garde art, for instance. In addition, symbolic capital is also by definition misrecognised: for example, for Marcel Duchamp's *Fountain* to be recognised as art required forgetting that it first needed to be consecrated and named as such. Also in relation to misrecognition, for Bourdieu the conditions of domination must be internalised:

domination must be seen as normal, inevitable or natural before it can be accepted (Swartz, 2010: 48). Bourdieu would not suggest that people consent to their domination, rather only that they adapt to it.

Mapping the structure of objective relations in a research field (vis-à-vis the field of power) entails the identification of what is and is not valued in the field (i.e. the types of capital), who is in possession of the preferred forms of capital and the amount of capital they possess. Here, it might be determined that what constitutes a social class 'on paper' might be different from what exists in reality. For example, and relevant in the context of corporate social responsibility research, on paper social and environmental reports evince transparency and progress on the part of corporations. Yet it is remiss to talk about these initiatives without mentioning the larger space of social relations and the exchange of capital that goes on within it. The work of corporate lobbyists and PR firms and their considerably effective efforts to undo or stall legislation aimed at changing behavior can easily offset paper-based claims of improvement. Corporate social responsibility (and social and environmental reporting) constitute a field of struggle, which is located within a much larger and highly important field of power that should not be ignored.

Having established what are the preferred forms of capital in a field, who is (and who is not) in possession of them and having traced the field's structural relations back to the field of power, it remains to study the dispositions of the field's key agents, the third of the three sub-stages in Bourdieu's second stage of research. Understanding their backgrounds, formal education, socialisation and life trajectories – or *habitus* – is important because habitus organises the agent's practices and the agent's perceptions of practices (Malsch *et al.*, 2011: 198). To not understand or at least have an idea of the interpretive schema that drives powerful social agents in a field greatly weakens the insights that can be attained regarding the operation and transformation of a field. This stage typically requires in-depth interviews with agents, though with the right research design it can even involve the use of quantitative methods (see Robson and Sanders, 2009).

It goes without saying that these three sub-stages alone – mapping the symbolic and material resources in a field, identifying who possesses those resources and understanding the dispositions of capital-rich actors – all require a great deal of effort. Yet, Bourdieu's prescriptions do not stop there, as he asks one more thing, and that is for the researcher to reflect upon how the social conditions of thinking set limits on one's thought (Grenfell, 2010). This stage is similar to the first in that one is still required to reflect upon the field's academic orthodoxies, why the object of study was chosen and what brought it about, and how the object is constructed in the discipline. Thus, for instance, capital market researchers should reflect upon why exactly they view financial reports as decision-useful products circulated in an information economy both before and after the research is carried out. The *post-hoc* act of 'reflexivity' or 'participant objectivation' is designed to do nothing more than draw out the implicit associations or biases that invariably shaped the knowledge-production process. That one's research is sponsored or funded means that it can never be truly disinterested. Competitiveness in a research field, careerist ambitions, institutional pressures to publish and even just having the time and privilege to observe the social world, all effect the knowledge that is ultimately produced. Reflexivity is not optional either, because researchers belong to a *collective* community (Grenfell, 2010: 24; Bourdieu, 2004). Insofar as they are invested in the game of science and the (endless) pursuit of universal truth, researchers have a responsibility to that community to understand exactly how certain interests affect the symbolic goods that they produce.

Bourdieu (2004) is unabashed in his commitment to science, reason and the pursuit of truth. Yet, he was also committed to social justice and change. These twin objectives put him in a difficult and some would say unmanageable position – attempting to produce disinterested knowledge, but with a purpose. The way he balanced these two objectives was, however, really quite straightforward: he pursued phenomena of public interest (with a decided bent towards the more disenfranchised and dominated members of the public) and he pursued their understanding with academic rigour. The idea was that he would undertake an analysis of the highest academic standards, but that analysis must be something political activists could actually use (Swartz, 2010: 56). Yet he didn't stop at producing social science that mattered. Especially towards the end of his life, he also engaged politically; signing petitions, setting up research centers, writing op-eds, manning picket lines and taking part in public policy debates (Bourdieu, 1998, 2003, 2008). Converting his significant academic and symbolic capital into political capital, he became one of France's best-known critics of the establishment. As a rule, however, he always believed that it was his (hard-earned) scholarly expertise that gave him the right to intervene politically, and not his individual conscience (Bourdieu, 2008). His inclination to fire back against the tyranny of the market (Bourdieu, 2003) was premised on his belief that he had more to offer than simply his "attachments and roots, passions and interests, positions and thus points of view… and misview" (Bourdieu, 2008: 148).

4 Bourdieu and accounting research

In the final section of this chapter, I would like to discuss the manner in which Bourdieu's work has been used in accounting. Building upon the comprehensive review provided by Malsch *et al.*, (2011), the point I wish to make is that not only is a more holistic use of Bourdieu's concepts possible, but there are likely benefits to be had in more closely following the three stages (and sub-stages) of his methodology. This is especially the case when it comes to the construction of the research object (stage 1) and participant objectivation (stage 3), which few address in their work, at least explicitly. Moreover, while Bourdieu was an advocate of measuring when appropriate, there is an almost complete lack of quantitative or combined quantitative–qualitative analysis in the critical accounting literature (Everett *et al.*, 2015). Given the greater (though not-always-deserved) legitimacy that quantitative research has in the public sphere, it would seem that this is yet another reason that critical accountants might wish to turn to Bourdieu.

My review of the use of Bourdieu's work is based on work published in the following accounting journals: *Critical Perspectives on Accounting*; *Accounting, Organizations and Society*; the *Accounting, Auditing and Accountability Journal*; and *Accounting Forum*. In these journals, 62 papers were found that cite Bourdieu. Among these, eleven were excluded from further analysis as the references to Bourdieu were only for tangential purposes, for example mentioning Bourdieu in the context of French social theory or mentioning his name alongside that of Giddens. I then closely examined and conducted a word search of the remaining 51 papers using the following terms: 'capital'; 'field'; 'habitus'; 'symbolic violence'; 'doxa'; 'illusion'; 'misrecognition'; 'domination'; and 'power'. These are terms which I believe are key to Bourdieu's theory. While the notions of *practice* and *structure* are also frequently used by Bourdieu, he uses them in a rather general way, for example he labels his approach a theory of practice. A number of other terms were also searched to gain a sense of the general context within which Bourdieu's work was used, including: 'inequality', 'ethics', 'suffering', and 'critical'. Other terms that might have been included in my enumeration of his concepts include 'resistance', 'reflexivity', 'class', 'social justice', 'alienation', 'classification' and 'elite'. However, I do not feel these are among his core concepts.

In each of the 51 papers analysed, Bourdieu was cited 36 times on average, though with a range of between 2 (Everett and Neu, 2000) and 235 citations (Malsch *et al.*, 2011), it is clear that there is a more-or-less heavy reliance on his work. Moreover, the author's name does not have to be mentioned frequently for a paper to be inspired by Bourdieu, though it is probably fair to say that a higher frequency is associated with a closer engagement with his work.

Regarding the 13 concepts used, these were mentioned a total of 9,015 times, at an average of 177 times per paper or 14 times per concept per paper. Some papers that stand out in regard to a heavy reliance on Bourdieu include Alawattage (2011); Carter and Spence (2014); Cooper and Joyce (2013); Cooper, Coulson and Taylor (2011); Hamilton and Ó hOgartaigh (2009); Jayasinghe and Wickramasinghe (2011); Malsch *et al.* (2011); and Shenkin and Coulson (2007). Regarding the notion of capital, the work of Alawattage (2011); Andon, Free and Sivabalan (2014); Carter and Spence (2014); Xu and Xu (2008), and, especially, Chenhall, Hall and Smith (2010) and Thompson (1999) are noteworthy. Regarding the notion of field, this concept is featured strongly in Alawattage (2011); Andon *et al.* (2014); Carter and Spence (2014); Cooper and Joyce (2013); Gracia and Oats (2012); Jayasinghe and Wickramasinghe (2011); Neu (2006); and Stringfellow, McMeeking and Maclean (2015). In respect of the third concept in Bourdieu's triad, habitus is central in the work of Alawattage (2011); Goddard (2004); and Hamilton and Ó hOgartaigh (2009).

There is, however, a great deal of variation in the use of Bourdieu's concepts, with capital and field comprising over half of all mentions (see Figure 7.1). Indeed, concepts such as misrecognition, doxa and illusio are seldom mobilised in accounting research, despite their being three of his more innovative and powerful ideas – all are central to his theory of the individual, and all would seem to be applicable in an analysis of accounting or accounting-related actors. Challenges exist in operationalising these ideas, and some might be better viewed through competing lenses, for example relying on Foucault's notion of discourse rather than Bourdieu's idea of doxa. However, until they are mobilised it is hard to say what these challenges and comparative weaknesses really are. And while Malsch *et al.* (2011) correctly observe that habitus is not employed as often as is probably warranted, I would add that this is also the case with the notion of symbolic violence. Insofar as critical accounting deals with topic areas involving injustice and inequality, that analysis should probably be as concerned with the use and abuse of soft power as hard power. As Weber points out, the state wields a monopoly over the legitimate use of force – power – and, following Weber, Bourdieu notes that force is manifested in symbolic and not only material acts. Symbolic or soft power is also important, perhaps more so because it is often not

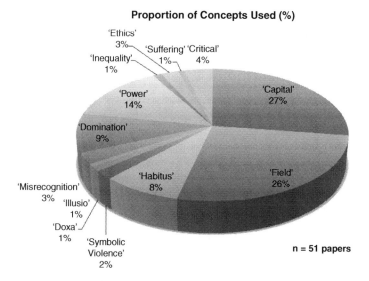

Proportion of Concepts Used (%)

'Ethics' 3%
'Suffering' 1%
'Critical' 4%
'Inequality' 1%
'Power' 14%
'Capital' 27%
'Domination' 9%
'Misrecognition' 3%
'Habitus' 8%
'Field' 26%
'Illusio' 1%
'Doxa' 1%
'Symbolic Violence' 2%

n = 51 papers

Figure 7.1 Use of Bourdieu's concepts in accounting research.

visible. Moreover, and as the efficacy of the media, think-tanks and PR firms makes clear, it is not just the state that wields symbolic capital in today's world. That members of the public – an increasing number of whom have become investors (at times unwittingly) – are largely unable to properly interpret financial statements suggests that accounting itself might be complicit in significant acts of symbolic violence. This is also the case with audit engagements, symbolic acts *par excellence* that should warrant concerns over how material resources are at times redistributed away from those whose distance from economic necessity is not great.

A number of papers that position these less widely used concepts more centrally include Alawattage (2011), Cooper et al. (2011), Farjaudon and Morales (2013) and Stringfellow et al. (2015) (symbolic violence); Alawattage (2011), Cooper et al. (2011), Gracia and Oats (2012) and Stringfellow et al. (2015) (doxa); Andon et al. (2014), Cooper and Johnston (2012), Cooper and Joyce (2013), Farjaudon and Morales (2013) and Gracia and Oats (2012) (illusio); and Archel (2011), Chabrak and Craig (2013), Everett (2003), Everett and Neu (2000), Neu et al. (2001) and Stringfellow et al. (2015) (misrecognition). It is worth pointing out that a number of papers rely on a wide variety of Bourdieu's concepts. Employing a more holistic approach, these include Chabrak and Craig (2013); Cooper et al. (2011); Farjaudon and Morales (2013); Gracia and Oats (2012); Jayasinghe and Wickramasinghe (2011); Malsch et al. (2011); and Stringfellow et al. (2015).

In analysing the papers, I was also interested in the extent to which the use of Bourdieu equates to a *critical* engagement with his work. For that reason I considered the manner in which the authors relying on Bourdieu focused on the notions of domination and power. Here, the work of Alawattage (2011); Archel et al. (2011); Cooper and Joyce (2013); Farjaudon and Morales (2013); Goddard (2004); Jayasinghe and Wickramasinghe (2011); Malsch et al. (2011); and Stringfellow et al. (2015) are notable. A study need not focus heavily on Bourdieu's concepts to be either useful to the public or take as its object of concern an area of critical interest, though one would expect that concepts such as inequality, equity, ethics, morality, misery and suffering might be relied upon. Indeed, a number of papers relying on Bourdieu incorporated these terms, such as Alawattage (2011); Chabrak and Craig (2013); Cooper (2005); Fourcade and Healy (2013); Neu, Friesen and Everett (2003); and Sargiacomo, Ianni and Everett (2014). Given the importance of the act of classification in accounting, and given the manner in which accounting tends to serve elite rather than dominated groups in society, two other papers worth mentioning that rely on these concepts include Edwards, Dean, Clarke and Wolnizer (2013) and Fourcade and Healy (2013), respectively. Finally, a number of authors also mobilise the idea of the 'critical' and use Bourdieu as a means of helping them do this. These papers include Chabrak and Craig (2013); Chiapello and Baker (2011); Cooper (2002); Jacobs and Evans (2012); Lukka and Granlund (2002); Malsch et al. (2011); Neu et al. (2001); and Sargiacomo et al. (2014).

One of Bourdieu's main research areas was the education system, wherein he was able to show that despite its claims to being a meritocracy – the system was open to all and so success was merely a function of hard work and intelligence, and not income – the system continued to discriminate against those belonging to lower-income groups on account of their lack of the right cultural capital and consequent tendency to self-exclude. It is not surprising then that accounting researchers have used Bourdieu to examine accounting education, for example Chabrak and Craig (2013) and McPhail, Paisey and Paisey (2010), though this area is still very much in its infancy. The questions of whether individuals from capital-poor backgrounds have a fair chance of succeeding in the field of accounting, and what the obstacles that they face are, remain very much unresolved questions.

Bourdieu was also interested in the association between cultural capital and economic capital amongst elites, another area that has received relatively little attention in the accounting literature. Although numerous studies rely on Bourdieu to explore the professional field – for example Andon et al. (2014); Carter and Spence (2014); Dambrin and Lambert (2012); Edwards

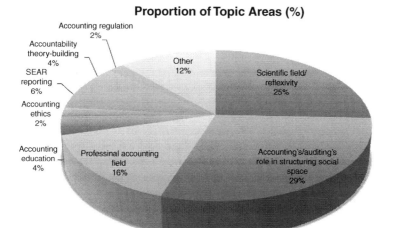

Proportion of Topic Areas (%)

Accounting regulation 2%

Accountability theory-building 4%

SEAR reporting 6%

Accounting ethics 2%

Accounting education 4%

Professinal accounting field 16%

Other 12%

Scientific field/ reflexivity 25%

Accounting's/auditing's role in structuring social space 29%

n = 51 papers

Figure 7.2   Areas of use of Bourdieu's work.

and Walker (2010); Farjaudon Morales (2013); Gracia and Oats (2012); Ramirez (2001); and Stringfellow *et al.* (2015) – there is still much work remaining in this area, especially work that considers the cultural homologies that exist among elite accountants and also work that employs quantitative measures (see Robson and Sanders, 2009).

The two main areas, however, that have incorporated Bourdieu's work are self-reflexive examinations of the accounting research field and examinations of the manner in which accounting and accounting-related actors shape and affect the social space (see Figure 7.2) Bourdieu often called on researchers to turn the tools of analysis back upon themselves, and some have found Bourdieu's ideas useful in this regard, for example Chiapello and Baker (2011); Cooper (2002; 2005); Edwards *et al.* (2013); Everett and Neu (2000); Lee (1997), (1999); Lukka and Granlund (2002); Malsch and Tessier (2015); Malsch *et al.* (2011); Neu *et al.* (2001); and Raineri (2015). In relation to how accounting as a form of symbolic capital or accounting actors as 'consecrators' of capital have the power to re-shape and transform a field, a good deal of work has been carried out using Bourdieu's ideas. This is a particularly important area of concern for Neu and colleagues (Everett, 2003; Neu, 2006; Neu, Everett, Rahaman and Martinez, 2013; Neu, Silva and Ocampo-Gómez, 2008; Rahaman, Everett and Neu, 2007), though many others have also undertaken research in this area (Alawattage, 2011; Chenhall *et al.*, 2010; Fourcade and Healy, 2013; Goddard, 2004; Jacobs and Kemp, 2002; Jayasinghe and Wickramasinghe, 2011; Kurunmäki, 1999; Oakes and Young, 2010; Sargiacomo *et al.*, 2014).

One area in which Bourdieu's work would appear to offer a good deal of untapped potential is the area of accounting regulation and accounting standard setting. To date, only Hamilton and Ó hOgartaigh (2009) and Xu and Xu (2008) have incorporated Bourdieu's insights in this area, which seems remiss since the state, state power and the state's monopoly over symbolic violence are reoccurring themes in his work. Work that examines the capital endowments, backgrounds and life trajectories of accounting regulators and standard setters and their structural relations and connections to other capital-rich actors would also seem a natural extension of Bourdieu's ideas in accounting.

Given the importance that Bourdieu places on the idea of legitimacy and the process of legitimation, it is perhaps no surprise that Bourdieu's insights have also been applied in the area of social and environmental accounting research (Archel *et al.*, 2011; Everett, 2004; Lodhia and Jacobs, 2013). With the importance that Bourdieu also places on activism and neo-liberal discourse and practice, neither is it surprising that his work has been applied in the context of enhanced accountability theory (Cooper and Johnston, 2012; Shenkin and Coulson, 2007). Yet other accounting-related studies have used Bourdieu in new and imaginative ways, for example, examining how accountants are represented in popular music or in the case of workplace rights violations (Cooper *et al.*, 2011; Jacobs and Evans, 2012; Smith and Jacobs, 2011), suggesting that Bourdieu's rich set of ideas and works remains an exceptionally worthwhile resource for critical accountants.

This chapter was submitted by the author with the following title: "Accounting research and Bourdieu's 'Scholarship with Commitment'."

Notes

1 Commentaries related to the idea of critical accounting appear in a variety of accounting journals. For the purposes of illustration, I have limited myself to the review of papers appearing in journals that tend to publish this work, namely: *Critical Perspectives on Accounting*; *Accounting, Organizations and Society*; the *Accounting, Auditing and Accountability Journal*; and *Accounting Forum*.
2 As a reviewer of this chapter pointed out, critical researchers need to be aware that Bourdieu's concepts are also susceptible to institutionalisation and the effects of the taken for granted.
3 Unusual in the sense that he combined the two perspectives in an attempt to achieve the best that each had to offer.

References

Alawattage, C. (2011). "The calculative reproduction of social structures: the field of gem mining in Sri Lanka," *Critical Perspectives on Accounting*, 22(1): 1–19.
Andon, P., C. Free and P. Sivabalan (2014). "The legitimacy of new assurance providers: making the cap fit," *Accounting, Organizations and Society*, 39(2):75–96.
Archel, P., J. Husillos and C. Spence (2011). "The institutionalisation of unaccountability: loading the dice of corporate social responsibility discourse," *Accounting, Organizations and Society*, 36(6): 327–43.
Bourdieu, P. (1984). *Distinction: A Social Critique of the Judgment of Taste*. Cambridge, MA: Harvard University Press.
Bourdieu, P. (1990). *The Logic of Practice*, translated by R. Nice, Stanford: Stanford University Press.
Bourdieu, P. (1996). *On Television*, translated by P. P. Ferguson, New York: The New Press.
Bourdieu, P. (1998). *Acts of Resistance: Against the Tyranny of the Market*, London: Verso.
Bourdieu, P. (2000). "For a scholarship with commitment," *Profession*, 40–5.
Bourdieu, P. (2003). *Firing Back: Against the Tyranny of the Market 2*. London: Verso.
Bourdieu, P. (2004). *Science of Science and Reflexivity*. Chicago, IL: University of Chicago Press.
Bourdieu, P. (2008). *Political Interventions: Social Science and Political Action*, translated by D. Fernbach, London: Verso.
Bourdieu, P. and L. J. Wacquant (1992). *An Invitation to Reflexive Sociology*. Chicago, IL University of Chicago Press.
Carter, C. and C. Spence (2014). "Being a successful professional: an exploration of who makes partner in the Big 4," *Contemporary Accounting Research*, 31:(4): 949–81.
Carter, C. and T. Tinker (2006). "Critical accounting and the labour process," *Critical Perspectives on Accounting*, 17(5), 525–28.
Chabrak, N. and R. Craig (2013). "Student imaginings, cognitive dissonance and critical thinking," *Critical Perspectives on Accounting*, 24(1): 91–104.
Chimisso, C. (2001). *Gaston Bachelard: Critic of Science and the Imagination*. London: Routledge.
Chenhall, R. H., M. Hall and D. Smith (2010). "Social capital and management control systems: a study of a non-government organization," *Accounting, Organizations and Society*, 35(8): 737–56.
Chiapello, E. and C. R. Baker (2011). "The introduction of French theory into English language accounting research," *Accounting, Auditing & Accountability Journal*, 25(2): 140–60.
Cooper, C. (2002). "Critical accounting in Scotland," *Critical Perspectives on Accounting*, 13(4): 451–62.

Cooper, C. (2005). "Accounting for the public interest: public ineffectuals or public intellectuals?" *Accounting, Auditing & Accountability Journal*, 18(5): 592–607.

Cooper, D. J. and M. J. Sherer (1984). "The value of corporate accounting reports: arguments for a political economy of accounting," *Accounting, Organizations and Society*, 9(3–4): 207–32.

Cooper, D. J. and T. M. Hopper (1987). "Critical studies in accounting," *Accounting, Organizations and Society*, 12(5): 407–14.

Cooper, C. and J. Johnston (2012). "Vulgate accountability: insights from the field of football," *Accounting, Auditing & Accountability Journal*, 25(4): 602–34.

Cooper, C. and Y. Joyce (2013). "Insolvency practice in the field of football," *Accounting, Organizations and Society*, 38(2): 108–29.

Cooper, C., Coulson, A. and P. Taylor (2011). "Accounting for human rights: doxic health safety practices – the accounting lesson from ICL," *Critical Perspectives on Accounting*, 22(8): 738–58.

Dambrin, C. and C. Lambert (2012). "Who is she and who are we? A reflexive journey in research into the rarity of women in the highest ranks of accountancy," *Critical Perspectives on Accounting*, 23(1): 1–16.

Dobbin, F. "The poverty of organizational theory: comment on *Bourdieu and Organizational Analysis*," *Theory and Society*, 37(1): 53–63.

Dobbin, F (2008). "The poverty of organizational theory: comment on 'Bourdieu and organizational analysis'," *Theory and Society*, 37(1): 53–63.

Edwards, J. R. and S. P. Walker (2010). "Lifestyle, status and occupational differentiation in Victorian accountancy," *Accounting, Organizations and Society*, 35(1): 2–22.

Edwards, J. R., G. Dean, F. Clarke and P. Wolnizer (2013). "Accounting academic elites: the tale of ARIA. *Accounting, Organizations and Society*, 38(5): 365–81.

Everett, J. (2002). "Organizational research and the praxeology of Pierre Bourdieu," *Organizational Research Methods*, 5(1): 56–80.

Everett, J. (2003). "The politics of comprehensive auditing in fields of high outcome and cause uncertainty," *Critical Perspectives on Accounting*, 14(1–2): 77–104.

Everett, J. (2004). "Exploring (false) dualisms for environmental accounting praxis," *Critical Perspectives on Accounting*, 15(8): 1061–84.

Everett, J. and D. Neu (2000). "Ecological modernization and the limits of environmental accounting?" *Accounting Forum*, 24(1): 5–29.

Everett, J., D. Neu, A. S. Rahaman and G. Maharaj (2015). "*Praxis, doxa*, and research methods reconsidering critical accounting," *Critical Perspectives on Accounting*, 32: 37–44.

Farjaudon, A. L. and J. Morales (2013). "In search of consensus: the role of accounting in the definition and reproduction of dominant interests," *Critical Perspectives on Accounting*, 24(2): 154–71.

Fourcade, M. and K. Healy (2013). "Classification situations: life-chances in the neo-liberal era," *Accounting, Organizations and Society*, 38(8): 559–72.

Gaffikin, M. (2009). "Twenty-one years of critical resistance – almost: a reflection," *Accounting Forum*, 33(4): 268–73.

Gallhofer, S., J. Haslam and A. Yonekura (2013). "Further critical reflections on a contribution to the methodological issues debate in accounting," *Critical Perspectives on Accounting*, 24(3): 191–206.

Goddard, A. (2004). "Budgetary practices and accountability habitus," *Accounting, Auditing and Accountability Journal*, 17(4): 543–77.

Gracia, L. and L. Oats (2012). "Boundary work and tax regulation: A Bourdieusian view," *Accounting, Organizations and Society*, 35(5): 304–21.

Gray, R., J. Dillard and C. Spence (2009). "Social accounting research as if the world matters," *Public Management Review*, 11(5): 545–73.

Grenfell, M. (2010). "Working with *habitus* and *field*: the logic of Bourdieu's practice," in E. Silva and A. Warde (eds): *Cultural Analysis and Bourdieu's Legacy*, London: Routledge.

Grenfell, M. J. (2012). *Pierre Bourdieu: Key Concepts*. London: Routledge.

Hamilton, G. and C. Ó hÓgartaigh (2009). "The Third Policeman: 'The true and fair view', language and the habitus of accounting," *Critical Perspectives on Accounting*, 20(8): 910–20.

Jacobs, K. and S. Evans (2012). "Constructing accounting in the mirror of popular music," *Accounting, Auditing and Accountability Journal*, 25(4): 673–702.

Jacobs, K. and J. Kemp (2002). "Exploring accounting presence and absence: case studies from Bangladesh," *Accounting, Auditing and Accountability Journal*, 15(2): 143–61.

Jayasinghe, K. and D. Wickramasinghe (2011). "Power over empowerment: encountering development accounting in a Sri Lankan fishing village," *Critical Perspectives on Accounting*, 22(4): 396–14.

Kaidonis, M. A. (2009). "Critical accounting as an epistemic community: hegemony, resistance and identity," *Accounting Forum*, 33(4): 290–97.

Kurunmäki, L. (1999). "Professional vs financial capital in the field of health care– struggles for the redistribution of power and control," *Accounting, Organizations and Society*, 24(2): 95–124.

Laughlin, R. (1999). "Critical accounting: nature, progress and prognosis," *Accounting, Auditing and Accountability Journal*, 12(1), 73–8.

Lee, T. (1997). "The editorial gatekeepers of the accounting academy," *Accounting, Auditing and Accountability Journal*, 10(1): 11–30.

Lee, T. A. (1999). "Anatomy of a professional élite: the executive committee of the American Accounting Association," *Critical Perspectives on Accounting*, 10(2): 247–64.

Lodhia, S. and K. Jacobs (2013). "The practice turn in environmental reporting," *Accounting, Auditing and Accountability Journal*, 26(4): 595–615.

Lukka, K. and M. Granlund (2002). "The fragmented communication structure within the accounting academia: the case of activity-based costing research genres," *Accounting, Organizations and Society*, 27(1–2): 165–90.

Macintosh, N. B. and T. Shearer (2000). "The accounting profession today: a poststructuralist critique," *Critical Perspectives on Accounting*, 11(5): 607–26.

McPhail, K., C. Paisey and N. J. Paisey (2010). "Class, social deprivation and accounting education in Scottish schools: implications for the reproduction of the accounting profession and practice," *Critical Perspectives on Accounting*, 21(1): 31–50.

Malsch, B. and S. Tessier (2015). "Journal ranking effects on junior academics: identity fragmentation and politicization," *Critical Perspectives on Accounting*, 26: 84–98.

Malsch, B., Y. Gendron and F. Grazzini (2011). "Investigating interdisciplinary translations: the influence of Pierre Bourdieu on accounting literature," *Accounting, Auditing and Accountability Journal*, 24(2): 194–228.

Mouritsen, J., H. T. Larsen and A. Hansen (2002). "'Be Critical!' critique and naïvete - Californian and French connections in critical Scandinavian accounting research," *Critical Perspectives on Accounting*, 13(4): 497–513.

Nash, R. (1999). "Bourdieu, 'habitus', and educational research: is it all worth the candle?" *British Journal of Sociology of Education*, 20(2): 175–87.

Neu, D. (2006). "Accounting for public space," *Accounting, Organizations and Society*, 31(4): 391–414.

Neu, D., D. J. Cooper and J. Everett (2001). "Critical accounting interventions," *Perspectives on Accounting*, 12(6): 735–62.

Neu, D., Everett, J., A. S. Rahaman and D. Martinez (2013). "Accounting and networks of corruption," *Accounting, Organizations and Society*, 38(6–7), 505–24.

Neu, D., C. Friesen and J. Everett (2003). "The changing internal market for ethical discourses in the Canadian CA profession," *Accounting, Auditing and Accountability Journal*, 16(1): 70–103.

Neu, D., L. Silva and E. Ocampo-Gómez (2008). "Diffusing financial practices in Latin American higher education," *Accounting, Auditing & Accountability Journal*, 21(1): 49–77.

Oakes, L. and J. J. Young (2010). "Reconciling conflict: the role of accounting in the American Indian Trust Fund debacle," *Critical Perspectives on Accounting*, 21(1): 63–75.

Oats, L. (ed.) (2012). *Taxation: A Field Research Handbook*, London: Routledge.

Poullaos, C. (2004). "Globalisation, accounting critique and the university," *Critical Perspectives on Accounting*, 15(4–5): 715–30.

Rahaman, A. S., J. Everett and D. Neu (2007). "Accounting and the move to privatize water services in Africa," *Accounting, Auditing and Accountability Journal*, 20(5): 637–70.

Raineri, N. (2015). "Business doctoral education as a liminal period of transition: comparing theory and practice," *Critical Perspectives on Accounting*, 26: 99–107.

Ramirez, C. (2001). "Understanding social closure in its cultural context: accounting practitioners in France (1920-1939)," *Accounting, Organizations and Society*, 26(4–5): 391–418.

Reiter, S. A. and P. F. Williams (2002). "The structure and progressivity of accounting research: the crisis in the academy revisited," *Accounting, Organizations and Society*, 27(6): 575–607.

Robbins, D. (2007). "Framing Bourdieu's work on culture," in T. Edwards (ed.) *Cultural Theory: Classical and Contemporary Positions*. London: Sage Publishers.

Robson, K. and C. Sanders (2009). *Quantifying Theory: Pierre Bourdieu*. New York: Springer.

Sargiacomo, M., L. Ianni and J. Everett (2014). "Accounting for suffering: calculative practices in the field of disaster relief," *Critical Perspectives on Accounting*, 25(7): 652–69.

Sayer, A. (2010). "Bourdieu, ethics and practice",. in E. Silva and A. Warde (eds) *Cultural Analysis and Bourdieu's Legacy*, London: Routledge.

Shenkin, M. and A. B. Coulson (2007). "Accountability through activism: learning from Bourdieu," *Accounting, Auditing and Accountability Journal*, 20(2): 297–317.

Silva, E. and A. Warde (2010). "The importance of Bourdieu," in E. Silva and A. Warde (eds) *Cultural Analysis and Bourdieu's Legacy*, London: Routledge.

Smedley, A. and B. D. Smedley (2005). "Race as biology is fiction, racism as a social problem is real: anthropological and historical perspectives on the social construction of race," *Psychologist*, 60(1): 16–26.

Smith, D. and K. Jacobs (2011). "Breaking up the sky," *Accounting, Auditing and Accountability Journal*, 24(7): 904–31.

Stringfellow, L., K. McMeeking and M. Maclean (2015). "From four to zero? the social mechanisms of symbolic domination in the UK accounting field," *Critical Perspectives on Accounting*, 27: 86–100.

Swartz, D. (1997). *Culture and Power: The Sociology of Pierre Bourdieu*. Chicago, IL: University of Chicago Press.

Swartz, D. (2010). "Pierre Bourdieu's political sociology and public sociology," in E. Silva and A. Warde (eds) *Cultural Analysis and Bourdieu's Legacy*, London: Routledge.

Thompson, G. D. (1999). "Cultural capital and accounting," *Accounting, Auditing and Accountability Journal*, 12(4): 394–412.

Tinker, T. (1991). "The accountant as partisan," *Accounting, Organizations and Society*, 16(3): 297–310.

Tinker, T. and R. Gray (2003). "Beyond a Critique of Pure Reason: from policy to politics to praxis in environmental and social research," *Accounting, Auditing and Accountability Journal*, 16(5): 727–61.

Webb, J., T. Schirato and G. Danaher (2002). *Understanding Bourdieu*. London: Sage Publishers.

Wilkinson, B. R., and C. H. Durden (2015). "Inducing structural change in academic accounting research," *Critical Perspectives on Accounting*, 26: 23–36.

Williams, P. F. and S. P. Ravenscroft (2015). "Rethinking decision-usefulness," *Contemporary Accounting Research*, 32(2): 763–88.

Xu, Y. and X. Xu (2008). "Social actors, cultural capital, and the state: the standardization of bank accounting classification and terminology in early twentieth-century China," *Accounting, Organizations and Society*, 33(1): 73–102.

SECTION III

8

THE ACCOUNTANCY PROFESSION

Alan Richardson

1 Introduction

During the Industrial Revolution new products, technologies and modes of organisation emerged that allowed markets to expand significantly, while new institutions such as the Limited Liability Corporation and stock exchanges developed to facilitate the exploitation of those markets. As product and capital markets expanded, new occupational specialties also emerged (Stigler, 1951) including financial accounting, cost accounting and auditing (Chandler and Daems, 1979). These occupational specialties resulted in the emergence of the world's largest professional service firms and high-profile professional associations that have existed for almost 200 years (Richardson, 2008). The ways that these occupational specialties were organised was not preordained or immutable; rather the professional form adopted by auditors and later financial and management accountants (for convenience, all of these specialists will be referred to hereafter as 'accountants') reflected a culturally and historically specific institution; that is, a distinctive feature of UK society in the mid to late 1800s, which had profound effects on the way that accounting and auditing was practised. The critical accounting literature begins with the basic premise that the professionalisation of accounting was a strategic choice embedded within a particular social and historical context and has explored the emergence of the professional model, the implications of this model for society and practitioners, and its effective[1] abandonment in the late twentieth century.

This chapter reviews the critical literature on the emergence, development and demise of the professional model in accounting and auditing. While the critical accounting literature is broad and amorphous (Laughlin, 1999), in this chapter the focus is on those studies that present an "immanent critique" of professionalisation (i.e. an analysis of the contradictions of this institutional form) or which place the accountancy profession within a political economy framework that examines its position at the nexus of the economy, civil society and the state. The chapter is structured as a stylised[2] history of the accounting profession beginning with the emergence of professional associations, the closure of the profession through the use of ascriptive criteria for membership, the profession's engagement with the power of the state and the embedding of accounting expertise in regulation, the globalisation of the profession and the rise of a commercial model of accounting practice.

The chapter concludes by identifying pressing research issues that arise from the emergence of accounting as a 'post-professional' (Suddaby, Cooper and Greenwood, 2007; Burns, 2007) occupation. This perspective assumes that the commercial model of accounting does not simply replace the professional model but rather generates diverse hybrid institutions (Dacin, Goodstein and Scott, 2002) with emergent features that will require empirical and theoretical work to fully appreciate. As Dacin *et al.* (2002: 50) observe:

> Diversity is introduced both through the variety of carriers and their connections and by the differing attributes of the host systems: societies, fields, and organizations (Djelic, 1998). Global change is not necessarily about uniformity or oppression or progress; nation-states and organizations and managers are not sponges or pawns, but actors responding to challenges under the guidance of existing institutions (Guillen, 2001). The resulting changes thus often appear as hybrids, forms combining new and old elements constructed through bricolage (Campbell, 1997).

2 Accountancy as a profession

Traditional sociological accounts held that the professions were a distinct class of occupations recognisable by their traits (e.g. the use of codes of ethics, self-regulation, systems of education and credentialing), and their reliance on specialised and arcane knowledge. This approach however runs into difficulty when occupational groups who are not commonly held to be professions (e.g. hairdressers) begin to adopt the same traits as the classic professions and when differences in the knowledges underlying practices are recognised, such as when the scientific basis of medical knowledge is compared with the conventional basis of legal knowledge. A more productive approach to the professions is to regard this form of occupational structure as simply a means "to translate one order of scarce resources – knowledge and skills – into another – social and economic rewards" (Larson, 1977: xvii). This approach allows the adoption of professional traits to be seen as a strategy to gain advantage in the marketplace (material rewards) and in society (legitimacy). As a strategy, its success is contingent on specific circumstances and there is no reason to assume that an occupation would restrict itself to this strategy should circumstances change.

This logic leads critical accounting researchers to examine the individuals that formed the first accounting associations (Anderson and Walker, 2009; Carnegie, Edwards and West, 2003; Kedslie, 1990; Lee, 1996, 2000; McMillan, 1999; Richardson, 1989, 2000; Romeo and Rigsby, 2008; Zelinschi, 2009) and the reasons they chose to use the professional model rather than to simply practice accounting as a commercial enterprise. In general, the founders of accounting associations were the highest status members of the occupation. They saw accounting as part of a moral order and sought to separate themselves from less qualified practitioners. The issue of qualifications, however, is not an objective aspect of professional practice (Anderson, Edwards and Chandler, 2005, 2007). The elite practitioners also sought to institutionalise a definition of expertise and to establish a hegemonic regime in which others would accept this definition and hence accept the elite's position within the status hierarchy (Goddard, 2002; Richardson, 1987b). They used the professional form to bring closure to the profession (i.e. to use ascriptive criteria to determine fitness for entry to the profession; see the next section for further details). These criteria established a homophily with other social elites (Richardson, 1989; see also Ramirez, 2001; and Bailey, 1992, for examples of failure to establish this relationship and hence the failure to establish the profession). The professional model was an established institution for knowledge-based occupations at this time in the United Kingdom and notably was the model used by lawyers who initially competed with accountants for certain roles particularly in trustee (bankruptcy) work (Edwards, 2001; McClelland and Stanton, 2004).

The professional model was thus institutionalised as a means of organising high-status knowledge-based occupations at the time and place that accounting was gaining a critical mass of practitioners; it was the established model of the legal profession with whom accountants competed for work within a particular institutional field; and it combined a moral and ascriptive dimension that allowed the founders of early accounting associations to develop their connection to other social elites and to enact their social values in organisational form. These characteristics made it a reasonable strategic choice for the status enhancement project undertaken by the founders of the early accounting associations.

3 The closure of the accountancy profession

The professions are, in theory, meritocracies where entry to the profession is based on possession of a defined body of technical skills and advancement in the profession is based on the demonstrated ability to apply those skills to clients' problems. This normative model for professions opens itself to an immanent critique. An immanent critique is a mainstay of critical empirical work that identifies the contradictions between the assumptions and claims of any social institution and the actions that sustain those institutions. In the case of accounting, the claimed desire to limit entry to the profession to those qualified to practice and to establish professional standards in order to protect the public, that is to attain closure, have been the primary targets of immanent critique. The principal criticism was that professional associations used criteria unrelated to merit to exclude people from the practice of accounting.

In some cases the existence of exclusionary practices was explicit, for example, most early accounting associations had an explicit ban on women members that was unrelated to the potential competency of women as accountants (Emery, Hooks and Stewart, 2002). This was claimed to reflect the definition of a "person" as a man in some legal systems (McKeen and Richardson, 1998) making it impossible to grant professional status to a "non-person." The role played by gender within accounting goes well beyond a narrow reading of legal precedents. In other cases, residency or citizenship requirements were used to exclude otherwise qualified persons. This form of exclusion, that is "nativism" (Miranti, 1988; Dyball, Poullaos and Chua, 2007), reflected the competition between local accountants and expatriates from countries with more established professions during the formative years of the profession in some colonies. In some cases, nativism was supported by the state as a form of resistance to imperial influence (Dybal *et al.*, 2007). This relationship will be discussed again when dealing with the globalisation of the accountancy profession in Section 5 below.

Other forms of exclusionary practice might not be explicit (Walker, 1991). In most cases, the accounting profession required serving articles (a form of apprenticeship) with a member already in practice prior to being accepted into membership of the professional association. This meant that the hiring practices of public accounting firms could serve as an exclusionary process without the visibility of professional rules. In addition, if the profession requires formal education prior to candidates sitting professional examinations, then the entry criteria of colleges and universities may have the effect of closing the profession. These practices might exclude groups based on race, religion or other criteria (Hammond, 1997, 2002; Hammond, Clayton and Arnold, 2009; Annisette and O'Regan, 2007). Similarly, the requirement that a professional accountant be of "sound moral character" (as attested to by existing members) and to pass examinations or attend education programs that might reflect biased cultural norms as much as technical knowledge (Hoskin and Macve, 1986) could have exclusionary effects.

It is important to note that not all exclusionary effects are intentional. In some cases, using one's own unacknowledged cultural biases can inadvertently encourage exclusionary practices.

Kanter (1977) for example, notes that the male dominated C-suite in private companies was continued by incumbents selecting replacements with similar traits; what she refers to as "homo-sexual reproduction." It may not be a conscious act of exclusion as much as acting based on feelings of familiarity with candidates and hence having confidence in their ability to do the job. In other cases, however, closure was explicitly about maintaining the material interests of incum-bents. For example, the entry of women into the profession was opposed because of its assumed effect on the value of male labour (Roberts and Coutts, 1992; McKeen and Richardson, 1998).

The claim that the profession serves the public interest in restricting entry and in it the style of practice has been subject to extended debate starting with the definition of the con-cept of the public interest itself (Parker, 1994; Baker, 2005; Dellaportas and Davenport, 2008). A primary way that the 'public interest' has been operationalised in the accounting profession has been through codes of ethics. This topic is considered in greater length by Paul Williams in this volume. Several studies have deconstructed these codes examining the way in which they serve to reduce competition among members, prevent non-members from participating in professional activities and reinforce a character-based image of professional practice (Neill, Stovall and Jinkerson, 2005; Neu, Friesen and Everett, 2003). Codes of ethics thus become a means of enforcing the behaviour of members in keeping with the dimensions of closure applied to the profession. Again, however, it is important not to assume that codes of ethics are self-consciously designed to achieve exclusionary ends. Cohen, Pant and Sharp (1992) and Jakubowski, Chao, Huh and Maheshwari (2002), for example, illustrate how the cultural and social institutions of a country constrain the content of accounting associations' codes of ethics. This is to say, patterns of exclusion (or patterns of the allocation of social roles and rewards) are embedded in broader social institutions, and professional associations are limited in what they can do, for better or worse, by the values of the society in which they operate (Simmons and Neu, 1997).

The attempt to close the profession by a private voluntary organisation has limitations. While the professional associations might be able to bring together high-status accountants and further reinforce their dominant position in the profession by creating a designation to signal member-ship in an exclusive group, this approach could not prevent other groups of accountants from attempting to replicate these institutions (Shackleton, 1995). In some cases these alternative groups provided an immanent critique of the dominant group through their existence and struggle to be recognised as professionally equal (Richardson, 1987a). This process may have encouraged the first associations to refine their processes and implement their claimed values more fully than they might have otherwise.

In some cases the rise of alternative accounting associations was tied to the division of labour in accounting (i.e. the separation of auditing or public accounting and management accounting in particular) (Loft, 1986; Anderson, 1996). The first accounting associations focused on auditing and public practice. They were not interested in organising accountants working in other areas of practice or as employees within business organisations. However, as associations representing accountants outside of public practice developed, the public accounting associations recognised that these alternative associations could challenge their hegemony and needed to be managed. The problem for these associations is that there is significant overlap in the knowledge on which different specialties might practice and their members would drift into the domains claimed by other associations (e.g. an auditor becoming a corporate accountant) without changing their professional affiliation. This tended to bring associations into competition even though the orig-inal intent was to stake out complementary domains (Abbott, 1988). In most cases, analyses of competition between accounting associations suggest that this would have positive effects for clients (Dunmore and Falk, 2001; Richardson, 1987a) but the existence of multiple associations reduces the ability of accountants to gain social rewards for their skills by making the profession less exclusive.

The rise of alternative accounting associations can be accommodated through the merger of associations or the "consolidation of the profession" as it has been described (Lee, 2010). This would create a monopoly association that retains its private sector character. There have been repeated attempts to consolidate the profession in several countries including Canada (Richardson and Kilfoyle, 2012), the United Kingdom (Wilmott, 1986), the United States (Previts and Merino, 1979) and Australia (Carnegie *et al.*, 2003). But merging associations is a problematic process given the different demographics each association serves and the specific entry standards, educational programs and organisational forms that have been adopted to serve members (Richardson and Jones, 2007). The recent merger of the profession in Canada, for example, retains within it the former diversity of the profession with specialties and regional organisational structures, and has established procedures that have disenfranchised some elements of the profession (Richardson and Kilfoyle, 2012; Richardson, 2017). It will be a challenge for the new organisation to overcome these internal divisions and to prevent new associations from being created to represent excluded groups of practitioners.

The reconsideration of the professionalisation of accounting as a process of status enhancement moved researchers in this area beyond immanent critique into a political economy–informed analysis. In this mode of analysis the key issue is to understand the complex linkage between accounting, the economy, civil society and the state. In particular, concern with understanding the process of closure lead researchers to examine the relationship between the profession and the state in its various forms.

4 The accountancy profession and the state

As noted in the previous section, the attempt to close the profession through the formation of private organisations has limitations. These limitations encouraged the early associations to reinforce their positions using the power of the state.[3] In part this might be done simply by incorporating the professional association and registering a 'reserved' title (i.e. a designation limited to members of that association). A stronger signal of state support however was chosen by the first accounting associations in the United Kingdom who sought to be 'chartered'. The term 'chartered' signals that the association has been formally created by a Royal Charter rather than simply under acts of incorporation. This designation reflects the political connections and social status of the group (Chua and Poullaos, 1993: 700). These approaches attempt to close the profession by establishing the superior abilities of a particular group and developing a trademark or brand to signal these abilities. If, however, the tasks accountants are hired for in the market do not require this level of skill, or clients are price sensitive, then consumers are unlikely to develop brand loyalty, with further steps being needed to ensure the rewards to the profession.[4]

The limitation may be overcome by having the accounting association specified in legislation as the group capable of providing certain legislated functions. For example, an act might require that a company produce audited financial statements; a professional association might then try to close the profession by having the act define an 'auditor' as someone possessing the designation of that association. This was an approach followed in the Canadian audit market (Richardson, 2000). The Institutes walked a fine line, although they succeeded in having their designation cited in legislation but also added "or other expert accountant" or similar terminology because of fear that a monopoly in legislation would require taking all accountants into membership of the association thus undermining their elite status (Anderson *et al.*, 2007). This tension between closure and status is evident in numerous settings.

The power of the state can be further harnessed by restricting the creation of reserve title organisations or regulating the profession to create a single designation. Ultimately the profession can be 'registered'; that is, it can secure mandatory possession of a state-sanctioned designation for entry to the profession. The experience of the profession with registration has been diverse. In the United States the certified public accountant (CPA) designation has become a state designation that signals that a person has the minimum level of competence thought necessary to protect the public interest. In Canada, by contrast, the state has used existing designations as a basis for restricting access to certain tasks. This means that aspirational standards, rather than minimum standards, are employed to register auditors which could be argued to raise the average cost of audits above what might be seen in competitive markets. These kinds of differences create problems when nations agree to free trade in services or where cross-border competition among accountants exists (Arnold, 2005; Yapa, 2006). The argument is made that under free trade agreements standards must fall to the lowest common denominator (under the assumption that this level reflects the minimum needed for the protection of third parties).

The profession's engagement with the state had a reciprocal effect. Although the associations may have approached the state as a source of power to enhance their position in society and with respect to competing associations or practitioners, they found that the state saw in the accounting profession a means to deal with issues in the regulation of the economy. In particular, as the idea of transparency as a means of regulation grew in the United States and other countries after the Great Depression (Fung, Graham and Weil, 2007), the accountancy profession was increasingly drawn into state functions. Such a relationship is often referred to as 'corporatism'.

4.1 The accountancy profession and corporatism

'Corporatism' refers to the organisation of social interests into groups that facilitate interaction with the state, which allows the state to delegate certain functions to these groups. Corporatism thus allows the state to avoid dealing with certain areas/topics that might create political unrest if raised to the level of the polity as a whole (e.g. labour relations in certain industries) or where the capacity to act lies in the hands of technical experts rather than political representatives (e.g. professional regulation).

As accounting associations turned to the state for the power to close the profession, the associations found that they were entering into a corporatist relationship with the state. This meant, in part, that certain private functions of the association were now subject to greater public scrutiny and transparency, and that the functioning of the profession (for example, in standard setting, education and entry standards) was expected to isolate the state from sectoral conflicts (Richardson, 1989; Walker and Shackelton, 1995; Yee, 2012). The profession was expected to act in contested areas where the outcome affected the interests of various stakeholders. For example, the relative claims of debt holders, equity holders and labour on the firm are affected by definitions of assets, liabilities and profit. The state avoids taking on the political cost of defining these constructs by delegating them to the profession in return for allowing the profession to self-regulate (Suddaby and Viale, 2011).

The use of corporatist structures was most common among auditors and financial accountants given the importance of these functions in mediating the relationships between the firms' stakeholders. Cost accountants also had opportunities to use corporatist arrangements to advance their statuses but were less successful in taking advantage of them. This appears to have been due to the temporary circumstances, for example during major wars (Loft, 1986) or during prolonged economic depressions (Fleischman and Tyson, 1999), when cost became a public issue rather than the demand for cost information being derived from financial reporting requirements. But even in planned economies where cost might have been expected to be a focus of state intervention in the economy, there is little evidence of the rise of a distinct cost accounting profession. Further research is needed on this phenomenon. Even among audit associations, however, corporatist arrangements are related to economic and political changes such that in Portugal, for example, distinct periods of liberal professionalism and corporatism are evident (Rodrigues, Gomes and Craig, 2003).

In a number of settings the history of professional formation operated in the opposite direction to that assumed in the stylised history just provided, with the state being the initiator of professional formation. This was a common pattern in continental Europe and in some colonies and communist countries (Ballas, 1998; De Beelde, 2002; Poullaos and Sian, 2010; Mihret, James and Mula, 2012; Rodrigues, Schmidt, dos Santos and Fonseca, 2011). The difference may be related to differences in legal systems (code law versus common law) and to the degree of state intervention in the economy. But, regardless of the context, the underlying motivation for the state appears to have been the same: to create a body distinct from the state to take on the problematic legitimacy of clients and to isolate the state from these conflicts (Dedoulis and Caramanis, 2007).

The development of a corporatist relationship with the state meant that some forms of closure that might have been allowed within a private body received much greater scrutiny and legal challenge. This led to "protecting the public interest in a self-interested way" (Lee, 1995; Canning and O'Dwyer, 2003). The corporatist relationship with the state was thus both empowering and limiting as a form of closure (Thornton, Jones and Kury, 2005).

5 The globalisation of the accountancy profession

Accounting and auditing are primarily used in the service of capital and hence when capital moved from the centre of imperial networks to the colonies during the Industrial Revolution, accountants, or at least accounting skills, moved with them (Johnson and Caygill, 1971; Chua and Poullaos, 2002; Poullaos, 2009). The global flow of capital during the twentieth century has shifted from the United Kingdom to the United States resulting in a shift of hegemonic influence. While the United Kingdom developed a network of colonies and diffused its institutions around the world, the United States focused on economic and cultural hegemony resulting in a more diffuse impact on the accounting profession (Mihret and Bobe, 2014; Richardson, 2010). This is a very broad topic and will be considered at greater length, and with a different focus, in this volume by Cameron Graham.

The initial wave of the globalisation of the accounting profession in the later 1900s took three forms. First, there was a mimicry of the professional names and structures that had been established in the United Kingdom (Parker, 2005). In some cases, this reflected the migration of accountants from the United Kingdom into the colonies (Sian, 2011) but often simply reflected the knowledge of a successful model of advancement for the occupation. It is notable, for example, that there are many 'Institutes of Chartered Accountants' across the British Empire that formed without a Royal Charter. The term 'chartered' had become a valuable brand or trademark and was used regardless of the legitimacy of the term in a particular jurisdiction (Bakre, 2005, 2006). The mimicry of the British model was subject to variation in local settings based on political constraints or the absence of the educational infrastructure capable of fully implementing the United Kingdom model (Poullaos and Sian, 2010).

Second, some associations at the centre of imperial networks used the colonies to further their aspirations at home and in some cases established colonial branches of their association or offered their examinations in remote locations (this was most notable among some of the later UK entrants to the profession such as the Association of Chartered Ceritified Accountants [ACCA]) (Briston and Kedslie, 1997; Annisette, 1999, 2000). Chua and Poullaos (1993) document the complex relationship between the attempt by an association to achieve closure while also positioning itself with respect to competing colonial and imperial accounting associations. The global population of the holders of a designation provides legitimacy to the originator of that designation in its home jurisdiction and in other jurisdictions into which it plans to expand (Verhoef, 2014). There has not yet been a sustained examination of the ACCA's global strategy but this would be useful to fully appreciate the attempt to create a transnational accounting designation by a single association (see Annisette and Trivedi, 2013).

Finally, there have been aspirations to create a global profession with a credential that would transcend political boundaries either through the negotiation of mutual recognition agreements that would allow the free flow of accountants between countries or the creation of a global accounting designation (Shafer and Gendron, 2005). The use of mutual recognition agreements allowed the UK associations to come to terms with associations in the colonies using the same name (i.e. 'Chartered Accountants') since the primary objective was to ensure that British accountants were not denied work opportunities in the colonies. The creation of a unique transnational designation has a more recent history and will be discussed later in this chapter.

Poullaos and Sian (2010) identify the lingering effects of the British Empire on accounting institutions throughout the world. The volume illustrates the variation in patterns of professionalisation depending, in part, on the nature of the colony (settler versus exploitation) and the nature of the economy (particularly the extent to which there were capital intensive export industries). Brock and Richardson (2013) expand this focus to mandate territories, such as the Holy Lands after the First World War, administered but not colonised by the United Kingdom. While the focus of Poullaos and Sian (2010) is on the contribution of the British Empire, the papers included in that volume also note the effect of other imperial influences on accounting (such as the French Empire and the cultural and economic hegemony of the United States after the Second World War). They also note that the British Empire created opportunities for accountants from other countries in the periphery to relocate in search of opportunities. In particular they call for further exploration of the diaspora of Indian and Chinese accountants across the Empire; a topic developed by Annisette and Trivedi (2013) who examine the attempt by Indian CAs to enter the Canadian accounting profession.

In spite of the similarities in the structure of the profession and the professional regulation across the globe created by imperial links, there remain variations related to the nature of the societies in which accounting associations appear (Puxty, Willmott, Cooper and Lowe, 1987; Richardson and MacDonald, 2002). Parker (1989) suggests that the most important export from the United Kingdom was in fact the *idea* of accountancy as a profession regardless of the way that this idea was expressed in particular contexts. This idea has considerable longevity even though, as discussed further on, it is not clear that it is still the dominant model of practice or the strategic frame within which professional associations plan activities.

The modern global aspirations of the profession reflect the expansion of the accounting firms into new markets and the cost efficiencies that would flow from a harmonisation of professional models (in the same way that a harmonisation of financial reporting standards reduces their costs) (Cooper, Greenwood, Hinings and Brown, 1998). The expansion of the firms and their influence in matters of professional development led Cooper and Robson (2006) to urge researchers to consider the place of accounting firms as sites of professionalization. The work of Caramanis (1999, 2005) on the influence of the big accounting firms on the regulation and structure of the audit profession in Greece provides evidence of the importance of this relationship.

One interesting aspect of the modern globalisation of the profession was the attempt to create a global credential (Shafer and Gendron, 2005) known initially as the XYZ project and ultimately suggesting that the global profession use the 'cognitor' label to signal the move of accountants from traditional roles into a role of thought leadership. Although the project came to an abrupt end when US state societies rejected the concept, the recent adoption of the CPA designation in Canada (although a chartered professional accountant rather than a certi-fied public accountant as in the United States), and the merger of the UK Chartered Institute of Management Accountants (CIMA) and the American Institute of CPAs (AICPA), suggests that some level of global harmonisation remains part of the strategy of the profession's leaders (Richardson and Kilfoyle, 2012).

This pressure to harmonise the global profession is reflected in the increasing importance of transnational bodies, such as the International Accounting Standards Board (IASB) and the International Federation of Accountants (IFAC), in the organisation of the profession (Humphrey, Loft, Jepperson and Turley, 2006; Humphrey, Loft and Woods, 2009; Loft, Humphrey and Turley, 2007). Individual states have used the models propagated by the transnational bodies as a guide to their own operations and have delegated important standard-setting roles to them. It will be suggested further on in the chapter that this trend reflects the combined impetus of globalisation and the commercialisation of the profession.

6 The commercialisation of accountancy

Richardson (1997) suggests that the professionalisation of an occupation requires the successful implementation of four strategies: market enhancement; market closure; professional closure; and professional influence. The first two strategies reflect the profession's base in the market and the need to encourage the expansion of that market for their services (either in depth or scope) while limiting access to these market opportunities to members of the profession. The second two strategies reflect the profession's embeddedness in political institutions and the need to gain state sanction to close entry to the profession and to establish the profession's legitimacy in defining the relationship between society and professional technologies. He concludes that the market in which accounting attempted to professionalise has been too dynamic to allow these strategies to reach maturity resulting in the incomplete professionalisation of accounting:

> [T]he profession has failed to gain statutory recognition of a task domain in which accountants are uniquely qualified to practice; the profession has failed to develop a cognitive basis sufficient to standardize the training of practitioners and close the pro-fession; and, the market for public accounting services has shifted away from those core activities that the institutional structure was designed to support and protect.
>
> *(Richardson, 1997: 635)*

The accounting firms, of course, have been quicker to respond to the dynamics of the markets than professional associations and have been shifting from a professional model to a commercial model for some time (Hanlon, 1994; Greenwood and Suddaby, 2006). Hanlon (1994) links the commercialisation of the profession to the changing nature of capitalist economies (see also critique and commentary on the commercialisation thesis by Wilmott and Sikka, 1997; Dezalay, 1997; and Hanlon, 1997). If the model of practice is shifting then one would expect that the structure of the profession and its regulation would also shift (Citron, 2003). Evidence suggests that public perceptions of accountants have already shifted (Carnegie and Napier, 2010). The rise of oversight bodies for the accounting profession after the collapse of Enron clearly shows the shift in regulatory thinking from viewing the profession as a self-regulating profession to a regulated industry.

One major shift associated with the commercialisation of the profession has been the rise of multidisciplinary partnerships (Greenwood and Suddaby, 2006). These partnerships bring together whatever set of skills are needed to meet client needs. Of greatest concern has been the integration of accounting and legal firms where differences in the rules regarding client confidentiality versus the duty to report have highlighted potential paradoxes in these firms (specifically in the context of tax work). Both the legal profession and accounting profession historically barred the creation of partnerships outside of their own community partly as a means of establishing disciplinary boundaries and establishing clear lines of oversight between the professional bodies and practices (Abbott, 1988).

The shift in the preferred model for organising the occupation of accounting from commercial to professional and back to commercial over the last 150 years suggests that our understanding of accounting needs to evolve beyond models of professionalization. Yet our understanding of accounting cannot simply return to a basic commercial model. The history of professionalism continues to exert its influence over accounting; it is necessary to consider the organisation of accounting from a post-professional perspective.

7 Accountancy and professionalisation redux

The stylised history recounted thus far has one major complication that has not been adequately studied. While the large accounting firms have commercialised and globalised their practices, there remains a strong local component to accounting practice and local professional associations continue to serve local market needs (Ramirez, 2009). The divide between large firms and small firms has been a standard part of most studies of audit market behaviour (e.g. studies of audit pricing, quality and ethics) but the institutional consequences of this divide have not been theorised. Too much emphasis has been placed on the global accounting firms and the markets they serve resulting in a lack of understanding of the local relevance of professional models. However, with this caveat, I accept that accounting is moving into a post-professional model (Suddaby *et al.*, 2007) which will have dramatic consequences.

The professions, in general, may be seen as occupational groups who, historically, took on and resolved the problematic legitimacy of their clients. This was done performatively; that is, by using their social mandate to "define what is right and wrong within a specific sphere of activity" (Richardson, 1987b: 341). But if the accounting profession has lost its status as a liberal profession and practice has become commercialised, on what basis does accounting continue to claim the right to be an agent of legitimation? The entry of the state into a direct oversight role for audit firms (Zeff, 2003a,b) and the delegation of national standard-setting processes to a transnational body (Porter, 2005; Carmona and Trombetta, 2008) suggest that a new social order for the practice of accounting is emerging, one which will be anchored in a different institutional order than it had been previously. West (1996: 91) suggests that professionalisation provides an enduring status and that examples of deprofessionalisation are hard to find (see Velayutham and Perera, 1996; Fogarty 2014). This view may be correct concerning the institutional trappings of professionalism but the social status, privileges and expectations of professionalism are subject to greater challenge and are being eroded in many of the traditional professions. The questions of what accounting, as an occupation, will become and what roles society may allocate to the occupation are open.

If accounting is moving beyond its traditional professional models and aspirations, then we need to begin the development of a post-professional model for accounting. A post-professional model will have to account for the changing discourses by which accounting legitimates its status in society (the shift from professional to commercial discourses in particular), for the increasing diversity of organisational forms through which accounting services are delivered to clients (including forms that are not mediated by professional accountants), for the mechanisms by which accounting retains its normative claims to expertise (and perhaps most importantly the separation of knowledge production, particularly standard-setting, from the provision of services based on that knowledge), for the potential bifurcation between global and local mechanisms, and for what strategies will be adopted by accounting at an occupational level to continue to pursue its status-enhancement project.

8 Conclusion

The critical literature on the professionalisation of the accounting profession has developed from an immanent critique of the accounting profession – holding the profession's actions up against the ideal professional model – to a full political economy analysis of the position of accounting within the state, civil society and economy. This literature has documented the ways in which accounting sought to control market opportunities through various strategies related to the implementation of the professional model, and the failure of this model in the late twentieth century. The challenge for critical researchers dealing with these issues is to better understand the way that the commercialisation of accounting will affect the process of professionalisation and regulation.

Our understanding of professionalisation processes is reasonably well developed with regard to the major developed economies but there is still work to do to understand the lingering effects of Empire on the diffusion and variation of professional models across the globe. With the fall of communism and the expansion of market economies to Eastern Europe, there is an opportunity to study the role of the profession in the transition between planned and market economies and the effect of that transition on the professionalisation process and professional institutions in those countries. There is also a need to understand the local variations in professional processes as the economy separates into global and local markets.

Perhaps the most pressing issue for the literature on professionalisation and the institutional structure of accounting is to identify a model that can guide research in a post-professional world.

This chapter was submitted by the author with the following title: "Professionalization and the accounting profession."

Notes

1   This is not to say that professional associations have ceased to exist nor that accountants are no longer regarded as professionals. As will be argued in this chapter, accounting practice has commercialised, society has reduced the self-regulatory power of the accountancy profession through independent oversight mechanisms and the classic model of professional organisation is no longer driving the strategy of professional associations. In this sense, accounting has moved into a new phase of development where the professional model is less relevant to our understanding of accounting as an occupation.
2   A 'stylized' set of facts is often used in economics to connect models to an empirical reality. It is equivalent to an 'ideal type' in Weberian sociology and is intended to provide an analytic or organising model rather than to describe any particular circumstance. The model used reflects the experience of the UK and settler colonies. Variations on this theme are observed in non-settler countries (Poullaos and Sian, 2010), in centrally planned economies (Gilles, 2014), and in code law countries. The development of transnational financial and product markets is leading to a convergence of national systems consistent with the mixed model of state regulation and market competition that underlies the model described here.

3   In some countries the state was instrumental from the initial formation of the profession. This will be discussed further on in the chapter. The relationship between the profession and the state is a key difference between the model used in this chapter and the development of the profession in code law and centrally planned economies.

4   The alternative explanation is that clients are unable to distinguish between accountants of different skill/quality levels, that they are unable to determine the services they need and that society is harmed by the failure of clients to make the right choice. This leads to a public interest rationale for closing the profession.

References

Abbott, A. (1988). *The System of Professions. An Essay on the Division of Expert Labor*, Chicago, IL: University of Chicago Press.

Anderson, M. and S. P. Walker (2009). "'All sorts and conditions of men': the social origins of the founders of the ICAEW," *British Accounting Review*, 41(1): 31–45.

Anderson, M., R. J. Edwards and R.A. Chandler (2005). "Constructing the 'well qualified' chartered accountant in England and Wales," *The Accounting Historians Journal*, 32(2): 5–54.

Anderson, M., R. J. Edwards and R.A. Chandler (2007). "'A public expert in matters of account': defining the chartered accountant in England and Wales," *Accounting, Business & Financial History*, 17(3): 381–423.

Anderson, R. H. (1996). "The transfer of cost accounting institutions to New Zealand," *Accounting History*, 1(2): 79–93.

Annisette, M. (1999). "Importing accounting: the case of Trinidad and Tobago," *Accounting, Business & Financial History*, 9(1): 103–33.

Annisette, M. (2000). "Imperialism and the professions: the education and certification of accountants in Trinidad and Tobago," *Accounting, Organizations and Society*, 25(7): 631–59.

Annisette, M. and P. O'Regan (2007). "Joined for the common purpose: the establishment of the Institute of Chartered Accountants in Ireland as an all-Ireland institution," *Qualitative Research in Accounting & Management*, 4(1): 4–25.

Annisette, M. and V. U. Trivedi (2013). "Globalization, paradox and the (un) making of identities: immigrant Chartered Accountants of India in Canada," *Accounting, Organizations and Society*, 38(1): 1–29.

Arnold, P. J. (2005). "Disciplining domestic regulation: the World Trade Organization and the market for professional services," *Accounting, Organizations and Society*, 30(4): 299–330.

Bailey, D. (1992). "The attempt to establish the Russian accounting profession 1875–1931," *Accounting, Business & Financial History*, 2(1): 1–24.

Baker, C. R. (2005). "What is the meaning of "the public interest"? examining the ideology of the American public accounting profession," *Accounting, Auditing and Accountability Journal*, 18(5): 690–703.

Bakre, O. M. (2005). "First attempt at localising imperial accountancy: the case of the Institute of Chartered Accountants of Jamaica (ICAJ) (1950s–1970s)," *Critical Perspectives on Accounting*, 16(8): 995–1018.

Bakre, O. M. (2006). "Second attempt at localising imperial accountancy: The case of the Institute of Chartered Accountants of Jamaica (ICAJ)(1970s–1980s)," *Critical Perspectives on Accounting*, 17(1): 1–28.

Ballas, A.A. (1998). "The creation of the auditing profession in Greece," *Accounting, Organizations and Society*, 23(8): 715–36.

Briston, R. J. and M. J. M. Kedslie (1997). "The internationalization of British professional accounting: the role of the examination exporting bodies," *Accounting, Business & Financial History*, 7(2): 175–94.

Brock, D. M. and A. J. Richardson (2013). "The development of the accounting profession in the Holy Land since 1920: cultural memory and accounting institutions," *Accounting History Review*, 23(3): 227–52.

Burns, E. (2007). "Positioning a post-professional Approach to Studying Professions," *New Zealand Sociology*, 22(1): 69–98.

Campbell, J. L. (1997). "Mechanisms of evolutionary change in economic governance: interaction, interpretation, and bricolage," in L. Magnusson and J. Ottosson (eds): *Evolutionary Economics and Path Dependence*, Cheltenham, UK: Edward Elgar.

Canning, M. and B. O'Dwyer (2003). "A critique of the descriptive power of the private interest model of professional accounting ethics: an examination over time in the Irish context," *Accounting, Auditing and Accountability Journal*, 16(2): 159–85.

Caramanis, C.V. (1999). "International accounting firms versus indigenous auditors: intra-professional conflict in the Greek auditing profession, 1990-1993," *Critical Perspectives on Accounting*, 10(2): 153–96.

Caramanis, C.V. (2005). "Rationalisation, charisma and accounting professionalisation: perspectives on the intra-professional conflict in Greece, 1993–2001," *Accounting, Organizations and Society*, 30(3): 195–221.

Carmona, S. and M. Trombetta (2008). "On the global acceptance of IAS/IFRS accounting standards: the logic and implications of the principles-based system," *Journal of Accounting and Public Policy*, 27(6): 455–61.

Carnegie, G. D. and C. J. Napier (2010). "Traditional accountants and business professionals: portraying the accounting profession after Enron," *Accounting, Organizations and Society*, 35(3): 360–76.

Carnegie, G. D., J. R. Edwards and B. P. West (2003). "Understanding the dynamics of the Australian accounting profession: a prosopographical study of the founding members of the Incorporated Institute of Accountants, Victoria, 1886 to 1908," *Accounting, Auditing and Accountability Journal*, 16(5): 790–820.

Chandler, A. D. and H. Daems (1979). "Administrative coordination, allocation and monitoring: a comparative analysis of the emergence of accounting and organization in the USA and Europe," *Accounting, Organizations and Society*, 4(1): 3–20.

Chua, W. F. and C. Poullaos (1993). "Rethinking the profession-state dynamic: the case of the Victorian charter attempt, 1885–1906," *Accounting, Organizations and Society*, 18(7): 691–728.

Chua, W. F. and C. Poullaos (2002). "Empire Strikes Back? an exploration of centre–periphery interaction between the ICAEW and accounting associations in the self-governing colonies of Australia, Canada and South Africa, 1880–1907," *Accounting, Organizations and Society*, 27(4): 409–45.

Citron, D. B. (2003). "The UK's framework approach to auditor independence and the commercialization of the accounting profession," *Accounting, Auditing and Accountability Journal*, 16(2): 244–74.

Cohen, J. R., L. W. Pant and D. J. Sharp (1992). "Cultural and socioeconomic constraints on international codes of ethics: lessons from accounting," *Journal of Business Ethics*, 11(9): 687–700.

Cooper, D. J. and K. Robson (2006). "Accounting, professions and regulation: locating the sites of professionalization," *Accounting, Organizations and Society*, 31(4): 415–44.

Cooper, D. J., R. Greenwood, B. Hinings, B. and J. L. Brown (1998). "Globalization and nationalism in a multinational accounting firm: the case of opening new markets in Eastern Europe," *Accounting, Organizations and Society*, 23(5): 531–48.

Dacin, M. T., J. Goodstein and W. R. Scott (2002). "Institutional theory and institutional change: introduction to the special research forum," *Academy of Management Journal*, 45(1): 45–56.

De Beelde, I. (2002). "Creating a profession 'out of nothing'? The case of the Belgian auditing profession," *Accounting, Organizations and Society*, 27(4): 447–70.

Dedoulis, E. and C. Caramanis (2007). "Imperialism of influence and the state-profession relationship: the formation of the Greek auditing profession in the post-WWII era," *Critical Perspectives on Accounting*, 18(4): 393–412.

Dellaportas, S. and L. Davenport (2008). "Reflections on the public interest in accounting" *Critical Perspectives on Accounting*, 19(7): 1080–98.

Dezalay, Y. (1997). "Accountants as "new guard dogs" of capitalism: stereotype or research agenda?" *Accounting, Organizations and Society*, 22(8): 825–29.

Djelic, M. L. (1998). *Exporting the American Model: The Postwar Transformation of European Business*, New York: Oxford University Press.

Dunmore, P.V. and H. Falk (2001). "Economic competition between professional bodies: the case of auditing," *American Law and Economics Review*, 3(2): 302–19.

Dyball, M. C., C. Poullaos and W. F. Chua (2007). "Accounting and empire: professionalization-as-resistance: the case of Philippines," *Critical Perspectives on Accounting*, 18(4): 415–49.

Edwards, J. R. (2001). "Accounting regulation and the professionalization process: an historical essay concerning the significance of PH Abbott," *Critical Perspectives on Accounting*, 12(6): 675–96.

Edwards, J. R., M. Anderson and R. A. Chandler (2007). "Claiming a jurisdiction for the 'Public Accountant' in England prior to organisational fusion," *Accounting Organizations and Society*, 32(1–2): 61–100.

Emery, M., J. Hooks and R. Stewart (2002). "Born at the wrong time? an oral history of women professional accountants in New Zealand," *Accounting History*, 7(2): 7–34.

Fleischman, R. K. and T. Tyson (1999). "Opportunity lost? chances for cost accountants' professionalization under the National Industrial Recovery Act of 1933," *Accounting, Business & Financial History*, 9(1): 51–75.

Fogarty, T. J. (2014). "The bloom is off the rose: deprofessionalization in public accounting," in S. Mintz (ed.): *Accounting for the Public Interest: Perspectives on Accountability, Professionalism and Role in Society*, Springer Netherlands.

Fung, A., M. Graham and D. Weil (2007). *Full Disclosure: The Perils and Promise of Transparency*, Cambridge: Cambridge University Press.

Gillis, P. (2014). *The Big Four and the Development of the Accounting Profession in China (Vol. 16)*, Bingley, Yorkshire: Emerald Group Publishing.

Goddard, A. (2002). "Development of the accounting profession and practices in the public sector-a hegemonic analysis," *Accounting, Auditing and Accountability Journal*, 15(5): 655–88.

Greenwood, R. and R. Suddaby (2006). "Institutional entrepreneurship in mature fields: the big five accounting firms," *Academy of Management Journal*, 49(1): 27–48.

Guillen, M. F. (2001). *The Limits of Convergence: Globalization and Organizational Change in Argentina, South Korea, and Spain*, Princeton, NJ: Princeton University Press.

Hammond, T. (1997). "From complete exclusion to minimal inclusion: African Americans and the public accounting industry, 1965–1988," *Accounting, Organizations and Society*, 22(1): 29–53.

Hammond, T. (2002). *A White Collar Profession: African American Certified Public Accountants Since 1921*, Chapel Hill, NC: University of North Carolina Press.

Hammond, T., B. M. Clayton and P. J. Arnold (2009). "South Africa's transition from apartheid: the role of professional closure in the experiences of black chartered accountants," *Accounting, Organizations and Society*, 34(6): 705–21.

Hanlon, G. (1994). *The Commercialization of Accountancy: Flexible Accumulation and the Transformation of the Service Class*, New York: St Martin's Press.

Hanlon, G. (1997). "Commercialising the service class and economic restructuring—a response to my critics," *Accounting, Organizations and Society*, 22(8): 843–55.

Hoskin, K. W. and R. H. Macve (1986). "Accounting and the examination: a genealogy of disciplinary power," *Accounting, Organizations and Society*, 11(2): 105–36.

Humphrey, C., A. Loft, K. K. Jeppesen and S. Turley (2006). "The international federation of accountants: private global governance in the public interest?" in G. F. Schuppert (ed.): *Global Governance and the Role of Non-state Actors*, Baden-Baden: Nomos Verlag.

Humphrey, C., A. Loft and M. Woods (2009). "The global audit profession and the international financial architecture: understanding regulatory relationships at a time of financial crisis," *Accounting, Organizations and Society*, 34(6): 810–25.

Jakubowski, S. T., P. Chao, P., S. K. Huh and S. Maheshwari (2002). "A cross-country comparison of the codes of professional conduct of certified/chartered accountants," *Journal of Business Ethics*, 35(2): 111–29.

Johnson, T. J. and M. Caygill (1971). "The development of accountancy links in the Commonwealth," *Accounting and Business Research*, 1(2): 155–73.

Kanter, R. M. (1977). *Men and Women of the Corporation*, New York, NY: Basic Books.

Kedslie, M. J. (1990). "Mutual self interest—a unifying force: the dominance of societal closure over social background in the early professional bodies," *The Accounting Historians Journal*, 17(2): 1–19.

Larson, M. S. (1977). *The Rise of Professionalism: A Sociological Analysis*, Berkeley, CA: University of California Press.

Laughlin, R. (1999). "Critical accounting: nature, progress and prognosis", *Accounting, Auditing and Accountability Journal*, 12(1): 73–8.

Lee, T. (1995). "The professionalization of accountancy: a history of protecting the public interest in a self-interested way," *Accounting, Auditing and Accountability Journal*, 8(4): 48–69.

Lee, T. (1996). "Identifying the founding fathers of public accountancy: the formation of the Society of Accountants in Edinburgh," *Accounting, Business & Financial History*, 6(3): 315–35.

Lee, T. (2000). "A social network analysis of the founders of institutionalized public accountancy," *The Accounting Historians Journal*, 27(2): 1–48.

Lee, T. (2010). "Consolidating the public accountancy profession: the case of the proposed Institute of Chartered Accountants of Great Britain, 1988-9," *Accounting History*, 15(1): 7–39.

Loft, A. (1986). "Towards a critical understanding of accounting: the case of cost accounting in the UK, 1914–1925," *Accounting, Organizations and Society*, 11(2): 137–69.

Loft, A., C. Humphrey and S. Turley (2007). "In pursuit of global regulation: changing governance and accountability structures at the International Federation of Accountants (IFAC)," *Accounting, Auditing and Accountability Journal*, 19(3): 428–51.

McClelland, P. and P. Stanton (2004). "'An ignorant set of men': an episode in the clash of the legal and accounting professions over jurisdiction," *Accounting History*, 9(2): 107–26.

McKeen, C. A. and A. J. Richardson (1998). "Education, employment and certification: an oral history of the entry of women into the Canadian accounting profession," *Business and Economic History*, 27(2): 500–21.

McMillan, K. P. (1999). "The Institute of Accounts: a community of the competent," *Accounting, Business & Financial History*, 9(1): 7–28.

Mihret, D. G. and B. J. Bobe (2014). "Multiple informal imperial connections and the transfer of accountancy to Ethiopia (1905 to 2011)," *Accounting History*, 19(3): 309–31.

Mihret, G. D., K. James and J. M. Mula (2012). "Accounting professionalization amidst alternating state ideology in Ethiopia," *Accounting, Auditing and Accountability Journal*, 25(7): 1206–33.

Miranti, P. J. (1988). "Professionalism and nativism: the competition in securing public accountancy legislation in New York during the 1890s," *Social Science Quarterly*, 69: 361–80.

Neill, J. D., O.S. Stovall and D. L. Jinkerson (2005). "A critical analysis of the accounting industry's voluntary code of conduct," *Journal of Business Ethics*, 59(1–2): 101–08.

Neu, D., C. Friesen and J. Everett (2003). "The changing internal market for ethical discourses in the Canadian CA profession," *Accounting, Auditing and Accountability Journal*, 16 (1): 70–103.

Parker, L. D. (1994). "Professional accounting body ethics: in search of the private interest," *Accounting, Organizations and Society*, 19(6): 507–525.

Parker, R. H. (1989). "Importing and exporting accounting: the British experience," in A. G. Hopwood (ed.): *International Pressures for Accounting Change*, London: Prentice Hall.

Parker, R. H. (2005). "Naming and branding: accountants and accountancy bodies in the British Empire and Commonwealth, 1853-2003," *Accounting History*, 10(1): 7–46.

Porter, T. (2005). "Private authority, technical authority, and the globalization of accounting standards," *Business and Politics*, 7(3): 1–32.

Poullaos, C. (2009). "Professionalisation," in J. R. Edwards and S. P. Walker (eds): *The Routledge Companion to Accounting History*, London: Routledge.

Poullaos, C. and S. Sian (eds). (2010). *Accountancy and Empire: The British Legacy of Professional Organization*, London: Routledge.

Previts, G. J. and B. D. Merino (1979). *A History of Accounting in America: An Historical Interpretation of the Cultural Significance of Accounting*, New York: John Wiley & Sons Inc.

Puxty, A. G., H. C. Willmott, D. J. Cooper and T. Lowe (1987). "Modes of regulation in advanced capitalism: locating accountancy in four countries," *Accounting, Organizations and Society*, 12(3): 273–91.

Ramirez, C. (2001). "Understanding social closure in its cultural context: accounting practitioners in France (1920–1939)," *Accounting, Organizations and Society*, 26(4): 391–418.

Ramirez, C. (2009). "Constructing the governable small practitioner: the changing nature of professional bodies and the management of professional accountants' identities in the UK," *Accounting, Organizations and Society*, 34(3): 381–408.

Richardson, A. J. (1987a). "Professionalization and intraprofessional competition in the Canadian accounting profession," *Work and Occupations*, 14(4): 591–615.

Richardson, A. J. (1987b). "Accounting as a legitimating institution", *Accounting, Organizations and Society*, 12(4): 341–355.

Richardson, A. J. (1989). "Canada's accounting elite: 1880-193," *The Accounting Historians Journal*, 16(1): 1–21.

Richardson, A. J. (1997). "Social closure in dynamic markets: the incomplete professional project in accountancy," *Critical Perspectives on Accounting*, 8(6): 635–53.

Richardson, A. J. (2000) "Building the Canadian Chartered Accountancy profession: a biography of George Edwards, FCA, CBE, LLD, 1861-1947," *The Accounting Historians Journal*, 27(2), 87–116.

Richardson, A. J. (2008). "Strategies in the development of accounting history as an academic discipline," *Accounting History*, 13(3): 247–280.

Richardson, A. J. (2010). "Canada between empires," in C. Poullaos and S. Sian (eds): *Accountancy and Empire*, London: Routledge.

Richardson, A. J. (2017). "Merging the profession: a social network analysis of the consolidation of the accounting profession in Canada," *Accounting Perspectives*, 15(4), 83–104.

Richardson, A. J. and D. B. Jones (2007). "Professional "brand", personal identity and resistance to change in the Canadian accounting profession: a comparative history of two accounting association merger negotiations," *Accounting History*, 12(2): 135–64.

Richardson, A. J. and E. Kilfoyle (2012). "Merging the profession: a historical perspective on accounting association mergers in Canada," *Accounting Perspectives*, 11(2): 77–109.

Richardson, A. J. and L. D. MacDonald (2002). "Linking international business theory to accounting history: implications of the international evolution of the state and the firm for accounting history research," *Accounting and Business Research*, 32(2): 67–77.

Roberts, J. and J. A. Coutts (1992). "Feminization and professionalization: a review of an emerging literature on the development of accounting in the United Kingdom," *Accounting, Organizations and Society*, 17(3): 379–95.

Alan Richardson

Rodrigues, L. L., D. Gomes, D. and R. Craig (2003). "Corporatism, liberalism and the accounting profession in Portugal since 1755," *The Accounting Historians Journal*, 30(1): 95–128.
Rodrigues, L. L., P. Schmidt, J. L. dos Santos and P. C. D. Fonseca (2011). "A research note on accounting in Brazil in the context of political, economic and social transformations, 1860-1964," *Accounting History*, 16(1): 111–23.
Romeo, G. and J. T. Rigsby (2008). "Disseminating professionalism: the influence of Selden Hopkins on the USA accounting profession," *Accounting History*, 13(4): 415–50.
Shafer, W. E. and Y. Gendron (2005). "Analysis of a failed jurisdictional claim: the rhetoric and politics surrounding the AICPA global credential project," *Accounting, Auditing and Accountability Journal*, 18(4): 453–91.
Shackleton, K. (1995). "Scottish chartered accountants: internal and external political relationships, 1853-1916," *Accounting, Auditing and Accountability Journal*, 8(2): 18–46.
Sian, S. (2011). "Operationalising closure in a colonial context: The Association of Accountants in East Africa, 1949–1963," *Accounting, Organizations and Society*, 36(6): 363–81.
Simmons, C. and D. Neu (1997). "Re-presenting the external: editorials and the Canadian CAs (1936–1950)," *Accounting, Organizations and Society*, 22(8): 799–824.
Stigler, G. J. (1951). "The division of Labor is limited by the extent of the market," *Journal of Political Economy*, 61(1): 185–93.
Suddaby, R. and T. Viale (2011). "Professionals and field-level change: institutional work and the professional project," *Current Sociology*, 59(4): 423–42.
Suddaby, R., D. J. Cooper and R. Greenwood (2007). "Transnational regulation of professional services: governance dynamics of field level organizational change," *Accounting, Organizations and Society*, 32(4): 333–62.
Thornton, P. H., C. Jones, C. and K. Kury (2005). "Institutional logics and institutional change in organizations: transformation in accounting, architecture, and publishing," *Research in the Sociology of Organizations*, 23: 125–70.
Velayutham, S. and H. Perera (1996). "Recent developments in the accounting profession in New Zealand: a case of deprofessionalization?" *International Journal of Accounting*, 31(4): 445–62.
Verhoef, G. (2014). "Globalisation of knowledge but not opportunity: closure strategies in the making of the South African accounting market, 1890s to 1958," *Accounting History*, 19(1–2): 193–226.
Walker, S. P. (1991). "The defence of professional monopoly: Scottish Chartered Accountants and 'Satellites in the Accountancy Firmament' 1854-1914", *Accounting, Organizations and Society*, 16(3): 257–83.
Walker, S. P. and K. Shackleton (1995). "Corporatism and structural change in the British accountancy profession, 1930–1957," *Accounting, Organizations and Society*, 20(6): 467–503.
West, B. P. (1996). "The professionalisation of accounting: a review of recent historical research and its implications," *Accounting History*, 1(1): 77–102.
Willmott, H. (1986). "Organising the profession: a theoretical and historical examination of the development of the major accountancy bodies in the UK," *Accounting, Organizations and Society*, 11(6): 555–80.
Willmott, H. and P. Sikka (1997). "On the commercialization of accountancy thesis: a review essay," *Accounting, Organizations and Society*, 22(8): 831–42.
Yapa, P. S. (2006). "Cross-border competition and the professionalization of accounting: the case of Sri Lanka," *Accounting History*, 11(4): 447–73.
Yee, H. (2012). "Analyzing the state-accounting profession dynamic: some insights from the professionalization experience in China," *Accounting, Organizations and Society*, 37(6): 426–44.
Zeff, S. A. (2003a). "How the US accounting profession got where it is today: Part I," *Accounting Horizons*, 17(3): 189–205.
Zeff, S. A. (2003b). "How the US accounting profession got where it is today: Part II," *Accounting Horizons*, 17(4): 267–86.
Zelinschi, D. (2009). "Legitimacy, expertise and closure in the Romanian accountant's professional project, 1900-16," *Accounting History*, 14(4): 381–403.

142

9

THE AUDIT PROFESSION

Richard Baker

1 Introduction

In the wake of the worldwide financial crisis of 2008, the European Commission (EC) addressed the regulation of auditing through the issuance of a Green Paper that called for a review of the role of the statutory audit as well as the wider environment within which statutory audits are conducted (EC, 2010). The purpose of this Green Paper was to question whether the role of auditors could be enhanced to mitigate future financial crises. In particular, the Commission sought to address whether audits provide the right kind of information for participants in capital markets, whether there are issues around the independence of audit firms, whether there are risks linked to a concentrated market for audit services, and whether supervision at a European level might be useful. In addition to the EC's Green Paper, various academic experts on the regulation of statutory auditing have argued that the reputation of corporate reporting has been in crisis (Quick, Turley and Willekens, 2007).

Trust in the process of financial accounting and auditing has been undermined by high-profile scandals involving major corporations, such as Enron, Parmalat, Ahold and Worldcom. Professional bodies of accountants have responded in various ways to the EC Green Paper and academic criticism, including the Institute of Chartered Accountants in England and Wales (ICAEW). In a document entitled *International Consistency: Global Challenges Initiative: Providing Direction*, issued by the ICAEW in 2010, the Institute concluded that there are limits to the global regulation of auditing arising from cultural differences among countries. The Institute further concluded that historical traditions and differences in the ways that auditing has been practiced in different countries are important. These observations inform the basic premise of this chapter, which is that expectations for increased global regulation of auditing may be difficult to achieve so long as definitions regarding the purpose of regulating corporate activity, as well as the role of statutory auditing within that regulation, differ among countries. The following discussion of the history of the evolution of the auditing profession in the United Kingdom, France and Germany seeks to demonstrate this premise.

The remainder of the chapter is organised as follows. The next section addresses theoretical issues related to the evolution of auditing as a professional practice. The three subsequent sections discuss the evolution of professional auditing in the United Kingdom, France and Germany, respectively. A discussion and conclusion follow.

2 Theoretical issues related to the discussion of auditing as a professional activity

Abbott (1988) has indicated that the process of professionalisation involves competition among occupational groups for the opportunity to become recognised as a profession. Professional recognition is typically achieved when the governing authority of the state grants recognition as a profession to an occupational group along with monopoly rights in a particular area of occupational practice. In the case of the auditing profession it was the right to perform statutory audits, which was restricted to the members of certain identifiable accountancy bodies. No other aspect of accountancy has been similarly recognised or regulated by the state. Hence it was the creation by the state of the monopoly right to perform statutory audits that prompted the growth in size and status of the auditing profession.

The sociology of the profession's literature also indicates that the regulation of professional activity differs among countries, and that in particular, there is a higher expectation in code law countries (such as France and Germany) with respect to the importance of state regulation of the professions (Abbott, 1988). This higher expectation in code law countries regarding regulation of professional activity by the state derives from the fact that the state often plays a role in creating professions in code law countries (Abbott, 1988). Consequently, there is a major distinction between the status of professions in code law countries such as France and Germany and common law countries such as the United Kingdom, with the state playing a more prominent role in the regulation of professional activity in code law countries.

This distinction in the role and status of professions among countries leaves open the question of precisely what the definition of the auditing profession is in different countries. The answer to this question ranges from one that defines the auditing profession to include *only* persons who are authorised to perform statutory audits, through a definition that includes persons who are members of recognised professional bodies, to a definition that includes all persons engaged in accounting or auditing work. The second and third definitions are beyond the scope of this chapter, as a result of which the following discussion concentrates on those aspects of the accountancy profession pertaining to the provision of auditing services.

A second theoretical issue that arises in a discussion of the evolution of auditing as a profession relates to the origins of the practices which are now referred to as professional. Prior to the nineteenth century, accounting and auditing were not considered to be professional activities. Pursuant to Abbott's model of the system of professions (Abbott, 1988), various groups of occupational practitioners competed with one another and against other occupational groups to become recognised as professionals in the rapidly growing industrial nations of the nineteenth century, including the United Kingdom, France, Germany and the United States (the latter case is not discussed here, however) (Edwards and Walker, 2010; Ramirez, 2001; Quick, 1994).

In the United Kingdom, the accountancy profession emerged in the form of private sector accountancy bodies (Parker, 2005; Ramirez, 2009). While these accountancy bodies were able to achieve recognition from the British Crown through royal charters, they were not formally regulated by the British state. In France, the regulation of the auditing profession emerged initially through the appointment by royal edict of *inspecteurs* and *censeurs* as early as the seventeenth century. After the French Revolution, there was a period of economic liberalism during the nineteenth century when the French state had little involvement with the regulation of accounting or auditing (Lemarchand, 1995; Ramirez, 2001). This period of economic liberalism was followed, after the Second World War, by the current period in which the regulation of the accounting and auditing profession is divided between the Ordre des Experts Comptable (for professional accountants) and the Compagnie Nationale des Commissaires aux

Comptes (CNCC) (for statutory auditors), with both bodies having been created by the French state. In Germany the regulation of the auditing profession has been conducted through quasi-governmental bodies (e.g. the *Wirtschaftsprüferkammer*) that operate pursuant to law and regulation. However, the role and status of the auditing profession in Germany developed in a manner different from that of the United Kingdom and France in that the *Wirtschaftsprüfer* has been traditionally considered to be an advisor to the Supervisory Board within a two-tiered system of corporate governance.

A third issue that arises when discussing the evolution of the auditing profession relates to the classification of financial reporting systems in different countries. This classification is important because the primary subject matter of external audits of financial statements is based on financial accounting theory and principles. A great deal of prior research has compared differences in financial accounting and reporting systems among countries (see, for example: Bloom and Naciri, 1989; Doupnik, 1987; Hopwood, 1989; Hopwood, Burchell and Clubb, 1979; Nobes and Parker, 1995; Taylor, Evans and Jay, 1986; Willmott, Puxty, Robson, Cooper and Lowe, 1992). Nobes and Parker (1995) maintain that two types of financial reporting systems have developed through time, the "micro/professional" system (Model A) and the "macro/uniform system" (Model D). In the micro/professional system (Model A), the primary providers of capital are individuals, while in the macro/uniform system (Model D), the primary providers of capital are banks and governments. In the micro/professional system, corporate governance is delegated to professional managers and directors, while in the macro/uniform system, corporate governance is the responsibility of supervisory boards consisting of representatives of shareholder and creditor groups, trade unions and government. In the micro/professional system the legal framework is provided by common law, while in the macro/uniform system the legal framework is based on codified law derived from Roman antecedents. Model A represents the extreme end of the micro/professional system, and Model D represents the extreme end of the macro/uniform system. There are also intermediate Models B and C which can be placed between these extremes. Nobes and Parker have used their classification scheme to categorise the financial reporting systems of the United Kingdom, France and Germany, among other countries (see Figure 9.1).

Within the Nobes and Parker model, the United Kingdom and Germany stand at opposite ends of a spectrum, with the classification of France being closer to that of Germany.[1] The differences between the financial reporting systems of countries can be traced to various factors, including differences in legal systems; traditional sources of capital; roles played by banks;

CLASSIFICATION OF COUNTRIES ACCORDING TO ENVIRONMENTAL FACTORS							
Factor	A	B	C	D	United Kingdom	France	Germany
Providers of finance	Individual/ institutional investors			→ Bank/state/family	A	C	D
Corporate governance	Managers/ Directors			→ Supervisory board/state	A	D	D
Legal system	Common law			→ Codified/Roman	A	D	D
Taxation	Little influence			→ Large influence	A	C	D
Profession/ state	Large/powerful profession			→ State dominance	A	D	D

Figure 9.1 Classification of countries according to environmental factors.

accounting and auditing standards setting practices; corporate governance practices; and the impact on financial reporting of laws regarding income taxation and dividend payments (see for example Mueller, 1967; Nair and Frank, 1980; Nobes, 1983, 1992; Gray, 1988; Perera, 1989; Evans and Nobes, 1998a,b).

A primary argument of this chapter is that the historical factors which led to differences in financial reporting systems also led to differences in the regulation of the auditing profession. Individual shareholders have been the traditional providers of capital in the United Kingdom, and even before the involvement by the British state in the regulation of auditing United Kingdom shareholders demanded the issuance of audited financial statements (Benston, 1973). As a result, the United Kingdom auditing profession developed in the private sector by means of institutes of professional accountants. In Germany, banks and insurance companies have been the traditional providers of capital. These entities have legal rights to representation on the supervisory boards of companies and the ability to obtain private information directly from company management. Consequently, the regulation of the auditing profession in Germany developed in response to the needs of large institutional investors such as banks and insurance companies. The experience in France has been mixed, with historical periods during which the French government encouraged capitalist development and periods in which the state nationalised major enterprises. Consequently, the regulation of both the accounting and auditing professions in France developed largely through legislation and government decree.

In summary, differences in historical factors, which led to differences in the development of financial reporting systems, also led to differences in the regulation of the auditing profession. In the United Kingdom, the regulation of the auditing profession has been conducted through private-sector professional bodies. In both Germany and France the regulation of the auditing profession has been conducted pursuant to law and regulation.

3 The United Kingdom

The development of accountancy in the United Kingdom has been previously addressed by many researchers, including such authors as Kedslie (1990), Cornwell (1991, 1993), Walker (2004), Boys (1994, 2011), Maltby (1999), Edwards, Anderson and Matthews (1997), Edwards (2001, 2010), Edwards, Anderson and Chandler (2007) and Lee (2011), among others. Most of these authors have focused on the development of the accountancy profession and not on the auditing profession as a separate or distinct element of the accountancy profession. This is because, unlike France, there is no distinction made in the United Kingdom, between the accountancy and auditing professions. The remainder of this section reviews some of the findings of the prior literature, with a focus on the development of the auditing profession as a specific element of the accountancy profession.

3.1 Historical background of accountancy and auditing in the United Kingdom

Micklethwait and Wooldridge (2003: 20) suggest that the practice of auditing in Great Britain may be traceable to the rise of the joint-stock company during the reign of Elizabeth I. Dobija (2011: 2) points to the separation of ownership and control in the East India Company as providing an impetus for the rise of auditing. Audits of joint-stock companies during the sixteenth through the eighteenth centuries, were primarily what may be referred to as 'amateur' audits in which certain shareholders (or members) of the company were appointed to conduct audits on behalf of their fellow shareholders.

The development of the auditing profession appears to have emerged at a later point in British history, perhaps towards the end of the eighteenth century or early in the nineteenth century. However, it is important to emphasise that there is little recognition of either accountancy or auditing as professions during that period and no distinction was made between accountancy and auditing; the professional services of accountancy and auditing were considered to be provided by one occupational group. Based on an examination of trade directories, Edwards *et al.* (2007: 67) provide evidence regarding the number of "accomptants" or "accountants" offering services to the public in the larger English cities in different decades of the nineteenth century, with numbers ranging from 20 in the 1800s, to 301 in the 1830s, to 499 in the 1850s, to 1,248 in the 1870s. The listings in the trade directories often identified "accounting" rather than "auditing" services (Edwards *et al.*, 2007: 68); thus, auditing was not distinguished as a separate aspect of accountancy services. The significance of this point is, as Boys (1994, 2011) points out, there were practicing accountants and auditors in the United Kingdom during the early nineteenth century but these emerging professional accountants and auditors were not regulated by the British state.

Edwards *et al.* (2007: 82) indicate that two positive acts on the part of the British state emerged in the 1830s and 1840s which led to an increased demand for auditing services. The first was the Joint Stock Companies Act 1844, which included a requirement that joint-stock companies issue audited financial statements to their shareholders. Subsequent to this Act, there was an increased use of joint-stock companies to fund the construction of the British railway network. The second legal action on the part of the British state was the creation in 1835 of municipal corporations for the purpose of supplying civic improvements. These municipal corporations were also required to have external audits. Matthews, Anderson and Edwards (1998: 139–41) indicate that audit work during this period was of great importance to the growth of the accountancy profession in the United Kingdom. Corporate failures and financial manipulations during the 1830s and 1840s during the formation of capital-intensive railway companies, demonstrated a need for "an expert and independent audit" (Parker, 1986: 8).

Interestingly, the British state appears to have taken a relatively *laissez faire* approach to audit regulation during the latter half of the nineteenth century (Lee, 2013). This may have been due to the growing strength and importance of the accountancy profession in Britain, and the ability of certain professional bodies to resist regulation by the state. Rather than imposing direct regulation by the government, there was Crown recognition of professional bodies of accountants in different cities of the United Kingdom, who were permitted to regulate themselves. In addition to providing other accountancy services, the members of these recognised professional bodies also came to be acknowledged as experts in auditing (Maltby, 1999).

In 1854 the prototype of the Institute of Chartered Accountants of Scotland, referred to as the Society of Accountants in Edinburgh, was followed by the Glasgow and Aberdeen societies, all known as 'chartered accountants'. These societies eventually merged to become the Institute of Chartered Accountants of Scotland (ICAS) in 1951. In 1880, there was also a fusion of several English societies of accountants to form the Institute of Chartered Accountants in England and Wales (ICAEW). On the basis of the emergence of these recognised professional bodies, the regulation of the auditing profession developed largely in the hands of the profession (Walker, 1993, 2004).

It is interesting to note that while the existence of an auditing profession was evident by the end of the nineteenth century,[2] the Companies Act 1856 removed the requirement for joint-stock companies to have an audit, replacing this requirement with a model set of articles of incorporation which included a balance sheet format and a proposed series of procedures to audit the balance sheets. Thus, while the provisions of the 1856 Act facilitated the creation of limited liability joint-stock companies in the United Kingdom, it was not until the Companies Act 1948 that external audits of financial statements were required by law to be performed by qualified professional auditors, and it was not until the Companies Act 1976 that the three primary institutes of chartered accountants (ICAEW; ICAS; and Institute of Chartered Accountants in Ireland – ICAI); and the Association of Cost and Certified Accountants (subsequently renamed as the Association of Chartered Certified Accountants – ACCA), were specifically mentioned by law as the only bodies whose members were authorised to perform statutory audits.

3.2 Structures regulating statutory auditing in the United Kingdom

The structures regulating statutory auditing in the United Kingdom have been modified several times since the mid-1970s. In 1976, the Auditing Practices Committee (APC) was established in the private sector by several recognised professional bodies in order to formalise cooperation on auditing practices. In 1978, the APC published a preliminary codification of auditing best practices, with more formal publication of auditing standards and guidelines beginning in 1980. In 1989 the APC began to issue a series of "Practice Notes" which were intended as practice guidelines to assist auditors in applying auditing standards for particular circumstances or industries. The APC was restructured in 1991 and renamed the Auditing Practices Board (APB).

With respect to the regulation of statutory auditing by the state, the Companies Act 1989 included provisions designed to "ensure that only persons who are properly supervised and appropriately qualified are appointed as company auditors, and that audits are carried out properly, with integrity and with a proper degree of independence." This requirement in the Companies Act 1989 was influenced by the Eighth European Directive on Company Law issued in 1984 regarding the approval of persons responsible for carrying out statutory audits. The manner in which this was implemented in the United Kingdom was to designate the historical professional bodies as Recognised Qualifying Bodies (RQBs) and Recognised Supervisory Bodies (RSBs). As a consequence, the recognised professional bodies include ICAEW, ICAS, ICAI, ACCA and also the Chartered Institute of Public Finance and Accountancy (CIPFA) and the Association of International Accountants (AIA) (see Figure 9.2).

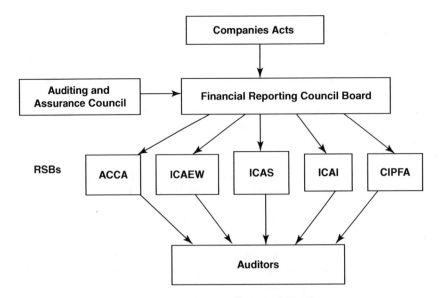

Figure 9.2   Regulation of statutory auditors in the United Kingdom.

Following the passage of the United States' Sarbanes-Oxley Act of 2002, and the creation of the Public Companies Accounting Oversight Board (PCAOB) as the primary regulatory body for audits of companies with publicly traded shares, the British Government felt it necessary to follow suit by reorganising the regulatory structures for financial services in the United Kingdom, including those of professional auditing. This led to the UK Financial Reporting Council's (FRC) role being expanded to become the single independent regulator of auditing. Following the Companies Act 2006, the FRC (and its audit arm) is no longer independent of the state. It is required to report annually to the Secretary of State for Business and to Parliament on how it has conducted its oversight of the regulation of statutory auditors, including regular visits to the recognised professional bodies.

Additional reforms were carried out in July 2012 to enable the FRC to operate as a unified regulatory body with enhanced independence. A new structure was implemented to ensure effective governance of all the FRC's regulatory activities under the responsibility of the FRC Board. As part of the reforms, the APB was replaced by the Audit and Assurance Council. Responsibility for setting auditing standards was assumed by the FRC Board, with the Audit and Assurance Council acting in an advisory role to the FRC Board. In addition, the Audit Quality Review (AQR) team, formerly known as the Audit Inspection Unit, monitors the quality of the audits of listed companies and other major public interest companies in the United Kingdom. This means that the AQR team has a mission very similar to that of the PCAOB in the United States. However, the RSBs of the various professional institutes continue to play an important role in the regulation of their members, thus retaining a greater degree of self-regulation on the part of the profession than in the United States, France or Germany.

In summary, the historical development of the auditing profession in the United Kingdom occurred primarily in the private sector, with education and admission requirements, disciplinary practices and professional standards being conducted through recognised professional bodies. Beginning in 2006, the FRC (and effectively the British Parliament) assumed a greater role in the regulation of the auditing profession, thus confirming the predictions of both Abbott (1988) and Larson (1977) that it is difficult for professions to maintain their independence in the face of regulation by the state. This pattern of historical development of professional auditing through private sector professional bodies contrasts with the way that the auditing profession developed in France, as will be seen in the following section.

4 France

Miller (1990) provides an extensive analysis of interrelationships between accounting practices and the state during the Colbert (1661–83) period in France. The legal technologies employed during that period focused on the regulation of company accounts pursuant to the Ordinance of 1673. An official publication of instructions explaining this Ordinance was issued by the French state in order to instruct merchants on the proper presentation of accounts. In addition, there was an increase in the role of *intendants*[3] appointed by the King, as well as the inception of systematic and detailed accounting information flows from the provinces to the centre (Miller, 1990). The keeping of exact books of accounts (Savary, 1676) was required not only to promote the success of business enterprises, but also to enhance control over companies and promote commercial order within the French state. Miller (1990) maintains that the Colbert period was a significant time of innovation in the calculative practices of accounting and for a wide range of other practices of government. He also argues that it was through a particular political rationality of creating 'order' that a distinct set of accounting and governmental practices were linked (1990: 315). At the same time, it is important to acknowledge that throughout much of Louis

XIV's reign, France was the leading European military power, engaging in three major wars and two minor conflicts. Thus, an important political rationale based on military competition cannot be discounted with respect to this period. In other words, the creation of economic order and a unified set of commercial practices throughout France facilitated economic prosperity which enhanced the military power of the French state.

4.1 Background of accounting and auditing in France

Hilaire (1989) indicates that when the Compagnie des Indes was reorganised in 1723 during the Regency Period, *inspecteurs* were designated by royal authority, and *syndics* were elected at the general meeting of shareholders to review the stewardship of the directors. Lefebvre-Teillard (1982) states that during the nineteenth century *censeurs* were given the task of checking the operations of an enterprise, visiting locations and examining books. The *censeurs* reported to the members of the company (i.e. shareholders). The same author indicates that before 1863 the organising documents of companies provided for the appointment of a *commissaire* whose role was to examine the accounts and report on his findings to the members of the company.

The key legislation pertaining to the development of the auditing profession in France is as follows:

> *Law of 23 May 1863*: created *commissaires*, usually called *commissaires de surveillance* or *censeurs*, which provided protection for shareholders for the first time in French history;
>
> *Decree of 8 August 1935*: required competence and independence of statutory auditors and specified incompatible occupations;
>
> *Law of 24 July 1966* and the *Decree of 12 August 1969*: specified the organisational structure for the profession of *commissaires aux comptes*.

The Law of 23 May 1863 specified that

> [t]he annual general meeting designates one or more *commissaires*, members or not, who are given the responsibility of preparing a report to the annual general meeting of the following year on the situation of the company, on its balance sheet and on the accounts presented by the administrators. The resolution approving the balance sheet and accounts is null if it has not been preceded by the report of the *commissaires* (article 15).
>
> The *commissaires* have the right, to be exercised whenever they think it appropriate, in the interests of the members, to review the books, to examine the operations of the company and to call for a general meeting (article 16).

Standards of independence and competence, and a requirement for the exercise of professional secrecy were not included in the 1863 Act. The Act specified only that "the extent and the effects of the *commissaires*' responsibility towards the company are determined according to the general rules of the mandate" (article 26). This article was subsequently repeated word for word in article 43 of the Law of 24 July 1867. The commissaire, usually referred to at that time as *commissaire de surveillance*, or *censeur* (Houpain and Bosvieux, 1935), could be chosen from among the shareholders, relatives of the directors or even from the employees of the company. Members of the board of directors could not be appointed as commissaires. No knowledge of accounting and finance was required. Education in accounting was not recognised by the French government until the *brevet d'expert compatable* was created in 1927 by the Ministry of Public Instruction, and the *brevet professionnel de comptable* in 1931 (Boqueraz, 2000; Degos, 2004: 9).

Leduc (1982) indicates that with respect to the appointment of commissaires:

> There were flagrant cases where the job was entrusted to an ageing, and particularly incompetent, shareholder, from which derives the image which is found too often, of the *commissaire* signing a report prepared by the accounting department of the company.

Bouteron (1953: 110) writes that: "as far as the *commissaires* were concerned, it was clear that they lacked both technical training and independence from the management." Hémard, Terre and Mabilat (1974: 50) note:

> [I]f it is to be fulfilled in a satisfactory manner, the task entrusted to auditors requires that the individuals who undertake it should have two essential qualities: on the one hand competence, and on the other independence from those who manage the company, qualities to which one should naturally add intellectual and moral probity. Unfortunately these prerequisites completely escaped those who drafted the law.

While there was general agreement about the incompetence and lack of independence of commissaires under the 1863 Act, the regulation of the auditing profession in France was not fundamentally changed until the Decree of 8 August 1935, which required publicly traded companies to select at least one of their commissaires from a list maintained by the Courts of Appeal. A Decree of 29 June 1936 established the conditions for admission to the Court lists which was made dependent on a technical examination; however, many persons were exempted from the examination because of their status as practicing accountants, while the examination itself was not set at a high level (Bocqueraz, 2010). The 1935 Decree introduced several changes to audit regulation which remain in force today:

- a definition of conflicts of interest prohibiting any employee of the company or relative of the directors from being appointed as an auditor;
- a requirement that the commissaire receive no income other than that arising from the audit engagement;
- a prohibition against the commissaire becoming a director of the company within five years of the expiry of the audit engagement;
- an obligation for the commissaire to observe professional secrecy;
- any breaches of the law on the part of audit clients were to be reported to the public prosecutor;
- any publication of false information by the commissaire would be a criminal offence.

The concept of a *co-commissariat* (i.e. two auditors for each annual audit) was also established in 1935 with respect to financial institutions accepting savings from the public. The 1935 decree mandated that there should be two auditors, including one who was considered to be competent by virtue of having been registered with the Appeal Court. It was possible, therefore, for a company, to have several commissaires. It was only with the law of 24 July 1966, however, that listed companies were explicitly obligated to appoint two qualified commissaires, although this was already the practice of most large French companies (Bennecib, 2004).

4.2 Structures regulating statutory auditing in France

Since the end of the Second World War, the French accounting and auditing professions have been divided into two separate professions, both of which are regulated by the state. French law restricts a statutory auditor and a public accountant from working for the same client. The auditing profession is regulated by the Compagnie Nationale des Commissaires aux Comptes (CNCC), and the accounting profession is regulated by the Ordre des Experts-Comptables (OEC). The CNCC is in turn supervised by the Ministry of Justice (*Garde des Sceaux*), while the OEC is supervised by the Ministry of Economy and Finance. Although the Commissariat aux Comptes has existed as an institution since 1863, rapid economic expansion in the post-Second World War period and the concomitant growth of the financial markets in France, established the obligation to inspect accounts, enforced under the Companies Act of 24 July 1966. A subsequent decree of 12 August 1969 created the Compagnie Nationale des Commissaires aux Comptes (CNCC) under the aegis of the Ministry of Justice (CNCC, 1994).

All statutory auditors must be enrolled in the official list of the CNCC. The CNCC is organised on a regional basis and members can be registered in any one of the 34 offices throughout France. The CNCC has seen its role greatly enlarged over the years to cover the inspection of accounts in all categories of organisations, both profit-making and not-for-profit entities. Beyond the statutory mission of attesting that the financial statements present a true and fair view of the financial positions and results of operations of the company, the French auditor is also called upon to intervene when companies seek additional capital or to provide an early warning procedure for companies likely to encounter financial difficulties (CNCC, 1994).

In 1967, beginning with the establishment of the Commission des Opérations de Bourse (COB, the French equivalent of the US Securities and Exchange Commission), now replaced by the Autorité des Marchés Financiers (AMF), discussions emerged regarding the competence of auditors and the effectiveness of the *co-commissariat* arrangement (COB, 1994). It was believed that the co-commissariat arrangement provided a higher level of audit quality. In addition, elimination of the co-commissariat could have led to a loss of audit engagements by French auditors in favour of the large international accounting firms. Consequently, even though the idea of a co-commissariat arose initially in 1935 due to a perceived lack of competence among auditors, the requirement was maintained because removing it would be detrimental to French audit firms, particularly with respect to large audit clients.

As a result of the Law of 24 July 1966 and the Decree of 12 August 1969 the role, duties and status of the statutory auditor in France were significantly modified. The requirement to preserve professional secrecy was retained, independence was reinforced, entry to the profession was made conditional upon passing exams of a very high level, and the purpose of the audit was clearly defined. In short, the 1966 Law marked the end of amateur auditors. As far as competence and independence were concerned, the Decree of 12 August 1969, and the modifications of the Law of 24 July 1966, anticipated the Eighth European Company Law Directive of 1984 concerning the qualification of statutory auditors. The Law of 24 July 1966 maintained the obligation to have two commissaires for listed companies and for limited liability companies with a capital of more than five million francs. In addition, there was a requirement for a change of statutory auditors every six years.

An important historical event which has had significant impact on statutory auditing in France was the creation of the Plan Comptable. This legal requirement established a specific chart of accounts and a mandatory format for financial statements. Thus, what was to be audited became specified by law. The origins of the Plan Comptable are interesting in that it was in effect a cultural intrusion imposed by the Goering Plan during the German occupation of France in the 1940s (Standish, 1990). The Plan Comptable continued to be the legal framework for accounting standards in France into the post-Second World War period. Following various amendments, it is now called the Plan Comptable Générale (PCG), as defined by Regulation 99-03 of the Comité de la Réglementation Comptable (CRC), and validated by the Ministry

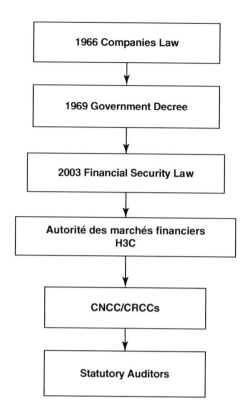

Figure 9.3 Regulation of the statutory auditor in France.

of the Budget. Changes to the PCG are now recommended by the Autorité des Normes Comptables (ANC) which was created by the Ordonnance No. 2009-79.

In summary, the evolution of the auditing profession in France has been associated with legal requirements for the appointment of auditors, ranging from *inspecteurs,* to *syndics,* to *censeurs* and finally to *commissaires.* The law of 23 May 1866 required limited liability companies to appoint a commissaire to audit the accounts and report to the shareholders; however, there were no requirements concerning who could be appointed to this position, nor any education and experience requirements. It was not until 1935 that a legal requirement specified that two commissaires must be appointed, at least one of whom must be enrolled in a list of professional auditors maintained by the Court of Appeal. Finally, the law of 1966 marked the end of the amateur auditor, with commissaires being required to be enrolled in an organisation that subsequently came to be called the CNCC, operating under the direct supervision of the Ministry of Justice. Consequently, the evolution of the auditing profession in France has been closely associated with political rationalities and legal technologies related to the goals and objectives of the state.

5 Germany

The commercial history of Germany can be traced to the Hanseatic League which emerged in the thirteenth century when the cities of Hamburg and Lubeck formed an agreement to protect their merchants against Baltic pirates (Funnell and Robertson, 2011). The Germanic state consisted of the various city states, which joined together for trading and military protection purposes, rather than as a nation state *per se*. The Hanseatic League eventually came to include city states located throughout Northern Europe. A common language – Low German – and a common set of trading laws and regulations prevailed throughout the Hanseatic League. Merchants conducted their trading businesses through agents located in member cities, but they operated primarily through sole proprietorships or short-lived partnerships rather than limited liability companies (De Roover, 1956). Thus corporate governance and external auditing were not required due to the close internal control exercised by owner/traders.

Germany remained a dispersed and divided political entity until the nineteenth century, when it was unified under Chancellor Bismarck in 1871. During the following 40 years leading up to the First World War, Germany quickly surpassed the United Kingdom in terms of industrial power. The focus of Germany's industrial enterprises was on manufacturing, primarily in metallurgy, chemicals and machinery. In addition, the form of capitalism that developed in Germany during this period was quite different from that of the United Kingdom and France. Four distinct differences can be identified (Micklethwait and Wooldridge, 2003). First, German law did not prohibit monopolies. In fact, German law explicitly allowed contractual agreements that regulated prices, production output and market sharing. Consequently, the number of cartels in Germany increased from four in 1875 to 385 in 1905. The second difference with respect to German capitalism was the unique system of corporate governance based on a two-tier system of corporate control. The 1870 law that introduced the ability to form joint-stock companies also required such entities to have two levels of control: management boards, responsible for day-to-day decisions; and supervisory boards, made up of significant shareholders and other interested parties.

The third difference related to the role and influence of banks, which continues to this day. Instead of share markets, major banks provided most of the capital for industrial expansion. These banks were universal banks, combining aspects of commercial and investment banking as well as investment trusts. Bankers sat on the supervisory boards of Germany's largest industrial companies. The fourth distinction was the emphasis on the social role of corporations. This was influenced by the German guilds that had survived much longer than their counterparts in other parts of Europe. The guilds had preserved the system of apprenticeships. Beginning in the 1880s, a comprehensive system of social insurance developed that required companies to pay pensions, and provided representation for labor unions on the supervisory boards of companies.

The modern structure of corporate governance in Germany, which developed after the Second World War, is based on the *Aktiengesellschaft* (AG), which is the German term for 'public stock company'. *Aktiengesellschaften* (the plural form) are corporations with publicly traded shares listed on stock exchanges. An AG is one of two major forms of business organisation prevalent in Germany. The AG requires a specified minimum amount of capital, the annual issuance of audited financial statements, and a two-tiered corporate governance structure that includes a supervisory board and a management or executive board. The second organisational form, which is more common than the AG, is the *Gesellschaft mit beschrankter Haftung* (GmbH), which translates as 'company with limited liability'. GmbHs constitute approximately 95 per cent of German companies.

The supervisory board is charged with establishing the corporation's overall goals and objectives, while the management board focuses day-to-day operations of the company. The supervisory board must include among its members certain representatives of the corporation's employees to ensure that employees are directly involved in the direction of the corporation's activities. This requirement derives from the fact that until the twentieth century, many German companies were family owned and therefore privately held, with no involvement by the company's employees in the direction of the companies. During the period when the concept of the corporation was developing in Germany, socialist political parties sought to democratise the corporate structure by requiring AGs to have representatives from the employees. Consequently, the supervisory board of large, public corporations must include 20 members, 10 of which are elected by the shareholders, the other 10 being employee representatives. For smaller corporations, the minimum number of board members is three. The total number of members of the board must be divisible by three.

5.1 The role of the statutory auditor in Germany

Evans (2005) points out that while the history of the accountancy profession has given rise to extensive research in the Anglo-American sphere, there is little published in English on developments in Germany. She also supports the idea that there are considerable differences in the role and status of professions and the regulation of the accountancy profession among countries. In addition, she maintains that there is a lack of common terminology and a lack of conceptual equivalency among the words 'professions' and 'professionalisation' in English and in German (see e.g. Jarausch, 1990; Kocka, 1990: 68). Beginning in the late nineteenth and early twentieth centuries, for example, auditing firms in Germany consisted primarily of large corporate entities with primarily outside ownership, as distinct from the traditional partnership form in the United Kingdom. The first of these corporate entities (Deutsche Treuhand-Gesellschaft) was initially set up as a trust company. The Deutsche Treuhand-Gesellschaft moved into the increasingly lucrative audit market, providing competition to sole practitioners who could not compete with the large and well-connected firms. Quick (1994) has examined the early history of these corporate audit firms and their distinctive features, which to some extent survive to the present day.

In addition, the role of the statutory auditor in Germany has historically been different from that in the United Kingdom, where all limited liability companies are required to be audited, and also different from France, where all legal business entities are required to be audited. In Germany, only AGs and some GmbHs are required to be audited. Another difference as compared with the United Kingdom is that German companies primarily obtain capital from banks and insurance companies, and the banks and insurance companies are often important shareholders. This entitles them to participate in the general meetings of the companies in which they own shares and to obtain private information. Finally, a system of proxy voting allows banks to vote on behalf of smaller shareholders in the annual general meeting of shareholders. Historically it was the job of the supervisory board to audit the financial statements. The demand for external audits was prompted by the failure of the supervisory boards to perform proper audits. The basic function of the statutory auditor in Germany has therefore been to assist the supervisory board. The audit report is addressed to the supervisory board. The statutory auditor is engaged by the supervisory board and afterwards formally elected by the general assembly of the shareholders. Since the supervisory board supervises the activities of the board of management, the German statutory auditor may feel less role conflict than the auditor in the United Kingdom. This is because the German statutory auditor is less beholden to the management of the company for their appointment.

5.2 Structures regulating the statutory auditor in Germany

Statutory auditors in Germany are required to be members of the Wirtschaftsprüferkammer (WPK), a public law body created in 1961 pursuant to the Wirtschaftsprüferordnung (WPO), the law regulating the profession of auditors. The WPK is supervised by the Ministry of Economics of the German government. There are two professional qualifications in auditing:

the *Wirtschaftsprüfer* (WP) and the *vereidigter Buchprüfer* (vBp). The vBp is a lower level qualification. A vBp is allowed to audit only medium-sized, private limited-liability companies (GmbH).
Both the WP and the vBp must be members of the WPK. Certain aspects of the auditor's role
and responsibility in Germany are also defined by the *Handelsgesetzbuch* (HGB) (similar to the
company laws in the United Kingdom and France).

In Germany audits can be performed by audit corporations; that is, firms of auditors incorporated with limited liability. Audit corporations must also be members of the WPK. Members
of the WPK therefore include qualified individuals (WP and vBp sole practitioners, partners or employees of audit firms) and auditing firms (Wirschaftsprüfungsgesellschaften and
Buchprüfungsgesellschaften) (see Figure 9.4).

The function of the WPK is to regulate statutory auditors in accordance with the provisions
of the WPO. The WPK enforces standards prescribed by law and participates in disciplining
auditors who violate those standards. If the violations are serious then the special chambers and
senates of the German courts dealing with WP matters become involved in the disciplinary
process. In addition to the WPK, there is also an *Institut der Wirtschaftsprüfer in Deutschland* (IDW).
Membership in the IDW is voluntary and is restricted to WPs. The IDW is involved in training,
continuing professional education and the establishment of auditing standards. In comparing
the roles of the WPK and the IDW, the WPK is responsible for ethical standards and the IDW is
responsible for technical standards.

It can be seen that the regulation of statutory auditors by the German government is more
direct than it is in the United Kingdom but probably comparable to that of France. This observation supports the classification scheme proposed by Nobes and Parker (1995). In Germany, the
education and training of auditors are prescribed by law. Disciplinary actions for violations of
professional standards are also prescribed by law, but most disciplinary actions are conducted in
an administrative manner. One aspect of the regulation of auditors in Germany that is also quite
different from that of the United Kingdom is the idea that the auditor is viewed as having a
public function under law. Various German commentators have suggested that the auditor has a
political responsibility (Lutter, 1977) and that the auditor exercises certain functions under public law (Schulze-Osterlow, 1977). These ideas would be quite foreign to the United Kingdom
context but would probably be better understood within the French context. Another notice-

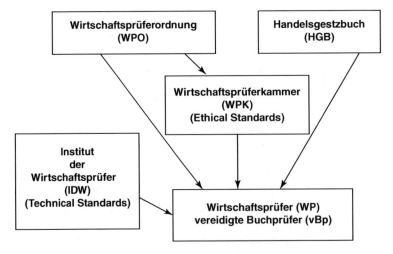

Figure 9.4 Regulation of the statutory auditor in Germany.

156

able difference between Germany and the United Kingdom is in the area of self-regulation. In Germany self-regulation occurs only within the strict boundaries of the law.

6 Discussion

Table 9.1 summarises the regulatory structures for the auditing professions in the United Kingdom, France and Germany. Based on the discussion of the historical evolution of the profession in these three countries, it can be seen that the regulatory structures differ in substantial ways. During the last 20 years, however, there have been efforts to harmonise the regulatory structures for the auditing profession in the European Union.

6.1 Initiatives to harmonise the regulation of statutory auditing

The regulation of statutory auditors was affected by the Eighth Directive of the European Commission (EC, 1984; Evans and Nobes, 1998a) issued in 1984. The purpose of the Eighth Directive was to harmonise regulation within the EU, in particular with regard to entry into the auditing profession and qualifications to become a statutory auditor. In response to the Eighth Directive, the member states of the EU modified their company laws or state regulations (i.e. government decrees) to comply with the provisions of the Directive (Evans and Nobes, 1998a; Cooper, Puxty, Puxty, Robson and Willmott, 1996; Buijink, Maijoors, Meuwissen and van Witteloostuijn, 1996). However, compliance with the Directive did not mean that the regulation of statutory auditors is the same in every country (Buijink *et al.*, 1996; Margerison and Moizer, 1996). Moreover, the Eighth Directive did not cover all aspects of audit regulation; it focused primarily on reducing barriers to intra-European trade in audit services. A subsequent Council Directive of 21-12.88 required mutual recognition of higher education accounting diplomas and mandated professional training of at least three years' duration.

In October 1996, the EC issued a Green Paper entitled *The Role, The Position and The Liability of the Statutory Auditor Within The European Union* (EC, 1996). Green Papers of the Commission provide the basis for the discussion of issues among the member states of the EU. Following the issuance of the Green Paper, a conference was held in Brussels in December 1996. The objective of the conference was to discuss the regulation of statutory auditors in Europe and the regulatory role of the EU. There was general agreement that the EU should provide a common regulatory framework (EC, 1998). Among the topics discussed in the Green Paper and at the conference, were the following: the definition of the statutory audit; contents of the audit report; the competence of the statutory auditor; the independence of the statutory auditor; the role of the statutory auditor in corporate governance; the auditor's civil liability; and the freedom of establishment and the freedom to provide services across national borders.

One important point contained in the first paragraph of the Green Paper reads as follows:

> The requirement to have the annual and consolidated accounts of certain companies audited by a qualified professional which was introduced for the Community as a whole by the Accounting Directives, is designed to protect the public interest.
>
> *(EC, 1996: 4)*

It is precisely in defining what constitutes the public interest that the regulation of statutory auditors comes to be of great importance. The protection of the public interest is viewed somewhat differently in the three countries investigated. In the United Kingdom the public interest is defined primarily in terms of a well-functioning capital market, while in Germany the statutory

Table 9.1 Differences in regulation of statutory auditors in the UK, France and Germany

	UNITED KINGDOM	FRANCE	GERMANY
WHAT STRUCTURES REGULATE THE STATUTORY AUDITOR?	Private Sector Professional Bodies.	Government decree and CNCC.	Wirtschaftsprüfer -ordnung (WPO) and -kammer (WPK).
WHAT IS THE ROLE IN CORPORATE GOVERNANCE?	To provide a true and fair view opinion of financial statements.	As an adjunct to governmental regulation of corporations.	As an advisor to the supervisory board.
WHO CAN BECOME A STATUTORY AUDITOR?	3 yrs.	5 yrs.	6 yrs.
–EDUCATION	University.	University or Business School.	University.
	No accounting required.	Pass a series of examinations in accounting.	Accounting, Economics, or Business required.
–TRAINING	3 yrs. Under a RQB.	3yrs. To become an expert comptable. Then admission to CNCC.	4 yrs. under supervision of a WP.
–EXAMINATION	Set by each professional body.	Set by a national curriculum.	Set by each German state.
WHO DISCIPLINES THE STATUTORY AUDITOR?	Private Sector Professional Bodies.	The regional CNCC.	The WPK and disciplinary courts.

auditor is viewed as assisting the supervisory board with respect to the proper functioning of corporate governance. In both Germany and France the statutory auditor is deemed to act on behalf of the state in certain circumstances.

In late 2010, the EC addressed the regulation of the statutory auditor in a direct manner by issuing a further Green Paper calling for consultation on the role of statutory audit as well the wider environment within which statutory audits are conducted (EC, 2010). The purpose of this Green Paper was to question whether the role of auditors could be enhanced to mitigate future financial crises. Apparently, the EU Commission believed that the financial crisis of 2008 implied weaknesses in statutory auditing. In particular, the Commission wanted to address whether audits provide the right kind of information for participants in capital markets, whether there are issues around the independence of audit firms, whether there are risks linked to a concentrated market for audit services, and whether supervision at a European level might be useful and how to best meet the specific needs of small and medium-sized businesses.

The Green Paper made several specific statements about statutory audits that may or may not be generally accepted. It defined statutory audits as audits of company accounts as required by EU law. Auditors are entrusted by law to conduct statutory audits. The aim of an audit is to offer an opinion on the truth and fairness of the financial statements of the companies audited in complete independence of the audited company. To this extent, the independence of auditors should be the bedrock of the audit environment. In the wake of the banking crisis of 2008–09, questions have arisen on whether the role of auditors can be enhanced to mitigate financial risk in the future. In contrast, the premise of this chapter has been that expectations for increased regulation of statutory auditing may be difficult to meet so long as definitions regarding the purpose of regulating corporate activity, as well as the role of statutory auditing within that regulation, differ among countries. The previous discussion of the history of the evolution of the auditing profession in the United Kingdom, France and Germany has sought to demonstrate this premise.

7 Summary and conclusion

Beginning in the mid-nineteenth century, a gradual removal of restrictions against the formation of limited liability companies, and other positive acts on the part of the state, provided linkages between political rationalities which favoured economic liberalism and legal technologies which facilitated capital formation. Thus, the origins of the auditing profession as an important component of corporate governance can be linked with the emergence of the limited liability company as a principal form of business enterprise. Legal requirements for audited financial statements provided an opportunity for the growth of an auditing profession but historical differences among nation states regarding the role and status of professions led to differences in the ways that the profession evolved in different countries. These differences have comprised the primary focus of the chapter.

Abbott (1988) has argued that professional recognition is achieved when the governing authority in a nation state grants recognition of something as a profession. Recognition by the state is accomplished through a specific action taken by the state to grant monopoly rights in a certain area of occupational practice. The restriction by the state of the right to perform audits to members of certain specifically identified bodies of accountants is the primary characteristic of the auditing profession. No other aspect of accountancy is similarly recognised or regulated by the state. The arguments of the chapter confirm Abbott's contention that professions seek state support to confirm their legitimacy. Abbott also indicates that the regulation of professional activity differs among countries, and that, in particular, there is a higher expectation in code law countries (such as France and Germany) regarding the importance of the state in the regulation of professions. The arguments of the chapter are that there is a distinction between the role and status of professions in code law countries such as France and Germany and common law countries such as the United Kingdom, with the state playing a more prominent role in the regulation of professional activity in code law countries.

The purpose of this chapter has been to explore the evolution of the auditing profession in the United Kingdom, France and Germany. The focus has been on the regulation of auditing and the way in which the regulatory structures differ in several countries. The importance of this topic lies in its implications for regulatory harmonisation. If the differences in regulation are based on established laws and historical traditions relating to the training of auditors and their role in corporate governance, then expectations for increased harmonisation may be difficult to achieve. As long as the definition of the purpose of regulating corporate activity differs among countries, then regulatory structures will differ. As the importance of the global capital market activity increases, the definition of the role and purpose of regulating corporate activity increases the perceived need for regulatory harmonisation. Indeed, it may well be that interest in this topic on the part of the EC will improve the regulatory structures for statutory auditing; however, given the propensity for political actors and political motives to enter into the regulatory process, it seems unlikely that improved regulatory structures will emerge in the near-term future.

This chapter was submitted by the author with the following title: "A critical look at the emergence of the auditing profession."

Notes

1   In this chapter we do not include an empirical example of Model B, but the United States might be considered to be an example of mixed model somewhat close to Model B.
2   According to Anderson *et al.* (1996: 366), by 1896, 76.2 per cent of UK listed companies were audited by Chartered Accountants.
3   Intendants were royal civil servants in France under the Ancien Regime. They were appointed by the king to serve in a specific regional area with respect to fiscal matters such as taxation, policing and judicial affairs.

References

Abbott, A. (1988). *The System of Professions: An Essay on the Division of Expert Labor*, Chicago, IL: The University of Chicago Press.
Anderson, M., J. R. Edwards and D. Matthews (1996). "A study of the quoted company audit market in 1886," *Accounting, Business & Financial History*, 6(3): 363–87.
Bennecib, J. (2004). "De l'efficacité du co-commissariat aux comptes," *Thèse de sciences de gestion*, Université Paris IX-Dauphine.
Benston, G. (1973). "Required disclosure and stockmarkets: an evaluation of the Securities Exchange Act of 1934," *American Economic Review*, 63:132–55.
Bloom, R. and M. Naciri (1989). "Accounting standard setting and culture: a comparative analysis of the United States, Canada, England, West Germany, Australia, New Zealand, Sweden, Japan and Switzerland," *International Journal of Accounting*, 24: 70–97.
Bocqueraz, C. (2000). "The professionalisation project of French accountancy practitioners before the Second World War," *Thèse de sciences de gestion*, Université de Nantes.
Bocqueraz, C. (2010). "France," in G. Previts, P. Walton and P. Wolnizer (eds): *A Global History of History of Financial Reporting and Public Policy: Europe*, Bingley, Yorkshire: Emerald Group Publishing.
Bouteron, J. (1953). Origines et évolution du contrôle exercé par les Commissaires de Sociétés, *Revue de la Compagnie des Commissaires de Sociétés Agréés par la Cour d'Appel de Paris*: 103–22
Boys, P. (1994). "The origins and evolution of the accountancy profession," in W. Habgood (ed.) *Chartered Accountants in England and Wales: A Guide to Historical Records*, Manchester: Manchester University Press.
Boys, P. (2011). *A Study of Practising Accountants Listed in London Trade Directories Published Before 1840*, London: Institute of Chartered Accountants in England and Wales.

Buijink, W., S. Maijoor, R. Meuwissen and A. van Witteloostuijn (1996). *The Role, Position and Liability of the Statutory Auditor Within the European Union*, Maastricht: Maastricht Accounting and Auditing Research Center.

CNCC (1994). *The Statutory Auditors: Status and Mission*, Paris: Compagnie Nationale des Commissaires aux Comptes.

COB (1994). *Rapport du Groupe de Travail Sur La Déontologie des Commissaires Aux Comptes Dans Les Sociétés Qui Font Appel Public à L'Épargne*, Paris: Commission des Opérations de Bourse and Compagnie Nationale des Commisaires aux Comptes.

Cooper, D., A. Puxty, K. Robson and H. Willmott (1996). "Changes in the international regulation of auditors: (in)stalling the Eighth Directive in the UK," *Critical Perspectives on Accounting*, 75(6): 589–616.

Cornwell, S. V. P. (1991). *Curtiss Jenkins Cornwall & Co.: A Study in Professional Origins*, London and New York: Garland Press.

Cornwell, S. V. P. (1993). "The nature of Bristol accountancy practice during the 1820s: some comments," *Accounting, Business & Financial History*, 3(2): 155–64.

De Roover, R. (1956). "The development of accounting prior to Luca Pacioli according to the account-books of medieval merchant," in A. C. Littleton and B .S. Yamey (eds) *Studies in the History of Accounting*. London: Sweet & Maxwell.

Degos, J. G. (2004). Un aspect trop peu connu de l'histoire financière: les diplômes d'expertise comptable, *Revue du financier*, 146: 33–48.

Dobija, D. (2011). "Early evolution of corporate control and auditing: the British East India Company (1600-43)," Available at SSRN: http://ssrn.com/abstract=1886945.

Doupnik, T. (1987). "Evidence of international harmonization of financial reporting," *Journal of Accounting*, 23(1): 47–68.

Edwards, R. J. (2001). "Accounting regulation and the professionalization process: an historical essay concerning the significance of P.H. Abbott," *Critical Perspectives on Accounting*, 12(6): 675–96.

Edwards, J. R. (2010). "Researching the absence of professional organisation in Victorian England" *Accounting, Business & Financial History*, 20(2): 177–208.

Edwards, J. R. and S. P. Walker (2010). "Lifestyle, status and occupational differentiation in Victorian accountancy," *Accounting, Organizations and Society*, 35(1): 2–22.

Edwards, J. R., M. Anderson and D. Matthews (1997). "Accounting in a free market economy: the British company audit in 1886," *ABACUS*, 31(1): 1–25.

Edwards J. R., M. Anderson and R. Chandler (2007). "Claiming a jurisdiction for the "Public Accountant" in England prior to organizational fusion," *Accounting, Organizations and Society*, 32(1–2): 61–100.

EC (1984). *Eighth Council Directive of 10 April 1984 based on Article 54 (3) (g) of the Treaty on the approval of persons responsible for carrying on the statutory audits of documents (84/253/EEC)*. Brussels: Office of the European Commission.

EC (1996). *Green Paper: The Role, the Position and the Liability of the Statutory Audit Within the European Union (OJ No C 321, 28.10.96)*. Brussels: Office of the European Commission.

EC (1998). *Communication from the Commission: The Statutory Audit in the European Union: The Way Forward*. Brussels: Office of the European Commission.

EC (2010). *Green Paper: Audit Policy: Lessons from the Crisis*. (COM(2010) 561 final). Brussels: Office of the European Commission.

Evans, L. (2005). "Editorial: Accounting history in the German language arena," *Accounting, Business & Financial History*, 15(3): 229–33.

Evans, L. and C. Nobes (1998a). "Harmonization in the structure of audit firms: incorporation in the UK and Germany," *European Accounting Review*, 7(1): 125–48.

Evans, L. and C. Nobes (1998b). "Harmonization relating to auditor independence: the Eighth Directive, the UK and Germany," *European Accounting Review*, 7(3): 493–515.

Funnell, W. and J. Robertson (2011). "Capitalist accounting in sixteenth century Holland: Hanseatic and the Sombart thesis," *Accounting, Auditing and Accountability Journal*, 24(5): 560–86.

Gray, S. (1988). "Towards a theory of cultural influence on the development of accounting systems Internationally," *ABACUS*, 24(1): 1–15.

Hémard, J., F. Terré F and P. Mabilat (1974). *Sociétés Commerciales*. Paris: Dalloz Hilaire, J. (1989). La formation du commissariat aux comptes, in *Le Commissariat aux Comptes, Renforcement ou Dérive?* 1: 13–42.

Hopwood, A. G. (1989). "International pressures for accounting change," in A. G. Hopwood (ed.): *International Pressures for Accounting Change*. London: Prentice-Hall Inc.

Hopwood, A.G., S. Burchell and C. Clubb (1979). "The development of accounting in its international context: past concerns and emergent issues," in A. Roberts (ed.). *An Historical and Contemporary Review of the Development of International Accounting*, Atlanta, GA: Georgia State University.

Houpain, A. and B. Bosvieux (1935). *Traité général théorique et pratique des sociétés civiles et commerciales et des associations*, 7e, Paris: Sirey.

ICAEW (2010). *International Consistency: Global Challenges Initiative: Providing Direction*, London: Institute of Chartered Accountants in England and Wales.

Jarausch, K. H. (1990). "The German professions in history and theory," in G. Cocks and K. H. Jarausch (eds): *German Professions 1800–1950*, New York and Oxford: Oxford University Press.

Kedslie, M. J. (1990). *Firm Foundations: The Development of Professional Accounting in Scotland*, Hull: Hull University Press.

Kocka, J. (1990). "'Bürgertum' and professions in the nineteenth century: two alternative Approaches," in M. Burrage and R. Torstendahl (eds) *Professions in Theory and History: Rethinking the Study of Professions*, London: Sage Publishing.

Larson, M. S. (1977). *The Rise of Professionalism: A Sociological Analysis*, Berkeley, CA: University of California Press.

Leduc, E. (1982) Origines et évolution du contrôle légal des comptes en France. *Bulletin de la Compagnie Regionale des Commissaires aux Comptes de Paris*, 21: 9–10.

Lee, T. A. (2011). "Paul and Mackersy, accountants, 1818–34: public accountancy in the early nineteenth century," *Accounting History Review*, 21(3): 285–307.

Lee, T, A. (2013). "Reflections on the origins of modern accounting," *Accounting History*, 18(2): 141–61.

Lee, T. A. and R. H. Parker (1979). *The Evolution of Corporate Financial Reporting*, Nairobi Thomas Nelson & Sons.

Lefebvre-Teillard, A. (1982). *La Société Anonyme au 19ème Siècle*, Paris: PUF.

Lemarchand, Y. (1995). "1880-1914, l'échec de vérification des bilans. Le rendez-vous manqué de la normalization," *Comptabilité-Contrôle-Audit*, 1(1): 1–24.

Lutter. M. (1977). "Die Kontrolle der Kontrolleure," in W. Busse von Colbe and M. Lutter (eds): *Wirtschftsprüfung Heute: Entwicklung oder Reform?* Wiesbaden: Ein Bochumer Symposion.

Maltby, J. (1999). "A sort of guide, philosopher and friend: the rise of the professional auditor in Britain," *Accounting, Business and Financial History*, 9(1): 29–50.

Margerison, J. and P. Moizer (1996). "Auditor licensing in the European Union: a comparative study based on cultural differences," *European Accounting Review*, 5(1): 29–56.

Matthews, D., M. Anderson and J. R. Edwards (1998). *The Priesthood of Industry: The Rise of the Professional Accountant in British Management*, Oxford: Oxford University Press.

Micklethwait, J. and A. Wooldridge (2003). *The Company: A Short History of a Revolutionary Idea*, New York: Modern Library.

Miller, P. B. (1990). "On the interrelations between accounting and the state," *Accounting, Organizations and Society*, 15(4): 315–38.

Mueller, G. (1967). *International Accounting*, New York: Macmillan.

Nair, R. and W. Frank (1980). "The impact of disclosure and measurement practices on international accounting classification," *Accounting Review*, 55(3): 426–50.

Nobes, C. (1983). "A judgemental international classification of financial reporting practices," *Journal of Business, Finance and Accounting*, 10(1): 1–19.

Nobes. C. (1992). *International Classification of Financial Reporting*, 2e, London: Routledge.

Nobes, C. and R. Parker (1995). Comparative International Accounting, London: Prentice Hall.

Parker, R. H. (1986). *The Development of the Accountancy Profession in Britain to the Early Twentieth Century*. University of Alabama: Academy of Accounting Historians.

Parker, R. H. (2005). "Naming and branding: accountants and accountancy bodies in the British Empire and Commonwealth, 1853-2003," *Accounting History*, 10(1): 17–46.

Perera, M. (1989). "Towards a framework to analyse the impact of culture on accounting," *International Journal of Accounting*, 24(2): 42–56.

Quick, R. (1994). "Disciplinary actions against auditors in Germany," *Fourth Maastricht Auditing Research Symposium*, Maastricht, Netherlands: University of Limburg.

Quick, R., S. Turley and M. Willekens (2007). *Auditing, Trust and Governance: Developing Regulation in Europe*, London: Routledge.

Ramirez, C. (2001). "Understanding social closure in its cultural context: accounting practitioners in France (1920-1939)," *Accounting, Organizations and Society* 26(4–5): 391–418.

Ramirez, C. (2009). "Constructing the governable small practitioner: the changing nature of professional bodies and the management of professional accountants' identities in the UK," *Accounting, Organizations and Society*, 34(3–4): 381–408.

Savary, J. (1676). *Le parfait négociant ou instruction général pour ce qui regarde le commerce de toute sort de marchandises, tant France que des pays étrangers*. Paris: Chez la Veuve Estienne.

Schulze-Osterloh, J. (1977). "Stellung und Unabhängigkeit des Wirtschaftsprüfers," in W. Busse von Colbe and M. Lutter M (eds). *Wirtschaftsprüfung Heute: Entwicklung oder Reform?* Wiesbaden, Germany: Ein Bochumer Symposion.

Standish, P. (1990). "Origins of the Plan Comptable Général: a study in cultural intrusion and reaction," *Accounting and Business Research*, 20(80): 337–52.

Taylor, M., T. Evans and A. Jay (1986). "The impact of IASC accounting standards on comparability and consistency of international accounting reporting practices," *International Journal of Accounting*, 22(1): 53–67.

Walker, S. P. (1993). "Anatomy of a Scottish CA practice: Lindsay, Jamieson & Haldane 1818-1918," *Accounting, Business and Financial History*, 3(2): 127–54.

Walker, S. P. (2004). "Conflict, collaboration, fuzzy jurisdictions and partial settlements. Accountants, lawyers and insolvency practice during the late 19th century," *Accounting and Business Research*, 34(3): 247–65.

Willmott, H., A. Puxty, K. Robson, D. Cooper and T. Lowe (1992). "Regulation of accountancy and accountants: a comparative analysis of accounting for research and development in four advanced capitalist countries," *Accounting Auditing and Accountability Journal*, 5(2): 32–56.

10

ETHICS

Paul Williams

The glorification of warfare and machismo *may, indeed, be older in the history of human cultures than the emphasis on alleviating suffering regardless of the class or gender of the sufferer, but it is this latter outlook, which has deep roots in the great religious traditions of the world ... to which I shall refer by the name "ethics".* (Putnam, 2004: 23)

1 Introduction

Persons certified or chartered as accountants are generally presumed to be members of a profession as attorneys, medical doctors or clergymen are. They are learned, autonomous, committed to serving the public good and bound by a code of conduct to practice their profession ethically. Thus when we think about accounting and ethics we uncritically assume that the conjunction of these two concepts is the behaviour of individuals who practice the discipline of accounting. Ethics conjoined with accounting means nothing but the appropriate behaviour of individual practitioners. Much of the literature and most of the instruction in accounting that pertains to ethics is about what individuals should or should not do as practitioners. The purpose of this chapter is to provide a critique of that perspective on accounting ethics by arguing that a better perspective for understanding the ethicality of accounting is not a focus on the conduct of individual practitioners, which is certainly important, but a focus on the practice of accounting itself. The perspective provided on accounting ethics in this chapter is, rather than accounting as a practice of ethical professionals, one of practitioners of an ethical profession. The development of this perspective begins with a discussion of what constitutes a profession and what being a profession implies about the ethical conduct of its practitioners. This discussion is followed by a description of what the professional ethics of accountants are as they state them in their code, which, in turn, leads into an alternative portrayal of what are ethics more suitable to a profession. Following this is a lengthy explanation of how, by the ethical ends of the profession of accounting, accounting has failed to fulfill its ethical obligations and the reasons this is so. The chapter concludes with an argument for a different perspective on the accountant's actual role in society that is more compatible with accounting being a profession whose social function better resembles ethically that of medicine and law.

2 Professional ethics

According to Kultgen (1988) professions have certain defining characteristics.[1] The most common ones are that

1   a profession involves a skill based on theoretical knowledge;
2   the skill requires extensive and intensive training and education;
3   the professional must demonstrate competence by passing a test;
4   the profession is organised and it is represented by associations of distinctive character;
5   integrity is maintained by adherence to a code of conduct;
6   professional service is altruistic;
7   the professional assumes responsibility for the affairs of others;
8   professional service is indispensable for the public good;
9   professionals are licensed, so their work is sanctioned by the community;
10 professionals are independent practitioners, serving individual clients;
11 they have a fiduciary relationship toward their clients;
12 they do their best to serve their clients impartially without regard to any special relationship;
13 they are compensated by a fee or fixed charge.

(Kultgen, 1988: 60)

The essence of these basic characteristics is that a member of a profession applies a neutral, technical skill that requires considerable education and a certification of competence via a non-market process of legal certification. The skill provided by the professional is essential to the community and the skill is provided for its own sake and not instrumentally for profit: the service is regarded as being altruistic. Individual professionals are guided in their behaviour by a code of ethics or conduct designed to ensure that the profession consists of individuals who behave ethically when exercising their professional skills. What constitutes ethical conduct for most professions is an overarching mandate to practice professional skills in order to advance the public interest; that is, to contribute to advancing the general welfare.

Accounting seems to possess Kultgen's 13 characteristics but, importantly, there is ambiguity about three of them that makes status as a profession problematic for accounting. As we shall see later in this chapter characteristic number six is problematic since the professional code specifically indicates accounting is not altruistic in the ends it seeks. It is also questionable whether characteristic eight is apposite since, as will be demonstrated later, the current ends sought by the profession make it doubtful that accounting services are currently indispensible for the public good. Finally, characteristic ten is quite problematic since the accounting profession, whose professional status derives from the audit function, serves two masters: the auditee who pays them; and, allegedly, the public on whose behalf the audit is being performed.

Thus, what is (in) the public interest may be more problematic for the accounting profession than for others. The example of medicine presents perhaps the simplest case of a profession serving the public interest. Health is, if anything is, a pre-requisite to human happiness (Deaton, 2013). Every member of the public may be presumed to desire health and freedom from pain. Those few who may not so desire may easily avoid health and absence of pain with only the eventual assistance of nature. Thus, the skills that physicians possess, which are designed to restore health and alleviate pain, are skills essential to achieving something vital to the public interest. Physicians treat individual patients (clients) without regard to any consideration other than that the patient is in need of medical attention. There is egalitarianism to the plying of medical skills and it is that egalitarianism that contributes to what physicians do being in the public interest. This is captured in the Hippocratic Oath (modern version written by Louis Lasagna in 1964):

I swear to fulfill, to the best of my ability and judgment, this covenant:...

I will respect the hard-won scientific gains of those physicians in whose steps I walk, and gladly share such knowledge as is mine with those who are to follow.

I will apply, for the benefit of the sick, all measures which are required, avoiding those twin traps of overtreatment and therapeutic nihilism.

I will remember that there is art to medicine as well as science, and that warmth, sympathy, and understanding may outweigh the surgeon's knife or the chemist's drug.

I will not be ashamed to say "I know not," nor will I fail to call in my colleagues when the skills of another are needed for a patient's recovery.

I will respect the privacy of my patients, for their problems are not disclosed to me that the world may know. Most especially must I tread with care in matters of life and death. Above all, I must not play at God.

I will remember that I do not treat a fever chart, a cancerous growth, but a sick human being, whose illness may affect the person's family and economic stability. My responsibility includes these related problems, if I am to care adequately for the sick.

I will prevent disease whenever I can, for prevention is preferable to cure.

I will remember that I remain a member of society, with special obligations to *all my fellow human beings, those sound of mind and body as well as the infirm* (emphasis added).

If I do not violate this oath, may I enjoy life and art, respected while I live and remembered with affection thereafter. May I always act so as to preserve the finest traditions of my calling and may I long experience the joy of healing those who seek my help.

(Lasagna, 1964)

By adhering to this oath of virtues individual physicians might reasonably justify that they are acting in the public interest.

Law, another paradigmatic profession, serves a public interest but not in the same manner as a physician. The ethical practice of law requires the appropriate legal system if it is to serve the public interest. Presumably, justice is something desired by everyone. There is ample evidence from numerous fields including anthropology, evolutionary psychology, behavioural economics and so on, that humans possess an innate public good urge and that they are willing to incur substantial costs to achieve justice (Basu, 2011; Corning, 2011; Tomasello, 2009). As Adam Smith (1982: 85) notes: "Society may subsist, though not in the most comfortable state, without beneficence; but the prevalence of injustice must utterly destroy it." An attorney advocates for his or her client and justice is done because of the adversarial system of justice. A second attorney advocates for the opposing client (the State in the instance of those accused of a crime). It is through this adversarial process of single-minded focusing by attorneys on both sides that presumably leads to a just outcome. Thus, in many countries an attorney is provided to anyone accused of a crime, gratis, so that justice is not meted out by how much money one has.[2]

The profession of accounting is based on its control of the technique of double-entry accounting (DEA), which is a technology available since at least the fifteenth century (Soll, 2014), 300 years before there emerged a profession of accounting. This technology was part of the repertoire of well-educated persons, particularly European merchant-traders. Like mathematics, DEA was owned by everyone, like an open-source program, and this openness is the explanation for why we continue to refer to the body of accounting standards as GAAP – "generally accepted accounting principles." Today DEA consists of vast numbers of codified procedures created by formal regulatory organisations, so the process by which DEA develops over time is no longer one of the general acceptance of principles via an open-source process that is organic and embedded in the social practices of merchants, governments and so on. However, by the mid-eighteenth century the technique of DEA was captured by a group of practitioners of the craft who managed to become chartered, thus bringing the power of the state to bear in creating a nascent profession. Today DEA is owned by a collection of persons who refer to themselves as a profession (Chabrek, Cooper, Catchpole and Williams, 2016). In the fifteenth century DEA was a technique like plane geometry or calculus that could be adapted by anyone to their own particular circumstances. However, by the mid-nineteenth century, DEA had become a commodity controlled by an organised group of persons for whom DEA formed the foundation of a profession and a basis for regulating business toward certain ends.

As a profession, accounting has the responsibility to demonstrate how the ownership of DEA allows it to serve the public interest. Unlike medical technology or legal knowledge the connection between accounting technology and the public interest is more difficult to demonstrate. This makes accounting's claim to professional status via serving the public interest much more tenuous to make. The reason for this is that the clients of accounting professionals seek those services to gain an advantage over their fellow citizens. For an ailing client of a physician restoration of that client's health does not of necessity subtract from the health of others; for the client of an attorney, achieving justice for him or herself does not subtract necessarily from the justice available to others. As Williams (2014: 165) states:

> The clients served by professional accountants are mainly ones seeking through those services an advantage over everyone else. What is distinctive about accounting clients that is different from medicine or law is that they have the means to acquire accounting services and the interests to need them. Any person may get sick and need a physician; any person may get "in trouble with the law" and need an attorney who will be provided to them whether they can afford one or not. But clients seeking accounting services seek them to pursue interests that bear no *necessary* (emphasis in original) relationship to what society deems in its interest. Thus, for accountants "service to clients" does not automatically provide for the public interest....[3]

2.1 The professional ethics of accountants

That service to clients does not automatically provide for the public interest is readily discernible from the manner in which the Code of Professional Conduct of the American Institute of Public Accountants (AICPA) is structured. The Code is over 180 pages long – a manual that articulates what a professional accountant may and may not do. It is a code of conduct and not a code of ethics. The do's and do not's are allegedly derived from six basic principles, which may be intended as *ethical* principles. These principles are: responsibilities; the public interest; integrity; objectivity and independence; due care; and the scope and nature of services (AICPA, 2015: 5–7). The first two of these principles, responsibility and the public interest, are principles that effectively circumscribe the ethical burden of accountants relative to that of physicians or lawyers.

"Responsibilities" require professionals to "exercise sensitive professional and moral judgments in all their activities" (AICPA, 2015: 5). However, the requirements of responsibilities extend only to those who use the accountant's services. "The public interest" principle is a tour de force in circular definitions. For professional accountants who are members of the AICPA, "[t]he public interest is defined as the collective well-being of the community of people and institutions that the profession serves" (2015: 5). Unlike medicine and law, where the public whose interest is served is the community of all human beings because all need health care or justice, for accountants the public constituting the public interest is circumscribed to include only those persons (corporate as well as flesh and blood humans) the profession chooses to serve. Thus, unlike professions that, at least theoretically, provide to all equally something good for all, accounting provides something good to just those for whom the good provided is worth paying for. The element of altruism is decidedly absent from the accounting profession's reckoning of who its professional expertise serves.

The Code of Conduct derived from these principles specifies which actions, relationships and so on are permissible or not permissible for a member of the AICPA. The Code acts as a guide to permissible means through which an accountant may serve the profession's particular, limited specification of the public interest. So long as the professional accountant's behaviour comports with the mandates of the Code of Conduct, he or she may be construed to be acting ethically. Similarly, violating the provisions of the Code constitutes unethical behaviour, which is illustrated most vividly by the demise of Arthur Andersen, formerly the leading accounting services firm. The demise of the firm was brought on by Andersen employees' numerous violations of the Code provisions associated with Andersen's client Enron. Ironically, though numerous Code of Conduct violations were committed by Andersen's auditors of Enron, the case can be made that it is the rationale of the professional code of conduct that undermined that code. Because the Code stipulates the public interest as constituted of the interests of the entities it serves and Enron's was the interest being served, the Code failed to induce within Andersen auditors at Enron the ethical will to prevent Enron's fraud. The harm done to so many people, perhaps none more so than those who depended on Enron for their livelihoods, are the public yet the public's interest was not served.

The remainder of the chapter is devoted to an attempted explanation of why accounting professional codes of conduct aimed at serving the public interest ironically frequently fail to do so in often spectacular ways.

3 Ethics defined

In the Western tradition there has been an ongoing conversation about ethics for over two millennia. Ethical schools abound – deontology, virtue, intuitionism, utilitarianism (act or rule) – as do all manner of religious variations on what God expects of his minions. For the purposes of this chapter it is essential that some sense of what is meant by the ethical that is germane to the accounting profession is articulated. That accounting has significant effects on society has been noted by the sociologist Andrew Abbott who has extensively studied professions. He noted that in today's society there are neglected professions that have not been studied sufficiently to get a fuller understanding of the nature of professions. According to Abbott:

> The most important subjects for such investigations will be understudied professions like accounting and psychology. In particular, the jurisdiction of money requires the kind of attention long received by health. Perhaps sociologists and historians, as biological individuals, concern themselves more with the profession of life and death than with the profession of loss and profit, but surely *accounting is today far more socially important than medicine.*
>
> *(Abbott, 1988: 325; emphasis added)*

In what ways is it the case that accounting is more socially important than medicine? Certainly for most people the vast majority of their lives is lived in relative good health. Except for periodic episodes of ill health from accidents, encounters with certain bacteria or viruses and so on, most people live each day out from under the influence or control of the medical profession. Likewise, most people have but sporadic interactions with attorneys, the majority of which occur when real estate transactions are consummated, wills are signed or divorces granted. However, everyone everyday is concerned with making a living. Except in the rare case of a Ben Gunn or Robinson Crusoe, making a living entails social activity – the means of living for most human beings are provided collectively (Alperovitz and Daly, 2008; Milanovic, 2011; Corning, 2011) and the complex of economic relationships among people is to a substantial extent mediated through accounting. Indeed, how much wherewithal each of us has to live on is to no small extent determined by ukases written in the language of accounting. A simple, some would say sophomoric, example will help to illustrate the power and reach of accounting to affect peoples' well-being.

The following example is derived from Williams (2010: 27) and Bayou, Reinstein and Williams (2011: 121). Accounting reports are reports about entities. Even as individuals we represent an entity as a taxpayer and we are required to prepare accounting reports about our activities in order to ascertain how much tax we pay. According to accounting logic all economic activity is conducted by entities, because without entities accounting reports are not possible. All manner of entities affect our lives, but the most significant ones in the modern era are those upon which people are dependent for their livelihoods, mainly incorporated businesses. Corporations are by far the most significant economic actors in terms of their power and reach. The consequences of their actions extend to nearly everyone.

Piketty (2014: 315) reports that in the United States, at least, the factor contributing to the highly skewed distribution of income has been the returns to labor of corporate executives, the so-called "Supermanagers." Compensation of the managerial class in most Anglo-Saxon societies has grown exorbitantly relative to the compensation of the median labourer. Because corporations act as wealth concentrators they provide a reservoir of resources that may be distributed largely at the discretion of the managers who operate them (Reich, 2015). This reservoir of resources is defined largely by accounting conventions through the balance sheet: Assets = Liabilities + Net Assets. The Net Assets of any corporation represent the wealth of that corporation and signifies the distributable amount of that wealth. Periodic enhancements to that wealth are represented by the income equation: Net income = Revenues – Expenses, the components of which are defined by accounting conventions.

The seemingly simple and straightforward income equation, however, conceals a great deal about the corporate form's reach and influence over the lives of people. The conventional interpretation of Net Income = Revenues – Expenses is that net income is the result of activities that lead to describing it as being earned (net income is frequently referred to as 'earnings'). As earnings, net income is bestowed with an aura of virtue because net income is, after all, earned or deserved. Thus, the income equation is loaded with ethical significance since it is a statement about a morally desirable thing – profit which is earned. Friedman (1970) famously proclaims that the sole purpose of business is to make as much profit as it can within the rules of the game. A key tenet of the moral defense of capitalism lies in the belief that profit seeking in competitive markets leads to material prosperity for everyone so long as the rules of the capitalist game are confined to enforcing property rights, making for enforceable contracts, and for governments to provide for defense.[4] Other than that a society organised around markets will be optimal for producing prosperity and happiness for the most people. On the basis of this logic the income equation is an expression of a profoundly ethical nature.

However, as Bayou *et al.* (2011) and Williams (2010) demonstrate the income equation also hides a great deal about the ethical significance of accounting. As anyone who has completed a first course in accounting knows the elements of the income equation come with valences reflecting value judgments about good and bad. Net income is good. Revenues are good. Expenses are bad. Thus, to maximise net income, the ultimate good thing for a firm to seek, the firm must seek to increase its revenues and reduce its expenses. But what is happening when net income is being maximised? The components of the income equation can be expanded and labeled with more literal descriptions, thus:

Net Income = Revenues – Expenses
Gross income of shareholders = Cost to consumers of goods and services – gross incomes of workers – gross incomes of suppliers – gross incomes of creditors – gross incomes of governments – net externalities – capital allowance.

Viewed in this way, it is apparent that the income equation expresses just one particular preference for what good the business firm can do. Hidden from explicit consideration is that the avenues available for accomplishing that good are potentially significant bad things. In the world of utopian economics represented by general equilibrium theory everyone gets what they are worth because no one has more power than another, which implies markets price everything appropriately. In the world inhabited by flesh and blood human beings, however, where the bulk of economic activity is conducted by oligopolistic business corporations, power is not equally distributed and the simplistic assurances about the magical workings of invisible hands are, therefore, suspect.

Expressed as such, the income equation makes it clear that the "gross income of shareholders" is not by any necessity the thing that must occupy the left-hand side of the equation. The equation could be expressed, for example, as follows:

Net externalities = Cost to consumers of goods and services – gross incomes of shareholders, workers, suppliers, creditors and governments – capital allowance.

In this form the equation signifies that the role of the corporation is to maximise net externalities rather than shareholder income. In a different formulation the equation could be written:

Costs to consumers of goods and services = gross incomes of shareholders + workers + suppliers + creditors + governments – net externalities – capital allowances.

In this form the corporation is a producer of goods and services whose value is allocated among numerous stakeholders by whatever algorithm leads to a just outcome. Whatever form the equation takes requires some choice about the purpose of the corporation and that choice is invariably one fraught with ethical ramifications. That is so because the ends to be pursued are at issue, and ends, at least of human beings and institutions, are value laden. What is the good end or ends to which corporations are directed? That is the rub and a highly significant consideration for accounting not as a collection of ethical professionals, but collectively as an ethical profession.

Returning to the quote at the head of the chapter: what is ethics for an ethical profession? As Putnam defines ethics, it is in essence the alleviation of human suffering. Ethics or morality[5] involves relationships; it speaks in the second person (Darwall, 2006). No matter how meticulous an individual's conduct vis-à-vis some moral code, if the ends served by that conduct do not produce good outcomes for others or actually do others harm, then the individual is not serving a moral purpose even though following the code. In organisational contexts, Adams and Balfour (1998) describe the phenomenon of moral practitioners serving immoral ends as "administrative evil." One vivid example they use to illustrate the phenomenon is one involving the accountants who worked for the German Rail Authority; Adams and Balfours' chilling account is instructive of the distinction between an ethical professional and an ethical profession:

> Bureaucratic procedure had to be followed, however, and dictated that no agency, including the Gestapo or the SS, could simply use the trains as they saw fit. The German Rail Authority derived its revenue from individual clients and organizations requiring space on its trains. The client for the trains to the death camps was the Gestapo, and the travelers – one way only – were Jews. The fare, payable by Gestapo offices, was calculated at the passenger rate, third class, for the number of track kilometers, one way only, with discounts for children. Group rates were applied to transports exceeding 400 individuals. For the guards, the round trip fare had to be paid. It was in this routine, matter-of-fact way that whole communities were transported to their deaths.
>
> *(1998: 67)*

This potential evil residing in the conduct of accountants is derived from the central place of accounting in the bureaucratic administration of modern societies (Graeber, 2015). If the focus of professional ethics is confined to prescribing the conduct of individual practitioners as they ply their technical skills, then there arises the genuine danger that those technical skills will serve ends that are contrary to human well-being. As Bayou *et al.* (2011) argue, the essential role of accounting in contemporary society is situating corporate businesses in time and the more thorough the situating the more complete is the narrative about what a business has done. And the more complete the narrative, the more noble is the narrative. For good or ill the conscience of the corporate form of business lies in the laws and regulations that govern its conduct. Corporations may be persons in the eyes of the US Supreme Court, but they are not persons in the most fundamental sense of being capable of experiencing human moral emotions like guilt or shame and acting upon them. Accounting is thus a central element of the legal regulatory apparatus that guides corporate behaviour; accounting is part of any society's justice system and, thus, performs an essentially ethical function. It is on the basis of how well accounting performs this function that accounting must assess itself as an ethical profession. The next section discusses how, currently, the profession argues it is fulfilling that function and provides a critique of how that argument is inadequate for an ethical profession.

4 Practitioner means and a profession's ends

According to the AICPA Code of Conduct what imposes a public interest responsibility on members of the profession is the particular public "who rely on the objectivity and integrity of *members* to maintain the *orderly functioning of commerce*" (emphasis added) (AICPA 2015: 5). Of course what constitutes the "orderly functioning of commerce" is fraught with ambiguity and contentiousness. Since its inception in the nineteenth century, the profession has subscribed to a certain view of what is entailed for the profession to fulfill that basic aim. History, particularly recent history, calls that view into question and suggests it is time to seriously reconsider that view and whether the ends served by the profession can reasonably be considered ethical ones.

4.1 Accounting and financial crisis

The "orderly functioning of commerce" was recently disrupted by the onset of the Great Recession, sometime during 2008. While what caused it will be disputed forever many have already attributed it to the liberalisation of the financial markets in many countries of the world, most notably led by the US financialisation of many Western economies (Phillips, 2002), the dramatic increase in the complexity of financial instruments, and the *de jure* and *de facto* deregulation of financial markets created a dramatic increase in systemic risk across the global financial system (Posner, 2010). A major feature of the financial system erected over the last century and a half to cool speculative fevers (Shiller, 2000) and, thus, reduce the danger of excessive systemic risk has been the evolution of a system of financial reporting. This system has been constructed in accordance with certain presumptions of how and what to report that includes an attestation function performed by the accounting profession. When the profession refers to its end of providing for the orderly functioning of commerce, it is this attestation role by which the profession mainly accomplishes that end. The financial reporting system prominently features standard-setting bodies, the Financial Accounting Standards Board (FASB) in the United States and the International Accounting Standards Board (IASB) in most of the rest of the world, who assume the power to prescribe the content of financial reports to which the profession attests. Since the financial crisis, a decidedly disorderly functioning of commerce occurring in spite of this system, the financial reporting component of the financial system, prominently featuring the accounting profession, now merits some critical scrutiny. Just how might the accounting profession be implicated in the crisis?

One notable observation about accounting's role in the financial crisis is offered by the Nobel economist Paul Krugman:

> Let me quote from a speech that Lawrence Summers, then deputy Treasury secretary (and now the Obama administration's top economist), gave in 1999. "If you ask why the American financial system succeeds," he said, "at least my reading of the history would be that there is no innovation more important than that of generally accepted accounting principles: it means that every investor gets to see information presented on a comparable basis; that there is discipline on company managements in the way they report and monitor their activities." And he went on to declare that there is "an ongoing process that really is what makes our capital market work and work as stably as it does."
>
> So here's what Mr. Summers – and, to be fair, just about everyone in a policy-making position at the time – believed in 1999: America has honest corporate accounting; this lets investors make good decisions, and also forces management to behave responsibly; and the result is a stable, well-functioning financial system.
>
> What percentage of all this turned out to be true? Zero.
>
> *(Krugman, 2009:A27)*

Juxtapose Krugman's assessment with an apologia for the banking system's egregious failures, written by two very prominent US academics:

> Our analysis leads us to conclude, as have others, that contrary to what critics of fair value contend, fair value accounting played little or no role in the Financial Crisis. However, transparency of information associated with measurement and recognition of accounting amounts relating to, and disclosure of information about, asset

securitizations and derivatives likely was insufficient for investors to assess properly the values and riskiness of affected bank assets and liabilities.

(Barth and Landsman, 2010: 417)

On one hand Krugman explicates reporting did the obvious: financial reporting did not *prevent* the financial crisis. Barth and Landsman seem quite satisfied to argue that at least reporting didn't *cause* the financial crisis, so the financial reporting system is vindicated except for the failure to require even more disclosure "to enable market participants to assess the risks related to the assets to which the bank is exposed" (2010: 417).

Professional accountants whose professional purpose is to play the critical role in the financial reporting system may find solace in their not having caused the financial crisis, but surely the public would be dismayed at such an attitude since the cost of the financial reporting system is not inconsiderable. To the layman that cost might seem a particularly heavy price to pay for something that merely doesn't cause financial crises. Of course Krugman's reference to Larry Summers' approbation of financial reporting and Barth and Landsman's call for even more transparent financial reporting both imply that the presumed role of financial reporting is indeed to *prevent* financial crises since no one but classical economists would consider such massive disruption to millions of peoples' lives an orderly functioning of commerce. That the United States and parts of Europe have yet to recover from financial crises is fairly compelling empirical evidence that the current system of financial reporting has not succeeded in doing that.[6] One conjecture explored in the following pages is that accounting professionals (and scholars) have abandoned the metaphor that defined accounting for centuries of its development and adopted an inappropriate metaphor to define what end accounting is to play in the global financial system (Johnson, 1993).

4.2 The over-and-over again solution

Financial crises have recurred throughout the history of capitalism and the history of the accounting profession in the United States is intimately connected to these crises (Previts and Merino, 1998). Cycles of financial crises after the US Civil War prompted increased federal regulation of corporations engaged in interstate commerce and also encouraged the development of a public accounting profession. Developing a profession of accounting during the latter half of the nineteenth century was partially rationalised by the belief that part of the solution to financial crises was "publicity."[7] In spite of repeated financial scandals and crises, faith in the institution of self-correcting financial markets persists; that is, the market *per se* does not lead to financial crises, but simply a market in which some critical number of investors have too little information.[8] Thus the accounting remedy for financial crises relies on the market itself via greater disclosure of information into the market. A basic premise behind the publicity solution to financial crises is that financial market participants (investors [more aptly, speculators] and creditors), if provided adequate good information, would act rationally within the market and market forces themselves would mitigate the risk of financial crises. An independent public accounting profession acquires its legitimacy as a profession from the publicity solution since the profession provides the assurance that financial information about firms is sufficient and reliable. Following the standard economic assumption about the economic rationality of investors in the markets, firms have compelling incentives to provide such verified financial information so as to avoid the discounting of share prices that theoretically results when rational investors know less about a firm than they do about other firms.

In spite of the seemingly impeccable logic of this strategy for building a system of financial reporting, it has never worked effectively. The well-informed market alone as a failsafe against financial crisis has repeatedly failed to prevent crises. In the post-World War I period there occurred a drifting away from the nineteenth-century Progressive movement's skepticism of the self-regulating market and a re-emergence of anti-regulatory, free-market economic policies. The 1920s saw a period similar in substantive respects to the current period. There was greater concentration of wealth in a small proportion of the population. During the decade between the end of World War I (1919) and the Crash of 1929, the top 1 per cent of income recipients in the United States went from 15 per cent of the total income to 24 per cent of total income (Reich, 2010). Similarly, the anti-regulatory, free-market policies (the neo-liberal revolution) of the 1980s, in both the United States and United Kingdom led to an income distribution in both countries nearly identical to that preceding the Crash of 1929.[9] Greater income concentration in both epochs was accompanied by greater speculative investing and a larger role for finance in the economy (Phillips, 2002; Reich, 2010).

After the 1929 Crash, the publicity strategy re-emerged as a palliative for apparent market failure but was amended with respect to the role to be played by the accounting profession. Somewhat ironically, rather than relying only on market forces to provide demand for audited financial information, the US Congress enacted into law a *requirement* that a Certified Public Accountant (CPA) be employed by the auditee to provide assurances about financial information. The accounting profession was also empowered by the SEC via the Committee on Accounting Procedure to establish what the content of the financial reports was to be in order for sufficient publicity to prevent market breakdowns from occurring. Even though publicity, through the provision of audited financial statements, did not prevent the financial crisis of 1929, the belief persisted that publicity via the CPA attestation of information was still a viable solution and that mandating that CPAs be admitted through the doors of publicly traded companies was the necessary remedy to the financial reporting system.

The most recent financial crisis indicates that even an elaborate code of complex reporting standards and the legal mandate to purchase the services of CPAs to ensure publicity has, once again, not worked to prevent financial crisis. Even this system of complex reporting standards and the legal requirement that auditors be granted entry to the firm hasn't prevented WorldCom, Enron, Global Crossing, AIG, Bank of America, the housing bubble, Lehman Brothers, HSBC and so on. Once again the financial reporting system failed to provide the publicity that prevents financial crises, the disorderly functioning of commerce.

However, showing remarkable faith in the publicity solution, the US Congress' response to the most recent succession of financial crises was to enact the 2002 Sarbanes-Oxley (SOX) Act. SOX altered the financial reporting system once again by forcing auditees to pay CPAs not only for assurance about financial reports but also for assessment of their internal controls. In addition, the government will now regulate the profession directly (via the Public Company Accounting Oversight Board [PCAOB]) as well. The accounting profession is to lose a considerable amount of its ability to self-regulate, a key defining characteristic of a profession, in order to assure that the self-regulatory power of financial markets will work as persistently believed it will. A popular definition of insanity is to keep doing the same thing over and over again expecting a different outcome. Yet that is what the publicity strategy has amounted to over the last century and a half. At this juncture, if we are to learn anything from history, then we must begin to ask some very serious questions about why the strategy of publicity continues to fail us. Perhaps the accounting profession needs to seriously entertain the prospect that the basic premise behind the publicity solution is part of the problem, and that the problem is more serious than one of simply finding better methods of implementation. That is that the presumably good end served by the profession is not so good after all.

4.3 "Reckonings"

Soll's (2014) recent book on the history of DEA is entitled *The Reckoning*, which provides, probably unintentionally, keen insight into a basic confusion of the profession about the technology it owns. Through historical vignettes, chapter by chapter, Soll illustrates an inherent tension that exists within DEA as a system of reckoning. According to Soll, DEA may be understood as a system of reckoning in a calculative sense – a guide to rational behaviour – which is the sense on which the publicity solution is based. Simultaneously DEA also provides a record of that rational behavior which allows for a "reckoning" in another sense, that of rendering judgments about that behaviour by others. As Williams (2015: 1), in his review of the book, explains it:

> The title, *The Reckoning*, is a triple *entendre'*. Accounting is a system of gathering information for "reckoning," i.e., figuring out and charting a course. This is the sense of reckoning that dominates contemporary understanding of accounting epitomized by the official purpose of accounting being the provision of information useful for making rational economic decisions. Reckoning also connotes accountability, epitomized in the expression "the day of reckoning" which, in Christian lore, we all must face when we are confronted by St. Peter at the Heavenly Gates (where we find out what we have to pay for our sins). There is yet a third sense in which Soll uses the concept of reckoning and it is what the book aims to provide – a "reckoning" of a profession that has in substantial ways been a poor steward of the powerful tool it co-opted and commodified starting in the late nineteenth century.

The accounting profession's failure to prevent financial crises may be partly attributable to a failure to explicitly acknowledge this inherent tension in DEA and consequently to have opted for the wrong root metaphor for what accounting is vis-à-vis financial reporting and, thus, for what is the proper end to be served by the profession. Root metaphors are those metaphors that we use to "describe worlds" (Brown, 1989: 84). The importance of root metaphors lies in the way they structure and bound how the world may be viewed. Once a field of enquiry has adopted some root metaphor to describe what it is about, the results of its enquiries are predictable. For Brown: "root metaphors are frameworks for interpreting meaning within which sense become facts, facts become concepts, and concepts become discourse" (1989: 96). The publicity strategy is predicated on a root metaphor of information (Ravenscroft and Williams, 2009) – reckoning in the calculative sense. Accounting's function in society is thus an enabling one; its function in the capitalist financial system is to abet that system by providing it with an allegedly crucial input – information suitable for calculating the best course of action for a capital provider vis-à-vis a particular firm. Thus accounting is an activity that is analogous to any other activity whose purpose is to simply inform, for example journalism, weather forecasting, medical laboratory work and so on. The FASB (1978) (and IASB) explicitly states that the purpose of financial reporting is to provide useful information for making scarce resource allocation decisions and that the contribution financial reporting makes is to improve the efficiency with which capital is allocated. Therefore, the rules, principles, regulations and so on that comprise the technical corpus of professional, financial reporting knowledge are conceived as recipes for representing economic reality that enable prediction about future economic states, that is as guides for producing information that is useful for *rational* economic decision making (users reckon that they should do this rather than that). If accomplished sufficiently well then sufficient information to accomplish "publicity" will result, which, given the self-regulatory properties of markets, will prevent financial market failures that produce financial crises. Financial crises are largely the result of insufficient information for the market to reckon correctly.

4.4 Utopian economics

This wrong metaphor derives its current power over the financial reporting system and the accounting profession from the intellectual ascendance, starting in the late 1960s, of neo-liberal thinking in the economic and political realm (Ravenscroft and Williams, 2009). As Chabrak (2012) has shown, the rise of neo-liberal economic and political thinking was abetted by the investment of substantial sums of money by the corporate community into the creation of neo-liberal think tanks and political action groups set up to reverse the expansion of the New Deal welfare state in the United States and Fabian Socialism in the United Kingdom, and to create more market-driven societies around the world (Jones, 2012). The core intellectual substance of this neo-liberal movement is a utopian economics (Cassidy, 2009: 8) whose roots lie in the interpretations of Adam Smith inspired by Hayek and operationalised by Friedman's Chicago School of economists. That this Chicago school economics is utopian has been demonstrated by enumerable recent critiques by Friedman's fellow economists (e.g. Medema, 2009; Ormerod, 1994; Chang, 2010; Foley, 2006; Nelson, 2001; Shiller, 2000; Keen, 2001, Mirowski, 2013).

The utopianism of the economic foundations of the financial reporting system is explained by Marglin (2008). There are four basic premises that make up the ontology of Chicago's Friedman school of economics (and thus the information metaphor, publicity strategy link), all of which Marglin demonstrates are myths. These myths Stephen Marglin identifies (2008: 45) as individualism; knowledge as algorithm; community as equal to the nation state; and unlimited wants. According to Marglin these premises are not 'true' in the sense that they correspond to the world in which humans actually live. They are cultural myths that are based on a particular set of value judgments. There is historical precedent for the belief that the principal contributor to the recent Great Recession is the product of the re-ascendance of these very myths holding sway over economic and accounting policy makers over the last generation (Reich, 2010; Galbraith, 2008; Hacker and Pierson, 2010).

Considering each in turn: the myth of individualism is the familiar economic man who "is fixed and unchanging; he is a responsible actor at all times and places; his preferences are not up for discussion, evaluation, or analysis; finally, he is self-interested in a particularly narrow way" (Marglin, 2008: 45). This is the basis of the methodological individualism of economics – the supposition that all social phenomena can be explained from considering only the actions of individuals. Society is, thus, merely the summation of individual actions. Recent work in cognitive psychology and behavioural economics provides evidence for the mythical character of the individualism premise (Ariely, 2008). Basu (2011), citing recent economic research indicating that humans have a "public good urge," makes methodological individualism an untenable position.[10] Yet without a world populated by ubiquitous and persistent rational economic actors, the publicity strategy alone preventing financial crises is a remote prospect.

Knowledge as algorithm is the privileging of algorithmic forms of knowledge over knowledge that comes from experience (Marglin, 2008: 46). This myth is the claim that all valid knowledge must take a calculative form; that is, the form associated with the natural sciences. The problem with this particular mythology is that it exiles moral considerations from economic affairs and, ironically, condemns economics to fail as a discipline that has produced any such valid knowledge

(Flyvberg, 2001; Rosenberg, 1992; Mlodinow, 2008). The publicity strategy's allegiance to the myth of algorithmic knowledge sustains the illusion that financial reporting is simply a technical problem, which has a solution; that is, DEA can actually provide information sufficient for calculation for what is essentially an ethical problem. However, no such solution exists (Roberts, 2009).

The community being equal to the nation state myth is critical to economics' exclusive focus on efficiency; it allows economics to avoid considerations of power and the problem of distributive justice. Distribution is a problem for the nation state, not for economics, and is thus placed outside the purview of economics (Marglin, 2008: 46). The acceptance of this myth for the design of the financial reporting system is to likewise ignore the distributional consequences of that system by the singular focus on making markets only more efficient rather than also more just. The externalities imposed on the community by economic actors are not a problem for economics since they are dealt with by the state.

'Unlimited wants' is the myth that, "It is human nature that we always want more than we have and that there is consequently never enough" (Marglin, 2008: 47). Besides this being an overly simplistic and empirically invalid assertion about human nature (Corning, 2011), it makes the standard textbook definition of economics as the science of satisfying unlimited wants with limited resources an irrational end for the discipline to pursue since, by definition, it is impossible to satisfy unlimited wants with limited resources. From a practical, policy perspective, if resources are limited, wisdom would advise we limit our wants to what the resources can provide. The publicity strategy's acceptance of the unlimited wants myth deafens financial reporting policy to considerations of appropriate human ends and notions of common welfare.

Thus, the premises of utopian economics are highly implausible in the sense that they seem not to correspond to the world in which humans actually live. They are cultural myths; if relied upon for making policy they produce a financial reporting system based on a particular set of value judgments and not a system based on the world we actually inhabit. There is historical precedent for the belief that the principal contributor to the financial crisis in which we currently find ourselves is the result of pursuing policies based on these very myths.

As previously mentioned, the last time these myths were ascendant as foundations of economic policy Americans experienced the Great Depression. When these myths again came to dominate policy discourse as the result of the neo-liberal revolution, whose figureheads were Ronald Reagan in the United States and Margaret Thatcher in the United Kingdom (Harvey, 2005; Ravenscroft and Williams, 2009), just prior to the 2008 market crash the top 1 per cent of income recipients had regained that level of national income share they had just prior to the crash of 1929 (from a low of 8 per cent of national income in 1978) (Reich, 2010). Instead of a more efficient or prosperous economy, these myths produced the massive redistribution of wealth to a very small proportion of the population. The Congressional Budget Office (CBO) (2011) study of the distribution of household incomes from 1979 through 2007 shows that the top 1 per cent of income recipients experienced a 275 per cent increase in after-tax income, while the 60 per cent of the population in the middle of the income distribution experienced less than a 40 per cent increase. Not since the Gilded Age in American history has there been such a dramatic and rapid redistribution of income and wealth from the many to the few. One major contributor to this massive shift according to the CBO is

> [a] decrease in the share of total market income from wages and other labor compensation and an increase in the share from capital gains contributed to the increase in market income inequality because capital gains are much more concentrated among higher income households than is labor income.
>
> *(CBO, 2011: 7)*[11]

The role that financial markets have played in affecting this change in the relative prospects of the American people is considerable. The financialisation of the US economy has had more than just income distribution effects, as well. Kevin Phillips (2002) provides a historical account of how the financialisation of national economies has contributed to social decline (Soll's third sense of reckoning) – as wealth concentrates other indicators of social well-being like infant mortality, educational attainment, democratic institutions and so on decline. That the publicity strategy serves only the interests of participants in financial markets, which are not synonymous with human welfare, calls into question accounting's self-described function in society. It raises serious questions as to whether the professed end of professional accounting is as ethically defensible as is the case for medicine or law.

An important ethical lesson for accounting from the current financial crisis is that financial markets are not natural constants that produce often harmful outcomes we all must accept because we mistakenly or cynically believe they follow natural laws. Merely putatively serving the needs of investors and creditors constructed out of economic myths (Stout, 2012) without attention being paid to where the boundaries of those markets are drawn and what their consequences are is, at base, a value judgment that tacitly endorses the outcomes described in this section. The financial reporting system, constructed on a foundation of these myths, has failed to prevent financial crises (and never will) by merely providing publicity. Its inadequacy suggests that a more critical examination of the master metaphor underlying the system is in order, which has implications for what ends the accounting profession should serve in order to claim to be an ethical profession.

5 In conclusion: a more useful metaphor?

Ironically the basic structure of accounting information systems, double-entry bookkeeping, contains a more useful metaphor for designing a more ethically defensible financial reporting system. Ijiri (1975) elaborates at length on what distinguishes an accounting information system from other information systems. According to Ijiri (1975: 32) the nature of an accounting system makes little sense unless one accepts that "*accountability* has clearly been the social and organizational backbone of *accounting* for centuries." Schmandt-Besserat (1992) concludes that the first appearance of an accounting function in human society had as its purpose civic administration; Urton and Brezine (2005) note the same function was fulfilled by the accounting device of the khipu in Incan society. Benston provides a lexical ordering of accounting's ends based on his interpretation of the historical development of accounting:"The ends that accounting serves are *control*, information for decisions, and an overview, or conspectus, of the enterprise" (1984: 47, emphasis added). From the perspectives these scholars offer, accounting systems are not systems designed primarily to inform, but systems designed primarily to regulate, that is "financial statements are merely the tip of the iceberg; what is important is the system behind the statements" (Ijiri, 1975: x). Thus, financial statements are an artefact of, not the purpose of, a system constructed to regulate the conduct of firms and individuals within firms – to provide a reckoning in the sense of a judgment about the appropriateness of the behaviour.

Williams (2002, 2010) demonstrates that the discursive practice of accountants, vis-à-vis accounting rules (GAAP), indicates that rules are not simply prescriptions for creating information. They are directive; they tell people what they must and must not do. Thus, the financial reporting system consists mainly of moral directives; regulations designed to direct behaviours towards certain ends, which themselves are value judgments that are open to debate. These moral judgments are reflected in the regulations the FASB and the IASB promulgate. Standard setters are participants in the process of *regulating* the financial system. There is a certain weight-of-law lying behind the regulations accounting produces and, via the mandatory auditing process, enforces. As Ijiri (1975: 24, emphases added) comments:

> In accounting, the *rules* are in the form of generally accepted accounting principles and procedures which are *enforced* by auditors. *Violations* are *penalized* by an auditor qualifying or even disclaiming an opinion.[12,13]

Accounting's function in the realm of financial reporting is essentially regulatory, regardless of how the profession's justificatory rhetoric of "decision-useful information" elides this fact. Accounting is essentially an ethical discourse and is very much an element of any society's *justice system*. Standard setting is the writing of rules of conduct; auditing compliance with those rules is a law-enforcement activity. Accounting historically has far more to do with law and politics than it does with financial engineering. Accounting's adherence to economic myths and the solution of publicity cannot be claimed to have made accounting a particularly valuable activity so far as avoiding financial crises. Indeed, distancing accounting from economics and economic rationales may be essential.[14]

Explicit acknowledgement of the value of direct regulatory involvement in financial affairs seems called for. Though the myths of economics induce beliefs that regulating is never preferable to the self-regulatory power of markets, the evidence suggests otherwise. For example, Figure 10.1 is reproduced from Moss (2010). It illustrates, for the period near the end of the US

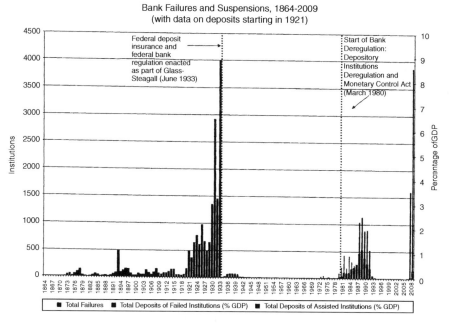

Figure 10.1 A unique period of calm amidst the storm.

Sources: *Historical Statistics of the United States*: Colonial Times to 1970 (Washington, D.C.: Government printing office. 1975), Series X-741.8(p. 1038): "Federal Deposit Insurance Corporation Failures and Assistance Transactions United States and Other Areas."Table BF01, FDIC website (http://www.fdic.gov/hsob); Sutch, Riached, "Gross domestic product: 1790-2002." Table Ca9-19 in *Historical Statistics of the United States, Earliest Times to the present: Millennial Edition*, eds. Susan B. Carter et al. (New York: Cambridge University Press, 2006); Bureau of Economic Analysis. "Gross Domestics Product." NPA Table 1.1.5. (http://www.bea.gov/national/nipaweb/SelectTable.asp).

Civil War through 2009, the dollar value of bank failures. Note that during the period when Glass-Steagall was the law of the land in the United States, there were virtually no bank failures.[15]

Beginning with the Reagan administration's deregulation of savings and loan institutions (Depository Institutions Deregulation and Monetary Control Act of 1980 and Garn-St. Germain Depository Institutional Act of 1982) and the subsequent repeal of Glass-Steagall in 1999, the frequency and magnitude of financial institution failures exploded.

The remarkable growth in the use of complex financial instruments or derivatives certainly contributed to the current financial crisis (McSweeney, 2009). Financial reporting understood as information has led standard setters to treat these complex financial assets as a naturally occurring economic phenomenon presenting standard setters with a 'technical' valuation problem. Even though there is no prospect of ascertaining the exact current value of such financial assets, standard setters have nevertheless prescribed that complex rituals be performed. These rituals are based on reasoning informed by economic myths in order to assign complex financial instruments a number reflecting a value based on their unknowable future outcomes. Financial reporting understood as regulating might have led to a different conclusion about the proliferation of complex financial instruments. Since there is no reliable way to value them perhaps the first question should be: should these financial instruments exist at all? Virtually every commodity must pass some regulatory test that it is, at worst, harmless. The Food and Drug Adninistration, for example, does not permit the sale of drugs until the prospective seller can prove there is a net benefit to society. In the case of financial products like derivatives, no such requirement exists. Perhaps the role of accounting standard setters should not be presumed to account for financial instruments but to bar the sale of those for which no accounting can be made. But this requires a much different metaphor and, perhaps, a bit more moral courage. Accountability (regulation) is a metaphor about the right behavior not the correct accounting measurement.

The important implication I wish to draw from the mythology that currently seems to govern standard setting and auditing is that accounting is as much about ethics, law and politics as it is about modernist finance and economics. Holding powerful economic interests in check is more likely to reduce the risks of financial crises than providing publicity to unregulated markets. If we want to improve the performance of accounting as a social practice we need to redirect our concern from achieving the impossible – an economically *correct* measurement – to one that is ethically more *right*.

This chapter was submitted by the author with the following title: "Accounting and ethics from one critical perspective."

Notes

1   These characteristics are based on attempts to define profession as a sociological term within a functionalist theoretic framework. These characteristics are provided only to serve the purpose of this chapter and are not intended to engage in theoretical debates about the nature of professions, for an introduction which see Abbott (1988) and Larsen (1977).

2   Obviously, the empirical reality is that in the case of both health care and justice the quality of each that one gets depends very heavily on how wealthy one happens to be. But that has more to do with the corrupting power of money and of the structure of the medical and legal professions than it does with the un-ethicality of doctors or lawyers.

3   The tax shelter industry epitomises why client service for accountants does not translate into public good since tax shelters pedaled by the Big 4 firms exploited loopholes in tax law to enable wealthy taxpayers to shift the burden of paying for public goods on to those unable to avail themselves of such shelters (Rostain and Regan, 2014). Also, unlike law and medicine there is no social provision of accounting services.

4   That this contention is psychologically and morally indefensible has been cogently argued by Foley (2006).

5 There is considerable variation among various scholars about whether there is a distinction between ethics and morality. One distinction that serves the purpose of this chapter is that ethics is the study and reasoning about what is moral or not moral.

6 Some economists now believe we will never recover in the sense we used to before the Great Recession. According to this thesis we have reached the "end of normal" and now face a new economic world the likes of which we have never experienced (Galbraith, 2014).

7 Publicity is the nineteenth-century jargon for what is currently captured by the term transparency. It is not within the scope of this essay to dwell on the etymological fine points of these terms and their historical association. Sufficient for the argument in this essay is that both terms have consistent connotations of opening to view the private goings on of publicly traded firms, i.e., making private financial behaviour more public which, in turn, allegedly leads to an orderly functioning of commerce (Roberts, 2009).

8 Applying non-linear modeling to the behaviour of financial markets shows that rather than being efficient as the EMH describes them they are fractal. What the data indicate is "…that the stock market is inherently *unstable*" (Keen, 2001, p. 246). In other words, crises are an inherent property of financial markets and markets produce crises by their own dynamics in spite of whatever information is or is not available to them.

9 Reich (2010, p. 6) reports that the richest 1 per cent of Americans received just 9 per cent of US income in the late 1970s. But by 2007, just before the Great Recession, the richest 1 per cent of Americans received 23.5 per cent of total US income. This period saw the most massive redistribution of income from the many to the few in US history (Piketty, 2014).

10 Methodological individualism is closely tied to Locke and other Enlightenment thinkers' explanation for the emergence of civil society which is labeled the social contract. Called one of the ten great philosophical mistakes (Adler, 1985), the fallacy of the social contract is aptly summed up by Putnam (2004: 103): "But the Enlightenment *derived* the idea of the consent of the governed from the mode of society as arising from a social contract. In effect, it derived sociability as well as morality from an idealized image of the law of contracts, from *property law*. And Dewey, like Hegel, thinks that this is ridiculous." Humans are social to start with; indeed we are the most social of all mammals (Shermer, 2004) and our "social contract" is written in our DNA.

11 Thomas Piketty (2014, p. 265) notes about the US: "…what primarily characterizes the United States at the moment is a record level of inequality in income from labor (probably higher than in any other society at any time in the past, anywhere in the world, including societies in which skill disparities were extremely large)…." This disparity Piketty attributes mainly to the remarkable relative growth in the compensation of corporate managers.

12 Sikka (2009) argues that a contributing factor to the financial crises bedeviling many Western economies is the failure of auditors to perform this basic professional responsibility. Auditors looked the other way as the excessively risky behaviour of many of their clients led to the failure of those clients.

13 Soll (2014: 176) quotes from an 1896 editorial in *The Bookkeeper* about how the earliest US CPAs viewed their responsibility: "The professional accountant is an investigator, a looker for leaks, a dissector and a detective in the highest acceptation of the term…. He is a reader of hieroglyphics, however written, for every erasure, altercation (sic), interlining, dot, dash or character may have meaning…. *He is the foe of deceit and the champion of honesty* (emphasis added). How quaint this seems today.

14 Summing up the performance of economics over the past thirty years the Cambridge University economist Ha-Joon Chang concluded: "In other words, economics has been worse than irrelevant. Economics, as it has been practiced in the last three decades, has been positively harmful for most people" (Chang, 2010: 249). Much the same can be said of professional accountants.

15 Canada, which maintained its strict regulation of banking activity, avoided the financial crisis that plagued its southern neighbor.

References

Abbott, A. (1988). *The System of Professions.* Chicago, IL: University of Chicago Press.

Adams, G. B. and D. L Balfour (1998). *Unmasking Administrative Evil,* Thousand Oaks, CA: Sage Publishing.

Adler, M. J. (1985). *Ten Philosophical Mistakes.* New York: Macmillan Publishing.

AICPA (2015). *Code of Professional Conduct,* Durham, NC: American Institute of Certified Public Accountants.

Alperovitz, G. and L. Daly (2008). *Unjust Deserts,* New York: The New Press.

Ariely, D. (2008). *Predictably Irrational*, New York: Harper Collins Publishers.

Barth, M. E. and W. R. Landsman (2010). "How did financial reporting contribute to the financial crisis?" *European Accounting Review*, 19(3): 399–423.

Basu, K. (2011). *Beyond the Invisible Hand*, Princeton, NJ: Princeton University Press.

Bayou, M. A. Reinstein, A. and P. F. Williams (2011). "To tell the truth: a discussion of issues concerning truth and ethics in accounting," *Accounting, Organizations and Society*, 36(2): 109–24.

Benston, G. J. (1984). "On the value and limitations of financial accounting", *Contemporary Accounting Research*, 1(1): 47–57.

Brown, R. H. (1989). *Social Science as Civic Discourse*, Chicago, IL: The University of Chicago Press.

Cassidy, J. (2009). *How Markets Fail*. New York: Farrar, Straus and Giroux.

CBO. (2011). "Trends in the distribution of household income between 1979 and 2007," The Congressional Budget Office.

Chabrak, N. (2012). "Money talks: the language of the Rochester School," *Accounting, Auditing and Accountability Journal*, 25(3): 452–485.

Chabrak, N., C. Cooper, L. Catchpole and P.F. Williams (2016). "Accounting and the third enclosure movement," *Working paper*, UAE University.

Chang, H.J. (2010). *23 Things They Don't Tell You About Capitalism*, New York: Bloomsbury Press.

Corning, P. (2011). *The Fair Society*, Chicago, IL: The University of Chicago Press.

Darwall, S. (2006). *The Second-Person Standpoint: Morality, Respect and Accountability.* Cambridge MA: Harvard University Press.

Deaton, A. (2013). *The Great Escape*, Princeton, NJ: Princeton University Press.

FASB (1978). "Statement of financial accounting concepts No. 1: objectives of financial reporting by business enterprises," Stamford, CN: Financial Accounting Standards Board.

Flyvbjerg, B. (2001). *Making Social Science Matter.* Cambridge: Cambridge University Press.

Foley, D. K. (2006). *Adam's Fallacy*, Cambridge, MA: The Belknap Press of Harvard University Press.

Friedman, M. (1970). "The social responsibility of business is to increase its profits," *New York Times Magazine*. September 13.

Galbraith, J. K. (2008). *The Predator State*, New York: The Free Press.

Galbraith, J. K. (2014). *The End of Normal*, New York: Simon and Schuster.

Graeber, D. (2015). *The Utopia of Rules*, Brooklyn: Melville House.

Hacker, J. S. and P. Pierson (2010). *Winner-Take-All Politics.* New York, NY: Simon and Shuster.

Harvey. D. (2005). *A Brief History of Neoliberalism*, Oxford: Oxford University Press.

Ijiri, Y. (1975). *Theory of Accounting Measurement*, Sarasota, FL: American Accounting Association.

Johnson, M. (1993). *Moral Imagination*, Chicago, IL: The University of Chicago Press.

Jones, D. S. (2012). *Masters of the Universe*, Princeton, NJ: Princeton University Press.

Keen, S. (2001). *Debunking Economics*, Annandale, NSW: Pluto Press.

Krugman, P. (2009). "The big zero," *The New York Times*, December 27: A27.

Kultgen, J. (1988). *Ethics and Professionalism*, Philadelphia, PA: University of Pennsylvania Press.

Larsen, M. S. (1977). *The Rise of Professionalism: A Sociological Analysis*, Berkeley, CA: University of California Press.

Lasagna, L. (1964). "Hippocratic oath," downloaded from Wikipedia, March 2016.

Marglin, S. A. (2008). *The Dismal Science*, Cambridge, MA: Harvard University Press.

McSweeney, B. (2009). "The roles of financial asset market failure denial and the economic crisis: reflections on accounting and financial theories and practices," *Accounting, Organizations and Society*, 34(6–7): 835–48.

Medema, S. G. (2009). *The Hesitant Hand*, Princeton, NJ: Princeton University Press.

Milanovic, B. (2011). *The Haves and the Have Nots*, New York: Basic Books.

Mirowski, P. (2013). *Never Let a Serious Crisis Go to Waste*, New York: Verso.

Mlodinow, L. (2008). *The Drunkards Walk*, New York: Vintage Books.

Moss, D. (2010). "Reversing the null: regulation, deregulation, and the power of ideas," Harvard Business School Working Paper, 10–080.

Nelson, R. H. (2001). *Economics as Religion*, University Park, PA: The Pennsylvania State University Press.

Ormerod, P. (1994). *The Death of Economics*, New York: John Wiley & Sons.

Phillips, K. (2002). *Wealth and Democracy*, New York: Random House, Inc.

Piketty, T. (2014). *Capital in the Twenty-first Century*, translated by A. Goldhammer, Cambridge, MA: Belknap Press of the Harvard University Press.

Posner, R. A. (2010). *The Crisis of Capitalist Democracy*, Cambridge, MA: Harvard University Press.

Previts, G. J. and Merino, B. D. (1998). *A History of Accounting in the United States: The Cultural Significance of Accounting*, Columbus, OH: The Ohio State University Press.

Putnam, H. (2004). *Ethics Without Ontology*, Cambridge, MA: Harvard University Press.

Ravenscroft, S. and P. F. Williams (2009). "Making imaginary worlds real: the case of expensing employee stock options," *Accounting, Organizations and Society*, 34(6–7): 770–86.

Reich, R. B. (2010). *After-shock*, New York: Random House, Inc.

Reich, R. B. (2015). *Saving Capitalism*, New York: Alfred A. Knopf.

Roberts, J. (2009). "No one is perfect: the limits of transparency and an ethic for 'intelligent' accountability," *Accounting, Organizations and Society*, 34(8): 957–70.

Rosenberg, A. (1992). *Economics – Mathematical Politics or Science of Diminishing Returns?*, Chicago, IL: The University of Chicago Press.

Rostain, T. and M. C. Regan (2014). *Confidence Games*. Cambridge, MA: MIT Press.

Schmandt-Besserat, D. (1992). *Before Writing, Volume I: From Counting to Cuneiform*, Austin, TX: University of Texas Press.

Shermer, M. (2004). *The Science of Good and Evil*, New York: Times Books, Henry Holt and Co.

Shiller, R. J. (2000). *Irrational Exuberance*, New York: Broadway Books.

Sikka, P. (2009). "Financial crisis and the silence of the auditors," *Accounting, Organizations and Society*, 34(6–7): 868–73.

Smith, A. (1982). *The Theory of Moral Sentiments*, Indianapolis, IN: Liberty Classics.

Soll, J. (2014). *The Reckoning: Financial Accountability and the Rise and Fall of Nations*, New York: Basic Books.

Stout, L. (2012). *The Shareholder Value Myth*, San Francisco, CA: Berrett-Koehler Publishers.

Tomasello, M. (2009). *Why We Cooperate*, Cambridge, MA: MIT Press.

Urton, G. and C. J. Brezine (2005). "Khipu accounting in early Peru," *Science*, 309(5737): 1065–67.

Williams, P. F. (2002). "Accounting and the moral order: justice, accounting and legitimate moral authority," *Accounting and the Public Interest*, 2:1–21.

Williams, P. F. (2010). "The focus of professional ethics: ethical professionals or ethical profession?" *Research on Professional Responsibility and Ethics in Accounting*, 14: 15–35.

Williams, P. F. (2014). "The IFAC framework: international accounting and the public interest," in S. Mintz (ed.): *Accounting for the Public Interest*, Dordrecht: Springer.

Williams, P. F. (2015). "Review of J. Soll: *The Reckoning*," New York: Basic Books, (2014) in *Accounting History Review*, 25(1): 69–73.

11
REGULATION

Lisa Baudot and Keith Robson

1 Introduction

The regulation of accounting has constituted a major area of research study for many decades (Cooper and Robson, 2006, provide a previous review). Many studies on the regulation of accounting and accountancy have given emphasis to three main themes. First, research on the genesis of accounting regulatory institutions and agencies in professional and national contexts has been a long-standing theme (Zeff, 1972; 1978; Haring, 1979; Robson, 1991; Young, 1994). A second theme has been the close examination of interventions, lobbying and other influences, including the organisational, linguistic and normative framing, involved in the setting of accounting standards and recommendations (Hope and Gray, 1982; Sunder, 1988; Puro, 1984; Francis, 1987; Robson, 1994; Young, 1996; 2003; Ravenscroft and Williams, 2009). Here the focus has tended to shift towards the political influences upon and the consequences of the activities of the major global players in accounting regulation. Third, there has been a growing awareness of the tensions between specific national or regional framings, and the imperatives for the harmonisation and merging of financial regulations both at the institutional and the policy levels (Puxty, Willmott, Cooper and Lowe, 1987; Camfferman and Zeff, 2007; Tamm-Hallstrom, 2004; Power, 2009; Richardson, 2009). While we do not review these research agendas in their entirety, this chapter touches upon issues within each theme, more specifically within the context of exploring the continuing spread of the influence of financial reporting regulation in the global arena. The regulation of accounting is increasingly a process enacted at a global level, this trend being evident in the changing character of studies on the regulation of accounting and accountancy.

In the field of accounting regulation many would argue that globalisation, however defined, has been central to the growth of important supranational accounting agencies, usually in the name of standardisation, harmonisation and "investors' needs" (Thorell and Whittington, 1994), of whom the latter, in practice, can be curiously quiet about the relationship between their information "needs" and further international accounting harmonisation (see Hopwood, 1994: 243). Yet less than 40 years ago the very idea of the need for standards to mediate and regulate accounting practices was controversial (Leach and Stamp, 1981; Zeff, 1972; Solomons 1978). The notions of professional judgement and autonomy seemed to hold more sway over the question of accounting policy choices (Baxter, 1984; Lyas, 1984). In this chapter we explore the literature on the regulation of financial reporting and financial accounting practices with particular reference to the growth and influence of international regulatory agencies. While our discussion will not address directly the extent to which the national regulatory bodies remain important, it is clear that since the 1970s the accounting professions of the major developed countries have initiated the construction of various supranational regulatory agencies ostensibly to harmonise and standardise accounting and auditing practices. National regulatory bodies, of course, persist and some, such as the Financial Accounting Standards Board (FASB) in the US, have emerged as global actors by virtue of the *de facto* influence of US Generally Accepted Accounting Principles (GAAP). Whereas 20 years ago it would have been difficult to see the producers of international accounting regulation as influential, the shifting alliances between national, regional and international intergovernmental organisations (IGOs) and non-governmental organisations (NGOs) have contributed to the increased global action of accounting regulation.

In their various ways these agencies serve as mediating agents in the globalising process (Boli and Thomas, 1999) and are therefore worthy, in our view, of further examination (Suddaby, Cooper and Greenwood, 2007). Our purpose in this chapter is to review the research that has explored, more or less critically, the emergence and the activities of the international agencies that operate in the regulatory spaces of financial reporting as well as the constitution of structures, relationships and ideologies by these agencies. We have organised our discussion into three empirical themes summarised in Table 11.1, although a number of studies inevitably overlap in terms of empirical subject. The three themes are (i) building and spreading regulatory institutions; (ii) the programmes and ideologies of accounting's regulatory spaces; and (iii) global imperatives, national contexts and regulatory contests. Across these studies, however, we also highlight, where significant, the nature of the conceptual frame that particular studies or authors deploy. With our interest in the critical studies of regulation, we do not speak specifically to the body of quantitative research on standard setting and regulation that considers the economic consequences and rationality of accounting policy choices or disclosure issues. That said, as a preliminary to our discussion we briefly elucidate the main conceptual frames, or groups of theory that have been drawn upon in the literature that we review.

2 Perspectives for understanding regulation

An important conceptual strand in the study of accounting regulation has been the work drawing upon political economy (Arnold, 2005, 2012). Here, there has been a clear critical focus upon the political contests among economic and political agencies as they attempt to pursue their economic interests by defining the terms and conditions upon which exchanges are shaped by financial reporting policies, including between developed and less developed nations and their professions (Arnold and Sikka, 2001). Studies drawing upon political economy consider how economic, social and political systems and structures impact on who benefits from accounting regulation, where specific systems and structures – those of capitalism and financialisation – work to advance vested interests (Cooper and Sherer, 1984). This focus goes hand in hand with a consideration of the organisations and groups in society who are advantaged, where specific societal interests – usually those of financial and shareholder capital – are consistently recognized to benefit to the detriment of others (Cooper and Sherer, 1984).

A close relative of the political economy perspective involves a consideration of accounting as embedded within a complex inter-state economy and society (Arnold, 2009). This alternative is based on the world systems theory of Wallerstein (2004), which views individual nations or economic units as peripheral elements from which powerful world empires and world economies at the core of the system extract goods and services. Wallerstein's work focuses on the relationship

Table 11.1 Main Ideas

Topic Descriptions	Exemplary References	Main Ideas
Building and spreading regulatory institutions		
Emergence of institutions, actors and organising principles– IASB, IFAC	Tamm-Hallstrom (2004), Chiapello and Medjad (2005), Loft et al. (2006), Botzem and Quack (2006, 2009), Chua and Taylor (2008), Botzem (2012)	In gaining/maintaining legitimacy, a particular set of organising principles are mobilised in the formation/structuring of private institutions.
		These organising principles reflect economic rationales which best serve the organisers themselves.
		The organisers reflect a particular network of actors and interests whose commitments are aligned with certain (neo-liberal) principles.
Global accounting profession and audit interests – in standardisation projects, in global regulatory architecture and so on.	Arnold and Sikka (2001), Caramanis (2002), Arnold (2005), Humphrey et al. (2009), Arnold (2012)	The role of the nation state in global regulation is compromised by domestic politics/interests while role of private global institutions, including the global accountancy profession, grows.
		The role of the accountacy profession as a key actor in accounting debates and a site of accounting regulation itself.
		Global accountancy professions (firms) as sources of regulation in countries with un(der)developed regulatory and professional institutions.
Programs and ideologies of accounting's regulatory spaces		
Discourses and linguistic or rhetorical appeals employed in accounting debates	Robson (1993), Young (1996), Young (2003), Walters and Young (2008), Young and Williams (2010)	Actors' interests are demonstrated in terms of their discourse – meanings they give, emphasis they place, categorization, use of persuasion, rhetoric, metaphors.
		Experts' assertions about solutions to accounting issues, reflected in discourses and texts of standards, establish boundaries and constrain action.
Deconstruction of concepts (decision-usefulness, public interest, true and fair view, materiality)	Young (2006), Dellaportas and Davenport (2008), Hamilton and Ó hÓgartaigh (2009), Edgley (2014)	Concepts and notions with links to neo-liberal economic ideology are often uncontested and taken for granted.
		Despite being vague, flexible and open to interpretation, concepts take on a life of their own, becoming powerful enough to be mobilised in justifying (or criticising) accounting phenomenon.

| Financialisation/neo-liberalisation | Froud et al. (2004), Power (2009), Zhang et al. (2012), Arnold (2012), Muller (2014) | The increasingly central role of financial capital and power of financial sector produced profound regulatory change, including support for global accounting/auditing standards.
From the end of the twentieth century, accounting regulation has shaped and been shaped by highly financialised forms of capital embedded within the wider economic and political system.
Different forms of capital for which different organising principles appear appropriate. |
| Financial economic expertise and order | Ravenscroft and Williams (2009), Murphy et al. (2013), Zhang and Andrew (2014), Erb and Pelzer (2015) | Accounting has become subservient to neoclassical economics, with the traditional accounting objectives and qualitative characteristics of financial information being displaced by principles of financial economics.
Traditional accounting objectives, stewardship and accountability, can/should be mobilised to challenge the neo-liberal agenda. |

Global imperatives, national contexts and regulatory contests

Shift of responsibility to private (global) standard-setting organisations Role of public authorities in (re-)exerting influence	Chiapello and Medjad (2005), Chua and Taylor (2008), Bengtsson (2011), Crawford et al. (2014)	Economic rationales for globalising institutions are unsupported by empirical evidence, more likely the consequence of an increasingly powerful global accounting culture. Private (global) standard setting as a mechanism which distances accounting from state-level politics while allowing the state to retain final say. Despite the trend towards a shift of responsibility for standard setting to the global private sector, governmental powers are still contenders in regulatory affairs.
The development of global standards in distinct national contexts	Chand and White (2007), Menniken (2008), Richardson (2009), Peng and Bewley (2010), Baker et al. (2012), Albu et al. (2014)	The impracticality and potentially negative impact of global standardisation projects in economies whose needs and systems may differ from developed economies. Differences in the application of global standards linked to aspects of economic, professional and political systems that may not facilitate certain accounting technologies (for example, fair value accounting).

between territorial and capitalist logics of power and attempts to make explicit that the position that economies hold must be considered relative to these logics and the world system in which economies are embedded. The literature informed by Wallerstein's approach therefore focuses attention upon the path by which global political and economic powers become central players in contemporary systems. It also recognises the ideologies and arrangements underlying those powers by engaging directly with the economic domination influencing processes of globalisation, often in the name of economic liberalisation. A similar strand of theory is also seen in the work on accounting and financialisation, and the reach of financial capital in setting the agenda for regulatory processes of standardisation, and structuring the frameworks for accounting policies in the name of, for example, fair value and the rational investor.

Wallerstein's work focuses on relations between global and political powers and ideologies and provides a theoretical framework for analysing the asymmetrical balance of power between the core and the periphery, while speaking much less to cultural and institutional dimensions or the development of world culture. Postcolonial studies on regulation, and on governance more generally, go even deeper in exploring this power asymmetry, often between the North and the South, considering in particular the roles, experiences and perspectives of the peripheral economies (Santos, 2002). This includes a focus on how the periphery is constrained by the hegemonic core and the development of movements and associations of feminist, indigenous, ecological and other minorities (e.g. Annisette, 2004, 2006; Annisette and Neu, 2004). According to Santos (2002), the weaker states are now threatened not only by the more powerful, but also by a select group of international financial agencies and private transnational actors which make up a new world financial architecture (Wade, 2007). This architecture includes

> Western governments and multilateral organizations such as the IMF, the Basel Committee on Banking Supervision, the Financial Stability Forum, the G20 of finance ministers and a gamut of non-official bodies, as well as financial firms and think-tanks from the advanced capitalist states.
>
> *(Wade, 2007: 116)*

Research has looked at accounting regulatory phenomena in the context of the international flows of capital, products, information, practices and people that these organisations serve to regulate as well as potential resistance by anti-hegemonic and anti-capitalist NGOs (e.g. Graham and Neu, 2003; Annisette, 2004; Abu, Everett and Neu, 2007; Neu Shiraz Rahaman, Everett and Akindayomi, 2010). The voice of the periphery, and particularly the global South, in organising this new world system is almost non-existent.

At the same time, cultural convergences across the globe are discernible. Societies the world over continue to see an explosion of organisations and organising through social, community and religious movements as well as education, healthcare, business and government agencies that are increasingly complex, standardised and formal (Drori, Meyer and Hwang, 2006). While postcolonial perspectives touch on cultural and institutional dimensions, development of cultural convergence on a universal scale (Meyer, Boli, Thomas and Ramirez, 1997) is emphasised by Meyer (1980) as being transmitted through a 'world polity'. A world polity refers to a governance system in which a global citizenship is interconnected with broad cultural systems embedded in Western societies and globally reflected (Meyer, 1980). According to Meyer *et al.* (1997), from the post-World War II period, a world society has crystallised through this polity, resulting in universally applicable cultural models and structural patterns that shape states, organisations and individual identities. Central to world polity theory is the assertion that institutional forms copy structural models and patterns introduced at the level of world society leading to worldwide diffusion and the adaptation of institutionalised values (DiMaggio and Powell, 1983). As a consequence, certain affinities can be recognised in world polity theory and institutional theory. Both, for instance, see increasing similarity in structural patterns as driving norms and standards despite differences in economic configurations, power relationships and local traditions.

In exploring the growth of regulatory institutions, we have noted, unsurprisingly, that a number of variants of institutional theory have tended to be important sources of problematisation, insight and inspiration. Themes of regulatory and normative diffusion and isomorphism have been drawn upon to elaborate changes in the institutional arenas of accounting and auditing. The growth and spread of regulatory agencies in accounting has been shown to indicate many commonalities with studies of isomorphism and the search for legitimate authority (Tamm-Hallstrom, 2004). As such, the emergence of regulatory organisations such as the International Accounting Standards Board (IASB) has followed familiar patterns of legitimate structure and organisation. Such work may be seen by some within the critical accounting community as minimally critical of regulatory initiatives and developments. Indeed, as Willmott (2014) notes, aside from institutional theory's obvious critique of the rationalist economic framing of human behaviour and the debunking of objectivism, it might well be that institutional theories struggle to engage with critical discussions of power and emancipation (Lawrence, 2008; Cooper, Ezzamel and Willmott, 2008). Nevertheless, there are studies within the institutional tradition that do suggest the power and influence of particular (Western) national (and normative) models of authority and influence in the constitution and evolution of new regulatory organisations in financial reporting and auditing.

A final tradition of theory evident in research on regulation adopts a more genealogical approach found in studies of regulatory institutions and particular policy debates. Such research steps back a little from the focus upon key organisations and political contests in accounting to explore the processes of 'problematisation' at the margins of accounting practices. Here the concern, which is not entirely uncritical, has been to explore how wider practices flow into and help reconstitute accounting's roles and missions (Young, 1994; Robson, 1994). Adopting a more constructionist ontology, such work has helped highlight the conditions of possibility and spaces that help form the regulatory agenda for accounting. Much of the emphasis of such research has been upon the discursive or 'programmatic' components (transparency, innovation, governance) of changes in accounting regulation. Further work has attempted to explore how state activities impact sometimes directly, but often indirectly, upon the rationalities that might inform regulatory initiatives.

In the concluding section we will reflect upon these conceptual threads in the context of research on accounting regulation, and suggest where research might yet go to explore the unfolding processes of accounting regulation and evolution of regulatory agencies in the global arena. In the next section we pick up the first of the empirical themes that characterise research on the international dimensions of accounting regulation.

3 Building and spreading regulatory institutions

Financial accounting and auditing arrangements were organised initially by the professional associations and, latterly, by national regulators for most of the twentieth century. For many researchers the exploration of the forging of accounting institutions and principles and the birth of standard-setting regimes at the national level constituted the bulk of social and political research into the regulatory and standard-setting processes (Zeff, 1972; Robson, 1991, 1994; Young, 1994). However, since the mid-1990s these arrangements have experienced rapid changes and a growth in influence (Arnold, 2012). This rapid internationalisation has inspired a body of research aimed at charting and accounting for the institutionalisation of international, if not global, accounting and auditing organisations and standards.

Accounting research has aimed to understand, explain and critique this phenomenon in several ways. For instance, research has focused on the emergence of the IASB (and the International Accounting Standards Committtee, IASC, as it was), its structure and governance, and the factors and circumstances leading to the acceptance by public authorities (states) of the transfer of norms to private NGOs (Tamm-Hallstrom and Bostrom, 2010). Camfferman and Zeff (2007) offer an exhaustive history of the origins of the IASC with particular reference to the apparent quest for accounting harmonisation in Europe. Similarly, the work of Tamm-Hallstrom (2004) explores in detail the emergence of the IASC and its search for authority in the late twentieth century. The author's focus on the configuration (i.e. governance structures and procedural models) of the IASC contributes to our understanding of the strategies and processes employed to enhance the legitimacy and authority of groups that develop worldwide models and standards. As opposed to focusing on the diffusion of IASC's standards, Tamm-Hallstrom's work reflects on the IASCs potentially conflicting goals of rule-making and organising principles, including user needs; financial (capital market) interests; expertise; and representativeness.

Likewise, the work of Botzem and Quack (2006, 2009) extends Tamm-Hallstrom's studies on expertise and representativeness to the initial years of the IASB, highlighting the particular backgrounds and associations of the individuals involved in the reorganised and rebranded international standard-setting body. Botzem and Quack (2006, 2009), and later Botzem (2012), see these backgrounds and associations as reflecting a specific set of actors (and interests) whose ideological commitments are aligned with the principles of user needs and financial interests. This set of actors, as a set of self-designated accounting experts comprised of members of the profession and, particularly, of global audit firms and their lobbying arms, such as the Federation des Expertes Comptable (FEE), operates in a largely closed forum which monopolises and constrains the input of 'other interests' in the development of accounting standards (Hopwood, 1994; Botzem and Quack, 2006; Botzem, 2012). This work echoes that of Loft, Humphrey and Turley, (2006) which analyses the emergence of the International Federation of Accountants (IFAC) as an international auditing standard setter and highlights a trend towards governance by experts with significant reliance on the seemingly technical influence of the large accounting firms.

These mainly institutional approaches provide important insight into how international non-government institutions are structured and mobilise a particular set of organising principles (Puxty *et al.*, 1987) in order to gain (and maintain) recognition. Such studies also critique certain taken-for-granted economic rationales underlying the purpose of these institutions – their aim to increase cross-national comparability/quality and improve market coordination – without explicitly breaking down those rationales. In addition, an alternative view challenges these economic rationales as explaining the push for international accounting standards by highlighting that these rationales are relatively unsupported by empirical evidence (Chua and Taylor, 2008).

A further stream of research on the institutionalisation of international accounting and auditing standards has focused on the presence and power of particular interests in the construction of the private standard-setting process, including national interests and the interests of the global accounting profession and the way in which the development of accounting standards plays out at the hands of these interests in different contexts. Relative to national interests, research has focused specifically on situations in which public authorities attempt to (re-)exert influence on the standard-setting process. Much of the debate in the accounting literature centered on the building of accounting institutions has explored the so-called harmonisation of accounting standards in Europe and, more broadly, of the convergence of standards worldwide (Ordelheide,

1993; Walton, 1993; Chua and Taylor, 2008). In 2005, regulation requiring companies publicly listed in the EU to comply with accounting standards established by a private standard-setting organisation, the IASB, signaled a relinquishment of public authority over accounting standard setting. However, the EU member states were neither the first nor the last to relinquish this authority. In fact, the EU grouping exists among countries now numbering over 100 that have embraced some form of the convergence of standards through the recognition of the IASB in domestic standard-setting processes while in many cases retaining little, if any, means of control over the process. Indeed, this potential weakening of domestic (even regional) sovereignty and the transfer of regulatory responsibility to NGOs has been the topic of significant debate (e.g. Danjou and Walton, 2012; Burlaud and Colasse, 2011).

Chua and Taylor (2008: 463), in particular, argue that

> [t]he move towards a single set of standards under the auspices of a private sector international issuing organization independent of state-sponsored national bodies is more about the political and social dimensions of globalization than it is about the alleged economic benefits of convergence in international accounting standards.

They suggest that this move could be the consequence of an increasingly prominent and powerful global accounting culture characterised by expertise-based rather than nationally based interests, as the work of Botzem (2012) and Botzem and Quack (2006, 2009) contends (see also Power, 2009). At the same time, Chua and Taylor (2008) indicate that moving standard-setting just outside of national boundaries may be seen as a way to distance accounting standards from national-level political conflict and debate while retaining final say over which standards are adopted, a sentiment that is similarly expressed by Chiapello and Medjad (2009).

In addition to research on nationally based interests, a number of studies have shed light on the interests of the global accounting profession in the development of accounting and auditing regulation. For instance, in their study of the state–profession relation in response to the failure of a major international bank, Arnold and Sikka (2001) find specific nation states, and especially major Western states, to be important movers and players in the regulation of global banking. At the same time, the authors noted that a nation state's global regulatory capacity is compromised by "history, domestic concerns and relationships with class and capitalist interests" (Arnold and Sikka, 2001: 475), while the regulatory capacity of non-governmental (private) 'global' institutions, including the accountancy profession, grows.

In this regard, Caramanis (2002) examines how developing patterns of global interconnections between the US, the EU and other powerful international organisations impacted accounting policy decisions at the level of the nation state in Greece. Among these organisations, the author finds the global auditing firms themselves to be capable of mobilising their relations with powerful political-economic actors to prevent the Greek government from re-establishing a state monopoly over accounting services after the market was liberalised in the early 1990s. This is one example of how the self-identified global accounting firms, within their US and EU power base, play a pivotal role in encouraging and enabling the conditions for 'global' professional service and labor markets by lobbying for agreements designed to encourage the harmonisation of accounting practices, promote mutual recognition of professional credentials through standard audit practices and dismantle national regulatory boundaries to trade in services (Suddaby, Cooper and Greenwood, 2007).

On the globalisation of accounting firms, Arnold (2005) analyses the efforts by non-government institutions, including professional accountancy firms and lobbying groups in Europe and the US, to create a global market for accounting and auditing services through international trade agreements. Arnold's research shows how such agreements were used to eliminate regulations that were viewed as

> barriers to trade and investment, such as diverse national and sub-national licensing and qualification requirements, regulations limiting scope of practice and forms of business organization and non-harmonized technical standards.
>
> *(Arnold, 2005: 299)*

Arnold (2012) employs a similar perspective in examining how the response of Western powers to the East Asian financial crisis of the late 1990s impacted the diffusion of international accounting and auditing standards. More specifically, Arnold (2012) shows how the increasingly central role of financial capital and the power of the financial sector in capital accumulation processes has provided support for the global reach of international accounting and auditing standards.

When the centrality of financial capital and the financial sector came under scrutiny during the most recent financial crisis, so did interactions between the international accounting profession and accounting bodies. For instance, in questioning the relative silence of the accounting profession during the crisis, Humphrey, Loft and Woods (2009) focus on less obvious interactions between the large audit firms, IFAC and international regulators. The authors caution that the accounting profession's silence should perhaps not be interpreted as a loss of relevance but rather as a question of whether the large audit firms have succeeded in a form of regulatory partnership with (or capture of?) the international accountancy bodies and public oversight boards.

Despite our initial specification of distinctions in the conceptual approaches to the study of accounting regulation, in these contributions we observe a blend of political economy and world systems perspectives. For instance, we can see how governmental organisations and NGOs become individual units of analysis within the context of the interconnected world political and economic system. We can also view the role of ideologies and arrangements underlying that system. In this way, the world systems perspective fits well with political economy's consideration of how specific economic, social and political systems and structures – in particular, the rise of capital markets and their ongoing financialisation – work to advantage certain interests to the detriment of others. Over many years, the power and influence acquired by capital markets has produced profound changes in regulation as well as new forms of competition that have reworked the balance between productive, market and financial goals (Froud, Johal, Papazian and Williams, 2004). Alongside this, the introduction of financial economics into financial accounting, from discounting in valuation methods to the expansion of mark to market and fair value measurement, has made financialisation a significant organising discourse (Power, 2009). As a result, accounting research has focused on how accounting regulation has shaped and been shaped by the highly financialised, shareholder value form of capitalism now observed in the world state at the end of the twentieth century.

4 Programmes and ideologies of accounting's regulatory spaces

In this section we examine more closely the research on accounting regulation that has explored the discourses and rationalities of the projects of accounting regulation (Miller, 1994). These include exploring the political ideologies and broader social movements that both articulate and rationalise accounting regulation. Central to many such studies are closer and more critical examinations of the discourses underpinning the globalising aspirations of accounting regulations, in particular, the discourse of neo-liberalism, the global financial economy and the needs of investors.

The programmes of the liberalisation of economies require a commitment to a broad set of ideas about how modern capitalist societies should operate. As such, the process of the standardisation of accounting and auditing services has been increasingly articulated in the name of the shareholder, capital market efficiency, market liberalisation and competition policy. Strands of accounting research on regulation have proffered critiques of neo-liberal commitments indicating for whom capitalist societies operate and the purpose of accounting regulation in those societies (e.g. producing decision-useful information for investors; Young, 2003, 2006; Ravenscroft and Williams, 2009). In addition, the growth of accumulation through financial markets has produced particular commitments to mechanisms that further normalise financial markets. These mechanisms include market valuations and measures of fair value, which have also been the subject of debate in contemporary research on accounting regulation. We discuss critical research touching on these issues in the paragraphs that follow.

For instance, Froud *et al.*, (2004) provide a politico-economic analysis of the events surrounding the collapse of Enron, in which this corporate case study is used to illustrate the power of the capital market and the finacialisation of corporate evaluations in the contemporary economic system. The authors argue that Enron's failure was not only a result of failed corporate governance, but also a result of the failure of the wider economic and political system in which Enron was embedded (Froud *et al.*, 2004). This system connected Enron to a particular web of interests and power that allowed, even encouraged, its behavior in the name of imaginary financial markets and success. Ravenscroft and Williams (2009: 770) develop this 'global imaginary' in arguing that accounting has been "transformed into a sub-discipline of financial economics, a servant of the imaginary world of neo-classical economics". These authors critique the information-useful objective of financial statements as a principle of financial economics that acting as a naturalising instrument for a neo-liberal ideology, displaces more traditional accountability objectives (Ravenscroft and Williams, 2009).

The role of these more traditional objectives is also the focus of Murphy, O'Connell and Ó hÓgartaigh's (2013) work on stewardship and the primary users of financial statements. Murphy *et al.* follow the evolution of stewardship and accountability and argue that, despite the language of standard setting, which suggests otherwise, these traditions remain embedded in the "living law" of accounting. The authors encourage scholars to build upon the stewardship and accountability traditions inherent in this living law in order to challenge the neo-liberal agenda of decision usefulness for investors as the sole objective of accounting (Murphy *et al.*, 2013). Relatedly, Zhang and Andrew (2014) examine how a newly configured conceptual framework for international accounting legitimises key concepts and characteristics of the neo-liberal agenda and works to sustain the centrality of finance and economics to accounting, emphasising the capacity of the political economy of accounting to refocus accounting from broader societal concerns towards the needs of capital markets. The authors show how narrowing the definition of users and the purpose of financial reporting, as well as shifting the qualitative characteristics of financial reporting within the conceptual framework, signifies a shift towards the interests of finance capital (Zhang and Andrew, 2014).

Expanding on this idea, Erb and Pelger (2015), show how the shifting qualitative characteristics of financial reporting, in particular the abandonment of the construct of 'reliability' in favour of 'faithful representation', has extended the boundaries of financial accounting and reporting even further in the direction of financial capital, primarily through current fair values. At the same time, Müller (2014) evaluates the political economy of the fair value revolution in standard setting over the last two decades, arguing this shift will likely never be complete as fair value accounting reflects a form of capital – one that is financial in nature – distinct from historical productive capital, for which a different form of accounting based on historical cost may remain more appropriate (Müller, 2014). Regardless of whether fair value takes over the accounting world, its prominence in accounting regulation and role as a technology of neo-liberalism and financialisation is apparent. For instance, Zhang, Andrew and Rudkin (2012) explore the role of fair value in the Chinese setting in the process of the neo-liberalisation and financialisation of political and economic systems. The authors show how claims regarding the convergence with international standards and the implementation of fair value have legitimised market transformation in China through the appearance of an efficient market in terms established by Western capitalist countries. At the same time, these claims remain disconnected from the underlying political and economic architecture operating within China (Zhang *et al.*, 2012). According to Zhang *et al.*, this discourse benefits powerful political and economic elites both inside and outside of China rather than advancing the public interest and is indicative of the constructed nature of accounting regulation.

Another characteristic of the impact of liberalising rationalities upon international accounting regulation has been the tying-in of trade agreements, mutual recognition processes and the liberalisation of accounting services (Arnold, 2005). Here the key focus has been upon the role that regulatory-approved accounting devices have had in enabling wider processes of economic liberalisation. Part of this concern has inevitably focussed upon the role of accounting regulation in extending the activities and legitimate jurisdiction of the large professional service and auditing firms. As the story of the formation of the IASC indicates, the impact of international regulations upon professional certifications and entry requirements was a key motivation for the British profession's action, even if such commercial motivations were implicit. And the interventions of the World Bank, World Trade Organization (WTO) and Organisation for Economic Cooperation and Development (OECD) in the liberalisation of accountancy services has seen rationales of competition and the removal of free trade restrictions brought explicitly into the service of the transnational regulation of accounting (Hegarty, 1997; Trolliet and Hegarty, 2003).

To take one prominent example of this process, the WTO's General Agreement on Trade in Services (GATS) sought to remove barriers to trade and investment in services including accountancy and the other activities of the multinational professional service firms (Arnold, 2005). As part of a general commitment to trade liberalisation, the WTO was established by the Marrakesh Agreement in 1994. Part of the WTO's work has been the implementation of GATS in domestic regulation. As Hegarty (1997: 85) points out, Article VI of GATS requires governments to apply regulations affecting service industries and professions such that they do not function as barriers to trade. In so doing governments are expected to review qualification requirements and credentials, and the potential of such licensing requirements to act as barriers to trade (WTO, 1998). In assessing this possibility, governments are instructed to take into account relevant international standards as benchmarks for the adequacy or restrictiveness of their service regulations. As such, the arena of international accounting and auditing standards has become a legitimating device for affirming the appropriate degree of liberality of a nation or that nation's professional association accounting and auditing standards.

The Working Party of Professional Services (WPPS) has applied the principles of GATS to all professions (Arnold, 2005), although according to Hegarty, accountancy was given a special priority. In implementing GATS the WPPS explicitly "encourage[d] the use of international standards through co-operation with the relevant international governmental and non-governmental organizations" (Hegarty, 1997: 86). With respect to accountancy this is an explicit recognition of the work of the IASC and IFAC. In 1997 the OECD joined the process, publishing a report highlighting recommendations for "adapting systems of national regulations to enable countries to compete better in a global economy" (Hegarty, 1997: 86).

In short, research by Arnold and others has shown how the standard-setting process is now tied into the rationale of global trade liberalisation and competition policy. GATS mandates successive rounds of negotiations aimed at further liberalisation of trade in services. GATS had as one objective the fixing of trade liberalisation to make it irreversible, but in general terms another iteration of the GATS intended to allow WTO members to bargain with each other and make commitments of new services. With regard to the case of accountancy, Gould (2002) argues that it is possible that the restrictions on US audit firms introduced by the 2002 Sarbanes Oxley Act, introduced in the wake of the Enron collapse, could be deemed a restraint on trade, given that the WTO secretariat has described the "compartmentalization/scope of practice limitations/incompatibilities" as one of the "most significant barriers to international trade in accountancy services" (WTO, 1998; Gould, 2002).

In addition to focusing on the way in which accounting issues are problematised and solutions to those issues constructed, another stream of research has focused on the underlying moral and social orders and meaning systems that form the foundation for standard-setting actions. Accounting has long been recognised, at least by a significant segment of the academic community, as a set of conventions, not facts, which are socially constructed and reconstructed over time. While the political economy view acknowledges the politics of this social construction through an exploration of powerful interests and ideologies, Burchell *et al.'s* (1985) theorisation of accounting takes a somewhat broader view of constructing accounting (regulation). This view sees the representation (and intervention) of accounting as contingent on the particular constellation of organisations, processes and models/ideas present within various arenas in any given period of time (Burchell *et al.*, 1985). Such a perspective has inspired research aimed at unraveling the problematisation of (taken-for-granted) programs, issues and rationalities of accounting regulation as well as their linkages to the discourses surrounding such programmes, issues and rationalities, the emergence of the legitimate subjects and actors constructing them and the time and space in which they are constructed (Robson and Young, 2009).

This discursive element, in terms of the language and rationales actors employ in accounting debates and the way in which such discourse establishes the boundaries of the debate, has been a significant topic of research (Robson, 1993; Young, 1994, 1996, 2003; Young and Williams, 2010). Building on the work of Burchell *et al.* (1985), Robson (1991) suggests that accounting phenomena are subject to a process of translation (Latour, 1987) within its wider social, economic and political context, through a legitimising discourse often not associated with the language of accounting. Robson (1991) illustrates this process of translation through the formation of the UK accounting standard-setting program and institution as the profession's own solution to the problems of accounting practice. Later, Robson (1994) explores the intersecting arenas that help to constitute how inflation accounting came to be seen as a problem that finally resulted in UK government intervention in the 1970s. In studying these arenas, Robson (1994) elaborates the importance of studying the relationships between accounting tools/techniques and policy discourses and rationales.

Young and Williams (2010) demonstrate how assessments and assertions of 'things that are similar' and 'things that are dissimilar' allow the standard setters to make judgments regarding the way in which particular categories of things should (or should not) be accounted for as well as whether they are relevant (or irrelevant) to investors. Indeed, the whole notion of relevance, or usefulness, to investors that forms the foundation for solutions and actions as currently proclaimed by the standard-setting bodies is a socially constructed notion, which is unpacked in the work of Young (2006). The author argues that the idea of information usefulness to individual investors in making decisions is a relatively recent notion, one that emerged despite not only little participation by users in the standard-setting process but also a lack of practical understanding of the decision-making processes employed by this category of actors (Young, 2006). Yet somehow this notion, with its links to the economic ideology discussed in the preceding section, has become powerful enough for standard setters to mobilise it in justifying and criticising particular accounting solutions.

Set within the broader context in which accounting regulation occurs, Young (1994) employs a "regulatory space" metaphor, which bears some resemblance to the "accounting constellation" (Burchell *et al.*, 1985) and a version of the concept of "arena" (Burchell *et al.*, 1985; Robson, 1991, 1994). Young's (1994) regulatory space contains people, organisations and events that construct and interpret accounting problems, actions and solutions as "appropriate or inappropriate" for standard setting. Young (1996) shows how appropriate actions and solutions to accounting problems, in this instance the problem of accounting for financial instruments, are advanced or constrained by reference to what standard-setting experts assert is "good or bad" accounting. Building on this idea, Young (2003) denotes the text of accounting standards itself as designed to express a particular view about both the "goodness" of the standard-setting process and the standard-setting body. That view, according to Young (2003), involves rhetorical strategies to persuade readers of accounting standards that the proposed standard (and the standard setter) is good, while silencing criticisms of the proposed standard (and the standard setter). Such strategies are elaborated by Walters and Young (2008) in their exploration of the way in which different metaphors have been mobilised by the professional and business press in relation to the issue of accounting for stock options. This work supports the value of rhetoric in revealing or suppressing the underlying construction of (solutions to) accounting issues.

In a similar fashion, a further line of research has emerged that aims to understand other powerful, constructed notions, including the public interest, materiality and the true and fair view, and the particular role of the accounting profession in the process of construction. The work of Dellaportas and Davenport (2008) reflects on the notion of "accounting for the public interest" highlighting how, despite being vague and open to interpretation, regulators continually mobilise this concept in standard setting and expect the accountancy profession to champion this notion. Other research identifies the profession as less passive in the construction of accounting concepts. Edgley (2014) sheds light on the concept of materiality showing the malleable nature of the concept and how that malleability has allowed the accountancy profession to adapt the signification of the concept in response to shifts in the broader environment. Finally, Hamilton and Ó hÓgartaigh (2009) explore the way in which the constructed notion of a true and fair view is further loaded with meaning through the routines of the accountancy profession, showing how accounting concepts are affected by practice. These papers highlight the role of the accountancy profession as a key actor in the construction of accounting discourse, reminding us of the insight Cooper and Robson (2006) provide when they reconceptualise the professional firms as sites of accounting regulation.

5 National contexts, regulatory contests and the implementation of accounting regulation

The apparent onward march of globalisation has left in its wake an impressive level of disagreement as to its significance for nation states, economic development, community and communitarian practices (Held and McGrew, 2002). For some the forces of globalisation undermine national governments and yet through the effects of economic trade may contribute to an increase in economic wealth and 'freedom' (Ohmae, 1995). Others contend that the extent of globalisation has been exaggerated, that there is less global trade now than in, for example, the nineteenth century and that the nation state retains considerable powers of influence and discretion (Hirst and Thompson, 1995).

No doubt reflecting in part the dispute over the significance of globalisation, two competing views have marked the consideration of the role of the nation state in accounting regulation and whether its power, function and authority to regulate can be maintained in light of certain globalising forces. In part, one critical discussion for globalisation and regulation is the democratic legitimacy, or lack of it, that international regulatory agencies have to adjudicate upon matters of accounting representations and the resource allocation processes that may accrue from them. One view claims a reduced role for the nation state against increasingly powerful (and efficient) private (and economic) institutions, while a second claims nation states adapt and restructure and, in doing so, remain important players. However, the differential role of government and non-government bodies in international standard-setting processes and, in turn, the local impact of such processes also depends on the historical, cultural and institutional specificities of any given setting and a number of studies have set out to shed light on this, in particular relative to emerging and developing countries.

Early research on the potential for global accounting regulation focused on the comparative analysis of the social and institutional context within which accounting is organised within nation states. Such studies, which helped to highlight the problems international standards faced in the implementation and the enforcement of standards. Puxty *et al.*'s (1987) work shows the contradictory nature of the way in which these principles exist in relation to one another, arguing that any apparent integration between them is potentially "illusory". Extending Puxty *et al.*'s analysis, Willmott *et al.* (1992) examine a specific accounting regulation within the context of the same four countries, contrasting a similar set of organising principles. Despite cross-national contextual differences and contradictions between organizing principles, Willmott *et al.* (1992) find remarkable convergence in the ways that the accounting regulation had developed in each setting.

Both of these analyses reveal how cross-national differences – historically, culturally and institutionally embedded factors – mediate accounting regulation with respect to these differences leading, on the one hand, to a certain skepticism about the prospects of convergence between settings (Puxty *et al.*, 1987) and, on the other, to more confidence in such prospects (Willmott *et al.*, 1992). In addition, both Puxty *et al.* (1987) and Willmott *et al.* (1992) emphasise the role of the nation state in facilitating the development of accounting while at the same time highlighting increasingly prominent international and transnational institutions in regulatory activities. These two themes, the role of the nation state and its links to international, even so-called transnational, accounting institutions, have become a significant focus of research on the globalisation and institutionalisation of accounting and professional regulation.

In this regard, Menniken (2008) advocates that researchers examine how globalised standards are articulated in local settings and how those settings connect the local back to the global. In doing so, her case study of the diffusion of international auditing standards within a large post-Soviet Russian professional accountancy firm draws attention to the way in which local practices were redefined and translated in a context in which professional approaches, programs and ethical attitudes towards work impact the manner in which international standards are put into practice. Similarly, in another case study, this time of Romania's translation and application of international standards, Albu *et al.* (2014) contend that local responses to these standards depend on the specific configurations among the regulators, professional associations and global accountancy firms. In particular, the authors suggest that these relationships are more 'internally confused' in developing economies, such as Romania, where underdeveloped accountancy professions are still searching for legitimacy and therefore play a significant role in institutional pressures to conform out of their own self-interest.

In considering the role of the nation state in international accounting regulation, Chiapello and Medjad (2009) discuss the EU case and the apparent desire to constitute the EU single market, to overcome conflicts between member states and to address budget difficulties (i.e. endogenous factors) as the primary drivers for delegating authority for accounting standards to the private sector. At the same time, the authors also refer to subsequent actions by the EU to (re)assert its authority as a sign that governmental powers are still contenders in regulatory affairs (Chiapello and Medjad, 2009). This argument is shared by Bengtsson (2011) who argues that, prior to the financial crisis, the IASB had been able to establish accounting standards with relatively little influence, over either its governance structure or standard-setting process, from the governmental arena while global institutions, and in particular the accountancy profession, had significant input. In focusing on the fair value debate, Bengtsson (2011) outlines how macro-events that implicated accounting as a contributor to the crisis enabled a shifting of power in which government actors regained influence through a process that allows them the final word (through endorsement) on the adoption of standards established by the IASB.

Crawford, Ferguson, Helliar and Power (2014) delve more deeply into the political contestation of the endorsement process in focusing on the debate surrounding the reporting of operating segments. This debate saw the EU attempt to contest the IASB's authority by initiating a consultation process separate from that of the IASB as part of EU endorsement on the issue of operating segments. While Crawford *et al.* (2014) consider that government-level influence over standard setting remains relatively weak, they highlight the potentially crucial role of a regional governmental forum in which proposals emanating from the IASB can be contested in the future.

Several studies have addressed the challenges faced by developing countries' regulatory regimes in adjusting to the supranational network of accounting regulation. Chand and White (2007) explore the willingness of a developing country with a limited capital market to accept international accounting standards. The authors indicate that non-state forces, in particular the international accounting firms, effectively determine Fiji's accounting regulatory processes as the country does not have the resources to consider generating its own domestic standards, and the professional institute is therefore obliged to imitate international best practice as dictated by the firms (Chand and White, 2007). At the same time, according to Chand and White (2007) the application of international accounting standards, with their focus on fair value, is impractical in developing economies whose needs may differ from those of developed capital markets, and that this serves only to create and sustain asymmetries and imbalances within and between countries.

These differential needs are also investigated by Peng and Bewley (2010) who study the challenge of applying international standards, and the desirability of converging local standards with international standards, with a specific focus on how China, as a major emerging economy, implements fair value accounting as codified in IFRSs. The authors find that differences in China's application of international fair value standards are linked to complex aspects of the economic and political system that need to be developed in order to facilitate fair value accounting, including infrastructure to support understanding, provide oversight and enforce application (Peng and Bewley, 2010; Zhang *et al.*, 2012). Such divergence is unlikely to be resolved in the near future and is also noted in the work of Baker *et al.* (2012) on China's decision to allow an option in accounting for business combinations that is prohibited by international (and US) accounting standards. According to Baker *et al.*, this decision highlights a differential understanding of the claimed fundamental objectives of financial reporting – to benefit the global capital markets – indicative of potential "disharmony" with such objectives across settings. One might consider this disharmony through the lens of political economy with its emphasis on

[t]he infrastructure, fundamental relations between class in society, the institutional environment which supports the existing system, and critical scrutiny of issues that are frequently taken for granted.

(Cooper and Sherer, 1984: 208)

The problematical position of nation states in international standard setting also surfaces in the work of Richardson, who uses social network analysis to depict the linked organisations in the (Canadian) accounting regulatory environment "as a network of interacting bodies rather than a hierarchy of state power" (2009: 572). He shows the integration of accounting and auditing standard-setting institutions with domestic securities regulators and international governance organisations (IOSCO/World Bank) and how this integration weakens domestic sovereignty over accounting regulation while providing advantages to specific private organisations to influence the outcome of regulatory processes both domestically and internationally (Richardson, 2009). Richardson's study is one of the very few to attempt to study the ensemble of regulatory bodies operating on a global stage within a framing that explores the articulation of Canada's standard-setting agencies to such a global network.

6 Summary

As we noted in the introduction, from the late twentieth century onwards, the emergence, expansion and progression of regulatory agencies in the global arena has been striking. While not the focus of this chapter, it is also true that the agenda of accounting research in mainstream 'archival' studies has been increasingly shaped by global development in IFRSs and the rise of fair value approaches to balance sheet items. In this chapter, we have reviewed studies of accounting regulatory change from three perspectives: building and spreading regulatory institutions; the programmes and ideologies of accounting's regulatory spaces; and the global imperatives, national contexts and regulatory contests that occur in these spaces. Much of this 'critical' research has drawn upon institutional, political economic and discursive, constructionist frameworks. Inevitably, the degree of critical intent embodied within each approach has varied, but we would maintain that studies less concerned to explore vested interests and agenda setting in global accounting regulation still have critical moments in showing the dispersed sites of accounting regulation, the discourses and programs underlying regulatory initiatives, and the growing rationalisation of accounting and auditing practices.

In revealing something of the discourses and rationales that structure accounting rules and regulation, we see the sponsoring role of political and programmatic movements and the ideals of, for example, neo-liberalism in the, perhaps paradoxical, growth of regulatory institutions. Moreover, it is also true that explorations of the programmatic ideals of regulatory agencies have shown commonalities that exist between the adoption of 'user-decision' and 'value-relevant' rationales for the construction of regulatory standards (Young, 1996; Power, 2010). Yet more work could be done in exploring evolutions in programmatic ideals as they rise to a level of taken-for-grantedness. Such work may include perhaps deconstructing the notion and role of transparency as an apparent justification for an ever-expanding suite of financial reporting disclosures, or of professional skepticism as a mysterious scapegoat for enduring issues with poor audit quality.

Relative to the emergence and evolution of regulatory institutions and standards, most studies have tended to explore individual instances of organisational establishment and growth, or specific accounting standards. This is, of course, understandable in that it is perhaps only in the past few years that we have tended to see more evidence of the contests that can arise (between the IASB and the EU, for example) and the connections forged (the convergence agendas of the FASB and the IASB, for example) between regulatory institutions. However, as the world's financial architecture seems to grow ever more entangled and opaque, our understanding of accounting and auditing regulatory contests and connections and the wider implications they have for world society become increasingly important. More attention can be devoted to the multiplicity of regulatory institutions that have appeared on the accounting and auditing landscape in the last two decades, and in particular, to the ways in which these institutions affect accounting boundaries, ideas and processes, and the key players within these institutions and their relations across the field.

Moreover, the research we have explored here has seemingly drawn less upon world culture (Meyer *et al.*, 1997), world systems (Wallerstein, 2004) and related postcolonial theories to understand aspects of the multiplication of accounting and auditing standards and institutions. Pursuing studies of the way in which globalising accounting regulatory institutions impact world cultural values and practices – gender, ethnicity, religion, family, class, sovereignty – and the contestation and confrontation these regulatory institutions may provoke is one avenue to be explored (Halliday and Osinsky, 2006). In addition, we agree with these authors that closer empirical inquiry could be made into the core agents, mechanisms and power structures that seek to institutionalise global accounting norms, not to mention the local and peripheral actors who adopt, adapt or reject them. The power of peripheral actors and organisations should not be minimised and could be further elaborated as could the factors which affect local/peripheral responses to global/core initiatives.

Finally, on the topic of key institutions and relationships, only a few studies have followed the lead of Richardson's study of the 'networks' that exist among the global institutions of regulation and national standard setters. Such work speaks also to critical issues of power and influence by uncovering the central nodes of decision making, or 'obligatory passage points' that exist in the global arena for accounting policy decision making. While, as Chiapello and Medjad (2009) show, disputes may arise between governmental and non-governmental institutions, Richardson's study of the 'interlocks' linking regulatory organisations in accounting and auditing offers one approach to studying in more detail the common agendas and mutual support that exists. Moreover, one critical dimension so far relatively underexplored is that of the connections and social networks that exist between the bureaucrats of accounting regulation on the internnational stage and the sponsorship of the Big Four in terms of staff secondment and research support. On the one hand, it is clear that the staffing of bodies such as the IASB, the IFAC and its International Accounting and Auditing Standards Board, has relied significantly upon the employment of former partners of the large professional service firms. On the other hand, while Hopwood remarked over 20 years ago that "[r]elatively few people are involved with the key regional and international accounting institutions, many serving on several of them, sometimes even representing seemingly different interests on each" (Hopwood, 1994: 242), it is not clear whether extent research studies understand well this community of 'professional' accounting regulators (Botzem, 2012; Botzem and Quack, 2006, 2009). In addition, the role of audit firm–sponsored bodies of expertise that can monopolise the inputs to regulatory discussions at a supranational level and the drafting of regulatory discussion and agenda-setting documents, such as in Europe the FEE, is also as Hopwood suggested relatively unknown. As Cooper and Robson (2006) suggest, the role of professional firms in the enactment of professional regulations has been underexplored, a state of affairs also matched by the lack of attention given to the close linkages between the Big Four and influential support for accounting regulatory initiatives.

References

Abu, S. R., J. Everett and D. Neu (2007). "Accounting and the move to privatize water services in Africa," *Accounting, Auditing and Accountability Journal*, 20(5): 637–70.

Albu, C., N. Albu and D. Alexander (2014). "When global accounting standards meet the local context: insights from an emerging economy," *Critical Perspectives on Accounting*, 25(6): 489–510.

Annisette, M. (2004). "The true nature of the World Bank," *Critical Perspective on Accounting*, 15(3): 303–23.

Annisette, M. (2006). "People and periods untouched by accounting history: an ancient Yoruba Practice," *Accounting History* 11(4): 399–417.

Annisette, M. and D. Neu (2004). "Accounting and Empire: an introduction," *Critical Perspectives on Accounting*, 15(1): 1–4.

Arnold, P. (2005). "Disciplining domestic regulation: the World Trade Organization and the market for professional services," *Accounting, Organizations and Society*, 30(4), 299–330.

Arnold, P. (2009). "Institutional perspectives on the internationalization of accounting," in C. Chapman, D. Cooper, P. Miller (eds): *Accounting, Organizations and Institutions: Essays in Honour of Anthony Hopwood*, Oxford: Oxford University Press.

Arnold, P. (2012). "The political economy of financial harmonization: the East Asian financial crisis and the rise of international accounting standards," *Accounting, Organizations and Society*, 37(6): 361–81.

Arnold, P. and P. Sikka (2001). "Globalization and the state-profession relationship: the case of the Bank of Credit and Commerce International," *Accounting, Organizations and Society*, 26(6): 475–49.

Baker, C. R., Y. Biondi and Q. Zhang (2012). "Disharmony in international accounting standards-setting: the Chinese approach to accounting for business combinations," *Critical Perspectives on Accounting* 21(2): 107–17.

Baxter, W. (1984). *Inflation Accounting*, London: Philip Allan.

Bengtsson, E. (2011). "Repoliticalization of accounting standard setting – The IASB, the EU, and the global financial crisis," *Critical Perspectives on Accounting*, 22(6): 567–80.

Boli, J. and G. M. Thomas, G. M. (1997). "World culture in the world polity: a century of international non-governmental organization," *American Sociological Review*, 62(2): 171–90.

Botzem, S. (2012). *The Politics of Accounting Regulation: Organizing Transnational Standard Setting in Financial Reporting*, Cheltenham: Edward Elgar Publishing.

Botzem, S. and S. Quack (2006). "Contested rules and shifting boundaries: international standard setting in accounting," in M. L. Djecli and K. Sahlin-Andersson (eds): *Transnational Governance: Institutional Dynamics of Regulation*, Cambridge: Cambridge University Press.

Botzem, S. and S. Quack (2009). "(No) limits to Anglo-American accounting? Reconstructing the history of the International Accounting Standards Committee: a review article," *Accounting, Organizations and Society*, 34(8): 988–98.

Burchell, S., C. Clubb and A. G. Hopwood, A. (1985). "Accounting in its social context: towards a history of value added in the United Kingdom," *Accounting, Organizations and Society* 10(2): 381–413.

Burlaud, A. and B. Colasse (2011). "'International' accounting standardization: is politics back?" *Accounting in Europe*, 8(1): 23–47.

Caramanis, C. (2002). "The interplay between professional groups, the state and supranational agents: Pax Americana in the age of 'globalization'," *Accounting, Organizations and Society* 27(4–5): 379–408.

Camfferman, K. and S. Zeff (2007). *Financial Reporting and Global Capital Markets: A History of the International Accounting Standards Committee, 1973-2000*, Oxford: Oxford University Press.

Chand, P. and M. White (2007). "A critique of the influence of globalization and convergence of accounting standards in Fiji," *Critical Perspectives on Accounting*, 18(5): 605–22.

Chiapello, E. and K. Medjad (2009). "An unprecedented privatization of mandatory standard-setting: the case of European accounting policy," *Critical Perspectives on Accounting*, 20(4): 448–68.

Chua, W. F. and S. L Taylor (2008). "The rise and rise of IFRS: An examination of IFRS diffusion," *Journal of Accounting and Public Policy*, 27(6): 462–73.

Cooper, D. J., and M. Sherer (1984). "The value of corporate accounting reports: arguments for a political economy of accounting," *Accounting, Organizations and Society*, 9(3–4): 207–32.

Cooper, D. J. and K. Robson (2006). "Accounting, professions and regulation: locating the sites of professionalization," *Accounting, Organizations and Society*, 31(4–5): 415–44.

Cooper, D. J., M. Ezzamel and H. Willmott (2008). "Examining "institutionalization": a critical theoretic perspective," in R. Greenwood, C. Oliver, K. Sahlin and R. Suddaby (eds): *SAGE Handbook of Organizational Institutionalism*, London: Sage Publications.

Crawford, L., J. Ferguson, C.V. Helliar and D. M. Power (2014). "Control over accounting standards within the European Union: the political controversy surrounding the adoption of IFRS 8," *Critical Perspectives on Accounting*, 25(4–5): 304–18.

Danjou, P. and P. Walton (2012). "The legitimacy of the IASB," *Accounting in Europe*, 9(1): 1–15.

Dellaportas, S. and L. Davenport (2008). "Reflections on the public interest in accounting," *Critical Perspectives on Accounting*, 19(7): 1080–98.

DiMaggio, P. J. and W. W. Powell (1983). "The iron cage revisited: institutional isomorphism and collective rationality in organizational fields," *American Journal of Sociology*, 48(2): 147–60.

Drori, G., J. W. Meyer and H. Hwang (2006). *Globalization and Organization: World Society and Organizational Change*, Oxford: Oxford University Press.

Edgley, C. (2014). "A genealogy of accounting materiality," *Critical Perspectives on Accounting*, 25(3): 255–71.

Erb, C. and C. Pelger (2015). "Twisting words"? A study of the construction and reconstruction of reliability in financial reporting standard-setting," *Accounting, Organizations and Society*, 40: 13–40.

Francis, J. (1987). "Lobbying against proposed accounting standards: the case of employers' pension accounting," *Journal of Accounting and Public Policy*, 6(1): 35–57.

Froud, J., S. Johal, V. Papazian, V. and K. Williams (2004). "The temptation of Houston: a case study of financialization," *Critical Perspectives on Accounting*, 15(6–7): 885–909.

Gould, E. (2002). *TACD background paper on trade in services*, prepared for the Trans-Atlantic Consumer Dialogue, October 2002.

Graham, C. and D. Neu (2003). "Accounting for globalization," *Accounting Forum*, 27(4): 449–65.

Halliday, T. and P. Osinski (2006). "Globalization of law," *Annual Review of Sociology*, 32: 447–70.

Hamilton, G. and C. Ó hÓgartaigh (2009). "The Third Policeman: true and fair view, language and the habitus of accounting," *Critical Perspectives on Accounting*, 20(8): 910–20.

Haring, J. (1979). "Accounting rules and 'The Accounting Establishment'," *Journal of Business*, 52: 507–19.

Hegarty, J. (1997). "Accounting for the global economy: is national regulation doomed to disappear?" *Accounting Horizons*, 11(4): 75–90.

Held, D. and A. McGrew (2002). *Governing Globalization: Power, Authority and Global Governance*, Cambridge: Cambridge University Press.

Hirst, P. and G. Thompson (1995). "Globalization and the future of the nation state," *Economy and Society*, 24(3): 408–42.

Hope, R. and R. Gray (1982). "Power and policy making: the development of an R&D Standard," *Journal of Business Finance and Accounting*, 9(4): 531–58.

Hopwood, A. G. (1994). "Some reflections on 'The harmonization of accounting within the EU'," *European Accounting Review*, 3(2): 241–54.

Humphrey, C., A. Loft and M. Woods (2009). "The global audit profession and the international financial architecture: understanding regulatory relationships at a time of financial crisis," *Accounting, Organizations and Society*, 34(6–7): 810–25.

Latour, B. (1987). *Science in Action: How to Follow Scientists and Engineers Through Society*, Boston, MA: Harvard University Press.

Lawrence, T. (2008). "Power, institutions and organizations," in R. Greenwood, C. Oliver, R. Suddaby, K. Sahlin-Andersson (eds): *The SAGE Handbook of Organizational Institutionalism*, London: Sage Publications.

Lyas, C. (1984). "Philosophers and accountants," *Philosophy*, 59: 99–110.

Leach., R, and E. Stamp (1981). *British Accounting Standards. The First 10 Years*, Cambridge: Woodhead-Faulkner.

Loft, A., C. Humphrey and S. Turley (2006). "In pursuit of global regulation: changing governance and accountability structures at the International Federation of Accountants (IFAC)," *Accounting, Auditing and Accountability Journal*, 19(3): 428–51.

Menniken, A. (2008). "Connecting worlds: translation of international auditing standards into post-Soviet audit practice," *Accounting, Organizations and Society*, 33(4): 384–14.

Meyer, J. W. (1980). "The world polity and the authority of the nation-state," in A. Bergesen (ed.): *Studies of the Modern World-System*, New York: Academic Press.

Meyer, J. W., J. Boli, J., G. M. Thomas and F. O. Ramirez (1997). "World society and the nation state," *American Journal of Sociology*, 103(1): 144–81.

Miller, P. (1994). "Accounting as social and institutional practice: an introduction," in P. Miller and A. G. Hopwood (eds): *Accounting as Social and Institutional Practice*, Cambridge: Cambridge University Press.

Müller, J. (2014). "An accounting revolution? The financialization of standard setting," *Critical Perspectives on Accounting*, 25(7): 539–57.

Murphy, T., V. O'Connell, V. and C. Ó hÓgartaigh, C. (2013). "Discourses surrounding the evolution of the IASB/FASB Conceptual Framework: what they reveal about the living law of accounting," *Accounting, Organizations and Society*, 38(1): 72–91.

Neu, D., A. Shiraz Rahaman, J. Everett and A. Akindayomi (2010). "The sign value of accounting: IMF structural adjustment programs and African banking reform," *Critical Perspectives on Accounting*, 21(5), 402–19.

Ohmae, K. (1995). *The Evolving Global Economy: Making Sense of the New World Order*, Boston MA: Harvard Business School Press.

Ordelheide, D. (1993). "True and fair view: a European and a German perspective," *European Accounting Review*, (2)1: 81–90.

Peng, S. and K. Bewley (2010). "Adaptability to fair value in an emerging economy: a case study of China's IFRS convergence," *Accounting, Auditing and Accountability Journal*, 23(8): 982–1011.

Power, M. (2009). "Financial accounting without a state," in C. Chapman, D. Cooper and P. Miller (eds), *Accounting, Organizations and Institutions: Essays in Honour of Anthony Hopwood*, Oxford: Oxford University Press.

Power, M. (2010). "Fair value accounting, financial economics and the transformation of reliability," *Accounting and Business Research*, 40(3): 197–210.

Puro, M. (1984). "Audit firm lobbying before the Financial Accounting Standards Board: an empirical study," *Journal of Accounting Research*, 22(2): 624–46.

Puxty, A. G., H. C. Willmott, D. J. Cooper, D. J. and T. Lowe (1987). "Modes of regulation in advanced capitalism: locating accountancy in four countries," *Accounting, Organizations and Society*, 12(3): 273–91.

Ravenscroft, S., and P. Williams (2009). "Making imaginary worlds real: the case of expensing employee stock options," *Accounting, Organizations and Society*, 34(6–7): 770–86.

Richardson, A. J. (2009). "Regulatory networks for accounting and auditing standards: a social network analysis of Canadian and international standards setting," *Accounting, Organizations and Society*, 34(5): 571–88.

Robson, K. (1991). "On the arenas of accounting change: the process of translation," *Accounting, Organizations and Society*, 16 (5–6): 547–70.

Robson, K. (1993). "Accounting policy-making and "interests": accounting for research and development," *Critical Perspectives on Accounting*, 4(1): 1–27.

Robson, K. (1994). "Inflation accounting and action at a distance: the Sandilands episode," *Accounting, Organizations and Society*, 19(1): 45–82.

Robson, K. and J. J. Young (2009). "Socio-political studies of financial reporting and standard setting," in C. Chapman, D. Cooper and P. Miller (eds): *Accounting, Organizations & Institutions: Essays in Honour of Anthony Hopwood*, Oxford: Oxford University Press.

Santos, B. D. S. (2002). "The processes of globalization," *Revista Crítica de Ciências Sociais and Eurozine*, 1–48.

Solomons, D. (1978). "The politicization of accounting: the impact of politics on accounting Standards," *Journal of Accountancy*, 146(6): 65–72.

Suddaby, R., D. Cooper, D. and R. Greenwood (2007). "Transnational regulation of professional services: governance dynamics of field level organizational change," *Accounting, Organizations and Society*, 32(4–5): 333–62.

Tamm-Hallstrom, K. (2004). *Organizing International Standardization – ISO and the IASC in Question of Authority*, Cheltenham: Edward Elgar.

Thorell, P. and G. Whittington (1994). The harmonization of accounting within the EU. *European Accounting Review*, 3(2): 215–40.

Trolliet, C. and J. Hegarty (2003). "Regulatory reform and trade liberalization in accountancy Services," in A. Mattoo. A. and P. Sauve (eds): *Domestic Regulation and Service Trade Liberalization*, World Bank Publications.

Wade, R. (2007). "A new financial architecture?" *New Left Review*, 46(July/August): 113–29.

Wallerstein, I. M. (2004). *World-Systems Analysis: An Introduction*. Durham, NC: Duke University Press.

Walters, M. and J. J. Young "Metaphors and accounting for stock options," *Critical Perspectives on Accounting*, 19(5): 805–33.

Walton, P. (1993). "Company law and accounting in nineteenth-century Europe," *European Accounting Review*, 2(2): 286–91.

Willmott, H. (2014). "Why institutional theory cannot be critical," *Journal of Management Inquiry*, 24(1): 1–7.

Willmott, H., A. Puxty, K. Robson, D. Cooper and T. Lowe (1992). "Regulation of accountancy and accountants: a comparative analysis of accounting for research and development in four advanced capitalist countries," *Accounting Auditing and Accountability Journal*, 5(2): 31–54.

WTO (World Trade Organization) (1998). *Council for Trade in Services* S/C/W/50, September 18, 1998.

Young, J. J. (1994). "Outlining regulatory space: agenda issues and the FASB," *Accounting, Organizations and Society*, 19(1): 83–109.

Young, J. J. (1996). "Institutional thinking: the case of financial instruments," *Accounting, Organizations and Society*, 21(5): 487–512.

Young, J. J. (2003). "Constructing, persuading and silencing: the rhetoric of accounting standards," *Accounting, Organizations and Society*, 28(6): 621–38.

Young, J. J. (2006). "Making up users," *Accounting, Organizations and Society*, 31(6): 579–600.

Young J. J. and P. Williams (2010). "Sorting and comparing: standard-setting and 'ethical' categories," *Critical Perspectives on Accounting*, 21(6): 509–21.

Zeff, S. A. (1972). *Forging Accounting Principles in Five Countries: A History and an Analysis of Trends*, Champaign, IL: Stipes Publishing Co.

Zeff, S. A. (1978). "The rise of economic consequences," *Journal of Accountancy*, 146(6): 56–63.

Zhang, Y. and J. Andrew (2014). "Financialization and the conceptual framework," *Critical Perspectives on Accounting*, 25: 17–26.

Zhang, Y., J. Andrew and K. Rudkin (2012). "Accounting as an instrument of neoliberalization?: Exploring the adoption of fair value accounting in China," *Accounting, Auditing and Accountability Journal*, 25(8): 1266–89.

12

ACCOUNTING AS COLONISATION

Jane Broadbent and Richard Laughlin

1 Introduction

Colonisation can be intuitively understood by going back to its roots and can be defined as a process where people "settle among and establish control over (the indigenous people of an area)" or when talking of a plant or animal it will "establish itself in (an area)."[1] This chapter reflects the view that whilst colonisation may be imposed, the colonisers may well have a positive intention – leaving open whether this is misguided or not – to achieve what they see as a positive outcome. Our main assumption, however, is that many colonisation attempts are unwelcome, often resisted and not guaranteed to succeed. We are particularly concerned with the use of 'accounting' as a tool of colonisation. Our concern is the manner in which accounting, as a way of thinking and a set of values, is used by one set of actors (the attempted colonisers) to try to reshape the thinking, values and actions of another set of actors (the target group to be colonised). The chapter unpacks this complexity, as it manifests itself in the context of public services, particularly those supplied through public sector organisations.[2] To provide an empirical grounding to this analysis the focus will be primarily on public sector organisations in the UK,[3] which have, for many years, been subject to a wide range of accounting-driven requirements coming from a range of societal regulatory bodies.

Public sector organisations, in the UK, and in a number of other countries, have been subject to a range of control intentions that have been referred to as the 'New Public Management' (NPM) (Hood, 1991, 1995) or, more accurately, the 'New Public *Financial* Management' (NPFM), as Olson, Guthrie and Humphrey (1998) label it. This latter descriptor highlights the significance of finance and accounting in the substance of these intentions to control. Whilst NPFM is neither 'new' nor unified in its nature, it does possess a set of mutable but generic characteristics, which, in countries such as the UK, have intensified over recent years. This intensification, we would argue, is due to the increasing use of accounting technologies to enable the controls of the would-be colonisers to become more focussed and sophisticated.

The nature of the would-be colonisers and those resistant to colonisation will be explored in the course of the chapter. They will be refined by using our development (cf. Broadbent, Laughlin and Read, 1991; Broadbent and Laughlin, 1998, 2013) of the analytical framework of Jurgen Habermas's Critical Theory (cf. Habermas, 1984, 1987). Habermas (1984, 1987) sees complex modern societies as made up by interconnected 'lifeworlds', 'steering media' and 'systems'. Lifeworlds are the underlying and changing shared values that constitute society at any point in time. These lifeworlds find expression in and through tangible systems that exist in society, again at a particular time point. Steering media, on the other hand, are the intervening bodies that ensure the societal systems do indeed adequately reflect the values contained in the lifeworld (again at a particular moment of time), using specific 'steering mechanisms' to achieve these purposes. Drawing from this framework Broadbent *et al.* (1991) argue that steering media (such as governments) and systems (such as public sector organisations) are respectively 'societal steering institutions' and 'organisations' with their own micro-lifeworlds (called 'interpretative schemes'), their own micro-steering mediums (called 'design archetypes') and systems (called operational 'sub-systems').

This institutional and organisational development of Habermas's model helps to make clear that these bodies can be driven by different values and concerns, and work independently of each other. Habermas does recognise this to a degree in his notion of the *internal colonisation of the lifeworld* (Habermas, 1987: 332ff). This is the situation where steering media break away from lifeworld demands and feed back into and reshape the lifeworld. However, he does not clarify why or how this might happen. Broadbent *et al.*'s (1991) recognition of institutional and organisational structures, that give the power and possibility for independent action and development, provides this clarification. It also provides the basis for understanding why and how societal steering institutions can deviate from a societal lifeworld direction and attempt to steer, using a range of steering mechanisms, organisations in ways that could lead to them not expressing lifeworld demands. It also helps to explain why, if this occurs, organisations may resist impositions of this sort even though societal steering institutions have a societally sanctioned role to regulate, through steering mechanisms, the behaviour of these organisations.

To explore these complex themes, the chapter is divided into three sections followed by a reflective conclusion. The second section provides a conceptual elaboration of the contents of this introduction that will be used as a *middle-range* (cf. Laughlin, 1995, 2004; Broadbent and Laughlin, 2013) theoretical language for exploring the more empirical sections that follow. The third section explores the changing nature of NPFM and the steering mechanisms it encompasses, with particular emphasis on the UK situation, over time. The fourth section explores some of the resistance strategies that we have observed in a range of public sector organisations, intended to prevent colonisation by the steering mechanisms of NPFM. The chapter concludes with a critical analysis of both the NPFM steering mechanisms of societal steering institutions and the resistance strategies of public sector organisations, as well as identifying pointers towards an alternative way forward.

2 A middle-range conceptual analytical framework

As indicated in the introduction the steering mechanisms used by societal steering institutions in an attempt to control (colonise?) public sector organisations, and the resistance strategies that these controls engender, are the main focus of this chapter. We describe these societal steering mechanisms where regulators seek to control an organisation as 'inter-organisational steering'. The internal steering mechanisms set up in reaction to inter-organisational steering, (including various forms of resistance) we see as 'intra-organisational steering', (Broadbent and Laughlin, 2013: 6ff). Figure 12.1 depicts these complex interrelationships. What the figure also makes plain is that societal steering institutions and public sector organisations have their own interpretative schemes, design archetypes and systems, which allow them to act independently of each other and possibly also of the societal lifeworld. This means that, despite the positional power of societal steering institutions, and whatever the colonising intent of the inter-organisational steering

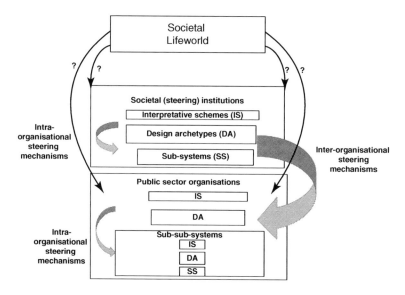

Figure 12.1 Steering Linkages between society and the public sector organisations.
Source: Broadbent and Laughlin, 2013.

mechanisms – which may not necessarily be driven by societal lifeworld demands – the success in changing the thinking and behaviour of public sector organisations is not guaranteed. This is because unless the inter-organisational steering mechanisms are in some way accepted by these organisations and become embedded, through force or by choice, in the intra-organisational steering mechanisms that drive the thinking and behaviour of these organisations, then any colonisation intentions will not be realised.

In our view, the key steering mechanism, whether of an inter-organisational or intra-organisational nature, is *money*. Habermas did not make the distinction between steering media and steering mechanisms but in his early work he identifies money and power as, in our terms, key steering mechanisms. However, in later work power through law displaces the role of money as the key steering mechanism (Habermas, 1996). The reason for this, according to Habermas, is because law "calls for a *more demanding normative anchoring* than money" (Habermas, 1987: 271 [emphasis in the original]). As Dodd (1994), Power and Laughlin (1996) and Broadbent and Laughlin (2009, 2013) argue, this downplaying of the significance of money and according a superior role to law is misplaced. To Simmel (1978: 211) money is a 'pure instrument' upon which any values can be implanted and thus it is a more powerful, more all-pervasive and a more flexible steering mechanism than law could ever be.

Our argument is that the power, flexibility and the consequent meaning given to money is provided by accounting. Accounting, in its many forms, provides the information 'codes' that make the 'pure instrument' of money into something that has meaningful intent. This, leads to a definition of accounting as

> the *ex ante* and *ex post* information 'codes' accompanying direct and indirect money transfers, which collectively constitute the key steering mechanisms of societal (steering) institutions and organisations.
>
> *(Broadbent and Laughlin, 2013: 10, emphasis as in the original)*

The significance of *ex ante* and *ex post* in this definition registers the important point that within this understanding accounting has both a proactive power – to guide actions to be taken through the use of money – and a reactive power – to see whether intended actions have been undertaken. This broad understanding of accounting encompasses not only those activities that are referred to as accounting – such as management accounting and financial accounting, which we call 'traditional accounting' in Broadbent and Laughlin (2013) – but also other forms of information that possess the characteristics of accounting but are often not referred to as such. In Broadbent and Laughlin (2013) we refer to these additional accounting-related information codes that are related to money as 'accountability' and 'accounting logic'. Accountability is an increasingly visible concept, linked to but going beyond the narrative-reporting extensions of traditional financial accounting, with a strong *ex post* emphasis. Accounting logic, however, is more complex and more insidious:

> Accounting logic's main characteristic relies on the traditional accounting assumption '….that it is possible to evaluate each and every financial flow in terms of outputs, and preferably outcomes achieved' (Laughlin, 2007, p. 280). All money transfers, under the direction of accounting logic, are seen rather like transactions, which are, of course, the bedrock of traditional accounting. This is a way of thinking about money transfers that assumes it is possible to forecast the expected outcome to be achieved as a result of this transfer. It also guides the required contents of the *ex post* report which relates to whether these defined expectations have been realised. It is as though *all* financial transfers can, in the final analysis, be seen as simple transactions where something (money) is given for something in return.
>
> *(Broadbent and Laughlin, 2013: 14, emphasis as in the original)*

Accounting logic has its roots in accounting, although is often not referred to as accounting, and is invariably not practised by recognisable qualified accountants. It has been influential on the thinking of many, including those who are regulators and politicians. It has led to the highly problematic but unquestioned norm that all money transfers can be seen as simple transactions and that *ex ante* and *ex post* information codes accompanying these transfers can be accurately defined and measured.

Broadbent and Laughlin (2009, 2013) provide a comprehensive account of our argument that links this understanding of steering mechanisms and money and accounting, accountability and accounting logic to alternative performance management systems (PMSs). This builds on and develops the extensive literature on management control systems and particularly the insightful understanding of PMSs by Otley (1999) and Ferreira and Otley (2009). A summary of our thinking in diagrammatic form is provided in Figure 12.2. We will not explore the detail of this in depth in this chapter but it is introduced for two purposes. First, to clarify the nature of transactional PMSs that are driven by accounting logic. Second, to highlight alternative relational PMSs to this form of steering mechanism, which finds its roots in different underlying assumptions that are not driven by accounting logic but are still expressed through money transfers and alternative accounting-related codes.

In broad terms Figure 12.2 highlights that PMSs seek to steer the nature of the ends and the means of actions and activities (of those they are intended to steer) in and through money transfers and accounting information codes. The nature of these can vary substantively. The nature of the context and the adopted and taken-for-granted model of rationality will affect the nature of the PMSs that are developed. Ferreira and Otley (2009) highlight 12 questions that need to be answered in the context of developing PMSs concerning, in the main, issues related to the ends

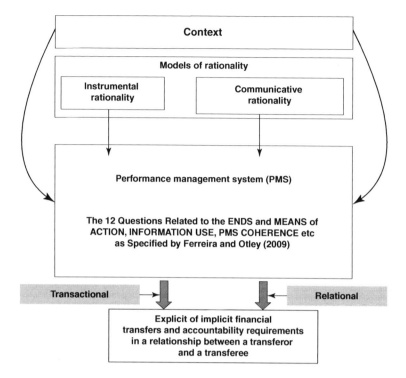

Figure 12.2   PMS: A conceptual model.

(adapted from Broadbent and Laughlin, 2009)

to be achieved and the means to achieve them. The context and mode of rationality adopted will impact on how these questions are addressed and hence upon PMS design. The nature of the systems may be transactional or relational (the explanation of which we give in the subsequent paragraphs), but whatever their orientation they will be expressed in and through money and the accompanying different forms of accounting information codes.

We highlight rationality because, in the words of Townley, Cooper and Oakes (2003: 1045) the discussion and decision about ends and means of actions involves the "pursuit of reason in human affairs," which is reliant on alternative models of rationality. As Figure 12.2 indicates, two fundamentally different models of rationality can be identified resulting in a distinction between

> [a] communicative approach that adopts a view that the understanding of ends and means comes out of an open discourse between parties leading to discursive agreement or are instrumental and determined by forms of discourse-constrained specification leading to a "rational calculation about the specific means of achieving definite ends" (Allen, 2004: 78).
> *(Broadbent and Laughlin, 2013: 75)*

As noted earlier, we argue that it is these alternative forms of rationality that lead to very different PMSs/steering mechanisms which we label 'transactional' and 'relational'. Transactional PMSs have

> a high level of specificity about the ends to be achieved (e.g. through performance measures, targets etc.) and often a clear specification of the means needed to

achieve these defined ends. Transactional PMSs are often organised as projects, with requirements linked to contracts over a defined period of time. It is for this reason that a PMS defined as 'transactional', at its simplest, is similar to a simple, in effect, 'exchange transaction' to achieve a particular end state through a defined set of means.

(Broadbent and Laughlin, 2009: 289)

The confidence to assume that transactional PMSs are possible, appropriate and the only steering mechanisms that are justifiable is arguably due to the power of accounting logic. This guides the thinking implicit in this approach, finding its full expression through the money transfer and the accounting codes that accompany this transfer. Sadly, due to the power of accounting logic's pervasive presence in the thinking of a wide spectrum of humanity, particularly those in Western democracies, transactional PMSs are pervasive. There is however an alternative – relational PMSs, which have the following characteristics:

> When a PMS is categorised as 'relational' the expectation is that ends and means are deliberately subject to a discourse between the stakeholders and chosen by them. Specificity of the sort demanded by a transactional PMS is possible but only if chosen and subject to the agreement of stakeholders. The key factor in this is the extent of choice and ownership of the specific ends and particular means of achieving them. Often the specific focus will be less like a defined project, less short-term in nature and more concerned with the long-term survival and sustainability of the organisation/ unit through which the stakeholders are working.
>
> *(Broadbent and Laughlin, 2009: 77)*

Transactional inter-organisational steering mechanisms[4] are more directional, more likely to have colonising intent and, therefore, more likely than relational inter-organisational steering mechanisms to be the subject of resistance strategies by public sector organisations. The reason quite simply is that the information codes in the money transfers in transactional steering mechanisms are intentionally prescriptive about what public sector organisations should be trying to achieve, and what *ex post* reports should be delivered. Invariably the nature of these *ex ante* and *ex post* requirements will not have been agreed with the stakeholders in public sector organisations leading to a sense of what right have 'they' (as in the societal steering institutions) to tell 'us' (as in the public sector organisations) what to achieve, how we should do this and what *ex post* reports should be provided. Fear of colonisation is, therefore, highly likely, leading, in most cases, to some form of resistance to this perceived intrusion.

This is an empirical claim that requires amplification through empirical cases, although there are some things that can be said at the conceptual level. What is known is that any inter-organisational steering mechanisms are intended to steer organisations in society. That is their role and thus they have positional power. If change is desired they must 'disturb' the equilibrium of organisations to achieve that organisational change. From an organisational perspective, undesired change will require a response, which begs the question: What responses are possible? Laughlin (1991) answers this question conceptually suggesting four alternative pathways. Thus, a disturbance, provided by inter-organisational steering mechanisms of a transactional or relational form, will 'track' their way through any organisation's interpretative schemes, design archetypes and sub-systems in different ways.

Two of these four pathways lead to second-order change. This particularly involves changes to the underlying values and genetic codes of the organisational interpretative schemes (although other changes will impact on other levels). These two change pathways are labelled 'evolution' and 'colonisation'. Evolution is the result of changes in the organisational interpretive schemes that emerge organically from changes in discourse; this might itself be engendered as a response to the inter-organisational steering mechanisms. Evolution does however lead to a state that is chosen and agreed (by all stakeholders). Colonisation, on the other hand, involves second-order changes but changes that are forced through by some of the organisational stakeholders, rejecting any opposition along the way until the values of the colonising group, reinforced and given legitimacy through the inter-organisational steering mechanisms become the new underlying values of the organisation as a whole.

The other two pathways that are conceptually possible according to Laughlin (1991) lead to what he designates as 'first-order change'. First-order change involves the organisation changing in response to inter-organisational steering mechanisms but in a way that does not affect the underlying values and genetic code of the organisation no matter how challenging these steering mechanisms may be to these values. These are referred to as 'rebuttal' and 'reorientation' forms of organisational change. Rebuttal, as its name suggests, involves trying to actually reject the inter-organisational steering mechanisms even though they may already exist and are in operation. Reorientation, on the other hand, involves changing the design archetypes and sub-systems in the organisation to accommodate the demands of these steering mechanisms but in such a way that the underlying values and genetic code of the organisation is unaffected.

These four pathways provide a powerful conceptual language for empirical investigations into the actual levels of change that occur in organisations, but they are not predictive. Thus, which of these four pathways will be followed in relation to attempts at inter-organisational steering is an empirical question. It is to this we now turn, starting with an analysis of the actual nature of these steering mechanisms over public sector organisation that have been developing over the last few decades in the UK. We will use the conceptual language we have introduced, particularly the nature of and distinction between transactional and relational steering mechanisms, to inform our analysis.

3 Societal steering mechanisms: the role of the New Public Financial Management (NPFM)

Hood (1991: 4–5) identifies seven key 'doctrinal components' of NPM:

1   *Hands-on professional management* in the public sector;
2   *Explicit standards and measures of performance*;
3   Greater emphasis on *output controls*;
4   Shift to *disaggregation* of units in the public sector;
5   Shift to greater *competition* in the public sector;
6   *Stress on private sector styles of management practice*;
7   Stress on greater *discipline* and *parsimony* in resource use.

(emphasis as in the original)

Hood argues that these NPM components reflect key underlying 'sigma-type values' (Hood, 1991: 15) which he typecasts as "keep it lean and purposeful" (Hood, 1991: 11). This can be distinguished from alternative core values in public management that Hood (1991: 11) refers to as 'lambda-type values' ("keep it robust and resilient"). In simple terms, sigma-type values lead to transactional steering mechanisms whereas lambda-type values are key in relational steering mechanisms.

To Hood (1995: 93) the move away from "progressive public administration" (PPA) to NPM involves "a shift towards 'accountingization' (a term coined by Power and Laughlin, 1992, p. 133)." This link to accountingization, however, only occurs when NPM evolves into what can be referred to as 'New Public Financial Management' (NPFM) following Olson, Guthrie and Humphrey (1998). Dunleavy and Hood (1994: 10) refer to this move from PPA to NPM – and into NPFM – as moving 'down group' and 'down grid'. What they mean by going down group involves a move to stressing the importance of the private sector in providing a lead on how to supply and manage the public services. Going down grid is more subtle, and involves stressing the importance of decentralisation and devolution but always coupled with an increase in the use of all manner of accounting controls to ensure that the devolved units follow centralised values and concerns. NPFM, as an intensified form of NPM, gives particular emphasis to three of Hood's seven characteristics, namely discipline and parsimony in resource use (Hood's component seven) through the use of explicit standards and measures of performance (component two) and a greater emphasis on output controls (component three). The other categories all remain important but, in the case of NPFM, there is an intensification of the importance of components two, three and seven of Hood's (1991) listing of characteristics.

The adoption of NPM and the subsequent change to NPFM across nation states varies. Hood (1995) provides one of the first important analyses of this variability and leads to the following conclusion:

> From the fragmentary literature on public management reform over the 1980s, the high NPM group in the OECD countries would be likely to include Sweden, Canada, New Zealand, Australia and the UK with France, Denmark, the Netherlands, Norway and Ireland also showing a number of marked shifts in the direction of NPM. At the other end, the low NPM group would be likely to include Germany, Greece, Spain, Switzerland, Japan and Turkey.
>
> *(Hood, 1995: 99)*

The focus of this chapter is on high adopters of NPM and NPFM, with a particular emphasis on the UK. This progressive development of NPM to NPFM in the UK is summarised in Figure 12.3, which represents the development of NPFM in the UK in three key stages: moving from PPP to NPM to NPFM and becoming ever more transactional in nature.

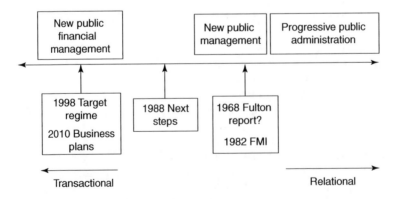

Figure 12.3   The intensification of transactional societal steering mechanisms over public sector organisations: the UK experience.

Source: Broadbent and Laughlin, 2013: 98, figure 4.1.

The Financial Management Initiative (FMI) in 1982 is often seen as a watershed event in the development of NPM in the UK, although Zifcak (1994: 12) traces its origins earlier, notably to the Fulton Report (1968). Jackson (1988) traces it back even further to the 1950s. Origins are always difficult to pinpoint yet there is no disputing that the emergence of the study on the efficiency and effectiveness of the civil service (Treasury and Civil Service Committee, 1982) that launched the FMI in the UK was significant. The FMI had clear intentions to

[p]romote in each Department an organisation and system in which managers at all levels have

1   a clear view of their objectives; and assess and wherever possible measure outputs or performance in relation to these objectives;
2   well defined responsibility for making the best use of their resources including a critical scrutiny of output and value for money; and
3   the information (including particularly about costs), training and access to expert advice which they need to exercise their responsibilities effectively.

(Treasury and Civil Service Committee, 1982: 21)

In Jackson's view:

[T]he FMI embodied the rational model of decision-making, in which objectives and constraints are set clearly, decision-making within the organisation is devolved, and financial management information is generated that will enable managers to manage resources efficiently.

(Jackson, 1988: vi)

Thus FMI was intended to bring new forms of rationality into public services management yet it had limited success, necessitating the introduction of the 1988 Next Steps initiative:

[W]hile the civil service was much more conscious of the cost of its activities than it has ever been, the essential features of management in Whitehall had remained untouched by five years of intensive administrative reform. Short-term political priorities still squeezed out long-term planning. Policy and ministerial support dominated civil service structure and function to the neglect of the effective delivery of government services. Government programmes were focussed on the expenditure of money rather than the achievement of results.

(Zifcak, 1994: 72)

Zifcak argues that Next Steps was an outgrowth of the FMI but was more robustly geared towards fundamental change. It saw "structural change as the precondition for attitudinal change" (Zifcak, 1994: 89), involving the establishment of agencies "to carry out the executive functions of government" (Zifcak, 1994: 73).

The proposals culminated in the Next Steps Report and were of concern to HM Treasury due to the increasing possibility for the move to agencies to lead to a "relaxation of central control" (Zifcak, 1994: 81). However, an increased emphasis on output and outcome controls was seen as offering a solution to resolve these concerns:

The Treasury was considerably more prepared than it had been to delegate some of its financial controls, particularly input controls .... But for this relaxation it had extracted

a price. The price was a greater role in setting targets and monitoring agency performance. The ground it lost on inputs it made up on outcomes.

(Zifcak, 1994: 83)

This emerging relationship involved 'management by contract' (Zifcak, 1994: 86); yet as he
observes "the reality was that no enforceable contracts existed." The seeds of a different emphasis
in NPM were planted at this point but its realisation was still to come. However, the *Next Steps*
initiative ensured that a greater transactional emphasis was guaranteed. Output and outcome
control aligned to financial transfers to delegated agencies became the primary focus for operationalising this required structural change. The intensification of the move to transactional and
sigma-type values, from NPM to NPFM, became ever more developed after the election of a
Labour Government in 1997. In 1998, the Labour Government published a Comprehensive
Spending Review (CSR) and introduced Public Service Agreements (PSAs). This was a step
change in a move from the NPM developments of the 1980s to a strong and clear NPFM
emphasis.

The CSR and PSAs were made possible as a result of the introduction of Resource
Accounting and Budgeting (RAB), which was in a well-advanced stage in 1998 even
though it only became fully operational in the early 2000s. At its simplest, RAB involves
a move from cash-based accounts and budgets to ones that are based on accruals principles so as to provide a distinction between capital and current expenditure. RAB involves
both resource accounts as well as resource budgeting that largely mirror private sector
practices:

> Resource accounts differ from the traditional cash accounts, both in their format and
> in the way they measure spending. Rather than being a simple statement of cash spent
> and received, they take broadly the same form as commercial accounts, with a balance
> sheet, the equivalent of a profit and loss statement, and information on cash flow, along
> with some additional information specific to the public sector.... Resource budgeting
> uses this information as the basis for planning and controlling public spending. Under
> the new system, these new costs are included in budgets.
>
> *(Likierman, 2003: 45–6)*

The introduction of RAB allowed a number of developments to occur. First and foremost,
RAB allowed Government expenditure to be categorised as either capital or current using
traditional accounting's understanding of these distinctions. Second, it allowed Government to
formulate capital and resource budgets – referred to as 'Capital and Resource Departmental
Expenditure Limits' (DELs). Third, RAB provided an opportunity to formalise the expectations
to be achieved from Capital and Resource budgets – referred to as 'Public Service Agreements'
(PSAs), as befits the 'something for something' accounting logic driver for this change. Fourth,
RAB allowed those societal steering institutions concerned with regulating the *ex post* reporting
of organisations to use the regulatory requirements for private sector organisations as the base
for public sector organisations as well. It thus gave traditional financial accounting and particular
forms of accountability, which had evolved over many years in and for the private sector, a new
domain of influence in the public sector.

Under the Labour Government, and up until the Coalition Government came to power in
2010, it was only DELs[5] that featured in the CSRs and Spending Reviews (SRs). The first CSR
in 1998 provided a wide-ranging review and a rolling three-year finance-led and outcomes-
based plan for all Government Departments. The 1998 CSR contained plans for the 1999/20006

to 2001/02 cycle. The first SR was issued in 2000 covering the period 2001/02 to 2003/04. A second SR in 2002 covered the period 2003/04 to 2005/06. This was the first SR where RAB was fully operational allowing full resource and capital budgets to be in place. A third SR, published in 2004, covered the period 2005/06 to 2007/08. A further wide-ranging CSR was published in 2007 to cover the period from 2008/09 to 2010/11. The Global Financial Crisis was to strike soon after the 2007 CSR was issued opening up considerable gaps in the income to cover these expenditure plans.

The Labour Government was defeated in a General Election in May 2010 and subsequently there were changes in the nature of these CSRs and SRs. A new Coalition Government was formed following this defeat, bringing together the Conservative and Liberal Democrat parties. As a result a new, rather more austere SR was issued, revising the 2010/11 plans of the Labour Government and setting out further plans for four years from 2011/12 to 2014/15. The Labour Government's CSRs and SRs had overlapping years to add some rigour to the budgeting process. The 2010 SR, however, moved to a four-year planning cycle, and for the first time included budgets not only for DELs but also AMEs yet it seemingly loosened the ties to outcomes through PSAs.

Before looking at what seemed to be a loosening of ties to PSAs, however, it is important to know something about their nature. The Labour Government's submission to the House of Commons' Public Administration Select Committee's (PASC) report on targets (PASC, 2003) provides some indicators of this nature and why they involved such a major change when they were first introduced in the CSR of 1998:

> The targets set out in Public Service Agreements … provide:
>
> – a clear statement of what the Government is trying to achieve;
> – a clear sense of direction and ambition;
> – a focus on delivering results;
> – a basis for monitoring what is and isn't working; and
> – better public accountability.
>> The PSAs have contributed to a real shift in culture in Whitehall away from inputs and processes towards delivering outputs and results.
>
> *(PASC, 2003: Minutes of Evidence, PST60)*

The structure of PSAs was made clearer in the 2002 SR, which began to reveal more direct links with the aims and objectives behind the targets. In the 2004 SR, PSAs evolved and changed yet again with a reduction in the number of these targets – to 110 – with an increasing outcome focus. The 2007 CSR reduced the PSAs even further – from 110 to 30. The 2007 PSAs were seen as the culmination of the use of PSAs "with 30 new PSAs setting a vision for continuous and accelerated improvement in the Government's priority outcomes over the CSR period" (taken from Archived Content of the 2007 Pre-Budget Report and Comprehensive Spending Review).

What is interesting about the Coalition Government's 2010 SR was its seemingly deliberate ending and abandonment of PSAs. The new Coalition Government made clear in June 2010 that "the Government's approach" (taken, along with the other quote in this paragraph from www.hm-treasury.gov.uk/press_10_10.htm) was to

> end the previous administration's complex system of Public Service Agreements that relied too heavily on rigid targets and instead ask departments to publish business plans

that show the resources they need to put in place in order to protect key frontline services and deliver on their objectives.

At one level this could be seen as a reversal of the intensifying of the transactional emphasis of NPFM to a more relational form. Closer inspection would suggest something rather different. The first tranche of Business Plans was published in November 2010. A cursory look at any of these Business Plans makes clear that they are driven by a long list of 'Coalition Priorities' that have a strong target-driven emphasis, with listings of actions to be undertaken with start and end times for completion and with clear 'milestones' to be met in relation to these targets and actions. This led Colin Talbot, in his Whitehall Watch (http://whitehallwatch.org/), to conclude that actually the new Business Plans are "new wine in old bottles" (this quote and others in this paragraph are taken from http://whitehallwatch.org/2010/11/08/department-business-plans-new-wine-in-old-bottles/). As Talbot makes plain:

> These plans are supposed to be "revolutionary" in several ways. But this 'revolution' is more spin than substance, with much of what they are doing simply following in the footsteps of previous governments – Conservative as well as Labour.

In conclusion, and referring back to Figure 12.3, these changes in the UK have involved a move from PPA to NPM to NPFM. This has led to an increasing transactional emphasis in the resulting inter-organisational steering mechanisms over public sector organisations, which have reacted very negatively to these increasing transactional steering mechanisms as the following section demonstrates.

4 The reaction of public sector organisations to new public financial management

As indicated in the previous section, societal steering institutions, due to their role in society, have positional power. Thus the steering mechanisms they produce cannot be ignored by public sector organisations. Something has to happen at the organisational level to deal with them. Conceptually these steering mechanisms are disturbances that need to track their way through organisations. Our argument is that these tracks can be of four types – two leading to second-order change (evolution and colonisation) and involving changes in the underlying values and genetic code of any organisation as well as at the design archetype and subsystems levels; and two leading to first-order change (rebuttal and reorientation), where the intra-organisational changes – in the design archetypes and subsystems – are such that the underlying interpretative scheme values remain unchanged.

Transactional inter-organisational steering mechanisms cannot be ignored by a public service reliant on funding from the steering organisation. These mechanisms are also, in their extreme form,[7] very directional in nature, making the organisational reactions inevitably more focused. When money is transferred with a clear information code that says that some specific objectives need to be achieved then it is difficult not to take such requirements very seriously. This is given added impetus by the use of *ex post* reporting requirements that necessitate making clear whether these objectives have or have not been achieved. This does not mean, even when these requirements are tightly defined, that public sector organisations do not attempt to resist these intrusions. This is particularly the case if the requirements are perceived as a direct and unwanted challenge to the nature of the underlying interpretative schemes of these organisations.

Resistance would appear to be the normal response of public service organisations. There is no indication, conceptually or empirically, that transactional steering mechanisms have provided the spur for the acceptance of the 'something for something' accounting logic of these steering mechanisms. Instead, as our research (e.g. Broadbent and Laughlin, 2013) has demonstrated, these steering mechanisms are perceived as potentially dangerous intrusions that need to be managed in some way to prevent the potential undermining of the underlying values of public sector organisations occurring.

Gorz (1989) with his critique of economic reason provides pointers as to why this is the case. His analysis recognises that economic reason, which is equivalent to our understanding of accounting logic and transactional steering mechanisms, despite its extension into new areas of societal life, is "unaware of how narrow its proper limits are" (Gorz, 1989: 2). In this regard Gorz's major concern is to clarify

> which activities can be subordinated to economic rationality without losing their meaning and for which activities economic rationalization would be a perversion or a negation of the meaning inherent in them.
>
> *(Gorz, 1989: 132–3)*

Gorz's answer to this is to unpack what he means by economic reason, or 'economic rationality' as he often refers to it, or transactional steering mechanisms to us, and to see which activities have these characteristics and which do not. His view is that

[e]conomic rationality seems properly applicable to activities which:

1 Create use value;
2 For exchange as commodities;
3 In the public sphere;
4 In a measurable amount of time, at as high a level of productivity as possible.

> *(Gorz, 1989: 138–9)*

His argument is that there are many activities that he terms 'commodity activities' which are "activities performed for remuneration" (Gorz, 1989: 139) but that not all commodity activities are the same in the sense that they all should be subject to economic rationality. His analysis is that the efficiency and effectiveness of "all those activities which meet a need for care, assistance or help" (Gorz, 1989: 143), which are invariably provided through public sector organisations,

> is impossible to quantify. Not only because the nature of demands for assistance are independent of the people providing care or assistance but because the reasons for these demands are impossible to plan. A doctor's productivity cannot be measured in terms of the number of patients she or he sees per day; nor that of a home-help in terms of the number of disabled people's houses he or she cleans; nor that of a childminder in terms of the number of children in her or his care, and so on. It is possible for the efficiency of 'carers' to be in inverse proportion to their visible quantifiable output.
>
> The service they provide cannot be defined in itself independently of the people whose individual needs they cater for. The point is not, as in manufacturing work, to produce predetermined acts or objects, which can be separated from the actual person producing them but to define the acts and objects to be produced according to other people's needs. Adjusting supply to suit demand, in other words, depends on a person-to-person relationship, not on the execution of predetermined, quantifiable actions.

It is for these reasons that those in the caring professions, and the public sector organisations in which they work, commonly find transactional steering mechanisms not to be an evolutionary possibility but rather a threat that is to be resisted in some way.

Colonisation is a constant possibility, however. Despite the resistance of stakeholders to the values encapsulated in transactional steering mechanisms, forced change of a colonisation nature can occur. Our research has not discovered this outcome. There is, however, other research evidence of colonisation; for example, as provided by Dent (1986, 1991) in his study of what he refers to as 'European Railways'. This is not the place to provide a detailed explication of Dent's analysis but there are three generic lessons that can be drawn from his case study.[8] First, that colonisation is achieved where a group of the stakeholders of any public sector organisation become staunch advocates of it, who find whatever ways possible to force the other stakeholders to accept the new way of thinking until the organisation as a whole expresses these values. De Board (1978) notes the existence of what he describes as a 'revolutionary change group', which invariably starts off as a 'specialist work group' that in time becomes

> 'budded off' from the main group, whose main task is to deal with the basic assumptions on behalf of the main group, thereby allowing the work group function of the main group to proceed effectively.
>
> *(de Board, 1978: 43)*

The 'basic assumptions' de Board refers to are those "latent anxieties that can come to the surface and affect the real work of the organization unless kept at bay" (Laughlin, Broadbent, Shearn and Willig-Atherton, 1994: 65). These latent anxieties in the current context are the transactional steering mechanisms. The creation of a 'specialist work group' to, in effect, handle these steering mechanisms and allow the perceived real work to proceed unhindered is, as we will see, a common organisational response. In the case of colonisation this specialist work group, although initially formed to handle the transactional steering mechanisms and allow the real work to continue, becomes the vehicle for redefining its nature. De Board recognises this possibility pointing out that specialist work groups are "continually in danger of actually doing something, working as a work group rather than a basic assumption group" (1978: 43).

Second, if the specialist work group does move away from fulfilling its intended absorbing role to become a colonising force it will use the significance and importance of the societal steering institution issuing the transactional steering mechanisms as a way to give power and legitimacy for their actions. Third, whilst the colonising group will look to the societal steering institutions to provide legitimacy, and will use the contents of the transactional steering mechanisms to guide their actions and thinking, they will stamp their own content and their own authority in their colonising endeavours. Clearly the colonising group will be at pains to make sure that the requirements contained in the transactional steering mechanisms are actually achieved but this does not mean that their actions and intentions will be limited to these requirements. Colonisation is therefore always possible but it does require the existence of a specialist work group who are willing and able to achieve this colonising intent making this more of an exception rather than the rule. The more normal change pathways, where the specialist work groups are fulfilling their more normal functions, albeit in different ways, are the rebuttal and reorientation first-order change pathways.

Rebuttal of transactional inter-organisational steering mechanisms is possible, certainly conceptually, yet, based on the empirical cases we have observed, very difficult to accomplish. Once the societal steering institutions have decided that particular transactional steering mechanisms are appropriate, and are perceived to be relevant and needed for public sector organisations any attempt at rebuttal is likely to be seen as reactionary and negative and often deemed backward looking. Yet as Broadbent, Jacobs and Laughlin (2001) demonstrate, through their analysis of the emergence of primary care 'commissioning groups' in the UK as a replacement for 'GP Fundholding', rebuttal is possible but requires certain key characteristics to be in place. In Broadbent and Laughlin (2013: 202) we draw from this analysis and highlight a number of these characteristics. First, to be successful the transactional inter-organisational steering mechanisms needs to be both not too tightly defined as well as accompanied by doubts at the societal level about the appropriateness of these steering mechanisms in the longer term. Second, successful rebuttal will involve a convincing demonstration that the transactional steering mechanisms are undermining key values that the societal steering institutions believe are important. Third, a viable convincing alternative for the societal steering institutions to use as the focus for their regulatory endeavours needs to be put forward. Fourth, successful rebuttal requires the emergence of a national body drawn from public sector organisation to argue and negotiate with the societal steering institutions. Fifth, the outcome of the rebuttal is uncertain. There is no guarantee that the preferred alternative (see the third characteristic) will be the final outcome. Given the positional power of the societal steering institutions they will have the final say on what is appropriate, which may be different from their original intentions but not a complete acceptance of the alternative. These characteristics do need to be in place for rebuttal to be successful but our view is that there are only limited circumstances when this will be the case. As a result, our view is that reorientation is the normal change pathway that is pursued by public sector organisations to deal with transactional inter-organisational steering mechanisms.

Reorientation can assume two forms, which in Broadbent and Laughlin (2013: 212) we refer to as 'reorientation through absorption' and 'reorientation through boundary management'. Both involve the transactional inter-organisational steering mechanisms being handled in public sector organisations in such a way as to prevent them intruding into the underlying values and genetic codes of these organisations – their interpretative schemes in other words. Both also involve the development of 'specialist work groups' (de Board, 1978: 43) to do this handling albeit in different ways. These differences are due to the different levels of intensity of the transactional steering mechanisms resulting in different ways they are handled. In the cases we have seen to date we have observed two different forms of reorientation through absorption in schools and GP practices (see Broadbent and Laughlin, 1998) and one form of reorientation through boundary management in higher education (see Broadbent, Gallop and Laughlin, 2010) and in relation to Private Finance Initiative hospitals (see Broadbent, Gill and Laughlin, 2008).

The two forms of reorientation through absorption both occur when the transactional inter-organisational steering mechanisms can indeed be absorbed by the specialist work group so as to leave the real work to continue unhindered. The rather less intrusive UK Local Management of Schools (LMS) Initiative in the late 1980s involved delegated budgets but without too demanding a set of requirements as to what should be achieved through these budgets. Even though these changes were accompanied with increased accountability demands, dealing with the requirements became more of an extra administrative burden than something more challenging. Our observations of schools were that, certainly in the early days of LMS, headteachers and deputy headteachers took it upon themselves to be the specialist work group and set themselves aside to handle LMS. The effect of this on these senior staff varied leading to the various colourful descriptors that we used such as 'absorber soaker sinkers' and 'absorber wheeler dealers' (Laughlin *et al.*, 1994) but, in all cases, handling the LMS requirements absorbed a considerable amount of energy and time of this senior staff inevitably taking them away from fulfilling their senior education role in their schools. This in turn caused problems for other staff and curriculum development more generally.

The other form of reorientation through absorption that we have observed came from the implementation of the rather more demanding new GP contract in the early 1990s in the UK. This new GP contract redefined what GPs should be doing using monetary reward structures to enable this redefinition. In simple terms this new contract delivered greater rewards if GPs undertook a range of defined preventative medical practices rather than the curative medical work that GPs considered was their real contribution. Rather than rebut these demands or absorb them as headteachers and deputy headteachers had done in schools, GPs decided to employ practice nurses and practice managers and give these preventative responsibilities and the management of them to these new professional groups. This allowed the GPs to continue with curative medicine, which they deemed to be their real work. Unlike schools, whose budgets were hard pressed, GPs were not quite as constrained financially and could employ these practice nurses and practice managers. This not only allowed this specialist work group to satisfy the new contract requirements but gave these primarily female practice nurses and practice managers new professional roles and presences (Broadbent, 1998) which they wouldn't have had otherwise. Whilst this is a positive outcome, the dangers of preventing these nurses and managers from doing anything other than facilitating these GP contract requirements, and on the payrolls of GPs to fulfil these functions, rather than becoming an evolving professional body, was great and remains so.

Reorientation through boundary management arises when the transactional inter-organisational steering mechanisms are intrusive and tightly defined and cannot be handled through the absorption processes described in the previous paragraphs. These steering mechanisms are such that they need to permeate the 'real work' of the public sector organisations. Yet this permeation needs to be such that the underlying values and genetic codes of these organisations remain unchanged. If this does not occur then it is no longer reorientation in terms of first-order change. We call this 'reorientation through boundary management' in Broadbent and Laughlin (2013) since to do this requires some skilful and careful management of the transactional inter-organisational steering mechanisms. This occurs at the 'boundary', in a systems sense, between what is 'within' the system that can be 'significantly influenced' and what is 'outside' that cannot be significantly influenced but, as with transactional inter-organisation steering mechanisms, is impinging upon the system (see Lowe, 1971). The examples of reorientation through boundary management that we have observed are in higher education (cf. Broadbent, 2011; Broadbent *et al.*, 2010).

A number of important conclusions can be drawn from this discussion. First, that due to the need to filter the transactional inter-organisational steering mechanisms, this invariably is the concern of senior management. Thus the specialist work group, in reorientation through boundary management, will be senior management whose primary role is to manage the real work of public sector organisations. It is they who have to filter these steering mechanisms into the real work but in such a way that the underlying values and genetic codes of the public sector organisations remains unchanged. Second, that to achieve this purpose is exceptionally complex and can cause problems if not understood by those doing the real work in these organisations. Third, that in some circumstances, senior management can become believers in, rather than filters of, the transactional inter-organisational steering mechanisms and thereby become a colonising force. If this should occur then due to the positional power of these senior managers in charge of the real work of any public sector organisation, the possibilities for colonisation are very considerable.

5 Some concluding thoughts

The contents of this chapter make sober reading. On the one hand they highlight a persistent attempt by a range of societal steering institutions over a long period of time to influence the behaviour of public sector organisations through a range of inter-organisational steering mechanisms. These steering mechanisms have involved money transfers and have increased in their intensity over time. They have been led by transactional thinking and enabled by forms of accounting to provide clear direction on what public sector organisations should be doing. They have had a deliberate intent to colonise. On the other hand, the public sector organisations have not welcomed these perceived intrusions. They have certainly not seen them as a spur to how these public sector organisations should evolve. Ideally they would like to rebut them but this is difficult when the transactional logic in the steering mechanisms is tightly defined and they are reliant on the resource provided by the steering institutions. In some cases, and under certain circumstances, the intent to colonise will by realised and second-order change will be achieved in these organisations. The more common outcome for public sector organisations is to reorient their systems to, in effect, comply with these required transactional inter-organisational steering mechanisms but in such a way that the underlying values and genetic codes of these organisations remains intact and unchanged. In some cases this reorientation can be achieved through various forms of absorption by a specialist work group set aside or employed to mop up the requirements and demonstrate compliance, but in such a way that the 'real work' remains unaffected. In other cases the reorientation needs to be enacted through boundary management, whereby there are attempts to filter the transactional steering mechanisms affecting the real work of the public sector organisation in a way that it does not lead to major second-order change in the values and genetic code– the interpretative schemes – of the organisation.

Whichever way this is looked at, it entails a colossal waste of energy in need of critical analysis and evaluation. As indicated in the introduction we accept that the colonising intentions of the societal steering institutions may well have positive intent. Yet all stakeholders in public sector organisations do not share this positive intent and resistance to them is the norm. These forces and counter-forces are extremely costly, in a broad sense, achieving either little in the way of real change or in relation to improving the delivery of public services. There are, as a result, two key, and maybe rather obvious, questions that need to be asked and answered of this sad state of affairs. First, are the societal steering institutions justified in their intention to colonise as expressed through their transactional inter-organisational steering mechanisms? Second, are the public sector organisations justified in their negative approach expressed in their resistance to these colonising intentions?

There is no easy answer to these questions but the place to start is with an analysis of the transactional inter-organisational steering mechanisms. To do this we need to analyse whether they demonstrate juridification at work. Teubner (1987: 3–4) points out that 'juridification' is an ugly word – as ugly as the reality it describes, since it refers to overregulation. Regulation, or steering, as we have argued is the role of societal steering institutions, but if steering is not guided by lifeworld demands to ensure that societal organisations express these lifeworld values, then it is overregulation and juridification. Teubner, drawing from his analysis of law, argues that this happens when laws breach structural coupling (Teubner, 1987: 26). We take the view that the points he raises apply to all forms of steering mechanisms. Teubner (1987: 26) provides some key pointers to when this is the case:

The fundamental limits of structural coupling are reached either when relevance criteria are not met or when the conditions of self-reproductive organisation are endangered.

According to Habermas (1987: 365–6) if, in our terms, the inter-organisational steering mechanisms are constitutive and legitimised only by and through procedure, then the relevance criteria are not met. On the other hand, if these steering mechanisms are regulative and amenable to substantive justification, then the relevance criteria are met. From the perspective of the public sector organisations, transactional inter-organisational steering mechanisms are constitutive and legitimised only by procedure. They fail the relevance test and they are also, again from the perception of the public sector organisations, endangering the self-reproductive organisation (Teubner, 1987: 26) that is achieved if the interpretative schemes of the public sector organisations are allowed to evolve through deliberate stakeholder choice. They thus fail this test as well. The question still remains whether these perceptions, which are biased to the views of public sector organisations, have legitimacy. Laughlin and Broadbent (1993: 343) address this by opening up the public sector organisations to wider societal views and make clear

> [t]hat once an organisation has been created, and a degree of autonomy of action has been granted, there needs to be a *demonstrable abuse* defined in the context of a *full democratic debate* before … [it is possible to justify] … an attack on the organizational lifeworld.
>
> *(Emphasis in the original. Authors' addition in square brackets)*

Our argument is that, based on this analysis, the transactional inter-organisational steering mechanisms are forms of overregulation, which is not justified since the public sector organisations have not demonstrably abused their freedom to determine their own evolutionary ways forward and there has been no full democratic debate to indicate otherwise.

This, however, does not mean that there should be no direction or regulation over public sector organisations and they should be just left to evolve in any way they choose, and without any interference from societal steering institutions. What is required is that public sector organisations be enabled to evolve their interpretative schemes through deliberate critical discourse between stakeholders through the use of relational communicative rationality. This can and should be enabled by societal steering institutions, not through highly specific and questionable transactional inter-organisational steering mechanisms that are resented, but rather through the use of what Teubner (1983) terms 'reflexive law', which will

> neither authoritatively determine the social functions of other sub-systems nor regulate their input and output performances, but will foster the reflexion structures within social sub-systems.
>
> *(Teubner, 1983: 275)*

With this enabling role for societal steering institutions, accompanied by a watching brief that public sector organisations are actively evolving through critical engagement with all stakeholders, they can return to their fundamental agenda of improving the delivery of public services and forget forever the problems and costs involved with needless colonisation attempts and the inevitable resistance that they engender.

This chapter was submitted by the authors with the following title: "Accounting colonisation and resistance: the case of the public services."

Notes

1 Quotes from Oxford Dictionaries online.
2 As Broadbent and Guthrie (2008) indicate, many public services are supplied through private sector organisations for a range of complex reasons, not least the unsubstantiated belief in the importance of the private sector in this provision. These 'public private partnerships' (see Broadbent and Laughlin, 2004), as they are referred to, will not, however, be the main focus of this chapter.
3 Leaving aside the upcoming (at the time of writing) referendum on Scottish independence, devolved powers have already been given to Scotland, Wales and Northern Ireland making it difficult to talk about changes in the United Kingdom as a whole. However, some of the more historical changes recounted in the following certainly did apply to the United Kingdom as a totality.
4 For the remainder of this chapter we will refer to transactional or relational steering mechanisms (of an inter-organisational or intra-organisational form) as a shorthand title. Whilst the linkages to PMSs may not be mentioned their presence is not forgotten.
5 There is an important distinction between DELs and Annually Managed Expenditure (AME). AME constitutes, in the main, social welfare payments and, according to the Labour Government, were deemed to be a moral obligation of society and should not be subject to the new budget and PSA constraints that applied to DELs.
6 The financial year runs from 1 April to 31 March.
7 This is increasingly the case in the UK and specifically so in England.
8 See Broadbent and Laughlin (2013: 239–42) for more details on the Dent case and these generic lessons.

References

Allen, K. (2004). *Max Weber: A Critical Introduction*, London: Pluto Press.
Broadbent, J. (1998). "Practice nurses and the effects of the New General Practitioner Contract in the British NHS: the advent of a professional project?" *Social Science and Medicine*, 47(4): 497–506.
Broadbent, J. (2011). "Discourses of control, managing the boundaries," *British Accounting Review*, 43(4): 1–14.
Broadbent, J. and R. Laughlin (1998). "Resisting the 'New Public Management': absorption and absorbing groups in schools and GP practices in the UK," *Accounting, Auditing and Accountability Journal*, 11(4): 403–35.
Broadbent, J. and R. Laughlin (2004). "Public Private Partnerships: nature, development and unanswered questions," *Australian Accounting Review*, 14(2): 4–10.
Broadbent, J. and J. Guthrie (2008). "Public sector to public services: 20 years of "contextual" accounting research," *Accounting, Auditing and Accountability Journal*, 21(2): 129–69.
Broadbent, J. and R. Laughlin (2009). "Performance management systems: a conceptual model," *Management Accounting Research*, 20(4): 283–95.
Broadbent, J. and R. Laughlin (2013). *Accounting Control and Controlling Accounting: Interdisciplinary and Critical Perspectives*, Bingley, Yorkshire: Emerald.
Broadbent, J., R. Laughlin and S. Read (1991). "Recent financial and administrative changes in the NHS: a Critical Theory analysis," *Critical Perspectives on Accounting*, 2(1): 1–29.
Broadbent, J., K. Jacobs and R. Laughlin (2001). "Organisational resistance strategies to accounting and finance changes: the case of general medical practice in the UK," *Accounting, Auditing and Accountability Journal*, 14(5): 565–86.
Broadbent, J., J. Gill and R. Laughlin (2008). "Identifying and controlling risk: the problem of uncertainty in the Private Finance Initiative in the UK's National Health Service," *Critical Perspectives on Accounting*, 19(1): 40–78.
Broadbent, J., C. Gallop. and R. Laughlin. (2010). "Analysing societal regulatory control systems with specific reference to higher education in England," *Accounting, Auditing and Accountability Journal*, 23(4): 506-531.
de Board, R. (1978). *The Psychoanalysis of Organizations*, London: Tavistock.
Dent, J. (1986). "Accounting and organisational cultures: a field study of the emergence of a new organisational reality," unpublished discussion paper, London Business School.
Dent, J. (1991). "Accounting and organisational cultures: a field study of the emergence of a new organisational reality," *Accounting, Organizations and Society*, 16(8): 705–32.
Dodd, N. (1994). *The Sociology of Money: Economics, Reason and Contemporary Society*, Cambridge: Polity Press

Dunleavy, P. and C. Hood (1994). "From old public administration to New Public Management, *Public Money and Management*, 14(3): 9–16.

Ferreira, A. and D. Otley (2009). The design and use of performance management systems: an extended framework for analysis," *Management Accounting Research*, 20(4): 263–82.

Fulton Report (1968). *Report of the Committee on the Civil Service* (Cmnd 3638), London: HMSO.

Gorz, A. (1989). *Critique of Economic Reason*, translated by G. Handyside and C. Turner, London: Verso.

Habermas, J. (1984). *The Theory of Communicative Action. Vol. 1: Reason and Rationalisation of Society*, translated by T. McCarthy, London: Heinemann.

Habermas, J. (1987). *The Theory of Communicative Action. Vol. 2: The Critique of Functional Reason*, translated by T. McCarthy, London: Heinemann.

Habermas, J. (1996). *Between Facts and Norms: Contributions to a Discourse Theory of Law*, tanslated by W. Rehg, Cambridge, MA: MIT Press.

Hood, C. (1991). "A public management for all seasons," *Public Administration*, 69(1): 93–109.

Hood, C. (1995). "The 'New Public Management' in the 1980s: variations on a theme," *Accounting, Organizations and Society*, 20(2–3): 93–109.

Jackson, P. (1988). "Forward" in P. Jackson (ed.): *The Financial Management Initiative*, London: Chartered Institute of Public Finance and Accountancy.

Laughlin, R. (1991). "Environmental disturbances and organisational transitions and transformations: some alternative models," *Organization Studies*, 12(2): 209–32.

Laughlin, R. (1995). "Empirical research in accounting: alternative approaches and a case for 'middle range' thinking," *Accounting, Auditing and Accountability Journal*, 8(1): 63–87.

Laughlin, R. (2004). "Putting the record straight: a commentary on 'methodological choices and the construction of facts: some implications from the sociology of knowledge'," *Critical Perspectives on Accounting*, 15(2): 261–77.

Laughlin, R. (2007). "Critical reflections on research approaches, accounting regulation and the regulation of accounting," *British Accounting Review*, 39(4): 271–89.

Laughlin, R. and J. Broadbent (1993). "Accounting and law: partners in the juridification of the public sector in the UK?" *Critical Perspectives on Accounting*, 4(4): 337–68.

Laughlin, R., J. Broadbent, D. Shearn and H. Willig-Atherton (1994). "Absorbing LMS: the coping mechanisms of a small group," *Accounting, Auditing and Accountability Journal*, 7(1): 59–85.

Likierman, A. (2003). "Planning and controlling UK public expenditure on a resource basis," *Public Money and Management*, 23(1): 45–50.

Lowe, A. E. (1971). On the definition of 'systems' in systems engineering," *Journal of Systems Engineering*, 2(1): 95–8.

Olson, O., J. Guthrie and C. Humphrey (eds) (1998). *Global Warning: Debating International Developments in New Public Financial Management*, Bergen: Cappelen Akademisk Forlag.

Otley, D. (1999). "Performance management: a framework for management control systems research," *Management Accounting Research*, 10(4): 363–82.

Power, M. and R. Laughlin (1992). "Accounting and Critical Theory," in M. Alvesson and H. Willmott (eds): *Critical Management Studies*, London: Sage Publishing.

Power, M. and R. Laughlin (1996). "Habermas, law and accounting," *Accounting, Organizations and Society*, 21(5): 441–65.

Public Administration Select Committee (PASC) (2003). *On Target? Government by Measurement*, HC61-1 (Main Report) and HC62 – II (Appendices: Minutes of Evidence), London: HMSO.

Simmel, G. (1978). *The Philosophy of Money*, London: Routledge.

Teubner, G. (1983). "Substantive and reflexive elements in modern law," *Law and Society Review*, 17(2): 239–85.

Teubner, G. (1987). "Juridification: concepts, aspects, limits, solutions," in G. Teubner (ed.) *Juridification of Social Spheres*, Berlin: Walter de Gruyter.

Townley, B., D. J. Cooper and L. Oakes (2003). "Performance measures and the rationalization of organizations," *Organization Studies*, 24(7): 1045–72.

Treasury and Civil Service Committee (1982). *Efficiency and Effectiveness in the Civil Service* (HC236), London: HMSO.

Zifcak, S. (1994). *New Managerialism: Administrative Reform in Whitehall and Canberra*, Buckingham: Open University Press.

13

ACCOUNTABILITY

John Roberts

1 Introduction

The aim of this chapter is to provide a review of the various ways in which I have sought to explore and understand accounting as an instrument of accountability. As such its primary focus will be on a variety of different papers through which I have sought to explore this theme over the years. My hope is that this review provides a useful, condensed but easily understandable introduction to what is arguably one of the central purposes that accounting information serves – that is creating accountability both within and beyond organisations.

To think about accounting as an instrument of accountability seems quite fundamental but in my initial work on this – a paper with Bob Scapens published in 1985 and entitled "Accounting systems and systems of accountability: understanding accounting in its organizational contexts" – accountability emerged as a theme more by accident than design. The Economic and Social Research Council project that Bob Scapens had designed was motivated in part by the then recent call of Burchell, Clubb, Hopwood, Hughes and Nahapiet (1980) to explore accounting in its organisational contexts. Their paper, which defined a field of research in which many have worked ever since, insisted that extant research was primarily normative in character, and as such largely ignorant of accounting's actual uses in organisations. Burchell *et al.* (1980: 11) put it as follows:

> [T]he roles that have been attributed to accounting may tell us a great deal about how people have come to see accounting, the influences on accounting discourse and the bases from which people have sought to publicly influence accounting. However, that is not to say that they are descriptive of practice.

In the project to which I had been recruited as an organisational researcher, Bob and I set out to explore the uses of accounting information in a variety of large established UK companies in the north of England. As an undergraduate student I had struggled through first year accounting, and the seemingly bizarre rituals of double-entry bookkeeping, which was almost the full extent of my technical accounting knowledge. As such there was little option but for me to talk to our interviewees not about the detail of their accounting treatments of costs or revenues, but rather of how accounting information was (or was not) used. In the doctoral thesis I had just finished I had drawn extensively on the work of Anthony Giddens. In this work, following Garfinkel and ethnomethodology, Giddens talks of accountability – the giving and demanding of reasons for conduct – as "a chronic feature of daily conduct" (Giddens, 1979: 57). It was this that provided me with a clue as to how, as a non-accountant, I might nevertheless be able to explore the uses of accounting in organisations.

As a chronic feature of daily life accountability could be seen as pervasive, as largely taken for granted, but nevertheless as central to social life. We are not autonomous atoms but instead must expect that others will routinely ask us to offer some explanation for what we have or have not done, and likewise will make similar demands upon others to explain themselves to us. Whilst routine, such practices of accountability are nevertheless very powerful. Accountability expresses and enacts a social bond: my obligations to others and theirs to me. It insists that my conduct makes a difference to others, and thereby reminds me of my existence. It makes a claim upon me which I can contest or accept. In the classroom I often seek to illustrate the power of these processes through asking students who are seeking to steal invisibly into the room why they have arrived late? The question alone is enough typically to improve punctuality in subsequent weeks, even when there are good reasons for lateness.

In the field research with Bob Scapens, which spanned a number of different companies, there were a whole variety of ways in which accounting information seemed, or at least aspired to be, central to such processes of accountability in organisations. On the one hand what was immediately obvious was that the mere existence of accounting information did not signify either its use or usefulness; acres of data seemed to be produced only to languish untouched in cupboards or in piles on desks. On the other hand, the absence of accounting information seemed to make it almost impossible to enact any form of accountability beyond immediate colleagues. In one case company, we followed an attempt to introduce a new production and control system into a cable manufacturing operation. Jobs entered the shop floor but were then largely lost from sight until they emerged at the other end; both customer goodwill and valuable copper were apparently prone to regularly disappearing along the way (Scapens and Roberts, 1993). At the time of the research accounting was far from omnipresent in the organisations we studied. Different functional areas had their own bespoke languages; salesmen talked to each other about book ordering and customer demand, works managers of production schedules and efficiency. It was accounting information, however, that then sought to translate these different functional activities into a set of common financial metrics. Even in this early work it was evident that the peculiar power of accounting information lay in its capacity to realise control at a distance; the accounting numbers were mobile and combinable and informed the actions, decisions and expectations of distant managers. In the particular contexts we studied, however, accounting for the most part was still struggling to assert its authority over shop floor activities. The struggle was consequential and subsequently many of the companies failed or were taken over as a result.

In abstracting from these field experiences in the 1985 paper, we suggested that if we wanted to see accounting in action then research should focus not on the assumed capabilities of abstract accounting systems, but rather on how, in practice, these enabled systems of accountability within an organisation. Here, following Giddens' threefold characterisation of structures, we suggested that accounting is effective in organisations through being drawn upon as a particular structure of signification, legitimation and domination. Accounting reads the world, or makes the world visible through a very particular frame of *meanings* that in capitalist organisations is tied to an interest in the realisation of a return on capital. These frames of meanings as they are drawn upon come to define the significance of not only what has happened – profit, loss and so on – but also what *should* happen. Budgeting processes and performance reviews define a set of *norms* for acceptable performance, against which individual performance can be judged and plans appraised. Insofar as accounting establishes its authority to define what is and should be, it thereby also realises its *dominance* in structuring interactions between people in organisations. But these micro structuring effects also accumulate in myriad ways such that accounting can acquire the capacity to define what will count in and for an organisation even in the absence of consent, and in this respect has the capacity to represent distant but powerful financial interests and bring them to bear upon relations at every level of a hierarchy.

What then was gained through this early formulation of the role of accounting in structuring organisational accountability? The attractive thing for me about Giddens is the emphasis he gives, following Marx, to agency. Organisations do not have an existence that is independent of those who work for them. Instead, organisational reality, like social reality more broadly, is only produced and reproduced through our own and others' agencies – albeit in ways that are neither wholly understood nor intended. In common sense, accounting still manages to cling to a self-image which suggests that it is no more than a neutral mirror of organisational reality. Seen as a resource for the endlessly reiterated processes of accountability through which organisations are produced and reproduced, accounting loses this image of passive neutrality, and instead becomes a key resource that is drawn upon in the structuring of organisational relationships. That its categories and expectations seem self-evident speaks only of the power it has acquired to routinely define what does, should and will count in organisational life.

However, in conceiving of accounting as a resource for accountability, more than the contingency of the world is brought into sight. Accounting's passive self-image as a neutral mirror of reality means that a great deal of accounting research has been preoccupied simply with using accounting information to investigate features of economic reality – capital market research – or alternatively with exploring how different accounting techniques might allow us to see more clearly or more sharply – historical cost versus fair value (Hopwood, 2008). The focus here is on the capacities of accounting to 'faithfully represent' what is assumed to be a reality beyond and independent of its representations. To insist that accounting is central to the structuring of organisational accountability – to the definition of what is and should be in interaction between people – is to point in an altogether different direction to the neglected realm of accounting's subjective effects; the way that accounting information and its use comes to shape us as 'subjects'. Accounting structures the world through structuring selves.

2 Accounting as subjection – accounting's individualising effects

I first explored accounting's subjective effects in a 1991 paper entitled "The possibilities of accountability," in which I sought to contrast and explore the interpenetration of what I termed the 'individualising' and 'socialising' *effects* of different forms of accountability. The focus of the 1984 paper had been predominantly on interaction; scenes of accountability between, say, a manager and his or her subordinate and the way that accounting information might be drawn upon within this scene to structure the interaction. Towards the end of the paper, again drawing on Giddens' (1991) work on disembedding and re-embedding mechanisms and what he calls "time-space distantiation," I tentatively explored how accounting information travels from one local context to another in a way that makes my conduct visible and subject to control at a distance. With Giddens, however, there is an awkward disjunction between the micro and macro which he only manages through proposing two forms of analysis – the analysis of strategic conduct or institutional analysis – each of which is made possible only by bracketing the other. At the same time as we were writing the 1984 paper, I was also reading Foucault's *Discipline and Punish* and here the notion of surveillance seemed to offer a much more powerful way to conceive of the cumulative, systemic effects of accounting (see Roberts, 2014 for a more detailed discussion). Central to Giddens is an insistence on the power of agency 'to make a difference', and yet, for me, it is Foucault rather than Giddens that offers the clearest sight of how we come to practice power upon ourselves and each other, and in this way subvert or eclipse the power of our own agency.

A key quotation from *Discipline and Punish* to which I have repeatedly returned is this:

> He who is subject to a field of visibility, and who knows it, assumes responsibility for the constraints of power, he makes them play spontaneously upon himself. He inscribes in himself the power relation in which he simultaneously plays both roles.
>
> *(Foucault, 1979: 202–3)*

One way to think about accounting information is to see it as creating such a field of visibility. The accountability relationships that had been our focus in the 1984 paper were themselves nested in a wider field of visibility, to which both manager and subordinate were subject, and of which both were aware, such that distant interests also achieved a presence in the local scene of accountability. Accounting information is powerful in organisations to the degree to which it establishes itself as the most important and authoritative way in which activity is made visible. Given accounting's central values of profit and return on capital, one aspect of this is that people scarcely appear in recognisable form within the mirror of our activity that it offers. Instead we appear as elements of cost or measures such as value added per employee. But accounting then becomes powerful through the way that the knowledge of the ways in which accounting makes my conduct visible comes to shape my sense of self and relationship to others. Within accounting and finance, agency theory assumptions of the self-interested and opportunistic nature of the individual remain highly influential. Such assumptions are taken to capture an *essential* aspect of human nature. The merit of Foucault's work lies in the way that it allows us to explore the entirely *social* processes through which such an *individualised* sense of self is fabricated. Here he points to processes of comparison, differentiation, hierarchizing, homogenising and exclusion which together serve both to 'normalise' and 'individualise'.

Such processes are perhaps most evident in how we come to even be employed by an organisation. When Foucault writes of the way that, within a field of visibility, we make the constraints of power "play spontaneously upon the self," he is describing the ways in which many of the (subjective) effects of power are realised in anticipation of its exercise. Whilst the employment relation is framed legally as an exchange between equals, in practice power is weighted heavily towards the employer. As a would-be employee, getting a job then becomes a process of trying to see myself as if through the eyes of the employer and then seeking to present myself as already meeting the standards and expectations that the employer has advertised. Such processes are homogenising in the sense that as a job applicant I am viewed, and view myself, not in terms of my uniqueness but rather in terms of the degree to which I meet the advertised criteria. Such processes involve my being compared with others but only in relation to my fit with the employer's expectations. To be successful in what is typically a competitive process I must somehow differentiate myself from these others. The competition ensures that for most the process ensures an experience of failure; the self is discovered as somehow lacking some desired qualities which only reinforces their authority. The discipline of the labour market is thus a scene in which I come to play both roles in the power relation as I seek to craft and present myself in the image of what the employer wants. However, even for those who succeed in such processes of recruitment, success is only momentary for, once employed, the value of the self is then subject to continuous re-appraisal in the routine processes of hierarchical accountability to which, as employee, I am then subject.

Accounting information typically plays a key role within such processes both by advertising the standards of performance upon which my continued employment depends, and through enabling processes of homogenisation, comparison, differentiation, hierarchization and exclusion which together serve to normalise and individualise the employee. Accounting homogenises in the way in which the diverse activities of production, sales, marketing, research and development and so on, are thereby re-presented in purely economic terms – as costs, revenue, investment and so on. Activities and their consequences are only recognised in these economic instrumental terms. In this homogenised, monetised form the results of activity can be summed, allowing the comparison of one period with another, or one department or division with another, or even one company with another (Robson, 1992, Vollmer, 2007). In this way performance can be ranked and differentiated. Such processes then provide the script for routine processes of hierarchical accountability in which I can be called upon to account for my performance, or the performance of those for whom I am responsible. In the extreme, such processes can result in exclusion either through, say, the sacking of an individual or the closure of a plant. Whilst such extremes are rare, their main effect is upon those that remain for whom they advertise the contingency of employment and the boundaries of acceptable performance. The effects of such accountability, however, are not confined to the particular scene or occasion of accountability – the performance review. Instead, most of their effects are realised in anticipation of such processes in the ways in which, to avoid blame or garner praise to the self, I work continuously upon the self in order to ensure I meet my performance targets. Budgets seek not only to make the future predictable and plan-able, but also, by turning measures into targets, advertise the standards of utility I am expected to meet. In Foucault's words they normalise; advertising the performance expectations (norms) that, as a good employee, I will not only be judged against by others but against which I *should* also judge myself.

In the 1991 paper I sought to express how these processes of accountability individualise by suggesting that they create a sort of anxious 'self-absorption' which leads to attempts to stand as if outside oneself in order to anticipate the expectations of others: "In adopting this stance, the standards and values of accounting are internalised. In adopting this stance the self is discovered as singular and solitary" (Roberts, 1991:360). Such self-absorption can be purely defensive in character – what do I need to do to keep my job – or more assertive in character. Alongside the spectre of exclusion lie the more positive potentials of winning the recognition and praise of superiors, and their promise of future promotion:

> The individualized self can aspire to an ever more complete autonomy, and each level of the hierarchy apparently offers a move towards this; position in the hierarchy serving as an objective confirmation of relative value and worth. In practice of course one is thereby drawn further and further into conformity with the standards of utility upon which one's 'success' depends. Once in a management position, one's security depends crucially on being able to secure others' conformity, and hence one is led increasingly to view not only the self but also others in the light of the instrumental concerns that accountability advertises.
>
> *(1991: 360)*

Accounting, and its use within routine processes of hierarchical accountability, individualises then in the way that it creates this self-absorption with how one is seen by powerful others, and leads to constant attempts to compare and differentiate the self from others in their eyes.

3 Socialising forms of accountability

For Foucault such individualising effects are far from automatic and always contain the possibility of resistance arising from what he calls the 'adverse force of multiplicity'. In the 1991 article I sought to explore such possibilities by contrasting the individualising effects of hierarchical accountability with what I termed *socialising* effects. The image of a self-centred, ambitious, narcissistic individual that is perhaps the archetype of such individualising processes does not describe the only possibilities of self-hood at work. In talking of socialising effects I had in mind those social ties – both of friendship and enmity – that are almost invariably formed in the routine interactions of people at work. In a way this takes us back to Giddens' notion of accountability as a chronic feature of everyday life; accountability which articulates and enacts my sense, not of solitariness, but rather of interdependence with others. The sharp contrast here is between the exclusively instrumental relation with both self and others that characterises the individualised mentality and the possibility of a fuller and reciprocal relationship to others as relationships overflow the confines of this instrumentalism.

If there is an Achilles heel to the individualised mentality it lies in the distortions to communication that arise in hierarchies. The hierarchy is used to assert one view over another in a way that is silencing, or induces the sycophantic desire to say only whatever might please the boss. By contrast socialising forms of accountability seem most able to flourish in lateral work relationships; in relationships with those with whom one works, or upon whom one's own work depends. In such contexts there is both more opportunity and less inhibition to what I can say. I both depend and am depended upon by others and yet this interdependence can only be secured through a sort of pervasive accountability in which we constantly remind each other of the difference we each make to the other. Such concrete relationships offer an alternative source of recognition grounded in open dialogue to that which is offered by the hierarchy.

> Rather than treating others narcissistically as a mere mirror for self, or instrumentally merely as means or obstacles to my private projects, unrestrained talk draws me into relation with others. In the process I am drawn to recognition of other as other beyond my instrumental interest in them – as a fellow subject. At the same time my own understanding is engaged and elaborated only through and in relation to others, so that understanding takes the form of a 'shared operation' of which no one is identifiably the author.
>
> *(Roberts, 1991: 363)*

The form of complex organisations is that of a complex web of interdependencies. Even if only local in scope, socialising forms of accountability both acknowledge and allow us to articulate such interdependence, in sharp contrast to the imagined autonomy of the individualised self.

The value of this contrast between the individualising and socialising effects of different forms of accountability lies in the way that it allows us to explore how these subjective effects interpenetrate each other. One aspect of this concerns the way that socialising forms of accountability can provide a space in which employees can come to question and challenge the official rhetoric of management. As such socialising forms of accountability can create a form of solidarity between colleagues and the opportunity to collectively seek to discuss the contradictions, inconsistencies and occasional idiocies of managerial discourse. In this way socialising forms of accountability do much to humanise the experience of work. But one can also suggest that they do much to secure the routine interdependence of action upon which organisation depends. In this sense they are an essential, if typically unacknowledged, supplement to hierarchical forms of accountability.

Writing in 1991 I imagined such socialising effects both as a valuable source of sanity at work but also as the possible site of organised resistance. How times change. At about the same time a whole new literature was emerging – *In Search of Excellence* (Peters and Waterman, 1982) being perhaps its most famous and influential embodiment – that sought to offer to Western managers the lessons that might be drawn from Japanese forms of organisation. One way to characterise this movement is to suggest that it consists of attempts to colonise the powerful effects of loyalty and reciprocal obligation that socialising forms of accountability create, and then put this to work for corporate purposes. There are a host of more recent studies that describe such attempts at normative control from Townley's (1993) Foucauldian study of emergent human resource practices, through Willmott's (1993) study of organisational culture, to Alvesson and Karreman's (2004) various studies of what they call socio-ideological control in professional service firms. The common theme of such studies is the way in which managers seek to recast the hierarchical relationship with employees in terms of becoming more supportive coaches and mentors, and re-conceive the work group as a team.

For me one of the most lucid and disconcerting studies in this regard is Catherine Casey's 1999 paper: "Come join our family." Her oil company case study describes team members disciplining each other, extracting confessions of poor performance from individuals and demanding apologies from them for 'having let the team down'. Deprived of a space at work in which the ideology of 'family' might be critiqued with colleagues, employees instead turn upon themselves in a stress-inducing critique; as Casey chillingly observes, in this way anger is transposed into guilt as employees subject themselves to the demand for continuous improvement. Significantly there is reason to suggest that this borrowing of Japanese practices to elicit the commitment (Walton, 1985) of employees has been highly selective. In a recent study of Japanese management accounting practices in the Kyocera corporation, Sawabe and Honmachi (2015) explore the intricate balancing of controls used to mobilise the efforts of work groups – amoeba – to corporate survival and success. The absolute foundation of these practices is a corporate commitment to job security. The rhetoric of shared values which now pervades Western organisations is typically rendered hollow by the ways in which accounting's values of profit and return on capital continue to be given priority and indeed provide the rationale for not making such a commitment to employees.

4 Empirical studies

The good thing about accountability is that it is indeed a chronic feature of everyday life and as such is intimately tied to the day-to-day routines through which organisations are produced and reproduced along with the subjectivities that animate them. I personally find it easier to think with concepts when they are tied back to empirical realities and so in this section I want to touch on two empirical studies through which I have sought to understand and then illustrate the peculiar power of accounting and the processes of accountability it makes possible both within and around organisations.

The first was a study of accountability in a UK organisation that I called Conglom (Roberts, 1990). Management accounting texts routinely describe the adoption of profit or responsibility centres within organisations, but my experience at least is that this is typically taught merely as the adoption of a particular structure of accounting information rather than as a key innovation in organisational accountability. In this way the significance of what Williamson (1971) has described as American capitalism's most important single innovation of the twentieth century is largely lost on most students. The acquisition of ELB by Conglom was an opportunity to study a UK example of the power of this innovation. The research began a year or so after the acquisition and thereby provided an opportunity for me to ask people not only to describe the new ruthlessly efficient form of financial accountability that Conglom was introducing, but also to get managers to contrast this with their experiences of accountability in the failing years of ELB as an independent entity.

What managers described to me were the classical failings that accompany the success of functional or what Williamson (1971) and Chandler (1977) call 'U-form organisation'. It is easy for students to imagine that the present has no history and that what they are being taught are timeless truths. The development of M-form (multidivisional) organisation in Dow Chemicals and General Motors early in the twentieth century was however a momentous innovation, albeit one that was only widely copied after the Second World War when McKinsey began to sell its advantages to organisations around the world. The ELB case was of a UK battery company that had grown along the sinews of the British Empire. It had its origins in the demand for batteries during the First World War but by the time of the acquisition in the 1980s ELB had become a global company with operations in the UK, Europe, Africa and the near and far East. A huge and more recent boost to the business had been given in the 1970s by the Japanese invention of the portable transistor radio; demand for batteries had exploded. As the company had grown on the back of this new source of demand all sorts of operational difficulties began to emerge. Chains of decision making were long and tortuous, middle managers lacked any autonomy, senior functional managers defended the interests of their specialist functions, and the board was bogged down in managing the immediate demands of operations to the neglect of a longer term strategy. In the 1970s, with the advice of consultants, ELB had decided to adopt a new divisionalised structure with three profit centres based in the UK, Europe and the rest of the world. With this change came a new divisional board structure and three new reporting entities. Whilst the promise of these accounting changes was of faster decision making and greater operational efficiency, in practice nothing much at all changed beyond the proliferation of boards and accounting entities.

It was only with the acquisition of ELB by Conglom that new divisionalised forms of accounting information began *to be used* in such a way as to transform effective accountability. The key to this was the ruthless use of financial controls, or more precisely the credible threat of the ruthless use of financial metrics. The management of ELB was instructed to deliver a 20% return on capital if they wanted to survive within the new group. This performance rule was then cascaded down to individual plants and the sales operation. Over a five-year period no plant was actually closed, and ELB survived within the wider corporate group, but the credible threat of closure was enough to transform the organisation. Functional barons now had no choice but to cooperate intensely with each other in seeking to ensure that the business as a whole survived, factory managers now had autonomy but only if they delivered massive cost savings in a declining market. In the three-year course of my research the size of the management team declined by two-thirds and overall employment fell as profits were diverted to the launch of a new product. The remarkable thing for me, however, was that people were nevertheless excited and fully engaged in the process of turning the company around, even when this implied their own redundancy.

The turnaround was led by a new manager brought in by Conglom who remains one of the most skilful managers I have ever encountered. One formative experience for this man had been managing a strike early in his career. The experience had taught him the power of the group and the necessity of mobilising this in any change process. He was fearful of the individualising effects of the use of intense financial controls that set manager against manager, and factory against factory. He therefore developed his own process around an annual management conference that sought to build commitment first amongst the senior management team, and then, through the conference itself, amongst the entire management group. Survival came to define the shared goal to which all must contribute, but this then was translated into public reciprocal commitments between factories, marketing and sales on delivering what they each had promised to the other. Faced with such a coherent strategy even the shop floor participated in the change process, and, even where managers expected to lose their jobs, they spoke of how much they had learnt.

For me this study offered an example of how individualising and socialising effects could be engineered around a widely communicated strategic goal within ELB. The nasty paradox, however, lay in the sharp contrast between the imposed austerity within ELB and the overall health of Conglom. No longer were the fruits of corporate power shared equally between levels of the hierarchy – unions, management, investors. The changed use of accounting information to create accountability around profit centres within ELB, along with the sense of shared destiny that the project of company survival created, served only to increase the power of the small corporate head office of Conglom. The studied indifference of this group of senior managers to all but their promise to deliver shareholders a continually improving return on their investment, translated into a very powerful lever with which to maximise the value they extracted from their different acquired business units. Accountability for financial performance was installed in the minds of managers and employees at every level as the unavoidable condition of individual and collective survival. Over time, however, even the most enthusiastic of business managers began to question whether this exclusive interest in maximising return on capital would ultimately prove sustainable without new investment that the corporate centre refused to make.

The second empirical study that I want to touch upon here is of the pivotal link between senior corporate managers and their major investors. In a sense this was embarked upon to explore the scene of accounting's transformation in the recent years from an instrument to secure the stewardship of companies, into information oriented to informing the decision making of investors (Whittington, 2008). Unlike most capital market studies, however, this one was a qualitative study conducted with three colleagues that sought to understand the significance of the private meetings that the chief executive, finance director and investment relations managers of companies hold at least annually with their major investors. As the title of the paper suggests – "In the mirror of the market: the disciplinary effects of company/fund manager meetings" – this was a Foucauldian-inspired reading of these meetings (Roberts *et al.*, 2006). We were lucky enough to be allowed to sit in on these meetings and in the ones we attended there was a sharp contrast between the rather anxious performance of the executives and the measured indifference of the twenty- or thirty-year-old analysts and fund managers who were their audience. That even the most senior executives of major companies were subject to such scrutiny only reinforces the Foucauldian sense of power as operating within a field of visibility to which all are subject. The overt aim of the meetings for executives was to ensure that their major investors had an appropriate understanding of their businesses. For investors it was an opportunity to 'see the whites of the eyes' of executives, as a valued supplement to their own financial modelling of future performance.

Less obviously, however, we came to view the meetings as a rather ritual disciplinary process through which the norm of shareholder value was installed in the minds of executives. The clue to such a reading came from the descriptions that executives offered of the intense preparations made for these typically one-hour-long meetings. Every aspect of the meeting was rehearsed from the formal elements of what would be presented, to the answers to all possible questions that might subsequently be asked by investors. Even the chemistry between the CEO and finance director was rehearsed and aligned in order that together they were able to deliver their message to the investor. I was already alert to such anticipatory processes and there was indeed a sense in which the actual meetings were largely rendered redundant given that executives had already internalised investors' demands for shareholder value. By the time of the meetings themselves executives seemed if anything more committed than the investors to the ideal of delivering shareholder value; at least in their eagerness to present themselves as already wanting what the investors wanted. As the title of the paper suggests, the meetings could be seen to offer executives a mirror of themselves as reflected by investor sentiment. To avoid investors' criticism, and or to secure their good opinion, executives fashioned themselves and their companies in the image of the investors' desire. For advocates of shareholder value such disciplinary effects could be seen as positive, but the writing of the paper followed the collapse of the tech-stock bubble, and the confidence-shaking failures of Enron and Worldcom in the US, and for me explained something of how, as with ELB, the sustainability of businesses, which is overtly what accounting information claims to assure, had been sacrificed to the short-term financial interests of both executives and investors.

5 Transparency or intelligent accountability?

In a further paper, the theme of how accounting information and its use for accountability so easily leads us astray, is investigated (Roberts, 2009). It was written at the time of the global financial crisis which offered numerous illustrations of such self-deceptive effects. The focus of the paper is on how we interact with accounting numbers; or more specifically with how we come to collude in the illusion that accounting numbers simply faithfully represent economic reality. Its core themes are transparency and narcissism and the ways in which they can coalesce to lead us collectively astray. Transparency is often treated as if, by itself, it constitutes a form of accountability. The metaphor upon which it depends is that of light passing through an object to reveal what is beyond it; transparency in this sense is no more than a means of making 'what is' visible. The 2009 paper is not an argument against transparency; given the anticipatory effects of surveillance – the ways that my behaviour is changed by the knowledge that it is or may be observed by distant others – transparency is a vital check on local corruption, and an essential resource for the management of all but the smallest organisation. But if we cannot manage without transparency, my argument is also that we cannot manage *only with* transparency. In other words, we need to interact much more intelligently with the accounting information upon which we depend.

How then does the idea of transparency lead us astray? The simple images of revealing or discovering or laying bare, as if this involved no more than the shining of light upon an object, seriously misrepresent the complex labour involved in the construction of transparency through processes of measurement and recording. The challenges of measurement, and measurement choices, have long been recognised in this regard. The accounting profession continues to place faithful representation at the core of the conceptual framework, and has moved to fair value in the name of such faithfulness, and yet at the same time knows all too well that accounting representations continue to remain the product not only of such measurement but also of numerous assumptions, judgements and choices; for example, discount rates. New forms of transparency are offered as a way of making visible what is currently ignored, for example, the social and environmental consequences of economic activity. In the process, transparency is revealed as always involving both a way of seeing and a way of not seeing.

In a 2009 paper, the anthropologist Marylyn Strathern tries to bring our attention back to what is illusory about transparency by asking the question: what does transparency conceal? She insists that transparency always involves a process of abstraction from a context that conceals the complex web of practices and relationships that constitute any institution. Since from a distance we know much of the world only through the ways in which it is rendered transparent, it is all too easy to imagine that the representation is the reality, or at least to act as if this were the case. Yet still, when transparency fails, we typically respond not by questioning how we use transparency – how we interact with the numbers – but rather through seeking to create improved transparency through yet more indicators.

But if the metaphor of transparency is both alluring and deceptive in this way, to this must be added the effects of our own narcissism. Ask people about transparency and they typically give a rather ambivalent response, particularly in relation to areas or activities in which they are themselves expert. Transparency is somehow grasped as both a good thing and a gross and potentially misleading simplification. Strathern (2000) talks here of how 'realities are knowingly eclipsed'; we act as if the products of transparency are real and adequate whilst knowing that they are not. My own attempt to explain this 'ambivalent embrace' of transparency looks to the ways in which transparency plays upon our own narcissism – our desire to be and be seen to be perfect. These arguments are in a sense no more than an extension of Foucault's discussion of the individualising effects of disciplinary power, but my hope is that they more fully illuminate how we collectively come to interact so unintelligently with accounting representations.

The Greek myth of Narcissus is instructive here. The myth has Narcissus falling in love with his own image as this is reflected back to him in a pool. Poor Echo is next to him, like a loyal subordinate, condemned to repeat his own words back to him. Narcissus drowns on the basis of this confusion as he seeks to join his image in the water. The power of accounting representations, or rather their power over us, lies in the way that I am prone to identify with the numbers and take them as a reflection of the value or worth of myself. 'Being in the red' is in this sense shameful and taken as a mark of my own inadequacies, whilst a 'profitable' result confirms my love-ability. Either way this is to confuse the self with its image as the numbers are treated as a reflection of the self. Even if I don't identify with the numbers, as my transparent self-travels, others will know me only through these, and this knowing will attract consequences regardless of its inadequacies. As a result, even if I know them to be misleading, I am prone to act as if the numbers are real; to secure the good opinion of the boss, or the boss's boss, effort and energy will be put into managing the indicators. As Tsoukas (1997: 838) puts it:

> [M]anagement becomes tantamount to keeping up appearances, and fighting shadows; managing via league tables leads to managing the league tables themselves.

A tool supposed to enable management becomes an end in itself.

An infinite array of corporate scandals have had this form; an organised collusion, sometimes illegal, to manufacture the appearance of 'good' results even if this is at the expense of longer term sustainability. Roberts (2009) was written in the aftermath of the global financial crisis which, in hindsight, revealed numerous examples of how individuals and organisations had colluded in producing the illusion of the profitability of securitised mortgage products. A reliance on value-at-risks models which were completely misleading, on historical default rates to structure collateralised debt obligations (CDOs), on credit ratings to inform investment decisions, on indices to value over-the-counter products, and on the apparent profitability of CDOs to inform strategy, all combined to produce first highly leveraged profits and then similarly leveraged losses.

If we seek to manage only with transparency we are effectively allowing ourselves and others to be mesmerised by the numbers either in the mistaken belief that the truth of the self is revealed in them, or for fear that others will believe that this is the case, or since our sense of being in control depends upon them. Is a more intelligent relationship with indicators possible? This chapter was inspired by Judith Butler's *Giving an Account of Oneself* (Butler, 2005) (see also Messner's [2009] very different ethical reading of Butler in relation to accountability). One of her core arguments here is to insist that even at the level of my own actions, I can never quite know what it is that I am doing. As Giddens argues, my rationalisations of my actions – my presentation of self as knowledgeable and competent – are always somewhat at odds with the understanding embodied in what I do. Deliberate deceit – the self-interested opportunism so loved by agency theorists – is only one possibility here, since for the most part my agency is either habitual or grounded in taken-for-granted or unconscious assumptions of which I am simply unaware. Butler's innovation here is to suggest that, if we are able to acknowledge this fact, then it can serve as the ground for a different ethic in relation to both self and others. In Butler's view:

> Precisely my opaqueness to myself occasions my capacity to confer a certain kind of recognition on others. It would be, perhaps, an ethics based on our shared invariable, and partial blindness about ourselves. The recognition that one is, at every turn, not quite the same as how one presents oneself in the available discourse, might imply a certain patience with others that would suspend the demand that they be self-same at every moment.
>
> *(Butler, 2005: 42)*

Rather than defend my transparent self as if indeed I did know what I was doing, or believe in my own perfection or perfectibility, the suggestion here is of a more compassionate attitude both to myself and others grounded in the all-too-real certainty that I can never quite know what I am doing, or the consequences of my actions for others. Accountability on this basis has a number of different potentials. It could take a more reflexive form – becoming an essential opportunity for learning and thought rather than a defensive or assertive display of the self as being in control. Collectively this in turn would serve as the basis for a greater shared resilience within organisations based on reciprocal understanding. Whilst individualised forms of accountability keep me preoccupied with myself, as discussion and debate, accountability might then better allow us to manage the interdependencies on which each depend. In all this we must still depend upon transparency but only as the stimulus for discussion rather than its final arbiter. For Butler (2005: 13):

> What emerges in this space is something of the weight of our practical dependence upon each other which accountability as talk, listening and asking questions then allows us to explore and investigate. Accountability is thereby reconstituted as a vital social practice – an exercise of care in relation to self and others, and an ongoing necessity as a social practice through which we insist upon and discover the nature of our responsibility to and for each other.

One way to read my work on accountability is as a sustained critique of agency theory assumptions (Roberts and Ng, 2012). Agency theory offers a given and idealised image of the self-interested and opportunistic individual that continues to be taught to new generations of accounting and finance students. The financial crisis offered a vivid illustration both of the performativity of these ideas – of how we had made a financial system on the back of its assumptions – as well as a very powerful illustration of their inadequacies. Highly incentivised mortgage salesmen, brokers, investment bankers, credit rating agents and institutional investors had all aggressively pursued their own self-interests, secure in the belief that risks had been passed on to others (Roberts and Jones, 2009). Accounting joined in by allowing the calculation and capture of associated profits by all the discrete economic entities involved. With the unanticipated housing downturn the self-interested opportunists panicked as they realised their own exposure to now leveraged losses, but then only made matters worse by clinging to the illusion that they could protect themselves from the systemic processes of which they were a part. The value of Foucault's work for me lies in pointing to the entirely social processes whereby the illusion of being a separate 'individual' is created. There is nothing given or fixed about an individualised self; rather this mindset is produced and reproduced only through the routine disciplinary processes of individualising forms of organisational accountability. What the financial crisis illustrated so powerfully was that the assumed gap or separation between individuals, and between individual accounting entities, was manufactured and largely illusory. There is no safe place outside the system and our only choice is to find ways to effectively manage the interdependencies within which our own agency is always nested. If there is a weakness to accounting information it is that its representations seem only to be capable of capturing or depicting a world in pieces and individualising forms of accountability only reinforce this sense. But we cannot blame accounting for the crisis but only our rather unintelligent use of the signals that it was providing.

6 Accountability as a core point of focus for future accounting research

Since I first started researching, increased transparency and accountability have become the standard remedies for almost all organisational ills. This period coincided with the adoption of new public management and an ever-increasing dominance of the neo-liberal ideology within which the accountable individual is critical. The instruments of transparency and accountability have since become central not only to private sector organisations but also to both public and third sector organisations as an intended instrument for the realisation of enhanced efficiency, value for money, together with numerous other context-specific key performance indicators. Pessimists see only an ever-increasing prevalence of these instruments (Power, 2015), ensuring that we will all be increasingly plagued and persecuted by these normative traces of our activity. Accountability then is likely to remain a core area of interest for research into the future.

Compared with mainstream accounting research, research on accountability has the peculiar merit of allowing us to explore accounting in use. Whilst mainstream accounting research still clings to the illusion that, with sufficient analytic skill, accounting numbers can be read both as a neutral mirror of the present and the means to render the future reliably predictable, to explore accounting in use opens us to a much more productive and performative view of accounting representations. The numbers participate not only in shaping decisions that have objective effects in the world, but critically they also shape us, the users and our relationships to others. They become the way in which I see or understand not only what I do and its effects, but also what it is to be a self; furnishing me with the standards against which both I and others should judge myself. Accountability makes us as subjects and realises subjection, and its endlessly reiterated routines play powerfully with feelings of greed, fear, hope, success and failure as we see our value reflected in the numbers (Boedker and Chua, 2013). Critically, accountability shapes my sense of my relation to others; it enacts my subjection to some, casts others as competitors or rivals and yet others with the cloak of indifference in the ways in which it leaves me preoccupied only with my securing of 'my' results.

Surprisingly, given its centrality, there remains a relative dearth of fine-grained empirical studies of accountability. Of great promise and relevance for accounting research has been the advent of studies which draw upon actor–network theory (ANT). The agency ANT grants to non-human actants allows us to acknowledge and explore very directly, and in fine detail, how our own agency is shaped – or 'pushed around' – by accounting numbers and artefacts that have typically been assumed to be the mere servants of human agency (Justesen and Mouritsen, 2011; Robson, 1992). Accounting numbers mediate almost all organisational relationships and herein lies the importance of accounting research. But typically absent in this ANT-inspired research is the human subject or any clear observation of the different potentials of the reflexivity of human and non-humans, such that the agency of accounting is possibly ceded a deterministic, if contingent, power. To recognise that accounting can never faithfully represent – that no representation can ever 'capture' reality or render the future knowable – in no way diminishes the importance of accounting but instead merely emphasises the importance of greater attention, both in practice and theory, to how we interact with accounting representations. Given the elusive nature of practice itself, such interaction – the synchronous and contingent objective and subjective effects that arise within the practice of accountability – happily offers an almost infinite horizon for future research.

This chapter was submitted by the author with the following title: "Accounting for accountability."

References

Alvesson, M. and D. Karreman (2004). "Interfaces of control: technocratic and socio-ideological control in a global management accounting firm," *Accounting, Organizations and Society*, 29(3–4): 423–44.

Boedker, C. and W. F. Chua (2013). "Accounting as an affective technology: a study of circulation, agency and entrancement," *Accounting, Organizations and Society*, 38(4): 245–67.

Burchell, S., C. Clubb, A. G. Hopwood, J. Hughes and J. Nahapiet (1980). "The roles of accounting in organizations and society," *Accounting, Organizations and Society*, 5(1): 5–27.

Butler, J. (2005). *Giving an Account of Oneself*, New York: Fordham University Press.

Casey, C. (1999). "Come join our family; discipline and integration in corporate organizational culture," *Human Relations*, 52(1): 155–78.

Chandler, A. (1977). *The Visible Hand: The Managerial Revolution in American Business*, Cambridge, MA: Belknap Press.

Foucault, M. (1979). *Discipline and Punish*, Harmondsworth, UK: Penguin Books.

Giddens, A. (1979). *Central Problems in Social Theory: Action, Structure and Contradiction in Social Analysis*, London: Macmillan.

Giddens, A. (1991). *Modernity and Self-Identity*, Cambridge: Polity Press.

Hopwood, A. G. (2008). "Changing pressures on the research process: on trying to research in an age when curiosity is not enough," *European Accounting Review*, 17(1): 87–96.

Justesen, L. and J. Mouritsen (2011). "Effects of actor network theory in accounting research," *Accounting, Auditing and Accountability Journal*, 24(2): 161–93.

Messner, M. (2009). "The limits of accountability," *Accounting, Organizations and Society*, 34(8): 918–38.

Peters, T. and R. H. Waterman Jr. (1982). *In Search of Excellence: Lessons from America's Best-Run Companies*, New York: Harper and Row.

Power, M. (2015). "How accounting begins: object formation and the accretion of infrastructure," *Accounting, Organizations and Society*, 47: 43–55.

Roberts, J. (1990). "Strategy and accounting in a UK conglomerate," *Accounting, Organizations and Society*, 15(1): 107–26.

Roberts, J. (1991). "The possibilities of accountability," *Accounting, Organizations and Society*, 16(4): 355–68.

Roberts, J. (2009). "No one is perfect: the limits of transparency and an ethic for intelligent accountability," *Accounting, Organizations and Society*, 34(8): 957–70.

Roberts, J. (2014). "Testing the limits of structuration theory in accounting research," *Critical Perspectives on Accounting*, 25(2): 135–41.

Roberts, J. and R. Scapens (1985). "Accounting systems and systems of accountability – understanding accounting practices in their organisational contexts," *Accounting, Organizations and Society*, 10(4): 443–56.

Roberts, J. and M. Jones (2009). "Accounting for self interest in the credit crisis," *Accounting, Organizations and Society*, 34(6): 856–67.

Roberts, J. and W. Ng (2012). "Against economic (mis-)conceptions of the individual: constructing financial agency in the credit crisis," *Culture and Organization*, 18(2): 91–105.

Roberts, J. , P., Sanderson, R. R. Barker and J. Hendry (2006). "In the mirror of the market: the disciplinary effects of company-fund manager meetings," *Accounting, Organizations and Society*, 31(3): 277–94.

Robson, K. (1992). "Accounting numbers as 'inscription': action at a distance and the development of accounting," *Accounting, Organizations and Society*. 17(7): 685–708.

Sawabe, N. and Y. Honmachi (2015). "Core values and responsibility accounting – dynamic tensions generated by competing values embedded in the management control system," working paper, University of Kyoto Graduate School of Management.

Scapens, R. and J. Roberts (1993). "Accounting and control: a case study of resistance to change," *Management Accounting Research*, 4(1): 1–36.

Strathern, M. (2000). "The tyranny of transparency," *British Educational Research Journal*, 26(3): 309–21.

Townley, B. (1993). *Reframing Human Resource Management; Power, Ethics and the Subject at Work*, London: Sage.

Tsoukas, H. (1997). "The tyranny of light," *Futures*, 29(9): 827–43.

Vollmer, H. (2007). "How to do more with numbers: elementary stakes, framing, keying, and the three-dimensional character of numerical signs," *Accounting, Organizations and Society*, 32(6): 577–600.

Walton, R. (1985). "From control to commitment in the workplace," *Harvard Business Review*, 63(2): 77–84.

Whittington, G. (2008). "Fair value and the IASB/FASB Conceptual Framework project: an alternative view," *ABACUS*, 44(2): 139–68.

Williamson, O. E. (1971). "Managerial discretion, organizational form, and the multi division hypothesis," in R. Marris and A. Wood (eds): *The Corporate Economy*, Cambridge, MA: Harvard University Press.

Willmott, H. (1993). "Strength is ignorance, slavery is freedom: managing culture in modern organizations," *Journal of Management Studies*, 30(4): 515–52.

SECTION IV

14

SOCIAL AND ENVIRONMENTAL ACCOUNTING

Rob Gray, Carol Adams
and David Owen

1 Introduction

Social, environmental and, more recently, sustainability accounting and reporting, both as a practice and as an academic pursuit, have had an interesting and, at times, somewhat fraught relationship with critical accounting. *Social accounting* (which we will take, for the purposes of this chapter, as shorthand for social, environmental, and sustainability accounting and reporting) and critical accounting have, at times, ignored each other; have, at times, been at loggerheads; and, perhaps more interestingly, have sometimes found common purpose and grounds for coop-eration. It is these different relationships – and the reasons for them – that we explore in this chapter.

Critical accounting, whilst by no means homogeneous, is primarily concerned with expos-ing the ways in which accounting is deployed as a mechanism of social injustice or, at least, is "implicated in deindustrialisation, deskilling [..., the] bureaucratisation of society, environmental pollution and conflict in society" (Cooper and Hopper, 1990: 1). Whilst social accounting is also largely motivated by concerns over the systematic creation and maintenance of inequality, oppression, injustice and planetary appropriation – typically through the mechanisms of capi-talism – its response is different. Indeed, social accounting has typically been more reformist in orientation, looking to amend accounting to reduce these malign elements and seeking to produce new accounts that could be used to clarify and expose the negative consequences of accounting and corporate behaviours. We might tentatively suggest (for the time being at least) that, at its simplest, critical accounting is more radical in intent and more theoretically and politically motivated whilst social accounting tends to be (or at least has tended to be) more conservative and more ethically and pragmatically orientated. As we will show, this typification will prove to be rather too simple.

Social accounting has recently been defined as

> [t]he process of communicating the social and environmental effects of organisations' economic actions to particular interest groups within society and to society at large. As such, it involves extending the accountability of organisations (particularly companies), beyond the traditional role of providing a financial account to the owners of capital, in

particular, shareholders. Such an extension is predicated upon the assumption that companies do have wider responsibilities than simply to make money for their shareholders.

(Gray, Adams and Owen, 2014: 3)

It is a wide and fluid concept that we might think of as comprising three broad components. First, there are the attempts by organisations to recognise and account for the social and environmental interactions of their economic activities in such a way that the managers, employees, unions and other (broadly 'internal') stakeholders might try to control and limit those interactions. This aspect of social accounting is broadly analogous to management accounting and might include such things as reporting local accounting data to employees; environmental management systems that provide accounts of the waste and pollution produced; and plant-wide health and safety data built into all staff appraisals. Ultimately, such concerns are almost always organisation-centric and are typically *managerialist* in that the information is principally intended to support management in their running of the organisation.

Second, there are the reports and accounts that organisations might prepare for their external stakeholders such as investors, governments, customers, local communities and wider non-governmental organisations (NGOs) and interest groups. These reports and accounts are broadly analogous to financial accounting and reporting and comprise a vast array of activities including, most notably, public reports which might claim to focus on such things as social responsibility, employees, product safety, human rights, the environment or even sustainability. It is within this broad second category where the greatest attention by both practice and academe has been focused. The third category comprises 'accounts' that are not produced by the organisation of interest and, on occasions, may not even be focused on organisations at all. These are broadly referred to as 'external social audits' and embrace an almost infinite array of possibilities. An NGO's exposé of multinational company corruption; an environmental agency's report on corporate pollution; a children's charity's exposure of child labour and human rights abuses; when a journalist collates data about gender abuses, these are all illustrations of external social audits and, thereby, a crucial element in the social accounting universe.

At the outset, it is crucial to note that social accounting, if it ever was, is not a coherent entity. As both scholarship and practice have developed, as the world has become more complex and as social accounting has engaged more with critique, social accounting has become a broad church that cannot properly or usefully be spoken of in the singular. Some of the lack of clarity which follows arises from a tendency amongst many of those engaged in the critique of social accounting to treat social accounting as singular at best and, at worst, as some ill-defined straw person.

We will return to each of these elements in the following pages, which are organised as follows. Section 2 provides a very brief overview and history of social, environmental and sustainability reporting and accounting before we turn to the political context and the assumptions that typically underlie social accounting in Section 3. Section 4 then rehearses the lively critique and debate that developed between critical and social accounting; a debate, acrimonious at times, but which nevertheless left both areas stronger and richer. Section 5 looks at one of the most exciting developments of recent years, namely the ways in which critical and social accounting have merged their insights and expertise in the fashioning of external social audits. The final section provides a brief conclusion.

2 A brief history of social accounting

Although scholars such as Guthrie and Parker (1989), Adams and Harte (1998) and Maltby (2005) identify examples of social accounting and reporting in the nineteenth and early twentieth centuries, the earliest reference to 'social audit' is usually attributed to Bowen (1953), while modern social accounting is typically identified as emerging in the 1960s and 1970s in North America and Europe (Gray *et al.*, 2014: 73). The early examples of social accounting initiatives seemed to come equally from social groups who were anxious that big business was getting more isolated from society (Drucker, 1965) and from commercial organisations themselves. There are significant early experiments of social accounting by US commercial organisations which include examples of engaging with stakeholders, reporting on corporate performance against legal standards and even attempting holistic financial accounts that incorporate social and environmental impacts (for more detail see Gray *et al.*, 2014). In Europe and the UK the early emphasis tended to be on both employee (information for employees) and employment (information about employees) reporting and the emergence of, something known as, the 'value added statement'. The period also saw early attempts at accounting for the environment as well as experiments in energy accounting. Perhaps most arresting was the response of the leading accounting bodies which enthusiastically embraced and supported social accounting initiatives (see, for example, ASSC, 1975; AICPA, 1977). From the 1970s social accounting practice became more diverse, expanding to include such developments as reporting on discrimination in employment, recognition of environmental liabilities, the growth of ethical investment and the essential conflicts inherent in the plant closure audits (Harte and Owen, 1987; Harte, Lewis and Owen, 1991). Then in the 1990s companies and professional bodies led the way in the development of the stand-alone reports – initially as environmental reports, then social responsibility reports and now sustainability reports.[1]

Summarising these in excess of 40 years of practice, it can be argued that whilst this (predominantly) voluntary reporting by organisations is now widespread, and there appears to be an almost universal acceptance of the broad principle of social, environmental and sustainability reporting, the practice itself is by no means universal. Furthermore, the standard of reporting (from the point of view of such criteria as completeness and accountability) remains woeful whilst the underlying issues – whether inequality, sustainability or injustice – continue to worsen. It remains far from clear that all this reporting has had any substantive impact on the well-being of society and the planet.

Accounting as an academic endeavour, to the extent that it was developed at all in the 1960s, was dominated by the US and by academics who were predominantly economists and/or professional accountants. Academic interest in either social or critical accounting at this time was minimal. Social accounting had been led by practice and only slowly did academics begin to analyse these practices and begin to suggest new approaches. Academic engagement with the field grew from about the mid-1970s (see, for example, Estes, 1976; Ullmann, 1976; Dierkes and Preston, 1977) and, increasingly, academics sought not just to analyse and comment on social accounting practice but actually began to involve themselves with this practice and the profession in attempts to encourage more substantive developments and new ways of accounting (Adams, 2002; Bebbington, 2007; Owen, Swift, Bowerman and Humphrey, 2000; Gray, 1990). However, this increasing commitment to engagement with practice potentially came at a price and, by the turn of the century, academic accounting had reached the point where social accountants were seriously debating amongst themselves the desirability, even the necessity, of engagement with practice (Adams and Larrinaga-Gonzales, 2007). A key part of this autocritique arose from a recognition of the need to carefully explore the implicit beliefs and assumptions that had underlain much of the social accounting project to this point.

3 Social accounting and the optimistic liberal project

It is probably the case that virtually all of the early social accounting efforts were predominantly reformist in nature (although see Medawar, 1976). In essence, the proposals to develop a more social form of accounting – whether from the profession, the state, business or academe – seemed to share a common view that a reform of reporting and organisational practices in the interests of accountability and the environment was not only desirable but eminently practicable. In the context of an apparently almost universal concern about environmental degradation and the increasing tensions between companies and unions, employees and communities, it was possible to be optimistic that such matters as, for example, protecting habitats, communities and workforces were self-evidently 'good' (desirable). The optimism extended to the possibility that society, law and business would be able to find a way to evolve to a more harmonious and cooperative model of political economy. Even more theoretically nuanced commentators seemed able to share in the possibility of such an optimistic view (Lowe and Tinker, 1977; Tinker and Lowe, 1980).

The neo-liberal explosion of the 1980s set about shattering this apparent consensus on the possibilities of a social democratic and fair future. Social accounting began to reflect, at least to some degree, this emerging tension. At the risk of over-simplification, two broad strands began to emerge.

On the one hand, academe and the accountancy profession began to see social accounting in its broadest sense as something which could perhaps make markets more efficient (Benston, 1982a,b), and which could actively support organisations in their pursuit of efficiency and profit. Amongst the most remarkable manifestations of (what we might call) this *neo-liberal social accounting*, were two very powerful components – albeit with very similar root motives. The first of these components was the emergence of the (now ubiquitous) *business case* literature (see, for example, Carroll and Shabana, 2010). Essentially, the argument was that conducting business in a socially responsible manner; adopting the highest standards of environmental probity; and, (as the environmental and sustainability debate grew in importance) acting 'sustainably'; were all good for the business; that is there was a 'business case' that led one to believe that there was no necessary conflict between pursuing business's traditional goals and maximising the returns to society, customers, employees and the environment. This misconception (Milne, Kearins and Walton, 2006; Gray, 2006a; Buhr, Gray and Milne, 2014) was lavishly supported by the second of these components and one of the most remarkable surges in academic attention: namely a plethora of research which sought to demonstrate that socially responsible/environmentally sound/sustainable corporations were also profitable ones ... and, indeed vice versa (Gray, 2006b; Gray *et al.*, 2014: chapter 8). For too many businesses, management consultants, accounting professionals and academics, social accounting had entered the promised land where virtuous accounting and accountability walked harmoniously hand in hand with large profitable business. For a great many this world still obtains: society and the planet are still safe in the hands of business. And for those who appear to believe this, both the critical accounting project(s) and much of the social accounting project(s) remain of no relevance or importance whatsoever.

Conversely, sections of academe and even parts of the profession, whilst recognising the demise of any apparent consensus about the purpose of business and society, continued in the belief that reforming accounting systems and, especially, systems of accountability was possible, practicable and desirable. It was considered possible because such new accounts were relatively easy and of low cost to produce. In addition, a full (say) stakeholder-orientated social account (see, for example, Gray, Dey, Owen, Evans and Zadek, 1997) would impose little or no direct restriction on conventional business activity but it *would* be a practical manifestation of those principles to which democracies (in general) and the accounting profession (in particular) claimed to subscribe – the principles of accountability and transparency. Accounts, as we know, create social reality (Hines, 1988) and new social and environmental accounts would create new social realities and offer stakeholders different insights into organisational activity. Such accounts were practicable in that theorising and experimentation had shown how such accounts might be constructed (Gray *et al*, 1997; Lamberton, 1998; Spence and Gray, 2008; Bebbington, 2007). Such new accounting was desirable because, the argument went, social responsibility and justice, environmental stewardship and, latterly, planetary sustainability were clearly values which needed to transcend simple economic rationalities if humanity and the planet were to survive. Indeed, there seemed to be the possibility of a new consensus emerging with the global concern for sustainability (see, for example, de Lange, Busch and Delgado-Ceballos, 2012; ACCA/ Accounting for Sustainability, 2015). The prospect of once again seeking to reform business and financial markets energised the social accounting project (see, for example, Burritt and Schaltegger, 2010).

The (typically) implicit vision which underpinned this optimism was that through a systematic production of new information for managers, and different suites of information for shareholders and other (non-financial) stakeholders, the juggernaut of capitalism might be slowly re-directed into a more benign direction. (For more detail see, for example, Owen, 1990; Schmidheiney and Zorraquin, 1996; Schaltegger and Burritt, 2010.)

Unfortunately, by about the turn of the century it was becoming more and more difficult to resist the conclusion that despite 40 years of experimentation and voluntary initiatives, business was largely unchanged in substance while the social and planetary problems were clearly growing. For some sections of the social accounting project this was not sufficient reason to abandon the reformist managerialist project and many colleagues, whether in academe, consultancy or the profession continue to seek ways of encouraging and guiding organisational change towards more social and environmental responsibility and accountability (see especially Schaltegger, Bennett Burritt and Jasch, 2008; Adams, 2015). For others though, the persuasive, if essentially assertive, arguments of the critical school increasingly chimed with the evidence that this marginalist approach to social accounting was simply not changing anything substantial, that it was increasingly being captured and deployed by capital and that maybe the problems were indeed essentially structural. It is here that the debates between the social accounting and critical schools began to seriously engage and, in the process, began to generate more subtle possibilities – at least for the social accountants.

4 The critical accounting critique

Critical accounting asks us to stand back from what we think we know, take a wider, more nuanced view of the larger accounting problematic and explore "what accounting could be" (Tinker, 1984: 156). It demands of us that we recognise the

> variety of ways in which accountants and auditors have become willing servants of partisan interests by supporting the exploitation of certain social constituencies on behalf of others.... [We are asked to recognise] the forms of alienation, perpetuated by accounting practice, that presently pass unrecognised by the public interest and social accounting literature.
>
> *(Tinker, 1984: 9)*

And although social accounting might insist that it too is concerned with "what accounting could be," social accountants, it is argued, have typically failed to take into account the systematic biases inherent in capitalism, the necessary limitations arising from an organisation-centred perspective and, crucially, how categories of meaning ("externalities" being a particular case in point) necessarily limit the level of analysis and the possibilities considered (see, for example, Tinker, 1985, especially pp. 200–01).

Puxty (1986, 1991) develops this critique, initially, in response to a paper by Parker (1986) and then later in response to papers from Parker (1991) and from Gray, Owen and Maunders (1991). Parker (1986) argues that given the observable rise in interest in social accounting in the 1970s and 1980s, it would make sense to respond to this manifestation of public opinion and sustain this development through the establishment of social accounting standards – similar in principle to conventional financial accounting standards. Puxty challenges the implicit assumptions in Parker's (and incidentally in much of social accounting's) arguments:

> Accounting information is part of a system of distorted communication within society that reflects the social system. Any extension of accounting developed through the processes of that system can thus be no more than an extension of that systematic distortion. Although to claim a deterministic control over accounting practice by the centers of power would be untrue in view of the internal dynamics of accounting as an independent technology with a force for its own survival and development, nevertheless the reproduction of those social relations is evidence that social accounting is no serious threat to it.
>
> *(Puxty, 1986: 108–9)*

That is, in essence, social accounting can only be allowed to flourish and to construct new and potentially radical truths if it does not challenge the major structures of capitalism. Further, social accounting is ambivalent about whether it wishes to challenge existing social relations or whether it does indeed wish to seek reform by working with the grain of the market and business. Puxty is arguing that social accounting can have no real value beyond its contribution to capital and profit. Indeed, in a later paper, Puxty (1991: 41) opines: "I reject the possibility of progress of society through current pluralist institutions, and corporate social information that might be generated through them." Crucially, his primary reason for this is less that class interests colonise and capture the communication that social accounting hopes to engender but rather that such communication is unable to show itself a contribution to valid discourse as Puxty argues it.

The essence of these sentiments is picked up by Tinker, Lehman and Neimark – in what is probably the most cited critique of social accounting. The core of their critique is that in social accounting's attempts (sometimes explicit, often implicit) to occupy a "middle ground" between, on the one hand, a conservative, traditional (Western) business position (typically growth and profit seeking above all) and, on the other, a radical, structural critique of capitalism, it unconsciously adopts a "relativistic philosophy, [a] conservative politics and [an] avowed commitment to pluralism [... which fails to recognise] the conflictual underpinnings of corporate activity" (1991: 28). Their argument is that social accounting, despite its frequent appeal and attachment to accountability, suffers (as the title of the paper alleges) a "political quietism" that allows some (highly dubious) notion of public opinion to be relied upon in order to establish what are, and what are not the concerns of the day. It is morally relativistic and fails to note that social and environmental concerns change with time, predominantly reflecting power and class interests. Here we see that the critical accounting critique is driving to the very heart of social accounting's optimistic search for reasonableness and consensus that we saw earlier in this chapter.

As if this were not enough to fatally wound the social accounting project(s), the growth of environmental concerns within social accounting attracted a major broadside from Cooper who, in an excoriating feminist critique speculated on

> [w]hy certain people (Gray, 1990, Porritt, 1989) in their desire (for achievement/ reflection, for self-perpetuation, or perhaps through a desire to be in control/get on top of *the* problem) believe that *accountants* with their phallogocentric binary opposition system can save the planet through accounting.
>
> *(1992: 33, emphasis in original)*

The *ad hominem* unpleasantness (which, one might note, pales beside the vitriol of Cooper *et al.*, 1992) should not be allowed to obscure the key issues of critique. When one accounts for something, there is a real danger that one profoundly reduces the essence of that which is accounted for: by measurement, by financialization, by singularity, by habit and so on, one takes only a single point of view of complex matters such as nature, life and society. The complexities and essences of a child's life or a threatened species are *not* captured by some cost-benefit number or a singular metric and any reliance upon such singularity profoundly and morally limits those things and perpetrates injustices and untruths. Furthermore, an essential component of any account is that whilst raising the visibility of one thing or person (or, more usually, one aspect of something or somebody) one is seriously in danger of making other things invisible. Thus any focus on essence or factor 'a' then makes it less likely that we will notice or even be aware of essence or factor 'not-a' (or as we now say, the 'other'). As with much of the critique, the arguments simplify and trivialise much that had been attempted by social accounting – however, the essential points always bear emphasis and repetition.

Such themes of critique can also be found in work such as that by Everett (Everett and Neu, 2000; Everett, 2004), which rehearses the critique that social accounting is essentially more reformist than it recognises; plays into the hands of the *status quo* and thereby strengthens the problems that have caused environmental crisis; and fails to properly address matters of structural and implicit power. These papers then go further, developing the feminist critique (that we see in Cooper's work) through the postmodern turn and use it to challenge social accounting for, amongst other things, failing to understand the performativity of language. Indeed, social accounting is charged that, by offering up alternative accountings, it continues and exacerbates the dualisms that are arguably at the heart of the environmental and social vandalism that we associate with modernity. Inevitably, there is some substance to these comments in that any proposed account – whatever its ambitions and allegiances – may well offer only singular views, thereby highlighting the question: Whose views are those? It is this, more than anything, that seems to drive the work of Brown and Dillard (see, for example, Brown and Dillard, 2013, 2014) who have directly attacked the singular and the realist in social (and especially environmental and sustainability) accounting and, employing what they call 'agonistic pluralism', argue for much greater links between social accounting and civil society discourses. The key point, which in and of itself is hard to dispute, is that

> [social] accountants have largely downplayed and/or under-theorized contingency and conflict and their implications for [social accounting …] civil society engagement. They typically ignore these aspects or deny them in various depoliticizing moves.
>
> *(Brown and Dillard, 2013: 3)*

By contrast, agonistic pluralism

> seeks to explicitly recognize and engage contestations among groups with divergent ideological perspectives in the interests of fostering progressive social change.
>
> *(Brown and Dillard, 2013: 3)*

This is a continuing element of Brown and Dillard's project and one which resonates with critique which challenges, *inter alia,* the Eurocentric nature of much (social) accounting work, (see especially Gallhofer *et al.*, 2000). However, an essential component of this work is that these authors, whilst continuing the critique of social accounting, are recognising the ambitions of that accounting and actively seeking to offer ways forward beyond only critique: namely through

> the development of dialogic/polylogic accountings that take pluralism seriously by addressing constituencies and perspectives currently marginalized in mainstream accounting.
>
> *(Brown and Dillard, 2014: 1120)*

This potential of a prospect of exploring cooperative possibilities between social and critical accounting is something we develop more in the following sections stimulated, at least in part, by what we see here in Brown and Dillard's work; what we learn from Tinker's recognition that successful political intervention is often a matter of judgement and instinct (Tinker and Gray, 2003); and from the inspiring later work of Cooper (Cooper *et al.*, 2005). Lest it be imagined that excoriating and ill-focused attacks are now a thing of the past, we have the more recent work of Spence and colleagues (Spence *et al.*, 2010) who could not be more keen to shake the social accounting soil from their early career sandals. In essence their critique is a return to the earlier arguments underlying Tinker's essential concerns:

> What accountability refers to is the demand that corporations become, if not responsible, at least transparent about their own irresponsibility. Thus, the SER project implicitly subscribes to some notion of Corporate Social Responsibility (CSR). Moreover, it projects this from a politically centrist position, problematically effacing wider power structures and failing to consider exactly how such processes of accountability might come about and what they might lead to (Tinker *et al.*, 1991). Moreover, because accountability reifies existing institutional arrangements, it precludes the possibility of linking up with other democratic demands in order to form a popular demand that would challenge those very same arrangements.
>
> *(Spence* et al.*, 2010: 78)*

Their critique also re-introduces the scornful and the *ad hominem* motifs in labelling social accounting as a "cargo cult" that has no understanding of a wider world outside of social accounting and, in particular, has no comprehension of the key components of the theories that social accounting so incompetently uses.

> Thus, in addition to the issue of how things are theorised, there is also the issue of whether they are theorised at all. In failing to conceptualise a context within which corporations operate, it becomes impossible to discuss whether accountability might be a realistic or desirable demand to make. Indeed, accountability is something that

increasingly preoccupies the SER project whilst it remains of no real significance to social movements.

(Spence et al.*, 2010: 79)*

5 Synthesising the critique?

Whilst the previous section, inevitably, is not a complete catalogue of the critiques of social, environmental and sustainability accounting it probably captures enough of the key challenges that elements of the critical accounting project(s) have brought to bear. At its most brutal, we might infer that we are thus asked to see social accounting (and indeed all social accountants) as politically quiet, naïve, captured, binary, insecurely masculine, reformist, vacillating, realist, illusory, facile, misguided, either slightly stupid or deliberately duplicitous and, more generally, either a total waste of time or engaged in self-delusory exercises that strengthen the very social, environmental and moral vandalism it claims to be seeking to challenge. That social accounting also finds itself heavily criticised by business and the more conservative *and* neo-liberal corners of accounting and finance (see, for example, Thornton, 2013; Gray, 2013) arguably places social accounting in an unusual position within the academy.

We are unable (and perhaps unwilling) to suggest why social accounting might be so subject to such severe critique but reviewing these critiques does allow some light to be shone upon the critical accounting project itself. Initially it is apposite to note that these critiques draw from a wide range of sources: sources which are not seamlessly harmonious themselves. Thus, for example, Puxty in these pieces is motivated mainly by Habermas's work, Tinker and colleagues draw more directly from Marx, Cooper from Cixous and Spence from Gramsci, whilst Gallhofer *et al.* and Brown and Dillard are examining different notions of culture and spirituality. In other work, for example, Dillard (2015) seeks to explore the byways of postmodern thought. They illustrate the diversity of the critical project(s) as well as that the critique of social accounting neither speaks with a consistent voice nor is necessarily the sole source of truth(s) and/or counter arguments. Most importantly, it seems very unlikely indeed that any activity, idea, artefact, language or proposal (whatever it is that one imagines social accounting to be) could withstand sustained critique from each and all of these differing points of view. Critical accounting is not homogeneous – nor should it be. *Equally, neither is social accounting.*

It is tempting to infer that social accounting offers diverse critical theorists a convenient straw person on which to practice and hone their critical skills, with more of an eye to publication and point scoring than to any emancipatory notion of deconstructing untruth or a manifest concern for life as it is lived. One wonders indeed whether some elements of the critical accounting project need to be reminded that they also may be subject to the critiques that they claim to be bringing. The words of Power and Laughlin (1992: 113) in their discussion of Critical Theory and accounting have a strange echo here:

> Categories of truth and falsehood have been displaced by predominantly instrumental conceptions of information. Knowledge has been replaced by information which 'sounds' true and establishes claims to credibility.

Rather than dwell upon this speculation here, it is more important for all of us to recognise that the quality of argument, evidence and scholarship are the means by which we engage in debate. Many of the critiques we have considered thus far in this chapter fail, for example, to distinguish between different strands of social accounting and frequently employ assertion, very unrepresentative selections of readings, or an almost deliberate misreading of texts in order to strengthen the straw person they are enjoying attacking. So, for example, it is simply not true that all social accountants subscribe to voluntary initiatives and are opposed to regulation as, for example, Gallhofer and Haslam (1997) or Everett and Neu (2000) claim. Neither is it true that notions of accountability necessarily presuppose notions of CSR, nor that all social accountants have no understanding of theory, as Spence *et al.* (2010) assert. Equally it is not indisputably the case that reformism has no worth (however doubtful we might be) or that critique will some-how necessarily hasten the fall of capitalism. Sadly, some of the debate has been characterised, possibly by both social and critical accountants, by lazy abuse and shoddy scholarship. This does not help the advance of understanding as far as we can see, which is rather a shame, since at the heart of the debates are useful and important insights.[2]

There have been a range of attempts to internalise the arguments from critical theorising into the social accounting canon, both as a direct response to comments and as reflections stimulated by the challenges (see, for example, Tinker and Gray, 2003; Gray, 2002, 2010; Owen, 2008). The most obvious effects of these have included a more widespread recognition of the political forces at work in social accounting; an increased diversity in the practices of social accounting research within the academy; and the more self-aware emergence of work which seeks explicitly to adapt to and overcome the limitations that critical theorists have identified. So, for example, whether social accounting necessarily needs to subscribe to social realism (Dillard, 2015) remains moot; whether social accounting can speak *for* nature and society as opposed to *of* nature and society seems to be a less exceptionable issue; and the evidence of over 25 years of voluntary initiatives demonstrates quite clearly that business, the accountancy profession and the state have no interest in adopting substantive social (or environmental or sustainability) accounts.

Equally, it is very relevant to draw attention to significant developments in social account-ing work that *have* emerged over the last decade or so in which corporate and professional claims are actively challenged and counter-narratives offered. This sort of engagement finds eloquent expression in the substantive and uncompromising analyses of the (especially) 'sus-tainababble' reports being published by companies and the whole cloud of language games that surround these reports (Buhr *et al.*, 2014; Adams, 2004). It is increasingly apparent that the narratives of sustainability presented in such reports are predominantly narrow and organisation-centric (Laine, 2010; Milne *et al.*, 2006; Cho *et al.*, 2015). They regularly focus on the business case (Laine, 2005; Spence, 2009), are overly optimistic and typically unreal-istic (Barkemeyer *et al.*, 2014), fail to address the tension between growth and sustainability (Tregidga *et al.*, 2013), and use rhetoric and metaphor to persuade the reader of the validity of their narrative (Castello and Lozano, 2011; Higgins and Walker, 2012). There is increasing awareness amongst social accountants that business has effectively captured the discourse of sustainable development, using its public utterances, including its sustainability reports, to legitimise its continuing pursuit of unsustainable 'business as usual' (Laine, 2010; Higgins and Walker, 2012; Tregidga *et al.*, 2013; Byrch *et al.*, 2015). As Byrch *et al.* (2015) suggest, there are still the reformists who advocate gradual change to business practices through eco-efficiency and ecological modernisation (Schaltegger and Burritt, 2010; Ferreira *et al.* 2010), although there is now a more widespread range of scholars who favour a transformative approach arguing for radical change to business, capitalism and accounting (e.g. Gray and Bebbington, 2000; Spence, 2009; Owen, 2008; Milne and Gray, 2013).[3] Perhaps this work does not qualify as critical accounting as such, but in its attempts to challenge claims and to expose duplicity and blatant misdirection, such elements of the social accounting project are no longer seek-ing any middle of the road.

So, arguably, there are areas within social accounting that have matured and developed in the light of some of the critique from critical accounting. There is one area essential to the social accounting projects where both critical and social accounting can find expression, which we previously designated as external social auditing.

6 Social audits, challenge and the niches of capitalism

External social audits, as Dey and Gibbon remark, are the diverse manifestations of the dissatisfactions of civil society with both "the moral deficiencies of corporate behaviour and, the associated 'grievances' against modern capitalism and globalization," which resonate "strongly with the work of the critical accounting community" (2014: 114). Such external social audits have long been a major component of the social accounting *oeuvre* and a wide range of examples comprise a significant component of its literature (see, for example, Harte and Owen, 1987; Medawar, 1976; Dey *et al.*, 2011; for more detail and some history see Gray *et al.*, 2014; Dey and Gibbon, 2014).

Dey and Gibbon make an interesting distinction between two types of such external social audits: those that react to and offer counter-narratives to the activities of the entities themselves; and those which are self-consciously acts of resistance (and which may not even use organisations as the accounting entity). Social accounting embraces both kinds.[4] The production of reactive counter-narratives is generally stimulated by an entity producing a report (maybe a social responsibility [sic] or sustainability [sic] report) which causes some individual(s), NGO or other body to react (often with outrage). Using both corporate and wider (typically media and internet) data the social audit might seek to challenge the viewpoints and the data expressed and/or offer alternative insights and emphases. Early examples include the 1977 Atlantic Richfield social audit and the 1980s shadow accounts produced for Barclays Bank (Gray *et al.*, 2014). More recent illustrations are provided by Adams' performance-portrayal gap analysis of a company (which for reasons connected with lawyers) was known only as 'Alpha' and the experimental attempts by Gray (1997 – based on the pharmaceutical company Glaxo) and Gibson *et al.* (2001a, b – based on HSBC and Tesco). These reactive examples are of interest to social accountants but they do not appear to capture the interests of the critical accountant.

It is the second of Dey and Gibbon's categories that excites the critical accounting community, however, and here there are a plethora of examples (see, for example, Geddes, 1991). Seminal to the field was the work of early independent bodies such as Social Audit Ltd and Counter Information Services, which publicly sought to challenge the claims and reputations of private and public entities (see, for example, Medawar, 1976; Ridgers, 1979). Their work remains inspirational. The work of Harte and Owen (1987) reported upon (and involved itself in) plant closure reports in which local authorities and trades unions produced data, evidence and argument to directly challenge government and corporate decisions to shut down industrial sites with the concomitant impact on employment and communities. The celebrated work of a group of UK academics in the conflict over the closure of the British coal mines in the 1980s stood as a widely reported challenge to the clear ideological basis of the reported government figures (Berry *et al.*, 1985; Neu *et al.*, 2001).

One of the harshest (early) critics of social accounting, subsequently produced one of the finest examples of social accounting as active intervention. Cooper *et al.* (2005) is a striking example of a constructive essay about the possibilities of social accounting from a critical theorist's point of view, which is then conjoined with a major intervention by the authors on the matter of student poverty. The combination of detailed and public engagement with reflective theorising illustrates just some of the possibilities that social accounting can achieve. Subsequent

Table 14.1 The Tip of the Interstitial Iceberg: Examples of external social audits and newer forms of accounts emerging from civil society

- Accounts of capitalism – e.g. Collison *et al.* (2007), (2010);
- critical National Accounts – WWF (2012);
- accounts of un-sustainability – e.g. Gray (2006);
- accounts of the oppressed/silenced – e.g. Cooper *et al.* (2005);
- accounts of the profession/corruption – e.g. Sikka (2010a); (2010b);
- silent + Shadow Accounts – Gibson *et al.* (2001); Dey *et al.* (2011);
- external Social Audits – e.g. Harte and Owen, (1987);
- counter Accounts – e.g. Gallhofer *et al.* (2006), Steiner, (2010);
- performance-portrayal gaps – e.g. Adams (2004);
- accounts for sustainability – e.g. Bebbington (2007);
- accounts as imagining – e.g. Davison and Warren (2009);
- accounts of Supply Chain + Accreditation – Locke *et al.* (2007);
- regional Accounts of Water, Air, Land, etc. – e.g. Lewis and Russell (2011).

Taken from Gray *et al.* (2014: 271).

work from Cooper on a range of social issues continues this thread. Relatedly, Thomson, Day and Russell (2015) illustrate how social movements can and do use a range of different accounts deployed in a variety of fora as part of a strategy of challenge and engagement.

Further examples abound, details of which can be found in Dey and Gibbon (2014) and Gray *et al.* (2014). In the academic sphere the work of Dey and colleagues particularly stands out (see, for example, Dey *et al.*, 2011; Thomson *et al.*, 2015), as they attempt to codify and extend the field through an exploration of social campaigns as examples of social accounting. As both Dey and Gibbon (2014) and Gray *et al.* (2014) illustrate, the field of external social audits has mushroomed and the range of examples that might be thought of as external social audits *and* of interest to both social and critical accountants has become vast. One attempt to offer a wider and more inclusive articulation of the field (and recognising that the Dey and Gibbon distinction does become somewhat blurred at the edges), is that of Gray, Brennan and Malpas (2014) who chose to re-envision the external social audits in such a way as to introduce the almost infinite array of possibilities that the field can offer. Informed by the work of Erik Olin Wright (2010), they suggest that most social accounting has sought (rightly or wrongly) symbiotic transformation – change that is broadly reformist. Whilst an established critical theorist himself, Wright is nowhere near as scornful of symbiotic initiatives as we have seen critical accountants can be, but he does suggest that the really interesting and potentially powerful transformations are those which he calls "interstitial" – initiatives which live in, develop and attack the niches within capitalism. External social audits of a more challenging nature can be seen precisely as examples of interstitial engagements – as new accounts forged precisely to challenge and to expose and explore conflict, injustice and degradation (for example). Such a concept allows us to conceive of accounts in quite the widest way imaginable, which in turn suggests that we can embrace the very considerable range of new accounts that academics in critical and social accounting – and indeed elsewhere – have suggested, developed or explored. A number of these possibilities are reported in Table 14.1.

Each of the examples in Table 14.1 represents a range of independent accounts which, in one way or another, seek to speak truth to power – of course, which power and how we speak are matters for debate. Furthermore, these interstitial accounts clearly represent attempts by scholars, NGOs, civil society activists and so on to explore, as Tinker suggests, what accounting (in its broadest sense) can be.

7 What do we learn and where next?

On an initial impression, it might be assumed that social and critical accounting have a great deal to say to each other in that both are motivated to some degree or other by the problems of/caused by conventional accounting and both have a concern for what accounting *can* be. However, as we have seen, the relationship in academe has not always been a harmonious one and such maturing that social accounting has managed has been because of – or despite – a diverse array of critical critique. We have not sought to counter and address each of the critical critiques – other work has done some of that already. Our aim has been to suggest the extent to which social and critical accounting might develop a greater synergy.

We have seen that social accounting has tended to privilege practice, pragmatics and possibilities over the greater immersion in social theory that typically characterises critical accounting. Equally, for many social accountants, cooperation, harmony and reformism are generally preferred (rightly or wrongly) over the placing of conflict at the heart of social relations as many critical accountants would prefer. Remembering that to a degree at least such preferences are just that, there is little question that critical accounting's central criticism of social accounting's political quietism and its lack of a nuanced understanding of assumptions and contexts has a real (and empirical) substance. For the most managerial social accountants, accounting's purpose is to help organisations do what they do better, with less negative social and environmental impacts. No critical accountant would see anything but problems in such immanent and un-analytical engagement.

For much social accounting, however, there remains genuine value in both the systematic deconstruction of false accounts and in the prospect of compiling accounts which do offer substantive and fundamental challenges to organisations, their activities, their claims and the systematic inequalities and destruction of which they are a part. That such social accountants' attachments typically embrace degrees of realism is not a criticism *per se* but a matter of difference: indeed, one to be celebrated and explored one might have thought. The determination that an organisation can be shown – empirically – to be irresponsible, dishonest, unsustainable and so on, seems to us to have value in and of itself. That organisations will successfully choose not to embrace such possibilities tells us even more. That critical accountants might well argue that they would have known these conclusions before the work was undertaken opens up a different, but crucial, sort of debate on matters of, *inter alia* epistemology.

Equally, despite the apparent dismissal, we (and many others) remain unconvinced that ideas such as accountability, the challenge of failures to be held to account and the speaking of truth to power are vacuous or without important social, political and moral moment. Indeed, as Lee and Cassels (2008) argue, such an approach to social disclosure has an important role to play in a Gramscian "war of position" as alliances and political blocs are mobilised and empowered to challenge the seemingly impenetrable power of capital (see also, Gray *et al.*, 2014: 151). There is more to be done here but it is far from clear that a critical theorist need dismiss such ideas out of hand (Wright, 2010; Owen, 2008; Dillard, 2015; Gray *et al.*, 2014).

Social, environmental and sustainability accounting is exceptionally unlikely to restrict itself to a focus only on the external social audits, but these new accounts and the almost infinite array of possibilities that they present have raised the prospect of potentially cooperative acts and actions between social and critical accountants, even if that appeal seems to resonate more strongly with social accountants than with critical accountants. It seems to us that a more cooperative engagement between social and critical accountants has a great deal to recommend it (see, for example, Tinker and Gray, 2003). If indeed critical accounting is concerned with what accounting can *be* then social accounting is principally concerned with exploring the actuality of what those accounts might be. In this case, the opportunities for constructive engagement seem both obvious and desirable if, indeed, we *do* want to know what new accounts that offer the prospects of emancipation, dialogue, the exposure of injustice/vandalism and the prospect of potentially more benign forms of economic organisation might actually look like (see Thomson *et al.*, 2015).

This chapter was submitted by the authors with the following title: "Social and environmental accounting and the critical accounting project(s): in search of creative tension."

Notes

1 For more detail and some critique of these developments see, Gray *et al.*, 2014; Buhr, Gray and Milne, 2014.
2 This is not the place to consider the possibility that some themes in social accounting may also be (unforgivably) guilty of such self-indulgence.
3 There is a sense in which these differences – which deserve more engaged debate than they currently enjoy – echo the earlier arguments between critical and social accounting. That is, the differences do not appear to be over matters of evidence but over differences in predisposition (towards matters which might include optimism and tolerance of conflict) and the level of resolution at which the matter is conceived (for example, globally or organisationally).
4 And examples from a range of sources and periods can be found on the CSEAR website at www.st-andrews.ac.uk/csear/sa-exemplars/

References

ACCA/Accounting for Sustainability (2015). *Sustainability and Business: The Next 10 years ACCA Students' Views on Sustainability*. www.accaglobal.com/content/dam/acca/global/PDF-technical.
AICPA (1977). *The Measurement of Corporate Social Performance*, New York: American Institute of Certified Public Accountants.
Adams, C. A. (2002). "Internal organisational factors influencing corporate social and ethical reporting," *Accounting, Auditing and Accountability Journal*, 15(2): 223–50.
Adams, C. A. (2004). "The ethical, social and environmental reporting-performance portrayal gap," *Accounting, Auditing and Accountability Journal*, 17(5): 731–57.
Adams, C.A. (2015). "The International Integrated Reporting Council: a call to action" *Critical Perspectives on Accounting*, 27(3): 23–8.
Adams, C.A.. and G. Harte (1998). "The changing portrayal of the employment of women in British banks' and retail companies' corporate annual reports," *Accounting Organizations and Society*, 23(8): 781–812.
Adams, C.A. and C. Larrinaga-González (2007). "Engaging with organisations in pursuit of improved sustainability accountability and performance," *Accounting, Auditing and Accountability Journal*, 20(3): 333–55.
ASSC (1975). *The Corporate Report*, London: Accounting Standards Steering Committee/ICAEW.
Barkemeyer, R., B. Comyns, F. Figge and G. Napolitano (2014). "CEO statements in sustainability reports: substantive information or background noise?" *Accounting Forum*, 38(4): 241–57
Bebbington, J. (2007). *Accounting for Sustainable Development Performance*, London: Chartered Institute of Management Accountants.
Benston, G. J. (1982a). "Accounting and corporate accountability," *Accounting, Organizations and Society*, 7(2): 87–105.
Benston, G.J. (1982b). "An analysis of the role of accounting standards for enhancing corporate governance and social responsibility," *Journal of Accounting and Public Policy*, 1(1): 5–18.
Berry, A.J., T. Capps, D. Cooper, P. Ferguson, T. Hopper and E.A. Lowe (1985) "Management control in an area of the National Coal Board: rationales of accounting practices in a public enterprise," *Accounting Organizations and Society*, 10(1): pp. 3–28.
Bowen, H. R. (1953). *Social Responsibilities of the Businessman*, New York: Harper & Row.
Brown, J. and J. Dillard (2013). "Agonizing over engagement: SEA and the 'death of environmentalism' debates," *Critical Perspectives on Accounting*, 24(1): 1–18.
Brown, J. and J. Dillard (2014). "Integrated reporting: on the need for broadening out and opening up," *Accounting, Auditing and Accountability Journal*, 27(7): 1120–56.

Buhr, N., R. Gray and M. Milne (2014). "Histories, rationales, voluntary standards and future prospects or sustainability reporting: CSR, GRI, IIRC and Beyond," in J. Bebbington, J. Unerman and B. O'Dwyer (eds): *Sustainability Accounting and Accountability*, London: Routledge.

Burritt, R. L. and S. Schaltegger (2010). "Sustainability accounting and reporting: fad or trend?" *Accounting, Auditing and Accountability Journal*, 23(7): 829–46.

Byrch, C., M. Milne, R. Morgan and K. Kearins (2015) "Seeds of hope? exploring business actors' diverse understandings of sustainable development," *Accounting, Auditing and Accountability Journal*, 28(5): 671–705

Carroll, A. B. and K. M. Shabana (2010). "The business case for corporate social responsibility: a review of concepts, research and practice," *International Journal of Management Reviews*, 12(1): 85–105

Castelló, I. and J. M. Lozano (2011). "Searching for new forms of legitimacy through corporate responsibility rhetoric," *Journal of Business Ethics*, 100(1): 11–29

Cho, C. H., M. Laine, R. W. Roberts and M. Rodrigue (2015). "Organized hypocrisy, organizational façades, and sustainability reporting," *Accounting, Organizations and Society*, 40: 78–94.

Cooper, C. (1992). "The non and nom of Accounting for (m)other nature," *Accounting, Auditing and Accountability Journal*, 5(3): 16–39.

Cooper, C., J. Dunn and A. Puxty (1992). "Anxious murderers: death drives in accounting," paper presented at Scottish Area BAA conference, Dundee.

Cooper, C., P. Taylor, N. Smith and L. Catchpowle (2005). "A discussion of the political potential of social accounting," *Critical Perspectives on Accounting*, 16(7): 951–74.

Cooper, D. J. and T. M. Hopper (1990) (eds). *Critical Accounts: Reorientating Accounting Research*, Basingstoke, UK: Macmillan.

de Lange, D. E., T. Busch and J. Delgado-Ceballos (2012). "Sustaining sustainability in organizations," *Journal of Business Ethics*, 110(2): 151–56.

Dey, C. and J. Gibbon (2014). "External accounts," in J. Bebbington, J. Unerman and B. O'Dwyer (eds): *Sustainability Accounting and Accountability*, London: Routledge.

Dey, C., S. Russell and I. Thomson (2011). "Exploring the potential of shadow accounts in problematising institutional conduct," in S. Osbourne and A. Ball (eds): *Social Accounting and Public Management: Accountability for the Common Good*, London: Routledge.

Dierkes, M. and L. E. Preston (1977). "Corporate social accounting and reporting for the physical environment," *Accounting, Organizations and Society*, 2(1): 3–22.

Dillard, J. (2015). "Accountability, social responsibility and sustainability: accounting for society and the environment," *Sustainability Accounting, Management and Policy Journal*, 6(3): 439–41.

Drucker, P. F. (1965). "Is business letting young people down?" *Harvard Business Review*, Nov/Dec: 49–55.

Estes, R. W. (1976). *Corporate Social Accounting*, New York: Wiley.

Everett, J (2004). "Exploring (false) dualisms for environmental accounting praxis," *Critical Perspectives on Accounting*, 15(8): 1061–84.

Everett, J. and D. Neu (2000). "Ecological modernization and the limits of environmental accounting," *Accounting Forum*, 24(1): 5–30.

Ferreira, A., C. Moulang and B. Hendro (2010). "Environmental management accounting and innovation: an exploratory analysis," *Accounting, Auditing and Accountability Journal*, 23(7): 920–48.

Gallhofer, S. and J. Haslam (1997). "The direction of green accounting policy: critical reflections," *Accounting, Auditing and Accountability Journal*, 10(2): 148–74.

Gallhofer, S., K. Gibson, J. Haslam, P. Nicholson and B. Takiari (2000). "Developing environmental accounting: insights from indigenous cultures," *Accounting Auditing and Accountability Journal*, 13(2): 381–409.

Geddes, M. (1991). "The social audit movement," in D. L. Owen (ed.) *Green Reporting*, London: Chapman Hall.

Gibson, K., R. Gray, Y. Laing and C. Dey (2001). *The Silent Accounts Project: Draft Silent and Shadow Accounts Tesco plc 1999-2000*, Glasgow: Centre for Social and Environmental Accounting Research. www.st-andrews.ac.uk/management/csear

Gray, R. (2006a). "Social, environmental and sustainability reporting and organisational value creation? whose value? whose creation?" *Accounting, Auditing and Accountability Journal*, 19(3): 319–48.

Gray, R. (2010). "Is accounting for sustainability actually accounting for sustainability…and how would we know? an exploration of narratives of organisations and the planet," *Accounting, Organizations and Society*, 35(1): 47–62.

Gray, R. (2013). "Back to basics: what do we mean by environmental (and social) accounting and what is it for? - a reaction to Thornton," *Critical Perspectives on Accounting*, 24(6): 459–68.

Gray, R., C. Adams and D. Owen (2014). *Accountability, Social Responsibility and Sustainability: Accounting for Society and the Environment*, London: Pearson.

Gray, R. H. (1990). *The Greening of Accountancy: The Profession after Pearce*, London: Association of Chartered Certified Accountants.

Gray, R. H. (1997). "The silent practice of social accounting and corporate social reporting in companies," in S. Zadek, R. Evans and P. Pruzan (eds): *Building Corporate Accountability: Emerging Practices in Social and Ethical Accounting, Auditing and Reporting*, London: Earthscan.

Gray, R. H. (2002). "The social accounting project and *Accounting Organizations and Society*: privileging engagement, imaginings, new accountings and pragmatism over critique," *Accounting Organizations and Society*, 27(7): 687–708.

Gray, R. H. (2006b). "Does sustainability reporting improve corporate behaviour? Wrong question? right time?" *Accounting and Business Research (International Policy Forum)*, 36(S): 65–88.

Gray, R. H. and K. J. Bebbington (2000). "Environmental accounting, managerialism and sustainability: is the planet safe in the hands of business and accounting?" *Advances in Environmental Accounting and Management*, 1: 1–44.

Gray, R. H., D. L. Owen and K. T. Maunders (1991). "Accountability, corporate social reporting and external social audits," *Advances in Public Interest Accounting*, 4: 1–21.

Gray, R. H., C. Dey, D. Owen, R. Evans and S. Zadek (1997). "Struggling with the praxis of social accounting: stakeholders, accountability, audits and procedures," *Accounting, Auditing and Accountability Journal*, 10(3): 325–64

Gray, R., A. Brennan and J. Malpas (2014). "New accounts: towards a reframing of social accounting," *Accounting Forum*, 38(4): 258–73.

Guthrie J. and L. D. Parker (1989). "Corporate social reporting: a rebuttal of legitimacy theory", *Accounting and Business Research*, 76: 343–52.

Harte, G. and D. L. Owen (1987). "Fighting de-industrialisation: the role of local government social audits," *Accounting, Organizations and Society*, 12(2): 123–42.

Harte, G., L. Lewis and D. L. Owen (1991). "Ethical investment and the corporate reporting function," *Critical Perspectives on Accounting*, 2(3): 227–54.

Higgins, C. and R. Walker (2012). "Ethos, logos, pathos: strategies of persuasion in social/environmental reports," *Accounting Forum*, 36(3): 194–208.

Hines, R. D. (1988). "Financial accounting: in communicating reality, we construct reality," *Accounting, Organizations and Society*, 13(3): 251–61.

Laine, M. (2005). "Meanings of the term 'sustainable development' in Finnish corporate disclosures," *Accounting Forum*, 29(4): 395–413.

Laine, M. (2010). "Towards sustaining the status quo: business talk of sustainability in Finnish corporate disclosures 1987-2005," *European Accounting Review,* 19(2): 247–74

Lamberton, G. (1998). "Exploring the accounting needs of an ecologically sustainable organisation," *Accounting Forum*, 22(2): 186–209.

Lee, B. and C. Cassell. (2008). "Employee and social reporting as a war of position and the union learning representative initiative in the UK," *Accounting Forum*, 32(4): 276–87.

Lowe, A. E. and A. M. Tinker (1977). "Siting the accounting problematic: towards an intellectual emancipation of accounting," *Journal of Business Finance and Accounting*, 4(3): 263–77.

Maltby, J. (2005). "Showing a strong front: corporate social reporting and the 'Business Case' in Britain, 1914-1919," *Accounting Historians Journal*, 32(2): 145–71.

Medawar, C. (1976). "The social audit: a political view," *Accounting, Organizations and Society*, 1(4): 389–94.

Milne, M. and R. Gray (2013). "W(h)ither Ecology? the Triple Bottom Line, the Global Reporting Initiative, and Corporate Sustainability Reporting," *Journal of Business Ethics*, 118(1): 13–29.

Milne, M. J., K. Kearins and S. Walton (2006). "Creating adventures in wonderland? the journey metaphor and environmental sustainability," *Organization*, 13(6): 801–39.

Neu, D., D. J. Cooper and J. Everett (2001). "Critical accounting interventions," *Critical Perspectives on Accounting*, 12(6): 735–62.

Owen, D. L. (1990). "Towards a theory of social investment: a review essay," *Accounting, Organizations and Society*, 15(3): 249–66.

Owen, D. (2008). "Chronicles of wasted time? personal reflection on the current state of, and future prospects for, social and environmental accounting research," *Accounting, Auditing and Accountability Journal*, 21(2): 240–67.

Owen, D. L., T. Swift, M. Bowerman and C. Humphrey (2000). "The new social audits: accountability, managerial capture or the agenda of social champions?" *European Accounting Review*, 9(1): 81–98.

Parker, L. D. (1986). "Polemical themes in social accounting: a scenario for standard setting," *Advances in Public Interest Accounting*, 1: 67–93.

Parker, L. D. (1991). "External social accountability: adventures in a maleficent world," *Advances in Public Interest Accounting*, 4: 23–34

Power, M. and R. Laughlin (1992). "Critical theory and accounting" in M. Alvesson and H. Willmott (eds): *Critical Management Studies*, London: Sage Publishing.

Puxty, A. G. (1986). "Social accounting as immanent legitimation: a critique of a technist ideology," *Advances in Public Interest Accounting*, 1: 95–112.

Puxty, A. G. (1991). "Social accountability and universal pragmatics," *Advances in Public Interest Accounting*, 4: 35–46.

Ridgers, B. (1979). "The use of statistics in counter-information," in J. Irvine, I. Miles and J. Evans (eds): *Demystifying Social Statistics*, London: Pluto Press.

Schaltegger, S. and R. L. Burritt (2010). "Sustainability accounting for companies: catchphrase or decision support for business leaders?" *Journal of World Business*, 45(4): 375–84.

Schaltegger, S., M. Bennett, R. Burritt and C. Jasch (2008) (eds). *Environmental Management Accounting for Cleaner Production*, Dordrecht, NE: Springer.

Schmidheiny, S. and F. J. Zorraquin (1996). *Financing Change: The Financial Community, Eco-efficiency and Sustainable Development*, Cambridge, MA: MIT Press.

Spence, C. (2009). "Social accounting's emancipatory potential: a Gramscian critique," *Critical Perspectives on Accounting*, 20(2): 205–27.

Spence, C. and R. Gray (2008). *Social and Environmental Reporting and the Business Case*, London: Association of Chartered Certified Accountants.

Spence, C., J. Husillos and C. Correa-Ruiz (2010). "Cargo cult science and the death of politics: a critical review of social and environmental accounting research," *Critical Perspectives on Accounting*, 21(1):76–89.

Thomson, I., C. Dey, C. and S. Russell (2015). "Activism, arenas and accounts in conflicts over tobacco control," *Accounting, Auditing and Accountability Journal*, 28(5): 809–45.

Thornton, D. B. (2013). "Green accounting and green eyeshades: twenty years later," *Critical Perspectives on Accounting*, 24(6): 438–42.

Tinker, A. M. (ed.) (1984). *Social Accounting for Corporations*, Manchester: Manchester University Press.

Tinker, A. M. (1985). *Paper Prophets: A Social Critique of Accounting*, Eastbourne, UK: Holt Saunders.

Tinker, A. M. and E. A. Lowe (1980). "A rationale for corporate social reporting: theory and evidence from organizational research," *Journal of Business Finance and Accounting*, 7(1): 1–17.

Tinker, T. and R. Gray (2003). "Beyond a critique of pure reason: from policy to politics to praxis in environmental and social research," *Accounting Auditing and Accountability Journal*, 16(5): 727–61.

Tinker, T., C. Lehman and M. Neimark (1991). "Corporate social reporting: falling down the hole in the middle of the road", *Accounting, Auditing and Accountability Journal*, 4(2): 28–54.

Tregidga, H., K. Kearins and M. Milne (2013). "The politics of knowing 'organizational sustainable development'," *Organization & Environment*, 26(1): 102–29.

Ullmann, A. E. (1976). "The corporate environmental accounting system: a management tool for fighting environmental degradation," *Accounting, Organizations and Society*, 1(1): 71–9.

Wright, E. O. (2010). *Envisioning Real Utopias*, New York: Verso Books.

15

EMERGING ECONOMIES

Trevor Hopper and Farzana Tanima

1 Introduction

Eighty per cent of the world population, of more than 7 billion people, live on less than $10 a day; nearly 50 per cent on less than $2.50 a day; and more than 1.4 billion receiving less than $1.25 live in extreme poverty. Worldwide, 870 million people have insufficient food to eat. According to the United Nations' Children's Fund (UNICEF) 22,000 children die daily due to poverty. In 1998, the United Nations (UN) estimated that it would cost $40 billion annually (about $58 billion today) to offer basic education, clean water and sanitation, reproductive health, and basic health and nutrition to everyone in every developing country.[1] In contrast, world military expenditure in 2012 is circa $1.756 trillion (Stockholm International Peace Research Institute Year Book, 2013). Many of these issues, especially poverty and hunger, can be alleviated by direct aid in the form of cash and provisions. This sometimes has merit, for example, a starving person cannot be more productive without greater sustenance, and immediate relief is essential for disasters whether caused by nature or humankind. However, it can only be a limited, temporary solution. If sustained it can create dependency, for example, with refugees refusing to return home when safe for fear that food and services may be more uncertain or lower than in camps. Longer-run development needs to be sustainable so, for example, capital donations such as mechanised boats for fishermen can become abandoned due to insufficient resources or expertise to maintain them. Direct aid may simply treat the symptoms rather than the causes of poverty, which vary between countries. These can include lack of natural resources and capital; unstable and/or ineffective governments; poor infrastructure such as transport and communications; inadequate education and expertise; corruption; barriers to trade; and dependence on foreign governments and/or businesses. Development goes beyond merely economic growth. Its benefits need to leverage up the resources of the poor, not just with respect to income but also, *inter alia*, their prospects of employment, an improved quality of life, education and literacy, and participation and influence in local and national politics.

At first sight accounting may seem peripheral to achieving this, which may explain the inattention paid to it by researchers in both development studies and accounting, indigenous politicians with more pressing matters on hand and, to a lesser degree, external institutions providing aid and finance. Solving poverty will not reside primarily in better accounting but it is an essential, if neglected or taken-for-granted, cog in mechanisms of development. Too often it has been seen as an unproblematic transference of essentially technical systems, regulations and concepts used in rich countries to poor ones. This masks a series of issues, however, including the alleged bias of such systems to particular Northern ideologies and interests, not least those of large multi-national corporations; insufficient recognition of indigenous circumstances, needs and participa-tion; implementation problems; inequities of power and an orientation towards financial rather than developmental ends. Hence many accounting policies recommended and/or imposed by external institutions fail in many underdeveloped countries (UDCs) (Andrews, 2013).

This chapter analyses these issues further. First, it traces how development policies since the 1950s when decolonisation gained momentum (most poor/UDCs are ex-colonies) have evolved. In so doing it identifies when and how accounting is integral to successive development policies, their repercussions, the actors and constituencies with (and without) influence and the problems and potential of current policies for development and accounting.

2 What is a developing country and what is development?

Defining a developing country is fraught with difficulty. The World Bank (WB) uses Gross National Income (GNI) criteria to categorise economies along four stages of development: (a) low income ($905 or less); (b) lower middle income ($906–$3,595); (c) upper middle income ($3,596–$11,115); and (d) high income ($11,116 or more) per head. This is a useful and objec-tive measure but it has problems. Taking a mean (or a median) may disguise wide income disparities within a country; for example, oil rich countries like Nigeria may have a high GNI per head but a high proportion of its populace live in poverty. Taking a snapshot of incomes per head can produce a static analysis and inadvertently bias findings towards accounting in problematic 'failing' states and thus deflect attention from more successful economies and how accounting may have aided their development. Moreover, there is a danger of 'ghettoising' accounting research by confining development to UDCs. Income differentials in many rich countries are increasing and pockets of poverty are becoming more widespread. Too often development policies implicitly assume that UDCs should learn from practices in rich coun-tries. However, the converse can be true, for example with respect to the role of microfinance and enabling poor and marginalised sectors of society to be more politically engaged. Many development aims for UDCs such as further empowering women, redistributing income and creating jobs for the poor and marginalised are, or should be, policy considerations in richer countries too. With these caveats in mind this chapter embraces income categories (a) to (b) but focusses primarily on lower income countries. Ex-communist countries in transition are excluded (see the special issue of *Management Accounting Research*, volume 13, issue 4 [2002] and Hopper and Hoque [2004]) as they are often relatively affluent, may lie within Northern political and economic systems, and have a legacy of Northern institutions under revival. Nevertheless, like rich countries, issues surrounding accounting and development in UDCs are relevant to transitional economies.

WB indices are cruder than two widely accepted UN indices. The human development index (HDI) measures three dimensions: life expectancy; educational attainment; and adjusted real income (dollar per person). The human poverty index (HPI) measures deprivation using four indices: the percentage of people expected to die before age 40; the percentage of illiterate adults; the percentage of people without access to health services and safe water; and the per-centage of underweight children under five. It classifies economies into four categories: (a) less developed countries (LDCs) (50); (b) developing economies (168); (c) economies in transition (20); and (d) developed economies (42). The inequality-adjusted human development index (IHDI) adjusts the HDI to take inequality into account. The focus of this chapter is on categories

(a) and (b) of the HDI but where relevant we have included data from countries in other categories since, as will be explained, rigid categorisation may preclude significant contributions and issues.

The UN indices recognise that development extends beyond economic growth and rising average incomes: greater prosperity may not trickle down to poorer sectors and development incorporates social and political factors not just economic ones. The HDI and HPI indices reflect the eight international Millennium Development Goals (MDGs) established after the UN Millennium Summit in 2000 involving 189 UN member states and at least 23 international organisations. All committed themselves to help achieving the MDGs by 2015. The MDGs were to eradicate extreme poverty and hunger; achieve universal primary education; promote gender equality and empower women; reduce child mortality; improve maternal health; combat HIV/AIDS, malaria and other diseases; ensure environmental sustainability; and develop a global partnership for development. These goals are critical to accounting research on development as they form the criteria against which accounting policies and practices should be evaluated. By contrast, stock market and economic measures that permeate so much accounting research and practice are woefully inadequate. Incorporating development criteria takes accounting into the realms of civil society, ecology, politics, inequality, gender, health and education, topics neglected by conventional mainstream accounting research but not its more critical and socially oriented counterparts. Moreover, as will be discussed, the universal adoption of MDG criteria, not least by the WB and its acolytes, has shifted development policies beyond market-oriented reforms to issues of governance, human rights and sustainability.

3 Accounting and development policies

In a review of management accounting research in UDCs (Hopper, Tsaneymi, Uddin and Wickramasinghe, 2009) found various factors influencing policies. Important institutions included international finance institutions (especially the WB, the International Monetary Fund [IMF], and their acolytes, e.g. the African Development Bank, stock exchanges and UN agencies). This review casts its accounting net wider to cover financial accounting and thus professional accounting bodies (indigenous and international), transnational accounting standard setters; the accounting industry especially the Big Four accounting firms; foreign donor countries; non-governmental organisations (NGOs); businesses, especially multinational organisations (MNOs); and the local state, especially its regulatory and legal institutions, and civil service. These operate in a dynamic milieu of international and domestic politics where issues such as culture, ethnicity, political leadership and civil society bear upon the implementation of policies emanating mainly from external institutions.

A comprehensive review of development policies emanating from academics, the various institutions involved, and individual countries lies beyond the scope of this chapter. However, most UDCs tend to be ex-colonies with a resultant colonial legacy and ties, and are aid dependant. Consequently, they must be sensitive to changing development policies emanating from the WB, the IMF and the UN. How these have changed since post-World War II, when many UDCs gained independence is chronicled below.

During the 1950s and 1960s, Marxist (e.g. Frank, 1972) and liberal economists such as Rostow (1960) provided different theories of development. Marxists stressed industrialisation through state central planning, public ownership of major enterprises and economic protection through tariffs and currency controls. In contrast liberal economists, drawing (arguably erroneously) from how development occurred in Northern economies, stressed free trade, markets and capital accumulation sometimes linked to democracy. The latter tended to be pursued in large countries, often with an abundance of natural resources. This had little resonance to most African and Asian economies, lacking capital and being predominately rural, traditional and agricultural. Consequently, especially after gaining independence from colonial rule, many adopted socialist regimes, often following external pressure and advice, but also due to indigenous rulers' ideological attachments to socialism and for pragmatic reasons such as shortages of private capital, underdeveloped product markets and limited human and physical resources. Parliamentary democracies were instituted but often were diminished or even abolished under systems of presidential one-party rule (civilian or military) or military dictatorships. Many UDCs took advantage of the Cold War and played off communist and Northern donor countries to secure aid, which was often oriented more towards securing the allegiance of political leaders rather than poverty alleviation. However, both development approaches were essentially economic, linear and modernist – local tradition and culture was perceived as an impediment and their sacrifice a necessary, if painful, necessity. Both stressed rational decision making to promote economic growth albeit through different means.

Whatever the development strategy, early accounting commentators emphasised the need for timely and reliable accounting information for investment and operational decisions by the state, for businesses and for national economic planning (Seidler, 1967a, b). Financial statements should trace economic transactions; monitor the performance of state-owned enterprises (SOEs) through reports to the minister concerned, parliament and potentially the public; audits should monitor and determine the accuracy of financial records and whether expenditure was sanctioned in private and public enterprises alike; internal accounting systems should provide economic data for rational decisions and monitor managers' achievements of plans; and budgeting between enterprises and planners should be the lifeblood of iterative central planning. Much of the accounting systems in place, adopted and supporting legislation stemmed from colonial times, while former colonial ties continued to be influential. However, there were recommendations to improve indigenous accounting's capacity and data provision, and gain greater recognition of accounting's importance by developing accounting education and professional development within a self-governed accounting profession (Seiler, 1966), and by institutions that transfer accounting technology (education bodies, international organisations, government agencies, MNOs, international accounting firms and local companies and accounting firms) creating a sub-plan within an overall economic plan to this end (Needles, 1976). Accounting was deemed to be vital as it "assists development programming in determining and improving efficiency and productivity," being accompanied by calls for an international, interdisciplinary theory that serves socio-economic aims (Enthoven, 1982: 109). In summary, the accounting proposed derived from, reproduced and reinforced legal rational authority and bureaucratic values to promote economic efficiency and growth through industrialisation.

Studies of successful accounting and development are sparse but drawing from work in accounting in countries that have successfully developed – for example, South Korea – such accounting changes were made and very likely contributed to this process. By contrast, events transpired differently from expectations in many UDCs often prone to economic, social and physical crises, political instability and regime changes. A recurring finding is that, whilst basically sound, accounting and accountability systems in government and state enterprises were often adopted and maintained, and in actuality they often played a ceremonial role to gain legitimacy from the populace and external funders. They played little role in ministerial and parliamentary scrutiny or in decisions at both the policy and operating levels, especially in state owned enterprises (SOEs). Instead, political rather than legal rational bureaucratic or economic criteria were dominant. Thus matters like filling positions, awarding contracts and operating decisions become subject to patronage by politicians seeking to bolster political support or to further their material interests. Officials, often poorly rewarded and trained, frequently responded by rule-bound behaviour or indulging in corrupt practices. A result was a failure to develop economically and recurrent fiscal crises caused, in part, by large accumulating losses of SOEs. This state of affairs has increasingly been attributed to neo-patrimonialism (to be discussed later), which creates market distortions harmful to long-run growth: its arbitrariness and instability is an anathema to capitalist investors (Kelsall, 2011).

During the 1980s and 1990s external funders, especially the WB and IMF, began to regard many states in LDCs as too big, corrupt and a block on, rather than facilitators of, development. The assumption was that state bureaucracies were inflexible, uncreative, rule-bound and corrupted by neo-patrimonial political leadership. Inspired by neo-classical economics, including agency theory, transaction cost economics and Friedmanite 'Chicago' neo-liberalism, and following the demise of the Cold War, the WB, the IMF and their acolytes began to advocate and enforce market-based solutions to development. Put crudely, the state was seen as the problem not the solution. Loans to rectify fiscal imbalances of LDCs often became conditional on adopting structural adjustment programmes (SAPs) stipulating free trade, competition, attracting private capital, limited government intervention and public sector reforms (Toye, 1994; Cook and Kirkpatrick, 1995; Hemming and Mansoor, 1988; Cook, 1986). SAPs tried to create conditions conducive for international finance capital and capital markets by eliminating subsidies, price controls and import barriers; reorganising and lessening public ownership of domestic banks; promoting private banks and domestic capital markets; privatising or closing SOEs; introducing new public management (NPM) in government agencies; and introducing legislation that forced trade unions (especially public sector ones) into collective bargaining, severing party links, and curtailed labour rights, especially in export zones. Rather than the government directly delivering services it was recommended that private firms or NGOs be contracted to do so. Consequently NGOs grew and multiplied. The aspiration was for a smaller state to play a greater supply-side role, follow legal-rational not partisan decision making, and create infrastructures conducive to market capitalism by promoting law and order, financial and commercial mobility, education and training congruent with market needs, and regulatory bodies, especially for privatised utilities where monopolies prevail, thereby protecting property rights, and for politics to consist of parties competing to deliver such regimes.

4 Market-based development policies and accounting

Effective accounting is crucial to such reforms, though often neglected by the IMF and WB whose policy officers have been, until recently, predominately macroeconomists. They tended to assume that accounting was essentially a technical matter that would flow from market reforms. Where accounting reforms were undertaken, they were usually based on the advice and reports of Northern accounting consultants.

Given the emphasis on privatisation, controlling indigenous banks, cutting subsidies and price controls, encouraging foreign business investment and private sector development generally, the adoption of international accounting and auditing standards was recommended, alongside company law reforms, building local professional accounting capacity and its regulation, and where possible strengthening stock exchanges and their regulations. In brief, the belief was that market-based development required the introduction of Northern accounting and auditing standards and reporting for private companies. It was presumed that competitive pressures and personal ownership in privatised companies would induce more commercial accounting systems; and the dictates of more vitalised capital markets, aided by government regulators and international audit standards, would improve auditing and external financial reports and thence better lubricate capital market transactions.

Government accounting, particularly new public management (NPM) (Hood, 1995), was a major focus. NPM promulgates private sector practices in government departments, especially tendering; decentralisation – often to local government; granting local managers greater discretion over means (subject to budget constraints); reconstructing civil service organisations around programmes; and appraising civil servants against key performance indicators. The belief was that viewing citizens as customers and reducing principal–agent conflicts facing civil servants through better internal auditing, the tight monitoring of results and performance-related rewards would improve accountability, reduce corruption and thus increase economic growth. Governments adopting NPM needed redesigned accounting systems that would break down costs and benefits to programs, individuals and sections; reinforce performance evaluation systems that reward achieving ends; and provide accurate costs and valuations to formulate and appraise bids for service contracts or state assets.

Judgments of such market-based reforms remain divided and their results are patchy and variable across jurisdictions. Nevertheless, they frequently experienced difficulties, for example exacerbating inequalities; neglect of poverty reduction, social goals and environmental issues; diminished local democracy; and failures to deliver the economic growth promised. The WB, IMF and Northern donors like the United States Agency for International Development (USAID) were accused of ignoring local resistance to privatisation; employing inadequate financial systems for equity sales; ignoring local needs; neglecting adequate regulation; and casting aside inconclusive evidence that private enterprises outperform SOEs (Commander and Killick, 1988; Cook and Kirkpatrick, 1995). Privatisations may bring more commercial controls but these can be at odds with broader development goals, for lower tax revenues, coercive controls, opaque accounting and tax evasion (Uddin and Hopper, 2003). Moreover, political intervention can continue sometimes in different guises, for example regulation (Wickramasinghe, Hopper and Rathnasiri, 2004).

Structural adjustment program (SAP) restructuring as a condition for loans had little success: on average, the performance of debtor country economies continued to lag behind UDCs that did not take out IMF loans, while environmental degradation and poverty frequently worsened (Structural Adjustment Programs, FPIF, April 1998). Stiglitz (2002) argued that IMF solutions worsen (even create) problems by unduly promoting global finance interests. Indeed, rather than stymying neo-patrimonialism the reforms could create fresh sources for it to feed from; for example, the distribution of privatised companies or politicians' capture of regulatory mechanisms. The results were similarly disappointing for accounting. It was not evident that adopting international accounting standards had much practical effect beyond resident international firms or indigenous firms seeking foreign listings: auditing often remained ignored, weak or corrupted; increased financial transparency and information did not materialise; policies, responsibilities and delivery of services became fragmented; accounting systems and regulations adopted to appease international agencies were often ignored in practice; and civil servants often suffering reductions in pay and numbers became at worst demoralised and more often less effective.

5 Development policy shifts: good governance and accounting

In retrospect it has been recognised that downsizing the state was an error (Chang, 2007; Stiglitz, 2002). In 1992 the WB identified that a country's governance quality; the type of political regime; how authority is exercised when managing economic and social resources for development purposes; and a governments' capacity to formulate and effectively implement policies, play a crucial role in development. Since 1997 international financial institutions, whilst not abandoning macroeconomic market-based reforms and encouraging private enterprise, have focussed on governance to address corruption, transparency, tax reform and other domestic concerns. Attention turned to the capable state and good governance to complement market-based policies (World Development Report, 1997). The agenda included strengthening the rule of law and protecting property rights; maintaining macro-economic stability; investing in human resources and infrastructure; protecting the most vulnerable, especially the poor and women; safeguarding natural resources and the environment; combatting corruption and mis-management; and integrating UDCs into the global economy. Thus whilst macroeconomic management and market-based reforms remained important there was a growing emphasis on building capacity and infrastructure to strengthen state institutions, businesses and civil society involvement.[2] Undemocratic tendencies and poor government were seen as liabilities given a more globalised economy wrought by reduced transportation and communication costs; and the erosion of artificial barriers to flows of goods, services, capital, knowledge and, to some extent, people. To increase the capacities of states, more donor funding has been directly placed into government coffers rather than to specific projects and delivery agencies, and there has been increased emphasis on improving planning and control systems including accounting ones; securing better motivated, trained and remunerated civil servants; and greater delegation of powers and resources to local governments and communities, for example through village development committees, commune accountability boards, citizen complaint procedures and so on.

Definitions of a capable state and good governance are often vague and varied, not least because some discretion is left with local policy makers (United Nations, 2006). Definitions can focus on means rather than ends. They do, however, tend to include more accountable public sector management responsive to other stakeholders and compliant with bureaucratic rules and regulations; free and transparent information; the rule of law; promotion of social justice and liberties; legitimate governments through free and fair elections with universal suffrage; and freedom of the press and voluntary association. Public sector reform often incorporates decentralisation to local governments and communities, specialisation according to programmes, redesigned management systems and capacity-building and civil service reforms through meritocratic recruitment and promotion, competitive pay, realistic staffing levels and performance appraisal to develop a workforce of the right size, skills mix, motivation and professional ethos.

The Seventh African Governance Forum Report (2007) provides an example of indigenous countries formulating what constitutes a capable state. In it African political leaders delineated its features which included (a) the creation, promotion and sustaining of an environment of peace, security and stability to enable people to engage in creative and productive activities; (b) the promotion and sustaining of constitutionalism, the rule of law and due processes of law; accountability and transparency; ensuring a better understanding of citizenship entitlements and obligations; (c) creating and maintaining an appropriate and continuously flexible balance between the efficiency of market forces and the availability and delivery of public goods and services; (d) creating an enabling environment and the appropriate policies, regulatory mechanisms and processes for the promotion of the private sector; ensuring good corporate governance; avoiding cronyism, and preventing corruption; (e) empowering the people to decide the form and composition of government; (f) managing diversities; (g) mobilising human and material resources; (h) promoting and consolidating gender equality; (i) promoting trust, understanding and the imperatives of national consensus amongst the political parties; and (j) promoting democracy and good governance.

WB Worldwide Governance Indicators (WGI), developed for 215 economies from 1996–2012, monitor in aggregate and by country six dimensions of governance: voice and accountability; political stability and the absence of violence; government effectiveness; regulatory quality; rule of law; and control of corruption. These derive from enterprise, citizen and expert survey respondents in industrial and UDCs, together with data from 32 survey institutes, think tanks, NGOs, international organisations and private sector firms. Indicators can be broken down by country across topics: agriculture and rural development; aid effectiveness; climate change; economy and growth; education; health; infrastructure; energy and mining; poverty; gender; environment; the private and public sectors; external debt; financial sector; science and technology; social development; social protection and labour; trade; and urban development. Space precludes a more detailed analysis of this exercise, which is not without its critics, but it denotes how the criteria and means of accounting extend into the social and political. The perceived route to development thus lies in increased accountability and accounting (defined broadly) that combines conventional, essentially Northern-state and market-based accounting, with concerns for greater democracy and decentralisation to local levels, and on sustainability and poverty reduction monitored by non-financial indicators. Paradoxically calls by social and environmental accounting researchers have been heeded more with respect to UDCs than rich ones, though how to integrate them into accounting systems still requires much work.

Critics allege that good governance policies mask donors' continued pursuit of neo-liberal objectives (Rowden and Ocaya-Irama, 2004), and the WB's 'prior actions' and 'triggers' detailed in loan agreements are simply SAPs renamed to give the illusion of change (Chang, 2007: 35). The donors' conception of civil society has been criticised as an elusive concept with many definitions serving plural interests. Similar suspicions abound about the WB's commitment to human rights. Critics argue that, "from its documents … the [WB's] notion of [human] rights is thin and somewhat incoherent, often expressed in legalistic [rather] than ethical terms" (McNeill and St. Clair, 2006: 36). Its small department responsible for ethical values is viewed as having a marginal role, its staff are unclear on what they can do about this and citizen participation in politics remains elusive (Harrison, 2004a; Lynch and Crawford, 2011). Repercussions for not meeting WB targets are unclear. For example, Harrison comments that:

> Tanzania, Mozambique and Uganda generally do not fare well on governance index-rankings; nevertheless, they enjoy very favourable judgements by the Bank and others as effective reformers.… [T]he generic concerns of governance can be employed to 'reward' or 'punish' African States.
>
> *(2004b: 72–3)*

Thus the question remains whether current changes in development policies promoted mainly but not exclusively by Northern institutions, and which largely mimic Northern practices and beliefs, will be effectively implemented – are they superior to previous market-based solutions? In addition, will they not suffer the fate of previous attempts at reform?

6 Donors, transnational institutions, globalised accounting and development

Much accounting change in UDCs flows from policies, advice and pressure from major transnational financial institutions, amongst which the IMF, the WB, the UN and the World Trade Organisation (WTO) are prominent. They form part of a complex nexus of interlocking transnational institutions covering banking supervision, payment and settlement systems, money laundering, insurance, the International Federation of Accountants (IFAC), securities commissions and the International Accounting Standards Board (IASB). Together they promote modernism whereby localities are more connected in time and space through modern communications, and free trade and capital flows (Giddens, 2000). Thus globalised trade and transactions, capital and investment movement, migration and the dissemination of knowledge are sought. Accounting figures prominently in this.

The WB and IMF tend to lay down practical general accounting recommendations but are not involved in technical detail. However, the WB's Framework International Financial Architecture (2001, 2005) seeks global standardisation through governments adopting international accounting and auditing standards, modified accounting regulations for small and medium-sized enterprises (SMEs), better human resources to implement standards and better public oversight of auditing. Saravanumthu (2004) argues that their bias towards financial measures incorporated in financial standards deflects attention from poverty reduction and environmental goals. The WB position can be contradictory – its ideology of globalisation, markets and support of MNOs may conflict with poverty reduction goals – leading to allegations that often the former is elevated above the latter, as exemplified in Mittel Steel's acquisitions in Algeria and Trinidad (Murphy, 2008).

The technical detail and delivery of the policies of transnational financial institutions often relies on inputs from Northern professional accounting associations, Big Four accounting firms and transnational regulation and standard setting agencies (IFAC and the IASB). Together they diffuse an Anglo-American model of universal professionalisation (Poullaos and Uche, 2012). They are not promoters of development. Northern professional accounting associations seek to expand their membership in the South, while the accounting industry seeks more consulting and auditing within UDCs and aid organisations. The Northern accounting organisations' commercial aims can produce conflicts of interest with development. The IFAC has an open membership, has emphasised the public interest and ethics and has consciously addressed the needs of UDCs, though it is being increasingly dominated by Northern accounting associations and the Big Four accounting firms (Samsonova-Taddei and Humphrey, 2014). The IASB is a private company and its membership over-represents Big Four firms. This raises questions as to its legitimacy to set standards, the constituencies they serve, asymmetries of power and the efficacy of the standards adopted (Cobham and McNair, 2012).

The IASB has neglected issues of concern to UDCs such as intra-company trade, transfer pricing, global consolidation, cross-border invoicing, tax confidentiality, not disclosing offenders and low penalties for tax transgressions (Botzem, 2014; Hopper, Lassou and Soobaroyen, 2016 forthcoming). For example, the IASB requirement for global consolidation obscures and obfuscates intra-company trade rather than making it transparent. Even the WB has had to ask the IASB to pay more attention to UDCs, SMEs and financial services to the poor, and the 2009 and 2010 G20 summits also recommended the IASB to pay more attention to UDCs (Fyson, 2012). Northern accounting agencies have a strong fiduciary interest in the globalisation of services sought by the WTO but this is highly political and linked to distributional issues. For example, there is persuasive evidence that whilst financial development improves asset allocation and is linked to economic growth in UDCs, it is not necessarily related to poverty reduction. It may even inhibit the latter by diverting more funding to larger enterprises and those with collateral rather than smaller, poorer firms (Hossain *et al.*, 2012).

Many donors and transnational financial institutions have adopted more sensitive development policies across a broader range of development issues but within accounting a Northern hegemony still prevails. As Arnold (2005) notes, the lower echelons of accounting have no voice in formulating global policies. For example, the Organisation for Economic Cooperation and Development (OECD) information-sharing agreements between countries and tax havens have proven ineffective for UDCs lacking the expertise to make their case and sufficient political clout to get a response. Resolution of this is complex. It requires greater political will, especially from the accountancy profession and Northern governments to legislate for and control tax havens, reduce financial secrecy by jurisdictions, reform multinational companies' accounting disclosures, and stymying illicit capital inflows. The latter often dwarf aid, for example in the case of Africa they totalled US$854 billion from 1970 to 2008 – more than four times sub-Saharan country debts (Cobham and McNair, 2012), while non-arms' length cross-border invoices lose tax revenue in UDCs and exceed total aid by 30 per cent. Tax havens encourage corruption in UDCs and Northern financial centres such as London are hubs of global offshore finance. A Financial Secrecy Index from Christian Aid and the Tax Justice Network finds, contrary to public opinion, that well-known tax havens like those in the West Indies are not as significant as thought. Switzerland, the Cayman Islands and Luxemburg were top but the US was in the top five and the UK thirteenth. Paradoxically cash-strapped Northern governments are focussing more on this given their losses in tax revenue from such manoeuvres.

Northern accounting professions, often with considerable membership in UDCs, and the IASB especially, need to pay greater heed to UDCs' accounting needs. Positive examples include the 2010 IFAC task force on public financial management to help private and public sector organisations in UDCs to harmonise, spread good practice and share knowledge; professional twinning such as the Society of Certified Accountants in Kosovo with the Royal Dutch Institute of Accounting; and a participative Department for International Development/ Chartered Institute of Public Finance and Accountancy development of the accounting profession in Lesotho. However, many UDCs failed to build a local accounting profession post-independence, with local professions remaining a colonial legacy. Those that sought to develop a local accounting profession often failed due to old Northern qualified elites preserving their status, especially as MNOs preferred foreign qualified accountants and Big Four audits. Local accountants' poor education and training, low professional standards, corruption and poor expertise, and accounting associations divided by class, race and ethnicity contributed to their poor reputation. The failure to create an effective local accounting that can articulate local needs and the subsequent reliance on Northern professions has exacerbated the neglect of accounting policies appropriate for UDCs, public sector and SME accounting, and of challenging an orientation that gears itself towards large international business over development within accounting generally.

Thus capacity needs to be built into UDCs' professional accounting institutions. However, the globalisation of services prevents this. If UDCs protect fledgling professional institutes and local accounting firms the WTO and international courts would likely dismantle this. The globalisation of financial services promotes Northern accounting as an elite profession not only amongst potential clients but also amongst Northern qualified members in UDCs wishing to protect their statuses and privileges. As a result, some UDCs require accounts to be audited by chartered accountants (Poullaos and Uche, 2012). Syllabuses offered by Northern accounting institutes, many of which are pursuing strategies of global expansion especially in UDCs, to candidates from the South are based on Northern practices, laws and locales and are often not taught by local universities and technical colleges. This further inhibits the creation of accounting attuned to development and local needs; for example, the Association of Chartered Certified Accountants' (ACCA's) syllabuses and examinations are UK based, allegedly to retain credibility. Regional organisations of accountants, as recommended by the IFAC, like the Pan African Federation of Accountants may help raise UDC voices and encourage joint professional schemes, and encourage more attention to training at the technician level and more accounting on trade courses both of which need enhancement. Whether this is occurring to the benefit of UDCs needs more research.

7 Accounting solutions: overspecified and oversimplified

A consequence of Northern hegemony is what Andrews (2013) labels 'overspecified but over-simplified solutions'. They are oversimplified as they commonly prescribe best accounting practices in the North as solutions to problems in the South regardless of local needs and capacities; and they are overspecified in that they contain considerable formal detail but fail to take account of different cultural norms and circumstances prevailing in many UDCs. Many accounting reforms, particularly in richer UDCs with strong institutions, have achieved significant success but the results in oil-rich and poor UDCs have been patchy and often disappointing (Andrews, 2013). Andrews examined 20 of the IMF and WB's Accounting and Auditing Reports of Standards and Codes in Africa since 2003. He found their emphasis on adopting international standards, and Northern laws and regulatory mechanisms, neglected the cultural and practical capacity of indigenous businesses and accountants to apply these to good effect. The result is high rates of adoption of formal systems that fail or are not complied with (exceptions are foreign companies with foreign stock exchange listings and local companies with or aspiring to such listings). Nevertheless, international institutions continue to judge accounting progress in individual countries by rates of the formal adoption of Northern systems. The issue is why are failing prescriptions often persisted with?

Other commentators criticise the overuse of Northern-centric prescriptions based on Northern practices for not having adapted to local needs, cultural differences and contexts; being too complex; and being overly geared towards capital markets and business rather than state or central planning. Their blanket recommendations prohibit UDCs choosing aspects most appropriate to them or tailoring them to local circumstances. Outside foreign experts, often flown in on short consulting contracts, tend to assume that effective regulatory mechanisms such as local security and exchange commission regulations and necessary legislations are in place, for example on transfer-pricing rules; and functioning capital markets regulated by staff in Ministries or the local agencies with adequate expertise and reliable and prompt information systems exist. This is often not so, as in the case of Ghana (CIPFA, 2010). Where education and training is given, it is often short run; for example week-long courses on specific systems rather than building skills that will ensure sustainable reforms. Often problems such as corruption, development aims, transparency and collecting tax revenues go unresolved, widely believed as being seen as intractable (Andrews, 2013).

Local accountants may not see the relevance, practicality or usefulness of global harmonised auditing standards or International Accounting Standards (IASs)[3] for the circumstances they face. Their underlying conceptual basis, based on common rather than civil law, may be alien to local auditors and their discretion to interpret standards rather than applying rules leaves many confused. These reporting and auditing standards may fail to reflect the needs of local family businesses with high ownership concentrations, or SMEs, or be incompatible with local cultures and business practices, such as guanxi. For example, in Bangladesh, businesses are characterised by high family ownership and ownership concentration, low audit fees (especially in the latter), weak accounting skills and competence of auditors, low incentives for public listing, weak capital markets and a lack of second-order institutions and poor legal enforcement. Easy access to cheap bank credit and default options are a bigger problem than shareholders' rights (Siddiqui, 2012). Thus there may be a case for relaxing the need for audits of owner-managed firms with no agency problems rather than increasing them. The wholesale promotion of Northern systems and solutions neglectful of UDCs' needs has often resulted in UDCs formally adopting IFAC auditing standards and IFRSs for expediency, especially if they are conditions for acquiring financial assistance from transnational financial institutions, but not applying or enforcing them locally (Fyson, 2012).

Policy changes regarding government accounting have been marked. Current policy still emphasises growth through the private sector, especially in SMEs, and attracting foreign investors. However, the WB *Framework* (2010) also emphasises local self-determination of programmes by strengthening governments and enhancing government officials' capacities to create infrastructure, implement legal and judicial systems conducive to business development and develop robust financial systems across endeavours ranging from micro credit organisations to large corporate ventures (Graham and Annisette, 2012).

Improving public financial management through transparent budgeting and accounting has become a cornerstone of international policy (OECD, 2005, 2008, 2012), not only to improve the quality of decisions, local planning and control and to reduce fiduciary risk, but also to monitor the effectiveness of aid against development goals and for donors to be accountable to their own constituencies, by demonstrating that aid is effective and spent for the purposes provided (Fyson, 2012). For example, the Copenhagen Accord pledged US$100 billion annually to offset climate change but managing this locally requires effective and innovative monitoring, not least with respect to financial matters. Perversely, donors' previous external monitoring had weakened the local development of public financial management. Each institution had its own requirements, which meant local officials were required to deal with many different, complex accounting requirements. Nevertheless, despite efforts to standardise and pool reporting to external aid givers, the pressures for aid-givers, especially donor government departments and international NGOs, to be accountable to their electorate or donors has meant that often demanding, conflicting accounting requirements remain. Many public financial management systems do not directly account for aid, thus donors need to maintain parallel accounting systems. Moreover, they often want quick results on specific tangible results to impress their own constituents, for example new schools built, whereas capacity building is long term, less tangible, multi-faceted and incremental. Thus the emphasis is on risk-minimisation and precluding local discretion and adaptability, contrary to stated policy objectives.

The switch by many Northern donors to building state capacity and placing their money directly into state revenue (i.e. into a single Ministry of Finance account rather than to specific projects) has increased the pressure to develop integrated, transparent and simple PFM systems (Fyson, 2012). A penchant for privatisations, contracting out services to private firms or NGOs remains, but this has become more pragmatic and limited given the realisation that the state may be the only feasible provider of large-scale services over many sectors, including health and education. Ironically previous SAPs had often brought severe cuts in the number of civil servants and reduced their pay, thereby weakening state capacity.

Within remaining government organisations NPM remains a model of reform. Accounting plays a central role. Adopting NPM–based auditing and accounting, integrated financial management information systems (IFMSs), developing a professional base of accountants and auditors, applying international government accounting and audit standards, and creating a strong legal framework to support modern accounting practices form part of broader economic reforms to eradicate corruption (Everett *et al.*, 2007: 520). The WB and the IMF continue to advocate NPM to encourage more focus on results not procedures; a customer orientation; innovation; quality standards and performance measurement; and using market players to deliver public services when more efficient and effective. NPM continues a shift from input and process accountability (bureaucracy, rules, regulations) to results (quantifiable outputs, measures and performance targets); devolution of management control; and improved reporting, accountability and monitoring mechanisms (Awio *et al.*, 2007). Two of the central accounting mechanisms are medium-term expenditure frameworks (MTEFs) and IFMSs. MTEFs, endeavour is to link policy, planning and practice, normally over three years, to try and achieve a balanced budget and shift resources to pro-poor activities within a poverty reduction strategy. Computerised budgeting and financial management seek to facilitate more flexible responses to macro-economic and cash flow changes; increased accountability, efficiency and effectiveness of public programmes and the application of external resources; decentralisation with adequate controls; and improved data quality. However, such systems require major preconditions including an ability to forecast accurately; clear national policies; government commitment; comprehensive budgets; coding that links results to inputs; transparent, accountable and effective civil service capacity; reliable indicators; local acceptance and involvement; a realistic and incremental change process; reasonably rewarded public servants; and cheap and reliable information technology. These are often absent in many UDCs.

Consequently the achievements of public financial management reforms can at best be patchy, for example in Uganda, Tanzania and Ghana (Wynne, 2005; Andrews, 2013). For example, the failure of IFMSs in Ghana has been attributed to politicians believing it a technical matter foisted on them but their support waned when they realised the political implications of greater transparency and accountability. The incentives for incorporating 'best practice' can be perverse. There is little evidence that improving public financial management, often introduced at the behest of the North, brings UDCs more aid and it may prove problematic. The benefits of a government's accrual of accounting over cash accounting are dubious; and the adoption of private sector IFMSs too complex to meet local needs and without substantial customisation can fail (Peterson, 2007). Moreover, the implicit assumption that poor public administration causes poverty, and thus the need for foreign experts, may be questionable. The indebtedness of many UDCs was often due to events beyond their control. Foreign consultants can exacerbate problems if they reduce the confidence of local managers and produce reforms not tailored to context and available resources. The inequities of experience, status and qualifications between the consultants and locals may prohibit locals from challenging and controlling consultants at the specification, tendering and implementation stages (Wynne and Lawrence, 2012), and thus inadvertently delimit developing local involvement and capacity.

Again, a frequent plea by commentators is for greater country ownership; more use of local knowledge; getting basic supporting requirements in place; better sequencing of reforms with a toleration of incremental muddling through and constant learning; building on existing and simple systems; and having realistic expectations – change is likely to be slow and spasmodic but not impossible. For example, there are numerous examples of successful donor projects directed at improving local capacity (Fyson, 2012).

8 Reconciling utopia with local context: accountability and civil society involvement

As recounted, many donors and major transnational financial institutions have come to promote good governance and broader development aims and criteria. Arguably, this is a more liberal stance to poverty and governance than in many Northern countries where income differentials and poverty are increasing, and there is growing disquiet with the accountability of politicians and public servants and the lack of local involvement in many facets of life. This is a curious state of affairs, for if good governance is commendable then why do predominately Northern institutions promote it in the South where its implementation is potentially more difficult? Consequently, it raises a series of important accounting issues for accounting policy and research more generally.

Accountability has come to the fore as a prerequisite of democratic or good governance. 'Triangle Accountability' (World Bank, 2004) claims that improved development emanates from (i) the state (politicians and policymakers) through greater democracy and more effective internal and external controls; (ii) service providers (managers and frontline workers) through market disciplines and increased public choice; and (iii) citizens and the clients of services through greater transparency, media and civil society involvement, and elections. The latter are important as this has encouraged the adoption of social accountability frameworks that monitor and publicly report planning and results for public policies and programmes transparently; and participatory[4] and pro-poor budgeting,[5] where citizens can be involved in budget formulation, implementation, monitoring and control. The aim is for civil society to participate more in government and hold officials responsible and answerable for their actions, activities and decisions. *Inter alia* the hope is that this will reduce corruption. Also capacity development involving community participation (including women) extends to other sectors, for example, NGOs, local government, professional associations, academics and community associations. The aspiration is to improve indigenous research and problem solving to meet local needs and priorities, and enable civil society to articulate and mobilise popular opinion, recruit and train new political leaders, disseminate information and hold governments to account.

Rights-based aid, which regards having access to water, food, shelter and education as basic human rights, is becoming more common. The recent broader WB indices reflect this and they raise a series of new accounting issues such as how to promote democratic forces and reduce corruption through transparent financial information and separated powers to provide checks and balances of power; increasing the participation of marginal poor clients; strengthening the voice and involvement of civil society organisations, political parties, the media and external organisations such as NGOs to make public servants and politicians more accountable; ensuring sustainability across a wide spectrum of social, economic, ecological and political indicators; and strengthening the capacity of the state nationally and locally to achieve these ends. For example, increasing a poor country's tax-raising capacity, especially through direct taxes, not only creates revenue but also heightens civil society scrutiny and ownership and accountability, and legitimises government (Holmes, 2012). Of course, the spectrum of broader non-financial indices raises a series of 'how best to' questions, in respect of how to measure the factors under scrutiny, carry the dangers of easily measurable factors dominating vital but less tangible ones and slavish devotion to what is measured rather than what is effective or manipulating data or actions to imperfect performance measures. Moreover, as Everett (2012) points out, indices and accounting can construct reality. For example, he argues that the widely followed Corruption Index of Transparency International suggests corruption is not a rich but a poor country problem and ignores the inequity of power relations between the North and South and the role of rich Northern interests regarding tax havens, tax avoidance by the accounting profession, defence spending and indebtedness.

Emergent approaches to development provide a sharp reminder to accounting researchers and practitioners generally that their remit should extend to constituencies beyond businesses and the state to civil society. This requires new means of evaluating performance that employ criteria beyond the merely financial and systems of reporting and accountability that are meaningful to poor and marginalised clients and permit their involvement in decisions. Presently, much financial accounting is too programme and time specific, which inhibits considerations of sustainability, reporting of and learning from failures and undertaking identity accountability (where members have moral commitments) and downward accountability, which describes the extent to which development organisations, such as NGOs, are accountable to those lower in the aid chain; generally intended beneficiaries (often poor, marginalised and women) (Jacobs and Wilford, 2010). For example, the illiterate, poor and marginalised sectors of society may require a simple, informal, oral and unusual accountability system that transcends current accounting to encourage dialogue, mutual learning and promote empowerment. Research shows that the latter is weak, frequently driven out by managerial targets, and often resisted or neglected by NGOs and other aid providers. NGOs are prone to being co-opted by the very (economic logic[6]) forces that they try to change (Lehman, 2007). The dilemma faced by NGOs concerns principally the nature of work they undertake, and the problems in relation to measuring performance, 'particularly if the objective is empowerment' (Edwards and Hulme, 1996: 968). NGOs tend not to have any evident 'bottom line' which often makes it harder to follow any sense of direction in relation to measuring their performance. Given the dominance of economic logic (predominantly shaped by aid providers), an 'obsession' with measuring performance, using narrow, superficial constructs such as size and growth, which give simplistic indicators of success, has emerged.

These problems are increasing issues of concern to Northern aid providers. It is well understood that that their accountability has been essentially upward[7] through traditional accounting means, which encourages a financial orientation to the exclusion of social accountability. Conventional accounting can reproduce and reinforce the dominance of financial and tangible, short-run achievements and drive out downward accountability, deflecting attention from broader development goals. However, donors must measure the efficiency and effectiveness of the aid they grant to justify their actions to their own funders. Development ministries in Northern countries must convince taxpayers that aid has been spent for the purposes allocated and has brought beneficial development. This is particularly difficult given the growing tendency to place aid directly into the government coffers of UDCs to encourage state building and local discretion rather than allocating funds to specific development projects. NGOs have similar concerns. Those that deliver services must demonstrate that they do this better than states, and their growing shift to advocacy on behalf of civil society, and especially the poor and marginalised sectors, similarly requires tangible demonstration. The danger is that given the lack of proven effective systems to reflect shifts in aid policies more conventional systems of financial reporting, accountability and performance measurement will continue to be employed with detrimental consequences for current development policies.

A manifestation of this concerns the role and provision of 'micro-finance'. Micro-finance is a term which refers essentially to a range of different financial services (such as credit, savings, insurance and pensions) provided in small or micro amounts to people who form the lower-income bracket(s) of society. While the term micro-finance connotes various types of financial services, it is often used interchangeably with the term 'micro-credit', given that credit is in greater demand, and hence in greater supply (compared with other services). Millennium development goals state that access to credit is a human right. In many circles microcredit is seen as the prime means of promoting development. However, there are two competing versions. One is Washington led, promoted by donor agencies such as USAID, the WB, the United Nations Development Programme (UNDP) Micro-Start Programme, the Consultative Group to Assist the Poorest (CGAP) and the Micro Credit Summit Campaign, which orchestrate an essentially market-based system of providers/organisers, be they private banks or NGOs, that contract with clients. The other is the Bangladesh (Grameen) approach that emphasises empowerment, education and promoting civil society political engagement via focusing on alleviating household poverty and vulnerability (Roy, 2010). This approach views the household as a cooperative site, where resources are pooled and shared equally and hence fails to pay attention to intra-household inequities. Both approaches recreate the poor as economic subjects and reduce poverty to being merely an economic issue, however, although the Bangladesh model does pay heed to improving the political engagement of poor clients. The danger is that both become new money-making opportunities for loan sharks to exploit the poor (Roy, 2010) regardless of civil society involvement and economic sustainability, and exploit the poor through high interest rates, shift the costs and processes of formal control and monitoring from the lender to the borrowers and make the poor the financiers of poverty reduction (Jacobs *et al.*, 2012).

In the view of the WB, 'corruption' is no longer a taboo word but has come to the fore in development policies (see WB Governance and Anti-corruption strategy, endorsed in 2007). Corruption and failed development initiatives are not attributable merely to the actions of external agencies but also involve local leadership. Many UDCs display outward signs of modern states including democracy (with more or less regular elections), a formal presidency and parliament, political parties, civil society organisations and a judiciary. Basically sound accounting and accountability systems are maintained but merely play a ceremonial role to gain legitimacy from the populace and external funders. They play little role in ministerial and parliamentary scrutiny or in policy and operating decisions. Instead, political rather than legal rational criteria are dominant. Thus matters like filling positions, awarding contracts and operating decisions become subject to patronage by politicians to bolster political support or to further their material interests. Officials, often poorly rewarded and trained, either respond by rule-bound behaviour, ignoring bureaucratic violations by elites or indulging in corrupt practices themselves. When rulers and their cronies make decisions informally through patronage networks outside formal state structures based on nepotism, clientelism and tribal, ethnic and regional ties (Hickey, 2003; Médard, 1982) corruption is fostered and renders formal systems of accountability redundant. Reforms to address this are likely to fail for those in power have little incentive for them to succeed. Development specialists frequently attribute this to neo-patrimonialism.

Weber (1947) saw patrimonialism as a traditional and legitimate form of authority (Pitcher *et al.*, 2009). He did not employ patrimonialism (where the state is the domain of one or a few leaders – often chiefs, elders or the 'big man') as a pejorative term for corrupt governance or a weak state. Rather it is a form of traditional domination often found in small-scale, traditional, sometimes tribal societies where relations between rulers and subjects are not governed by predictable economic calculations and codified laws. Instead, rulers distribute symbolic and material rewards (often unevenly) to fulfil reciprocal obligations in a shared culture. Relations are direct, dyadic and personal: there is no delineation of private and public realms, and no formal mechanisms of accountability or transparency. Nevertheless, leaders are accountable within traditional collective codes (Pitcher *et al.*, 2009).

Eisenstadt (1973), Médard (1982) and Clapham (1985) added the prefix 'neo' to distinguish contemporary patrimonialism from its traditional form. Neo-patrimonialism is a hybrid post-Weberian invention – "a creative mix of two Weberian types of domination: a traditional sub-type, patrimonial domination, and rational-legal bureaucratic domination" (Erdmann and Engel, 2007: 104). It is widely used to explain political and underdevelopment problems in UDCs (Roth, 1968; Le Vine, 1980). Officials commonly hold positions in bureaucratic organisations with formally defined powers which are exercised, so far as they can, not towards public service but as if they are private property (Erdman and Engel, 2007). Powerful position holders using informal means of patrimony personally distribute material resources ('rents' in modern economic terminology) to further their interests (Kelsall, 2011). The distinction between private and public spheres, at least formally, exists and is accepted, with public reference being made to it but in practice the distinction is blurred. Rational-legal formal rules may define authority and responsibilities and provide legitimacy for seemingly bureaucracies but within them patronage, clientelism, corruption, nepotism and ethnicity abound (Zolberg, 1969; Scott, 1969; Lemarchand and Legg, 1972). The exercise of power in neo-patrimonial regimes is erratic and incalculable.

Neo-patrimonialism is widely associated with corruption by rulers (i.e., the President, MPs, chiefs, party officials and government bureaucrats). In the view of Cammack:

> [I]t is no accident that neopatrimonial states are burdened by bureaucracies whose appointments are made according to tests of loyalty, and which *ineffectively account for public funds siphoned off* to spend on political projects.
>
> *(2007: 601–2, emphasis added)*

However, citizens, especially rural villagers, may expect patrimony from local leaders. Their scepticism of politics, politicians and the state combined with an orientation to traditional patrimonial leadership partly explains why civil society embraces quietism in many countries where "the overarching logic is to gain and retain power at all costs" (Cammack, 2007: 600). Democracy and multi-party elections can intensify neo-patrimonial governance (e.g. voters seek bribes and special favours from candidates). Although this contributes to poor PFM, public goods, governance and development (Kelsall, 2011) it is rational for subjects to gain favours as best they can.

Accounting reforms frequently fail due to neo-patrimonial leaders either ignoring them or using them for unintended purposes (Hopper, Tsmanyi, Uddin and Wickramasinghe, 2012). Weak government accounting and auditing facilitates corruption and renders financial planning difficult. For example, an IMF study on Anglophone Africa (Leonard, 1987) found data in accounting ledgers and monthly reports was not maintained, there were long delays in preparing and auditing the annual government accounts and there was corrupt expenditure. Instituting sound accounting reforms clashes with neo-patrimonial governance logic. Leaders may only support reforms if they can yield project-related resources for personal/political uses. Thus recommendations for government accounting improvement are often accepted but after implementation they are not used or are vehicles for leaders to pursue their interests. When anti-corruption commissions based on successful initiatives in Hong Kong and Botswana were introduced into post-Banda Malawi, its leaders used them to eliminate political rivals.

The wisdom of importing Northern accounting systems to eliminate neo-patrimonialism may be questionable if leaders and subjects calculate payoffs for participating according to their cultural beliefs and self-interests. Some progress may be possible if applying foreign political logics is avoided, however; otherwise accounting reforms will often fail. Rather they need to be based on knowledge of what accounting systems are effective, why and how. This requires grounded studies that link accounting to local circumstances and beliefs about legitimate governance, accountability and corruption, and the prevailing type of leadership. In states with non-developmental characteristics accounting reforms may achieve little unless the politics change. Thus political constraints must be recognised but not all forms of neo-patrimonialism preclude economic development absolutely. Local projects can benefit from leadership and coordination from benign neo-patrimonial leaders oriented to longer run development. Here incremental and selective accounting change may be the best option. Where state control has legitimacy and is strong, reforms may best concentrate on attributes of developmental states and societies. These include fostering strong central state authority and systems; political stability; all classes being taxable; regulated and disciplined labour; protection of the poor; a sense of nation and nationalism; and attracting domestic and foreign capital that contributes to promoting national development goals. Accounting reformers must think and act politically, and develop analyses and recommendations that take into account the political context of the country, how decisions are made and in whose interests? In those situations where formal accounting mechanisms are weak then where do networks of power reside; what logic drives policy; how is bureaucracy maintained and used; is tradition a factor; and how are elections won? Accounting reforms that fail to consider their political and cultural feasibility and realistic means of implementation may prove useless. In so doing it is important to distinguish political leaders from public servants. A powerful, competent and insulated bureaucracy may exist or can be nurtured that is stable; has the authority to create, direct and manage development; and is sufficiently competent, professional and autonomous to resist tests of political loyalty, even in many neo-patrimonial regimes.

This does not constitute an argument for maintaining the status quo; nor abandoning decentralisation, greater democracy and accountability; and eliminating corruption. The need for accounting systems, structures and processes that further development in its broadest sense remain. Such ventures include giving the poor and marginalised greater voice; aiding civil society organisations that monitor and report on government spending and activities; promoting government accountability, not least by increasing the transparency and volume of financial information; reducing corruption; and encouraging independent media. Critical accounting researchers should endeavour to promote positive social change and address institutional weaknesses but within an accommodation of indigenous political rationality, the national context and involvement of civil society in change rather than simply adopting Northern assumptions and practices. It is important to avoid stark dichotomies and constructing mutually exclusive solutions, for example the state versus markets; state centralisation versus decentralisation to local organisations; or civil society versus the body politic. Finally, it is important to develop indigenous accounting capacity through education, training and research so that elites, the intelligentsia, civil servants, the media and thus civil society can debate the problems and repercussions of neo-patrimonialism and increase awareness of transnational governance superstructures and emerging modes of regulation. Transforming public opinion may be more productive than insisting on compliance to externally prescribed accounting practices.

9 Conclusion

This chapter has explored how development policies since the 1950s have evolved, and how accounting shapes and is shaped by broader frameworks of development. While accounting is not the 'salvation of poverty', it is an essential ingredient in the development process, which warrants more attention from the various parties involved (Hopper *et al.*, 2012). The preoccupation of development approaches, emanating from the WB, IMF and UN, based on rational decision making to promote economic growth, and the inattention paid to accounting by actors[8] involved in development, have given accounting a predominantly economic logic. Further, underlying power asymmetries between Northern and poor countries have led to a hegemonic consensus around Northern development thought, whereby accounting best practices in the North are prescribed in the South, with insufficient regard to prevailing local cultural norms and circumstances. The blanket promotion of Northern solutions as prerequisites for financial assistance results in UDCs adopting IASs that are neglectful of UDCs' needs and reinforce power asymmetries between the 'developed' North and the 'developing' South. Moreover, given the periodic, results-oriented and upward focus of many accounting systems of aid givers such as donor government departments and international NGOs, they often concentrate on short-term indicators of success, rather than broader, less tangible structural (social, economic, political and legal) factors; for example, a donor organisation spending €1 million on educating female children reported on how many girls were educated through the project, but not less tangible factors such as "the kind of education provided to the girls," "their life stories" and "the barriers the teachers face" (Unerman and O'Dwyer, 2012: 150). Practices based on economic logic stifle alternative social logics and spaces with the potential to address the structural factors that foster poverty and inequality.

Given the dominance of neo-patrimonialism in many UDCs, often sprinkled with corruption, accounting reforms frequently fail, due to leaders either ignoring them, or using them for unintended purposes. As discussed, leaders may only support reforms if they can yield resources for personal/political gains. Thus, accounting reforms may be unsuccessful if local political constraints are ignored. UDCs are influenced by their historical legacy of colonialism and they are reliant on external agencies for aid, which has encouraged the uncritical and widespread adoption of Northern, market-based models. Northern accounting, auditing and corporate governance mechanisms require "efficient capital markets, investor sophistication, and effective second-order institutions such as efficient regulators and judiciary," however (Hopper *et al.*, 2012: 11). In many UDCs corporate governance may be characterised by high ownership concentration, weak incentives for companies to go public, poor perception of the skills of auditors and an absence of effective monitoring and second-order institutions. Whilst the current model emphasises the local self-determination of programmes by strengthening governments, and developing local capacity, its emphasis on NPM encourages a focus on results (and not process), together with effectiveness and efficiency criteria that neglect broader development indicators.

The chapter questions the wisdom of importing Northern accounting systems into the South, without establishing what accounting systems are effective, why and how. It stresses the importance of taking into account the social, economic, political, religious and legal contexts of specific countries; viewing accounting as a critical part of the development matrix; enabling local participation in the design process; and producing accounting and accountability systems that consider a wide range of complex factors such as the empowerment of the poor and marginalised. This requires accounting researchers to engage in collaborative dialogues with researchers in development studies, indigenous politicians, accounting standard-setting bodies and external agencies providing aid and finance, to help develop multidimensional indigenous accounting models through ongoing education, training and research.

These issues need careful consideration to foster a transformation from technocratic upward to multidimensional downward accounting and accountability systems. Greater indigenous participation should redistribute power from 'experts' to the lower echelons of users and designers whose voice in formulating global policies is currently minimal. This may well meet resistance from senior officials (within both Northern countries and UDCs) unwilling to accede to redistributions of power. Also supposed experts may regard the process of giving locals a voice, especially the marginalised, as too time consuming and costly (Brown, 2009), as a consequence of which subaltern voices become excluded. However, whilst recognising that engagement and dialogue between and within diverse groups with different power dynamics will not be without contestation and discontent, there is a need to better understand the discursive barriers that exist between elites and non-elites, and how power is mediated in the global socioeconomic order through expert languages such as economics and accounting (Kapoor, 2008). Our conclusion is that successfully developing accounting and accountability systems relevant to UDCs must be cognisant of factors such as "legacies of colonialism," "socioeconomic inequalities on democratic politics," "participation of the subaltern" and the "pivotal role of the state" (Kapoor, 2008: 98). This path is fraught with challenges and requires development and accounting experts to critically reflect upon and understand the difficulties of embarking on this journey. It may involve experts intentionally releasing some of their power, building safe spaces for people to foster accountings of their own voices, unlearning elite prejudices and constructing institutional forms that are "flexible, responsive, capable of cross-cultural translation" and "better listening" (Molisa, Vandagombo and Brown, 2012: 306). Such processes can facilitate longer term social transformations to enable the development industry (and accounting) to become part of a world not far removed from the world in which poor people presently live their everyday lives (Cornwall and Brock, 2005).

This chapter was submitted by the authors with the following title: "Accounting for less developed countries retrospectively and prospectively."

Notes

1   These statistics are taken from https://www.dosomething.org/facts/11-facts-about-global-poverty, 27/05/2014. These come from secondary sources, namely Global Issues, Statistic Brain, One, and World Food Programme. Debates over estimates exist but few would query their basic tenor. They are consistent with World Bank estimates.
2   Civil society organisations include non-governmental organisations, professional and private sector associations, trade unions, families, churches, neighbourhood groups, social and work groups.
3   International Financial Reporting Standards (IFRSs) are the new name for International Accounting Standards issued after 2001.
4   Participatory budgeting requires a set of interrelated conditions – legal, bureaucratic, fiscal, informational, political and cultural – that enables civil society organisations and other development actors to engage in budget processes in a sustained and effective manner.
5   Pro-poor budgeting focuses on budget priority setting, allocation and implementation for achieving pro-poor objectives as in the health, education, water and sanitation sectors. It involves legislative and executive branches, civil society, businesses and the media. It can be a bottom-up (when the initiative starts from the community) or top-down approach (when the initiative starts from the state).
6   The term 'economic logic' used in development studies literature (e.g. Battilana and Dorado, 2010) connotes a framework which primarily focuses on maximising profits and fulfilling fiduciary obligations to investors and depositors, as opposed to addressing broader development concerns. A predominantly economic logical framework within development organisations such as NGOs, may lead missions to drift from their original primary objectives.
7   The term 'upward' reflects the hierarchical mode of a relationship between the NGOs and aid providers, and also the power imbalance between the two parties (Fowler, 1996).
8   Such as researchers in development studies and accounting, indigenous politicians, accounting standard-setting bodies and external institutions providing aid and finance to UDCs.

References

African Press Organisation (2007). *The Seventh African Governance Forum* (AGF7). https://appablog.word-press.com/2007/10/24/the-seventh-african-governance-forum-agf7/.

Andrews, M. (2013). *The Limits of Institutional Reform in Development: Changing Rules for Realistic Solutions*, Cambridge: Cambridge University Press.

Arnold, P. J. (2005). "Disciplining domestic regulation: the World Trade Organisation and the market for professional services," *Accounting, Organisation and Society*, 30(4): 299–330.

Awio, G., S. Lawrence and D. Northcott (2007). "Community-led initiatives: reforms for better accountability?" *Journal of Accounting and Organizational Change*, 3(3): 209–26.

Battilana, J. and S. Dorado (2010). "Building sustainable hybrid organisations: the case of commercial microfinance organisations," *Academy of Management Journal*, 53(6): 1419–40.

Botzem, S. (2014). "Transnational standard-setting in accounting: organizing expertise-based self-regulation in times of crises," *Accounting, Auditing and Accountability Journal*, 27(6): 933–55.

Brown, J. (2009). "Democracy, sustainability and dialogic accounting technologies: taking pluralism seriously," *Critical Perspectives on Accounting*, 20(3): 313–42.

Cammack, D. (2007). "The logic of African neopatriamonialism: what role for donors?" *Development Policy Review*, 25(5): 599–614.

Chang, H. J. (2007). *Bad Samaritans: Rich Nations, Poor Policies and the Threat to the Developing World*, London: Random House Business.

CIPFA (2010). *Annual Report 2010*. http://www.cipfa.org/about-cipfa/annual-report/annual-report-2010.

Clapham, C. (1985). *Third World Politics: An Introduction*, London: Helm.

Cobham, A. and D. McNair (2012). "The role of rich countries in development: the case for reforms," in T. Hopper, M. Tsamenyi, S. Uddin and D. Wickramasinghe (eds), *The Handbook of Accounting and Development*. Cheltenham, UK: Edward Elgar Publishing Ltd.

Commander, S. and T. Killick (1988). "Privatization in developing countries: a survey of the issues," in P. Cook and C. Kirkpatrick (eds), *Privatization in Less Developed Countries*. New York: St Martin's Press.

Cook, P. (1986). "Liberalisation in the context of industrial development in less developed countries," Manchester, UK: *Manchester Discussion Papers in Development Studies*.

Cook, P. and C. Kirkpatrick (eds) (1988). *Privatisation in Less Developed Countries*, Brighton: Wheatsheaf Books.

Cook, P. and C. Kirkpatrick (1995). "Privatisation policy and performance," in P. Cook and C. Kirkpatrick (eds): *Privatisation Policy and Performance: International Perspectives*. London: Prentice Hall.

Cornwall, A. and K. Brock (2005). "What do buzzwords do for development policy? A critical look at 'participation', 'empowerment' and 'poverty reduction'," *Third World Quarterly*, 26(7): 1043–60.

Do Something (2015). "11 facts about global poverty." https://www.dosomething.org/facts/11-facts-about-global-poverty.

Edwards, M. and D. Hulme (1996). *Beyond the Magic Bullet: NGO Performance and Accountability in the Post-Cold War World*, West Hartford, CT: Kumarian Press.

Eisenstadt, S. N. (1973). *Traditional Patrimonialism and Modern Neo-Patrimonialism*, London: Sage Publications.

Enthoven, A. J. H. (1982). "International management accounting: its scope and standards," *International Journal of Accounting*, 17(6): 59–74.

Erdmann, G. and U. Engel (2007). "Neopatrimonialism reconsidered: critical review and elaboration of an elusive concept," *Journal of Commonwealth and Comparative Politics*, 45(1): 95–119.

Everett, J. (2012). "Corruption in developing countries: 'thinking' about the role of accounting," in T. Hopper, M. Tsamenyi, S. Uddin and D. Wickramasighe (eds): *The Handbook of Accounting and Development*, Cheltenham: Edward Elgar Publishing Ltd.

Everett, J., D. Neu and A. Rahaman (2007). "Accounting and the global fight against corruption," *Accounting, Organisation and Society*, 32(6): 513–42.

Fowler, A. (1996). "Demonstrating NGO performance: problems and possibilities", *Development in Practice*, 6(1): 58–65.

Frank, A. G. (1972). "The development of underdevelomemt," in J. D. Cockcroft, A. G. Frank and D. Johnson (eds): *Dependence and Underdevelopment*, Garden City, NY: Anchor Books.

Fyson, S. (2012). "Accounting and development: the role of donors from policy to practice," in T. Hopper, M. Tsamenyi, S. Uddin and D. Wickramasinghe (eds): *The Handbook of Accounting and Development*, Cheltenham: Edward Elgar Publishing Ltd.

Giddens, A. (2000). *Runaway World: How Globalisation is Reshaping Our Lives*, New York: Routledge.

Global Issues. (2015). "Poverty facts and stats." http://www.globalissues.org/article/26/poverty-facts-and-stats.

Graham, C. and M. Annisette (2012). "The role of transnational institutions in framing accounting in the global south," in T. Hopper, M. Tsamenyi, S. Uddin and D. Wickramasinghe (eds): *The Handbook of Accounting and Development*, Cheltenham: Edward Elgar Publishing Ltd.

Harrison, G. (2004a). "Why economic globalization is not enough," *Development and Change*, 35(5): 1037–47.

Harrison, G. (2004b). *The World Bank and Africa. The Construction of Governance States*. London, Routledge.

Hemming, R., and Mansoor, A. M. (1988). Privatisation and Public Enterprises. IMF Occasional Paper 56. Washington, DC, IMF.

Hickey, S. (2003). "Does politics keep people poor? Is reducing chronic poverty a political possibility?" *Insights*, 46.

Holmes, D. (2012). "Taxation and accounting issues in developing countries," in T. Hopper, M. Tsamenyi, S. Uddin and D. Wickramasinghe (eds): *The Handbook of Accounting and Development*, Cheltenham: Edward Elgar Publishing Ltd.

Hood, C. (1995). "The "New Public Management" in the 1980s: variations on a theme," *Accounting, Organizations and Society*, 20 (2–3): 93–109.

Hopper, T. and Z. Hoque (2004). "Accounting and accountability in emerging and transition economies," *Research in Accounting in Emerging Economies – Special Supplement 2*.

Hopper, T., P. Lassou and T. Soobaroyen (2016). "Globalisation, accounting and developing countries," *Critical Perspectives on Accounting* (forthcoming).

Hopper, T., M. Tsamenyi, S. Uddin and D. Wickramasinghe (2009). "Management accounting in less developed countries: what is known and what needs knowing," *Accounting, Auditing and Accountability Journal*, 22(3): 469–514.

Hopper, T., M. Tsamenyi, S. Uddin and D. Wickramasinghe (2012). "Introduction: accounting and development," in Hopper, T., M. Tsamenyi, S. Uddin and D. Wickramasinghe. (eds): *The Handbook of Accounting and Development*. Cheltenham: Edward Elgar Publishing Ltd.

Hussain, M., M. Hussain and K. Sen (2012). "Accounting standards and capital market development," in T. Hopper, M. Tsamenyi, S. Uddin and D. Wickramasinghe (eds): *The Handbook of Accounting and Development*, Cheltenham: Edward Elgar Publishing Ltd.

IFAC (2010). *Nurturing the Development and Growth of Accountancy*, New York: International Federation of Accountants.

Jacobs, A. and R. Wilford (2010). "Listen first: a pilot system for managing downward accountability in NGOs," *Development in Practice*, 20(7): 797–811.

Jacobs, K., M. Habib, N. Musyoki and C. Jubb (2012). "Empowering or oppressing: the case of microfinance institutions," in T. Hopper, M. Tsamenyi, S. Uddin and D. Wickramasinghe (eds): *The Handbook of Accounting and Development*, Cheltenham: Edward Elgar Publishing Ltd.

Kapoor, I. (2008). *The Postcolonial Politics of Development*, New York: Routledge.

Kelsall, T. (2011). "Rethinking the relationship between neo-patrimonialism and economic performance in sub-Saharan Africa," *IDS Bulletin*, 42(2): 76–87.

Lehman, G. (2007). "The accountability of NGOs in civil society and its public spheres," *Critical Perspectives on Accounting*, 18(6): 645–69.

Lemarchand, R. and K. Legg (1972). "Political clientelism and development: a preliminary analysis," *Comparative Politics*, 4(2): 149–78.

Leonard, D. K. (1987). "The political realities of African management," *World Development*, 15(7): 899–910.

Le Vine, V. T. (1980). "African patrimonial regimes in comparative perspective," *Journal of Modern African Studies*, 18(4): 657–73.

Lynch, G. and G. Crawford (2011). "Democratization in Africa 1990–2010: an assessment," *Democratization*, 18(2): 275–310.

McNeill, D. and A. St. Clair (2006). "Development ethics and human rights as the basis for poverty reduction: the case of the World Bank," in D. Stone and C. Wright (eds): *The World Bank and Governance: A Decade of Reform and Reaction*, London: Routledge.

Medard, J. F. (1982). "The underdeveloped state in tropical Africa: political clientelism or neo-patrimonialism?" in C. Clapham (ed.): *Private Patronage and Public Power*. London: Frances Printer Ltd.

Molisa, P., D. Vandagombo and J. Brown (2012). "Social and environmental accounting in developing countries – challenges, conflicts and contradictions," in T. Hopper, M. Tsamenyi, S. Uddin and D. Wickramsinghe (eds): *The Handbook of Accounting and Development*, Cheltenham, UK: Edward Elgar Publishing Ltd.

Murphy, J. (2008). "International financial institutions and the new global managerial order," *Critical Perspectives on Accounting*, 19(5): 714–40.

Needles, B. E. (1976). "Implementing a framework for the international transfer of accounting technology," *International Journal of Accounting Education and Research*, 12(1): 203–35.

OECD (2005). *The Paris Declaration on Aid Effectiveness: Five Principles for Smart Aid*. http://www.oecd.org/dac/effectiveness/45827300.pdf.

OECD (2008). *The ACCRA Agenda for Action* (AAA). http://www.oecd.org/dac/effectiveness/45827311.pdf.

OECD (2012). *The Busan Partnership for Effective Development Cooperation*. http://www.oecd.org/dac/effectiveness/Busan%20partnership.pdf.

One. (2015). "Join the fight against extreme poverty." http://www.one.org/international/.

Peterson, S. B. (2007). *Imperfect Systems IFMISs in Africa*, World Bank and Harvard University.

Pitcher, A., M. H. Moran and M. Johnston (2009). "Rethinking patrimonialism and neopatrimonialism in Africa. *African Studies Review*, 52(1): 125–56.

Poullaos, C. and C. U. Uche. (2012). "Accounting professionalisation in developing countries," in T. Hopper, M. Tsamenyi, S. Uddin and D. Wickramasinghe (eds): *The Handbook of Accounting and Development*, Cheltenham: Edward Elgar Publishing Ltd.

Rostow, W. W. (1960). *The Stages of Economic Growth: A Comparative Manifesto*, Cambridge: Cambridge University Press.

Roth, G. (1968). "Personal rulership, patrimonialism and empire-building in the new states," *World Politics*, 20(2): 194–206.

Rowden, R. and J. Ocaya Irama (2004). "Rethinking participation," ActionAid USA / ActionAid Uganda, discussion paper, Washington, DC: ActionAid International.

Roy, A. (2010). *Poverty Capital: Microfinance and the Making of Development*, London and New York: Routledge.

Samsonova-Taddei, A. and C. Humphrey (2014). "Transnationalism and the transforming roles of professional accountancy bodies," *Accounting, Auditing and Accountability Journal*, 27(6): 903–32.

Saravanamuthu, K. (2004). "What is measured counts: harmonized corporate reporting and sustainable economic development," *Critical Perspectives on Accounting*, 15(3): 295–302.

Scott, J. (1969). "The analysis of corruption in developing nations," *Comparative Studies in Society and History*, 11(3): 315–41.

Seidler, L. J. (1967a). *The Function of Accounting and Economic Development: Turkey as a Case Study*. New York: Praeger.

Seidler, L. J. (1967b). "International accounting: the ultimate theory course," *Accounting Review*, 42(4): 775–81.

Seiler, R. E. (1966). "Accounting, information systems and underdeveloped nations," *Accounting Review*, 41(4): 652–56.

Siddiqui, J. (2012). "Audit markets in less developed economies: caveats for globalisation?" in T. Hopper, M. Tsamenyi, S. Uddin and D. Wickramasinghe (eds): *The Handbook of Accounting and Development*, Cheltenham: Edward Elgar Publishing Ltd.

Stiglitz, J. E. (2002). *Globalisation and its Discontents*, London: Penguin Books.

Stockholm International Peace Research Institute (SIPRI) (2013). SIPRI *Yearbook 2013*. http://sipri/org/yearbook/2013

Toye, J. (1994). "Structural adjustment: context, assumptions, origin and diversity," in R. Van der Heoven and F. v. d. Kraaij (eds): *Structural Adjustment and Beyond in Sub-Saharan Africa*, London: James Currey.

Uddin, S. and T. Hopper. (2003). "Accounting for privatisation in Bangladesh: testing World Bank claims," *Critical Perspectives on Accounting*, 14(7): 739–74.

UN (2006). *Millennium Development Goals*. http://www.un.org/zh/millenniumgoals/pdf/MDGReport2006.pdf.

Unerman, J. and B. O'Dwyer (2012). "Accounting and accountability for NGOs," in T. Hopper, M. Tsamenyi, S. Uddin and D. Wickramasinghe (eds): *The Handbook of Accounting and Development*, Cheltenham: Edward Elgar Publishing Ltd.

United Nations, Economic and Social Council (2006). *Compendium of Basic Terminology in Governance and PublicA*, 06-20194 (E) 300106, Committee of Experts on Public Administration, fifth session, New York.

Weber, M. (1947). *The Theory of Social and Economic Organisation*, New York: The Free Press.

Wickramasinghe, D., T. Hopper and C. Rathnasiri (2004). "Japanese cost management meets Sri Lankan politics: disappearance and reappearance of bureaucratic management controls in a privatised utility," *Accounting, Auditing and Accountability Journal*, 17(1): 85–120.

World Bank (2004). *World Development Reports* 2004. http://web.worldbank.org/WBSITE/EXTERNAL/EXTDEC/EXTRESEARCH/EXTWDRS/0,contentMDK:23083461~pagePK:478093~piPK:4776 27~theSitePK:477624,00.html.

World Bank (2007). *The World Bank Governance and Anti-Corruption Strategy* http://web.worldbank.org/WBSITE/EXTERNAL/TOPICS/EXTGOVANTICORR/0,contentMDK:21096079~menuPK:30 65285~pagePK:210058~piPK:210062~theSitePK:3035864,00.html.

World Bank Group (1997). *World Development Report*. Retrieved 28/08/15 from https://openknowledge.worldbank.org/handle/10986/5980.

World Food Programme (2015). *What Causes Hunger*. http://www.wfp.org/hunger/causes.

Wynne, A. (2005). "Public financial reforms in developing countries: lessons from Ghana, Tanzania and Uganda," working paper 7. Harare Capacity Building Foundation.

Wynne, A. and S. Lawrence (2012). "Global accounting in the global south: the design, implementation and use of global solutions for local needs," in T. Hopper, M. Tsamenyi, S. Uddin and D. Wickramasinghe (eds): *The Handbook of Accounting and Development*, Cheltenham: Edward Elgar Publishing Ltd.

Zolberg, A. R. (1969). "Military role and political development in tropical Africa," J. Doorn (ed.): *The Military Profession and Military Regime*, The Hague: Mouton.

16

CORPORATE GOVERNANCE

Lee Parker

1 Introduction

Any inspection of accounting research conference programmes and accounting research journal literature will reveal a litany of studies designated 'corporate governance'. What this entails is often poorly defined or only implied, and has largely become captive to predictive, positivist, quantitative studies of corporate characteristics mapped against financial disclosure strategies and patterns, often linked to an obsession with the subject of earnings management. There seems no end to the volume of incremental research produced in this particular milieu, so that any reader could be forgiven for concluding that corporate governance has been thoroughly explored by accounting researchers and that the field has been well and truly ploughed.

However it can be argued that the plethora of incremental attention has been directed through very limited theoretical lenses, with simplistically predictive intent, focussing upon only a small subset of the accounting and accountability menu, and lacking any direct engagement with the central actors in the field. Furthermore, for many accounting researchers, the highest level of decision-making authority within the organisation to which their gaze has risen, has been that of the audit committee. The board of directors appears to have remained largely beyond their consideration, and yet it is at this level where arguably profound strategic, control and accountability, responsibility and influence lies. Thus, this territory represents a virtual lacuna to accounting researchers, and yet it is where such apparent absence and opaqueness pervades, that the possibility of important insights and knowledge expansion may lie (Choudhury, 1988; Arrington and Francis, 1989; Hines, 1992; Inkpen and Choudhury, 1995). Consequently, for both interpretive and critical researchers in accounting, from financial accountability, management accounting, auditing and social accountability perspectives, this field remains largely unexplored and presents considerable opportunity.

This chapter will first critique the preponderance of accounting literature on corporate governance emanating from outside the black box of governance processes and then will offer a review of corporate governance research approaches and challenges for accounting researchers. Current understandings of internal boardroom corporate governance processes will be considered. Our knowledge of directors' roles and behaviours in strategy and control will then be examined and critiqued, and related accountabilities explored. In setting a forward-looking corporate governance research agenda for critical accounting researchers, the question of available theoretical frames will be addressed. Finally, this chapter will envisage a direction and agenda for board-level corporate governance research from both critical and interpretive perspectives in the accounting literature.

2 Examining the black box

The dominant quantitative positivist genre of accounting research into corporate governance treats the organisation and/or the board as a virtual black box that contains some mystical processes into which key inputs are fed and from which outcomes emerge. The nature of those processes is largely unremarked upon, accounting researchers' focus being firmly fixed upon seemingly never-ending attempts to model and associate the inputs and outcomes. The fixed point in time snapshot of claimed relationships between these external variables is reified for its statistical generalisability, largely abstracted from the complexities of social, institutional, political and economic environments that both surround and interact with actors within the organisation and its board. The processes by which perceptions are conditioned, attitudes formed, behaviours practised and power and control are wielded (often being the prime interests of journalists, regulators and the wider community), are seemingly ignored by accounting researchers claiming to advance the cause of effective corporate governance. Could it be that the convenience of desk-based research, remote from engagement with field sites, actors and the messiness and complexity of live scenarios, holds a time and effort-saving attraction for many researchers? This could explain why so-called archival research has become their dominant currency (Rose, Mazza, Norman and Rose, 2013).

Positivist corporate governance researchers have examined a plethora of independent variables they have hypothesised as affecting the black box of corporate governance. The list of variables that has been examined is impressive. For example, Larcker, Richardson and Tuna (2007) classify such variables into seven general categories: directors' profiles; stock ownership by directors and senior executives; institutional stock ownership; activist stockholders; debt holders and preferred stockholders; an executive compensation mix; and anti-takeover devices. These are largely structural factors that are hypothesised to either influence or somehow proxy for corporate governance processes. They only require the researcher to access archival data procured at arm's length from any organisation. So what variables are examined to represent the outcomes of the corporate governance black box? The list is similarly impressive: abnormal accruals; accounting restatements; future operating performance narratives; future excess stock returns; voluntary non-mandatory information disclosures in management reports within the annual report; overall firm disclosures; CEO turnover; the cost of equity capital; dividend payouts; degree of leverage; the cost of debt; analysts' forecasting accuracy; and earnings quality (Eng and Mak, 2003; Larcker *et al.*, 2007; Brown, Beekes and Verhoeven, 2011). Researchers repeatedly strive to derive associations between these inputs and outputs as somehow representing a questionably defined amalgam of corporate governance drivers and outcomes. The focus is clearly upon corporate financial performance and stockholder benefits.

More recently the proclivity of boards towards and strategies for earnings management have attracted a veritable tsunami of studies. They are present in force at contemporary accounting research conferences around the globe. The list of perspectives examined is almost endless: the likelihood of directors opposing executive management's earnings management strategies; executive compensation impacts on earnings management; the audit committee's, executive committee's and board's roles in preventing earnings management; the profile and degree of independence of board and audit committee members; the number of analysts following firm performance; forecasts related to IPOs; the firm ownership structure; the extent of institutional investment in the firm; and proxies for board activity in relation to earnings management. Earnings management is also dissected through impacts on dimensions of earnings quality such as earnings timeliness, earnings informativeness, financial restatements and fraud (Xie, Davidson and Dadalt, 2003; Brown *et al.*, 2011; Rose *et al.*, 2013).

A key feature of positivist studies of corporate governance is their attention to the structural profile and activity proxies for the corporate board. These include board size, the percentage of executive and non-executive directors, stockholding versus non-stock holding directors, directors' expertise and experience profiles, the number of other boards on which directors serve, the number and frequency of board meetings, the number of directors serving on the audit committee and the executive compensation committee, the number and frequency of audit committee meetings, the age profile of directors, the executive or non-executive chair of the board, and the separate or dual holding of CEO and board chair positions (Xie *et al.*, 2003; Eng and Mak, 2003; Bushman, 2004; Larcker *et al.*, 2007; Brown *et al.*, 2011; Rose *et al.*, 2013). Such research may produce limited governance deliverables in the long run. For example, Nicholson and Kiel (2003) point to meta-analyses of such studies that overall can point to no substantive relationship between a board's compositional profile and corporate performance, and only a limited possible impact on corporate performance related to the proportion of non-executive directors (NEDs) on the board. Christopher (2010) also points to the inconclusive results across studies of numerous board and corporate performance variables.

From critical and interpretive accounting research perspectives, this accounting-based corporate governance research corpus presents a yawning lacuna of multiple dimensions. Effective corporate governance is defined and focussed solely in terms of financial management and disclosure in the interests of corporate stockholder wealth maximisation. The board of directors is conceptualised from a purely structural characteristics viewpoint. There is no attempt to focus on boardroom processes, other than simplistic proxies such as the number and frequency of board meetings. Board-level corporate governance remits such as regulatory compliance, accountability to employees and the community, operational efficiency and effectiveness, social responsibility, management control, strategic decision making, risk management and more, do not appear to be on researchers' radar. The breadth of corporate stakeholder groups and the board's representativeness, networking activity and consideration of stakeholder interests is almost entirely neglected. How directors conceive of and actually execute their roles and responsibilities, how boards actually conduct their affairs (both inside and outside the boardroom), how directors and senior executives interact and build relationships, how boards process information, conduct their internal discourse and arrive at strategy, policy, compliance and control decisions are all opaque to most positivist accounting researchers. Their research methodologies do not require nor allow them to engage directly with organisational actors in order to access such data or develop such understandings (Pettigrew, 1992; Leblanc and Gillies, 2003).

So the black box of director and boardroom corporate governance perceptions, attitudes, discourse, debate, decision processes, behaviours, actions, strategies, control and accountability construction remains a hidden world; truly black. Yet arguably, the nature, focus and impact of corporate governance and accountability emanating from the board is most effectively revealed and understood by penetrating the processual black box in which many contemporary accounting researchers appear to assume nothing exists. Yet that void most likely holds the key to our deeper understanding and critique of the corporate governance process (Choudhury, 1988). The special issue of the *Accounting, Auditing and Accountability Journal* on 'Corporate Governance, Accountability and Mechanisms of Accountability' (Brennan and Solomon, 2008), called upon accounting researchers to push the boundaries of corporate governance, employing a broader array of methodological approaches and theoretical perspectives as well as addressing a much broader spectrum of issues within a diversity of theoretical frameworks. It is to this challenge with respect to boardroom governance that the chapter now turns.

3 Interrogating the corporate governance process

Board-level corporate governance processes are the focal activity that most contemporary accounting and management research studies have bypassed. This has been even more prominently recognised by some leading researchers in the management research literature. They point to contemporary corporate governance researchers'"near universal focus on a direct relationship between corporate governance mechanisms and firm financial performance" (Dailey, Dalton and Cannella, 2003: 376), and their repeated focus on governance variables such as board size, executive/nonexecutive director ratios, directors' shareholdings and so on, in search of some optimal balance between these (Gabrielsson and Huse, 2005). As already argued in the previous section, Gabrielsson and Huse (2005: 24) contend that "most empirical studies treat the actual work of the board as a black box, assuming that the behaviour and conduct directors can be successfully inferred from the board's demographic characteristics." Dailey *et al.* (2003) and Gabrielsson and Huse (2005) see this trend as involving researchers making huge leaps in relying on proxies and statistical analysis to draw inferential relationships between such demographic variables and board and corporate financial performance. These copious studies produce results that are mixed. Yet researchers remain content to sit at a distance from actual boards and directors, employing archival methods to draw statistical inferences while remaining remote from the actors involved in the governance process (Pettigrew, 1992; Leblanc, 2004). Gabrielsson and Huse (2005) explain this as being driven by researchers' greater personal convenience in limiting themselves to desk-based secondary data research that fits the template for publishing in desirable journal targets, despite its marginal relevance to issues of corporate governance processes. Leblanc (2004: 437) describes this in vivid terms:

> To be self-critical of the academic work done in this area, trying to distill a relationship between governance and performance – from outside of a boardroom – is analogous to trying to find out what makes a sports team effective by sitting in a cafeteria reading the sports pages, without entering the arenas or locker rooms or interviewing the game's great teams or players.

So despite the welter of corporate governance research published in the accounting and management literatures, there has developed only a minimal understanding or critique of how boards actually work and how they do or do not contribute to effective corporate governance and accountability. Yet as Leblanc and Gillies (2003) point out, this is likely to be the most important factor in critically evaluating corporate governance and its outcomes. Corporate governance and context at the board level requires attention to past, present and future processes, investigations of linkages between context and action, engagement in holistic and not simply linear explanations of process, and the engagement of researchers both closely involved with as well as more distant from actors (Pettigrew, 1992). In penetrating and critiquing corporate governance from an accounting as well as management and accountability perspectives, we need a closer and more detailed understanding of who is actually and influentially involved in governance decision making, how they execute their roles and influence, why they act and react the way they do, where power lies and how it is mobilised (Pettigrew, 1992). Despite their legal- and regulatory-based powers, directors and boards wield power through their solidarity and action as a concerted group. The majority of corporate governance research in accounting has failed to recognise or address power differentials within boards and this may at least in part explain why much corporate governance research has failed to yield new or significant understandings and critiques of corporate governance and accountability (Clarke, 1998; Hambrick, Weredr and

Zadac, 2008). The exercise of power within boards can manifest itself in various actions and relationships including the relationships and relative roles of the board's chair and CEO, the relationships and communications between them and the other board members, the networks and expertise of particular board members as well as the interactions between the board and external contextual factors (Pettigrew, 1992; Hambrick *et al.*, 2008).

Boardroom process issues that may directly impact on corporate governance and accountability abound. They include questions of the manifestation and prevalence of group-think; the barriers and constraints upon candid discussion and debate; boardroom climate and directors' discussion and critique of executive plans and actions; the motivations, perceptions and behaviours of executive and non-executive directors; who assesses organisational, CEO and directors' performances and how; the manner in which the competencies and intellectual capital of board members is actually drawn upon; the nature of talk and discourse between board members both within and outside the boardroom; and the impact of relational dynamics between board members (Pettigrew, 1992; Samra-Fredericks, 2000; Leblanc, 2004; Gabrielsson and Huse, 2005; Hambrick *et al.*, 2008).

The pathway to accessing boardroom governance and accountability processes is available. It is most appropriately targeted through interview and participant observation (Clarke, 1998; Snow and Thomas, 1994; McNulty, Zattoni and Douglas, 2013). While there are sensitivities in trying to gain and maintain field access to directors and their boards, there is no substitute for direct engagement with the actors themselves if we are to penetrate the crucial process perspective on corporate governance. Arguably, it is a pathway to data collection more likely to be productive than securing agreement from directors to commit to written forms of personal reflection on their roles and practices (Leblanc, 2004). Tapping into directors' discourses and narratives permits the possibility of close-up insights into actors' behaviours, motivations and sense-making not otherwise possible (Samra-Fredericks, 2000; Ng and De Cock, 2002). Here also is the call and opportunity for participant observation within the boardroom as an active or complete member researcher, permitting longitudinal, holistic, contextualised analyses of live settings. Admittedly, gaining such access can pose challenges (Daily *et al.*, 2003); however, it has already been proven possible for researchers to take on these roles and to yield invaluable insights from within the sanctum of the boardroom (Collier, 2005; Parker, 2003, 2007a,b, 2008a,b; Leblanc and Schwartz, 2007).

One suspects that researchers are often tempted to discount the possibility of boardroom access, fearing the imagined barriers to be faced: specifically in terms of anticipated board-level resistance for reasons of confidentiality, risks of competitive disadvantage, fear of critique and so on. Yet little by little, studies involving boardroom observations and director interviews are gradually appearing in the accounting and management research literatures. Some potentially more available access routes can include approaching not-for-profit organisational boards, small enterprise boards and even public sector boards. Some such organisations can be found to appreciate the value of such research to their own ongoing governance developments, and to be open to an approach for research access. Furthermore, in the well-tried tradition of qualitative field research, access can be facilitated by personal introductions through connections researchers and their own networks may already have to such organisations and directors. Finally, the importance of how a study proposal is drafted and presented to such groups cannot be overestimated. It is still entirely practicable to pursue a critical agenda, but to construct clear project outlines and proposals which directors can readily understand and appreciate, and given the opportunity, meeting with them to explain clearly what the researcher seeks and how the partnership may deliver value to both parties.

4 Inside the boardroom

What have we learned from interview and participant observations of directors and boards at work? With respect to desirable board size, interviewees have tended towards arguing for a range between five and twelve members. The lower limit appears to be associated with a perceived minimum required for adequate representativeness of a spectrum of views as well as offering checks and balances, while the upper limit is associated with views on the quality of debate and decision making, potential for passive acquiescent board members and dominant members' grandstanding (Forbes and Milliken, 1999; Taylor and O'Sullivan, 2009). NEDs are seen as bringing independence, wider experience and skill sets, and network linkages outside the organisation. On the question of the executive director (ED) and NED balance, directors who have been interviewed appear to be comfortable with a range of proportions including a majority of NEDs (Chiu and Monin, 2003; Taylor and O'Sullivan, 2009). Importance can also be attached to diversity in the profiles of board members which can include functional expertise, age, gender and industry segment representation, with rotation being achieved when desired through fixed terms with maximum renewal periods for directors (Parker, 2007b). Board profiles and their manner of achievement, maintenance and change, however, remain open for much greater researcher scrutiny and critique, especially as board composition carries major accountability implications. Critical scrutiny has yet to be applied to this highest organisational accountability level by critical accounting researchers.

ED and NED roles and tasks have also come in for scrutiny. These range across strategising, monitoring, control, regulatory compliance, policy and accountability (Spira and Bender, 2004; Leblanc and Gillies, 2005; Parker, 2008b; Machold and Farquhar, 2013). The manner in which they carry these out can include their contribution of knowledge, expertise, market and industry intelligence, and access to their personal and professional networks. They may also offer the discipline of questioning, and supervising executive management, being both advisors and judges (Spira and Bender, 2004). However, we need much more insight into how boards actually go about these tasks. Studies already show how board meetings can be consumed with routine information dissemination, compliance discussions and routine report reviews, propelling boards towards transgressing into the micromanagement of executive management responsibilities and failing to address major strategic and policy issues (Leblanc and Gillies, 2005; Parker, 2007b, 2008a; Machold and Farquhar, 2013).

CEO–board relations are an important dimension of and influence upon the exercise of power and accountability. Generally there is support for separating the CEO and chair of board roles between two separate people to avoid conflict of interest between the two roles (Chiu and Monin, 2003; Taylor and O'Sullivan, 2009). Of interest from a critical accounting and accountability research viewpoint is the observation that the relationship between the CEO and chair of the board can be a crucial driver of board agendas, decisions and actions, since their relationship and strategies can often drive the issues that appear on the board's agenda and how they are led and addressed (Dulewicz, 1995). This reflects their degree of mutual respect and trust, the level of accountability required by the board chair, the chair's degree of independence and the ways in which each relate to and communicate with the rest of the directors (Parker, 2007b; 2008b). Whose interests the board chair and directors serve is also a matter for investigation. Only in the field can we critically assess this through penetrating their attitudes, behaviours and actions. For example, they may represent particular sectional groups or interests that are not immediately obvious from external scrutiny (Uddin and Choudhury, 2008).

In order to better understand and critique the exercise of power and influence and the commitment to organisational and personal accountability at board level, accessing the actors themselves and their processes of corporate governance becomes essential. It is not transparent to the simple purview from outside the organisation taken by the externally positioned quantitative researcher. Both formal and informal decision-making processes have been shown to co-exist in the boardroom setting, and much can be explained by the crucial informal governance processes that transpire both within and outside boardroom meetings (Dulewicz, 1995; Parker, 2007b). Indeed Parker's (2007a,b, 2008a) participant observations of boardrooms reveal that many crucial decisions can be triggered, evaluated and made entirely informally and with scant reference to formal protocols or documentation. Boardroom decision styles can reflect power differentials between board members, the leadership styles of the CEO and board chair, directors' concepts of their roles and the degree to which they share these. This can be summarised as the extent of shared mental models of operation and intent, and the balance of power relations within the board (Letendre, 2004; Bailey and Peck, 2013). It must also be said that NEDs are still to considerable extent at the behest of their ED counterparts with their greater inside knowledge of the organisation. The latter can influence what information and interpretations are presented to the board and can strongly influence boardroom discussions and judgements (Useem and Zellecke, 2006), yet execution of organisational accountability clearly demands that the board can exercise power and control over senior executives (Holland, 2001). Clearly again this calls for greater attention by critical accounting researchers, since both financial and management accounting processes, outputs and reporting effectively have their beginnings and their responses and public transmissions (if any) at the board level.

Inside the boardroom, directors interviewed tend to emphasise the importance of the receiving appropriate and critical information, being able to debate issues in an open and transparent manner, and operating with mutual trust and respect (Van den Berghe and Levrau, 2004; Letendre, 2004). This at first sight to the accounting researcher and reader concerned with corporate governance and accountability may seem far too 'soft', vague and unmeasurable. Nonetheless, it is the internal boardroom culture and dynamics that can have a profound effect, for good or ill, on the quality and effectiveness of corporate governance processes. Parker's (2007b, 2008a,b) participant observer boardroom studies found that a culture of informality and humour could assist board meetings in the vigour and candid nature of critique and debate brought to bear, lubricating communication and relationships between board members. Indeed some boards have been observed to deliberately develop both formal and informal social events and traditions to assist in building such relationships. This is essentially a contribution to group chemistry (Leblanc and Gillies, 2005). Balancing formality and informality in board processes, encouraging open and candid debate, developing proactive rather than passive director attitudes and actions, and exercising a self-critique of the board's own processes and performance of its duties (both as a board and as individual directors) are all seen as important elements of and contributions to board culture (Van den Berghe and Levrau, 2004; van Hamel, van Wijk, de Rooij and Bruel, 1998; Leblanc and Gillies, 2005). Yet as Brundin and Nodqvist's study (2008) reveals, emotions in boardroom debates and determinations are neglected at our peril, since they reflect and reveal the operation of power and status in director relations and interactions that can dramatically influence perceptions, decisions and actions emanating from the boardroom. These are factors ignored by most corporate governance researchers, and yet they can have significant impacts on the manner and outcomes of corporate governance processes. It is such processes within the sanctum of the boardroom that are ignored by the majority of corporate governance research, particularly in the accounting literature. As discussed earlier in this chapter, this has resulted in a plethora of published research on corporate governance which qualitative researchers and corporate governance practitioners recognise as predominantly statistical analyses conducted remote from the scene of organisational governance processes and generally failing to address those processes and their potent impact on actual corporate governance execution.

5 Boardroom strategising

Qualitative and mixed method boardroom corporate governance research provides a range of insights into the board's involvement in strategic planning and the strategic management dimensions of the governance process. The level of contributions to strategising can vary from minimal to substantial, reflecting a variety of influences such as governance traditions in the industry or sector, the organisation's own history, the manner of director selection, directors' strategic governance skills and experience, the information available to directors, and the structuring and chairing of board meetings and their agendas (Cornforth and Edwards, 1999). The type of strategic contributions made by boards has also been found to vary from reviewing and approving senior executives' plans and initiatives, to influencing the nature of the planning process, contributing to the discussion of missions and objectives, providing ideas that input into strategies and advising at points of an organisation's strategic transition such as mergers, acquisitions and divestiture (McNulty and Pettigrew, 1999). The interaction between EDs and NEDs is also an important strategic influence whereby EDs can become conditioned to pre-reviewing their strategic proposals in terms of likely acceptability to NEDs and where NEDs form the house of review that monitors, tests and challenges strategic proposals and their probity and feasibility. Thus the board becomes a filter that can both initiate strategy as well as review and approves strategy (Parker, 2003).

Parker's (2007a) participant observer study found that informal approaches to strategising are as prevalent as more formal approaches within boardroom meetings. These can take the form of informal, interactive strategic dialogues initiated by directors raising strategic issues and pursued by the board in calling for executives to present strategic proposals, offering feedback and monitoring progress. This is supported by Stiles' (2001) study which finds directors particularly taking proactive roles in reviewing and discussing strategy, and by McNulty and Pettigrew's (1999) study that observes directors to be shaping the context of strategic debate, influencing the preparation of strategy proposals, and reviewing and approving or rejecting proposals. Thus as Papadakis, Lioukas and Chambers (1998) report, formal strategic planning processes nonetheless still act as an important conduit for strategising. As others have found, however, that process also exhibits considerable degrees of informality.

Boards can nonetheless err on the side of shorter term decision horizons and planning, as has been revealed by Cowen and Osborne (1993) and Parker (2001). This can be produced by a focus upon and reaction to immediate past events, short-term crises and present circumstances. When this occurs, the board tends to then absent itself from anticipating longer-term developments or laying long-term strategic foundations (Parker, 2001). This can leave the board operating in a reactive posture, trying to defend the organisation against competitive pressures without taking proactive initiatives, instead aiming for survival in the twelve-month budgetary cycle. Furthermore, in association with such an orientation, boards run the risk of slipping from strategic management into micromanagement, where they trespass upon executive management's routine operational decision-making prerogatives, engaging in short-term operational decision-making at the neglect of their longer-term strategic responsibilities (Parker, 2007a). Observational and interview studies also point to the importance of resource pressure and financial focus on board strategic orientations and discussions. As Parker (2001) and Papadakis *et al.*, (1998) have found, such perceived resources' pressure can promote reactive short-term planning and decision-making tensions within the board. Multiple resource pressures can invoke a high degree of perceived financial constraint and hence an overriding financial focus in directors' conceptions and prioritisations of strategies (Parker, 2001, 2003).

As part of its strategic management orientation, the board may also engage in stakeholder relationships management and the proactive management of its accountability disclosures. This has been revealed, for example, by Parker's (2003) participant observer study, which observed directors cultivating their organisational profiles and relationships with the government, media, public and other groups, seeking to build support for and facilitate its strategic ambitions and strategic financing. At the same time, the study found directors struggling to execute transparent financial disclosure while operating in a highly competitive environment where the pursuit of financial resources and returns could be negatively impacted by the financial disclosures they authorised. Thus Parker (2003) finds that directors actually managed the definition of to whom they and their organisation were accountable, as well as the nature of the financial disclosure and accountability they delivered.

6 The crucial control process

In their review of management control research, Berry, Coad, Harris, Otley and Stringer (2009) call for more embedded and collaborative research in this field. This again lends further support to this chapter's argument that the processes of board-level corporate governance and control require such a qualitative, embedded, processual research perspective, as well as a critical eye. The limited number of observational and interview studies addressing board-level control processes suggest that for both profit and not-for-profit boards, there is a shifting balance struck between directors' attention to operational and financial control, but with a tendency towards a financial focus (Stiles and Taylor, 2001; Parker, 2008a). However, the manner in which both operational and financial control are exercised does not appear to accord with any presumed 'textbook' formal approaches through the linking and evaluation of formal strategic plans, business plans and budgets. Studies to date reveal that in fact boards may pay budgetary control systems and associated routine reports only limited attention, focussing upon them near the financial year's end when debating overall financial results and the coming year's budget drafting. Particular aspects of budget results might for example draw directors' attention through directors' dialogue, informal knowledge of organisational finances and operations, concern about particular organisational costs or profit centre performance, or interests in the financial progress of particular strategic projects rather than through their examination of the routine formal accounting reports (Marginson, 1999; Stiles and Taylor, 2001; Parker, 2008a).

Extant qualitative processual research suggests that the control currency in the boardroom is interactive and dialogically focussed and driven, rather than focussed on formal management control reports and their information sets. It is more often informally triggered through directors' particular strategic interests (Parker, 2008a). This somewhat resonates with Mundy's (2010) study which observes that interactive control appears to play a crucial role in balancing other control levers: belief control, boundary control and diagnostic control. In Parker's (2008a) study, control issues are more often triggered for discussion and review by particular directors or the CEO often raising them independently from any formal report. This was consistent with observations also made in Stiles and Taylor (2001) and Parker (2003). It also appears to echo, to some extent, Marginson's (1999) study that observes a greater recourse to social controls than administrative controls.

Such studies have also remarked upon boards' monitoring behaviours which at times appear to reveal a preference for directors advising and supporting the CEO rather than taking a more judgemental evaluative stance (Stiles and Taylor, 2001; Parker, 2008a). They have also observed limited apparent monitoring of budgetary performance or linkages between budget outcomes and business and strategic plans on a monthly or quarterly basis (Miller, 2002; Parker, 2008a). In a study of Belgian company boards, Van den Berghe and Baelden (2005) report a wide variance in boards' attention to their monitoring roles, with some allocating significant time while others allocate minimal time in favour of strategy-focussed discussions. Alternatively, boards' monitoring attention has been found to be attracted by significant and repeated exceptions from plans or excessive external causal attributions for below-target performance (Van Hammel *et al.*, 1998; Stiles and Taylor, 2001). Jonsson's (2005) study of Icelandic boards also reveals a variety of board roles spanning a changing spectrum in response to changes in ownership structures or management that includes the categories of watchdog, pilot, advisor and rubber-stamper.

Boardroom studies have also identified a degree of concern exhibited by directors about the quality, reliability and complexity of decision-making information (including financial) provided to them. These concerns can arise due to a variety of information sources and organisational circumstances, including the ability of the accounting information system to provide the relevant and appropriate information they need, questions of reliability in data collection and processing by the accounting system, the timeliness of reporting and its impact on maintaining an adequate early warning system, and the perceived complexity and volume of reports and data provided to them. The latter issue has on occasion prompted calls for and experiments with simplified summary highlight forms of reporting for board consumption (Van Hammel *et al.*, 1998; Parker, 2003, 2008a, b).

The picture just outlined, drawn from studies of boardroom control processes, presents an arguably different view of management and financial control system operation at the organisation's highest level than is assumed away, for example, by the plethora of quantitative corporate governance studies that treat the board-level governance process as a black box. From a critical research perspective this raises a host of concerns and research agendas. Formal accounting and reporting systems and formally tabled performance data may reach nothing like the levels of significance that accounting researchers may assume to be the case. Agency theorists may be wide of the mark in how they presume control is exercised, by whom and over what. The power of directors both within and beyond the boardroom appears as a malleable and elusive phenomenon, not easily constrained by formal accounting and accountability systems. Operating in such an individualised, dialogical and social form, control has the capacity to be dynamic, proactive and timely. On the other hand, it also carries the risk of severe dysfunction, with major impacts on organisations, employees and communities.

7 A question of accountability

It could be argued that to the extent that accounting researchers have directed their attention to stakeholder engagement mechanisms, they have couched their investigations from an accountability perspective without necessarily acknowledging the related governance dimensions. This has at times left research siloed into either accounting/accountability or governance when in actuality, the processes of accounting, auditing, accountability and stakeholder engagement are all mechanisms of governance. This vital link between governance, accounting and accountability is often misinterpreted, with accounting being mistakenly seen as a distinct professional process, with little or nothing to do with corporate governance.

While researchers have paid some recognition to the importance of considering board of directors' accountability issues, actual attention paid to this responsibility and relationship has been to date, scant (Brennan and Solomon, 2008). Issues of accountability have largely been addressed by accounting researchers in terms of corporate accountability to shareholders, with linkages between such aspects as accounting, governance and risk management being barely examined (Bhimani, 2009). Indeed overviews of corporate governance studies in the accounting literature, while naming the board as a dimension of importance, then actually proceed to focus upon and study the audit committee (Cohen, Krishnamoorthy and Wright, 2004). With respect to exercising their accountability roles and obligations, the manner in which boards approach their deliberations and decisions has also been only marginally addressed. Some work has been done on examining the characteristics of boardroom culture that may affect the creation and delivery of accountability. These have included studies identifying styles of director interaction that include 'challenging but supportive', 'independent but involved', 'openness and generosity', 'preparedness and involvement' and 'creativity and criticality' (Huse, 2005). Leblanc and Gillies (2003), for instance, argue that this lacuna limits the ability to draft effective regulations for improving corporate governance. Collier's (2008) study also suggests a board's concern with both accountability to salient external stakeholders and internal organisational relationships and accountabilities. This is one of the very few qualitative field studies in accounting applied to such issues at board level, however. Examinations of *how* boards actually select their members, develop policies and performance expectations of themselves, clarify their own responsibilities, decide on board subcommittees, and monitor organisational performance are very few indeed (Holland, 2002). In an interview study of 34 non-profit organisational boards, Holland (2002) finds that only a few explicitly address accountability issues such as detailing board member expectations and responsibilities, or discussing their policies regarding conflicts of interest. Some were found to approach their accountability responsibilities by focussing much of their discussion on strategic objectives and priorities but most were found to be content to simply review executives' plans and decisions. Self-evaluation of board group and individual director performance was also found to be only sporadically in evidence.

In addition to our limited understanding of internal boardroom accountability processes, there is the strong suspicion that entrenched corporate power lies unremarked beneath the surface of board functioning and accountability delivery. The dynamics of power inequalities, competition for influence and resistance to external demands for board-level accountability and change are all crucial features of board-level corporate governance and accountability that call for the attention of critical accounting researchers. Internationally, corporate scandals and accountability failures over the years have been legion, with copious media coverage having been afforded to them. Legislators have variously attempted to respond, and boards of directors have invariably been criticised and blamed (Christopher, 2010). Yet our knowledge of how boards have acted and why, how they came to be ineffective and how they failed in their corporate governance duties, remains minimal (Leblanc and Gillies, 2003; Parker, 2007c). Directors may become socialised into a preservation of their own power and resistant to any change in the *status quo,* or the emoluments their positions afford (Collier, 2005). Thus while corporate accountability scandals may generate periodic public angst and discussion, as well as reactive legislation and increased penalties, they may only prompt limited temporary reflection by most ongoing boards and hence have little influence on their approaches to and acquittal of their accountability roles (Holland, 2002; Marnet, 2007).

As should by now be evident, this section is aptly titled "A question of accountability". With respect to board-level corporate governance, the attitudes, roles, processes and delivery of boardroom accountabilities remain largely opaque to outside purview. Again, as already observed in this chapter, accounting researchers have largely been content to examine board structures and profiles from a distance. Engagement with directors and boards at the coalface, examinations of their attitudes and behaviours, and analysis of their governance processes has not attracted significant accounting researcher engagement. Yet it is here that both qualitative processual and critical accounting research is urgently needed. Without it, we are likely condemned to persist in the repetitive cycle of corporate board accountability failures.

8 A theoretical landscape

Accounting and management research in corporate governance and with respect to corporate governance at the board level has been informed by a variety of theories. The list is quite impressive, but studies have largely resorted to a particular group from among that list. Reflecting a dominant economics and finance paradigm, agency theory has often been invoked by corporate governance researchers focussing on contracting between board, senior executives and shareholders (Clarke, 1998; Becht, Bolton and Roel, 2003; Gabrielsson and Huse, 2005). The dominant appeal of agency theory has been attributed to its simplicity and its assumptions that corporate activity can be simplified down to contracting parties where participants are completely opportunistic and self-interested, the board acting to reduce the gap between management and shareholder interests (Daily *et al.*, 2003; Hendry and Kiel, 2004). Its focus is on market efficiency to be pursued through incentive systems and voluntary compliance (Letza, Sun and Kirkbride, 2004) and its accountability focus is directed effectively only towards one group, the shareholders (Christopher, 2010). Yet the non-alignment of board and shareholder interests and the failure of control via incentive schemes have been linked to many of the corporate scandals and crashes witnessed in recent decades (Christopher, 2010). Furthermore, it has been suggested that simplistic agency-based assumptions may not hold in varying social, economic and institutional settings and cannot cope with a diverse range of institutional contexts (Christopher, 2010).

Despite its ongoing fascination for many traditional accounting researchers, agency theory is highly suspect as an efficient and appropriate theoretical framework for analysing corporate governance in most national and international environments. It is exceedingly difficult to locate any contemporary economy or stock market that resembles Jensen and Meckling's (1976) market for corporate control, with its dispersed external shareholders, or with automatically 'bad' directors and 'good shareholders' who attempt to monitor and control those directors. Instead, markets are characterised by concentrated ownership exhibiting very different problems. Roberts (2001) clearly identifies the problems with any attempt to apply agency theory in today's context. It is simply a theory that is no longer fit for purpose.

A further key theoretical framework evident in governance research has been that of resource dependence theory which conceives of the board as a boundary spanner linking the organisation to its environment and assisting it to secure resources from that environment, through communicating, networking and legitimising (Clarke, 1998; Huse, 2005; Gabrielsson and Huse, 2005). The resources directors provide can also reflect their own personal expertise and networks such as legal, financial, marketing and other forms of intellectual capital (Daily *et al.*, 2003). The board thus draws resources from the environment and can also buffer the organisation from adverse external environmental changes (Hendry and Kiel, 2004). This theory privileges consideration of the quality and effectiveness of directors in executing their governance roles and the aggregate board capital that together they deliver (Christopher, 2010).

As with other areas of accounting research, corporate governance studies have often been framed by stewardship theory which casts the directors and senior executives as stewards of the organisation and its assets, the board collaborating with and mentoring senior management (Clarke, 1998; Huse, 2005; Gabrielsson and Huse, 2005). In contrast to agency theory, directors are considered more trustworthy and their interests are seen as more sympathetically related to those of the shareholders, encountering situations where they see their own interests as being consistent with shareholder interests, and also are motivated by the intrinsic satisfaction of their board roles and contribution (Daily *et al.*, 2003; Hendry and Kiel, 2004; Letza *et al.*, 2004). Achievement and responsibility needs are seen to be important director motivators, however, and as Turnbull (1997) argues, the degree of director selflessness and stewardship orientation may be culturally contingent.

Stakeholder theory extends stewardship theory in seeing the board's role as going beyond maximising shareholders' wealth to inclusively addressing the concerns of a wider range of stakeholders, thereby moving beyond a purely economic remit and involving non-market considerations and performance monitoring (Clarke, 1998; Letza *et al.*, 2004; Gabrielsson and Huse, 2005). The list of wider stakeholders extends across employees, government, customers, competitors, suppliers, activists, non-government organisations (NGOs) and communities. Indeed, NGOs are an example of institutions who are beginning to represent and give voice to the needs and concerns of marginalised societal groups who still do not attract the attention of researchers who, for example, may operate from an agency theory perspective. Stakeholder theory thus attempts to account for a wider range of forces that condition the board's corporate governance role and performance in both organisational and societal interests (Christopher, 2010).

In addition to agency theory, resource dependence theory, stewardship theory and stakeholder theory, other theories that have been applied to corporate governance issues and research at the board level include managerial hegemony theory, contingency theory, accountability theories, new institutional theory, sense making, discourse, control and social capital theories (Clarke, 1998; Hendry and Kiel, 2004; Huse, 2005; McNulty *et al.*, 2013; Subramaniam, Stewart, Ng and Shulman, 2013). Arguably there is room for more sociologically and critical theory–derived theoretical positions that can productively be applied to board-level corporate governance and accountability questions. There is a need to move beyond a simple obsession with economic markets and financial incentives if we are to penetrate boardroom processes and governance failures, recognising the potential importance of environments, institutions, clans, communities and more (Turnbull, 1997). The economics-based perspective has produced versions of corporate governance and its effectiveness or otherwise that diverge observably from how corporate governance works or does not work in the field (Davis, 2005). Indeed, the qualitative tradition of governance research tends to draw more often on sociological perspectives, as evidenced in some of the aforementioned theoretical perspectives (McNulty *et al.*, 2013). It is from the sociological perspective that we are better equipped to develop an informed critique of director behaviour and board performance (Pesqueux, 2005; Marnett, 2007). One example of this potential lies in attending to theories of power and political influence in board-level operations and deliberations (McNulty *et al.*, 2013). This can include attention to the balance and competition for power between executives and directors as well as shareholders, and the processual relationships and dealings between CEOs and boards (Daily *et al.*, 2003). How power is accrued and exercised by directors, management, shareholders and other stakeholders, the formal and informal sources of power and checks against its dysfunctional and inequitable use, and the roles of information and communication in its disposition, all call for greater attention by critical accounting researchers in the corporate governance field (Turnbull, 1997).

Board-level corporate governance research in the accounting literature urgently awaits the greater application of sociologically and critical theory–grounded perspectives that counter the illogical assumptions in rational, economically focussed views of the world of governance and can assist in penetrating and unpacking the wider range of agendas and behaviours embedded in the corporate governance process. As Letza *et al.* (2004) argue, economics-based theories have neglected or assumed away important dimensions of the governance process that include irrationality, beliefs, emotions and ideologies that often act as vital inputs to the governance process. Rather than static, abstract theorisations, we need theoretical models that relate to the idiosyncrasies of practices and their complex and often varying contexts. As Letza *et al.* (2004) also observe, corporate governance may best be served by the application of pluralist theorisations that furnish, better understand and critique the ideologies, politics, philosophies, conventions, social customs and institutional settings that make up governance at both the board and organisation-wide levels.

9 Setting the agenda

At the risk of stating a truism, we still have much to learn about corporate governance and accountability at the level of the board. As this chapter has outlined, an understanding and critique of the *processes* of corporate governance stand to offer us a far more penetrating engagement with corporate governance and accountability as it is practised by actors in the field. Rather than relying on static, externally derived and simplistic director profiles, we need to address director world views, attitudes and behaviours, as well as the dynamics of the boardroom including information processing, discourse, debate and decision making. Particularly from a critical perspective, we need a far more realistic, candid and theoretically informed critique of board-level relationships, communications and accountability to marginalised groups ranging from non-institutional shareholders through to local communities and NGOs.

We have the available armoury for undertaking this processual and critical research agenda. Among the qualitative research methods available are participant observation, interview, documentary analysis, discourse analysis, historical methodologies and more. They are essential to our moving from that disconnected world outside the corporate governance black box, to infiltrating the directors' world inside the boardroom black box. As has already been pointed out in this chapter, while not without its challenges, accessing that world is entirely possible. It more often involves searching for and being alert to organisational access opportunities and then seizing such access opportunities and building relevant projects to take advantage of them.

The critical agenda stands well positioned to address the many issues of sources, manifestations and impacts of the exercise of power within and beyond the boardroom. We need more closely engaged and more finely wrought accounts of relationships between the CEO and the board chair, the CEO/board chair and directors, as well as between EDs and NEDs. Particularly important is a better understanding and critique of the evaluative versus advisory roles and interactions between directors and executives on the board and between board members and the CEO. Positivist quantitative modelling studies relying on externally derived profiles tell us very little! It is only from within the heat of the boardroom that we can derive a more realistic understanding and produce a better located critique of power relationships and processes at the board level of corporate governance. That of course includes a more transparent engagement and reckoning of board member selection and rotation, board self-evaluation processes, directors' strategy versus control focuses, the relationship between strategic and policy focuses, director compliance with executives' strategic edicts and the tendency towards directors' engagement in micromanagement.

From an accounting and control perspective, we are woefully under-informed and hence constrained in our critical ability by our need for a clearer insider view of the actual linkages in directors' deliberations on strategy, business plans and budgets. We cannot merely assume that the presence of detailed or sophisticated formal accounting reporting and control systems automatically implies that such linkages are in place and effectively employed. To what extent are boardroom monitoring and performance evaluation processes actually occurring, regularly undertaken and effective? What types of strategic accounting information inputs are provided? Are they understood, actually employed or ignored? If the latter, what takes their place in conditioning directors' control discourse and decisions? We also need more informed impressions and then critiques of both the extent of financial versus operational control focuses that occur in the boardroom. In addition, our approach to this level of governance will be well served by determining from the actors themselves what triggers their monitoring and control discussions. How this is done can also reveal much for accounting researchers: unpacking the extent of formal versus informal control processes exercised within the board, rather than presuming that control discussions begin and end with formal accounting reports.

Finally, we arrive at the widely acknowledged need for a critical project with respect to board accountability. Already we have some evidence of deliberate disclosure management by boards. It is simply insufficient for earnings management scholars to repeatedly demonstrate that it happens and then proceed to offer predictive circumstances when it might happen again. For corporate governance policy and practice betterment, we need to enter the black box of the boardroom to reveal a broader suite of information types and their manipulation, penetrating the processes by which it is effected and the rationalisations declared by directors who so engage. The research agenda does not end there, however. So many corporate frauds and crashes have been linked to failings in the boardroom, and yet accounting scholars barely mention this in their research agendas. A critical and qualitative research agenda offers an opportunity to seek out an inside view of the modes of accountability exercised between directors themselves, between executives and board directors, and then in actuality between the board and its various stakeholder groups. What are the board's attitudes, communications, intentions, and then delivery or management of their accountabilities? To what extent are directors driven by their self-interest and their compliance with board chairs or CEOs who facilitate their board appointments? How much board deliberation and activity masks a preservation of the *status quo*, and consequentially, directors' personal benefits?

The accounting and management research communities have made significant beginnings in our responsibility to better understand and critique corporate board-level governance, control and accountability. However, those researchers who have moved in close to the coalface, engaging with directors and boards directly, are yet few in number. It is only from that close engagement with actors and their processes that we can begin to develop an informed basis for board-level governance and accountability process critique. If as critical researchers, we are serious about our commitment to *both* critique *and* change, then the necessary research trajectory is clear.

This chapter was submitted by the author with the following title: "Corporate governance and control: rediscovering boardroom processes."

References

Bailey, B. C. and S. I. Peck. (2013). "Boardroom strategic decision-making style: understanding the antecedents," *Corporate Governance: An International Review*, 21(2): 131–46.

Becht, M., P. Bolton and A. Röel (2003). "Corporate governance and control," in G. M. Constantinides, M. Harris and R. M. Stulz (eds): *Handbook of the Economics of Finance*, Burlington: Elsevier Science.

Berry, A. J., A. F. Coad, E. P. Harris, D. T. Otley and C. Stringer (2009). "Emerging themes in management control: a review of recent literature," *British Accounting Review*, 41(2): 2–20.

Bhimani, A. (2009). "Risk management, corporate governance and management accounting: emerging interdependencies," *Management Accounting Research*, 20(1): 2–5.

Brennan, N. M. and J. Solomon (2008). "Guest editorial: corporate governance, accountability and mechanisms of accountability: an overview," *Accounting, Auditing and Accountability Journal*, 21(7): 885–906.

Brown, P., W. Beekes and P. Verhoeven (2011). "Corporate governance, accounting and finance: a review," *Accounting & Finance*, 51(1): 96–172.

Brundin, E. and M. Nordqvist (2008). "Beyond facts and figures: the role of emotions in boardroom dynamics," *Corporate Governance: An International Review*, 16(4): 326–41.

Bushman, R., Q. Chen, E. Engel and A. Smith (2004). "Financial accounting information, organizational complexity and corporate governance systems," *Journal of Accounting & Economics*, 37(2): 167–201.

Chiu, P. and J. Monin (2003). "Effective corporate governance: from the perspective of New Zealand fund managers," *Corporate Governance: An International Review*, 11(2): 123–31.

Choudhury, N. (1988). "The seeking of accounting where it is not: towards a theory of non-accounting in organizational settings," *Accounting, Organizations and Society*, 13(6) 549–58.

Christopher, J. (2010). "Corporate governance: a multi-theoretical approach to recognizing the wider influencing forces impacting on organizations," *Critical Perspectives on Accounting*, 21(8): 683–95.

Clarke, T. (1998). "Research on corporate governance," *Corporate Governance: An International Review*, 6(1): 57–66.

Cohen, J., G. Krishnamoorthy and A. Wright (2004). "The corporate governance mosaic and financial reporting quality," *Journal of Accounting Literature*, 23: 87–152.

Collier, P. M. (2005). "Governance and the quasi-public organization: a case study of social housing," *Critical Perspectives on Accounting*, 16(7): 929–49.

Collier, P. M. (2008). "Stakeholder accountability: a field study of the implementation of a governance improvement plan," *Accounting, Auditing and Accountability Journal*, 21(7): 933–54.

Cornforth, C. and C. Edwards (1999). "Board roles in the strategic management of non-profit organisations: theory and practice," *Corporate Governance: An International Review*, 7(4): 346–62.

Cowen, S. S. and R. L. Osborne (1993). "Board of directors as strategy," *Journal of General Management*, 19(2): 1–13.

Daily, C. M., R. Dalton and A. A. Cannella (2003). "Corporate governance: decades of dialogue and data," *Academy of Management Review*, 28(3): 371–82.

Davis, G. F. (2005). "New directions in corporate governance," *Annual Review of Sociology*, 31: 143–62.

Dulewicz, V. (1995). "Appraising and developing the effectiveness of boards and their directors," *Journal of General Management*, 20(3): 1–19.

Eng, L. L. and Y. T. Mak (2003). "Corporate governance and voluntary disclosure," *Journal of Accounting and Public Policy*, 22(4): 325–45.

Forbes, D. P. and F. J. Milliken (1999). "Cognition and corporate governance: understanding boards of directors as strategic decision-making groups," *Academy of Management Review*, 24(3): 489–505.

Gabrielson, J. and M. Huse (2005). "Context, behavior and evolution," *International Studies of Management and Organization*, 34(2): 11–36.

Hambrick, D. C., A. V. Weredr and E. J. Zadac (2008): "New directions in corporate governance research," *Organization Science*, 19(3): 381–85.

Hendry, K. and G. C. Kiel (2004). "The role of the board in firm strategy: integrating agency and organisational control perspectives," *Corporate Governance: An International Review*, 12(4): 500–20.

Hines, R. D. (1992). "Accounting: filling the negative space," *Accounting, Organizations and Society*, 17(3–4): 313–41.

Holland, J. (2001). "Financial institutions, intangibles and corporate governance," *Accounting, Auditing and Accountability Journal*, 14(4): 497–529.

Holland, T. (2002). "Board accountability: lessons from the field," *Nonprofit Management & Leadership*, 12(4): 409–28.

Huse, M. (2005). "Accounting and creating accountability: a framework for exploring behavioural perspectives of corporate governance," *British Journal of Management*, 16(S): 65–97.

Inkpen, A. and N. Choudhury (1995). "The seeking of strategy where it is not: towards a theory of strategy absence," *Strategic Management Journal*, 16(4): 313–23.

Jensen, M. C. and W. H. Meckling (1976). "Theory of the firm: managerial behaviour, agency costs and ownership structure," *Journal of Financial Economics*, 3(4): 305–60.

Jonsson, E. I. (2005). "The role model of the board: a preliminary study of the roles of Icelandic boards," *Corporate Governance: An International Review*, 13(5): 710–17.

Larcker, D. F., S. A. Richardson and I. Tuna (2007). "Corporate governance, accounting outcomes and organizational performance," *Accounting Review*, 82(4): 963–1008.

Leblanc, R. and J. Gillies (2003). "The coming revolution in corporate governance," *Ivey Business Journal*, Sept–Oct: 1–11.

Leblanc, R. and J. Gillies (2005). *Inside the Boardroom: How Boards Really Work and the Coming Revolution in Corporate Governance*, Ontario: John Wiley & Sons Canada.

Leblanc, R. and M. S. Schwartz (2007). "The black box of board process: gaining access to a difficult subject," *Corporate Governance: An International Review*, 15(5): 843–51.

Leblanc, R. W. (2004). "What's wrong with corporate governance: a note," *Corporate Governance: An International Review*, 12(4): 436–41.

Letendre, L. (2004). "The dynamics of the boardroom," *Academy of Management Executive*, 18(1): 101–04.

Letza, S., X. Sun and J. Kirkbride (2004). "Shareholding versus stakeholding: a critical review of corporate governance," *Corporate Governance: An International Review*, 12(3): 242–62.

Machold, S. and S. Farquar (2013). "Board task evolution: a longitudinal fields study in the UK," *Corporate Governance: An International Review*, 21(2): 147–64.

McNulty, T. and A. Pettigrew (1999). "Strategists on the board," *Organization Studies*, 20(1): 47–74.

McNulty, T., A. Zattoni and T. Douglas (2013). "Developing corporate governance research through qualitative methods: a review of previous studies," *Corporate Governance: An International Review*, 21(2): 183–98.

Marginson, D. E. W. (1999). "Beyond the budgetary control system: towards a two tiered process of management control," *Management Accounting Research*, 10(3): 203–30.

Marnett, O. (2007). "History repeats itself: the failure of rational choice models in corporate governance," *Critical Perspectives on Accounting*, 18(2): 191–210.

Miller, J. L. (2002). "The board as a monitor of organizational activity: the applicability of agency theory to nonprofit boards," *Nonprofit Management and Leadership*, 12(4): 429–50.

Mundy, J. (2010). "Creating dynamic tensions through a balanced use of management controls," *Accounting, Organizations and Society*, 35(5): 499–523.

Ng, W. and C. De Cock (2002). "Battle in the boardroom: a discursive perspective," *Journal of Management Studies*, 39(1): 23–49.

Nicholson, G. J. and G. Kiel (2003). "Board composition and corporate performance: how the Australian experience informs contrasting theories of corporate governance," *Corporate Governance: An International Review*, 11(3): 189–205.

Papadakis, V. M., S. Lioukas and D. Chambers (1998). "Strategic decision-making processes: the role of management and context," *Strategic Management Journal*, 19(2): 115–47.

Parker, L. D. (2001). "Reactive planning in a Christian bureaucracy," *Management Accounting Research*, 12(3): 321–56.

Parker, L. D. (2003). "Financial management strategy in a community welfare organisation: a boardroom perspective," *Financial Accountability and Management*, 19(4): 341–74.

Parker, L. D. (2007a). "Boardroom strategizing in professional associations: processual and institutional perspectives," *Journal of Management Studies*, 44(8): 1454–80.

Parker, L. D. (2007b). "Internal governance in the nonprofit boardroom: a participant observer study," *Corporate Governance: An International Review*, 15(5): 923–34.

Parker, L. D. (2007c). "Financial and external reporting research: the broadening corporate governance challenge," *Accounting and Business Research*, 37(1): 39–54.

Parker, L. D. (2008a). "Boardroom operational and financial control: an insider view," *British Journal of Management*, 19(S): 65–88.

Parker, L. D. (2008b). "Towards understanding corporate governance processes: life at the top," *Indonesian Management and Accounting Research*, 7(1): 1–15.

Pesqueux, Y. (2005). "Corporate governance and accounting systems: a critical perspective," *Critical Perspectives on Accounting*, 16(6): 797–823.

Pettigrew, A. M. (1992). "On studying managerial elites," *Strategic Management Journal*, 13(S2): 163–82.

Roberts, J. (2001). "Trust and control in Anglo-American systems of corporate governance: the individualizing and socialising effects of processes of accountability," *Human Relations*, 54(12): 1547–72

Rose, J. M., C. R. Mazza, C. S. Norman and A. M. (2013). "The influence of director stock ownership and board discussion transparency on financial reporting quality," *Accounting, Organizations and Society*, 38(5): 397–405.

Samra-Fredericks, D. (2000). "Doing 'Boards-in-Action' research – an ethnographic approach for the capture and analysis of directors' and senior managers' interactive routines," *Corporate Governance: An International Review*, 8(3): 244–57.

Snow, C. C. and J. B. Thomas (1994). "Field research methods in strategic management: contributions to theory building and testing," *Journal of Management Studies*, 31(4): 457–80.

Spira, L. F. and R. Bender (2004). "Compare and contrast: perspectives on board committees," *Corporate Governance: An International Review*, 12(4): 489–99.

Stiles, P. (2001). "The impact of the board on strategy: an empirical examination," *Journal of Management Studies*, 38(5): 627–50.

Stiles, P. and B. Taylor (2001). *Boards at Work: How Directors View Their Roles and Responsibilities*, Oxford, Oxford University Press.

Subramaniam, N, J. Stewart, C. Ng and A. Shulman (2013). "Understanding corporate governance in the Australian public sector: a social capital approach," *Accounting, Auditing and Accountability Journal*, 26(6): 946–77.

Taylor, M. and N. O'Sullivan (2009). "How should national governing bodies of sport be governed in the UK? An exploratory study of board structure," *Corporate Governance: An International Review*, 17(6): 681–93.

Turnbull, S. (1997). "Corporate governance: its scope, concerns and theories," *Corporate Governance: An International Review*, 5(4): 180–205.

Uddin, S. and J. Choudhury (2008). "Rationality, traditionalism and the state of corporate governance mechanisms: illustrations from a less developed country," *Accounting, Auditing and Accountability Journal*, 21(7): 1026–51.

Useem, M. and A. Zelleke (2006). "Oversight and delegation in corporate governance: deciding what the board should decide," *Corporate Governance: An International Review*, 14(1): 2–12.

Van den Berghe, L. A. A and A. Levrau (2004). "Evaluating boards of directors: what constitutes a good corporate board?" *Corporate Governance: An International Review*, 12,(4): 461–78.

Van den Berghe, L. A. A. and T. Baelden (2005). "The monitoring role of the board: one approach does not fit all," *Corporate Governance: An International Review*, 13(5): 680–90.

Van Hamel, J. A., H. E. van Wijk, H. E., A. J. H. de Rooij and M. Bruel (1998). "Boardroom dynamics – lessons in governance," *Corporate Governance: An International Review*, 6(3): 193–201.

Xie, B., W. N. Davidson and P. J. Dadalt (2003). "Earnings management and corporate governance: the role of the board and the audit committee," *Journal of Corporate Finance*, 9(3): 295–316.

17

FINANCIALIZATION

Colin Haslam, Nick Tsitsianis and George Katechos

1 Introduction

This chapter is about the adoption of Fair Value Accounting (FVA) by the major accounting standards setting agencies, specifically the International Accounting Standards Board (IASB) and, in the US, the Financial Accounting Standards Board (FASB). FVA in contrast to historic cost accounting (HCA) involves a reorientation from the income statement to balance sheet and from historic costs to the disclosure of market values within a reporting entity's accounts. Hopwood (2009) observes that the move to fair FVA has been hotly debated. Hopwood's argument is that whilst one strand of the accounting and finance debate encouraged this shift in calculative and reporting practice, there are also "inherent ambiguities" that need to be explored, specifically, how has FVA been "operationalized in calculative terms" and what are the "wider consequences." In the following pages we argue that the adoption of FVA needs to be contextualised within the *financialized firm* in order to best understand its operational impact and wider consequences.

Both the FASB in the US and the IASB elsewhere now mandate the use of FVA within a range of extant financial reporting standards. This adoption of FVA is the outcome of an ongoing reorientation away from HCA, as a consequence of which the balance sheet rather that income statement becomes the focus of attention in terms of providing a relevant and faithful representation of a firm's financial condition to investors. HCA records realised revenues and how changes and movements in revenues and expenses impact upon the financial position of the firm on the balance sheet. FVA, in contrast, reveals how ongoing changes in the market value of assets (traded or estimated) impact upon a reporting entity's comprehensive income and reported shareholder equity. The accounting debate about HCA or FVA centres on "different conceptions of what it is for an accounting estimate to be reliable" (Power, 2010: 201). The monopolising conception, according to Power, is now grounded in financial economics, "with its dominant cultural and technical authority as a style of reasoning spanning academia and practice" (Power, 2010: 203). Opposing this conception and its acquired legitimacy involves challenging financial economics (Whitley, 1986) and the value relevance and reliability of information disclosed in a reporting entity's financial statements (Barth, 2007; Barth and Landsman, 2010).

The IASB's and the FASB's adoption and consolidation of the balance sheet approach is apparent in a range of accounting standards that permit FVA. However, International Financial Reporting Standard (IFRS) 13 and Financial Accounting Standard (FAS) 157: Fair Value

Measurements are the cornerstone accounting standards that set out the calculative and reporting principles governing FVA. These standards emphasise that FVA is a market-based and not an entity-specific measurement and that the financial statements of the firm should, where possible, reflect the market value of the assets employed. Where a market valuation/price is not available then judgements and modelling can be employed to mimic what market participants would have experienced when pricing the asset. Both IFRS 13 and FAS 157 promote the use of a fair value hierarchy that distinguishes between valuations based on market data obtained from sources independent of the reporting entity (observable inputs) and the reporting entity's own assumptions about market values based on the best information available in the circumstances (unobservable inputs). The notion of unobservable inputs is intended to allow for situations in which there is little, if any, market activity for the asset at the measurement date (IFRS 13[1]: 8 and FAS 157[2]: 3).

2 Perspectives on the financialized firm

In this chapter we argue that it is important to contextualise the adoption of FVA within the financialized firm to assess its operational impact and consequences. We draw upon three key elements from the financialization literature to frame our analysis and arguments about the operational and social consequences of adopting of FVA. Financialization is often deployed to describe the means by which capital market interests exert control over the stewardship of corporate resources. Epstein (2005) observes that

> [s]ome writers use the term 'financialization' to mean the ascendancy of 'shareholder value' as a mode of corporate governance (see also Palley, 2007); some use it to refer to the growing dominance of capital market financial systems over bank-based financial systems; some follow Hilferding's lead and use the term 'financialization' to refer to the increasing political and economic power of a particular class grouping: the rentier class.
>
> *(Epstein, 2005: 3)*

Orhangazi uses the term financialization to capture the complex relations between "financial markets and other aspects of the economy" (Orhangazi, 2008: xiv). Krippner (2005) argues that changes in the composition of corporate balance sheets from tangible to financial asset accumulations establish a situation where "[n]on-financial corporations are beginning to resemble financial corporations – in some cases, *closely* – and we need to take this insight to our studies of corporate behaviour" (Krippner, 2005: 201).

Lazonick (2013) observes that financialization is about the dominance of an ideology based on shareholder value, that is,

> [the] mode of corporate resource allocation has been legitimized by the ideology, itself a product of the 1980s and 1990s, that a business corporation should be run to "maximize shareholder value."
>
> *(Lazonick, 2013: 859)*

Lazonick's argument is that firms in the US have become preoccupied with maximising short-run returns on capital and distributing profit to shareholders to maximise their returns at the expense of a long-term commitment to innovation and workforce skills for product and process renewal. This, Lazonick argues, is undermining the competitiveness of the US economy because the interests of shareholders do not align with the broader stakeholder interests and the need to sustain competitiveness. For Lazonick:

The key to the problem is the compensation of US corporate executives with indexed stock options that reward them for stock-price movements that are driven by stock-market speculation and manipulation and that are justified by the ubiquitous ideology that the role of these corporate executives is to "maximize shareholder value."

(Lazonick, 2011: 1)

Froud, Johal, Leaver and Williams (2006) observe that financialization is about how the process of the ongoing recapitalisation of assets in speculative secondary markets conjoins both technical and rhetorical elements (Froud *et al.*, 2006: 71). That is, market valuations involve both a technical calculation together with a narrative rhetorical component that is often employed to exaggerate performance and transformation. Both the technical numbers and optimistic narratives combine to generate an intangible aspect to an assets market value and it is this intangible component, incorporated into the valuation of assets, that tends to "the widest and the freest" (Veblen, 2005: 76). The trading of financial assets involves buyers taking speculative positions with the intention to sell on to make a profit in an endless round of recapitalisation(s) that exploit a difference between the bid/ask spreads and motivations of complex financial intermediaries. This process of ongoing recapitalisation is fuelled by leverage whereby the collateral embedded in the value of assets takes on an increasingly intangible form. As a consequence, in a financialized world the capital market takes on added significance in terms of facilitating the vendibility of assets at the expense of maintaining the serviceability of this capital. The underlying current earnings from assets become a distant and less relevant factor determining the ongoing value of these assets (Haslam, Andersson, Tsitsianis and Yin, 2012).

Employing these various perspectives we can construct an understanding of the financialized firm: first, non-financial firms increasingly resemble financial firms; second, earnings distribution is prioritised over profit retention; and third, asset valuations recorded on balance sheets are speculative and volatile. In the following section we argue that professional bodies and accounting standard-setting agencies are actors that have influence over the regulatory process governing corporate behaviour. The accounting project is set out within a general conceptual framework and is one that from the outset prioritises the interests of investors. Zeff (1999) reminds us that the architects of the accounting conceptual framework have consistently taken the view that the financial statements should provide information to inform investors. For example, in its seminal *A Statement of Basic Accounting Theory* (ASOBAT), the American Accounting Association (AAA, 1966: 1) defined accounting as "[t]he process of identifying, measuring, and communicating economic information to permit informed judgments and decisions by users of the information," where the principal users are understood to be investors.

The justification for adopting FVA over HCA is that it enhances the provision of decision-useful information to investors and this, in turn, serves to promote capital market efficiency. An alternative perspective is advanced in this chapter, one that contextualises the impact of changed financial reporting standards within the financialized firm and uses this framing device to evaluate consequences in terms of firm-level financial fragility and instability. The following section offers a review of how the shift from HCA to FVA was informed by a motivation to enhance the provision of decision-useful information to investors and thereby promote capital market efficiency and lower the cost of capital (risk). In contrast our object is to set out an alternative framing that locates the shift from HCA to FVA within the financialized firm and employ this perspective to explore operational impacts and possible consequences (Hopwood, 2009).

3 Financial disclosure: informing investors for capital market efficiency

In its 2013 discussion document ASOBAT, the IASB invited readers to provide comments and responses to a series of questions asked. At the outset, whilst this is a discussion paper, it revealed the intentions and priorities of the reform agenda for financial reporting, namely, that the general purpose of financial reporting is to provide decision-useful information to investors and those providing financial resources to firms (Biondi, 2012). In the view of the IASB:

> The objective of general purpose financial reporting is to provide financial information about the reporting entity that is useful to users of financial statements (existing and potential investors, lenders and other creditors) in making decisions about providing resources to the entity.
>
> *(IASB, 2013: 20)*

This objective has been a long-standing guiding principle governing the purpose of general-purpose financial reporting:

> Financial reporting should provide information that is useful to present and potential investors and creditors and other users in making rational investment, credit, and similar decisions.
>
> *(FASB, 2008: 10)*

Although the primary objective is to provide information to investors that is decision useful this can be enhanced where the information provided is comparable, capable of being verified, timely and easy to understand:

> If financial information is to be useful, it must be relevant and faithfully represent what it purports to represent. The usefulness of financial information is enhanced if it is comparable, verifiable, timely and understandable.
>
> *(IASB, 2013: 21)*

Accounting standards, we are informed, serve to enhance transparency and inform investors about a firm's financial position and this, in turn, influences capital stock allocations (debt and equity), decisions about risk and adjustments to a firm's cost of capital. For Tarca (2012: 1):

> When the standards are applied rigorously and consistently, capital market participants will have higher quality information and can make better decisions. Thus markets allocate funds more efficiently and firms can achieve a lower cost of capital.

3.1 Arguments for the re-orientation from historic cost to fair value accounting

The reorientation in financial reporting from HCA to FVA was justified because it would enhance transparency and improve the quality of information disclosed to investors thereby influencing capital allocation decisions and reducing the cost of capital (risk). The US Chartered Financial Analysts (CFA) institute has observed: "We believe fair value measures are most relevant because they reflect the reality upon which the economic world operates: transactions take place at fair value" (CFA, 2010: 1). The debate about the costs and benefits of historic or fair value accounting has been long standing in both Europe and the US. In 1966, the AAA committee tasked with developing an integrated statement of basic accounting theory released its report, *A Statement of Basic Accounting Theory*, regarding which Emerson, Karim and Rutledge (2010) observe:

> ASOBAT is extremely pertinent to any discussion of fair value reporting, both through its emphasis on relevance, as well as through the inclusion of a proposal that would allow entities to provide multiple measures of transactional information. This "dual-reporting" proposal was seen as an effort to transition the industry away from historical cost toward the more relevant measure of fair value.
>
> *(Emerson et al., 2010: 79)*

Littleton (2011) makes a general observation that economists seek to capitalise future earnings expectations into current asset valuations but that accountants have been generally predisposed to measure costs actually incurred by an enterprise before the current date. Economists consider that it is important for a business enterprise to periodically recalibrate balance sheet valuations on the basis of changes to the market value of assets employed or the expected future earnings from these assets. Accountants, according to Littleton, find expected earnings unacceptable for most accounting uses because they are unwilling to

> cut loose their thinking and their service from the provable objectivity of accounts kept and financial statements made in terms of costs actually incurred by this enterprise before the current date.
>
> *(Littleton, 2011: 4–5)*

It is the case that with HCA the purchase cost of an asset at the transaction date will correspond to the market value of that asset. However, the difference between HCA and FVA is not concerned with what to do with the initial recorded measurement but what happens with the subsequent measurement of balance sheet assets. The difference between HCA and FVA centres on whether the information disclosed in a reporting entity's financial statements is subject to contemporary revaluations (Edwards and Bell, 1964, Chambers, 1965, 1966; Morgan, 1988) to reflect current economic realities where economic theory guides accounting practice (Barker and Schulte, 2017). In this regard FVA favours the recalibration of asset values informed by ongoing changes to market values or, in the absence of market values, expectations about changes to the future discounted earnings capacity of assets held on the balance sheet.

Ditchev and Penman (2007) also review the differences between these alternative and competing approaches to doing financial reporting, a balance sheet approach (FVA) and income statement approach (HCA). The balance sheet–based approach is focussed on the appropriate valuation of assets and liabilities as the primary goal of financial reporting, with the determination of other accounting variables considered secondary and derivative (Ditchev and Penman, 2007). By contrast, the income statement approach is focussed on the determination of revenues, expenses and the timing and magnitude of the revenue and expense amounts and residual earnings where "balance sheet accounts and amounts are secondary and derivative" (Ditchev and Penman, 2007: 4; see also Ronen, 2008). For an HCA perspective changes on the balance sheet drop out as a residual adjustment in periodic accruals. During the 1970s the FASB concluded, after considerable debate, that the balance sheet approach should inform standard setting and general financial reporting (Ditchev and Penman, 2007: 216). Penman (1973) summarises the difference between the income statement and balance sheet approaches to accounting in terms of the way in which assets are conceptualised: either as representing a "service-potential asset-in-use" or "asset-in-exchange." That is, the firm can either sacrifice or transform assets to generate revenues and profits or accumulate and recapitalise assets to capture realised or unrealised holding gains that inflate earnings (Dichev and Penman, 2007: 10).

IFRS 13 and FAS 157 are, as we have noted, the cornerstone accounting standards that outline the principles and techniques governing the process of FVA. Both IFRS 13 and FAS 157 employ a fair value hierarchy that prioritises the inputs that should be used to construct the fair value of an asset. Level one inputs are based on observable market data, level two inputs are those other than quoted market data and level three valuations are where the reporting entity can employ judgements and modelling. These judgements are based on best estimates about the behaviour of market participants and how they would price the asset or liability, specifically assumptions about future cash flows and the cost of capital employed to discount expected cash flows. Whether market prices or estimates are being employed, there is a speculative element attached to valuing assets at their fair value. The challenge for accountants is to estimate fair values accurately and this involves reducing the scope for discretion. Where identical assets trade in liquid markets this information provides a reliable valuation but discretion and judgement are often required where asset values have to be estimated or modelled (Ryan, 2008; Barker and Schulte, 2017).

EU Directive 2013/34 states:

> The recognition and measurement of some items in financial statements are based on estimates, judgements and models rather than exact depictions. As a result of the uncertainties inherent in business activities, certain items in financial statements cannot be measured precisely but can only be estimated. Estimation involves judgements based on the latest available reliable information.
>
> *(para. 22)*

While for the IASB:

> To a large extent, financial reports are based on estimates, judgements and models rather than exact depictions. The Conceptual Framework establishes the concepts that underlie those estimates, judgements and models.[3]
>
> *(IASB, 2013: 196)*

These judgements about the valuation of assets should be on the basis of how investors, creditors and other lenders would assess the contribution of an asset or liability. The IASB document continues:

> The IASB believes that the relevance of a particular measurement will depend on how investors, creditors and other lenders are likely to assess how an asset or a liability of that type will contribute to the entity's future cash flows.
>
> *(IASB, 2013: 108)*

There is a general understanding that investors are interested in knowing the current market value of a firm's assets and liabilities and net worth rather than the historic cost of a firm's balance sheet. Gigler, Kanodia and Venugopalan (2013: 2) suggest:

> While the arguments supporting fair value accounting are not based on any formal analytical models that we are aware of, the intuition underlying its support seems to be

the following. The current market values of a firm's assets and liabilities are much more descriptive of a firm's financial position/wealth than their historical acquisition cost.[4]

In terms of informing investors it is argued that fair value information provides valuations that reflect the fundamental performance of the firm and this contributes to informing investors and makes the capital market more efficient. This logic surrounding the use of fair values to adjust information recorded in financial statements and disclosures has, according to Gigler *et al.*, (2013) become "obvious and compelling" and thus a proliferation of accounting standards deal with the mechanics of fair value accounting for financial instruments, tangible and intangible assets, property, biological assets and business combinations.

The adoption of FVA by the FASB and the IASB was primarily justified in terms of informing investors so as to enhance capital market efficiency and thereby reduce the cost of capital. A recent comprehensive review of the academic evidence on financial reporting and its impact on capital market efficiency carried out by the Institute of Chartered Accountants in England and Wales (ICAEW) concluded:

> It is not possible, however, to draw indisputable conclusions on the overall effects of mandatory IFRS adoption based on the available research. Different researchers arrive at different conclusions.
>
> *(ICAEW, 2014: 6)*

In the next sub-section we argue that the adoption of FVA can be contextualised within an alternative framework of analysis that we describe as the financialized firm. This framing is employed to evaluate and reveal contradictions and ambiguities that can arise from the adoption of FVA in terms of firm-level financial fragility and stability.

3.2 Installing FVA in the financialized firm

Our argument here is that the adoption of new forms of accounting disclosure need to be stress tested within the context of the financialized firm. Krippner (2005) observes that non-financial firms increasingly resemble financial firms in terms of the structure of their balance sheets and it is important to understand how this impacts on corporate behaviour. Our argument is that the adoption of FVA allows firms to adjust the value of their assets to a market value informed by active market prices or judgements and modelling about market values. The outcome is that the asset structure of a firm's balance sheet blends both assets at cost and increasingly assets at a market valuation. Thus asset values recorded on balance sheets of non-financial firms increasingly resemble that of financial firms that trade in financial instruments. FVA adjustments to a firm's assets are essentially speculative values extracted from active secondary markets that trade assets or estimates and modelling that mimics these speculative market conditions. Thus asset values recorded on a firm's balance sheet have the potential to become unstable because they are increasingly connected to stock and bond prices, securitized asset prices, property market conditions and other volatile capital markets.

FVA adjusts the reported value of a firm's assets but these line items are not isolated; rather they are interconnected by virtue of double-entry bookkeeping that adjusts assets in line with liabilities. We could envisage a relatively immaterial adjustment to the market value of a firm's assets triggering off a material financial disturbance elsewhere in the accounts. For example, a relatively small adjustment in the value of a firm's marketable securities could undermine reported profits and thereby also undermine retained earnings reserves reported within shareholder equity. Plihon (2002), for example, consolidates this understanding about accounting as a networked transmission system observing that when adjustments are made to one-line item changes these are not confined to a single set of accounting records but trigger compound effects. Plihon makes the point that financial fragility results from relatively immaterial adjustments to one-line items translating into material impacts elsewhere in the financial statements. This connectivity between line items can generate unintended consequences. For example they can undermine liquidity; compromise solvency; damage credit ratings; force the sale of assets; and amplify downsizing (Plihon, 2002).

In the financialized firm Lazonick (2011, 2013) draws attention to the fact that US and European firms are now distributing more of their profit as dividends and share buy-backs for treasury stock. These distributions are so high that there is very little surplus profit carried forward into the firm's shareholder equity to accumulate as retained earnings. This means that the financial fragility of firms is heightened because potential asset value impairments would be charged to retained earnings reserves but these are being hollowed out. Table 17.1 reveals that the Standard and Poor's (S&P) 500 group of companies distributed approximately 90 per cent of their earnings as dividends and share buy-backs over the period 2011–2016.

Froud *et al.* (2006) argue that the potential for speculative asset values to become impaired is amplified because numbers and optimistic narratives combine to justify and inflate market values. On the technical side of things numbers are employed to represent the growth in an asset's earnings and also construct the discount rate for the cost of capital. However, these technical calculations are also supplemented with narratives that tend to exaggerate the capacity for financial transformation. There is therefore a tendency for asset markets to promote the vendibility of assets at the expense of their serviceability, with the result that the underlying earnings of these assets bear only a distant relation to their current market valuations.

To construct our framework of analysis we employ a series of key ratios to evaluate the adoption of FVA within the financialized firm (see Figure 17.1). Our investigation focuses on the S&P 500 group of firms which have adopted FVA since 2001 and specifically focuses on the recording of goodwill which reflects the difference between an acquired company's book value and its stock market value. The adoption of FVA accounting modified how goodwill is accounted for because this line item now accumulates on the asset side of a firm's balance sheet and is periodically tested to establish whether this is impaired[5] (see also KPMG, 2014). Previously goodwill would have been amortised as an annual charge against earnings and absorbed by a reduction in retained reserves in shareholder equity. Goodwill therefore represents the absorption of market value into the acquiring firm's accounts and is at risk if it is assessed to have become impaired (Biondi, 2013).

A first key ratio describing the financialized firm is the earnings distribution ratio which reveals the extent to which the share of earnings distributed as dividends and share buy-backs is increasing. A further important ratio reveals the relation between retained earnings held in reserves and goodwill. Specifically, the ratio of goodwill to retained earnings minus treasury

Table 17.1 US S&P 500 dividends and share buy-backs out of earnings

	Operating earnings mill $	Dividends mill $	Share Buy-backs mill $	Dividends and Share buy-backs mill $	As a share of earnings %
2011–2016	$4,596.21	$1,605.74	$2,476.56	$4,082.30	89

Source: www.spdji.com/indices/equity/sp-500

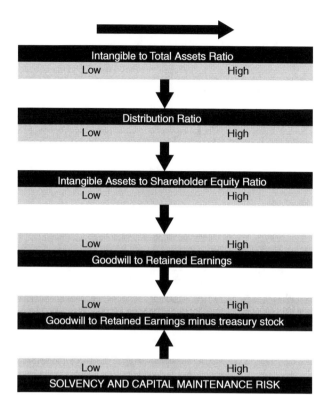

Figure 17.1 Key ratios employed to review the adoption of FVA within the financialized firm.

Source: adapted from Haslam, Tsisianis, Hoinaru, Andersson and Katechos, 2016.

Notes: For definitions of data employed to construct these ratios see Endnote.[6]

stock reveals the extent to which a firm is accumulating a reserves that could absorb goodwill impairment. Our argument is that the net retained earnings after deducting treasury stock provides an important financial buffer, similar to a bank's regulatory capital, thereby acting to contain or hedge the risk of insolvency.

4 Asset impairment risk: fragility and instability in the financialized firm

The absorption of goodwill into the S&P 500 continues to accumulate as firms also continue to acquire other firms in an active market for corporate control. In the US the typical market to book value multiple averages 3:1; that is, the market value of acquisitions is roughly three times that of their recorded book value. Goodwill arising out of corporate acquisitions will continue to accumulate on the acquiring firm's balance sheet because it is not amortised. In 2014 we estimate that the US S&P 500 group of firms had an accumulated goodwill on balance sheet amounting to $2.2 trillion (see Figure 17.1). Although this goodwill was only equivalent to 8 per cent of the total assets recorded on the balance sheet of the S&P 500 it is, as we will now argue, a significant item relative to the annual net income and stock of retained earnings reserves held within shareholder equity.

In the year 2000 the ratio of goodwill to net income in the S&P 500 stood at 2:1, and by the year 2014 this had increased to 2.5:1 (see Figure 17.2). A relatively minor goodwill impairment would have a significant impact on S&P 500 net income, for example, just a 10 per cent impairment of goodwill in 2014 would have reduced net earnings per share (EPS) by one-quarter and this, in turn, would immediately have a negative impact on stock market valuations because EPS is employed to construct equity valuations.

Figure 17.3 shows the distribution of net income to dividends and share buy-backs for a matched group of firms, that is, the same firms for which we have data for both years. The banded ratio reveals the share of firms in the sample of 444 that distribute between *x* and *y* per cent of their net incomes. The general pattern observable in this chart is for an increased number of firms listed in the S&P 500 to distribute more of their net income to shareholders over the

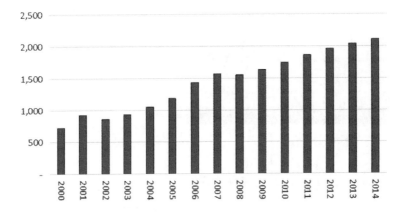

Figure 17.2 S&P 500 goodwill accumulation 2000–2014 in dollars.

Source: Thomson Analytics Datastream S&P 500 data.

Note: Sample consists of 444 paired S&P 500 firms; that is, all firms for which we have data on total assets and intangible assets over the complete period.

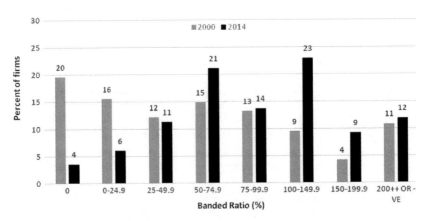

Figure 17.3 S&P 500 disbursements to shareholders out of net income (distribution of firms).

Source: Thomson Analytics Datastream S&P 500 data.

Note: Sample consists of 444 paired S&P 500 firms with all firms having data on net income, dividends and share buy-backs across both time periods.

period 2000–2014. In 2000, 24 per cent of firms in our S&P 500 matched sample distributed dividends and share buy-backs in excess of their net income but by 2014 some 44 per cent of firms were distributing more to shareholders than their net income generated. Lazonick (2014: 46) argues that this high distribution of profit to shareholders leads to a culture of downsizing and distributing because, in an era of shareholder value, there is very little headroom for productive re-investment:

> Consider the 449 companies in the S&P 500 index that were publicly listed from 2003 through 2012. During that period those companies used 54% of their earnings—a total of $2.4 trillion—to buy back their own stock, almost all through purchases on the open market. Dividends absorbed an additional 37% of their earnings. That left very little for investments in productive capabilities or higher incomes for employees.

Our findings also confirm that the S&P 500 group of firms are distributing a higher proportion of net income as dividends and share buy-backs during the period 2000 to 2014 and this, we argue impacts upon the accumulation of profit reserves in shareholder equity. The accumulation of profit reserves, after deducting dividends and treasury stock, is accumulating at a slower rate than the accumulation of goodwill. In Figures 17.4 and 17.5 we estimate the number of firms listed in the S&P 500 that have recorded goodwill that exceeds their accumulated reserves reported in shareholder equity. The information employed to construct these charts is outlined in Table 17.2. For the first group of firms we are able to subtract accumulated treasury stock balances from retained earnings but for the second group we are estimating the retained earnings minus treasury stock by subtracting from the total shareholder equity the accumulated original paid in capital including share premiums.

The analysis for both Figures 17.4 and 17.5 reveals a similar pattern. Roughly 50 per cent of firms listed in the S&P 500 are operating with accumulated goodwill that exceed their retained earnings after deducting treasury stock. If these firms were to write down their goodwill this could potentially erode paid-in capital exacerbating financial fragility and amplifying financial instability.

Our aggregate analysis reveals that US firms are absorbing market value onto their balance sheets as they account for the difference between the market and book values of acquisitions as goodwill. These financialized firms are aggressively distributing more of their profits as

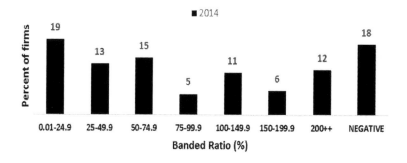

Figure 17.4   Goodwill/retained earnings minus treasury stock.

Source: Thomson Analytics Datastream S&P 500 data.

Note: Sample consists of 257 paired S&P 500 firms with all firms having data on treasury stock and retained earnings. A negative ratio results because the retained earnings after deducting treasury stock are negative.

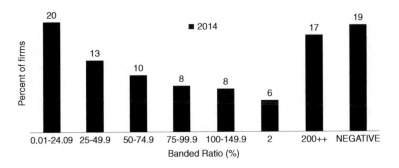

Figure 17.5 Goodwill/retained earnings minus treasury stock (approximated).

Source: Thomson Analytics Datastream S&P 500 data.

Note: Sample consists of 159 paired S&P 500 firms with all firms having data on paid-in capital including premiums and total shareholder equity (see Table 17.1). A negative ratio results because the deduction of paid-in capital from shareholder equity results in a deficit figure.

Table 17.2 Data employed to construct Figures 17.4 and 17.5

For the year ended 2014 for S&P 500 firms	Figure 17.4	Figure 17.5
Accumulated common stock and additional paid in capital	X	X
Plus accumulated retained earnings	X	Approximation for retained earnings minus treasury stock
Minus accumulated treasury stock	(Y)	
Plus/minus other comprehensive income	X or (Y)	
= Total shareholder equity	Z	Z
Number of firms with data	257	159

Notes: Figure 17.4 employs the data for 257 matched firms where we have both accumulated retained earnings and treasury stock disclosed in 2014. For Figure 17.5 we have subtracted accumulated common stock and additional paid-in capital (including share premiums) from total shareholder equity to obtain an estimate of the retained earnings after deducting treasury stock (noting that this will also capture comprehensive income adjustments).

dividends and share buy-backs and this is reducing the accumulation of retained earnings to the point where many firms could not absorb a significant goodwill impairment. In circumstances where retained earnings reserves are completely hollowed out, asset impairments would immediately need to be written off against paid-in capital. In Table 17.3 we employ three company cases to reveal the extent to which retained earnings reserves are being hollowed out relative to goodwill: Microsoft; Pfizer; and Hewlett-Packard.

These three company cases illustrate the extent to which retained earnings can be hollowed through the distribution of dividends and share buy-backs for treasury stock. In the case of Pfizer retained earnings are negative and there is also a negative comprehensive income reserve arising out of charging pension fund deficits and currency translation losses. In this specific case any goodwill impairments would immediately erode paid-in capital and a relatively modest 10 per cent goodwill impairment would reduce net income by one-quarter. Companies like Microsoft have also pursued aggressive dividends and share buy-back policies, which has eroded retained earnings to $2.3bn with goodwill standing at $18bn and so

Table 17.3 Goodwill and retained earnings reserves in Pfizer, Microsoft and Hewlett-Packard

	Pfizer $ mill	Microsoft $ mill	Hewlett-Packard $ mill
For Year 2015–6			
Paid-in capital	81,501	68,178	1,981
Retained earnings	-7,259	2,282	32,089
Other comprehensive income	-9,522	1,537	-6,302
Retained earnings plus comprehensive income	-16,781	3,819	25,787
Goodwill	48,242	17,872	32,941
Net income	16,700	6,960	4,554

Source: Edgar Securities and Exchange Commission datasets. www.sec.gov

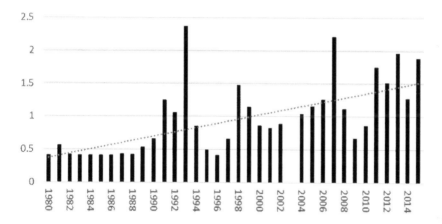

Figure 17.6 Pfizer dividends and share buy-backs to net income ratio from 1980 to 2015.
Source: Thomson analytics datastream S&P 500 data.

a relatively small goodwill impairment charge would erode paid-in capital and undermine reported net income. Hewlett-Packard has maintained retained earnings to a level that would absorb a significant goodwill impairment but even a relatively small write-down would significantly damage reported net earnings.

In the Pfizer case we observe that over the period 1980 to 2015 the ratio of distributed net income increases from roughly 50 per cent of profits to levels that are consistently in excess of profits generated by the company (see Figure 17.6). During the period 1980 to 2015, Pfizer's accumulated net income was roughly $100 billion with dividends roughly $100 billion and share buy-backs $105 billion. In order to maintain the payment of dividends and purchase of stock buy-backs that exceeded net income, Pfizer was using debt to finance equity distributions. When a firm makes share repurchases these are recorded at their market value and shown as reducing retained earnings in shareholder equity on the balance sheet.

The Pfizer case also illustrates that treasury stock is a fluid balance because repurchased shares can subsequently be employed to finance future acquisitions; that is, Pfizer's deals have been financed by a mix of cash plus its own treasury shares. For example, the deal to purchase the Wyeth pharmaceuticals company in 2010 for $68 billion involved Pfizer paying for the deal with a mix of borrowing, cash reserves plus its own shares issued from treasury stock. The market value of these treasury stock shares was $17.19 per share and accounted for roughly 34 per cent of the deal.

Under the terms of the deal, Pfizer would pay $50.19 a share for the company — $33 a share in cash and 0.985 Pfizer shares worth $17.19 a share based on Pfizer's closing price on Friday. That is roughly a 29 percent premium over the share price before word of the deal leaked on Friday.

(Sorkin and Wilson, 2009)

After the acquisition of Wyeth, Pfizer's earnings per share (EPS) deteriorated but the promise to investors was that a more aggressive stock buy-back campaign would strengthen its EPS. Within two years of the acquisition roughly $20 billion had been spent on share buy-backs, a figure roughly equivalent to the company's spending on R&D during the same period:

Pfizer has begun buying back stock following a hiatus after its $68 billion purchase of Wyeth in 2009, but the purchases have been modest so far, at $1 billion in 2010. A more aggressive buyback of $5 billion to $6 billion annually in the next five years could lift the company's profit to more than $2.60 a share by 2015, speculates one shareholder. An even bigger buyback program of $8 billion to $9 billion annually could lift profit to almost $2.90 a share.

(Bary, 2010)

Treasury stock and goodwill are interconnected line items. This is because the treasury stock employed to finance acquisitions such as for Wyeth would be reported as reducing the balance of treasury stock. If the balance of treasury stock is reduced then this would serve to inflate shareholder funds (see jump in shareholder equity from 2008 to 2009). However, the subsequent aggressive buy-back of shares to replenish treasury stock and inflate the reported EPS would then show up as a progressive reduction in shareholder equity from 2010 onwards. In Figure 17.7 Pfizer's goodwill ratchets relative to shareholder equity because goodwill is accumulating after each acquisition whilst retained earnings are being depleted by an aggressive dividends and buy-back program. In Pfizer retained earnings balances reduce relative to goodwill accumulations as the process of financial engineering sets these two line items on divergent trajectories contributing to financial fragility and heightening the risk of financial instability.

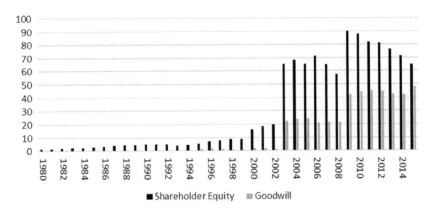

Figure 17.7   Pfizer shareholder equity and goodwill in dollars from 1980 to 2015.
Source: Thomson Analytics Datastream S&P 500 data.

5 Discussion and concluding observations

In this chapter we have argued that changes to accounting practise and disclosure should be evaluated within the context of the financialized firm, in order to reveal contradictions and a heightened risk to society. The reorientation of accounting practise from HCA to FVA has been widely justified within an investor-capital market frame that focuses on the provision of decision-useful information to investors so as to promote capital market efficiency and reduce the cost of capital. The users and preparers of firm financial statements are generally supportive of the adoption of FVA because it records 'real' transactions at their market value and this is information that investors tell the regulatory agencies they want to see produced. That is, accounting disclosures now reflect current economic realities where economic theory guides accounting practice (Barker and Schulte, 2017). The adoption of FVA, by way of contrast, troubles accountants because, according to Littleton, it shifts the focus of financial statements from the income statement to the balance sheet and the adjustment of balance sheet asset values to their market values. This objection is also founded upon the argument that accounting disclosures should both reflect and inform a conservative and prudent stewardship of resources in order to ensure capital maintenance (Hoogervorst, 2012; FRC, 2014). Others, including Biondi (2011) and Maystadt (2013), have argued that the adoption of FVA, and specifically with regards to the valuation of financial instruments, may have contributed to the financial crisis in the banking sector.

In this chapter we argue that it is necessary to stress test changes to accounting standards in relation to firm financial fragility and stability rather than adhere to the narrow requirements of investors and the promotion of capital market efficiency. To reinforce this conceptual shift we also argue that it is necessary to contextualise the installation of new accounting practices and the disclosure requirements within financialized firms. Drawing on three elements from the financialization literature we construct an understanding of the financialized firm: (i) Krippner's (2005) observation that non-financial firms are becoming more like financial firms; (ii) Lazonick's (2013) argument that US firms and their European counterparts are aggressively distributing earnings at the expense of re-investing; and Froud *et al.'s* (2006) argument that numbers and narratives combine to inflate capital valuations ahead of their putative earnings capacity where this intangible component of an assets value is volatile (Veblen, 2005; Haslam *et al.*, 2012).

In line with Krippner's argument the adoption of FVA makes non-financial firms more like financial firms, that is, the non-financial firm's balance sheet increasingly resembles a bundle of speculative financial instruments. Asset values are being adjusted on the basis of future earnings discounted back in time to generate a current market value (Palea, 2015). This process of adjusting asset values to a market value conjoins the firm's asset values to secondary markets that by their nature are volatile. In this chapter we focus on accounting for goodwill which records the difference between the book and the market values of acquired firms. This goodwill is no longer amortised but is accumulating on the balance sheet whilst being periodically assessed to establish if it is impaired.

Our analysis also confirms that US firms in the S&P 500 are distributing a higher proportion of their net income (Lazonick, 2013), and many are paying out more than they earn as profit in a given year. Thus many firms are now using borrowings to finance dividends and share buy-backs. This aggressive distribution of earnings is, we argue, hollowing out retained earnings which, like a bank's regulatory capital, is intended to serve as a buffer to absorb any adverse changes to the market value of assets held on balance sheet. What now matters is the interconnectivity between one accounting line item and another as identified by Plihon (2002) who observes that relatively immaterial adjustments to one line item could compromise another line item which also happens to be a key signifier for credit rating agencies, a key financial element in a bond covenant or solvency test.

Our analysis of the S&P 500 reveals that the goodwill recorded on the balance sheet is accumulating ahead of the retained earnings component of shareholder equity which is a financial buffer available to absorb asset value impairments. From a position of relatively robust reserves, in relation to asset value at risk, the S&P 500 is drifting further towards a situation of financial fragility and impending financial instability. Asset impairments can also undermine reported net income and again we argue that relatively small adjustment to a line item like goodwill would undermine earnings and trigger corporate restructuring. The company cases also reveal a different perspective on the interconnectedness of line items and although goodwill and treasury stock are interrelated line items, with one feeding the inflation of the other, these line items are on different trajectories in the financialized firm.

The adoption of FVA was justified on the basis that it would provide decision-useful information to investors and thereby would also contribute to making capital markets more efficient. The central argument of this chapter is that it is necessary to evaluate and stress test changes in accounting standards and their impact on reported firm financials. Specifically, we argue that changes to accounting disclosure need to be contextualised within the financialized firm. On the financialized firm's balance sheet assets now congeal speculative valuations at risk of being impaired but this risk is not being hedged by reserves because these are themselves being hollowed out. In the context of the financialized firm the adoption of FVA is leaving firms financially fragile and at heightened risk of instability.

This chapter was submitted by the authors with the following title: "Stress testing the adoption of fair value accounting (FVA): fragility and instability in financialized firms."

Notes

1   www.ifrs.org/use-around-the-world/education/fvm/documents/educationfairvaluemeasurement.pdf
2   www.fasb.org/cs/BlobServer?blobkey=id&blobwhere=1175823288587&blobheader=application/pdf
    &blobcol=urldata&blobtable=MungoBlobs
3   www.ifrs.org/Current-Projects/IASB-Projects/Conceptual-Framework/Discussion-Paper-
    July-2013/Documents/Discussion-Paper-Conceptual-Framework-July-2013.pdf
4   http://laef.ucsb.edu/pages/conferences/aae13/papers/kanodia.pdf
5.   *Common equity* Shareholders' equity data represents common shareholders' investment in a company. It
    includes but is not restricted to: common stock value; retained earnings; capital surplus; capital stock
    premium; and goodwill written off. *Retained earnings*. Retained earnings represent the accumulated
    after tax earnings of the company which have not been distributed as dividends to shareholders or
    allocated to a reserve account. *Treasury stock* Treasury stock represents the acquisition cost of shares
    held by the company. This stock is not entitled to dividends, has no voting rights and does not share
    in the profits in the event of liquidation. *Paid-in capital = common stock + capital surplus* Common stock
    represents the par or stated value of the issued common shares of the company. It includes the value
    of all multiple shares. Capital surplus represents the amount received in excess of par value from the
    sale of common stock. *Goodwill/Cost in excess of assets purchased*, net goodwill represents the excess cost
    over the fair market value of the net assets purchased. It is included in other intangible assets.
6   www.fasb.org/jsp/FASB/Document_C/DocumentPage?cid=1218220124961&acceptedDisclaimer=true

References

AAA. (1966). *A Statement of Basic Accounting Theory*, Evanston, IL: American Accounting Association.
Barker, R. and Schulte (2017). "Representing the market perspective: fair value measurement for non-
    financial assets," *Accounting, Organizations and Society*, 56: 55–67.

Barth, M. (2007). "Standard-setters, measurement issues, and the relevance of research," *Accounting and Business Research*, 37(3): 7–15.

Barth, M. and W. R. Landsman (2010). "How did financial reporting contribute to the financial crisis?" http://www.bde.es/f/webpi/SES/seminars/2010/files/sie1007.pdf.

Bary, A. (2010) "A prescription for growth." *Barron's*. http://www.barrons.com/articles/SB500014240529 702046502045760038022131336870

Biondi, Y. (2011). "The pure logic of accounting: a critique of the fair value revolution," *Accounting, Economics and Law*, 1(1): article 7.

Biondi, Y. (2012). "What do shareholders do? Accounting, ownership and the theory of the firm: implications for corporate governance and reporting," *Accounting Economics and Law: A Convivium*, 2(2): 2152–820.

Biondi, Y. (2013). "Hyman Minsky's financial instability hypothesis and the accounting structure of economy," *Accounting, Economics and Law: A Convivium*, 3(3): 141–66.

Chambers, R. (1965). "Measurement in accounting," *Journal of Accounting Research*, 3(1): 32–62.

Chambers, R. (1966). *Accounting, Evaluation and Economic Behavior*, Upper Saddle River, NJ: Prentice Hall.

Ditchev, I. and S. Penman (2007). On the Balance Sheet Model of Financial Reporting, Columbia Business School, Centre for Excellence in Accounting and Security Analysis. http://www8.gsb.columbia.edu/sites/ceasa/files/files/Dichev_final.pdf.

Edwards, E. and P. Bell (1964). *The Theory and Measurement of Business Income*, Berkeley, CA: University of California Press.

Emerson, T., K. Karim and R. Rutledge (2010). "Fair value accounting: a historical review of the most controversial accounting issue in decades," *Journal of Business & Economics Research* 8(4): 77–86.

Epstein, G. (2005). *Financialization and the World Economy*, Northampton, MA: Edward Elgar, USA.

FASB (2008). *Statement of Financial Accounting Concepts No. 1: Objectives of Financial Reporting by Business Enterprises*. http://www.fasb.org/resources/ccurl/816/894/aop_CON1.pdf.

FRC (2014). "True and Fair." https://www.frc.org.uk/FRC-Documents/Accounting-and-Reporting/True-and-Fair-June-2014.pdf.

Froud, J., S. Johal, A. Leaver and K. Williams (2006). *Financialization and Strategy: Narrative and Numbers*, London: Routledge.

Gigler, F., C. Kanodia and R. Venugopalan (2013). "Who benefits from fair value accounting? an equilibrium analysis with strategic complementarities." http://laef.ucsb.edu/pages/conferences/aae13/papers/kanodia.pdf.

Haslam, C., T. Andersson, N. Tsitsianis and Y. P. Yin, (2012): *Redefining Business Models: Strategies for Financialized World*, London: Routledge.

Haslam, C., N. Tstsianis, R. Hoinaru, T. Andersson and G. Katechos (2016). "Stress testing International Financial Reporting Standards (IFRS): accounting for stability and the public good in a financialized world," London: Queen Mary University.

Hoogervorst, H. (2012). "The concept of prudence: dead or alive?" FEE Conference on Corporate Reporting of the Future, September, Brussels. http://www.ifrs.org/Alerts/PressRelease/Documents/2012/Concept%20of%20Prudence%20speech.pdf.

Hopwood, A. G. (2009). "The economic crisis and accounting: implications for the research community," *Accounting, Organizations and Society*, 34 (6–7): 797–802.

IASB (2013). "A review of the conceptual framework for financial reporting," Discussion paper: DP/2013/1. http://www.ifrs.org/Current-Projects/IASB-Projects/Conceptual-Framework/Discussion-Paper-July-2013/Documents/Discussion-Paper-Conceptual-Framework-July-2013.pdf.

ICAEW (2014). "The effects of mandatory IFRS adoption in the EU: a review of empirical research." http://www.icaew.com/~/media/Files/Technical/Financial-reporting/Information%20for%20better%20markets/IFBM/effects-of-mandatory-ifrs-adoption-oct2014-execsum.pdf.

IFRS (2013). "The Conceptual Framework," Capital Markets Advisory Committee meeting. http://www.ifrs.org/Meetings/MeetingDocs/Other%20Meeting/2013/March/AP%203%20conceptual%20framework.pdf.

KPMG (2014). "Who cares about goodwill impairment? a collection of stakeholder views." http://www.kpmg.com/CN/en/IssuesAndInsights/ArticlesPublications/Documents/Who-cares-about-goodwill-impairment-O-201404.pdf.

Krippner, G. (2005). "The financialization of the American economy," *Socio-Economic Review*, 3(2): 173–207

Lazonick, W. (2011). "Reforming the financialized business corporation." http://50.87.169.168/Documents/EPRN/Lazonick-Reforming-the-Financialized-Corporation.pdf.

Lazonick, W. (2013). "The financialization of the U.S. corporation: what has been lost, and how it can be regained." https://www.google.co.uk/search?hl=en&q=lazonick+financialization&ei=dHDsVLqPGd GO7Qa5qoCgAQ.

Lazonick, W. (2014). "Profits without prosperity," *Harvard Business Review*, 92(5): 46–55.

Littleton, A. (2011). "Economists and accountants," *Accounting, Economics and Law: A Convivium*, 1(2), article 2.

Maystadt, P. (2013). Should IFRS standards be more "European"? http://ec.europa.eu/finance/accounting/docs/governance/reform/131112_report_en.pdf.

Morgan, G. (1988). "Accounting as reality construction: towards a new epistemology for accounting practice," *Accounting, Organizations and Society*, 13(5): 477–85.

Orhangazi, O. (2008). *Financialization and the US Economy*, Northampton, MA: Edward Elgar Publishers.

Palea, V. (2015). "The politics of fair value reporting and the governance of the standards-setting process: critical issues and pitfalls from a European perspective," *Critical Perspectives on Accounting*, 29: 1–102.

Palley, T. (2007). "Financialization: what it is and why it matters," Working Paper No. 525, Levy Economics Institute and Economics for Democratic and Open Societies, Washington, D.C. http://www.levyinstitute.org/pubs/wp_525.pdf.

Penman, S. (1973). "A framework for the development of a theory of financial accounting," *University of Queensland papers*, volume 2. https://espace.library.uq.edu.au/view/UQ:221172/HF5625_P46_1973_v2no4.pdf.

Plihon, D. (2002). "Rentabilite´ et risque dans le nouveau régime de croissance." Commissariat Général du Plan – No. 69, October. http://www.ladocumentationfrancaise.fr/var/storage/rapports-publics/024000552.pdf.

Power, M. (2010). "Fair value accounting, financial economics and the transformation of reliability," *Accounting and Business Research*, 40(3): 197–210.

Ronen, J. (2008). "To fair value or not to fair value: a broader perspective," *ABACUS*, 44(2): 181–208.

Ryan, S. (2008). "Fair value accounting: understanding the issues raised by the credit crunch". Council of Institutional Investors. www.sib.wa.gov/information/pr/white_paper.pdf40. Sorkin, A. R. and D. Wilson (2009). "Pfizer agrees to pay $68 for rival drug maker Wyeth," *New York Times*. www.nytimes.com/2009/01/26/business/26drug.html?_r=0.

Tarca, A. (2012). "The case for global accountings: arguments and evidence." www.ifrs.org/use-around-the-world/documents/case-for-global-accounting-standards-arguments-and-evidence.pdf.

Whitley, R. (1986). "The transformation of business finance into financial economics: the roles of academic expansion and changes in US capital markets," *Accounting, Organizations and Society*, 11(2): 171–92.

Veblen, T. (2005). *The Theory of Business Enterprise*, New York: Cosimo Inc.

Zeff, S. (1999). "The evolution of the conceptual framework for business enterprises in the United States," *Accounting Historians Journal*, 26(2): 89–131.

18

GLOBALISATION

Cameron Graham

1 Introduction

Globalisation has now become an underlying theme in critical accounting research. This is to say, in the past decade it has to a certain extent ceased to be a distinct topic and has become embedded as an assumption in a broad range of critical accounting studies. In this chapter, I will attempt to unpack this new, indirect perspective on the topic to see how accounting theories of globalisation have developed since my previous essay on this theme, Graham and Neu (2003).

In 2003, we argued that accounting researchers seeking to understand globalisation should attend to the roles of supranational institutions. We argued that these institutions, such as the World Bank and the World Trade Organization, facilitate the various flows across national boundaries that characterise globalisation at the operational level. While there have been several important studies of supranational institutions during the past decade or so, much has changed in the world since that essay was written. Accounting researchers have, as a result, moved in a number of important new directions. I will try to make sense of this growing and diverse set of studies, and then consider the question of where we might seek to go next. I will argue that critical accounting research on globalisation must come to terms, in some way, with Foucault's (2008) notion of biopolitics and the theorisation of globalisation developed by Hardt and Negri (2000). Building on Martinez (2011), I will argue that Hardt and Negri draw our attention to the micro-processes of globalisation that occur beyond disciplinary enclosures like corporations and factories, and that it is these that we must attend to if we are to understand the mechanisms of globalisation today.

In our 2003 paper, Dean Neu and I reviewed the globalisation literature in accounting to that point in time. We argued that 'globalisation' had become something of a catchphrase for research on the spread of consumer capitalism across the globe. A significant emphasis of accounting research on globalisation at that time was on institutions that enabled flows of capital and the territorial extension of market principles. We said that a closer examination of detailed accounting practices, particularly within supranational institutions like the World Bank, was needed to enrich our understanding of how accounting facilitates globalisation. Using a Foucauldian theorisation of accounting as a social technology, we proposed that accounting researchers should look beyond the obvious topics of capital market expansion and accounting regulation harmonisation, to see how accounting was implicated in various flows across national boundaries. These flows, we suggested, included not just flows of capital and products, but flows of information, policies and people.

Since the paper was published, critical accounting research has itself become more global in scope. Studies of non-Western countries are increasingly common. For instance, researchers have in the past decade or so examined accounting practices in South Asia (Ahmed, Hopper and Wickramasinghe, 2012; Belal, Spence, Carter and Zhu, 2017; Mir and Rahaman, 2005), Southeast Asia (Yapa, Jacobs, Huot and Parker, 2016), Latin America (Neu and Ocampo, 2007; Neu, Ocampo, Graham and Heincke, 2006; Neu, Silva and Ocampo Gomez, 2008), the Middle East (Al-Twaijry, Brierley and Gwilliam, 2003; Kamla, 2012), the South Pacific (Chand, 2005; Chand and White, 2007) and Africa (Neu, Rahaman, Everett and Akindayomi, 2010; Rahaman, Everett and Neu, 2007). Some attention has also been paid to Russia (Mennicken, 2008; Samsonova, 2009). Studies of China, which represents a special case because of its enormous influence on the global economy, have become prevalent (Ezzamel and Xiao, 2015; Ezzamel, Xiao and Pan, 2007; O'Connor, Chow and Wu, 2004; Yee, 2012; Zhang, Andrew and Rudkin, 2012). This diversity is promising because attention to regional and local mechanisms of globalisation is very much needed if we are to avoid unhelpful generalisations.

Regional and country-specific studies have thus examined a wide range of ways that accounting is implicated in globalisation in these countries. The traditional broad topics of accounting research are, of course, well represented. These include financial reporting and its regulation (*inter alia*, Arnold, 2012; Bozanic, Dirsmith and Huddart, 2012; Chiapello and Medjad, 2009; Ezzamel *et al.*, 2007); management accounting (Cooper and Ezzamel, 2013; Hopper, Tsamenyi, Uddin and Wickramasinghe, 2009; Macintosh, Shearer and Riccaboni, 2009; Martinez, 2011); auditing (Barrett, Cooper and Jamal, 2005; Mennicken, 2008; Okike, 2004; Samsonova, 2009; Sikka, 2009); and the accounting profession (Annisette and Trivedi, 2013; Boussebaa, 2015; Cooper and Robson, 2006; Sikka, 2008). Other studies on less traditional topics have also appeared. To dig deeper into this diverse collection of studies, I turn first to critical accounting studies of supranational organisations, as we had advocated in 2003. Then I will explore the various ways in which critical accounting scholars have moved well beyond what we had considered to be of paramount importance at that time.

In developing the following brief review, I have tried not to be too critical about what it means to be 'critical'. That is, I have not imposed too strict a definition on what counts as critical research. Instead, I have looked for research that has stretched the boundaries and pushed the assumptions of globalisation research in the field of accounting. This is consistent with a pragmatist's approach to research, wherein the goal is not to achieve convergence but instead to foster a proliferation of ideas (Rorty, 1991). I have therefore sought out examples of interesting research rather than attempting an exhaustive review of globalisation literature. The purpose here is to understand better where accounting research on globalisation can go, rather than to document every contribution to where it is.

2 The roles of supranational organisations

Recent work on supranational organisations has been led by Dean Neu and his various co-authors. Others have also studied the activities of these organisations, of course. Murphy (2008), for instance, looks at how the World Bank and other financial institutions influenced the growth of Mittal Steel Corporation. Annisette (2004) argues that the World Bank, along with the International Monetary Fund (IMF), has been a key player in the imposition of accounting standards on nation states and, moreover, was subject to financial and political pressures that have led it to pursue the interests of private capital at the expense of the public interest. Such studies have offered important insights into the roles of supranational organisations in the field of accounting. However, Neu's body of work has arguably provided the most detailed examination of how supranational institutions influence the field of government within nation states, paving the way especially for global flows of capital, information and policy.

Four Neu papers in particular stand out. Neu *et al.* (2010) examine the role of the IMF in 'reforming' the African banking sector. Rahaman *et al.* (2007) provide a detailed critical study of the Ghanaian government's privatisation of water services, under the influence of the World Bank and other supranational creditors. In Latin America, Neu and Ocampo (2007) look at the diffusion of particular financial practices into national governments by the World Bank, and at the efforts by the World Bank to reform the basic education system in the region (Neu *et al.*, 2006). It is this latter article, for which I was a co-author, that I wish to examine in more detail, because it so clearly highlights the local impact of global institutions, and the impact of localisation on global projects.

In this study of the World Bank, we examine how accounting technologies were used to render the field of education governable across Latin America. The set of theoretical tools that were employed were drawn from the work of Foucault and Bourdieu. We argue that accounting and other financial expertises furnished the basis for 'informing' technologies through which the behaviour of individuals is regulated in globalisation. Accounting plays a key role in this process of informing. By capturing local social realities in inscriptions, which are then brought to centres of calculation to inform policy decisions, accounting permits intervention at the national and local levels by organisations such as the World Bank. We argue that these interventions in the lives of individuals occur by altering the necessary habitus (Bourdieu, 1990) that pertains to a field of practice such as education, and by encouraging self-disciplining activities (Foucault, 1984a) on the part of individuals in the field. Through an analysis of lending agreements and other documents pertaining to 15 of the World Bank's basic education projects in Latin America, as well as interviews with participants in the field, we argue that accounting was instrumental in implanting new technologies and in creating new visibilities to restructure the field, and most importantly in creating within the field a network of mutually monitoring agents. Amongst these agents were auditors and various agencies created for the purpose of operationalising the education reforms.

One of the key insights of this study was that accounting is used to translate and retranslate information flowing across national boundaries and into specific sites. This translation suggests how globalisation must be localised in order to successfully take root within a field of practice, and that such translations open globalisation projects to local reinterpretation. The study therefore emphasises the need for accounting researchers to study local practices in order to understand globalisation (e.g. Albu, Albu and Alexander, 2014; Cruz, Scapens and Major, 2011).

3 The roles of the accounting profession

The past decade has also seen the publication of a number of studies exploring the link between supranational institutions and the accounting profession. Of particular importance is Arnold's (2005) examination of the role of the World Trade Organization (WTO) in altering the field of accounting practice in sovereign states. Arnold shows how the WTO is opening up domestic accounting service markets to competition, in the name of free trade. She shows that the WTO effectively has been working on behalf of the Big 4 accounting firms, which lobby against domestic barriers to trade in services and then move in when these barriers are lowered.

Arnold's 2005 study demonstrates that supranational institutions are actively involved in creating markets, beneath a guise of 'natural' market demand and the rhetoric of inevitability that characterises globalisation discourse. In this particular instance, Arnold examines how the WTO, in the name of liberalising international trade, places restraints on domestic trade in accounting services. The WTO, as the final arbiter of international trade disputes (Arnold, 2005: 304), governs accounting services under the umbrella of the *General Agreement on Trade in Services* (GATS). Arnold also demonstrates how the GATS affects all domestic regulations on accounting services, even when those regulations do not discriminate against foreign accounting firms (2005: 314). The GATS, through its *Disciplines on Domestic Regulation in the Accountancy Sector* document, released in 1998, affects the ability of domestic regulators to determine the necessary qualifications for accountants and the licensing of accountants. The *Disciplines* also require that all proceedings to determine qualifications and licensing requirements be open to comment. This ensures that well-funded international firms and other lobbyists can exert influence on domestic decision making. The *Disciplines* specifically prohibit the creation of 'unnecessary' barriers to trade in accounting services beyond those that fulfill legitimate objectives. Arnold cites the Canadian Bar Association as an example of a body that has expressed concern about the impossibility of satisfying the WTO, that restrictive requirements are necessary and legitimate (2005: 317). Arnold argues that economic integration in globalisation efforts, without corresponding political integration, has led to a fragmentation of the sovereignty of nation states, a process in which accounting firms have directly participated.

The accounting profession plays a number of other significant roles in facilitating globalisation. Barrett *et al.* (2005), for example, examine the crucial role of auditing in enabling multinational companies to maintain legitimacy and attract capital. Drawing on Giddens, they argue that globalisation is dialectically related to localisation. Their theorisation of the relationship between the global and the local is consistent with the argument I am making here, that accounting researchers must study the local in order to comprehend the global.

4 The regulation of financial reporting

The accounting profession is an active player in creating the regulatory and legal apparatuses on which globalisation depends. The roll-out of regulations that facilitate capital flows has been key to globalisation, while the continuing harmonisation of accounting standards has obviously been an important part of this process. The notion of harmonisation suggests that benign global processes are at work to bring countries into alignment. Recent accounting research, however, has recognised that in order to understand these global processes, one must examine the specific processes of accounting regulation at the national level. For indeed, it is the variety of ways in which nation states have acceded to or resisted transnational influences on their autonomy that makes globalisation such a complex process.

Most recent attention given to regulation by critical accounting scholars has, therefore, been at the level of the individual nation state. Bakre (2008) examines the case of Jamaica, arguing that financial reporting not only played a crucial role in the domination and exploitation of Jamaica during the colonial period, but continues to function as a tool of exploitation in the postcolonial period. Chand and White (2007) look at the convergence of accounting standards in Fiji, arguing that important International Financial Reporting Standards (IFRS) concepts like "relevance," which means relevance to the needs of absentee owners, are poorly suited to economies like that of Fiji, where less than 4 per cent of equity in publicly traded companies is held by absentee owners (Chand and White, 2007: 611). Ezzamel *et al.* (2007) examine the relationship between political ideology and accounting regulation in China, combining a discourse analysis of public documents with the insights resulting from a set of difficult-to-obtain interviews with a wide range of actors. These document how changes in ideology since the time of Mao have made China amenable to certain modes of accounting regulation. Mir and Rahaman (2005) examine the case of Bangladesh, where international lenders pressurised the government to adopt international standards.

Mennicken (2008) and Samsonova (2009) both look at auditing regulation in post-Soviet Russia. These studies highlight the importance of local adaptation processes in the adoption of international standards. Mennicken's Latourian study is particularly important because it examines adaptation processes at the level of the audit firm. She argues that auditing standards, being less detailed than accounting standards, offer a clear opportunity to see adaptations in action. By examining how accounting firms used the notion of 'standards' to achieve institutional legitimacy and market advantage in the field of audit in Russia, she shows that, "Dreams of sameness had become enmeshed in problems and practices of exclusion" (Mennicken, 2008: 409). Thus, the notion of standardisation is shown to be a complex political process, wherein both global and local networks of interests come to determine just how and where international standards convey legitimacy and advantage.

Perhaps the most provocative critical study of regulation is the critique of European accounting standard–setting by Chiapello and Medjad (2009). It documents the fragile legitimacy of the International Accounting Standards Board (IASB), which is privately funded and unaccountable to any government oversight. According to this study, a third of its funding comes from the Big 4 accounting firms, which also occupy two of the IASB's trustee positions (2009: 453). Chiapello and Medjad also document the convoluted process by which the European Union (EU) ratifies the standards determined by the IASB, a process whereby the EU seeks to come to terms with the fact that it has no oversight of the IASB yet depends on it for its accounting regulations. By virtue of this process, member nations of the EU have effectively ceded part of their sovereignty to the IASB, argue the authors, partly because the only alternatives would be to adopt American standards (i.e. International Accounting Standards [IAS]) or to fund a costly and bureaucratic alternative to the IASB. The paper documents quite thoroughly the mechanisms by which the EU and the IASB depend on each other to provide legitimacy to the IFRS. The paper is provocative because it draws attention to the questionable legitimacy of international accounting standards, simply by documenting the 'backstage' arrangements by which the EU effectively sits standard settings.

These studies of regulation show how tenuous and artificial the processes of global regulation and harmonisation are in the field of accounting. The effort to produce accounting standards that facilitate the flow of capital across international borders, on which global capitalism depends, is constantly in tension with the need to adapt the standards to local needs, while maintaining the appearance of neutrality and independence from private interests. Yet the funding mechanisms behind these standards are largely dependent on private sources, which themselves need their funding to appear freely given and without strings attached, else the legitimacy of the standards will be called into question.

5 Accounting and the global corporation

One of the primary ways through which accounting shapes and is shaped by globalisation has to do with the embeddedness of accounting in corporations. As corporate operations extend to the transnational scale, they outstrip the capacity of individual nation states to govern them. Corporations, rather than nations, become significant contributors to the flows of capital, products, information, policies and people that characterise globalisation. Accounting plays a central role in the governance of global corporations, and hence in the governance of global capitalism. While much attention has been given by critical accounting research to financial reporting and its regulation, arguably the two most important topics are rather unexplored. These are the internal governance of global corporations through management accounting and the coordination of increasingly complex supply chains, and the taxation of the global corporations.

5.1 Management

Within the multinational corporation, accountants shape these flows in direct, practical ways. This raises questions for researchers of how globalisation actually works inside large corporations, and what accounting and accountants do there to perpetuate and extend globalisation. Various critical accounting researchers have addressed these questions over the past decade or more. The two articles that I want to draw attention to here are Macintosh *et al.* (2009) and Cooper and Ezzamel (2013), because together they demonstrate how complex the relationship is between globalisation and accounting when observed at the local level.

Macintosh *et al.* examine the management control systems of global corporations from an ethics perspective. Drawing on Levinas, they revisit the takeover of Nuovo Pignone by General Electric, as documented in the work of Busco, Riccaboni and Scapens (2006). Macintosh *et al.* argue that the imposition of the "GE Way" changed the ethos of the Italian subsidiary through the installation of a regime of financial and non-financial performance measurements. Employees were reclassified according to performance and behaviour, and those who did not fit the new ethos found themselves released by their employers. The authors use the ethics of Levinas, which recognises an immediate accountability between actors that exists before any intentionality, as a tool to critique the objectivising economic accountability implicit in the GE Way. The paper demonstrates ways in which the global economic discourse of capitalism obliterates regional cultural differences and non-economic forms of accountability in intra-corporate relationships.

Similarly Cooper and Ezzamel (2013) examine the way global economic discourses are operationalised inside multinational firms. Based on interviews conducted at corporate offices in the UK, Germany, China and Japan, as well as an analysis of corporate documents, the authors illustrate how globalisation discourses were translated into local terms. Drawing on Said (1997), they argue that 'molestation', which refers to restraints on the inventiveness of authors of corporate discourse, results in a conversion of notions like that of a 'balanced scorecard' and 'key performance indicators' into something practical at the local level, which may differ from the formal expression of these notions. Cooper and Ezzamel argue that this understanding of globalisation explains how local variations in global practices arise, while offering an alternative to explanations that emphasise power and resistance.

While these two papers examine large multinational corporations, it is important to note that global capitalism has now also begun to operate more and more through networks of smaller entities, not just large hierarchical organisations. Froud, Johal, Leaver and Williams (2014) offer an example of research into this complex form. The authors examine the financialization of supply chain arrangements between a Chinese supplier, FIH, and an American purchaser, Apple. The paper offers a fascinating analysis of labour's share of value added in the production of Apple's products. The authors argue that if the iPhone were to be manufactured in the US instead of China, Apple's gross margin would still remain at 50 per cent. Such detailed analyses of the profitability of global corporations are surprisingly rare in critical accounting research.

5.2 Taxation

As a result of excessive profits, the taxation of global corporations has received intense scrutiny in the media in the past couple of years. Global corporations have been widely criticised for the way they have (usually legally) avoided taxation through shell companies and subsidiaries that are located, or perhaps simply registered, in countries with extremely low corporate tax rates. Companies with well-recognised brands, such as Apple and Google, have received particularly adverse publicity for this (e.g. Groden, 2016; Rankin, 2016).

Critical accounting research on this topic began well ahead of the current media storm about corporate tax evasion. Killian (2006) examines how US multinationals took advantage of low Irish tax rates, while Otusanya (2011) examines the case of Nigeria. The most prominent critics of corporate tax avoidance, however, have been Sikka and Willmott (Sikka, 2008; Sikka and Willmott, 2010, 2013). They have been especially critical of the active role played by the accounting profession in creating and exploiting tax loopholes on behalf of their large corporate clients. For example, Sikka (2008) documents the role of Big 4 accounting firms operating in the UK in creating limited liability partnership legislation in Jersey, a UK Crown Dependency. This legislation enabled the clients of these firms effectively to move capital offshore to avoid taxation.

Tax avoidance by global corporations has reached the point at which it is safe to designate some of the methods employed as being blatant. As Murphy (2013) points out, the problem of tax avoidance is not a case of Western corporations exploiting poor nations with underdeveloped or corrupt taxation systems, as we might expect if we think of globalisation in the prototypical sense of outsourcing the production of Western goods to impoverished countries with dirt-cheap labour. Rather, tax avoidance by global corporations is exemplified by the exploitation of UK and EU tax laws by American global brands, such as Apple, Google, Starbucks, Ebay, Amazon, Microsoft, and Gap, joined by European firms such as Ikea (Chew, 2016). This work highlights the present inability of nation states, even in a tightly regulated environment such as the EU, to govern global corporations.

This topic deserves much more attention from critical accounting scholars. It presents a major challenge, however, because it is both highly technical and the details of the exploitative practices are hidden inside large accounting firms and corporate C-suites. Nevertheless, I would argue that corporate tax avoidance demands our attention because it offers an explicit demonstration of the contradictions of neo-liberalism. Global corporations do not simply exploit existing loopholes in regulation, as anti-globalisation protestors and the business media alike often suggest (see, for example, the photo accompanying the *Fortune* article by Chew, 2016). Rather, they manufacture these opportunities for tax avoidance through the direct lobbying of legislators and the active cooperation of the accounting profession (Sikka, 2008). Corporate efforts to avoid taxation involve the deliberate cultivation of favourable regulation, not an absence of regulation, in contradiction to the free market rhetoric we often associate with globalisation.

Just as importantly, tax avoidance by global corporations demonstrates the linkages between the global and the local, and between the economic and the social, because a lack of tax revenue from global corporations means either an increased tax burden on individual workers or a lack of funding for social programmes that mitigate the economic, social and health risks of globalisation borne by individuals. Coordinated efforts by global networks of corporations to avoid taxation draw a stark contrast between the highly structured social character of corporations and the economic individualism that underpins globalisation rhetoric. Tax avoidance is therefore a topic where research can have a profound effect on accounting practice and on the lived experience of people living locally in a globalised corporate world.

6 The production of risk

The propensity of global corporations for avoiding taxation arises because globalisation, which appears to depend on universal standards and uniform practices, actually depends on local differences. Discrepancies in national taxation rates and the competition of nations for corporate favour are just one example of this. Tensions between the global and the local in account-ing standards, noted earlier, are another. Such tensions leave the entire global infrastructure of accounting regulation fraught with risk. In this section, we will look at two ways in which these risks can materialise. First, we will discuss the risk of corruption. Then we will discuss the risk of financial crisis. Critical research has shown that in a globalised world, accounting is implicated in the production of both kinds of risk. It has also shown that these crises are not merely financial, but have profound humanitarian consequences.

6.1 Corruption

It would be a mistake to draw too much of a distinction between corruption and financial crisis. Both are related to systemic factors, and both provide ample opportunity for individual opportunism. Yet the notion of corruption alludes, I would argue, to personal morality, no matter how widespread the corruption may be, while the notion of financial crisis alludes to matters of the global economy. Everett, Neu, and Rahaman (2007) successfully problematise traditional assumptions about corruption and about the role of accounting in addressing it. They contrast two mentalities behind global anticorruption efforts. The orthodox mentality sees the fight against corruption as a noble cause. This is the view valorised by accounting and promoted by the major actors in the anti-corruption effort, including transnational institutions such as the World Bank. The radical mentality, in contrast, recognises the 'vices' implicit in this anti-corruption effort, which are related to problems of race, class and gender, and in which accounting plays a performative role.

A number of studies of corruption have focused on its criminal aspects. Compin (2008) analyses the role of accounting in criminal activities in terms of how organised is the crime and how illegal the activity. He compares money laundering, which is the legitimising of funds flowing from criminal activities, with money dirtying, which entails the funneling of funds into terrorist and other illegal activities. Lehman and Okcabol (2005) go further than Compin by questioning our assumptions about crime itself. They recognise crime as a social construction, similar to the way in which Everett *et al.* (2007) problematise assumptions about corruption. In particular, Lehman and Okcabol draw attention to discrepancies in how accounting crimes designated as being of the white collar variety are treated differently in our society than other types of crimes. Racial factors in particular are highlighted as leading to high incarceration levels for non-accounting crimes.

6.2 Financial crises

While corruption and other criminal activities related to accounting are difficult to research due to problems of access to data, the other major endogenous risk in globalisation is awash with data. The problem is to reduce the data to a manageable set that is amenable to analysis. We are talking about global financial crises. In 2003, when Dean Neu and I addressed the topic of globalisation, the world was just recovering from the 1997 financial crisis in South East Asia. Currency volatility, contagion and the flight of capital from various Asian countries had spooked investors in 1997, and confidence in foreign investment opportunities was just rebuilding. Today, the global economy is recovering from a different crisis, one that has had far longer effects. This was the financial crisis of 2008, set off by the sub-prime mortgage problems in the US. This crisis has led to a prolonged global recession and persistent volatility. The effects of this crisis persist in part because of sovereign debt problems in Europe, as well as the recent economic conditions in

China. The economy has now leveled off from its previous dramatic growth, which has had the result of leading to a reduced demand for raw materials from other nations.

The crisis of 2008 has therefore prompted much attention from critical accounting scholars, including Bengtsson (2011) in *Critical Perspective on Accounting*, and before that, a special section in volume 34 of *Accounting, Organizations and Society* in 2009. While one year is perhaps too short a time for academics to conduct original research and offer in-depth conclusions, this special section did offer a platform for leading accounting scholars (e.g. Sikka, 2009) to point the way towards much needed empirical studies. Indeed, Arnold took up her own challenge (Arnold, 2009) by later producing a political economy analysis of the roles of accounting in the East Asian financial crisis (Arnold, 2012). It is worth noting that this paper did not, of course, offer an analysis of the 2008 financial crisis, but rather of the previous 1997 financial crisis. This simply points to the difficulty of comprehending something as massive as a global financial crisis using the tools of academic research within a time frame more suited to journalism.

6.3 Humanitarian consequences

While the critical accounting academy may have had difficulty reacting in a timely fashion to the global financial crisis of 2008, it has succeeded somewhat better in coming to terms with other horrific consequences of globalisation. Of particular note is the way researchers have addressed the links between accounting and human rights. The editors and contributors to the special issue of *Critical Perspectives on Accounting* in 2011 deserve credit for their contribution on this topic. As the editors of the issue argue, although business activities in the globalised economy have often been linked with human rights abuses, unfortunately their governance and accountability implications "have largely passed the accounting profession and critical accounting community by" (McPhail and McKernan, 2011: 734).

Contributors to this special issue examined how accounting shapes a variety of human rights. They looked at the development of corporate reporting standards related to the rights of employees in the garment industry (Islam and McPhail, 2011), the link between human rights and foreign investment in globalisation (Sikka, 2011), the failure of workplace audits to protect the rights of workers to a safe work environment and the use of accounting to calculate the fine for violations of these rights (Cooper, Coulson and Taylor, 2011), and the implications for human rights of the accounting notion of transparency (Gallhofer, Haslam and van der Walt, 2011). Each of these papers demonstrates the power of critical accounting research to derive the logic of accounting practice from tightly focused case studies. They examine specific business activities related to globalisation, such as the outsourcing of production to low-cost countries and the vulnerability of workers in a global economy where capital can move much more quickly and effortlessly than people.

6.4 Migration

In the past year (it is 2016 at the time of writing), a different kind of humanitarian consequence has captured the attention of the world, one that does indeed involve the movement of people. It is the flight of Syrian refugees across international borders. This crisis presents a difficult challenge to accounting researchers, as the roots of the problems are pervasive and the requisite data for an accounting study are difficult to capture. It is part of a larger problem of migration in the globalised world, where people move to flee violence and seek employment, destabilising both the country from which they are fleeing and the country they (seek to) reach, while turning their own lives upside down.

In Graham and Neu (2003), we argue that flows of people through migration are an important part of globalisation, and that the constitutive role of accounting in immigration policies and the distribution of work require close examination. In the past few years, flows of people as refugees have often dominated the news. Reactions to these flows have become a prominent aspect of discourse in Western democracies, with the trope of "building walls" explicitly intended to keep out (undesirable) immigrants recurring in the 2016 US presidential election debates. The importance of flows of people in globalisation, both to seek work and to seek refuge from political instability, has become undeniable. Accounting researchers have barely begun to address this issue, however. Two contributions of note have appeared, however. Agyemang and Lehman (2013) argue that migration is a phenomenon shaped by a numbers game, the result of attempts to classify and quantify populations. The subaltern is most affected by this, that is, the person who without participating in the process is handed an identity not of their own choosing. Media reports and migration statistical studies are equally culpable in labeling individuals, assigning them moral and economic values, and imputing relationships to other populations and to causes of migration. Accounting, the authors argue, is complicit in this process through the valorisation of free market explanations for migration, the attribution of costs, and the audit of corporate compliance with immigration laws. The authors plea for engaged critical accounting research on this pressing social issue, and the abandonment by critical researchers of assumptions of accounting objectivity.

Annisette and Trivedi (2013) look at migration from a very different perspective. They examine the experience of immigrant accountants in Canada and the contradictions that neo-liberalism has created with respect to their identity. The authors consider not only the contradictions for the individual immigrant accountant, but the contradictions for the state, the labour market and the notion of 'place' that is implicit in the efforts of the accounting profession to erect barriers to entry in a globalised world. Besides the insights that it gives us into the professionalisation of accounting labour, the study is important for our present discussion, because it again reminds us of the mutually constitutive relationship between accounting and globalisation, and between the global and the local.

7 Globalisation, neo-liberalism and biopolitics

Critical accounting research on globalisation has had, over the past decade, to adapt to changes in globalisation itself. The advent of ever more extreme forms of neo-liberal capitalism has made the need for critical research urgent. In this section, I will set out what I believe are the most important opportunities for new and provocative research on accounting and globalisation. My argument is based on recent attempts to move critical accounting research beyond the disciplinary enclosures, such as factories, that have been addressed by many Foucauldian accounting scholars (Martinez, 2011).

The argument begins with Michel Foucault's notion of "biopolitics" (Foucault, 1978, 2008). Biopolitics is the endeavour to rationalise the government of populations. Foucault (2008) argues that the government of populations arises from the rationalities of liberalism, which include the aim of minimal intervention by the state. Foucault argued that neo-liberalism, which begins as a response to the problems of World War II, represented the extension of economic analysis and market rationalities into all areas of social policy (Foucault, 2008: 219). This is where the fetishisation of free markets, which has been with us since Thatcher and Reagan, begins. Foucault offered his critique of neo-liberalism in 1978 and 1979, before these two politicians were even elected. He argued that the realisation of the neo-liberal vision depends on subjectivising the individual as an entrepreneur. Neo-liberalism centres on the government of enterprises, so the government of populations requires that people be encouraged to think of themselves as enterprises. The result of this kind of thinking is the atomisation and individualisation of populations. Individuals must be made responsible for the development of their own human capital, and responsible, as economic producers, for their own earnings (Foucault, 2008: 226).

In contemporary neo-liberal practice, through technologies such as social impact bonds and micro-finance that are laced with accounting, this conception of the individual lays risk and responsibility on some of the most vulnerable in our societies. These technologies operate at the individual level, without consideration for the structural mechanisms that exclude the poor from full economic and political participation. They encourage the poor to become entrepreneurs, with undiversified financial risk and a limited capacity to escape either the cycle of indebtedness or the exploitative relations of existing social hierarchies (Rankin, 2001, 2002, 2008), yet leave them exposed to exploitation by financial institutions that can diversify their own risk. They construct individual subjectivity through accounting mechanisms that require them to become consumers of risk and objectivise them as sets of cash flows to be monetised for the benefit of the capital markets.

The question of how accounting is implicated in the construction of the individual has been a prominent theme in accounting literature, particularly in research drawing on Foucault's analysis of governmentality (1979, 1984b, 1991), beginning in the mid-1980s with Hoskin and Macve (1986), Knights and Collinson (1987) and Miller and O'Leary (1987). The focus of this prominent line of research has largely been on governmental and corporate settings congruent as disciplinary enclosures. Martinez (2011) argues that neo-liberalism today operates beyond disciplinary enclosures, and that accounting research must adapt to this change. He draws on the insights of Hardt and Negri (2000), who argue that the extension of economic thinking under neo-liberalism now transcends both political and conceptual boundaries, permeating and producing all areas of life, such that "the economic, the political, and the cultural increasingly overlap and invest one another" (Hardt and Negri, 2000: xiii).

Hardt and Negri suggest that the global order has bypassed the national state and has become an unbounded society founded on the biopolitical production of social reality, a global version of what Deleuze (1992) calls a "society of control." While disciplinary society operates through networks of apparatuses and technologies that regulate customs and habits, the society of control operates more immanently, through the "brains and bodies of the citizens" (Hardt and Negri, 2000: 23). This means that power in the society of control is enacted through individual relationships. This is a radical intensification of the kind of discipline that only takes place at work, for instance. This kind of discipline permeates all aspects of everyday life (Hardt and Negri, 2000: 24).

For Hardt and Negri, one consequence of this is that resistance to global society is individualised and thereby neutralised and absorbed into culture. Protest is commodified as nothing but a singular expression of culture (Hardt and Negri, 2000: 25). This is the political counterpart to the economic notion of the individual as an entrepreneur of the self. Through culture, the production of the subjectivity of the individual connects the political and economic modes of neo-liberalism. The economic aggregation of individual production replaces the political aggregation of democratic participation as the primary concern of government. This is what links the macro- and micro-issues of accounting today. The global and the local are dialectically related through the biopolitical government of populations, which is the same under neo-liberalism as the biopolitical production of life. The global order feeds itself through the production of local differences. Local differences are the source of profit, as even the most elementary analysis of outsourcing to countries with low wage structures can demonstrate.

8 Paths for future research

This chapter has argued that while critical accounting research has responded to changes in the mechanisms and trajectories of globalisation, through investigations of supranational organisations, the role of the accounting profession and the regulation of financial reporting, it is yet to grapple fully with the two primary challenges of globalisation. These are the new global corporation, operating through networks of corporate actors and coordinating accounting flows to evade governance by individual states, and the micro-level impacts of globalisation on the individual.

Critical accounting research can address the global order by attending to its micro-processes. To do this, it must recognise how dynamic the mechanisms are for the micro-production of life. As Neu *et al.* (2009) argue, the "assemblages" (Deleuze and Guattari, 1987) of technologies and people that characterise contemporary life are constantly changing, constantly becoming something new. This means that the roles of accounting in society are constantly adapting and localising, constantly producing new accounting practices and presenting new challenges to accounting theory. Accounting researchers will find the analysis of these changing roles of accounting challenging. The collection of internal corporate data is difficult because of problems of access to confidential records. The collection of micro-level individual data in poor countries is costly and sometimes difficult to fund through traditional sources of research funding, and connecting this local data to global processes is not easy, particularly within the confines of journal contributions.

The disparity in power between global corporations on the one hand and the very poor on the other challenges our objectivity. We will need to avoid being either cheerleaders or cynics, as the effects of globalisation are complex. Lives are changing at the micro-level, and in many cases for the better. Attention is clearly needed to the damaging and oppressive consequences of globalisation and the roles of accounting in facilitating and even actively promoting these negative consequences. However, to understand accounting fully, we must attend as well to the positive effects of globalisation and the potential for accounting to facilitate and promote these effects (Gallhofer and Haslam, 2006). This is particularly necessary, I would argue, if critical accounting research on globalisation is to reach a wider audience.

Nonetheless, attention can be given to the asymmetrical distribution of any positive consequences. If the poor see any benefit from the capillary flows of global capital, the rich see enormous benefits through arterial flows. The rich also have the capacity to diversify risk through ownership of portfolios of corporations, and through hedging instruments, along with the benefit of enjoying influence on financial regulation that the poor do not. Accounting permits micro-flows of capital to be aggregated into massive wealth for the few. It does little to aggregate the political micro-capital of the poor into a voice that can be heard on the global stage. For this reason, critical accounting research on globalisation must make explicit the connections between the global and the local, the macro and the micro, in order to expose the exploitative corporatised relationship between the rich and the poor. If it does not do this, it does not deserve the name "critical."

References

Agyemang, G. and C. R. Lehman (2013). "Adding critical accounting voices to migration studies," *Critical Perspectives on Accounting*, 24(4–5): 261–72.
Ahmed, Z., T. Hopper and D. Wickramasinghe (2012). "Hegemony and accountability in BRAC – the largest hybrid NGO in the world," Auckland University of Technology.
Al-Twaijry, A. A., J. A. Brierley and D. R. Gwilliam (2003). "The development of internal audit in Arabia: an institutional theory perspective," *Critical Perspectives on Accounting*, 14(5): 507–31.

Albu, C. N., N. Albu and D. Alexander (2014). "When global accounting standards meet the local context—insights from an emerging economy," *Critical Perspectives on Accounting*, 25(6): 489–510.

Annisette, M. (2004). "The true nature of the World Bank," *Critical Perspectives on Accounting*, 15(3): 303–23.

Annisette, M. and V. U. Trivedi (2013). "Globalization, paradox and the (un) making of identities: immigrant Chartered Accountants of India in Canada," *Accounting, Organizations and Society*, (1): 1–29.

Arnold, P. J. (2005). "Disciplining domestic regulation: the World Trade Organization and the market for professional services," *Accounting, Organizations and Society*, 30(4): 299–330.

Arnold, P. J. (2009). "Global financial crisis: the challenge to accounting research," *Accounting Organizations and Society*, 34(6): 803–809.

Arnold, P. J. (2012). "The political economy of financial harmonization: the East Asian financial crisis and the rise of international accounting standards," *Accounting, Organizations and Society*, 37(6): 361–81.

Bakre, O. M. (2008). "Financial reporting as technology that supports and sustains imperial expansion, maintenance and control in the colonial and post-colonial globalisation: the case of the Jamaican economy," *Critical Perspectives on Accounting*, 19(4): 487–522.

Barrett, M., D. J. Cooper and K. Jamal (2005). "Globalization and the coordinating of work in multinational audits," *Accounting, Organizations and Society*, 30(1): 1–24.

Belal, A., C. Spence, C. Carter and J. Zhu (2017). "The Big 4 in Bangladesh: caught between the global and the local," *Accounting, Auditing and Accountability Journal*, 30(1): 145–163.

Bengtsson, E. (2011). "Repoliticalization of accounting standard setting – the IASB, the EU and global financial crisis," *Critical Perspectives on Accounting*, 22(6): 567–80.

Bourdieu, P. (1990). *The Logic of Practice*, translated by R. Nice, Cambridge: Polity Press.

Boussebaa, M. (2015). "Professional service firms, globalisation and the new imperialism," *Accounting, Auditing and Accountability Journal*, 28(8): 1217–33.

Bozanic, Z., M. W. Dirsmith and S. Huddart (2012). "The social constitution of regulation: the endogenization of insider trading laws," *Accounting, Organizations and Society*, 37(7): 461–81.

Busco, C., A. Riccaboni and R. W. Scapens (2006). "Trust for accounting and accounting for trust," *Management Accounting Research*, 17(1): 11–41.

Chand, P. (2005). "Impetus to the success of harmonization: the case of South Pacific Island nations," *Critical Perspectives on Accounting*, 16(3): 209–26.

Chand, P. and M. White (2007). "A critique of the influence of globalization and convergence of accounting standards in Fiji," *Critical Perspectives on Accounting*, 18(5): 605–22.

Chew, J. (2016). "Corporate giants accused of evading billions in taxes," *Fortune*. http://fortune.com/2016/03/11/apple-google-taxes-eu/.

Chiapello, E. and K. Medjad (2009). "An unprecedented privatisation of mandatory standard-setting: the case of European accounting policy," *Critical Perspectives on Accounting*, 20(4): 448–68.

Compin, F. (2008). "The role of accounting in money laundering and money dirtying," *Critical Perspectives on Accounting*, 19(5): 591–602.

Cooper, D. and M. Ezzamel (2013). Globalization discourses and performance measurement systems in a multinational firm," *Accounting Organizations and Society*, 38(4): 288–313.

Cooper, D. J. and K. Robson (2006). "Accounting, professions and regulation: locating the sites of professionalization," *Accounting, Organizations and Society*, 31(4–5): 415–44.

Cooper, C., A. Coulson and P. Taylor (2011). "Accounting for human rights: doxic health and safety practices – the accounting lesson from ICL," *Critical Perspectives on Accounting*, 22(8):738–58.

Cruz, I., R. W. Scapens and M. Major (2011). "The localisation of a global management control system," *Accounting, Organizations and Society*, 36(7): 412–27.

Deleuze, G. (1992). "Postscript on the Societies of Control," *October*, 59(Winter): 3–7.

Deleuze, G. and F. Guattari (1987). *A Thousand Plateaus: Capitalism and Schizophrenia*, Minneapolis, MN: University of Minnesota Press.

Everett, J., D. Neu and A. S. Rahaman (2007). "Accounting and the global fight against corruption," *Accounting, Organizations and Society*, 32(6): 513–42.

Ezzamel, M. and J. Z. Xiao (2015). "The development of accounting regulations for foreign invested firms in China: the role of Chinese characteristics," *Accounting, Organizations and Society*, 44: 60–84.

Ezzamel, M., J. Z. Xiao and A. Pan (2007). "Political ideology and accounting regulation in China," *Accounting, Organizations and Society*, 32(7): 669–700.

Foucault, M. (1978). *History of Sexuality Volume 1: An Introduction*, translated by R. Hurley, New York: Pantheon Books.

Foucault, M. (1979). *Discipline and Punish: The Birth of the Prison*, New York: Vintage Books.

Foucault, M. (1984a). "The means of correct training," in P. Rabinow (ed.), *The Foucault Reader*, New York: Pantheon.

Foucault, M. (1984b). "Panopticism," in P. Rabinow (ed.): *The Foucault Reader*, New York: Pantheon.

Foucault, M. (1991). "Governmentality," in G. Burchell, C. Gordon and P. Miller (eds): *The Foucault Effect*, Chicago, IL: University of Chicago Press.

Foucault, M. (2008). *The Birth of Biopolitics: Lectures at the Collège de France, 1978-79*, translated G. Burchell, Houndmills: Palgrave Macmillan.

Froud, J., S. Johal, A. Leaver and K. Williams (2014). "Financialization across the Pacific: manufacturing cost ratios, supply chains and power," *Critical Perspectives on Accounting*, 25(1): 46–57.

Gallhofer, S. and J. Haslam (2006). "The accounting–globalisation interrelation: an overview with some reflections on the neglected dimension of emancipatory potentiality," *Critical Perspectives on Accounting*, 17(7): 903–34.

Gallhofer, S., J. Haslam and S. van der Walt (2011). "Accountability and transparency in relation to human rights: a critical perspective reflecting upon accounting, corporate responsibility and ways forward in the context of globalisation," *Critical Perspectives on Accounting*, 22(8): 765–80.

Graham, C. and D. Neu (2003). "Accounting for globalization," *Accounting Forum*, 27(4): 449–71.

Groden, C. (2016). "European Union calls for global companies to disclose more tax data," *Fortune*. http://fortune.com/2016/04/12/european-union-tax-eu/

Hardt, M. and A. Negri (2000). *Empire*, Cambridge, MA: Harvard University Press.

Hopper, T., M. Tsamenyi, S. Uddin and D. Wickramasinghe (2009). "Management accounting in less developed countries: what is known and needs knowing," *Accounting, Auditing and Accountability Journal*, 22(3): 469–514.

Hoskin, K. W. and R. H. Macve (1986). "Accounting and the examination: a genealogy of disciplinary power," *Accounting, Organizations and Society*, 11(2): 105–36.

Islam, M. A. and K. McPhail (2011). "Regulating for corporate human rights abuses: the emergence of corporate reporting on the ILO's human rights standards within the global garment manufacturing and retail industry," *Critical Perspectives on Accounting*, 22(8): 790–810.

Kamla, R. (2012). "Syrian women accountants' attitudes and experiences at work in the context of globalization," *Accounting, Organizations and Society*, 37(3): 188–205.

Killian, S. (2006). "Where's the harm in tax competition?: lessons from US multinationals in Ireland," *Critical Perspectives on Accounting*, 17(8): 1067–87.

Knights, D. and D. Collison (1987). "Disciplining the shopfloor: a comparison of the disciplinary effects of managerial psychology and financial accounting," *Accounting, Organizations and Society*, 12(5): 457–77.

Lehman, C. R. and F. Okcabol (2005). "Accounting for crime," *Critical Perspectives on Accounting*, 16(5): 613–39.

Macintosh, N. B., T. Shearer and A. Riccaboni (2009). A Levinasian ethics critique of the role of management and control systems by large global corporations: the General Electric/Nuovo example," *Critical Perspectives on Accounting*, 20(6): 751–61.

McPhail, K. and J. McKernan (2011). "Accounting for human rights: an overview and introduction," *Critical Perspectives on Accounting*, 22(8): 733–37.

Martinez, D. E. (2011). "Beyond disciplinary enclosures: management control in the society of control," *Critical Perspectives on Accounting*, 22(2): 200–11.

Mennicken, A. (2008). "Connecting worlds: the translation of international auditing standards into post-Soviet audit practice," *Accounting, Organizations and Society*, 33(4): 384–414.

Miller, P. and T. O'Leary (1987). "Accounting and the construction of the governable person," *Accounting, Organizations and Society*, 12(3): 235–65.

Mir, M. Z. and A. S. Rahaman (2005). "The adoption of international accounting standards in Bangladesh: an exploration of rationale and process," *Accounting, Auditing and Accountability Journal*, 18(6): 816–41.

Murphy, J. (2008). "International financial institutions and the new global managerial order," *Critical Perspectives on Accounting*, 19(5): 714–40.

Murphy, R. (2013). *Over Here and Undertaxed: Multinationals, Tax Avoidance and You*, New York: Random House.

Neu, D., E. Ocampo, C. Graham and M. Heincke (2006). "'Informing' technologies and the World Bank," *Accounting, Organizations and Society*, 31(7): 635–62.

Neu, D. and E. Ocampo (2007). "Doing missionary work: the World Bank and the diffusion of financial practices," *Critical Perspectives on Accounting*, 18(3): 363–89.

Neu, D., L. Silva and E. Ocampo Gomez (2008). "Diffusing financial practices in Latin American higher reducation: understanding the intersection between global influence and the local context," *Accounting, Auditing and Accountability Journal*, 21(1): 49–77.

Neu, D., J. Everett and A. S. Rahaman (2009). "Accounting assemblages, desire, and the body without organs: a case study of international development lending in Latin America," *Accounting, Auditing and Accountability Journal*, 22(3): 319–50.

Neu, D., A. S. Rahaman, J. Everett and A. Akindayomi (2010). "The sign value of accounting: IMF structural adjustment programs and African banking reform," *Critical Perspectives on Accounting*, 21(5): 402–19.

O'Connor, N. G., C. W. Chow and A. Wu (2004). "The adoption of 'Western' management accounting/controls in China's state-owned enterprises during economic transition," *Accounting Organizations and Society*, 29(3–4): 349–75.

Okike, E. (2004). "Management of crisis: the response of the auditing profession in Nigeria to the challenge to its legitimacy," *Accounting, Auditing and Accountability Journal*, 17(5): 705–30.

Otusanya, O. J. (2011). "The role of multinational companies in tax evasion and tax avoidance: the case of Nigeria," *Critical Perspectives on Accounting*, 22(3): 316–32.

Rahaman, A. S., J. Everett and D. Neu (2007). "Accounting and the move to privatize water services in Africa," *Accounting, Auditing and Accountability Journal*, 20(5): 637–70.

Rankin, J. (2016). "Europe pressures multinationals to declare taxes and profits," *The Guardian*. http://www.theguardian.com/business/2016/apr/12/brussels-pressures-multinationals-to-declare-taxes-and-profits

Rankin, K. N. (2001). "Governing development: neoliberalism, microcredit, and rational economic woman," *Economy and Society*, 30(1): 18–37.

Rankin, K. N. (2002). "Social capital, microfinance, and the politics of development," *Feminist Economics*, 8(1): 1–24.

Rankin, K. N. (2008). "Manufacturing rural finance in Asia: institutional assemblages, market societies, entrepreneurial subjects," *Geoforum*, 39(6): 1965–77.

Rorty, R. (1991). "Science as solidarity," *Objectivity, Relativism, and Truth: Philosophical Papers* (Vol. 1). Cambridge: Cambridge University Press.

Said, E. W. (1997). *Beginnings: Intention and Method*, London: Granta Books.

Samsonova, A. (2009). "Local sites of globalisation: a look at the development of a legislative framework for auditing in Russia," *Critical Perspectives on Accounting*, 20(4): 528–52.

Sikka, P. (2008). "Globalization and its discontents: accounting firms buy limited liability partnership legislation in Jersey," *Accounting, Auditing and Accountability Journal*, 21(3): 398–426.

Sikka, P. (2009). "Financial crisis and the silence of the auditors," *Accounting, Organizations and Society*, 34(6): 868–73.

Sikka, P. (2011). "Accounting for human rights: the challenge of globalization and foreign investment agreements," *Critical Perspectives on Accounting*, 22(8):811–27.

Sikka, P. and H. Willmott (2010). "The dark side of transfer pricing: its role in tax avoidance and wealth retentiveness," *Critical Perspectives on Accounting*, 21(4): 342–56.

Sikka, P and H. Willmott (2013). "The tax avoidance industry: accountancy firms on the make," *Critical Perspectives on International Business*, 9(4): 415–43.

Yapa, P., K. Jacobs, B. C. Huot (2016). "The field of accounting: exploring the presence and absence of accounting in Cambodia," *Accounting, Auditing and Accountability Journal*, 29(3): 401–27

Yee, H. (2012). "Analyzing the state-accounting profession dynamic: some insights from the professionalization experience in China," *Accounting, Organizations and Society*, 37(6): 426–44.

Zhang, Y., J. Andrew and K. Rudkin (2012). "Accounting as an instrument of neoliberalisation? Exploring the adoption of fair value accounting in China," *Accounting, Auditing and Accountability Journal*, 25(8): 1266–89.

19

POPULAR CULTURE

Ingrid Jeacle

1 Introduction

This chapter provides an overview of an emergent research theme within critical accounting research. Popular culture has been recognised as an insightful new field of scholarly inquiry (Jeacle, 2012). The call to pursue an accounting and popular culture research agenda recognises the increasingly significant role of popular culture in economic and social life. Social media sites, such as Facebook, are an obvious example of this situation; these internet businesses are not only powerful global concerns, they are also inherently integrated into the rhythms of daily life (Ellison, Steinfield and Lampe, 2007). An accounting and popular culture perspective encourages scholars to investigate such dominant components of popular culture and explore the accounting angle. In other words, recognises a popular phenomenon and unravels the 'accounting story' therein. This represents a departure from traditional modes of accounting research which seek to interrogate the latest professional pronouncement on international standard setting or analyse the market's reaction to a recent disclosure of accounting information. It involves stepping outside predetermined boundaries that have traditionally defined the scope of accounting scholarship. Hence, it represents a further attempt to push the boundaries of critical accounting research into ever new territories. An accounting and popular culture research agenda also requires a broad understanding of what constitutes accounting. Drawing on the work of Miller (2001), the notion of calculative practices or calculative technologies provides a valuable means of understanding the often far-reaching role of accounting. Regimes of calculation are increasingly pervasive in contemporary life. An awareness of the myriad modes of calculative accountability provides a powerful basis on which to unravel the interlinkages between accounting and popular culture.

It is important to recognise the foundation stone for the new research agenda of accounting and popular culture. In 1994, Anthony Hopwood identified a particularly interesting arena for furthering our understanding of accounting and the social; he devoted a special issue of the journal *Accounting, Organizations and Society* (*AOS*) to the theme of "Accounting and Everyday Life" (Hopwood, 1994). The editorial to this special issue is short in length but potent in content. Essentially, Hopwood calls for scholarly attention to be paid to the rituals of everyday life and their interlinkages with accounting. This represented a pioneering step within critical accounting research. Traditionally research themes had been grounded in manufacturing practices, capital markets or professional accounting standard setting. Hopwood recognised the opportunity to move beyond these domains and open up new critical spaces in which to explore the role of accounting. Engaging with everyday life represented a brave proposal that would challenge existing perceptions of the scope of accounting research. Hopwood acknowledged that the linkage between this new territory and the practice of accounting was not immediately perceptible – the rituals that pervade the everyday do not have an obvious point of connection with the business of accounting. Yet if scholars could surmount this hurdle, rich returns lay in wait. Research in this field held the potential to reveal the expansive power of accounting in the shaping, not only of economic factors, but the more mundane aspects of daily life. The study of accounting in a popular culture context is a natural extension of Hopwood's vision for engagement with the everyday.

It is important to acknowledge that the pursuit of new agendas within critical accounting research, whether it be accounting and popular culture or some other theme, is not an end in itself. The capture of new spaces or domains is meaningless unless it offers a fresh understanding of accounting as a social and organisational practice. The aim of critical accounting research has always been to question and to probe, and to provide alternative insights into accounting's role. Consequently, the value of a research agenda embedded in popular culture lies in its ability to further our understanding of accounting more generally. Popular culture is well placed to illuminate the wider impact of accounting because popular culture itself is so dominant a feature of contemporary life. Hence, by revealing the interlinkages between popular phenomena and calculative technologies, we potentially gain insights into the powerful transformative effects of accounting. From this perspective, accounting does not merely react to popular fashions and trends but rather, also plays a role in the shaping of such popular phenomena.

Such an argument regarding the power of accounting has already been persuasively made in the theoretical contributions of a number of scholars. For example, Miller (2001), drawing on the governmentality work of Foucault (1991) and Miller and Rose (1990), suggests the influential role of calculative technologies in the deployment of programmes of government. This linking of mundane micro-practices of calculation with broader social and economic agendas celebrates the influence of humble technologies in shaping daily life. Similarly, Power's (1994, 1997) seminal work on audit society captures the contemporary fascination with rituals of checking and verification, highlighting the significant legitimating role of audit in society. Popular culture is merely one more domain in which we may witness the power of accounting as suggested by these scholars. Popular culture provides another locale to observe the linking of micro-technologies to wider social agendas, and a space in which we may easily observe the myriad variants of audit society. Yet it is a domain, which due to its sheer scale and speed of responsiveness, is especially apt at showcasing the power of accounting in shaping everyday life.

This leads us to a particularly pertinent point. Chapman, Cooper and Miller (2009) have noted how accounting scholarship is increasingly gaining attention within the wider social science community. In other words, social theorists who might previously have regarded the discipline of accounting as a practice remote from their own concerns are now recognising the impact of calculative regimes and audit rituals. The work of sociologists Espeland and Sauder (2007) is an example of this genre. Drawing on Power's audit society argument, these authors deliberate upon the proliferation of ranking mechanisms in contemporary society. This is only one example of the influence of Power's scholarship across the social sciences (Hopwood, 2009). Similarly, Miller and Rose's (1990, 2008) work on governmentality has made a significant impact within sociology (Heidensohn and Wright, 2010). Hence, the challenge, but also the opportunity, for critical accounting scholars is to highlight the wider role of accounting, to make that leap beyond the confines of our own community. As will be discussed in the next section, popular culture is already a central feature of sociology, and consequently any examination of the interlinkages between accounting and popular phenomena should be insightful to both domains.

The remainder of this chapter is structured as follows. In order to set the context for deliberations regarding accounting and popular culture, an overview of the key themes in the sociology of popular culture is first provided. This is followed by a review of the extant accounting literature which has engaged with the themes of popular culture and everyday life. The next section suggests some further research avenues for critical accounting scholars working in the field of popular culture. The final section offers some concluding observations.

2 The phenomenon of popular culture

'Popular culture' is the term traditionally used to distinguish the cultural pursuits and preferences of the mass populace from those of the elite (Burke, 1994; Strinati, 2004). The distinction between high and low cultures, however, is becoming increasingly blurred (McRobbie, 1999). Such blurring of boundaries is evident, for example, in the work of English artist Damien Hirst, whose latest addition to the art world was a re-interpretation of the Walt Disney character Mickey Mouse.[1] Consequently, the significant debates within cultural studies are not concerned with the relative position of popular to high culture, but rather the influence of factors such as globalisation and the media on popular culture itself. Globalisation, in particular innovations in technology, has had a profound impact on the spread of popular culture (Storey, 2003). With the aid of internet sites such as YouTube, local trends can instantly become global phenomena; the Korean dance craze (Gangnam Style) that entered the public consciousness in 2012 provides a vivid illustration of how popular culture has gained a global audience. Indeed, the media, in all its guises, postmodern theorists argue, is one of the most dominant influences on popular culture. Through its production and dissemination of popular culture, the media, is seen as the defining means by which reality is constructed in contemporary life (Harvey, 1989; Lash, 1990; Lash and Urry, 1994). Once again, advances in technology have promulgated this process and created a sense of ubiquitous media (Featherstone, 2009). With the advent of Web 2.0 internet sites, the media is no longer the preserve of traditional cultural purveyors, such as national broadcasters. Rather, media is now also produced by the 'ordinary people' (Turner, 2010) through a myriad array of blogs, video uploads and user reviews. Essentially, we are witnessing a democratisation with regard to media access (Napoli, 2010). As a consequence, popular culture is not only disseminated through these new media forms but is also actively "shaped and constituted" by the social data itself (Beer and Burrows, 2013: 67).

Given the prominence of popular culture in contemporary life, it is perhaps unsurprising that its study is a central feature of cultural studies more generally (Hall, 1992; Storey, 2009). While initially its trivial and low-brow connotations may have impeded its serious intellectual consideration (Schudson, 1987), the rituals of everyday life ultimately gained recognition within social theory (de Certeau, 1984). Scholars such as Gramsci (1971) have been influential in establishing the significance of popular culture as a research topic; Gramsci's particular contribution is his conception of popular culture as a consequence of a prevailing hegemony, and the role of the media in that process of consensus. Gramsci's work was also highly influential with the members of the Centre for Contemporary Cultural Studies at the University of Birmingham. This institutional forum became a celebrated centre for culture studies from the 1960s, with Hoggart's (1990) seminal work on working class popular culture and Hall's (1980) prescient views on the role of television both emanating from this theoretical base. More recently, research into popular culture has been a particularly attractive choice for young researchers (McRobbie, 2005). In terms of specific research topics examined within this genre, they are as varied and "elusive" (Fiske, 1989: 45) as the concept of popular culture itself. However, it is useful to mention some of the key themes within the popular culture movement and hence identify possible sites for future accounting research.

Consumerism has occupied a great deal of debate within cultural theory. The shopping experience is now viewed as akin to a recreational activity (Shields, 1992). Social commentators have explained consumption practices using a range of theoretical lenses, from a means by which the individual distinguishes his or herself (Bourdieu, 1984), to a medium of communication (Baudrillard, 1970). Consuming has become tightly tied to identity construction (Featherstone, 1991; Bocock, 1993) and most notably in the case of fashion consumption (Wilson, 1985). Fashion is a vivid illustration of a project of the self (Finkelstein, 1994), a project played out in the ritual trip to the shopping mall. Such rituals have become defining aspects of contemporary life and hence fashion is no longer viewed as a trivial topic, but rather as a legitimate and scholarly subject of inquiry within popular culture (Barnard, 1996; Breward, 2000). This shift in emphasis has been important, not only for the domain itself, but also for opening up further research avenues for women, who perhaps not surprisingly, have been drawn to the study of fashion and its gendered associations (Modleski, 1986; Rakow, 1986).

Popular culture is also synonymous with popular music (Storey, 2003). The relationship between pop music and the media is a particularly fruitful field of research within cultural studies (Frith, 1994). The influence of American culture, as with many aspects of popular culture more generally (Strinati, 2004; Webster, 1988), is important to recognise here. In the field of cinema too, one of the most powerful cultural innovations of the twentieth century (Branston, 2000), American produced movies were consistently more popular with early audiences (Sharpe, 1969). Cinema has always been a popular entertainment form for the masses (Miles and Smith, 1987), but with the advent of television such experiences could become embedded in everyday home life (Stokes, 1999). Indeed, everyday life (or an escapism variant of it) quickly became the context for the television soap opera (Ang, 1985). Hence television is perceived as a particularly significant presence in popular culture, a forum through which meanings can be produced and disseminated in a postmodern world (Fiske, 1987; Hall, 1980), and through which social interactions and everyday conversations are moulded (Bausinger, 1984; Morley, 1986). Increasingly, television is now the vehicle through which popular sporting pursuits, such as football (Horrall, 2001), are accessed. Another manifestation of popular culture, which feeds off music, cinema and television in equal measure is the cult of celebrity (Turner, 2004). Indeed, popular fame is even in the reach of the 'ordinary' citizen through the medium of the ubiquitous reality television show (Holmes, 2004), a form of entertainment now enjoyed by the masses (Bauman, 2007). Whether it takes the shape of the reality television show or celebrity magazine, tabloid culture is now pervasive in contemporary life (Glynn, 2000; Gripsrud, 1992; Winship, 1987). The advances in technology discussed earlier have fuelled this particular podium of popular culture, with sites such as Twitter producing a live stream of wide-ranging comment from celebrities themselves. Such innovations will no doubt provide rich fodder for future cultural theorists.

In summary, the scholarly study of popular culture merely reflects the sweeping changes in everyday life over the last century. Industrialisation loosened traditional ties and networks and in so doing created the autonomous citizen who embraced mass culture (Leavis, 1933; MacDonald 1957). Hence, the classical concerns of sociology, encompassing religion, class and gender, have been supplemented by new debates which capture contemporary events. It is important that the discipline of accounting is not left behind in this movement. As will be discussed in the next section, research into the micro-processes of accounting can provide rich insights into the macro phenomena of popular culture.

3 Accounting studies in popular culture

Given that accounting and popular culture is a relatively new research field, a body of literature is still emerging. Some of this work is presented under the specific banner of accounting and popular culture, such as those papers hosted within a 2012 special issue of the *Accounting, Auditing and Accountability Journal* on the theme. Others, while coming under the broader umbrella of critical accounting, engage with popular themes in contemporary life and hence are also included in this section's review.

The context of cinema is a useful place to begin this review as it constitutes, as noted earlier, one of the classic vehicles for discerning and disseminating the popular trends of an era. A populist pursuit in its own right, it both captures and reflects contemporary popular culture. One of the earliest accounting studies set within the context of the cinema is Beard's (1994) examination of the portrayal of accounting/accountants in Anglo-American movies during the time period between 1957–1994. This fascinating study provides important insights into how the accountant/accounting is portrayed in popular culture. We witness, for example, how the role of the accountant is used within the movie plot to convey character attributes, from conservatism to dysfunctionality. The study also reveals the scope for ridicule and satire that seems inherently bound up in popular perceptions of the accountant. A subsequent study by Dimnik and Felton (2006) of twentieth-century North American movies provides further insights into the representation of the accountant in popular culture, from hero to villain, and dreamer to eccentric. More recently, Jeacle (2009) has shown how an examination of the cinema's box office ledger can reveal the mores and cultural mood of an audience over time. Spanning a period from the early days of the silver screen right up to the 1970s, an accounting ledger provided a lens from which to view the popular likes and dislikes of a cinema-going audience. In a more contemporary study, Jeacle (2014) has drawn upon Goffman (1956) to examine the scrutineering role of the auditor at the BAFTA cinema awards ceremony. At these popular entertainment events, the spectacle of the auditor provides an important legitimating function, providing symbolic assurance over the process of the award-giving ceremony.

Like cinema, pop music is another medium of popular culture. While the links between pop music and accounting are not immediately obvious, a number of innovative studies have recently emerged to break down any lingering conceptions about the far-reaching scope of critical accounting. In a similar vein to the early studies of cinema just noted, Smith and Jacobs (2011) examine the characterisation of accountants and accounting in pop music. From an analysis of song lyric databases, the authors identify a number of key representations of the accountant/accounting in pop music. Perhaps worryingly for the accounting profession, the authors found that there is a dark side to this representation with accountants often characterised in song as perpetrators of fraud and deception. Jacobs and Evans (2012) turn to the lyrics of the Beatles to explore the tensions between the bourgeois world of the accountant and the purity of the artist. Drawing on Bourdieu, the authors examine how the accountant is characterised by the music artist and how the latter balances the need for the former's economic expertise against the desire for creative credibility.

Bourdieu's work, and in particular his concept of a field, is enrolled in Cooper and Johnston's (2012) study of Manchester United Football Club. This icon of popular culture forms a fascinating backdrop to exploring the meaning of the term 'accountability' in the twenty-first century. The authors use the hostile takeover bid of the Club by the Glazer family as a case from which to discuss the ways in which accountability is used to maintain the position of the powerful. Calls for accountability are easily made, they argue, but those in positions of power tend to be immune from the resulting performance measures. Risaliti and Verona (2013) use the context of

Italian football to examine the valuation of players' registration rights in the financial statements. The paper provides an illustrative example of the interlinkages between accounting technologies and broader popular phenomena by identifying the repercussions of the overestimation of player registration rights on the Italian football crisis of the 2001/2002 season. The case of football provides a further example of the significance of sociopolitical processes, one of the central tenants of critical accounting, in the shape of Cooper and Joyce's (2013) analysis of the insolvency of a Scottish football club.

Rugby, another popular sporting spectacle, provides the context for a series of insightful papers by Andon and Free (2012, 2014). The authors use the case of the Melbourne Storm salary cap breach to illustrate the manner in which auditing is mobilised as a legitimating tool. A crisis arose in 2010 when it was discovered that the rugby club Melbourne Storm had breached the National Rugby League's (NRL) salary cap for a number of years. Examining the manner in which audit was subsequently deployed by the NRL to ensure future enforcement of the salary cap, led Andon and Free to come to some important conclusions regarding the role of auditing in crisis management. Broadening their context to also include the Canadian Football League, Andon, Free and Sivabalan (2014) again draw on Bourdieu to explore how auditors establish legitimacy in such new audit spaces. Hence by stepping beyond the traditional domain of financial audit, into the popular world of sport, these auditors have generated fresh insights into the scope of the professional audit.

Another popular pastime of the masses in contemporary life is consumerism. In particular, as noted earlier, the purchase of clothes has become a leisure lifestyle choice. Fashion is inherently embedded in popular culture as its defining feature is that it follows the latest trends. Like other domains of popular culture, there has been a relative dearth of critical accounting studies in the field of fashion. However, some recent papers have revealed the role of calculative technologies in shaping the contours of the fashion industry. Jeacle (2015) and Jeacle and Carter (2012), for example, examine the world of the United Kingdom fashion chain store. These papers suggest the significance of accounting as a mediating instrument between the demands of creativity and cost control within the fashion design process, and also highlight the role of calculative technologies in sustaining the fast pace of chain store fashion. In a further study of the low-price fashion chain, but this time from the perspective of Central America, Neu, Rahaman and Everett (2014) provide valuable insights into the role of accounting in maintaining (often inadvertently) sweatshop conditions within the fashion industry.

The virtual world holds infinite possibilities for actively engaging with or merely observing popular culture in contemporary society. As a site of commerce, the web serves as a purveyor of all things popular. As a site of information, it hosts a mammoth archive of the minutiae of the latest popular trends. Prior accounting research has already revealed the value of the virtual space for our understanding of what constitutes accountability (MacKenzie, Buckby and Irvine, 2013), and the development of accountability projects (Lowe, Locke and Lymer, 2012). Virtual platforms can play a significant role in disseminating official corporate accounts (Gallhofer and Haslam, 2006). Twitter, the favourite of the celebrity, is now a popular medium through which organisations can regularly update their shareholders (Blankespoor, Miller and White, 2013). Equally important are the 'counter accounts' (Gallhofer, Haslam, Monk and Roberts, 2006) facilitated by the virtual space. From an accounting and popular culture perspective, the accounts which emanate from 'popular' websites are a source of interest. In particular, as Jeacle and Carter (2011) have argued, the accounts, opinions and perspectives that are aired in the myriad array of online user review sites can offer the accounting scholar new insights on the concepts of auditing and accountability.

A final theme to consider within this review is that of the popular stereotyping of the account-ant. Literature on the accounting stereotype is broad in scope, and predates the emergence of a specific accounting and popular culture research agenda. Yet it is important to mention some of these studies here as often a key element in stereotype construction is the representation of the character in contemporary popular culture. For example, Carnegie and Napier (2010) examine how the media, in the form of books targeted at a populist audience, portrays accountants in the wake of Enron. Their study of generalist books on corporate failure finds potentially negative consequences for the accountancy profession. In setting out a research agenda for investigating the accountant's professional identity, Parker and Warren (2009) stress the importance of a visual perspective, particularly in the context of media stereotyping. Photographic imagery is clearly a central element to how popular culture is communicated. Hence a popular culture context can offer a rich tapestry of visual imagery from which to view movements in the strength of the stereotype.

More recent studies of the accounting stereotype which have engaged directly with the accounting and popular culture research agenda include the works of Miley and Read (2012), Evans and Fraser (2012) and Czarniawska (2012). The latter two studies draw upon popular fiction to explore the nuances of the accounting stereotype. The focus of Czarniawska's (2012) paper is the detective novels of David Dodge in which the character of James "Whit" Whitney stars. Set in the 1940s United States, Whit is a certified public accountant who also dabbles in detective work, from catching drug smugglers to tracking down German spies. Detective novels are also a feature of Evans and Fraser's (2012) paper which examines the thrillers of Alexander Clark Smith. In these novels, the Scottish chartered accountant, Nicky Mahoun, becomes embroiled in all manner of murder and corruption in 1950s Britain. As with cinema and music, popular fiction forms a frame from which aspects of the accounting stereotype, both positive and negative, can be very effectively viewed. While critics may frown on this form of fiction, there is nothing trivial about it in terms of its mass reach and popular influence (Gelder, 2004; Longhurst, 1989). In place of fiction, Miley and Read (2012) draw upon jokes in popu-lar culture to gain insight into the accounting stereotype. Their analysis of an internet website devoted to jokes about accounting/accountants allowed them to draw comparisons between the characterisation of the accountant and the stock character of the professional man in *commedia dell'arte*, a form of improvisational theatre. All of these studies are significant in that they capture how the accountant is portrayed in the popular imagination, which has important consequences for the future of the accountancy profession and the image it wants to construct.

4 Frontiers in the study of accounting and popular culture

Given the continually shifting nature of popular culture, new opportunities for researching its interlinkages with accounting are constantly emerging. It is useful though to identify some areas of research which may prove particularly insightful in furthering an understanding of how accounting engages with popular trends. In this section, four potential new sites of research are suggested: the virtual world; the media; globalisation; and popular culture–producing organisa-tions. Each area will be considered in the following paragraphs.

Accounting scholars have increasingly suggested that an examination of assurance projects in realms beyond the traditional financial audit can shed further understanding on the nature and meaning of the audit process (Andon and Free, 2012; Chapman and Peecher, 2011; Cooper and Morgan, 2013). The realm of the virtual user review offers one such alternate arena. As noted earlier, with the advent of Web 2.0 technology, internet users are no longer passive voyeurs of digital data but rather are active participants in its creation. This scenario has facilitated the rise of the online user review where web users share their personal experiences of products and services. Some review sites have reached a level of sophistication that such personal accounts are converted into numerical scores and rankings. There are, of course, numerous issues to consider with regard to the credibility of the user review – critics have questioned their biased nature (Van Dijck, 2009) and the reliability of the reviewer's lay knowledge over credentialed expertise (Keen, 2007). Nonetheless, the user review has become an increasingly popular presence with the source of its trust appearing to be embedded in the high degree of trust placed in fellow members of their virtual community (Schmallegger and Carson, 2008). From a critical account-ing perspective, the user review is a fascinating occurrence because it allows us to consider issues such as trust and assurance – issues which are central to the nature of the audit process. In this manner, examining a popular phenomenon allows insights into traditional accounting concerns. Perhaps more importantly, however, accounting can in turn tell us something about the virtual user review and its rise to prominence. For example, is the popularity and prevalence of the user reviewer a reflection of the power of audit society and the need for checking in contemporary life (Power, 1996)? Are the opinions of fellow web users trusted because they inherently tap into notions of objectivity and independence that are associated with the professional audit (Power, 2003)? Jeacle and Carter (2011) have explored some of these themes from the perspective of the travel advice website TripAdvisor, but a great deal more work in this field needs to be done. More generally, the internet offers the popular culture accounting scholar a rich vista of research opportunity.

The media, in all its guises, is a crucial element in both the dissemination and construction of popular culture. It is a vehicle by which meanings can be communicated and signified in popular culture (Barthes, 1973). For example, cinema and television create the characters who provide a ready fodder for tabloid gossip and whose lifestyles are minutely displayed in the celebrity maga-zine. However, there is nothing particularly new in the nature of this form of popular culture. Since the advent of the silver screen, the lives of movie stars have attracted attention through the medium of the fan-based magazine or newspaper feature (Shafer, 1997). What is different about the relationship between popular culture and contemporary media, however, is its continual, twenty-four-hour presence. The ubiquitous nature of contemporary media (Featherstone, 2009) has been fuelled by a digital revolution which has spawned social media sites such as Twitter and Facebook. The consequence of this scenario is that a popular trend can now be initiated and globally transmitted in mere minutes, hence creating an intrinsic relationship between social media and popular culture (Beer and Burrows, 2013; Hansen, 2010). This makes social media an incredibly powerful forum in contemporary society. It also makes it an important site of research for critical accounting. Of course, there are myriad avenues of research which the critical scholar can travel down when engaging with social media. The way in which corporations increasingly use social media to provide accounts of their actions, for example, provides an alternative angle to more traditional modes of accountability (Jeacle and Carter, 2014). For actor–network theo-rists influenced by the thoughts of Latour (1986, 1987) and Callon (1986), the vast connected sites of Twitter and Facebook should surely offer a framework for examining the mobilisation of both actors and popular trends across time and space and the role of calculative technologies in that process.

Beyond the novelty of new media forms, the traditional mediums of television, cinema, radio and print offer fertile grounds for understanding the ways in which accounting influences, and in turn is influenced by, popular culture. As noted earlier, the cinematic lens has been a use-ful means to explore the accounting stereotype in popular culture, yet further insights can be gleaned from an examination of the cinematic industry more generally. For example, to what extent do the costing schedules and production budgets of film operations impact upon the nature of what gets filmed, and hence what actually becomes popular culture? To what extent does the choice of film star, location and set become determined by calculative technologies? Is box office success reliant on good publicity or simply tight budgetary control? Similar issues exist in the arena of television. As Carter and McKinlay (2013) argue, the cost savings associated with making a reality show over a period drama has consequences for the content of popular prime-time viewing. The subject matter of popular print media and its relationship with accounting also need to be examined; the cover feature in the weekly glossy magazine spread is no doubt a careful calculation between the celebrity fee and sales distribution statistics. In this manner, a focus on the media allows us to capture how accounting may play a central role in what gets played out as popular culture in our daily lives.

Globalisation has been the subject of intense academic inquiry for many years now. Organisational, social and cultural theorists have examined the origins and impact of the global corporate firm and pondered the meaning of a global culture for our sense of nationalism and identity (Beck, 2000; Featherstone, 1990; Sassen, 1998). With the exception of the recent work of Cooper and Ezzamel (2013), accounting scholars have remained relatively immune to this global trend. Our conception of the global has tended to revolve around the state of harmonisation of international accounting standards or the expansion of the audit profession into new territories. Consequently, globalisation has remained rooted at the professional rather than the organisational level. An engagement with accounting and popular culture, however, immediately brings the issue of globalisation to the fore. Global brands such as Starbucks, IKEA and McDonald's are icons of popular culture (Lyons, 2005; Ritzer, 1983; Rosenberg, 2005). To understand their role in contemporary life is to also understand the manner in which they deploy their accounting systems. Recent press attention in the United Kingdom has criticised the fact that the coffee chain Starbucks had managed to avoid paying British corporation tax for several years.[2] Clearly there lies a financial reporting angle to this controversy. At a deeper managerial level, what role does accounting play in shaping the goals and strategic directions of these organisations? When expanding their territorial scope, for example, what costing scenarios and budgetary predictions are enrolled in the decision-making process? Equally, beyond the traditional accounting debates on brand valuation, what role might accounting technologies play in the creation and sustenance of the brand in the first instance? To what extent has the global success of these ventures been centred on their performance measurement or management control systems? This leads neatly on to a final avenue of future research.

There is a need for investigation into the forms of management control systems used within popular culture organisations. Previous work on the role of accounting within 'high culture' organisations, for example the work of Zan, Blackstock and Cerutti (2000), has highlighted the delicate balancing act that accounting must play where the dominant mission of the organisation is cultural rather than profit making. The culture clash between artists and business can generate a potentially challenging environment for the operation of an accounting system. We know little, however, of the role of accounting within the purveyors of popular culture. Do such organisations, for example, use traditional accounting systems to manage their business, or does the dynamic nature of popular culture require the deployment of particularly flexible measures of performance and control? To what extent does accounting feed into the decision-making processes in such fast moving and changeable contexts? A particularly important feature of these investigations is not only to understand the nature of accounting practices within popular culture organisations, but more importantly to gain some insight into whether accounting actually influences or moulds popular phenomena. For example, does the information revealed by accounting technologies, or calculative practices more generally, shape decisions which orient popular culture in one direction versus another? For of course, organisations involved in the selling of popular culture, such as music labels, magazines and television broadcasters, are not neutral vehicles in the distribution of popular culture. Rather they are active participants in the creation of that culture – fashion chain stores, for example, not only follow popular fashion trends but also play a central role in influencing perceptions of what is deemed fashionable and unfashionable (Jeacle, 2014b). Consequently, an understanding of how costing data or budget projections may influence decisions in favour of one trend over another reveals important information about how popular culture is created or sustained. This provides an opportunity, therefore, to showcase the power of accounting and its contribution to fields beyond the realm of its own discipline. Explanations of popular culture have traditionally been concentrated within cultural studies. This literature can now be supplemented and even enhanced by new insights from within the accounting domain.

When undertaking investigations in any of the new fields of inquiry just outlined, it is useful to be open to the role of accounting technologies beyond the immediate confines of the finance function. Prior scholarship has witnessed the rise of the hybrid accountant (Burns and Scapens, 2000; Kurunmäki, 2004), which has important implications for conducting empirical accounting research. As critical accounting scholars, our scope of inquiry should not be limited to the traditional jurisdiction of professional accounting practice; rather we must engage with a host of actors across the organisational space. While some of these characters may not feel that they are immediately acquainted with accounting operations, or indeed see any resemblance between their role and that of the accountant (see, for example, the stereotypical perceptions of the merchandiser in the fashion chain store [Jeacle and Carter, 2012]), their use of calculative practices is revelatory. It reveals the reach of accounting throughout the organisation and beyond its boundaries. Hence by adopting a broad notion of what constitutes accounting, the critical accounting community has opened up new and fascinating vistas of knowledge. This defining feature of critical accounting research is particularly important in investigations of accounting's interlinkages with popular culture. Such a flexible and open approach will facilitate a full appreciation of the myriad ways in which accounting engages with popular phenomena.

5 Concluding comments

Amongst the seminal contributions to accounting research are the defining statements set out by Hopwood (1983) and Miller (1994) with regard to the social and organisational context of accounting. These works delivered a simple, yet immensely powerful message, and one that was to alter the shape of subsequent accounting research. To engage fully with accounting required a recognition of its role; not only of its ability to recast power relations within an organisation, but also recognition of the impact of social and institutional pressures on the practice itself. That an accounting technique can shape, and in turn be shaped by, such exogenous factors was a novel departure from a vein of research that had traditionally focused on the micro-technicalities of the craft rather than its wider ramifications. Indeed, so persuasive has been the shift in emphasis pioneered by Hopwood and Miller that 'the context' has become a prominent feature of contemporary investigations. The notion that accounting can operate in a vacuum is anathema to current qualitative accounting researchers. Consequently, Hopwood and Miller were amongst a small number of key academics who created a new space within accounting research.

Further seminal roles during this era were played by Tony Lowe and colleagues at the University of Sheffield, who effectively coined the term 'critical accounting'. The term was further formalised in 1990 with the launch of David Cooper and Tony Tinker's journal *Critical Perspectives on Accounting*. The creation of Lee Parker and James Guthrie's *Accounting, Auditing and Accountability Journal* and the organisation of the first Interdisciplinary Perspectives on

Accounting Conference (see Cooper and Hooper, 1987) were other pivotal moments in the construction of a new agenda for accounting research. Roslender and Dillard (2003) provide a comprehensive and insightful review of this fascinating period of transition within accounting research. More importantly, they delineate between the oft used terms of 'interdisciplinary' and 'critical' accounting, and argue that the latter is most appropriately understood to be a subset of the former that exhibits a commitment to a radical political praxis. Notwithstanding the differing positions adopted by those who favoured the critical as opposed to the Hopwood and Miller Foucauldian-inspired camps (Foucault, 1977), the pioneering pronouncements of all of these scholars opened up an alternative domain for accounting scholarship and created a firm foundation for future innovative studies.

Accounting and popular culture is one such new domain of accounting research. By moving beyond traditional fields of accounting scholarship we realise the opportunity to unveil the far-reaching influence of accounting in everyday life. The notion of discipline boundaries is critical here. One of the core features of critical accounting research has been its interdisciplinarity. By engaging with other disciplines, the critical accounting scholar is exposed to new ideas and schools of thought. The repercussions of this for the subject of accounting are that it staves off the staleness of operating in a vacuum. Indeed, as Miller (1998) has so persuasively argued, accounting is most interesting at the margins. It is at the margins of a discipline where new, fresh insights and novel approaches become most readily apparent. This is not to denigrate the central ground of a discipline, but merely to recognise that disciplinary boundaries are never fixed. The inevitable blurring of boundaries at the margins offers up the vistas of new territories and hence opportunities for a subject area. Popular culture is one such new domain.

In this regard, there is an inherent creativity at the heart of critical and interdisciplinary accounting research – as Parker and Guthrie aptly observe, it "requires a preparedness to venture into the unknown and to grapple with the unfamiliar" (2014: 3). Indeed, the ability to view accounting in new and creative ways has been a consistent trademark of critical accounting scholarship (Jeacle and Carter, 2014). As a community of scholars we have been fortunate to have several outlets in which to expound such creativity, from conferences such as the Interdisciplinary Perspectives on Accounting Conference, Critical Perspectives on Accounting Conference and Asia Pacific Interdisciplinary Perspectives on Accounting Conference, to journals such as *Accounting, Organizations and Society*, *Critical Perspectives on Accounting* and the *Accounting, Auditing and Accountability Journal*. Indeed, the editors of the latter journal see "championing intellectual pluralism" as one of the central foundations of their journal (Parker and Guthrie, 2009). For creativity to flourish, however, it is important that new domains of inquiry, such as the field of popular culture, receive an open and unbiased hearing. The peer review process is a crucial point of passage in this process of induction. Scholarly criticism is an essential element of evaluating and refining a paper's argument and contribution. Yet, while acknowledging this vital function, it is also expedient to express a cautionary word with regard to the nature of such a review process. Reviewers and journal editors hold influential positions in ensuring that critical accounting retains its creativity. In exercising such power, these actors have extremely important roles in facilitating new ideas and fields of research, and hence securing the future of critical accounting scholarship.

It is also useful to note in these concluding comments that the emergence of a literature on accounting and popular culture is of its time. It is reflective of the general mores, interests and concerns of the individual and enterprise alike. For example, the innovations in cost accounting in the early decades of the twentieth century were a product of the surge of interest in efficiency and scientific management initiatives. The drive for international accounting standards during the late twentieth century was a response to the increasing globalisation of business. More recently, the rise of social and environmental accounting research mirrors the ecological concerns of the populace. Hence, an interest in the interlinkages between accounting and popular culture similarly reflects an awareness of the increasing pervasiveness of popular culture in contemporary life. A related point is that as a research theme, accounting and popular culture is particularly appealing to young researchers as it is a context to which they inherently relate. Indeed, there are few corners of the globe left where the youth of today remain untouched by the bombardment of popular text and imagery. Their innate understanding of popular phenomena bodes well for their ability and eagerness to engage with accounting practice within this domain. Consequently, accounting and popular culture has the potential to provide a rich and rewarding contribution to critical accounting research. As they say in popular parlance: watch this space!

Notes

1 www.telegraph.co.uk/culture/art/art-news/10558497/Damien-Hirst-creates-Mickey-Mouse-portrait-for-charity.html.
2 See www.bbc.co.uk/news/uk-politics-23019514, accessed August 2014.

References

Andon, P. and C. Free (2012) "Auditing and crisis management: the 2010 Melbourne Storm salary cap scandal," *Accounting, Organizations and Society*, 37(3): 131–54.
Andon, P. and C. Free (2014). "Media coverage of accounting: the NRL salary cap crisis," *Accounting, Auditing and Accountability Journal*, 27(1): 15–47.
Andon, P., C. Free and P. Sivabalan (2014). "The legitimacy of new assurance providers: making the cap fit," *Accounting, Organizations and Society*, 39(2): 75–96.
Ang, I. (1985). *Watching Dallas*, London: Methuen.
Barnard, M. (1996). *Fashion as Communication*, London: Routledge.
Barthes, R. (1973). *Mythologies*, London: Paladin Books.
Baudrillard, J. (1970). "La societe de consummation" reprinted and translated in M. Poster (ed.): *Jean Baudrillard: Selected Writings*. Stanford, CA: Stanford University Press.
Bauman, Z. (2007). "Liquid art," *Theory, Culture & Society*, 24(1): 117–26.
Bausinger, H. (1984). "Media, technology and everyday life," *Media, Culture and Society*, 6(4): 343–51.
Beard, V. (1994). "Popular culture and professional identity: accountants in the movies," *Accounting, Organizations and Society*, 19(3): 303–18.
Beck, U. (2000). *What is Globalization?*, London: Polity Press.
Beer, D. and R. Burrows (2013). "Popular culture, digital archives and the new social life of data," *Theory, Culture & Society*, 30(4): 47–71.
Blankespoor, E., G. S. Miller and H. D. White (2013). "The role of dissemination in market liquidity: evidence from firms' use of Twitter," *Accounting Review*, 89(1): 79–112.
Bocock, R. (1993). *Consumption*, London: Routledge.
Bourdieu, P. (1984). *Distinction*, London: Routledge and Kegan Paul.
Branston, G. (2000). *Cinema and Cultural Modernity*, Buckingham: Open University Press.
Breward, C. (2000). "Cultures, identities, histories: fashioning a cultural approach to dress" in N. White and I. Griffiths (eds.): *The Fashion Business: Theory, Practice, Image*, Oxford: Berg.
Burke, P. (1994). *Popular Culture in Early Modern Europe*, Aldershot: Scolar Press.
Burns, J. and R. Scapens (2000). *The Changing Nature of Management Accounting and the Emergence of 'Hybrid' Accountants*, New York: IFAC Publications.
Callon, M. (1986). "Some elements of a sociology of translation: domestication of the scallops and the fishermen of St Brieuc Bay," in J. Law (ed.): *Power, Action and Belief: A New Sociology of Knowledge?* London: Routledge and Kegan Paul.
Carnegie, G. D. and C. J. Napier (2010). "Traditional accountants and business professionals: portraying the accounting profession after Enron," *Accounting, Organizations and Society*, 35(3): 360–76.
Carter, C. and A. McKinlay (2013). "Cultures of strategy: remaking the BBC, 1968-2003," *Business History*, 55(7): 1228–46.

Certeau, M. de (1984). *The Practice of Everyday Life*. Berkeley, CA: University of California Press.

Chapman, C. and M. Peecher (2011). "Worlds of assurance," *Accounting, Organizations and Society*, 36(4–5): 267–68.

Chapman, C., D. Cooper and P. Miller (2009). "Linking accounting, organizations and institutions," in C. Chapman, D. Cooper and P. Miller (eds): *Accounting, Organizations and Institutions*. Oxford: Oxford University Press.

Cooper, D. and T. Hooper (1987). "Critical studies in accounting," *Accounting Organizations and Society*, 12(5): 407–14.

Cooper, C. and J. Johnson (2012). "Vulgate accountability – insights from the field of football," *Accounting, Auditing and Accountability Journal*, 25(4): 602–34.

Cooper, D. and M. Ezzamel (2013). "Globalization discourses and performance measurement systems in a multinational firm," *Accounting, Organizations and Society*, 38(4): 288–313.

Cooper, C. and Y. Joyce (2013). "Insolvency practice in the field of football," *Accounting, Organizations and Society*, 38(2): 108–29.

Cooper, D. and W. Morgan (2013). "Meeting the evolving corporate reporting needs of government and society: arguments for a deliberative approach to accounting rule making," *Accounting and Business Research*, 43(4): 418–41.

Czarniawska, B. (2012). "Accounting and detective stories: an excursion to the USA in the 1940s," *Accounting, Auditing and Accountability Journal*, 25(4): 659–72.

Dimnik, T. and S. Felton (2006). "Accountant stereotypes in movies distributed in North America in the twentieth century," *Accounting, Organisations and Society*, 31(2): 129–55.

Ellison, N., C. Steinfield and C. Lampe (2007) "The benefits of Facebook "friends": social capital and college students' use of online social network sites," *Journal of Computer-Mediated Communication*, 12(4): 1143–68.

Espeland, W. N. and M. Sauder (2007). "Rankings and reactivity: how public measures recreate social worlds," *American Journal of Sociology*, 113(1): 1–40.

Evans, L. and I. Fraser (2012). "The accountant's social background and stereotype in popular culture: the novels of Alexander Clark Smith," *Accounting, Auditing and Accountability Journal*, 25(6): 964–1000.

Featherstone, M. (1990). *Global Culture: Nationalism, Globalization and Modernity*, London: Sage Publications.

Featherstone, M. (1991). *Consumer Culture and Postmodernism*, London: Sage Publications.

Featherstone, M. (2009). "Ubiquitous media," *Theory, Culture & Society*, 26(2–3): 1–22.

Finkelstein, J. (1994). "Fashion, taste and eating out," in *The Polity Reader in Cultural Theory*. Cambridge: Polity Press.

Fiske, J. (1987). *Television Culture*, London and New York: Methuen.

Fiske, J. (1989). *Understanding Popular Culture*, London: Routledge.

Foucault, M. (1977). *Discipline and Punish, The Birth of the Prison*. London: Allen Lane.

Foucault, M. (1991). "On governmentality," in G. Burchell, C. Gordon and P. Miller (eds): *The Foucault Effect: Studies in Governmentality*, London: Harvester Wheatsheaf.

Frith, S. (1994). "Music for pleasure," in *The Polity Reader in Cultural Theory*. Cambridge: Polity Press.

Gallhofer, S. and J. Haslam (2006). "Online reporting: accounting in cybersociety," *Accounting, Auditing and Accountability Journal*, 19(5): 625–30.

Gallhofer, S., J. Haslam, E. Monk and C. Roberts. (2006). "The emancipatory potential of online reporting: the case of counter accounting," *Accounting, Auditing and Journal*, 19(5): 681–718.

Gelder, K. (2004). *Popular Fiction: The Logics and Practices of a Literary Field*, London: Routledge.

Glynn, K. (2000). *Tabloid Culture: Trash Taste, Popular Power and the Transformation of American Television*, Durham, NC: Duke University Press.

Goffman, E. (1956). *The Presentation of Self in Everyday Life*, Edinburgh: University of Edinburgh Social Sciences Research Centre.

Gramsci, A. (1971). *Selections from the Prison Notebooks*, translated by Q. Hoare and G. Nowell Smith, London: Lawrence and Wishart.

Gripsrud, J. (1992). "The aesthetics and politics of melodrama," in P. Dahlgren and C. Sparks (eds): *Journalism and Popular Culture*, London: Sage Publications.

Hall, S. (1980). "Encoding and decoding in the television discourse," in S. Hall, D. Hobson, A. Lowe and P. Willis (eds): *Culture, Media, Language*. London: Routledge.

Hall, S. (1992). "Cultural studies and its theoretical legacies," in L. Grossberg, C. Nelson, and P. Treichler (eds): *Cultural Studies*. London: Routledge.

Hall, S. and P. Whannel (1964). *The Popular Arts*, London: Hutchinson.

Hansen, M. (2010). "New media," in W. Mitchell and M. Hansen (eds): *Critical Terms for Media Studies*, Chicago, IL: University of Chicago Press.

Harvey, D. (1989). *The Condition of Postmodernity*, Oxford: Basil Blackwell.

Heidensohn, F. and R. Wright (2010). "The British Journal of Sociology at sixty," *British Journal of Sociology*, 61(s1): 1–6.

Hoggart, R. (1990). *The Uses of Literacy*, London: Chatto and Windus.

Holmes, S. (2004). "'All you've got to worry about is the task, having a cup of tea, and doing a bit of sun-bathing': approaching celebrity in Big Brother," in S. Holmes and D. Jermyn (eds): *Understanding Reality TV*, London: Routledge.

Hopwood, A. G. (1983). "On trying to study accounting in the contexts in which it operates," *Accounting, Organizations and Society*, 8(2-3): 287–305.

Hopwood, A. G. (1994). "Accounting and everyday life: an introduction," *Accounting, Organisations and Society*, 19(3): 299–301.

Hopwood, A. G. (2009). "On striving to give a critical edge to Critical Management Studies," in M. Alvesson, T. Bridgman and H. Willmott (eds): *The Oxford Handbook of Critical Management Studies*, Oxford: Oxford University Press.

Horrall, A. (2001). *Popular Culture in London c.1890-1918: The Transformation of Entertainment*. Manchester: Manchester University Press.

Jacobs, K. and S. Evans (2012). "Constructing accounting in the mirror of popular music," *Accounting, Auditing and Accountability Journal*, 25(4): 673–702.

Jeacle, I. (2009). "'Going to the movies': accounting and twentieth century cinema," *Accounting, Auditing and Accountability Journal*, 22(5): 677–708.

Jeacle, I. (2012). "Accounting and popular culture: framing a research agenda," *Accounting, Auditing and Accountability Journal*, 25(4): 580–601.

Jeacle, I. (2014). "'And the BAFTA goes to ...': the assurance role of the auditor in the film awards ceremony," *Accounting, Auditing and Accountability Journal*, 27(4–5): 778–808.

Jeacle, I. (2015). "Fast fashion: calculative technologies and the governance of everyday dress," *European Accounting Review*, 24(2): 305–28.

Jeacle, I. and C. Carter (2011). "In TripAdvisor we trust: rankings, calculative regimes and abstract systems," *Accounting, Organizations and Society*, 36(4–5): 293–309.

Jeacle, I. and C. Carter (2012). "Fashioning the popular masses: accounting as mediator between creativity and control," *Accounting, Auditing & Accountability Journal*, 25(4): 719–51.

Jeacle, I. and C. Carter (2014). "Creative spaces in interdisciplinary accounting research," *Accounting, Auditing and Accountability Journal*, 27(8): 1233–1240.

Keen, A. (2007). *The Cult of the Amateur: How the Democratization of the Digital World is Assaulting Our Economy, Our Culture, and Our Values*, New York: Doubleday Currency.

Kurunmäki, L. (2004). "A hybrid profession – the acquisition of management accounting expertise by medical professionals," *Accounting, Organizations and Society*, 29(3–4): 327–47

Lash, S. (1990). *The Sociology of Postmodernism*, London: Verso Press.

Lash, S. and J. Urry (1994). "Postmodernist sensibility," in *The Polity Reader in Cultural Theory*, Cambridge: Polity Press.

Latour, B. (1986). "The powers of association," in J. Law (ed.): *Power, Action and Belief: A New Sociology of Knowledge?* London: Routledge and Kegan Paul.

Latour, B. (1987). *Science in Action*, Milton Keynes, UK: Open University Press.

Leavis, F. R. (1933). *Mass Civilisation and Minority Culture*, Cambridge: Minority Press.

Longhurst, D. (1989). "Introduction: reading popular fiction," in D. Longhurst (ed.): *Gender, Genre and Narrative Pleasure*, London: Unwin Hyman.

Lowe, A., J. Locke and A. Lymer (2012). "The SEC's retail investor 2.0: interactive data and the rise of calculative accountability," *Critical Perspectives on Accounting*, 23(3): 183– 200.

Lyons, J. (2005). "Think Seattle, act globally," *Cultural Studies*, 19(1): 14–34.

MacDonald, D. (1957). "A theory of mass culture," in B. Rosenberg and D. White (eds): *Mass Culture*, Glencoe, IL: The Free Press.

MacKenzie, K., S. Buckby and H. Irvine (2013). "Business research in virtual worlds: possibilities and practicalities," *Accounting, Auditing & Accountability Journal*, 26(3): 352–373.

McRobbie, A. (1999). *In the Culture Society: Art, Fashion and Popular Music*, London and New York: Routledge.

McRobbie, A. (2005). *The Uses of Cultural Studies*, London: Sage Publications.

Miles, P. and M. Smith (1987). *Cinema, Literature and Society: Elite and Mass Culture in Interwar Britain*, London: Croom Helm.

Miley, F. and A. Read (2012). "Jokes in popular culture: the characterisation of the accountant," *Accounting, Auditing and Accountability Journal*, 25(4): 703–18.

Miller, P. (1994). "Accounting as social and institutional practice: an introduction," in A. G. Hopwood and P. Miller (eds): *Accounting as Social and Institutional Practice*. Cambridge: Cambridge Studies in Management.

Miller, P. (1998). "The margins of accounting," *European Accounting Review*, 7(4): 605–21.

Miller, P. (2001). "Governing by numbers: why calculative practices matter," *Social Research*, 68(2): 379–396.

Miller, P. and N. Rose (1990). "Governing economic life," *Economy and Society*, 19(1): 1–31.

Miller, P. and N. Rose (2008). *Governing the Present: Administering Economic, Social and Personal Life*, Cambridge: Polity Press.

Modleski, T. (1986) "Femininity as mas(s)querade: a feminist approach to mass culture," in C. MacCabe (ed.): *High Theory/Low Culture*, Manchester: Manchester University Press.

Morley, D. (1986). *Family Television*. London: Comedia.

Napoli, P. (2010). "Revisiting 'mass communication' and the 'work' of the audience in the new media environment," *Media Culture Society*, 32(3): 505–16.

Neu, D., A. S. Rahaman and J. Everett (2014) "Accounting and sweatshops: enabling coordination and control in low-price apparel production chains," *Contemporary Accounting Research*, 31(2): 322–46.

Parker, L. and J. Guthrie (2009). "Championing intellectual pluralism," *Accounting, Auditing and Accountability Journal*, 22(1): 5–12.

Parker, L. D. and S. Warren (2009). "Bean counters or bright young things? Towards the visual study of identity construction among newly qualified professional accountants," *Qualitative Research in Accounting and Management*, 6(4): 205–23.

Parker, L. and J. Guthrie (2014). Addressing directions in interdisciplinary accounting research," *Accounting, Auditing and Accountability Journal*, 27(8): 1–7.

Power, M. (1994). *The Audit Explosion*, London: Demos.

Power, M. (1996). "Making things auditable," *Accounting, Organizations and Society*, 21(2–3): 289–315.

Power, M. (1997). *The Audit Society: Rituals of Verification*, Oxford: Oxford University Press.

Power, M. (2003). "Auditing and the production of legitimacy," *Accounting, Organizations and Society*, 28(4): 379–94.

Rakow, L. (1986). "Feminist approaches to popular culture: giving patriarchy its due," *Journal of Communication Inquiry*, 9(1): 19–41.

Risaliti, G. and R. Verona (2013). "Players' registration rights in the financial statements of the leading Italian clubs: a survey of Inter, Juventus, Lazio, Milan and Roma," *Accounting, Auditing and Accountability Journal*, 26(1): 16–47.

Ritzer, G. (1983). "The McDonaldization of society," *Journal of American Culture*, 6(1): 100–07.

Rosenberg, B. (2005). "Scandinavian dreams: DIY, democratisation and IKEA," *Transformations*, 11.

Roslender, R. and J. Dillard (2003). "Reflections on the interdisciplinary perspectives on accounting," *Critical Perspectives on Accounting*, 14(3): 325–51.

Sassen, S. (1998). *Globalization and its Discontents: Essays on the New Mobility of People and Money*, New York: The New Press.

Schudson, M. (1987). "The new validation of popular culture: sense and sentimentality in academia," *Critical Studies in Mass Communication*, 4(1): 51–68.

Schmallegger D. and D. Carson (2008). "Blogs in tourism: changing approaches to information exchange," *Journal of Vacation Marketing*, 14(2): 99–111.

Shafer, S. (1997). *British Popular Films 1929-1939: The Cinema of Reassurance*, London: Routledge.

Sharpe, D. (1969). *The Picture Palace and Other Buildings for the Movies*. New York: Praeger.

Shields, R. (1992). "Spaces for the subject of consumption," in R. Shields (ed.): *Lifestyle Shopping: The Subject of Consumption*, London and New York: Routledge.

Smith, D. and K. Jacobs (2011). "'Breaking up the sky': the characterisation of accounting and accountants in popular music," *Accounting, Auditing and Accountability Journal*, 24(7): 904–31.

Stokes, J. (1999). *On Screen Rivals: Cinema and Television in the United States and Britain*, London: Macmillan Press.

Storey, J. (2003). *Cultural Studies and the Study of Popular Culture*, Edinburgh: Edinburgh University Press.

Storey, J. (2009). *Cultural Theory and Popular Culture: A Reader*, Harlow: Pearson.

Strinati, D. (2004). *An Introduction to Theories of Popular Culture*, London and New York: Routledge.

Turner, G. (2004). *Understanding Celebrity*, London: Sage Publications.

Turner, G. (2010). *Ordinary People and the Media*, London: Sage Publications.

Van Dijck, J. (2009). "Users like you? theorizing agency in user-generated content," *Media Culture Society*, 31(1): 41–58.

Webster, D. (1988). *Looka Yonder: The Imaginary America of Populist Culture*, London: Routledge.

Wilson, E. (1985). *Adorned in Dreams: Fashion and Modernity*, London: Virago.

Winship, J. (1987). *Inside Women's Magazines*, London: Pandora.

Zan, L., A. Blackstock, G. Cerutti and C. Mayer (2000). "Accounting for art," *Scandinavian Journal of Management*, 16(3): 335–47.

SECTION V

20
ACCOUNTING HISTORY

Richard Fleischman, Thomas Tyson and David Oldroyd

1 Introduction

At the turn of the century Enron Inc. was one of the largest and wealthiest corporate enterprises in the US. Arthur Andersen (AA), its public accounting firm, was widely regarded as the premier international accounting firm by virtue of its ethics, the expertise of its staff and the longevity of its associations with the world's most prestigious clients. It is now clear that for Enron's senior management cadre, and especially its CEO, its power and wealth were insufficient, resulting in actions being taken that clearly violated the rules and ethics of accounting. The degree to which Enron's accounting staff were complicit in the episode is unclear but all of the company's employees experienced an initial loss of employment nevertheless. The fate of AA was just as grim as it collapsed in the aftermath. The extent of its own leadership's collusion is unknown since it was the misstatement of the value of Enron's foreign subsidiaries that was the major defalcation. In hindsight, a major issue that should probably have been handled differently was the US government's rush to justice, arguably precipitated by one employee's overly quick finger on a shredding machine. Much of what has subsequently been written about Enron suggests that AA could have survived the debacle, since the former Big Eight accountancy firms reduced to the Big Four through consolidations over recent decades is, in retrospect, less than an ideal outcome. It was particularly shortsighted on the part of the US government to accentuate further an already oligarchic situation within a vital industry, especially as virtually all of AA's staff quickly found new employments with former competitors.

A crucial lesson that the Enron episode, among many others, offers anyone contemplating a career in accountancy is the desirability of taking any elective theory, ethics or history course that may be on offer as part of their educational program. The study of accounting's history is arguably doubly valuable since from an ethics perspective, more often than not, it reveals the baser side of human behavior, an assertion that the present chapter seeks to document with some force. The field of accounting history itself has a long and distinguished history, characterised by increasingly high levels of sophisticated scholarship. It is widely canvassed that with the advent of Critical Accounting Historical Research (CAHR) in the 1980s, the field experienced a significant change in both the extent and richness of the insights generated. These in turn are viewed as holding out the promise of an enhanced self-awareness on the part of those who practice or seek to practice accountancy in some way. CAHR has deployed a number of historical paradigms,[1] which it shares with the broader corpus of critical accounting research, that are designed to further our understanding of events in accounting history and to sensitise the awareness of accounting practitioners and academicians to their obligations to maintain high ethical standards and the protection of the public interest.

The broad designation CAHR is probably better understood to also encompass a number of subcomponents variously referred to as "alternative research," "paradigmatic theorising" "enabling accounting research, "interventionist accounting" and "the new accounting history," notwithstanding the confusion that persists over the meaning of these terms (Oldroyd, 1999). The resultant departure from traditional historiography is considerably broader with respect to topics investigated, methodologies utilised and explanatory paradigms deployed. Its progress has in no small part also been facilitated by the emergence of new journals, again committed to promoting the broader critical accounting project, most importantly *Critical Perspectives on Accounting* (*CPA*), the *Accounting, Auditing and Accountability Journal* (*AAAJ*) and *Accounting, Organizations and Society* (*AOS*), all competing to attract the best of the papers reflecting these new directions.

2 Critical accounting historical research: general underlying principles

A valuable point of departure is to provide an overview of how a number of prominent critical accounting scholars identify the parameters and goals of their research. Laughlin encourages engagement with the accounting profession in an attempt to achieve consensus with respect to

> [a] critical understanding of the role of the accounting processes and practices and the accounting profession in the functioning of society and organizations with an intention to use that understanding to engage (where appropriate) in changing those processes, practices and the profession.
>
> *(1999: 73)*

In contrast Sikka and Willmott (1997: 158) go further and urge confrontation with the profession and its leadership:

> The accountancy profession has surrounded itself with narratives of even-handed public behaviour, professional ethics and discipline through which it rehearses and sustains the dominant fable of "progress" embedded in accounting history. … Heroic professional bodies and their leaders battle against the odds and, amidst this chaos, introduce and protect the public from diverse troubles and dangers. Such myths can be questioned by involving alternative sources, exhuming buried documents, reviving forgotten and abandoned histories (Said, 1994) to question whether the profession is all that it claims to be.

Broadbent (2002: 436) cautions that "critical accounting should … argue for the provision of information sets that resist the *status quo*." Of great value is work that "has demonstrated resistance to the patriarchal and gendered values that lie behind accounting's taken-for-granted construction." Baker and Bettner likewise support the concept that accounting is not the value-free, neutral portrait of reality that many would have us believe:

> Critical researchers have convincingly and repeatedly argued that accounting does not produce an objective representation of economic "reality," but rather pursues a highly contested and partisan representation of the economic and social world.
>
> *(1997: 305)*

In their founding editorial in the newly established *CPA* journal, Cooper and Tinker observe:

> Most of all, we reject methodological secularism and academic obscurantism, and support new forms of dialogue and tolerance that encourage catholic, eclectic and interdisciplinary approaches. The only methodological endorsement we will make is that "anything and everything" should be open for "Critique."
>
> *(Cooper and Tinker, 1990: 1)*

Accordingly, Moore (1991: 770) defines critical accounting as

> [a] set of discursive practices… embodying a radical epistemology (or political) state which questions objectivity in the first place, finds "accurate representation" an impossible goal, and seeks alternative descriptions for what accountants do and the role accounting plays.

The ultimate aim is a better world, to which end Gallhofer and Haslam note the important characteristic of accounting's

> enabling ability to act as a force for radical emancipatory social change through making things visible and comprehensible and helping engender dialogue and action towards emancipatory change.
>
> *(1997: 82)*

To achieve this, it is necessary to question the role of accounting and our preconceptions about it.

Turning now to accounting history, Merino and Mayper observe that "the term *traditional* refers to historical inquiries that attempt to render the past familiar, the term, *critical*, refers to those inquiries that try to render the familiar unfamiliar" (1993: 238, emphasis as in the original). Most historians, whatever their persuasion, would probably not admit to the level of intent to interpret the past in a certain way that is implicit in this quote. Indeed, the dichotomy expressed here between critical historians and so-called traditionalists is too simplistic as one could equally argue that writing to a paradigm, as discussed in the next section, is also about rendering the world familiar in the mind's eye of the proponent (Oldroyd, 1999). A more accurate description of the essence of critical accounting history is that it challenges our preconceptions about the present through analysis of the mix of historical contingencies that have created it (Hoskin and Macve, 2000; Parker, 2004).

3 The major paradigms: a fruitful literature

Contributions from within three paradigms – Economic rationalism (Neoclassicism); Foucauldianism; and Marxism (Labour Process) – have shaped the greatest part of the CAHR literature. Each is briefly introduced in this section, identifying the basic tenets of the paradigm, their founders and the key players who have kept the paradigms contemporary and reinvigorated through recent decades. The work of many other scholars will also be noted later in the chapter in a survey of a range of fields wherein CAHR practitioners have exposed past injustices, and in which those performing the accounting function may have been complicit.

3.1 *Economic Rationalism (ER)*

This, the oldest of the three paradigms, is understood to have evolved from neoclassical economics, particularly from Adam Smith's *An Inquiry into the Nature and Causes of the Wealth of Nations*

(1776). Smith's key concept was that individuals are guided by an "invisible hand" in the direction of their own best economic self-interest. This theory justified *laissez-faire* economics as a fundamental dictate for governmental policy at both the domestic and foreign policy levels. Since Smith predated many of economics' other founding fathers by over a century, and as a result of which his contribution was less well known, much of his relevance in the economic world of the late nineteenth and twentieth centuries needed to be re-established. This task was accomplished primarily by Chandler (1977), a Harvard business historian, who chronicled how "the visible hand" of managerial decision making had replaced the "invisible hand" of market forces, explaining in part the advent of the modern business enterprise and the new accounting methods devised to record and control its activities and calculate its profits. Williamson (1985) extended Chandler's vision to organisation theory by introducing transaction cost analysis, claiming that the main purpose of capitalism's economic institutions is to economise on transaction costs.

ER scholars as a group have been very interested in the evolution of the factory system, particularly in the US and the UK. This is an area of human experience in which Foucauldian and Marxist scholars have often disagreed but sometimes have crossed paradigmatic lines and worked together with ERs. Perhaps the most famous contribution to grace an ER library is Johnson and Kaplan's *Relevance Lost* (1987), which builds upon research the authors had pursued at the DuPont and General Motors archives. The authors claim that virtually all the management accounting techniques in use at the time of writing in the US industrial sector had been known to the two giants in the 1920s, and that the stagnation over the half-century that followed appeared to explain the loss of American industrial hegemony in the aftermath of World War II. They incorporate in their book suggestions they claim will get US industry back on track. While many economic historians, including the present authors, disagreed with some of the claims made, many did concur with Foucauldians Ezzamel, Hoskin and Macve (1990) that the book propelled accounting history to centre stage.

A propensity for ER scholars has been the gathering of historical information. Flesher has assembled an immense collection of archival documents at the University of Mississippi Library, which is now available online to researchers from around the globe. Edwards (2000) and Fleischman (2006) have each re-republished a multi-volume set of CAHR papers. Parker and Yamey (1994) compiled an excellent collection of articles written by British authors. Fleischman, Walker and Funnell (2012) republished a more modest collection of CAHR papers. All of these references include historical work by scholars influenced by a variety of paradigms. For anyone seeking an accessible source of accurate information on a variety of accounting topics, historical and current, Chatfield and Vangermeersch's (1996) *The History of Accounting: An International Encyclopedia* cannot be beaten. If one's wish is specifically accounting history research worldwide, Mattessich (2008) comes highly recommended. Finally, the *Routledge Companion to Accounting History*, edited by Edwards and Walker (2008a), is another well-received recent collection.

3.2 *Foucauldianism*

Michel Foucault, a central figure in French postmodern theory who stressed the centrality of language, was identified by Habermas as "*the* theorist of power" (1987: 287). The disciplinary paradigm he established to study the control practices evident in closed institutions, including asylums, prisons, barracks and schools, appears in many ways to parallel the factory system and other facets of modern life in which accountancy is implicated. In the factory and in other environments mediated by managerial action, it seems that accounting techniques serve as a vehicle for 'normalising the gaze' required to accommodate discipline at a micro-level, and thereby labour control, to render it observable, calculable and accountable.

As founder and editor-in-chief of *AOS* Hopwood, himself an outstanding Foucauldian theorist, used the pages of the journal to promote Foucauldian accounting history research. Many seminal contributions are associated with several of his colleagues at the London School of Economics, including Miller, and Napier. Macve was also an LSE colleague, albeit of a different Foucauldian slant, although his long-term collaborator and co-author, Hoskin, was not. Together Hoskin and Macve have produced a flow of prominent articles continuing from the partnership's formation in the mid 1980s to the present day.

Hoskin and Macve's first major project was to demonstrate their conviction that the "genesis of modern management" occurred at the Springfield Armory, an American munitions establishment (Hoskin and Macve, 1986, 1988). After considerable archival research, they concluded that the key factor was the arrival of Daniel Tyler who brought with him West Point connections, disciplinary techniques and the knowledge necessary for time-study methodology to establish systems of grading that rendered workers observable and accountable. A similar analysis was subsequently applied to the early New England textile industry. Developments at both sites were extensively debated with Tyson for over a decade (Hoskin and Macve, 1988, 1996, 2000; Tyson, 1993, 1998, 2000). In what may or may not be construed an amazing coincidence, seminal work appeared in the late 1980s or early 1990s from theorists representing each of the three major paradigms. For ER, it was *Relevance Lost* (1987); for Foucauldianism, it was a superbly crafted article by Miller and O'Leary (1987) in which outside disciplines (psychology and sociology) are brought into basically an accounting discussion of how the industrial labourer was turned into a "governable person." The Marxist contribution to this trio of papers will be outlined in the next section.

Two further Foucauldian authors instrumental in establishing the paradigm as a major force are Loft (1986), who documents the ways in which the British government conducted World War I domestically, and in a small but revealing book, *Coming into the Light* (1990), how this impacted on the formation of a cost accounting association, the Institute of Cost and Works Accountants (ICWA), in the aftermath of the war.[2] A second significant contribution to the paradigm is Stewart, whose 1992 paper highlights the particular and extraordinarily valuable Foucauldian contribution to accounting historiography. More recent works by authors either supporting or challenging Foucauldian interpretations include Carter, McKinlay and Rawlinson (2002), McKinlay (2006) and Tinker (2005).

3.3 Marxism

The first volume of Marx's classic *Das Kapital* was published in German in 1867. His economic theories are undoubtedly better known than those of the other paradigmatic forefathers, Smith and Foucault. Unfortunately, much of what passes for the received wisdom thereon is both erroneous and widely rejected because of Marx's posthumous association with class struggle, Soviet Russia and the Cold War. Marx's philosophy of history was derived from the Hegelian dialectic, according to which an existing reality (the thesis) generates the thought in the minds of people that the opposite might be more desirable (the antithesis). The interaction between the two produces a changed reality (the synthesis). The Marxist dialectic (dialectical materialism) features class struggle between the bourgeoisie, those who own the modes of production, and the proletariat, those who have nothing to offer economically but the labour of their own two hands. 'Struggle' between these two classes, coupled with technological innovation, produces new economic realities, with new combatants, but in the same two highly unequal positions of economic power. Class conflict continues until a "classless society" eventuates wherein each contributes according to their ability and receives in return according to their needs.

One of the many strengths of Marxism as a paradigm has been its ability to respond and adapt to changing economic and industrial environments. It is said that one of the obligations of Marxist historians is updating the paradigm as new stages of capitalism wax and wane. Marxist historians, although not having lost contact with Marxist views of class conflict, have moved away from an older economic reductionism, in the guise of "vulgar Marxism" into a wider investigation of the social, cultural and broader underpinnings that define industrial relations. This breadth of focus is evident in the seminal works of Hobsbawm (1972), Thompson (1964, 1967) and Hill (1986). Braverman (1974) provides a penetrating analysis of the progressive deskilling of American industrial labour with the advent of new managerial hierarchies in the later nineteenth century, taking Marxist thinking into its labour process phase, a term subsequently frequently appended to the name of the paradigm itself. The heterogeneity and subjectivity of the labour force became crucial issues.

Labour process theory was very quickly embraced by a number of the leading advocates of critical accounting research, one consequence of which was that Marxism soon became established as a major CAHR paradigm. In these early years, Tinker and his co-authors were the most prominent voices for exposing the evils of big business and the accounting that supported its malevolent operations (Tinker, 1985; Tinker, Merino and Neimark, 1982). Bryer is another prolific Marxist accounting historian who has analysed a range of topics from English feudalism to the development of capitalism in the US. A relatively recent arrival on the scene is Toms (2006), who as a moderate subscriber to the paradigm, prefers to be known as a "Marxian." Some labour process scholars have urged a broadening of managerial innovations beyond the "conspiratorial, one dimensional concept" (Knights and Willmott, 1986: 4) to an evolution of labour processes that feature different control techniques, even consensual ones (Burawoy, 1985; Edwards, 1989). Finally, Hopper and Armstrong (1991) provide a detailed Marxist analysis of the evolution of the American labour movement that builds to a penetrating critique of the Johnson and Kaplan's largely positive prognosis advanced in *Relevance Lost*. Hopper and Armstrong's paper is offered as a crowning achievement of reasonably recent Marxist-influenced accounting historiography.

To conclude this section, it is appropriate to note that many other paradigms have made their ways into accounting historical research from kindred disciplines including economics, philosophy, sociology and so on. A valuable source of information is Lodh and Gaffikin (1997), who provide details of these additional paradigms and their various influences on CAHR and critical historiography.

4 Unhappy beginnings

The early years of paradigmatic discourse inspired many traditional accounting historians to hope that it would afford the opportunity for a greater level of dialogue. Many felt their particular paradigm would be more universally recognised as contributing to the explanations of specific historical events or, at a more panoramic level, to adding richness to patterns of historical development. Others had cause to hope that the utilisation of multiple paradigms in combination would provide a deeper understanding of the crucial events and processes of history. Some very helpful discussions of paradigmatic issues have been sponsored in special issues of *CPA*, a process that continues, and to which the present authors enthusiastically contribute.

At this point it is useful to address a number of issues that are not particularly paradigmatic in nature but rather arise more intransigently perhaps, as reflective of differing opinions as to what is appropriate in the writing of history itself. For example, can the voices of the past be heard only as transmitted though primary sources? If some of the voices had no access to an accounting record, could a secondary source (an historian) be their advocate? If so, were these historians able to be objective or were they inescapably burdened by personal and societal prejudices? These are questions that virtually defy consensus. A truly vital issue is what, if any, should be the relationship between the past and the present in the writing of history?

Fleischman typifies the historian trained years ago in the mindset that historians had the fundamental obligation to report the past as it actually happened, without the intrusion of moral stances reflective of the author's personal prejudices. Only then, could the voices of the past be truly and accurately transmitted to contemporary listeners, without the confounding 'noise' of what exists only in the future. Napier (1989) divides the historical process into two functional categories: the "gatherers" of information who scoured archival repositories and reported their findings, providing grist for the paradigmatic mills, whereupon the "contextualizers" could supplement that information with paradigmatic theory to produce the finished historical product for publication. This observation led Fleischman to realise that his approach lacked objectivity because the process of selection of what to report from the archive was itself subjective. The picture is not all one-sided, however. Archival historians attempt to reduce subjectivity by validating the evidence in terms of the reliability of the sources, such as in terms of their closeness to events. Indeed, to criticise accounting historians for believing in "the overarching importance of primary sources," as Gaffikin (2011: 240) does, is highly questionable. In our view, the dichotomy between archival and contextual history is fallacious, as not to look for oneself leaves the historian at the mercy of someone else's interpretation of data, which they had probably selected with a completely different question in mind (Oldroyd, Tyson and Fleischman, 2015).

The past/present issue became a primary focal point of debate between critical and traditional accounting historians when Miller and Napier proclaim: "Within the traditionalist evolutionary model, the now is always present, if only *in utero* in the then" (1993: 639). Consequently, Miller and Napier were informing traditionalists that when the latter linked customs, idioms, conventions and/or prejudices to those that existed in their presents, but which were unbeknownst to those in the specific past they were reporting, they were committing "anachronisms," historiographic high crimes. In our view, they were out of step with the majority of historians and philosophers on this issue. Fleischman and Tyson (1997: 97–9) provide a lengthy list of scholars all of whom had previously spoken to the impossibility of achieving the past/present separation called for. Merino and Mayper (1993) observe that the dangers of "belief transference," ascribing current concepts to past historical figures, "increases exponentially when researchers use a theoretical framework to explain a particular historical phenomenon" (quoted in Fleischman and Tyson, 1997: 99). Most of the aforementioned scholars averred that bias in the writing of history is unavoidable. While we accept that view, we modify it, again agreeing with Merino and Mayper (1993) that the best we as historians can do is to minimise the problem by stating our biases forthrightly, thereby allowing the reader to judge who is speaking to them at key junctures, whether the voice from the past or the voice of the historian.

The issue of whether historians should, or even could, distance themselves from their own experiences and moral values, has proved vital in the teaching of accounting ethics. It was also a particularly poignant issue for the present authors when they embarked upon their slavery project that has subsequently resulted in some 15 papers in print. Previous papers on American slavery written by accounting historians had raised virtually no issues with respect to slavery's inherent immorality. In our first presentation on the topic at an American Accounting Association (AAA) regional meeting, we chose to take Fogel and Engerman (1974), perhaps the most famous and prolific historians on the subject of New World slavery, to task for failing to take a strong moral stance against the evils of the American South's "peculiar institution" in *Time on the Cross*, their most celebrated and prestigious work on the subject. In the discussion that followed the presentation, we were chastised by one of the Academy's most distinguished critical scholars for noting Fogel and Engerman's preeminence while also questioning their silence on the morality of New World slavery. Some years later, at a national AAA meeting, we presented a paper entitled "Somebody knows the trouble I've seen," in which we revealed some of the dehumanising aspects of slavery that we had identified in the course of research. On this occasion we received further criticism from several African-Americans in the audience who felt it presumptuous for Caucasian-Americans to truly appreciate how dehumanising slavery actually was. Taken together these episodes raise the question of what CAHR accomplishes if not to expose and voice outrage at evils that historians perceived in the past so as to forestall reoccurrence in the future? In a way this reaffirms what Santayana (1905) said years ago that if we do not study history, we are condemned to repeat it. Perhaps CAHR should add a corollary, if we do nothing to influence change in the present, nothing will change in the future.

This issue has massive ramifications not only for our slavery project, but for the teaching of ethics, accounting or otherwise. One of the present authors has used Hammond's provocative book, *A White Collar Profession* (2002), for classroom ethics discussion. The work poses the question of what is appropriate to say about the ethics of past societies in which the exclusion of African-Americans from licensure as accountants, on the basis of race alone, went unquestioned. A similar problem exists for users of Lippman's (2007) ethics case, designed specifically for classroom discussion, in which Nazi concentration camp accounts of income and expenditure were presented, followed by questions as to the responsibility of their compilers for the data generated. Here, at least, the Nuremburg war crimes tribunal presented some direction, as Nazi war criminals who had acted through what was a legitimate, albeit immoral, military chain of command, were not exonerated by the defense's argument that they were only following orders. Rather, they were held to a higher moral standard and suffered just punishments accordingly.

Three critical scholars, Miller, Hopper and Laughlin, (1991), penned an introduction to a special issue of *AOS* containing a collection of papers originally presented at a recent Interdisciplinary Perspectives on Accounting conference. Their paper was entitled, "The new accounting history: an introduction." At first some hackles were raised since paradigmatic theorists had already assumed this designation some years previously, to distinguish themselves from traditionalists, who by implication became "old accounting historians." It was easy to be taken in by welcoming phrases that proclaimed that "a heterogeneous range of issues and theoretical approaches" and a "proliferation of methodologies" were to be part of the new order. Many traditionalists were so blinded by this rhetoric and so desired acceptance by their "contextualizing" brethren that they failed to see that the invitation was shallow. It was apparent, reading between the lines, that various categories of "discoverers" were not accorded seats at the festive board. The "contextualizers" had once again distanced themselves from the archival researchers, and in the process, demoted the latter to antiquarianism, understood as an interest in antiquities, old books, antiques and so on. Although the term 'antiquarian' was unlikely to be viewed as demeaning within the British accounting academy, to Americans trained as historians, these were fighting words, and the frequency with which the "A word" was reiterated in the literature, evidences its pejorative intent.

While there have been some acrimonious exchanges between old and new historians, the paradigmatic debates of the 1990s and the first decade of the current century have generally advanced our understanding of the forces that have shaped accounting history. Laughlin appears the voice of reason among the "contextualization" forces that appeared hell-bent on marginalising traditional historiography. Laughlin (1995) argues that no one perspective can provide a more complete picture of accounting reality since choices have been made along multiple continuums – theory, methodology and change. Drawing inspiration from Feyerabend, Laughlin (2010) cautions that reducing accounting research to a single explanatory paradigm for all situations and circumstances would serve only to restrict innovation. Laughlin throws an additional spanner into monolithic paradigmatic positions by urging critical scholars to free themselves from total dependence on their philosophical fathers whether that be "Marx, Foucault, Habermas or whoever" (1999: 75), and supplement their wisdom with insights of their own. In the next section, we evaluate the degree to which this advice has been taken to heart within CAHR.

5 Paradigmatic conciliation

Fleischman, Kalbers and Parker (1996) argue for "expanding the dialogue" in expectation that the synergies and additive interactions between scholars of rival explanatory paradigms could expand our knowledge of history. Joint archival investigation and co-authorship is proposed. There has been some support for the concept from Davila and Oyon (2008) who feel that cross-paradigmatic collaboration would advance knowledge and would diminish the tendency of critical scholars to write to their paradigms. To date, there has been limited uptake of these suggestions, although examples can be identified. Fleischman and Macve (2002) and Toms and Fleischman (2015) undertake joint ventures to the archives of major British Industrial Revolution firms. Likewise, Parker (2008a) advocates theoretical and ideological pluralism in seeking the new and the risky. Funnell (1996; 1998b), at a practical level, points out the similarities between old and new accounting historians. Both Parker and Funnell use the same methodology (narrative and counter-narrative), and since all are ultimately seeking truth, different approaches should be tolerated, echoing Laughlin (1995). Chua (1998) writes that since history is allegory, grounded in values and faith, "overly zealous and evangelical stances should be avoided and interpretive differences celebrated." Arnold and McCartney (2003) claim that the gulf between 'old' and 'new' was a false dichotomy, occasioned by the newness of the accounting history discipline. Carmona, Ezzamel and Gutierrez (2004) contend that while traditional and normative history reflect different approaches, "both contribute significantly to the field, and indeed to the sharpening of each other's research agenda" (2004: 26).

A number of prominent accounting historians with feet in both camps have urged traditional historians to appreciate the value of their theory-based brethren. Merino (1998) urges tolerance and a willingness to listen because the new history brings diversity to the discipline, "making the familiar strange." Gaffikin (1998) opines that the discourses of the "new" accounting history are "not only desirable but essential for the survival" of the accounting history sub-discipline. Carnegie and Napier (2012) identify Fleischman and Macve as an example of researchers realising that theories (such as neo-classical economics and Marxist or Foucauldian perspectives) often emphasise different features of the historical phenomena rather than offering rival explanations; and conclude that "research in this area has demonstrated the need to tolerate theoretical diversity in order to avoid closing down areas of debate prematurely" (2002: 337).

In recent years, a number of papers have appeared in which a single author or multiple scholars with similar theoretical groundings have attempted to hypothesise the explanatory contribution of paradigms other than their own. Hooper and Pratt (1993) write of the process whereby the indigenous Maoris of New Zealand were dispossessed of their land by white colonists. While the paper is underpinned by the Foucauldian power/knowledge paradigm in an effort to understand this dispossession, Tinker's (1985) Marxist analysis that accountants do not function as neutral arbiters of social and economic conflict was likewise vital to the process.

Fleischman (2000) demonstrates that, contrary to common belief, Taylorism and scientific management theory predated its large-scale application in practice in the US by almost three decades, explaining the lag in terms of factors suggested by all three of the major paradigms. Walker's work (2008) is ostensibly an archival investigation of the origins of professional accounting societies in four major English cities that incorporates a literature search providing a goldmine of different paradigms that collectively explain the genesis of these societies. The sociology of professions paradigm suggests that the pursuit of monopolistic control is the primary motivation for seeking closure. In contrast, critical and conflict theory identifies lawyers, rival economic groups, lesser qualified practitioners and so on, as feasible opponents, justifying the attempts of accountants to close ranks. Walker's survey could well inspire the realisation that in explaining many episodes in accounting history, it is very helpful and perhaps vital to mention the paradigms that do not fit the particular situation. However, Walker concludes that conciliation is not necessarily a good thing given the important role controversy has played in historical debate. He also opines that paradigmatic literature is on the decline from its heyday in the 1990s. Perhaps that is true in quantitative terms as superficial theoretical groundings are not as *de rigueur* as was the case then.

Rodrigues and Craig (2007) deploy three familiar paradigms to assess the processes by which international accounting standard harmonisation might eventuate – the Hegelian dialectic, isomorphism as articulated by DiMaggio and Powell, and the Foucauldian power/knowledge theory. Carnegie and Napier (2010) contribute a comprehensive study of the black eye suffered by the accounting profession in the aftermath of Enron and the demise of Arthur Andersen (AA). Once again, their story involves a number of theoretical perspectives. The three featured in the paper are legitimacy theory, social contract theory and insights drawn from stereotyping literature. Legitimacy theory suggests that organisations do not possess an inherent right to exist and do so only as long as their values systems are congruent with societal values. Social contract theory assumes that understandings exist as to appropriate behaviour. Thus, when AA failed in its societal obligation, the contract was revoked. Subsequently both the AA stereotype and that of the profession as a whole changed as a result of Enron and other fiascos. The 'traditional' accountant stereotype since the formation of the company had been that of an honest (positive aspect) bean counter (negative aspect). Subsequently, the stereotype changed to that of the business professional who served the client, perhaps at the expense of the public interest. The eclipse of this stereotype signaled the "deprofessionalisation" of accounting, demoting it to the status of a mere occupation. The authors also provide a full disclosure of paradigms advocated by other scholars – agency theory, financialisation, Giddens' theories of late modernity and social closure drawn from the sociology of professions literature.

6 The suppressed voices

Despite the plethora of activity, accounting history is a relatively young academic discipline. Early practitioners of a half century ago were very much imbued with traditional beliefs that historians are able to objectively report the past, that primary source materials provide a non-partisan view of historical reality and that accounting's history has evolved progressively from past to present (the Whig interpretation of history). It was in the 1980s that accounting scholars in greater numbers began to appreciate the fact that those performing accounting functions have not universally operated as the guardians of the public interest that the profession has professed.

Accounting's actual failings are much more plentiful than the frauds and audit failures that have gained notoriety and darkened the profession's history. Arguably, the most significant accomplishment of CAHR has been manifested in the many books and papers that have exposed to the light of day the multitude of historical occasions when the discipline and its practitioners were not functioning in the best protective interests of all peoples. It is through these exposures that improvements have been manifest within those areas of the human experience that we have the power to impact and, hopefully, not repeat the mistakes of the past. Critical scholars have long and forcefully espoused the causes of groups oppressed, often with the complicity of accountants, whose voices had not been heard either because of the denial of access to accounting records, which meant they left no records, or no record was created about them.

6.1 The Holocaust

A poignant literature has exposed the complicity of German accountants in the Holocaust. A seminal CAHR paper by Funnell (1998a) chronicles how the Third Reich used accounting numbers to deny the humanity of Jewish prisoners, to render the "final solution" invisible and efficient, and to justify the actions and motives of those who sought the annihilation of European Jewry. Lippman (2007) and Lippman and Wilson (2009) relate the heartbreaking story of the calculations made by German accountants for cheapening the cost of gas used in the extermination process, although lengthening the suffering of the victims. Also, detailed records were kept of the maintenance costs of the forced labourers who toiled in concentration camp factories. The bottom line was a nine month life expectancy.

6.2 Slavery

US slavery was studied in the 1980s by accounting historians but this literature lacked a critical component until Cowton and O'Shaughnessy (1991) extended the focus to the British Caribbean, and Barney and Flesher (1994) pointed out in a study of the Locust Grove Plantation how owners dehumanised their slaves, treating them as mere instruments of capital wealth enhancement. A greater moral outrage of slavery was evident in a long series of publications by Fleischman, Tyson and Oldroyd, in many of which those performing accounting functions stand accused of complicity in sustaining the slavery regimes in the US and the British Caribbean (Fleischman, Oldroyd and Tyson, 2004; Tyson, Oldroyd and Fleischman 2005; Oldroyd, Fleischman and Tyson, 2008). One question to be asked is whether accountants should be held to a higher standard of justice for participating in what amounted to genocide, since the rigours of slavery often materially shortened the lives of the captive people. Another is if accountants should be accountable for the immoral acts of their employers. A recent verdict against the accountant at a Nazi death camp suggests that they are.

Other significant contributions to the slavery literature have been forthcoming from Vollmers (2003) on slavery in an urban, industrial setting, Hollister and Schultz (2010) who compare the accounting for the institution in New York State and the South, and Stuart (2010) in the Carolinas where the demographics of American slavery were at their worst because of the climactic conditions and the rigours of rice cultivation. McWatters and Lemarchand (2009) demonstrate the profitability of the slave trade and how the accounting methods used contributed to the rise of capitalism.

6.3 Imperialism

Numerous voices have been silenced under an imperialist yoke. The Aborigines of Australia and Maoris of New Zealand were dispossessed of their lands as documented by Gibson (2000), Hooper and Pratt (1995, 2003) and Hooper and Kearins (2004). Gallhofer Gibson, Haslam, McNicholas and Takiari (2000) reflect on the cultural gulf between European and indigenous cultures, urging Europeans to appreciate the valuable insights the latter can convey. Neu (1999, 2000a,b) and Neu and Graham (2004, 2006) have written extensively about the despicable process whereby Canada's indigenous population (its "first nations") was fashioned into a "governable people" through conquest, annihilation, containment and assimilation. Hoogvelt and Tinker (1978) and Elad (1998) provide case studies of colonial and post-colonial regimes in Africa as part of the widely documented "scramble for Africa".

Sian (2006a,b) offers extensive insights on the difficulties encountered by the indigenous population of Kenya trying to enter the accounting profession dominated by British professional societies. Sian is typical of critical scholars for whom a primary interest lies in a region to which they have close personal ties. Other examples are Annisette's (1999, 2000, 2003) works on Trinidad and Tobago, and Bakre's (2005, 2006) studies of the development of the Jamaican professional society which, even after independence, floundered because of internal and external interference from British accountants. Likewise, Davie (2000, 2005a,b) charts how the accounting methodology of the imperialist power was used to perpetuate racism and exclusion in Fiji. The work of Dyball, Poullaos and Chua (2007) asserts that the US delayed the coming of independence to the Philippines on the questionable pretext that the Filipino accounting profession was unable to manage the country's economic affairs without American supervision and oversight.

6.4 America's ethnic minorities

The US also has much to answer for in its treatment of minority populations. Hammond (2002) has been the pathfinder, tracking the difficulties African Americans have encountered entering public accountancy. Scholarship on Native Americans is centred at the University of New Mexico. Preston and Oakes (2001) document the disaster visited upon the Navajo by governmentally mandated herd reductions, while Oakes and Young (2010) tell the story of an 1887 act, designed to fracture the tribal system of land ownership.

6.5 Apartheid in South Africa

Unlike the slave economy of the American South, where the black and white populations were approximately of equal size, racist regimes in Africa were imposed by a small number of Europeans backed by distant military powers. The events of the post-apartheid quarter century in the Republic of South Africa are well within the memory of all but the youngest of us. Hammond has once again been in the vanguard of scholars researching this topic (Hammond, Arnold and Clayton, 2007; Hammond, 2012).

6.6 Gender issues

The early 1990s saw a number of powerful historical exposés of the genderisation of the accounting profession. Leaders here were Kirkham (1992, 1997), Loft (1992) and Kirkham and Loft (1993a,b), highlighting the time when US accountancy was in its infancy, when only men could aspire to be accountants, while women could not advance beyond bookkeeper or clerk roles. Walker (2003b) also finds sexual stereotyping and the exploitation of women in the UK. Cooper (2010) comes to the same conclusion of fear precipitating exclusion not only for the British accounting associations, but also in Australia. In the contemporary world, the entry-level difficulties faced by women have largely abated, only to be widely replaced by the "glass ceiling," however.

Ciancanelli, Gallhofer, Humphrey and Kirkham (1990) provide a quantitative analysis of female access to hierarchical positions in UK accountancy, reporting insufficient numbers of women in senior positions. Wootton and Kemmerer (1996, 2000) provide quantitative data on changing genderisation of the US accounting workforce 1930–90. A number of very prominent critical scholars of the 1990s suggested possible remedies for the environment that Lehman (1992) describes as one constructed by men in which women had to struggle culturally, educationally, economically and politically. Kirkham (1992) urges critical scholars to re-examine the hierarchical influence and power of the profession and its knowledge base with reference to gender. Hooks (1992) proposes a research agenda to expose the androcentric culture of public accounting.

Walker (1998, 2003a) spearheads an interesting gender-based project with a distinct and historical base – household accounting, primarily in Victorian England, but elsewhere as well. For example, Pallett and Oldroyd (2009) explore the contribution of household management guides to promoting the ethos of empire in India under British rule. Walker (1998, 2003a) discusses the distinction between private life (home) and the public realm (accounting work generally), and how genderised spheres of influence were created as a conequence. Closely related is the issue of motherhood and how it has contributed to the patriarchal nature of public accounting and the glass ceiling. Haynes (2000) and Lightbody (2009) employ oral histories to demonstrate how motherhood and career are intertwined, while Dambrin and Lambert (2008) point out that the economic cost of motherhood to accountancy firms forces women to seek alternative career trajectories.

Perhaps the way forward is for critical scholars of gender issues to stress the distinctive elements of female perspectives that render them valuable to accounting firms. This theme was picked up by Haynes (2000), Dillard and Reynolds (2008) and Parker (2008b). Conversely, Hammond and Oakes (1992) reject the proposition that a feminine perspective, initiative or talent could be defined since these attributes vary so greatly amongst women.

7 Accountancy under siege

Critical accounting scholars have scrutinised most constituencies that comprise what can be labelled 'accountancy', both historically and currently. Occupational groups include accountants in public practice, standard setters, management accountants, public sector accountants and accounting academicians. The resultant literature is sufficiently extensive to encompass charges for which all stand accused – subordination of the public interest, lack of accountability and the deployment of rhetoric to mask reality.

7.1 Accountants in public practice

Much has been written about the numerous audit failures and frauds that have punctuated accounting history from the South Sea Bubble to Enron and Madoff. In our recent memory, the savings-and-loans failures of the early 1990s resulted from inconsistent regulation that ran counter to GAAP, according to Margavio (1990). Merino and Kenny (1994) agree that the auditors of the savings and loans failed to transcend weak rules and assess the economic substance of transactions. Rather than detail the specific failures, it is perhaps more valuable here to explore what critical scholars have written about the way in which financial reporting and auditing have combined to produce infamous fiascos which seemingly became epidemic in the early twenty-first century. Fogarty, Helan and Knutson (1991) provide evidence that auditors sometimes failed to inform investors that the financial statements of clients should not be relied upon. Neu (1991) claims that the public was forced to put faith in auditors even though they were more likely to breach the public's trust than risk their clients' wrath. Mills and Bettner (1992) argue that the nature of the audit process and its standards mask conflict, maintain social order and legitimise professional actions.

This latter point, the establishment and maintenance of legitimacy rather than the protection of the public interest, has been a critical focus. The title of Power's (1997a) book is indicative – *The Audit Society: Rituals of Verification.* Young (1997) claims that the profession's domination of the process by which its own rules are determined is a device to preserve its legitimacy. Preston, Cooper, Scarborough and Chilton (1995) compare the 1917 and 1988 US codes of ethics to show how accountants have redefined legitimacy to a materially different society. Perhaps the strongest broadside against accountancy's legitimising efforts is found in Mitchell and Sikka (1993), who accuse the practice of assuming a god-like aura of impartiality and integrity when in actual fact it is truly collusive, undemocratic and committed to the status quo. Defending the auditing profession on the legitimacy issue, Guénin-Paracini and Gendron (2010) point out that legitimacy is hard to preserve when auditors become scapegoats for frauds, as AA learned with Enron. Carnegie and Napier (2010) also observe the negative stereotyping the profession has suffered post-Enron.

The accountancy profession commonly represents itself as the paragon of objectivity. Tinker and numerous co-authors have vehemently argued the partisan nature of accounting and accountants. In *Paper Prophets* (1985) he rejects the positivist notion that theories are dispassionate reflections of reality but should be viewed as grounded in social conflict. Lehman and Tinker (1987) aver that accounting practices are more productively regarded as ideological responses for parties participating in conflicts over wealth distribution. In his famous *AOS* debate with David Solomon, Tinker (1991) responds to Solomon's assertion that the absence of "representational faithfulness" would endanger the profession, that partisanship is inevitable in accounting since our actions are determined by social contradiction.

The range of accusations against the public accounting profession is even broader than the plethora of frauds and the unseemly tendency to preserve legitimacy at all costs. The prevailing approach to accounting ethics has been questioned by Chwastiak and Young (2003), who contend that annual reports are allowed to maintain silence on injustices as profit maximisation is seemingly the only measure of success. Many critical commentators have noted how the profession has also failed to close the expectations gap (Byington and Sutton, 1991; Olson and Wootton, 1991; Humphrey, Moizer and Turley, 1992; Young, 1997). Kluger and Shields (1991) discuss the failure to curb "opinion shopping," while Hendrickson (1998) chronicles post-1933 events in the US to show how self-regulation has failed with respect to independence issues. As Green (1999) points out, the problem of why audits fail remains unresolved.

The denial of access to the accountancy profession extends beyond the issues of race and gender discussed earlier in Britain, Africa, the Caribbean and the US. Exclusion was broader, however, with respect to the groups impacted and its worldwide parameters. Jacobs (2003) notes discrimination in hiring people from lower class origins. Duff and Ferguson (2007) report that the Big Four in the UK failed to employ people with disabilities while Fearfull, Carter, Sy and Tinker (2008) and Cooper and Taylor (2000) find that clerical workers were treated badly by firms. British interference also hampered the formation of professional bodies throughout the colonial empire – in Australia (Chua and Poullaos, 1998), Canada (Edwards and Walker, 2008b), New Zealand (Baskerville, 2006) and India (Verma and Gray, 2006), in addition to in Africa and the Caribbean. Comparable episodes are reported for France (Ramirez, 2001), Ireland (O'Regan, 2008) and Romania (Zelinschi, 2009).

7.2 *Standard setting*

Critical comment on specific standard-setting bodies is almost entirely focused on the Financial Accounting Standards Board (FASB), the International Accounting Standards Board (IASB) and the UK's Accounting Standards Board (ASB). Hines (1991) argues that conceptual frameworks are generally formulated to protect legitimacy and the status quo, while Zeff (1999) observes more specifically about FASB's conceptual framework that within a decade of its promulgation, there were no longer any board members who had participated in its deliberations. Young and Williams (2010) provide examples of FASB's value judgments that raise ethical issues about the standard-setting process. Fogarty (1994, 1998) has written extensively on US standard setting, covering topics as diverse as due process, political influences, research challenges and inconsistent theoretical approaches. Committee (1990) questions whether the whole regulatory power structure devolving from Congress to the Securities and Exchange Commission (SEC) to FASB is even constitutional. Briloff (1990, 2001) draws upon perceived decades of malfeasance to accuse the SEC of failing to mete out punishment evenhandedly and the FASB of issuing rules rather than standards. Samuelson (1999) argues that the body has only the strength to do what is "subjective and vague."

Across the Atlantic Jupe (2000) asserts that the UK's ASB was similarly weak, relying on voluntary compliance and being responsive only to the rhetoric of key allies to maintain its existence. Lee (1995), Noguchi and Edwards (2008) and O'Dwyer and Canning (2008) add fuel to the fire, claiming that professional bodies in the UK and Ireland lack commitment to their constituencies and the public interest. Camfferman and Zeff (2009) report that the Dutch profession tried to scuttle the Union Européenne des Experts Comptable Economiques et Financiers because of a perceived lack of rigor in European accounting standards.

Further papers have also criticised standard setters for failing to attend adequately to a number of key buzzwords vital to the process. For Zeff (1998), it is "independence," for Puxty and Laughlin (1983), it is "decision usefulness," and for Young and Mouck (1996), it is "objectivity."

7.3 Public sector accountants

A major public sector issue in the UK has been the nationalisation of industrial sectors and other enterprises under private control and the privatisation of what had been formerly nationalised. A *cause célèbre* was the nationalisation of the British coal industry that left critical scholars as "brassed off" as the colliery bands depicted in the movie of that name. Berry, Capps, Cooper, Ferguson, Hopper and Lowe, (1985), Hopper, Cooper, Lowe, Capps and Mouritsen (1986) and Cooper and Hopper (1988) all lent voices to the chorus of complaint. Arnold and Cooper (1999) relate events at the Medway Ports where privatisation was engineered by Price Waterhouse, resulting in half the workforce losing their jobs. Subsequently, the redundant workers were forced to sell their shares to the new owners at a ridiculously low price determined by KPMG. Jupe and Crompton (2006) observe that the Labour Government's promised regulation of the British railway industry was a smoke screen to mask a wealth transfer from taxpayers to the investment community.

7.4 The public interest

A delicate balance exists between accountants/auditors as the guardians of the public interest and their own self-interest and that of their firms. Miller (1999) takes the audit profession to task for failing to live up to the service tradition demanded by society. Threats to the public interest originate from a multitude of antagonists – the State, standard-setters, accounting associations, accounting firms and the capitalist class. Two works of the early 1990s attempted to set parameters: Miller (1990) observes that there were many possible congruencies between the roles of accounting and the objectives of the State and that these relationships needed to be researched;

and Broadbent and Guthrie (1992) call for more evaluative work in the public sector with an emphasis on making international comparisons. Two decades later Dellaportas and Davenport (2008) again call upon the profession to define what constituted the public interest and how to best serve it. Walker (2004b, 2008) relates how the Old and New Poor Laws stigmatised and denigrated the recipients of Britain's relief system in the nineteen century. Funnell (2001) reports how representatives of the British Treasury during the Irish Potato Famine cared little about relieving the suffering, with O'Regan (2010) offering similar insights on Poor Law administration in Ireland during the Famine.

There is much more that could be said about critical accounting's attempt to influence both governmental and accountancy profession reforms. In recent years, it has proved more productive to knock one's head against the wall than to generate reform action in the US. There have been notable efforts on the part of critical scholars to consider questions related to accountability and the efforts of accountants to mask governmental and corporate realities with rhetoric.

8 In conclusion: on the rare and unexpected joys of CAHR

Tyson and Fleischman (2006) report an investigation of the accounting ramifications of one of the most heinous episodes in American history – the mass "evacuation" of Japanese-American citizens from their homes along the West Coast to "concentration-like camps" further East. This was done out of fear, which later proved unfounded, that these Americans would provide aid and comfort to the enemy in World War II simply because of their ancestry. Meanwhile, their ethnic countrymen that served the war effort in the Pacific and Europe emerged as the most decorated battalion. The authors were surprised to discover through archival research that of all the governmental employees involved in the internment, accountants proved to be the most helpful to the uprooted people. Oldroyd enjoyed a similar experience with co-authors Funnell and Holden when undertaking archival work on the Newcastle Infirmary during mid-Victorian times. They were surprised to find the accounts being utilised by hospital management to justify rather than deny medical assistance to the poor in contravention of the dominant and politically correct self-help ethic of the time (Holden, Funnell and Oldroyd, 2009). It is a far greater pleasure to discover your discipline's forebears performing acts of goodness rather than pursuing the questionable actions you might have not unreasonably expected. In the case of traditional/ conventional accounting historians, finding four-leaf clovers in a field of grass and weeds reaffirms the joy of archival research – if your credentials have already been firmly established, such experiences become a true blessing.

Notes

1   A paradigm is a theory or a group of ideas about how something should be done, made, or thought about.
2   In 1972 the ICWA changed its name to the Institute of Cost and Management Accountants (ICMA), and subsequently to the Chartered Institute of Management Accountants (CIMA) in 1986.

References

Annisette, M. (1999). "Importing accounting: the case of Trinidad and Tobago," *Accounting, Business & Financial History*, 9(1): 103–34.
Annisette, M. (2000). "Imperialism and the professions: the education and certification of accountants in Trinidad and Tobago," *Accounting, Organizations and Society*, 25(7): 631–59.

Annisette, M. (2003). "The colour of accountancy: examining the salience of race in a professionalisation roject," *Accounting, Organizations and Society*, 28(7–8): 639–74.

Arnold, P. and C. Cooper (1999). "A tale of two classes: the privatisation of Medway Ports," *Critical Perspectives on Accounting*, 10(2): 127–52.

Arnold, A. and S. McCartney (2003). "'It may be earlier than you think': evidence, myths and informed debate in accounting history," *Critical Perspectives on Accounting*, 14(3): 227–53.

Baker, C. R. and M. S. Bettner. (1997). "Interpretive and critical research in accounting: a commentary on its absence from mainstream accounting research," *Critical Perspectives on Accounting*, 8(4): 293–310.

Bakre, O. (2005). "First attempt at localising imperial accountancy: the case of the Institute of Chartered Accountants of Jamaica (ICAJ) 1950s-1970s," *Critical Perspectives on Accounting*, 16(8): 995–1018.

Bakre, O. (2006). "Second attempt at localising imperial accountancy: the case of the Institute of Chartered Accountants of Jamaica (ICAJ) 1970s-1980s," *Critical Perspectives on Accounting*, 17(1): 1–28.

Barney, D. and D. L. Flesher (1994). "Early nineteenth century productivity accounting: the Locust Grove Plantation slave ledger," *Accounting, Business & Financial History*, 4(2): 275–94.

Baskerville, R. (2006). "Professional closure by proxy: the impact of hanging educational requirements on class mobility for a cohort of Big 8 partners," *Accounting History*, 11(3): 289–317.

Berry, A., T. Capps, D. Cooper, P. Ferguson, T. Hopper and E. Lowe (1985). "Management control in an area of the NCB: rationales of past practices in a public enterprise," *Accounting, Organizations and Society*, 10(1): 3–28.

Braverman, H. (1974). *Labor and Monopoly Capital: The Degradation of Work in the Twentieth Century*, New York: Monthly Review Press.

Briloff, A. (1990). "Accountancy and society: a covenant desecrated," *Critical Perspectives on Accounting*, 1(1): 5–30.

Briloff, A. (2001). "Garbage in/garbage out: a critique of fraudulent financial reporting 1987-1997 (the Coso Report) and the SEC accounting regulatory process," *Critical Perspectives on Accounting*, 12(2): 125–48.

Broadbent, J. (2002). "Critical accounting research: a view from England," *Critical Perspectives on Accounting*, 13(4): 433–49.

Broadbent, J. and J. Guthrie (1992). "Changes in the public sector: a review of recent 'alternative' research," *Accounting, Auditing and Accountability Journal*, 5(2): 3–31.

Burawoy, M. (1985). *The Politics of Production*, London: Verso.

Byington, R. and S. Sutton (1991). "The self-regulating profession: an analysis of the political monopoly tendencies of the audit profession," *Critical Perspectives on Accounting*, 2(4): 315–30.

Camfferman, K. and S. Zeff (2009). "The formation and early years of the Union Européenne des Experts Comptable Economiques et Financiers (UEC), 1951-63: or how the Dutch tried to bring down the UEC," *Accounting, Business & Financial History*, 19(3): 215–57.

Carmona, S., M. Ezzamel and F. Gutiérrez (2004). "Accounting history research: traditional and new accounting history perspectives," *De Computis*, 1(1): 24–52.

Carnegie, G. and C. Napier (2010). "Traditional accountants and business professionals after Enron: portraying the accounting profession," *Accounting, Organizations and Society*, 35(3): 360–76.

Carnegie, G. and C. Napier (2012). "Accounting's past, present and future: the unifying power of history," *Accounting, Auditing and Accountability Journal*, 25(2): 328–69.

Carter, C., A. McKinlay and M. Rawlinson (2002). "Introduction: Foucault, management and history," *Organization*, 9(4): 515–26.

Chandler, A. D. (1977). *The Visible Hand: The Managerial Revolution in American Business*, Cambridge, MA: Harvard University Press.

Chatfield, M. and R. Vangermeersch (eds) (1996). *The History of Accounting: An International Encyclopedia*, New York: Garland Publishing.

Chua, W. F. (1998). "Historical allegories: let us have diversity," *Critical Perspectives on Accounting*, 9(6): 617–28.

Chua, W. F. and C. Poullaos (1998). "The dynamics of closure amidst the construction of market, profession, empire and nationhood: an historical analysis of an Australian accounting association, 1886-1903," *Accounting, Organizations and Society*, 23(2): 155–187.

Chwastiak, M. and J. Young (2003). "Silences in annual reports," *Critical Perspectives on Accounting*, 14(5): 533–52.

Ciancanelli, P., S. Gallhofer, C. Humphrey and L. Kirkham (1990). "Gender and accountancy: some evidence from the UK," *Critical Perspectives on Accounting*, 1(2): 117–44.

Committee, B. (1990). "The delegation and privatization of financial accounting rulemaking authority in the United States of America," *Critical Perspectives on Accounting*, 1(2): 145–66.

Cooper, C. and P. Taylor (2000). "From Taylorism to Ms Taylor: the transformation of the accounting craft," *Accounting, Organizations and Society*, 25(6): 555–78.

Cooper, D. J. and T. M. Hopper (eds) (1988). *Debating Coal Closures*, Cambridge: Cambridge University Press.

Cooper, D. J. and T. Tinker (1990). "Editorial," *Critical Perspectives on Accounting*, 1(1): 1–3.

Cooper, K. (2010). "Accounting by women: fear, favour and the path to professional recognition for Australian women accountants," *Accounting History*, 15(3): 309–336.

Cowton, C. and A. O'Shaughness (1991). "Absentee control on sugar plantations in the British West Indies," *Accounting and Business Research*, 22: 33–45.

Dambrin, C. and C. Lambert (2008). "Mothering or auditing? the case of two Big Four in France," *Accounting, Auditing and Accountability Journal*, 21(4): 474–506.

Davie, S. (2000). "Accounting for imperialism: a case of British imposed indigenous collaboration," *Accounting, Auditing and Accountability Journal*, 13(3): 330–59.

Davie, S. (2005a). "Accounting's uses in exploitative human engineering: theorizing citizenship, indirect rule and Britain's imperial expansion," *Accounting Historians Journal*, 32(2): 55–80.

Davie, S. (2005b). "The politics of accounting, race and ethnicity: a story of a chiefly based preferencing," *Critical Perspectives on Accounting*, 16(5): 551–77.

Davila, T. and D. Oyon (2008). "Cross-paradigm collaboration and the advancement of management accounting knowledge," *Critical Perspectives on Accounting*, 19(6): 887–93.

Dellaportas, S. and L. Davenport (2008). "Reflections on the public interest in accounting," *Critical Perspectives on Accounting*, 19(7): 1080–98.

Dillard, J. and M. Reynolds (2008). "Green Owl and the Corn Maiden," *Accounting, Auditing and Accountability Journal*, 21(4): 556–79.

Duff, A. and J. Ferguson (2007). "Disability and accounting firms: evidence from the UK," *Critical Perspectives on Accounting*, 18(2): 139–57.

Dyball, M., C. Poullaos and W. F. Chua (2007). "Accounting and empire: professionalisation-as-resistance: the case of the Philippines," *Critical Perspectives on Accounting*, 19(1): 47–81.

Edwards, J. R. (1989). "Industrial cost accounting developments in Britain to 1830: review article," *Accounting and Business Research*, 19: 305–17.

Edwards, J. (ed.) (2000). *The History of Accounting*, 4 vols, London: Routledge.

Edwards, J. and S. Walker (eds) (2008a). *The Routledge Companion to Accounting History*, London: Routledge.

Edwards, J. and S. Walker (2008b). "Occupation differentiation and exclusion in early Canadian accountancy," *Accounting and Business Research*, 28(5): 373–91.

Elad, C. M. (1998). "Corporate disclosure regulation and practice in the developing Countries of Central Africa," *Advances in Public Interest Accounting*, 7: 51–106.

Ezzamel, M., K. Hoskin and R. Macve (1990). "Managing it all by numbers: a review of Johnson and Kaplan's *Relevance Lost*," *Accounting and Business Research*, 20: 153–66.

Fearfull, A., C. Carter, A. Sy and T. Tinker (2008). "Invisible influence, tangible trap: the clerical conundrum," *Critical Perspectives on Accounting*, 19(8): 1,177–96.

Fleischman, R. (ed.) (2006). *Accounting History*, 3 vols, London: Sage Publishing.

Fleischman, R. K. (2000). "Completing the triangle: Taylorism and the paradigms," *Accounting, Auditing and Accountability Journal*, 13(5): 597–623.

Fleischman, R. K. and T. N. Tyson (1997). "Archival researchers: an endangered species?" *Accounting Historians Journal*, 24(2): 91–109.

Fleischman, R. K. and R. H. Macve (2002). "Coals from Newcastle: alternative histories of cost and management accounting in north east coal mining during the British Industrial Revolution," *Accounting and Business Research*, 32(3): 133–52.

Fleischman, R. K., L. P. Kalbers and L. D. Parker (1996). "Expanding the dialogue: Industrial Revolution costing historiography," *Critical Perspectives on Accounting*, 7(3): 315–37.

Fleischman, R. K., D. Oldroyd and T. Tyson (2004). "Monetising human life: slave valuations on US and British West Indian plantations," *Accounting History*, 9(2): 35–62.

Fleischman, R. K., S. Walker and W. N. Funnell (eds) (2012). *Critical Histories of Accounting: Sinister Inscriptions in the Modern Era*, Abingdon: Routledge.

Fogel, R. and S. Engerman (1974). *Time on the Cross*, 2 vols, Boston: Little, Brown and Co.

Fogarty, T. (1994). "Structural-functionalism and financial accounting: standard-setting in the US," *Critical Perspectives on Accounting*, 5(3): 205–26.

Fogarty, T. (1998). "Accounting standard-setting: a Challenge for critical accounting researchers," *Critical Perspectives on Accounting*, 9(5): 515–23.

Fogarty, T., J. Helan and D. Knutson (1991). "The rationality of doing 'nothing': auditors' responses to legal liability in an institutionalized environment," *Critical Perspectives on Accounting*, 2(3): 201–26.

Funnell, W. (1998a). "Accounting in the service of the Holocaust," *Critical Perspectives on Accounting*, 9(4): 435–464.

Funnell, W. N. (1996). "Preserving history in accounting: seeking common ground between 'new' and 'old' accounting history," *Accounting, Auditing and Accountability Journal*, 9(4): 38–64.

Funnell, W. N. (1998b). "The narrative and its place in the new accounting history: the rise of the counter-narrative," *Accounting, Auditing and Accountability Journal*, 11(2): 142–62.

Funnell, W. (2001). "Accounting for justice: entitlement, want and the Irish famine of 1845-7," *Accounting Historians Journal*, 28(2):187–206.

Gaffikin, M. (1998). "History is dead, long live history," *Critical Perspectives on Accounting*, 9(6): 631–39.

Gaffikin, M. (2011). "What is (accounting) history," *Accounting History*, 16(3): 235–51.

Gallhofer, S. and J. Haslam (1997). "Beyond accounting: the possibilities of accounting and critical accounting research," *Critical Perspectives on Accounting*, 8(1): 71–95.

Gallhofer, S., K. Gibson, J. Haslam, P. McNicholas, and B. Takiari (2000). "Developing environmental accounting: insights from indigenous cultures," *Accounting, Auditing and Accountability Journal*, 13(3): 381–409.

Gibson, K. (2000). "Accounting as a tool for Aboriginal dispossession: then and now," *Accounting, Auditing and Accountability Journal*, 13(3): 289–306.

Green, D. (1999). "Litigation risk for auditors and the risk society," *Critical Perspectives on Accounting*, 10(3): 339–53.

Guénin-Paracini, H. and Y. Gendron (2010). "Auditors as modern pharmakoi legitimacy paradoxes and the production of economic order," *Critical Perspectives on Accounting*, 21 (2): 134–58.

Habermas, J. (1987). *The Philosophical Discourse of Modernity*, Cambridge, MA: MIT Press.

Hammond, T. D. (2002). *A White-Collar Profession: African-American CPAs since 1921*, Chapel Hill, NC: University of North Carolina Press.

Hammond, T. D. (2012). "An 'unofficial' history of race relations in the South African accounting industry, 1968-2000: perspectives of South Africa's first black chartered accountants," *Critical Perspectives on Accounting*, 23(–5): 332–50.

Hammond, T. D. and L. S. Oakes. (1992). "Some feminisms and their implications for accounting practice," *Accounting, Auditing and Accountability Journal*, 5(3): 52–70.

Hammond, T. D., P. Arnold and B. Clayton (2007). "Recounting a difficult past: a South African accounting firm's 'experiences in transformation'," *Accounting History*, 12(3): 253–82.

Haynes, K. (2010). "Other lives in accounting: critical reflections on an oral methodology in action," *Critical Perspectives on Accounting*, 21(3): 221–31.

Hendrickson, H. (1998). "Relevant financial reporting questions not asked by the accounting profession," *Critical Perspectives on Accounting*, 9(5): 489–505.

Hill, C. (1986). *The Collected Essays of Christopher Hill*, Amherst, MA: University of Massachusetts Press.

Hines, R. (1991). "The FASB's conceptual framework, financial accounting and the maintenance of the social world," *Critical Perspectives on Accounting*, 16(4): 313–31.

Hobsbawm, E. J. (1972). "Karl Marx's contribution to historiography," in R. Blackburn (ed.): *Ideology in Social Science*, New York, NY: Pantheon Books.

Holden, A., W. N. Funnell and D. Oldroyd (2009). "Accounting and the moral economy of illness in Victorian England: the Newcastle Infirmary," *Accounting, Auditing and Accountability Journal*, 22(4): 525–52.

Hollister, T. and S. Schultz (2010). "Slavery and emancipation in New York: evidence from nineteenth-century accounting records," *Accounting History*, 15(3): 371–405.

Hoogvelt, A. M. M. and A. M. Tinker (1978). "The role of colonial and post-states in imperialism—a case study of the Sierra Leone Development Company," *Journal of Modern African Studies*, 16(1): 67–79.

Hooks, K. (1992). "Gender effects and labor supply in public accounting: an agenda of research issues," *Accounting, Organizations and Society*, 17(3–4): 343–66.

Hooper, K. C. and M. J. Pratt. (1993). "The growth of agricultural capitalism and the power of accounting: a New Zealand case study," *Critical Perspectives on Accounting*, 4(3): 247–74.

Hooper, K. C. and M. J. Pratt. (1995). "Discourse and rhetoric: the case of the New Zealand Native Land Company," *Accounting, Auditing and Accountability Journal*, 8(1): 10–37.

Hooper, K. and K. Kearins (2004). "Financing New Zealand 1860-1880: Maori land and the wealth tax effect," *Accounting History*, 9(2): 87–105.

Hopper, T. and P. Armstrong (1991). "Cost accounting, controlling labour and the rise of conglomerates," *Accounting, Organizations and Society*, 16(5–6): 405–38.

Hopper, T., D. J. Cooper, E. A. Lowe, T. Capps. and J. Mouritsen (1986). "Management control and worker resistance in the National Coal Board," in D. Knights and H. Willmott (eds): *Managing the Labour Process*, Aldershot, UK: Gower.

Hoskin, K. W. and R. H. Macve. (1986). "Accounting and the examination: a genealogy of disciplinary power," *Accounting, Organizations and Society*, 11(2): 105–36.

Hoskin, K. W. and R. H. Macve (1988). "The genesis of accountability: the West Point connections," *Accounting, Organizations and Society*, 13(1): 37–73.

Hoskin, K. W. and R. H. Macve (1996). "The Lawrence Manufacturing Co.: a note on early cost accounting in US textile mills," *Accounting, Business & Financial History*, 6(3): 337–61.

Hoskin, K. W. and R. H. Macve (2000). "Knowing more as knowing less? Alternative histories of cost and management accounting in the US and the UK," *Accounting Historians Journal*, 27(1): 91–149.

Humphrey, C., P. Mozier and S. Turley (1992). "The audit expectations gap – *plus ca change, plus c'est la meme chose?*" *Critical Perspectives on Accounting*, 3(2): 137–61.

Jacobs, K. (2003). "Class reproduction in professional recruitment: examining accounting profession," *Critical Perspectives on Accounting*, 14(5): 569–96.

Johnson, H. T. and R. S. Kaplan (1987). *Relevance Lost: The Rise and Fall of Management Accounting*, Boston, MA: Harvard Business School Press.

Jupe, R. (2000). "Self-referential lobbying of the Accounting Standards Board: the case of Financial Reporting Standard No.1," *Critical Perspectives on Accounting*, 11(3): 337–59.

Jupe, R. and G. Crompton (2006). "'A deficient performance': the regulation of the train operating companies in Britain's privatised railway system," *Critical Perspectives on Accounting*, 17(8): 1035–65.

Kirkham, L. M. (1992). "Integrating He*r*story and Hi*s*tory in accountancy," *Accounting, Organizations and Society*," 17(3–4): 287–97.

Kirkham, L. M. (1997). "Through the looking glass: viewing sexual harassment within the accounting profession," *Critical Perspectives on Accounting*, 8(3): 273–83.

Kirkham, L. and A. Loft (1993a). "Accountancy and the gendered division of labour: a review essay," *Accounting, Organizations and Society*, 17(3–4): 367–78.

Kirkham, L.M. and A. Loft. (1993b). "Gender and the construction of the professional accountant," *Accounting, Organizations and Society* 18(6): 507–58.

Kluger, B. and D. Shields (1991). "Managerial moral hazard and auditor changes," *Critical Perspectives on Accounting*, 2(3): 255–272

Knights, D. and H. Willmott (1986). "Introduction," in D. Knights and H. Willmott (eds): *Managing the Labour Process*, Aldershot: Gower.

Laughlin, R. (1995). "Empirical research in accounting: alternative approaches and a case for middle-range thinking," *Accounting, Auditing and Accountability Journal*, 8(1): 63–87.

Laughlin, R. (1999). "Critical accounting: nature, progress and prognosis," *Accounting, Auditing and Accountability Journal*, 12(1): 73–8.

Laughlin, R. (2010). "A comment on 'Towards a paradigmatic foundation for accounting practice'," *Accounting, Auditing and Accountability Journal*, 23(5): 759–63.

Lee, T. (1995). "The professionalization of accountancy: a history of protecting the public interest in a self-interested way," *Accounting, Auditing and Accountability Journal*, 8(4): 48–69.

Lehman, C. (1992). "'Herstory' in accounting: the first eighty years," *Accounting, Organizations and Society*, 17(3–4): 261–85.

Lehman, C. and T. Tinker (1987). "The 'real' cultural significance of accounts," *Accounting, Organizations and Society*, 12(5): 503–22.

Lightbody, M. (2009). "Turnover decisions of women accountants: using personal histories to understand the relative influence of domestic obligations," *Accounting History*, 14(1–2): 55–78.

Lippman, E. (2007). "Accountants' responsibility for the information they report: an historical case study of financial information," *Accounting Historians Journal*, 36(1): 61–79.

Lippman, E. and P. Wilson (2007). "The culpability of accounting in perpetuating the Holocaust," *Accounting History*, 12(3): 283–303.

Lodh, S. and M. Gaffikin (1997). "Critical studies in accounting research, rationality, and Habermas: a methodological eflection," *Critical Perspectives on Accounting*, 8(5): 433–74.

Loft, A. (1986). "Towards a critical understanding of accounting: the case of cost accounting in the UK, 1914–1925," *Accounting, Organizations and Society*, 11(2): 137–69.

Loft, A. (1990). *Coming into the Light: A Study of the Development of a Professional Association for Cost Accountants in Britain in the Wake of the First World War*, London: Chartered Institute of Management Accountants.

Loft, A. (1992). "Accountancy and the gendered division of labour: a review essay," *Accounting, Organizations and Society*, 17 (3–4): 367–78.

McKinlay, A. (2006). "Managing Foucault: genealogies of management," *Management and Organizational History*, 1(1): 87–100.

McWatters, C. and Y. Lemarchand (2009). "Accounting for triangular trade," *Accounting, Business & Financial History*, 19(2): 189–212.

Margavio, G. (1993). "The Savings and Loan debacle: the culmination of three decades of conflicting regulation, deregulation and reregulation," *Accounting Historians Journal*, 20(1): 1–32.

Mattessich, R. (2008). *Two Hundred Years of Accounting Research*, New York NY: Routledge.

Merino, B. D. (1998). "Critical Theory and accounting history: challenges and opportunities," *Critical Perspectives on Accounting*, 9(6): 603–16.

Merino, B. and S. Kenny (1994). "Auditor liability and culpability in the Savings and Loan industry," *Critical Perspectives on Accounting*, 5(2): 179–93.

Merino, B. D. and A. G. Mayper (1993). "Accounting history and empirical research," *Accounting Historians Journal*, 20(2): 237–67.

Miller, M. (1999). "Auditor liability and the development of a strategic evaluation of going concern," *Critical Perspectives on Accounting*, 10(3): 355–75.

Miller, P. (1990). "On the interrelations between accounting and the state," *Accounting Organizations and Society*, 15(4): 315–338.

Miller, P. and T. O'Leary (1987). "Accounting and the construction of the governable person," *Accounting, Organizations and Society*, 12(3): 235–65.

Miller, P. and C. J. Napier (1993) "Genealogies of calculation," *Accounting, Organizations and Society*, 18(7–8): 631–47.

Miller, P., T. Hopper and R. C. Laughlin (1991). "The new accounting history: an introduction," *Accounting, Organizations and Society*, 16(5–6): 395–403.

Mills, S. and M. Bettner (1992). "Ritual and conflict in the audit profession," *Critical Perspectives on Accounting*, 3(2): 185–200.

Mitchell, A. and P. Sikka (1993). "Accounting for change: the institutions of accountancy," *Critical Perspectives on Accounting*, 4(1): 29–52.

Moore, D. C. (1991). "Accounting on trial: the critical legal studies movement and its lessons for radical accounting," *Accounting, Organizations and Society*, 16(8): 763–93.

Napier, C. J. (1989). "Research directions in accounting history," *British Accounting Review*, 21(3): 237–54.

Neu, D. (1991). "Trust, impression management, and the public accounting profession," *Critical Perspectives on Accounting*, 2(3): 295–313.

Neu, D. (1999). "'Discovering' indigenous peoples: accounting and the machinery of empire," *Accounting Historians Journal*, 26(1): 53–82.

Neu, D. (2000a). "Accounting and accountability relations: colonization, genocide and Canada's First Nations," *Accounting, Auditing and Accountability Journal*, 13(3): 268–88.

Neu, D. (2000b). "'Presents for the Indians': land, colonization and accounting in Canada," *Accounting, Organizations and Society*, 25(2): 163–84.

Neu, D. and C. Graham (2004). "Accounting and the holocausts of modernity," *Accounting, Auditing and Accountability Journal*, 17(4): 578–603.

Neu, D. and C. Graham (2006). "The birth of a nation: accounting and Canada's First Nations 1860-1900," *Accounting, Organizations and Society*, 31(1): 47–76.

Noguchi, M. and J. Edwards (2008). "Professional leadership and oligarchy: the case of the ICAEW," *Accounting Historians Journal*, 35(2): 1–42.

Oakes, L. and J. J. Young (2010). "Reconciling conflict: the role of accounting in the American Indian Trust Fund debacle," *Critical Perspectives on Accounting*, 21(1): 63–75.

O'Dwyer, B. and M. Canning (2008). "On professional accounting body complaints procedures: confronting professional authority and professional insulation within the Institute of Chartered Accountants in Ireland (ICAI)," *Accounting, Auditing and Accountability Journal*, 21(5): 645–70.

Oldroyd, D. (1999). "Historiography, causality and positioning: an unsystematic view of accounting history," *Accounting Historians Journal*, 26(1): 83–102.

Oldroyd, D., T. N. Tyson and R. K. Fleischman (2008). "The culpability of accounting practice in promoting slavery in the British Empire and Antebellum United States," *Critical Perspectives on Accounting*, 19(5): 764–84.

Oldroyd, D., T. N. Tyson and R. K. Fleischman (2015). "American ideology, socialism and financial accounting theory: a counter view," *Critical Perspectives on Accounting*, 37: 209–18.

Olson, S. and C. Wootton (1991). "Substance and semantics in the auditor's standard report," *Accounting Historians Journal*, 18(2): 85–111.

O'Regan, P. (2008). "Elevating the profession: the Institute of Chartered Accountants in Ireland and the implementation of social closure strategies 1888-1909," *Accounting, Business & Financial History*, 18(1): 35–59.

O'Regan, P. (2010). "A dense mass of petty accountability: accounting in the service of cultural imperialism during the Irish Famine 1846-1847," *Accounting, Organizations and Society*, 35(4): 416–30.

Pallett, S.D. and D. Oldroyd (2009). "Household management guides and cookery books for memsahibs: control in the home and promoting the ethos of empire," in B. H. Stroud and S. E. Corbin (eds): *Handbook on Social Change*, Hauppauge, NY: Nova Science Publishers.

Parker, L. D. (2004). "Presenting the past: perspectives on time for accounting and management history," *Accounting, Business and Financial History*, 14(1): 1–27.

Parker, L. D. (2008a). "Interpreting interpretive accounting research," *Critical Perspectives on Accounting*, 19(6): 9–14.

Parker, L. D. (2008b). "Strategic management and accounting processes: acknowledging gender," *Accounting, Auditing and Accountability Journal*, 21(4): 611–31.

Parker, R. H. and B. S. Yamey (eds) (1994), *Accounting History: Some British Contributions*, Oxford: Clarendon Press.

Power, M. (1997). *The Audit Society: Rituals of Verification*, Oxford: University of Oxford Press.

Preston, A., D. Cooper, D. Scarborough and R. Chilton (1995). "Changes in the code of ethics of the US accounting profession, 1917 and 1988: the continual quest for legitimation," *Accounting, Organizations and Society*, 20(6): 507–46.

Preston, A. and L. Oakes (2001). "The Navajo Documents: a study of the economic representation and construction of the Navajo," *Accounting, Organizations and Society*, 26(1): 39–71.

Puxty, T. and R. Laughlin (1983). "A rational reconstruction of the decision-usefulness criterion," *Journal of Business Finance and Accounting*, 10(4): 543–59.

Ramirez, C. (2001). "Understanding social closure in its cultural context: accounting practitioners in France (1920-1939)," *Accounting, Organizations and Society*, 26(4-5): 391–418.

Rodrigues, L. L. and R. Craig (2007). "Assessing international accounting harmonization using Hegelian dialectic, isomorphism and Foucault," *Critical Perspectives on Accounting*, 18(6): 739–57.

Samuelson, R. (1999). "The subjectivity of the FASB's conceptual framework: a commentary on Bryer," *Critical Perspectives on Accounting*, 10(5): 631–41.

Santayana, G. (1905). *Reason in Common Sense: The Life of Reason Volume 1* (republished 1980), New York: Dover Publications.

Sian, S. (2006a). "Inclusion, exclusion, and control: the case of the Kenyan accounting professionalization project," *Accounting, Organizations and Society*, 31(3): 295–322.

Sian, S. (2006b). "Reversing exclusion: the Africanization of accounting in Kenya 1963-70," *Critical Perspectives on Accounting*, 18(7): 831–72.

Sikka, P. and H. Willmott (1997). "Practising critical accounting," *Critical Perspectives on Accounting*, 8(1-2): 149–65.

Stewart, R. E. (1992). "Pluralizing our past: Foucault in accounting history," *Accounting, Auditing and Accountability Journal*, 5(2): 57–73.

Stuart, L. (2010). "Contingency theory perspectives on management control system design among U.S. Ante-Bellum slave plantations," *Accounting Historians Journal*, 37(1): 91–120.

Thompson, E. P. (1964). *The Making of the English Working Class*, New York: Pantheon Books.

Thompson, E. P. (1967). "Time, work-discipline, and industrial capitalism," *Past and Present*, 38: 56–97.

Tinker, T. (1985). *Paper Prophets: A Social Critique of Accounting*, New York: Praeger.

Tinker, T. (1991). "The accountant as partisan," *Accounting, Organizations and Society*, 16(3): 297–310.

Tinker, T. (2005). "The withering of criticism: a review of the critical renewal of professional, Foucauldian, ethnographic, and epistemic studies in accounting," *Accounting, Auditing & Accountability Journal*, 18(1): 100–35.

Tinker, A. M., B. D. Merino and M. D. Neimark (1982). "The normative origins of positive theories: ideology and accounting thought," *Accounting, Organizations and Society*, 7(2): 167–200.

Toms, S. (2006). "Asset policy models, the labour theory of value and their implications for accounting," *Critical Perspectives on Accounting*, 17(7): 947–65.

Toms, S. and R. K. Fleischman (2015). "Accounting fundamentals and accounting change: Boulton & Watt and the Springfield Amory," *Accounting, Organizations and Society*, 41(1): 1–30.

Tyson, T. (1993). "Keeping the record straight: Foucauldian revisionism and nineteenth century US cost accounting history," *Accounting, Auditing and Accountability Journal*, 6(2): 4–16.

Tyson, T. (1998). "The nature and environment of cost management among early nineteenth century US textile manufacturers," *Accounting Historians Journal*, 19(2): 1–24.

Tyson, T. (2000). "Accounting history and the emperor's new clothes: a response to knowing more as knowing less?" *Accounting Historians Journal*, 27(1): 159–71.

Tyson, T. N. and R. K. Fleischman (2006). "Accounting for interned Japanese-American civilians during World War II: creating incentives and establishing controls for captive workers," *The Accounting Historians Journal*, 33(1): 167–202.

Tyson, T., D. Oldroyd and R. K. Fleischman (2005). "Accounting, coercion, and social control during apprenticeship: converting slave workers into wage workers in the British West Indies, c.1834-1838," *Accounting Historians Journal*, 32(2): 201–31.

Verma S and S. J. Gray (2006). "The setting up of the Institute of Chartered Accountants of India: a first step in creating an indigenous accounting profession," *Accounting Historians Journal*, 33(2): 131–56.

Vollmers, G. L. (2003). "Industrial slavery in the United States: the North Carolina turpentine industry 1849-61," *Accounting, Business & Financial History*, 13(3): 369–92.

Walker, S. P. (1998). "How to secure your husband's esteem: patriarchy in the British middle class household during the nineteenth century," *Accounting, Organizations and Society*, 23 (5-6): 485–514.

Walker, S. P. (2003a). "Professionalisation or incarceration? household engineering, accounting and the domestic ideal," *Accounting, Organizations and Society*, 28(7–8): 743–72.

Walker, S. P. (2003b). "Identifying the woman behind the 'railed-in desk': the proto-feminisation of book-keeping in Britain," *Accounting, Auditing and Accountability Journal*, 16(4): 609–59.

Walker, S. P. (2004a). "The genesis of professional organisation in English accountancy," *Accounting, Organizations and Society*, 29(2): 127–56.

Walker, S. P. (2004b). "Expense, social and moral control: accounting and the administration of the old Poor Law in England and Wales," *Journal of Accounting and Public Policy*, 23(1): 85–127.

Walker, S. P. (2008). "Accounting, paper shadows and the stigmatized poor," *Accounting, Organizations and Society*, 33(4-5): 453–87.

Williamson, O. E. (1985). *The Economic Institutions of Capitalism*, New York: The Free Press.

Wootton, C. W. and B. E. Kemmerer. (1996). "The changing genderization of bookkeeping in the United States, 1870–1930," *Business History Review*, 70(4): 541–86.

Wootton, C. W. and B. E. Kemmerer (2000). "The changing genderization of the accounting workforce in the US, 1930-90," *Accounting, Business & Financial History*, 10(2): 169–90.

Young, J. (1997). "Defining auditors' responsibilities," *Accounting Historians Journal*, 24(2): 55-63.

Young, J. and T. Mouck (1996). "Objectivity and the role of history in the development and review of accounting standards," *Accounting, Auditing and Accountability Journal*, 9(3): 127–47.

Young, J. and P. Williams (2010). "Sorting and comparing: standard-setting and 'ethical' categories," *Critical Perspectives on Accounting*, 21(6): 509–21.

Zeff, S. (1998). "Independence and standard setting," *Critical Perspectives on Accounting*, 9(5): 535–43.

Zeff, S. A. (1999). "The evolution of the conceptual framework for business enterprises in the United States," *Accounting Historians Journal*, 26(2): 89–131.

Zelinschi, D. (2009). "Legitimacy, expertise and closure in the Romanian accountant's professionalization project 1900-1916," *Accounting History*, 14(4): 381–403

21

ACCOUNTING EDUCATION

Gordon Boyce

1 Introduction

As demonstrated throughout this volume, a substantial body of critical accounting knowledge, ideas and practices is well established within the accounting research community. However, the position of critical accounting in the accounting education domain is far less certain. This chapter explores the context for critical accounting education and considers key elements relating to its future development. Although the precise meaning and form of critical accounting may be contested, a generally well-accepted definition that applies nicely in the educational sphere is:

> A critical understanding of the role of accounting processes and practices and the accounting profession in the functioning of society and organisations with an intention to use that understanding to engage (where appropriate) in changing these processes, practices and the profession.
>
> *(Laughlin, 1999: 73)*

Dillard and Vinnari (2017) recently suggested an encompassing critical approach to accounting that may be thought of as centring on a 'public interest' orientation. In this vein, critical accounting strives to develop accounting in a way that serves the needs of 'pluralistic communities', considering "how accounting, accountants and accountability regimes facilitate more democratic institutions and processes that serve to enhance economic, social and environmental justice" (Dillard and Vinnari, 2017: 88). Thus, a critical lens with its "roots in social critique and praxis" recognises and critiques the existence and operation of power and gives "particular attention to ... underserved constituencies" (2017: 88–9). In all of these dimensions, critical accounting develops, nurtures and disseminates "accounting knowledges that are specifically designed to accomplish social change" (Roslender and Dillard, 2003: 338).

This chapter seeks to articulate an understanding of key theoretical and practical elements of critical accounting education, examining several essential dimensions that underpin endeavours to make accounting education more critical. Taking the notions just outlined as a starting point, it is clear that any notion of critical accounting education must represent a significant departure from the well-established conventional approaches to the accounting curriculum, teaching and learning. The critical approach represents a vastly different ethos to the traditional notion that limits the landscape of accounting education to meeting the perceived need for accounting graduates equipped to enter the domain of professional practice.

My own approach to critical accounting education simply takes education as a context for the practice of critical accounting as conceptualised thus far. In this setting, I hold that critical educational engagements must reflect, and reflect on, bodies of critical accounting knowledge. Importantly, this includes primary concerns with the meaning of accounting and accountability, which can be better understood, at least in part, through a consideration of the effects of accounting practice. Critical accounting must also challenge the way dominant and established forms of accounting "*promote, naturalise* and *universalise* economically rational, profit-centred, corporatist values" (Boyce, 2004: 572, original emphasis). In this light, critical accounting education should be an essential element or characteristic of any and all accounting education since it is not logically possible to 'properly' teach accounting unless this includes a clear conception of what accounting is and what it does in all its spheres of influence and effect, that is, including but extending beyond the realm of business and finance.

In preparing this chapter, I have reflected on my own subject position as an accounting researcher and educator. To help explicate the terrain of critical accounting education, I draw on some of my own published work together with that of a range of other researchers who have addressed critical and social aspects of accounting education. The chapter is organised in the following way. Section 2 examines six theoretical and practical guideposts for critical accounting education. First are three aspects of the context for critical accounting education: the ongoing official reform agenda, a perspective on the meaning of education and a consideration of the contemporary academic context within which critical accounting education is situated. Then, three foundations of critical accounting education are considered: praxis, reflexivity and re-thinking accounting critically. Section 3 brings the chapter together and reflects on the implications for further development of critical accounting education.

2 Theoretical and practical guideposts

This section examines six dimensions of theory and practice that contextualise and underpin critical accounting education.

2.1 *Accounting education reform*

Accounting education has been put under the microscope many times in recent decades by a range of significant institutional players in the US, UK and Australia. Numerous official reports emanating from the US have received global attention, including (but not limited to):

- the Bedford Committee on the Future Structure, Content and Scope of Accounting Education (Bedford *et al.*, 1986);
- the 'Big 8 White Paper' on Capabilities for Success in the Accounting Profession (Arthur Andersen and Co. *et al.*, 1989);
- the Accounting Education Change Commission (AECC) (1990) of the American Accounting Association (AAA);
- the Albrecht and Sack (2000) report, sponsored by the American Institute of Certified Public Accountants (AICPA), the Institute of Management Accountants (IMA), the AAA and the (then) 'Big 5' accounting firms;

- a PricewaterhouseCoopers (PwC) position paper on "Educating for the Public Trust" (PricewaterhouseCoopers 2003); and, most recently
- the Pathways Commission on Accounting Higher Education. (Behn *et al.*, 2012)

The need for educational reform has also been recognised elsewhere, including with Australia's Mathews Committee (Review Committee of the Accounting Discipline in Higher Education [1990]) and the UK's Long Range Enquiry into Education and Training for the Accountancy Profession (Solomons and Berridge, 1974). A consistent theme has been that the breadth and contemporary relevance of accounting education is severely lacking (see Black, 2012 and Sundem, 2014 for a pair of instructive overviews).

Sundem outlines how, following the impetus from debates that were prompted by the Ford and Carnegie Foundation reviews of business education in the US in the 1950s, and developments in articulating 'accounting theory' in the 1960s and 1970s, accounting education became "bogged down in techniques, rules, and regulations" in the 1980s (2014: 615). In the 1980s, the Bedford Committee reviewed developments in university accounting education programs over a sixty-year period (1925–85) and found that

> [t]he substance of accounting education has remained essentially the same over the last 50 years ... accounting education has not made significant efforts to improve its teaching methods over the last 60 years.
>
> *(Bedford and Shenkir, 1987: 84–6)*

The Committee found that "accounting education as it is currently approached requires major reorientation between now and the year 2000" (Bedford *et al.*, 1986). Similarly, the 'Big 8 White Paper' called for the "complete re-engineering of the educational process ... [including] objectives, content, design and methodology" (Arthur Andersen and Co. *et al.*, 1989). In the same period, a review of 17 different models for accounting education put forward over a 23-year period to the late 1980s (Needles and Powers, 1990) found that the broad categories of knowledge included in recommended curricula had generally remained static; there was little to suggest that there had been any substantive or systemic change in the approach to accounting education.

The AECC was constituted in 1989, with significant financial support from the large public accounting firms, to act as a catalyst for change flowing from the Bedford Report and the Big 8 White Paper. It produced an influential position statement on the "Objectives of Education for Accountants" (AECC, 1990) and, into the 1990s, funded a number of individual innovative projects, including one that produced "An accounting curriculum for the next century" (Albrecht *et al.*, 1994). The AECC's recommendations received significant attention and produced some positive outcomes in the US and elsewhere (Mathews, 1994; Calderon *et al.*, 1996). However, individual instances of change were generally not "successfully transferred to other universities" (Sundem, 2014: 617). The work of the AECC was itself criticised for focusing on the interests of a narrow range of stakeholders (Davis and Sherman, 1996), the unrepresentative distribution of AECC grants (Mintz, 1993) and failing to deal with the costs of change for different institutions (Sennetti and Dittenhofer, 1997).

Moving into the early 2000s, PricewaterhouseCoopers reviewed accounting education and optimistically suggested that a "transformation of accounting education is taking place ... moving education significantly beyond providing students only with technical training and specialized accounting knowledge" (PricewaterhouseCoopers, 2003: 6). This finding seemed to be based primarily on a handful of exemplar case studies. Despite some recognised improvements, including an increased emphasis on case studies, generic (soft) skill development and more attention to ethics within the curriculum, another influential review around the same time noted that previous warnings had gone "unheeded," again calling for accounting education to "transform itself" (Albrecht and Sack, 2000: 2, 66), and it was concluded that the "crisis in accounting education [was] growing" (Gabbin, 2002: 82). Gray and Collison suggested that "The problem is … *perhaps most importantly of all*, the very nature of accounting as it is currently understood and practiced (2002: 814, original emphasis).

The corporate, financial and accounting scandals of the 2000s (see Clarke *et al.*, 2014) prompted another "ethics revival" (see Cooper *et al.*, 2005: 374), although this tended to be characterised by a generally individualist, instrumentalist and often mechanistic approach to ethics that failed to consider broader social and systemic issues (Boyce, 2008, 2014a). The continuing malaise in accounting education ultimately resulted in the formation of the Pathways Commission to, yet again, consider "the future structure of higher education for the accounting profession" (Behn *et al.*, 2012: 9). Outlining its approach and mission, the Commission stated that "The educational preparation of accountants should rest on a comprehensive and well-articulated vision of the role of accounting in the wider society" (Behn *et al.*, 2012: 21). However, although the Pathways Commission report included "rhetorical flourishes about the importance of integrity to the profession and the social and economic purposes of accounting," it "largely reflected traditional accounting practice and ideology" (Boyce, 2014a: 549).

All of this suggests that the putative "revolution in accounting education" (Sundem, 1990) promoted by various accounting authorities must generally be regarded as a failure in terms of the objective to make accounting more relevant. There may be some sense in which accounting education "has come a long way in the last 50 years" (Sundem, 2014: 628), particularly in terms of some advances in contextualising accounting within the business context. Nevertheless, the overall conclusion is that decades of reform calls have been "rather unsuccessful" (Carmona, 2013: 117). The core accounting curriculum has "remained virtually unchanged" for more than 100 years (Merino, 2006: 370) and broader liberal and social aspirations for accounting education also represent "a century of failed efforts" (Willits, 2010: 20).

Well into the twenty-first century, a "general dissatisfaction with the state of accounting education persists" (Boyce *et al.*, 2015: 27). The seemingly endless succession of reviews and reform proposals has not produced fundamental change to educational practice. Taken as a whole, this represents an example of "complexly doing nothing" (Boyce, 2008: 260) within accounting. The failure "to challenge the traditional tenets of the discipline and the [continued prioritisation of] the perceived technical needs of professional practice" (Boyce *et al.*, 2012: 48) means that "fundamental questions concerning the content, the objectives and the central intellectual and moral values needed in accounting education remain profoundly unresolved" (Gray and Collison, 2002: 827).

This situation may partly be the product of the close ties between university accounting education and the professional bodies and accrediting agencies. This has resulted in a generally vocational and technical orientation within accounting education that tends to focus on detailed accounting procedures, standards, reporting requirements and the like – to the detriment of a broader consideration of accounting as a social and organisational phenomenon. To overcome this malady, a broader educational perspective is required – one that recognises, but looks beyond, the vocational and practice-oriented dimensions of accounting.

2.2 An educational perspective

Accounting education performs an important function in shaping the knowledge, skills and understandings both of accountants themselves and the wider group of business and political actors who use – and, recursively, shape – accounting (Laughlin, 2007). As Gray and Collison suggest, however, "the continuing 'debates' over accounting education," such as those reflected in Section 2.1, "are rarely debates at all," because they have not addressed "fundamental questions about education, the profession and accounting" (2002: 827).

Accounting practice, education and research are closely interconnected, as Williams (2004: 513) suggests, because of the "historical inter-connections" between the three domains, "and the questionable values that shaped their parallel developments." However, we may regard the university as representing the fulcrum of accounting where each of these three domains come together and (may) mutually inform each other. While much critical accounting activity has been undertaken in the research domain, the focus in this chapter is on *education* as pivotal in the production and reproduction of accounting, providing a key connector between research and practice. Education is the primary site where understanding of the practice dimension of accounting may be developed and challenged, and, over time, changed, starting with a broader understanding of the discipline's sociopolitical functioning and implications. Education plays a vital role because it is here that "it is clearly possible to create new foundational assumptions ... particularly in terms of the ability to influence tomorrow's accounting professionals" (Ravenscroft and Williams, 2005: 370).

The traditional technical, vocational and instrumental emphases within accounting education have sidestepped questions about the meaning of education and obviated tensions between different visions that have always been at play in universities. Preston's (1992: 50–1) characterisation of three broad perspectives on education helps delineate some of the debates:

1   *Vocational* education is primarily seen as training and related preparation for work. Uncritically accommodating the status quo and attendant social hierarchies, structures and modes of action, it is instrumental and extrinsic in orientation.
2   *Liberal* education is oriented to the development of the individual person, fostering individual potential and preparing the *whole* person for *life* (including, but not limited to, work).
3   A *socially critical* orientation to education focuses on the relationship between education and society and considers education as preparation for economic *and* social life. It accepts that education *cannot* be ideologically neutral, and commits to education as a lever to further social justice.

Considering education, broadly speaking, as "a continuous process of reconstruction of experience" (Dewey, 1997: 87), critical accounting can help to develop a balance between the humanistic/formative and vocational/instructive dimensions of education, thereby drawing on each of the three perspectives outlined. Gramsci (1971) makes an important distinction between being informed and being educated, seeking to break down the traditional divide between classical humanistic education and vocational or professional education, such that education could be "formative, *while* being 'instructive'" (Giroux, 1988: 200, emphasis added).

In many respects some of the major debates around education have reflected unresolved tensions between alternative educational perspectives *and* political interventions in public policy directions (Chronicle of Higher Education, 1986a). The role of education in social reproduction means that it is "a complex of meanings not all of which are consistent with the holistic view that education is an essentially positive element of the social structure" (Roslender, 1992: 8). Throughout their history, universities have been closely tied to the hegemonic order and subject to social, political and religious forces that seek social stabilisation and control in the interests of the social elite (Boyce, 2002). Indeed, education represents the dominant ideological state apparatus because of the way in which it reproduces prevailing ideologies (Roslender, 1992: 92). At the same time, universities provide a site where alternatives to the status quo can be thought and developed, producing a "dialectical tension between *education as domination* and *education as emancipation*" (Boyce, 2004: 567, original emphasis; see also Dillard and Tinker, 1996). It is in this sense that *critical* accounting education is therefore counterposed to approaches that reproduce and reinforce the existing social order.

It is generally accepted (at least at the level of rhetoric) that a rounded and complete education – including business and accounting education – should look beyond the vocational perspective and seek to prepare students for their "civic and social obligations," including "more transcendent issues that give meaning to existence and help students put their own lives in perspective" (the Carnegie Report, cited in the Chronicle of Higher Education, 1986b: 17). If education for "work, life and citizenship" is accepted as an important part of the wider responsibilities of a university (see White, 2013), broader education must be fostered "across the entire educational experience, and in the context of students' major fields" (National Leadership Council for Liberal Education and America's Promise, 2007: 2), including business and professional fields such as accounting (Colby *et al.* 2011; White, 2013).

Therefore, for critical accounting the key challenge is to create a suitable balance between the educational and training domains, so that students are both prepared to work within the world as it is, but also can understand that situation in all its contingency and possibilities for alternatives. Critical accounting provides a domain through which the examination and critique of real-life life problems and circumstances, from multiple perspectives, can build "connections between accounting education and the *lived experience* of students" (Boyce and Greer, 2013: 111, original emphasis). The development of technical and practical skills is not eschewed but contextualised and made meaningful through an understanding of how the practice of accounting impacts on daily life (see Hopwood, 1994). In practical terms, this is a "*fusion* between the academic and the technical" (Mayo, 2008: 427, emphasis added) – a Gramscian approach that rejects the immediacy of narrow vocationalism and "mere factuality," recognising the need to *concurrently* develop "in each individual human being an as yet undifferentiated general culture, the fundamental power to think and ability to find one's way in life" (Gramsci 1971: 26). As Roslender and Dillard point out:

> The University provides an admirable place to begin the process of persuading intending members of the accountancy profession that they are better served by adopting a questioning attitude. This should not be done at the expense of providing the expected level of technical training and accreditation.
>
> *(2003: 342)*

Thus, critical accounting education works with the "tension between … technical (vocational) expertise for future practice and … wider, critical, educational (transcendent) roles" (Gray and Collison, 2002: 800). This implies a capacity to critically examine the forces and influences that interact with organisations, critiquing, questioning and contesting received understandings of accounting (see Neimark, 1996). In the context of a field such as accounting, a critical approach is necessary to yield the "essential conditions" of *higher* education:

> The development of the student's autonomy as a self-sufficient rational inquirer. Following a process of higher education, a graduate (whatever his/her field of study) should have not just an understanding of the field—its key concepts, theories and findings—and be able to carry out the relevant operations, but should be able to engage with the field with a certain degree of detachment. He/she should be able to maintain a distance from the field, and be able to evaluate and be critical of it.
>
> *(Barnett, 1988: 245)*

In has been suggested that the "only … subject-matter for education … is Life … a particular body of knowledge which has peculiar reference to the life of the being possessing it" (Whitehead, 1959: 198, 202), and that "the college has an obligation to give students a sense of passage toward a more integrated, more coherent view of knowledge and life" (Carnegie Report, in Chronicle of Higher Education, 1986b: 18–19). If this is taken seriously, then seeking to develop the whole person and prepare students for full and meaningful participation in civic, socioeconomic and political activities must be seen as a central goal of education in accounting no less than in any other field (Neimark, 1996; Gray and Collison, 2002; Tinker and Gray, 2003; Boyce 2004).

In summary, accounting education should be oriented towards the twin goals of providing the knowledge and skills necessary to enter the world of work or a profession, *and* towards providing the critical knowledge and developing the capacities that are central to citizenship and full participation in democratic social and political life. In contrast to the traditional focus on the first of these two broad elements, to the significant neglect of the second, critical accounting education provides an important means to redress the imbalance. However, history shows that even relatively modest, progressively inspired reforms such as those referred to in Section 2.1, have been difficult to achieve in accounting education (see Merino, 2006), and as a consequence the contemporary academic context seems just as resistant to a genuine reform of accounting education as at any other time in its history.

2.3 The academic context

Parker (2002) provides an optimistic account of the opportunities and possibilities for accounting academics to engage in bottom-up debates about university futures. By contrast, Merino (2006: 377) is relatively pessimistic about the prospects for accounting education to address its societal obligations. In part this is because of the contemporary commodification of higher education, about which Boden and Epstein sound a significant note of caution suggesting that "the contemporary global transformation of higher education leaves little room for comfort" (2006: 224). Key among their concerns is the corporatisation of universities, to the extent that extant sociopolitical powers and interests are significant in shaping the function, form, activities and outputs of universities. In short, in the wake of neo-liberalism, universities have been captured by the interests of capital, undermining the traditionally conceived social functions of universities.

Sustained neo-liberal restructuring in recent decades has deepened and naturalised the relationships between universities and corporate interests, to the extent that knowledge produced and transmitted in universities is increasingly expected to conform to business and managerialist agendas, thus reinforcing existing economic and social structures (see Coady, 2000; Shear, 2008). The educational challenges suggested in Sections 2.1 and 2.2 are thereby magnified in the context of the contemporary neo-liberal business university that seems increasingly confounded regarding the purposes of its own existence (Beverungen *et al.*, 2008; Beverungen *et al.*, 2014). Critical academics in this environment face significant difficulties because of the "shrinking … space that academic intellectuals have for critical inquiry" (Shear, 2008: 56).

The experience inside academic institutions is contextualised by similar occurrences within the broader society. Just as the counter-hegemonic potential within society cannot be endlessly contained, so there are possibilities for resistance within universities themselves. While it is possible that universities are already "too deeply embodied within capital … to be sufficiently imaginative of different futures" (Boden and Epstein, 2006: 225), the hegemony of neo-liberalism is not yet total. There remain "contradictions and chinks within university systems" (2006: 234), providing an opening for the pursuit of the radical imagination of critical accounting, but these spaces are highly limited and constrained, particularly in business schools (Dunne *et al.*, 2008).

As with the history of reform efforts in accounting education, the present context may provide significant cause for pessimism, but it emphasises the need to reconsider the tenets of accounting education in such a way that the negative impacts of neo-liberalism can be countered – or at least ameliorated – in the name of genuine education. Social change will not result solely from change within accounting or accounting education; it must be recognised that accounting is both a condition *and* a consequence of the world as it exists and as it is made through intellectual and practical endeavours. The Gramscian understanding that all educators are "intellectuals, who as mediators, legitimators, and producers of ideas and social practices, perform a pedagogical function that is eminently political in nature" (Aronowitz and Giroux, 1993: 31) means that accounting educators must challenge the traditional tenets of their discipline.

Fundamentally, overcoming the institutionalised impediments to change must start with a reconception of accounting that moves beyond the narrow set of interests associated with business, the elevation of private property rights and the vested interests of the accounting profession (Owen, 2005). This kind of change implies the *imagination* and *real-isation* of a different kind of accounting – one that may be developed and constructed through praxis.

2.4 Praxis

Critical accounting education requires a "philosophy of praxis ... realised through the concrete study of past history and through present activity to construct new history" (Gramsci, 1971: 427). Praxis involves a relationship between theory and practice, and accordingly between knowledge, education, action and interaction. Knowledge itself emerges only "through ... the restless, impatient, continuing, hopeful inquiry human beings pursue in the world, with the world, and with each other" (Freire, 1996: 53). It is not transformed by chance, rather through "reflection and action upon the world in order to transform it" (1996: 33), that is, through praxis. Thus, critical accounting praxis works through knowledge "to describe and explain the world as thoroughly as possible in order to be better able to change it" (Buttigieg, 1986: 11). At the same time, educational praxis recognises that, because of the relationship between education and society, change cannot just be institutional but must also be societal.

Accounting plays a central role in creating and sustaining the particular economic discourses and actions that produce corporate and business scandals, environmental destruction and a variety of social problems. In this context the responsibilities of accounting educators are particularly significant because they directly affect the development of accounting knowledge and practice that relates to these outcomes. In developing a critical dimension, accounting education has the potential to offer alternatives to the dominant ideologies of the free market and to generate conceptions of *socially useful* accounting.

In the first instance, critical accounting must de-reify and denaturalise the present, which must come to be seen as a conjunction of particular historic interests rather than as an outcome of natural and immutable historical processes. Just as social reality is not a set of objective facts that are external to the individual knower or to social processes of knowledge production (Berger and Luckmann, 1984), so, too, the melange of individual and organisational realities created by and through accounting are mutable. Critical educational praxis recognises that universities have a key role in the reflection on and problematisation of persistent ideas of the day, operationalised through the development and nurturing of capacities for debating and contesting accounting ideas and practices, and promoting alternative conceptions of economy, society and politics (Craig *et al.*, 1999).

These goals are quite distinct from the general practice of accounting education in terms of its professional, vocational and business emphases, but critical accounting research has developed a significant body of knowledge on which educators may draw in developing their teaching. This extant knowledge of accounting and its effects should impel educational praxis – if only to grasp some of the conditions that characterise human existence and environmental degradation in the contemporary world, and accounting's role in them:

> In the countries of the North, we continue to be confronted with financial crises and economic restructuring—events where the economic burden continues to fall on the most vulnerable members of society. And in countries of the South and their equivalents, robber baron capitalism runs rampant, exacerbated by an increasingly globalised world that makes it difficult for impoverished governments to chart a path that is somehow independent of transnational capital and that adequately buffers its population from the vagaries of the market.
>
> *(Annisette et al., 2009: 1)*

This should produce an imperative that these issues be addressed within accounting – through the questions we ask and the issues we raise:

> Our conceptions, practices, and beliefs are not to be regarded as fixed and timeless, but rather as hypotheses in use … [thus] highlight[ing] their impermanence and allow[ing] us to more readily accept the importance of periodically examining their "goodness" by carefully attending to the consequences that they produce.
>
> *(Young, 2005: 10)*

Taking a broadly critical sociological perspective, Boyce *et al.* (2015) provide a wide range of theoretical and practical guidance for accounting educators. They outline relevant approaches to understanding accounting (chapter 5), sociological concepts and themes that are relevant to the accounting curriculum (chapter 6 – themes include power, control, pluralism ethics, value and history), and resources from the accounting literature (chapter 7). The latter included six themes around which an expanded consideration of scope and content could be built: thinking differently about accounting; languages of accounting; accounting in its social context; accounting, accountability and identity; examining the accountancy profession; and understanding the accounting field. These and related themes provide contexts for praxis in the sense of theory-informed action that is oriented towards social change.

Tinker and Gray suggest another important dimension of praxis:

> Praxis is a dual process: it recognizes the way we act on and change an external world "out there," yet in acknowledging that we are also part of that larger "out there," it also refers to the ways we ourselves are transformed, culturally, spiritually, cognitively, aesthetically, and emotionally. …
>
> *(2003: 737)*

> Praxis includes not just traditional activism of enabling changes "out there," but also the "in here" changes in the self-consciousness of actors, subjects, and their observers.
>
> *(2003: 751)*

Thus, critical accounting praxis also requires examination of the self as a subject of knowledge *and* an agent of action. This is the realm of reflexivity.

2.5 Reflexivity

Knowledge is the means through which students (and, indeed, teachers) come into "a valid relationship with the world, and so of knowing the world" (Barnett, 2009: 432), and it is a central role of higher education to deliver such knowledge, promoting the holistic development of students. All academic activity is intimately connected with our lives and ourselves (as individuals and communities of people). Each individual accounting practitioner, teacher, student and researcher is a product of social processes, and choices in accounting cannot be artificially separated from these processes. One aim of critical accounting praxis is "to know oneself better through others and to know others better through oneself" (Gramsci, in Forgacs, 1999: 59).

Little can be accomplished without recognising that the experience of accounting cannot be extricated from our material experience as social beings, and that a radically reformed accounting would therefore implicate concomitant change in the totality of social existence:

> Consciousness is ... from the very beginning a social product, and remains so as long as men exist at all. Consciousness is at first, of course, merely consciousness concerning the *immediate* sensuous environment and consciousness of the limited connection with other persons and things outside the individual who is growing self-conscious.
>
> *(Marx and Engels, 1970: 51, original emphasis)*

An objectified and reified reality is neither permanent nor immutable, and "people can come to understand how society operates, understand it as a social product, and understand that it is open to transformation. What is true of the existing order need not be true of the next" (Held, 1980: 190). However, change in accounting education is not a simple voluntaristic act because "[r]eality impinges upon, constrains individuals; it remains something seemingly 'non-human', objectified and reified."

As noted in Section 2.1, accounting education has remained remarkably resistant to change despite many significant reform endeavours. This situation has led Carmona to conclude that top-down reform is unlikely to happen:

> [R]ather than waiting for the implementation of some "grand" reform, I would encourage an *individual* approach to this important issue ... what can individual faculty members do.
>
> *(2013: 117, emphasis added; see also Hopper, 2013)*

Although change in accounting practice, education and research is, of necessity, a social accomplishment, Carmona's perspective suggests that an important responsibility for addressing accounting education change rests with academics themselves. Many systemic factors militate against reform at an official level, but change "also requires change to the self-consciousness of all actors involved" (Boyce *et al.*, 2012: 66). As Gramsci notes:

> The starting-point of critical elaboration is the consciousness of what one really is, and is "knowing thyself" as a product of the historical process to date which has deposited in you an infinity of traces, without leaving an inventory.
>
> *(1971: 342)*

Therefore, critical accounting education must instantiate a capacity for self-reflection in the subjects of accounting: teachers and students alike. This requires accounting educators to engage in some level of individual and collective reflexive self-examination:

> *Reflexivity* addresses the context of knowledge creation and application … through an "internal conversation" on the part of the knower … an examination *by* a knower of *the* knower – considering the self in relation to social context and vice versa. Thus, reflexivity requires an agent to actively reflect upon and recognise how their own socialisation and social context affect *what* and *how* they come to construct and apply knowledge – how they come to 'know'.
>
> *(Boyce et al., 2015: 169; see also Archer, 2010; Kaidonis, 2009)*

In accounting education, where ostensible accounting knowledge is presented and disseminated, reflexivity (for teachers and students) might start with a rejection of the apparent objectivity of accounting numbers, instead recognising them as socially constructed. This requires self-challenge on the part of accounting educators, whose 'internal conversation' might reflect on how "they have been socialised into the existing system through their own education" (Boyce, 2004: 579). Thus, reflexivity helps accounting educators to understand that they are themselves a product of social reproduction and that their own perspectives are "shaped by both their own personal values, attitudes and positioning, *and* the history and social context of those values, attitudes and positioning" (Boyce *et al.*, 2015: 169, original emphasis).

For students, reflexivity might start by considering themselves in relation to the educational context, which is likely to reflect an initial identification with a traditional conception of accounting (Boyce, 2004; Tinker, 1991; Sikka *et al.*, 1995). An internal conversation of reflexivity can open prior perceptions and self-understandings of students to critical scrutiny, but the educational context has to facilitate such self-examination. Critical accounting carries the potential to challenge conventional accounting standpoints and to help students to clarify their own positions and understandings of "the extent to which accounting is implicated in processes of social and political control" (Humphrey *et al.*, 1996: 80). This process undoubtedly challenges the individual, just as it helps to de-reify the apparent objectivity of accounting and its assumed natural and inevitable ties to the world of economics and commerce. Students can thereby be "equipped to develop their own personal and collective positions on accounting issues, and to discover possibilities for activating those positions through praxis" and an associated emergent self-consciousness (Boyce *et al.*, 2012: 66).

In summary, nurturing reflexivity in accounting education can help to "prepare students for *informed action in and on the world* … [including] an understanding of the relation of accounting to the mundane activities, language, and interactions of daily life engaged in by both academics and students, and how these relate to the larger social system within which they are embedded" (Boyce, 2004). This process should also generate insight into social reproduction and how it maintains the status quo, consequently facilitating re-examination of individual positioning in relation to the status quo:

> [A] social world where roles are inextricably intertwined and conflicting, and where the individual needs to develop a social self-consciousness for transcending conflicts. The same accounting individual often appears on several sides in the same dispute, and without a self-awareness about her role interdependencies, may ultimately contribute to her own repression and exploitation!
>
> *(Tinker, 1991: 305)*

Reflexivity in the critical accounting context opens up fundamental questions of the social contexts of accountability and associated identity formation. This is an important dimension of re-thinking accounting in a critical way.

2.6 Re-thinking accounting critically

In previous work, I have outlined a "tangential" approach to critical accounting education, suggesting that

> For accounting education to be socially relevant, it must be infused with an exploration of areas that may prima facie seem tangential to the "main game" of accounting" but are actually "an important part of the subject matter.
>
> *(Boyce, 2004: 572–3; see also Dillard and Tinker, 1996)*

Later, I opine that:

> Accounting research is sufficiently well-developed such that the conflicts and contradictions both within accounting and flowing from the practice of the discipline are well-known. Yet the effect of this body of knowledge on the content of teaching and learning within the accounting classroom remains limited. Accounting education has traditionally been narrowly defined within disciplinary boundaries that exclude consideration of anything outside the policies and practices of the discipline as such. In contradistinction, I outline a case for consciously adopting *tangential thinking* as a heuristic for the transcendence of mis-conceived, narrowly constructed disciplinary boundaries.
>
> *(Boyce, 2004: 567–8, italics in original)*

Thus, the tangential approach adopts a broader definition of accounting by reconsidering its boundaries and examining phenomena that are "positioned on the margins" where "the most interesting developments within the discipline are at play" (Boyce, 2014b: 117, 121; see Miller, 1998). It is at these margins that developing forms of critical, social and environmental accounting have brought to attention the role of technocratic and calculative forms of accounting in the perpetuation of environmental and social maladies. Tangential examination of accounting phenomena typifies a meaningful consideration of accounting in the contexts in which it operates (see Hopwood, 1983), and may be regarded as quintessential "attention to the various underserved constituencies" of accounting (Dillard and Vinnari, 2017: 88–9).

The tangential approach to accounting education also presents an ideal opportunity for dialogical approaches that admit alternative perspectives into the discourse and encourage critical reflection (see Freire, 1996). Accounting tangents also provide the opportunity to "bring the historical and contemporary social underpinnings of accounting practice into the classroom" facilitating the articulation of pre-existing 'common sense knowledge' with a more enlightened social consciousness that transcends the limitations of its pre-existing understandings (Boyce, 2004: 575; Hall, 1988). This process offers considerable scope, which

> may include locating the development and use of accounting systems, technologies, and associated policies, procedures, and practices in their organisational, social, and ethical contexts. It may involve identifying and questioning underlying assumptions and examining and interrogating the justifications and explanations offered by others. This should involve subjecting accounting systems, technologies, policies, procedures, and practices to scrutiny insofar as they have real direct and indirect consequences for social actors and groups. The interests of various (different) parties (including students, in varying aspects of their lives) should be considered and challenged.
>
> *(Boyce, 2004: 578)*

In addition to the more well-established critical accounting literature, as exemplified throughout the current volume, new and emerging critical research themes should impact on many areas of the accounting curriculum, providing an ever-renewing contemporary impetus for critical accounting education. Recent developments in the critical genre include:

- examination of the role of accounting in corruption, bribery, tax avoidance and other contemporary nefarious business practices, and related considerations (e.g. Sikka, 2010; Sikka and Willmott, 2010; Davids, 2014; Neu *et al.*, 2015);
- the provision of accounts that give voice to those who are marginalised or excluded from mainstream debates (e.g. Agyemang, 2015; Agyemang and Lehman, 2013; Lehman *et al.*, 2016; Neu, 2012);
- critiques of the spread of accounting practices and associated technologies such as public–private partnerships (PPPs) and the associated outcomes and effects (e.g. Shaoul *et al.*, 2011a, 2011b; Toms *et al.*, 2011; McDonald-Kerr, 2017);
- silent, shadow and counter accounting, which construct alternative forms of critical, social and environmental accounts (e.g. Moerman and van Der Laan, 2015; Boyce, 2014b; Dey and Gibbon, 2014; Boiral, 2013).

These areas position accounting education within the broader sociopolitical sphere. At the same time, they challenge the conventional financial/monetary logic of accounting:

> Accounting logic is the belief that it is possible to evaluate the use of financial transactions through the outputs or outcomes achieved and that these can be assessed, invariably in measurable form. Accounting logic is not something that is only exercised by accountants but is a way of thinking that permeates all of society. Its roots may be in accounting but its influence and practice goes way beyond the confines of practising accountants.
>
> *(Laughlin, 2007: 277)*

A critical re-thinking of accounting provides for a more encompassing accounting education that should resonate with a wide range of students and teachers alike, at the same time as it challenges them. It is through these multifaceted challenges that accounting education can garner meaning beyond the narrow aspirations of preparation for work in professional or related practices.

3 Implications: accounting education that makes a difference

The present state of accounting education is strongly influenced by socioeconomic and political tendencies, and its future development will continue to be so; these tendencies and their outcomes are neither inevitable nor predetermined, however. Marcuse (1964) draws attention to the manner in which societal development is a function of social choice, observing that the choice itself reflects "the play of the dominant interests" (Marcuse, 1964: xvi). Thus, it is important to note that the present state of accounting education, including its woeful history of efforts at reform, and an ongoing recognition of the crises of relevance, are all a contingent historical products of the interplay-dominant forces and tendencies within the field. In my view:

> Accounting exists not just *in* but *because of* its environment … it is part of a symbiotic process through which it mutually legitimates, and is in turn legitimated by, particular modes of economic activity.
>
> *(Boyce, 2014b: 118, fn 3)*

At the same time, these circumstances, and the periodic and cyclic scandals that erupt in the realms of business and professional accounting, provide

> historic junctures that allow 'critical' or 'positive' intellectuals the opportunity to use what capital they have to redefine what counts as legitimate in the field, and this has effects on the research problems that are studied and the curricula that are taught.
>
> *(Cooper et al., 2005: 377)*

Recognising that the present form, content and structure of accounting education is wholly inadequate, critical accounting education always starts with a *critical* understanding of *education* that is not limited to training for work or a profession, but relates to the broader society. Critical education is itself a multifaceted process of self-formation that is also committed to furthering social justice and may thereby challenge the extant power of social reproduction.

The role of universities in "furthering the social pursuit of 'goodness' (however defined) has always been a central feature of the justifying, legitimising language of the academy" (Morrison, 2001). Ultimately, it is broader educational goals that justify the presence of accounting in the university curriculum. Decades of official endeavours to reform accounting education to make it more relevant to its context have as yet produced very little substantive change. The persistence of extant processes, structures and curricula suggest that it is no longer viable for educators to rely on top-down or official pronouncements. Accounting educators must take responsibility for the state of the discipline, and bottom-up individual efforts are necessary. However, history shows that individual efforts, while necessary, are not sufficient. A greater collective endeavour on the part of the critical accounting community, as exemplified in the present volume, is required.

Journals such as *Critical Perspectives on Accounting* have played an exemplary role in recognising and promoting the importance of linking critical research and education. In recent years, the journal has published a number of special issues focusing on various aspects of accounting education in universities, and Dillard and Vinnari's (2016) review shows a significant quantum of articles examining accounting education. This literature is diverse: highlighting deficiencies in accounting programmes and curricula including in the areas of ethics and sustainability; critiquing the narrow scope of accounting education and its focus on financial quantification; examining issues associated with diversity; and critically exploring neo-liberalism and commercialisation in universities. In an exemplar article, Dillard argues for "the recognition of the political nature of both the teaching and the practice of accounting though the recognition and critical analysis of historical, economic and social context" (2002: 622). Arguing for a public interest, rather than commercial orientation, Dillard sees an "educational duty" to "include analyses and critical assessments of various business practices, thus emancipating both educators and students from the dominance of managerialism and capital in contemporary Western societies" (Dillard and Vinnari, 2017: 97).

Fundamentally, critical accounting education challenges the position of the neo-liberal business university, and does so in a manner that is actually consistent with the traditionally *espoused* "ideals" and "mission" of the university as a social institution. This is generally thought of as an institution that reflects on and problematises the pervasive ideas of the times and provides an institutional space for difference and debate (Newman, 1996; Craig *et al.*, 1999; Boyce, 2002).

Critical accounting education implies a much broader consideration of accounting and accountability by looking at and beyond the margins of accounting where perhaps the most interesting and important developments within the discipline lie. At the same time, it can influence future practice by raising the consciousness of students about the nature of accounting and its effects, and situating accounting in its socio-historical context. The *critical* relevance of this approach centres on the "critique of the given state of affairs on its own grounds—of the established system of life, which denies its own promises and potentialities" (Marcuse, 2007: 64). Equally important is its connection to lived experience and common sense, while transcending their limitations (Gramsci, 1971).

Enduring change in universities – and accounting education and practice – requires concomitant change in society, so critical accounting education must ultimately be linked to change in wider social spheres. Neither the nature, nor the future form, of accounting education, nor the nature of the institutions within which it is situated and that of the broader society, are pre-determined or inevitable. The future of critical accounting education, just as its present, is historically contingent. It will be a product of the "daily attention to teaching and learning that will form the focus of critical accounting educational practice. Intellectual involvement with students is perhaps the most important activity to be undertaken by educators with a commitment to social change" (Boyce, 2004: 570).

References

Accounting Education Change Commission (1990). "Objectives of education for accountants: position statement no. 1," *Issues in Accounting Education*, 5(2): 307–12.
Agyemang, G. (2015). "Perilous journeys across the seas: the accounting logic in Europe's agenda for migration," *Advances in Public Interest Accounting*, 19: 1–27.
Agyemang, G. and C. R. Lehman (2013). "Adding critical accounting voices to migration studies," *Critical Perspectives on Accounting*, 24(4–5): 261–72.
Albrecht, W. S. and R. J. Sack (2000). "Accounting education: charting the course through a perilous future," *Accounting Education Series: 16*, Sarasota, FL: American Accounting Association.
Albrecht, W. S., D. C. Clark, J. M. Smith, K.D. Stocks and L.W. Woodfield (1994). "An accounting curriculum for the next century," *Issues in Accounting Education*, 9(2): 401–15.
Annisette, M., C. Cooper and D. Neu (2009). "Editorial," *Critical Perspectives on Accounting*, 20(1): 1–2.
Archer, M. S. (2010). "Routine, reflexivity and realism," *Sociological Theory*, 28(3): 272–303.
Aronowitz, S. and H. A. Giroux (1993). *Education Still Under Siege*, Westport, CT: Bergin & Garvey.
Arthur Andersen and Co, Arthur Young, Coopers and Lybrand, Delloitte Haskins and Sells, Ernst and Whinney, Peat Marwick Main and Co, Price Waterhouse, and Touche Ross (1989). *Perspectives on Education: Capabilities for Success in the Accounting Profession ('The Big 8 White Paper')*, New York.
Barnett, R. (1988). "Does higher education have aims?" *Journal of Philosophy of Education*, 22(2): 239–50
Barnett, R. (2009). "Knowing and becoming in the higher education curriculum," *Studies in Higher Education*, 34(4): 429–40.
Bedford, N. and W. G. Shenkir (1987). "Reorienting accounting education," *Journal of Accountancy*, 164(2): 84–9.
Bedford, N., E. E. Batholemew, C. A. Bowsher, A. L. Brown, S. Davidson, C. T. Horngren, H. C. Knortz, M. M. Piser, W. G. Shenkir, J, K. Simmons, E. L. Summers and J. T. Wheeler (1986). "Future accounting education: preparing for the expanding profession (The special report of the American Accounting Association Committee on the Future Structure, Content, and Scope of Accounting Education)," *Issues in Accounting Education*, 1(1): 168–95.
Behn B. K., W. F. Ezzell, L. A. Murphy, M. Stith, J. Rayburn and J. R. Strawser (2012). *The Pathways Commission: Charting a National Strategy for the Next Generation of Accountants*, American Accounting Association and American Institute of CPAs.
Berger, P. and T. Luckmann (1984). *The Social Construction of Reality: A Treatise in the Sociology of Knowledge*, Harmondsworth: Pelican.
Beverungen, A., S. Dunne and B. M. Sørensen (2008). "University, failed," *Ephemera: Theory and Politics in Organization*, 8(3): 232–37.
Beverungen, A., C. Hoedemaekers and J .Veldman (2014). "Charity and finance in the university," *Critical Perspectives on Accounting*, 25(1): 58–66.
Black, W. H. (2012). "The activities of the Pathways Commission and the historical context for changes in accounting education," *Issues in Accounting Education*, 27(3): 601–25.
Boden, R. and D. Epstein (2006). "Managing the research imagination? Globalisation and research in higher education," *Globalisation, Societies and Education*, 4(2): 223–36.

Boiral, O. (2013). "Sustainability reports as simulacra? a counter-account of A and A+ GRI reports," *Accounting, Auditing and Accountability Journal*, 26(7): 1036–71.

Boyce, G. (2002). "Now and then: revolutions in higher learning," *Critical Perspectives on Accounting*, 13(5–6): 575–601.

Boyce, G. (2004). "Critical accounting education: teaching and learning outside the circle," *Critical Perspectives on Accounting*, 15(4–5): 565–86.

Boyce, G. (2008). "The social relevance of ethics education in a global(ising) era: from individual dilemmas to system crises," *Critical Perspectives on Accounting*, 19(2): 255–90.

Boyce, G. (2014a). "Ethics in accounting education," in R. M. S. Wilson (ed.): *The Routledge Companion to Accounting Education*, London and New York: Routledge

Boyce, G. (2014b). "Professionalism, the public interest and social accounting," in S. M. Mintz (ed.): *Accounting for the Public Interest: Perspectives on Accountability, Professionalism and Role in Society*, New York: Springer.

Boyce, G. and S. Greer (2013). "More than imagination: making social and critical accounting real," *Critical Perspectives on Accounting*, 24(2): 105–112.

Boyce, G., S. Greer, B. Blair and C. Davids (2012). "Expanding the horizons of accounting education: incorporating social and critical perspectives," *Accounting Education: An International Journal*, 21(1): 47–74.

Boyce, G., S. Greer, V. Narayanan and B. Blair (2015). *Sociologically Reimagining Accounting: A Scaffolded Framework of Research and Resources*, Melbourne. www.socialaccountingblog.wordpress.com.

Buttigieg, J. A. (1986). "The legacy of Antonio Gramsci," *Boundary* 2: 14(3): 1–17.

Calderon, T. G., A. L. Gabbin and B. P. Green (1996). "Summary of promoting and evaluating effective teaching," *Journal of Accounting Education*, 14(3): 367–83.

Carmona, S. (2013). "Accounting curriculum reform? he devil is in the detail," *Critical Perspectives on Accounting*, 24(2): 113–19.

Chronicle of Higher Education (1986a). "Carnegie study finds colleges are torn by divisions and confused over principles," November, 5: 1–16.

Chronicle of Higher Education (1986b). "Prologue and major recommendations of Carnegie Foundation's report on college," November, 5: 16–22.

Clarke, F., G. Dean and M. Egan (2014). *The Unaccountable and Ungovernable Corporation*, London and New York: Routledge.

Coady, T. (ed.) (2000). *Why Universities Matter: A Conversation About Values, Means and Directions*, Crows Nest, New South Wales: Allen & Unwin.

Colby, A., T. Erlich, W. M. Sullivan and J. R. Dolle (2011). *Rethinking Undergraduate Business Education: Liberal Learning for the Profession*, San Francisco, CA: Jossey-Bass.

Cooper, D. J., J. Everett and D. Neu (2005). "Financial scandals, accounting change and the role of accounting academics: a perspective from North America," *European Accounting Review*, 14(2): 373–82.

Craig, R. J., F. L. Clarke and J. H. Amernic (1999). "Scholarship in university business schools: Cardinal Newman, creeping corporatism and farewell to the 'disturber of the peace'?" *Accounting, Auditing and Accountability Journal*, 12(5): 510–24.

Davids, C. (2014). "Facilitation payments in international business transactions: law, accounting and the public interest," in S. M. Mintz (ed.): *Accounting for the Public Interest: Perspectives on Accountability, Professionalism and Role in Society*, New York: Springer.

Davis, S. W. and W. R. Sherman (1996). "The Accounting Education Change Commission: a critical perspective," *Critical Perspectives on Accounting*, 7(1): 159–89.

Dewey, J. (1997). *Experience and Education*, originally published in 1938, New York: Touchstone/Simon & Schuster.

Dey, C. and J. Gibbon (2014). "External accounts," in J. Bebbington, J. Unerman and B. O'Dwyer (eds): *Sustainable Accounting and Accountability*, London and New York: Routledge.

Dillard, J. F. (2002). "Dialectical possibilities of thwarted responsibilities," *Critical Perspectives on Accounting*, 13(5–6): 621–41.

Dillard, J. F. and T. Tinker (1996). "Commodifying business and accounting education: the implications of accreditation," *Critical Perspectives on Accounting*, 7(1–2): 215–25.

Dillard, J. F. and E. Vinnari (2017). "A case study of critique: critical perspectives on critical accounting," *Critical Perspectives on Accounting*, 43: 88–109.

Dunne, S., S. Harney, M. Parker, and T. Tinker (2008). "Discussing the role of the business school," *Ephemera: Theory and Politics in Organization*, 8(3): 271–93.

Forgacs, D. (ed.) (1999). *The Antonio Gramsci Reader: Selected Writings 1916–1935*, London: Lawrence and Wishart.

Freire, P. (1996). *Pedagogy of the Oppressed*, London: Penguin.

Gabbin, A. L. (2002). "The crisis in accounting education," *Journal of Accountancy*, 193(4): 81–6.

Giroux, H.A. (1988). *Teachers as Intellectuals: Toward a Critical Pedagogy of Learning*, Granby, MA: Bergin and Garvey.

Gramsci, A (1971). *Selections from the Prison Notebooks*, translated by G. N. Smith, London: Lawrence and Wishart.

Gray, R. and D. Collison (2002). "Can't see the wood for the trees, can't see the trees for the numbers? Accounting education, sustainability and the public interest," *Critical Perspectives on Accounting*, 13(5–6): 797–836.

Hall, S. (1988). "Gramsci and us," in S. Hall (ed.): *The Hard Road to Renewal: Thatcherism and the Crisis of the Left*, London: Verso

Held, D. (1980). *Introduction to Critical Theory: Horkheimer to Habermas*, Cambridge: Polity Press.

Hopper, T. (2013). "Making accounting degrees fit for a university," *Critical Perspectives on Accounting*, 24(2): 127–35.

Hopwood, A. G. (1983). "On trying to study accounting in the contexts in which it operates," *Accounting, Organizations and Society*, 8(2-3): 287–305.

Hopwood, A. G. (1994). "Accounting and everyday life: an introduction," *Accounting, Organizations and Society*, 19(3): 299–301.

Humphrey, C., L. Lewis and D. Owen (1996). "Still too distant voices? conversations and reflections on the social relevance of accounting education," *Critical Perspectives on Accounting*, 7(1): 77–99.

Kaidonis, M.A. (2009). "Critical accounting as an epistemic community: hegemony, resistance and identity," *Accounting Forum*, 33(4): 290–97.

Laughlin, R. (1999). "Critical accounting: nature, progress and prognosis," *Accounting, Auditing and Accountability Journal*, 12(1): 73–8.

Laughlin, R. (2007). "Critical reflections on research approaches, accounting regulation and the regulation of accounting," *British Accounting Review*, 39(4): 271–89.

Lehman, C., M. Annisette and G. Agyemang (2016). "Immigration and neoliberalism: three cases and counter accounts," *Accounting, Auditing and Accountability Journal*, 29(1): 43–79.

McDonald-Kerr, L. (2017). "Water, water, everywhere: using silent accounting to examine accountability for a desalination project," *Sustainability Accounting, Management and Policy Journal*, 8(1).

Marcuse, H. (1964). *One Dimensional Man: Studies in the Ideology of Advanced Industrial Society*, London: Routledge & Kegan Paul.

Marcuse, H. (2007). "A note on dialectic (1960)," in *The Essential Marcuse. Selected Writings Philosopher and Social Critic Herbert Marcuse*, A. Feenberg and W. Leiss (eds), Boston, MA: Beacon Press: 64–71.

Marx, K. and F. Engels (1970). *The German Ideology*, originally published in 1856, New York: International Publishers.

Mathews, M. R. (1994). "An examination of the work of the Accounting Education Change Commission 1989-1992," *Accounting Education: An International Journal*, 3(3): 193–204.

Mayo, P. (2008). "Antonio Gramsci and his relevance for the education of adults," *Educational Philosophy and Theory*, 40(3): 418–35.

Merino, B. (2006). "Financial scandals: another clarion call for educational reform – a historical perspective," *Issues in Accounting Education*, 21(4): 363–81.

Miller, P. (1998). "The margins of accounting," in M. Callon (ed.): *The Laws of the Markets*, Oxford and Malden, MA: Blackwell.

Mintz, S. M. (1993). "Concerns about the generalizability of results of the AECC grant program," *Journal of Accounting Education*, 11(1): 93–100.

Moerman, L. and S. van Der Laan (2015). "Exploring shadow accountability: the case of James Hardie and asbestos," *Social and Environmental Accountability Journal*, 35(1): 32–48.

Morrison, T. (2001). "How can values be taught in the university?" *Michigan Quarterly Review*, 40(2): 273–78.

National Leadership Council for Liberal Education and America's Promise. (2007). *College Learning for the New Global Century*, Washington, DC, Association of American Colleges and Universities.

Needles, B. E. and M. Powers (1990). "A comparative study of models for accounting education," *Issues in Accounting Education*, 5(2): 250–67.

Neimark, M. K. (1996). "Caught in the squeeze: an essay on higher education in accounting," *Critical Perspectives on Accounting*, 7(1): 1–11.

Neu, D. (2012). "Accounting and undocumented work," *Contemporary Accounting Research*, 29(1): 13–37.

Neu, D., J. Everett and A. S. Rahaman. (2015). "Preventing corruption within government procurement: constructing the disciplined and ethical subject" *Critical Perspectives on Accounting*, 28: 49–61.

Newman, J. H. (1996). *The Idea of a University*. New Haven, CT: Yale University Press.

Owen, D. (2005). "CSR after Enron: a role for the academic accounting profession?" *European Accounting Review*, 14(2): 395–404.

Parker, L. D. (2002). "It's been a pleasure doing business with you: a strategic analysis and critique of university change management," *Critical Perspectives on Accounting*, 13(5-6): 603–19.

Preston, N. (1992). "Computing and teaching: a socially-critical view," *Journal of Computer Assisted Learning*, 8(1): 49–56.

PricewaterhouseCoopers (2003). Educating for the Public Trust: The PricewaterhouseCoopers Position on Accounting Education, New York, PricewaterhouseCoopers.

Ravenscroft, S. and P. F., Williams (2005). "Rules, rogues, and risk assessors: academic responses to Enron and other accounting scandals," *European Accounting Review*, 14(2): 363–72.

Review Committee of the Accounting Discipline in Higher Education (1990). *Accounting in Education: Report of the Review of the Accounting Discipline in Higher Education. Volume 1: Main Report and Recommendations*, Canberra: Australian Government Publishing Service.

Roslender, R. (1992). *Sociological Perspectives on Modern Accountancy*, London: Routledge.

Roslender, R. and J. F. Dillard (2003). "Reflections on the Interdisciplinary Perspectives on Accounting Project," *Critical Perspectives on Accounting*, 14(3): 325–51.

Sennetti, J. T. and M. A. Dittenhofer (1997). "Changing the accounting curricula: which colleges and universities will accrue the higher economic costs?" *Issues in Accounting Education*, 12(1): 49–60.

Shaoul, J., A. Stafford and P. Stapleton (2011a). "NHS capital investment and PFI: from central responsibility to local affordability," *Financial Accountability & Management*, 27(1): 1–17.

Shaoul, J., A. Stafford and P. Stapleton (2011b). "Private finance: bridging the gap for the UK's Dartford and Skye bridges?" *Public Money and Management*, 31(1): 51–8.

Shear, B. W. (2008). "Gramsci, intellectuals, and academic practice today, *Rethinking Marxism*, 20(1): 55–67.

Sikka, P. (2010). "Smoke and mirrors: corporate social responsibility and tax avoidance," *Accounting Forum*, 34(3–4): 153–68.

Sikka, P. and H. Willmott (2010). "The dark side of transfer pricing: Its role in tax avoidance and wealth retentiveness," *Critical Perspectives on Accounting*, 21(4): 342–56.

Sikka, P., H. Willmott and T. Puxty (1995). "The mountains are still there: accounting academics and the bearings of intellectuals," *Accounting, Auditing and Accountability Journal*, 8(3): 113–40.

Solomons, D. and T. M. Berridge (1974). *Prospectus for a Profession: The Report of the Long Range Enquiry into Education and Training for the Accountancy Profession*, London: Advisory Board of Accountancy Education.

Sundem, G. L. (2014). "Fifty years of change in accounting education: the influence of institutions," in R. M. S. Wilson (ed.): *The Routledge Companion to Accounting Education*, London and New York, NY: Routledge.

Sundem, G. L., D. Z. Williams, and J. F. Chironna (1990). "The revolution in accounting education," *Management Accounting (US)*, December: 49–53.

Tinker, T. (1991). "The accountant as partisan," *Accounting, Organizations and Society*, 16(3): 297–310.

Tinker, T. and R. Gray (2003). "Beyond a critique of pure reason: from policy to politics to praxis in environmental and social research," *Accounting, Auditing and Accountability Journal*, 16(5): 727–61.

Toms, S., M. Beck and D. Asenova (2011). "Accounting, regulation and profitability: the case of PFI hospital refinancing," *Critical Perspectives on Accounting*, 22(7): 668–81.

White, M. (2013). "Higher education and problems of citizenship formation," *Journal of Philosophy of Education*, 47(1): 112–27.

Whitehead, A. N. (1959). "The aims of education," *Daedalus* 88(1): 192–205.

Williams, P. F. (2004). "Recovering accounting as a worthy endeavor," *Critical Perspectives on Accounting*, 15(4–5): 513–17.

Willits, S. D. (2010). "Will more liberal arts courses fix the accounting curriculum?" *Journal of Accounting Education*, 28(1): 1–42.

Young, J. (2005). "Changing our questions: reflections on the corporate scandals," *Accounting and the Public Interest*, 5: 1–13.

22

ORGANISATION STUDIES

Chris Carter and Alan McKinlay

1 Introduction

Governmentalist research has been as attracted to the nineteenth century as to the contemporary world. There are both historical and methodological reasons for this. Historical, in that the nature of politics and political authority is transformed after the Enlightenment: The population becomes a political object for the first time as it emerges as the source of the production of truths. Methodological, in that a population has to be defined conceptually as well as how it could be operationalised. Politics, power and knowledge become entangled.

We begin by outlining the main features of Foucault's concept of 'governmentality', a term that he introduced only in lectures and never in a finalised text. The sketchy nature of Foucault's conceptual outline has provided governmentalist scholars with an opportunity for theoretical and empirical innovation. We look at two conceptual developments that have used Foucault's governmentality as a point of departure. First, we consider the development of the concept of 'mediating instruments' to suggest that all sorts of social scientific techniques – including accounting – do not simply reflect some underlying, already existing reality but serve to create objects to be understood and, so, managed. Second, the related notion of 'management at a distance'; that mediating instruments allow the government of a diverse range of individuals, not *despite* their relative autonomy but *through* their capacity to exercise some degree of discretion, judgement and choice. Both of these concepts are borrowed from philosophers and historians of science, and not used by Foucault.

2 Governmentality

For Foucault, governing in the late twentieth century was increasingly about governing indirectly, through the "conduct of conduct" of social subjects (Foucault, 1982: 220–1). Across his writings on the genealogies of disciplinary power and governmentality, Foucault retains a concept of modern power as ubiquitous rather than exceptional; routine not spectacular; positive and productive in place of reactive and repressive. There are, however, important differences of emphasis. Where disciplinary power was fixed, most powerfully in architectures whose purpose was visible to all, its functioning was invisible to its target subjects. As a consequence, governmentality was mobile and unobtrusive in its operation, if not in its effects.

'Governmentality' was the term coined by Foucault to open up different ways of talking about the operation of power. Ironically, Foucault intended the term 'government' to be a way of *escaping* the state-centred analyses that dominated western Marxism. No less ironically, in the late 1970s Foucault suggested that the ambition of emerging, contemporary neo-liberalism could best be grasped by the re-appropriation of the open-ended, archaic meaning of government as any organised methods 'for directing human behaviour' (Foucault, 1997: 82; McKinlay and Pezet, 2017a). Here Foucault is registering the first moves of neo-liberalism, a political movement oriented towards reducing the state to its barest minimum in terms of direct delivery while expanding its strategic role in terms of expanding the role of the market. Foucault's project in writing about the prison, the hospital and the asylum had been about the formation of the human sciences and how these were entangled with disciplinary practices. In the twentieth century these disciplines could plausibly be read as expressions of a state logic. By the second half of the 1970s, however, this state logic was being challenged from the conservative new right. Ways of thinking about how individuals were required to manage themselves could not easily be squared with any analysis that persisted with placing the state at its core. At least for the moment, Foucault looked back towards these broader, more open ways of thinking about government.

The difference between disciplinary and governmentalist projects is not, in Foucault at least, categorical but of degree. Governmentality relies upon the individual's deliberate exercise of choice, a choice predicated upon autonomy. Even in the extreme case of the prison, achieving rehabilitation is not a function guaranteed by the architecture, sanctions and incentives of penology but by individuals bending to discipline, however reluctantly. The neo-liberal subject accepts full responsibility for him or herself. This relationship is not decided, far less imposed, by those who govern on those who are governed. Rather, Foucault argues, the relationship is worked out by the interaction of governors and the governed. The nature and dynamic of this relationship is not a theoretical question but always empirical and historical: 'by a series of conflicts, arguments, discussions and reciprocal concessions … between what is to be done and what is not to be done in the practice of governing' (Foucault, 2008: 12). Neo-liberal government acts by encouraging, imploring or incentivising individuals to manage themselves more effectively the better to meet new behavioural, psychological or moral standards. And, crucially, the liberal subject regards exercising personal choice solely in terms of his or her own utility as the way to express his or her care for others. Neo-liberalism 'governs through freedom', it requires the citizen to be active in the polity, the employee to assume the initiative rather follow orders, the patient to assume responsibility for their health (Rose, 1999: 61–97). *All* of these terms are, in principle, *measurable*. Indeed, without measurement, identifying thresholds, comparisons, ratios, deviations, changes in individual, group or population behaviours and beliefs would be impossible. Measurement is not, then, a second-order or merely operational issue but a necessary precondition of any governmentalist project. Measurement becomes necessary to neo-liberalism in action: management without managers, government without governors.

There is no sense in which a governmentalist project requires a comprehensive, far less a coherent, set of mediating instruments. For Foucault, the administrative logic of governmentality always depoliticises the exercise of power. Power becomes unremarkable, inscribed in administration and distant from those who aspire to govern. Here, Foucault was speaking on the eve of the neo-liberal experiment that has swept across Western democracies in the last three decades (McKinlay and Pezet, 2017b). We may question the extent to which this depoliticisation actually works in practice. At the very least, we can say that this depoliticisation has proved to be highly contingent. Time and again, governments and corporate executives have been asked to account not just for lapses in ethics or institutional failures but also for the routine efficacy of policies. A central methodological principle of governmentality is that it absolves specific factors, such as technology, class or culture, of the impossible burden of causality. Rather, the governmentalist objective is to examine effects, not causes and never the motivations of particular actors. Governmentalist research is typically expressed in language that is dense, that slaloms between theory and empiricism, and is somewhat hesitant. Linguistic complexity is intended to convey the dense interrelationships between actors, institutions and practices. The always hesitant tone is deliberate and reflects the provisional state of governmentalist theorisation; empirical and historical findings are, by contrast, expressed in more of a definite, declaratory form.

3 Mediating instruments

For Foucault, the process of knowledge creation is inherently expansive. Definition, codification and measurement all produce debate that overspills its initial limits. To explain this, Foucault discusses how through the mid to late nineteenth century, psychiatry moves from being exclusively about madness and monsters to a concern with much more mundane behaviours and practices. None of this is driven by malign motives but rather, a sense of societal emergency, on the one hand, or by a concern for the welfare of those not best served by existing schools, prisons or asylums. The deterioration in the social order was, for eugenicists, due to the deterioration in the human stock. This was a crisis because the abnormal bred faster than the general population. To arrest or reverse this deterioration, eugenicists advocated segregation. Segregation was also implicit in the demands of social reformers critical of institutions that failed the abnormal. To be made practical, segregation required definition, measurement and management of the abnormal:

> [The] nineteenth century is able to bring into the ambit of illness and mental illness all the disorders and irregularities, all the serious disorders and little irregularities of conduct that are not, strictly speaking, due to madness … it becomes possible to organize the whole problematic of the abnormal at the level of the most elementary and everyday conduct.
>
> *(Foucault, 2003: 132)*

In a seminal paper examining the links between science and capital budgeting in semiconductors, Peter Miller and Ted O'Leary (2007) provide a working definition of what they mean by mediating instruments:

> [T]hose practices that frame the capital spending decisions of individual firms and agencies, and that help to align them with investments made by other firms and agencies in the same or related industries.
>
> *(Miller and O'Leary, 2007: 702)*

The term 'instrument' is itself an implicit acknowledgement of their debt to philosophers of science, especially Ian Hacking (1983) and Mary Morgan and Margaret Morrison (1999). Mediating instruments are those practices that frame the decisions of quite distinct, autonomous institutions, providing sufficient commonalities to make their choices comprehensible, if not necessarily consistent, to one another. Mediating instruments link distinct, perhaps distant, institutions, fields and practices. Miller and O'Leary note the resonance of their work with that of Morrison and Morgan, especially around a model or mediating instrument being a "critical instrument of modern science" (Miller and O'Leary, 2007: 709). They argue that the notion of mediating instruments is a fruitful way of examining the ways in which science and the economy come to be linked, offering both ways of representing and intervening (2007: 711).

One of the central contributions of Miller and O'Leary is to demonstrate the importance of accounting as a mediating instrument. Notably it represents and establishes rather than uncovers 'facts'; creates 'quasi-objects' that gain local legitimacy while they enable predictions invested with sufficient plausibility to be acted upon in quite different contexts (Jordan, Jorgenson and Mitterhofer, 2013: 158). Accounting devices can be active rather than passive: constitutive of, rather than simply used by, strategy. Accounting numbers are flexible in their application, capable of linking diverse social objects; immutable and durable, capable of linking these social objects over time and distance while still claiming consistency and accuracy in definition and measurement. Mediating instruments are *necessary* to governing at a distance (Skaerbaek and Tryggestad, 2010; Qu and Cooper, 2011). Mediating instruments render abstract, visible and calculable that which is material, invisible or tacit, and social (Jeacle and Carter, 2012; Kurunmäki and Miller, 2011, 2013; Kurunmäki, Mennicken and Miller, 2016; Miller, Kurunmäki and O'Leary, 2008).

Mediating instruments are multiple and complex; complementary and contradictory; they are productive in that they can have an effectivity quite apart from their original 'strategic' purposes. Miller and O'Leary's example of Moore's Law as a mediating instrument that brought together economic and technical rationalities demonstrates how the mediating instrument transformed a sector far beyond anything Moore could have possibly envisaged when he came up with his original model. Here, again, mediating instruments are *designed* to meet a particular purpose and have specific categories, definitions, thresholds, timings and frequencies. These mediating instruments with their attendant languages, practices and ethical codes are not just productive in their own terms. Rather, mediating practices are constitutive of certain sorts of visibilities and knowledges that create social objects to be understood as well as the discursive terms with which subjects understand their own experience. The use of mediating instruments, similarly requires training, skill and interpretation, all of which can become constitutive of an abstract body of knowledge beyond the specific organisation and purpose of even a professionalising project. 'Mediating instruments' are those practices that offer predictability coupled with specific objectives for social actors that retain their autonomy even as they share a common future (Miller and O'Leary, 2007: 702–3).

For governmentality research, the importance of the philosophy of knowledge was not simply conceptual but also historical. As Hacking put it, the nineteenth century began with "an avalanche of numbers. The world was now conceived in a more quantitative way than ever before. The world is seen as constituted by numerical magnitudes" (Hacking, 1983: 242). The ultimate objective of calculation in the natural sciences and beyond was practical, to formulate the laws of nature, the better to understand the possibilities and limits of human interventions. Where Jeremy Bentham had clear ideas about how to diffuse new ways of organising, a second route to the diffusion of new forms of governmentality lay with a nexus of natural scientists, mathematicians and actuaries who shared a common project of the standardisation of measurement in the first three decades of the nineteenth century.

William Ashworth's pioneering work on the nexus of early nineteenth-century astronomers suggests that their collective – and international – quest for greater efficiency in data collection and processing rested upon calculation (Ashworth, 1994). Precise measurement and calculation required standard categories, agreed units of measurement, definitions and thresholds. The standardisation of celestial observations enabled the transformation of the observatory into a factory of measurement. The reformed observatory's stratified workforce of observers and computers were subject to limited tasks, themselves measured in terms of volume and accuracy (Schaffer, 1988: 119–20). Direct observation was no match for efficient administration. The analogues between the management of astronomical workers and those in the new factories were recognised, and developed by Charles Babbage amongst many others. Analogy gave way to principles that could travel to different organisational settings. The astronomers' and mathematicians' concerns for the discovery of universal natural laws were paralleled by those of actuaries and factory managers. Natural philosophy and political economy shared the same will to calculate. In the factory, just as in the observatory, direct observation merely provided the raw material for calculation. Calculation permitted experimentation and comparison, however flawed or partial: Direct observation could aspire to neither. Equally important, calculation was necessary to the production of abstract knowledge and rules that could be tested in various sites according to shared standards and measurement criteria. In turn, experimentation required a host of secondary innovations in measurement technologies. All of this complex debate, comparison and innovation constructed constituencies that shared key concepts and technologies, however much they may have used these to disagree with one another.

4 Governing at a distance

The sociology of science, especially the insights from John Law (1984, 1987), Bruno Latour (1986, 1987) and Michel Callon (1986), has provided important conceptual building blocks for governmentality's understanding of how coalitions of individuals, organisations and forms of knowledge have assembled behind more or less tightly coupled common projects. These complex projects are best understood in terms of their effects rather than how well their a priori truth claims fare under experimental scrutiny. Nor is there a hard and fast division between abstract knowledge and practical experimentation. Rather, knowledge and practice are entangled in more or less tightly coupled assemblages.

A central governmentalist concept is 'management at a distance'. The oblique management of individuals through standard operating procedures and accounting incentives and sanctions is, of course, a staple of post-1945 industrial sociology. However, industrial sociology understood formal organisational rules as a bureaucratic shell for everyday working life, as likely to be ignored or ridiculed as diligently obeyed. The distance between the sterility and unreality of formal rules and the rich vitality of organisational life was a hallmark of quotidian class struggle for Weberian and Marxist sociologists alike (Sennett, 2006). Governmentality takes a quite different approach. There is little point in looking at management in action or to the experience of managers and managed if one is to understand the logics of governmenalist projects. If one is to understand the changing logics of prisons one should attend to the meta-level debates between criminologists, prison governors and reformers and not look to the experience of those incarcerated or their warders. The arts of governing, argues Foucault (2001a: 313–14), are not hidden in "spontaneous, blind practices" but in expert debates that produce abstract and applied knowledges. This knowledge is formed in the grey literature of the professional press, not by philosophers detached from practice. The sweep of governmentality research loses – or, more accurately, sacrifices – the sense of contingency and choice that is the very stuff of historical research.

Law's classic 1984 study of the development of Portuguese naval power during the fifteenth and sixteenth centuries explores a host of parallel, interacting and cumulative innovations in material technologies and social practices. Together, these innovations formed a system of long-distance social control that allowed Portugal to dominate intercontinental naval routes. This is a classic text in actor–network theory. The systems of long-distance control were not designed to act as a coherent whole but gained coherence over decades; the centre exercises control over an important but dispersed periphery composed of distinct actors who necessarily enjoy a certain autonomy and agency. This system of long-distance social control cannot be understood as a projection of an imperial will to power but is, rather, constitutive of that power. The strategies of the centre are empty hubris without the mundane routines of long-distance social control. Here, actor–network theory and Foucault's understanding of power and knowledge intersect most directly. The influential 'London governmentalists', centred around Peter Miller and Nikolas Rose (see McKinlay, Carter, Pezet and Clegg, 2010), have drawn inspiration from actor–network theory in their development of Foucault's sketchy outline of governmentality. Crucially, a system of long–distance social control is a complex set of distinct but entangled material, technological and social elements, none of which is reducible to the other. Law identifies the categories – documents, devices and drilled people – that are important to *all* systems of long-distance social control. By 'documents' Law is referring to the navigational charts and instructions that guided Portuguese mariners but this category could also include the standard operating procedures of any bureaucracy. Technologies – or devices – allow the production and storage of relatively standardised data to be rendered meaningful, and translated into judgements, decisions and actions. Finally, drilled people are those with sufficient training to be able to follow instructions closely, to operate technologies precisely and exercise judgement where ambiguity remained.

In Law's account, 'distance' has an exclusively spatial meaning: long distance here means crossing oceans. But Law's vocabulary could be extended to temporal, psychological or social distance. The centre in Law's study is fixed and responsible for assembling the documents and devices, and drilled people for their journeys. The centre's role as an instigator – and prime beneficiary – could be extended. For example, various sorts of knowledge are dispersed across the network but only the centre is responsible for – and has the capacity to – collect, categorise and interpret data from the periphery as a whole. The periphery retains hidden and tacit knowledge, unknown, ignored or beyond the reach of the centre. Consistent centralised record keeping is a precondition of understanding change and continuity, patterns that identify deviations to be investigated, replicated or outlawed. This constitutes the temporality of power and knowledge in action. Techniques to render oneself knowable and so improvable require the creation of a psychological distance between the individual and the self or soul. Social distance could refer to developing systems to understand, manage and reform the poor or criminal. Distance is not necessarily spatial nor natural but can be constructed by documents, devices and drilled people.

Governmentality has underpinned significant research in the history of accounting. Accounting is the perfect vehicle for governmentalist systems in two ways. First, the will to count eases the diffusion of an organisational or technical innovation. Second, the authority of governmentality relies upon its claims to neutrality, to a technical logic that is beyond political contention. Only details can be contested, not the principle or objectivity of accounting. This, argues Roberts (1991: 359), is an important part of the peculiar, invisible power of accounting. Indeed, the professional legitimacy of particular accounting techniques may well precede their inclusion in a specific governmentalist project. The will to govern does not necessarily precede or cause the development of a particular accounting technique. That calculation does not necessarily – or, indeed, rarely – answer the functional requirements of institutional objectives is well established in organisation studies (Ahrens and Chapman, 2007: 2). Paradoxically, the power of accountability is inversely related to hierarchy: Surveillance and accountability is greatest in terms of depth and constancy at the base of organisations rather than at their peak (Roberts, 2001: 1553). Here is an echo of Foucault's various studies of how the objects and techniques of disciplinary and governmentalist projects are first defined by marginal or deviant types of individual, the sick, the criminal or the insane.

The distances covered by Portuguese mariners were real enough but 'distance' can also be made and may even be an effect of documents, devices and drilled people: "I am saying that 'governmentality' implies the relationship of the self to itself" (Foucault, 1997: 30). Psychological distance requires the making of a distance between the individual and the self or soul. The self has to be defined as an object to be studied, understood and reformed or its flaws accepted. Foucault wrote and lectured extensively on the technologies of the self that were used in classical Greece and on the dynamics of confession in the Roman Catholic church. For Foucault, the Catholic belief in the priest as confessor and on absolution was radically different from Protestantism. The Protestant belief in predestination eliminated the possibility of absolution while the confessional diary became 'a principle of rational action inside the writer himself' (Foucault, 2001b: 422).

The confessional diary was not a retreat from the bustle of public life and the ease of family life. Interrogating the self was not intended to be comfortable or reassuring. Quite the opposite: the confessional diary was where the individual confronted his or her weaknesses directly (Andrew, 2001: 31). The diary was, then, a device to create a distance between the individual and the self, the better to achieve objectivity. By acting as one's own confessor the objective was to enforce a stricter interrogation of the self than was possible through a priest. For Hugh Heugh, the diary was 'a system of intellectual and spiritual discipline' in which the individual should 'try thoroughly to know yourself, to watch', and to ask regularly 'what additional knowledge I have gained of myself'. Reflection required 'strict solitude' and a routinised examination – 'a labour' – of his life and work at home, in church and in the community. Above all, this was a hermeneutic of the self in which the individual's deepest feelings were to be interpreted through scripture. Salvation was not about secular achievement, even charity. Faith, tested by events, demonstrated through the small kindnesses of daily life and demeanour; and honed through the rigorous examination of one's soul. The diary was also an inventory of grace or, more commonly, of the faintest sign of God's benevolence. Equally pronounced was the diarists' tendency to lapse into a morbid introspection that served only as a daily reminder of the corruptibility of the self. Such melancholy solipsism was to be exorcised by reason and ritual. For Heugh, 'religious exercises and self-examination' were best conducted on the still of a Sabbath evening: 'to turn the eye of the mind inward upon itself'. In the protestant's textual form of the confession, the self cannot be hidden from view; only inadequate technique can leave 'the secrets of the heart' concealed from 'the application of reason' (see Foucault, 1980: 216). Confessional diaries were 'certainly not for the eyes of others', only for the individual author (Macgill, 1850).

For many years, Heugh largely wrote his diary in an idiosyncratic code to ensure that he never forgot that its purpose was *self*-improvement. The diary should be treated as a permanent record, an archive of the soul, to be reviewed periodically. Keeping a confessional diary was an exacting discipline that few could sustain continuously for many years. To meet Heugh's exacting standards required not just exceptional literacy and scriptural knowledge but a place of undisturbed solitude where the diaries could be stored securely. Most demanding of all, the confessional diary required the individual to make their activities and their most private feelings an object for scrutiny: The individual became both confessant and confessor. Writing the confessional diary should, then, be a ritual, a ritual in which the individual becomes both interlocutor and "the authority who requires the confession, prescribes and appreciates it, and intervenes in order to judge, punish, forgive, console and reconcile" (Foucault, 1990: 61–2). The paradox of this rigorous self-examination was that, to be effective, the individual had to use the confessional diary as a device to first render themself unknown in order to begin the labour of self-knowledge. Distance here was neither geographical nor natural but personal and psychological, and an effect of the confessional diary.

The devout Protestant's accountability of the self was based upon a pervasive system of church governance based on bookkeeping and accounting that stretched from the individual to the local to the national (Mutch, 2015). Church governance was not just a theological innovation nor merely a set of technical requirements on all spiritual and secular transactions, though it was certainly that. Accountability was woven into the fabric of daily life and accounting was a recurring metaphor for the calculation of the individual's spiritual worth. This is exemplified in the diary of the entrepreneur, Charles Cowan. Cowan meticulously tabulated his confessional diary, embedding his spiritual labours in the context of his family and business life. Indeed, Cowan, a paper maker, used a specially designed preprinted journal that kept a week over two pages, with the top left in a table in which days, tasks and hours were recorded. Cowan's categories were comprehensive and consistent over time: Time spent working for the church as an organisation was carefully distinguished from the time he spent on his solitary work on his own soul (McKinlay and Mutch, 2015: 243–5). The purpose was to assess the efficiency of his spiritual labours on himself and to ensure that these were not compromised by family or business responsibilities. Quite literally, Cowan was accounting for his soul.

The development of technologies to render individuals visible was a necessary precursor to making individuals and populations calculable. To render an individual visible did not necessarily involve sophisticated, large-scale or durable systems. Indeed, ways of revealing individuals to consistent scrutiny could be local, and for particular purposes. The first task Donald Sage, an energetic young Calvinist minister, set himself when he arrived at his new parish in 1822 was to inspect every family. He divided his parish into districts defined by distance and the number of families he could visit in a day. After a short confidential conference with the head of the family, each household member was examined in private about their knowledge of the Shorter Catechism. Finally, each parishioner, including any servants, was given 'a few admonitions' in front of the assembled household. In 1827 Sage wrote:

> I took up, at the same time, a census of the whole population, one column being devoted to the names of individuals, divided into families and numbered as such; another, setting forth their designation and places of residence; and a third, containing what might strictly be called the moral and religious statistics of the parish or remarks illustrative of the state, character and knowledge of each individual.

It would be all too easy to elide the practices of Calvinist ministers with a nascent form of governmentality, but their purpose was to know their parish comprehensively and their parishioners intimately. This practice of rendering individuals visible and knowable was personal to the minister rather than invested in an impersonal system comprehensible to others far beyond the parish. Nor could the spiritual capital of one parish be readily compared to another. Knowledge remained embodied in the individual minister and was not distributed across an anonymous system. Inspection regimes were prone to similar limitations in all sorts of institutions. The predictability of nightly prison visits by trustees, for instance, almost completely nullified their surveillant intent. These flaws were, of course, recognised in two central design principles of Jeremy Bentham's Panopticon. The first principle, constancy, is a *fiction* that is masked by the panopticon's second design principle, the *fact* of the invisibility of surveillance. Taken together, the fiction of constancy and the fact of invisibility produced uncertainty amongst prisoners induced to behave as if they were under watch at all times. Bentham's plans for a pauper kingdom through his National Charity Company suggested that accounting numbers were the heart of any system of management (Bahmueller, 1981: 191–3). Administration through comprehensive, standardised rules – coupled with central inspection – was the foundation of the management of anything and everything. The purpose of extremely detailed bookkeeping was not just comprehensiveness but to signify the intensity of surveillance. Bookkeeping could be simplified but the point was to make it more complex and detailed. In principle, this fetishisation of bookkeeping allowed comparisons across individuals, managers, institutions, time and space: the capacity to numericalise and visualise the social.

Early moral statisticians collected data on education and church attendance. Accountability need not be focussed internally or limited to the internal workings of the church. From the second decade of the nineteenth century, local statistical societies flourished, dominated by industrialists appalled at the amoral chaos of the settlements that grew around their factories (Marsh, 1985: 208). The anarchy of industrialising cities was understood as a *moral* problem. Public health and education, *not* government regulation of the factory system, should, argued these moral statisticians, be the target of the state. The degree of moral degradation was such that the poor could not be surveyed directly: Their role in creating their own squalor was inferred from institutional informants and ad hoc observation. The term 'moral statistics' gradually fell away during the nineteenth century. The decline of *moral* statistics paralleled the increased concern with quantification at the expense of eye-witness testimony and elite impressions (Cullen, 1975: 65, 146). 'Statistics' was now a hybrid term that signified that which was to be governed; and for which governors will be held accountable.

Virtue, not just vice, could be made visible through accounting numbers. The annual reports of mid-nineteenth century voluntary hospitals publicly reported the generosity of named benefactors. Individual philanthropy was made visible by accounting. The benevolence of individuals was laid open to the scrutiny of neighbours and peers. Analysing this data geographically permitted the targeting of fundraising collectors and a detailed spatial analysis of the relative generosity of districts and streets (Jackson, 2012: 47–72). We see a similar concern for moral geography in, for example, statistical studies of prostitution that turn on endless gradations of depravity and how these intersected with poverty and 'criminality' (Tait, 1840). The concern to construct an analytical moral economy of Magdalenism was tied to strategies for reform and rehabilitation that focused on *knowing* the individual and the population. Certainly, Magdalenism was to remain an amoral category. The efficacy and efficiency of different types of institutional intervention on different categories of individuals could, at least in principle, now be subject to abstract, rational calculation. The sharp binary of respectability and the fallen woman was overwritten by qualifications, exceptions and gradations. 'Fallen' begged the questions: how far, how often and how redeemable?

The Magdalen Asylums were nominally secular but were saturated by Christian precepts of work as *the* route to self-discipline and redemption. The accountability of the individual inmate mirrored that of donors, staff and the workings of the institution itself (Evans and Pierpoint, 2015: 669). The exception was that the Irish Magdalen laundries were marked by a singular and pervasive lack of internal and external accountability that amounted to a 'social silence' that deepened over time (Killian, 2015: 18). Statistics were a central feature of the Magadalens' annual reports but there was no attempt to categorise or interrogate this data in terms of, for example, age at admission, as a predictor of any potential reform of Magadalen practices. That said, the Magdalens did categorise their inmates by their success or failure: those women who defaulted on the promise of their reformation; those who were redeemed and left for domestic service. The authority of political arithmetic was derived from its capacity to observe, quantify and so redefine marginal and ordinary lives as a social fact, as a population. Following Foucault, power/ knowledge was productive in that it was no longer enough to identified – branded – a thief, a prostitute or an indigent. The individual had also to be understood as the population became known. Only through knowledge of individual motivations as part of aggregate data could the individual become rehabilitated (Foucault, 1977: 178).

From the late eighteenth century, debates about industry, institutions and the city gradually moved from being exclusively couched in terms of individual and collective moralities to include emerging notions of the social. Even those discourses that relied entirely upon moral categories began to include such categories as age, family and employment. This constituted an implicit grid of moral and social categories. Where statistics had been a moral arithmetic through the early nineteenth century other social factors, empty of normative judgment entered debates about the governance of industrial society (Hamlin, 1998: 52). The population – its health, morality and welfare – was now an object of administrative rationality (Poovey, 1995: 31–2, 52). It was not the individual's morality that caused them to be poor but poverty happened to people. "Poverty," as Dean (1991) puts it, had become "a condition which was distinct from its bearers ..., a site of theoretical and historical argument and conceptual elaboration." Establishing the case that poor relief should be a political right rather than left to the whims of charity turned upon statistical provenance. William Alison's 1840 statistical report on *The Management of the Poor* aspired to national coverage but was reliant upon clergy, missionaries and lay visitors. Alison's survey generated only 28 respondents and could not claim statistical provenance, only an authority derived from their profession and the consistency of their descriptions. Alison's firmest conclusion was his survey demonstrated the need for "a more judicious scrutiny" to understand poverty *statistically*. The absence of "regular, or official inspection, *and no record*" meant that social issues were not treated as technical matters of government but constantly collapsed into irreconcilable conflicts over first principles (Abrams, 1968: 13; Driver, 1993: 10). Statistical knowledge – social accounting – was predicated upon comprehensive, sophisticated and routine surveys of poverty:

> The grand desideratum is a regular and rigid surveillance of that part of the population which is necessarily dependent upon the assistance of the rest, in order that their real wants may be known, and their character and conduct watched.

Alison's vision of a medical police that treated poverty, hunger and employment as public health issues was marginalised by the success of the theologian Chalmers, the engineer Chadwick and the economics of Malthus. Both sides of this debate shared the assumption that the object of government was no longer the sovereign but the welfare of the population (McKinlay and Pezet, 2017b). A range of novel governmentalist projects emerged that shared this concern with the population: governmentalism was no longer reducible to, nor derived from, the state.

The development of technologies to make individuals visible was impersonal, analytical and comparative. Impersonal in that, in comparison to direct personal inspection or supervision, an individual could be known in himself, and, as a member of an abstract population, compared with others, over time and between locations. Knowledge was *possible* in terms of the individual and as a member of a population, a knowledge that was innovative, systemic and generative. Where *only* the individual could be known, *only* his or her productivity could be managed and, even then, *only* by the most intimate, labour-intensive supervision. Constructing accounts, by contrast, enabled individual productivity to be known as an ensemble of personal, task and technological characteristics. This analytical grid allows comparison not just of 'real' individuals but also of abstract categories. Abstract knowledge can be produced by recording and classifying real data and through rational manipulation so that projections are no longer reliant upon material changes in organisation. Otherwise incommensurable activities are rendered not just calculable but also comparable and open to abstract debate about alternatives. Technical developments in statistics were also important. Consider the experience of Adolphe Quetelet who is best known for his mathematical work on populations and the mean. Quetelet's technical contribution to statistics was only one element in his pursuit of a social physics, a search for the laws that governed society, a search that barely merits a footnote in the history of the social sciences. Quetelet shared the same background of observational astronomy as the scientific innovators who established standardised measurement as the precondition of progress. Based on the chest measurements of 5,738 Scottish soldiers, Quetelet calculated the distribution and the mean but concluded that deviations were not diversity but error. And error he equated with inferiority or abnormality; the 'average man' was the marker of ordered perfection. Utilising the 'average man' as the avatar for social policy would revolutionise 'the whole art of governing' by identifying the ends and the deviations that needed to be eliminated or suppressed (Porter, 1985: 60).

How, then, were the data necessary to understand – to make – populations to be collected? The most important way of collecting data was through inspection, carried out by an inspector drilled in how to recognise and categorise social characteristics, and equipped with standardised documents to be completed for storage and interrogation at a headquarters. In social work inspection assumed the form of home visits, an innovation that defined working class housing as a social and moral problem. Philanthropic intervention pivoted on increasingly fine-grained accounting, on the one hand, and on face-to-face inspection, on the other. Victorian social reformers regarded direct personal intervention as a way of collapsing the social and moral distance between the privileged charity worker and the slum dweller. All of the techniques developed by charity workers – from gentle door knocking to lowering the voice – were designed to reduce the social and moral distance between the inspector and the inspected, to domesticate stranger relations (Webb, 2007). Paradoxically, such empathetic inspection was necessary for regulation at a distance: only inspectors, not the inspected, compiled reports for headquarters; inspectors established the timing, duration and purpose of visits; and only the inspecting organisation defined the terms of inspection and had the possibility of developing knowledge of individuals and populations. With these innovations, inspection and inspecting organisations could begin to claim forms of knowledge as the basis of their authority, to buttress their social and moral claims. Walker (2006) points to the Victorian housing reformer Octavia Hill as an example of accounting as a device for maintaining tight, centralised control of an organisation and, no less important, as a mediating instrument for managing volunteer labour and tenants. For Hill, the possibility of large-scale organisation depended upon centrally set, tightly policed accounting procedures. If scale meant that direct personal control was impractical, then only standardised administration and accounting could ensure the consistency of interactions between her social workers and tenants. Repeatedly, Hill noted her anxiety about whether bookkeeping was an adequate substitute for her personal control. Accounting numbers did not extend beyond atemporal records that were incapable of statistical interrogation to register changing volunteer efficiency or client morality. (In this sense, Hill's accounting represented a way of organising that was no longer a form of sovereign power but not yet a disciplinary regime.) The drive to classify the poor was essential to shaping the operation of the late-Victorian Poor Law: administrative interventions were targeted at specific categories and the endless variety of their combination (Walker, 2008: 475).

5 In conclusion

It would be mistaken to consider governmentality only as the study of how *governors* govern, although this question has dominated governmentality studies. Just as Foucault regarded power and resistance not as cause and effect but as necessarily entangled so governmentality has to account for the awkward fact of resistance. Foucault's histories were written to serve as provocations to question the present. His histories were, then, to use his term, 'fictions' *and* histories of the present. The governmentality lectures were doubly exceptional, in that they were not developed into polished texts while offering a direct commentary on the present. The implicit assumption in notions such as the audit society is that the contemporary world is *saturated* with everyday accounting, that the audit society represents, if not an end point then certainly an unprecedented rationalisation of everyday life. And, moreover, that this has been an essential part of neo-liberalism in which institutions of all kinds, not just the state, require citizens to accept greater personal autonomy to meet simultaneously collective and individual goals. It is easy to slide from interrogating how different forms of calculation make ways of managing possible to argue that *only* the calculable can be managed; or that the calculable exhausts that which is to be managed. Accounting is *the* technology that enables control at a distance: to evaluate individuals, relationships and organisations, and to track their relative performance over time. Accounting numbers become the vehicle for managing organisations and for governing populations. A population need not be large in number but identifiable and definable, with, for instance, a specific place, characteristic or illness. Documents, devices and drilled people can create a separate, distinct – and so 'distant' – object rather than simply bridge a natural or real distance. 'Distance' is not necessarily natural or real but can be *created*: Assemblages of devices, documents and drilled people can *create* the object to be managed through their very operation.

The explosion of interest in accounting and everyday life has produced histories that suggest that the dual management of populations and the management of the self by the individual was constitutive of early nineteenth-century liberal common sense. Paradoxically, the very success of governmentalist research has risked de-historicising neo-liberalism by seeing it as a presence, albeit somewhat shadowy, long before its political rise from the late 1970s. Equally, a literal reading of conduct would suggest that governance knows precisely what behaviours need to be managed at a distance, and how this can best be achieved. The governmentalist research of, for instance, Miller, suggests that this trap can be avoided by stressing the inherently experimental – and so provisional - nature of organisation

Governmentality defined neo-liberalism much more broadly than being a tension or accommodation between the state and the market. Indeed, governmentality read the massive ambition of neo-liberalism seriously. The objective of neo-liberalism was the remaking of the individual, a determination to make individuals responsible for all aspects of their life. Neo-liberalism was, for governmentalists, not restricted to the economic but embraced all aspects of the social, from education and health to personal well-being. The market was not the objective of neo-liberalism, simply the vehicle to maximising individual autonomy and responsibility. Neo-liberalism redefined citizenship as a status that was neither universal nor unqualified. In their discussion of cultural assimilation and neo-liberalism, Schinkel and van Houdt (2010) recount the ways that the formal definition of citizenship was increasingly limited to the juridical and was a status granted only after the individual had demonstrated an adequate understanding of values and norms of society. The thin juridical status of citizen was achieved only after the individual had demonstrated their capacity to understand and live the thick moralised version of citizenship. A similar neo-liberal logic operates in economic life where individuals achieve some form of citizenship on condition that the they subscribe to and live out – embody – the organisation's values or philosophy. Individuals are no longer forced to conduct themselves in certain ways. Rather, organisations deploy processes that allow responsible subjects to embody and enact their moralised citizenship, whether that be expressed in terms of engagement, empowerment or commitment. The logic of governmentality suggests that measurement, particularly accounting numbers, enables marketisation. Only after categories, thresholds, rates of improvement or deterioration have been specified can contractual incentives and sanctions be specified. Measurement is not necessarily a result of marketisation but its corollary, if not a precondition. That which was political can be rendered technical and contractual.

This chapter was submitted by the authors with the following title: "Governing through numbers: Foucault, governmentality and accounting."

References

Abrams, P. (1968). *The Origins of British Sociology: 1883-1914*, Chicago, IL: University of Chicago Press.
Ahrens, T. and C. S. Chapman (2007). "Management accounting as practice," *Accounting, Organizations and Society*, 32(1–2): 1–27.

Alison, W. (1840). '"Illustrations of the Practical Operation of the Scottish System of Management of the Poor," *Journal of the Royal Statistical Society of London*, 3(3): 211–57.

Andrew, E. (2001). *Conscience and its Critics: Protestant Conscience, Enlightenment Reason, and Subjectivity*, Toronto: University of Toronto Press.

Ashworth, W. (1994). "The calculating eye: Baily, Herschel, Babbage and the business of astronomy," *British Journal for the History of Science*, 27(4): 409–41.

Bahmueller, C. (1981). *The National Charity Company: Jeremy Bentham's Silent Revolution*, Berkeley, CA: University of California Press.

Callon, M. (1986). "The sociology of an actor-network: the case of the electric vehicle," in M. Callon, A. Rip and J. Law (eds): *Mapping the Dynamics of Science and Technology: Sociology of Science in the Real World*, Basingstoke, UK: Palgrave Macmillan UK.

Cullen, M. (1975). *The Statistical Movement in Early Victorian Britain: The Foundation of Empirical Social Research*, Brighton, UK: Harvester Press.

Dean, M. (1991). *The Constitution of Poverty: Towards a Genealogy of Governance*, London: Routledge.

Driver, F. (1993). *Power and Pauperism: The Workhouse System, 1834-1884*, Cambridge: Cambridge University Press.

Evans, L. and J. Pierpoint (2015). "Framing the Magdalen: sentimental narratives and impression management in charity annual reporting," *Accounting and Business Research*, 45(6–7): 661–90.

Foucault, M. (1977). *Discipline and Punish: The Birth of the Prison*, London: Penguin.

Foucault, M. (1980). *Power/Knowledge: Selected Interviews and Other Writings*, London: Harvester Wheatsheaf.

Foucault, M. (1982). "The subject of power," in H. Dreyfus and P. Rabinow (eds): *Michel Foucault: Beyond Structuralism and Hermeneutics*, London: Harvester Wheatsheaf.

Foucault, M. (1990). *History of Sexuality, Vol. 1*, London: Penguin.

Foucault, M. (1997). *The Essential Works of Michel Foucault, 1954-1984, Vol. 1: Ethics, Subjectivity and Truth*, edited by J. D. Faubion, London: Allen Lane

Foucault, M. (2001a). "Omnes et singulatim," in *Michel Foucault Essential Work 3: Power*, edited by J. D. Faubion, London: Allen Lane.

Foucault, M. (2001b). "L'hermeneutique du sujet," Cours au College de France 1981-1982, Paris: Seuil/Gallimard.

Foucault, M. (2003). *Abnormal: Lectures at the College de France 1974-1975*, New York: Picador.

Foucault, M. (2008). *The Birth of Biopolitics*, New York: Macmillan Publishers.

Hacking, I. (1983). *Representing and Intervening: Introductory Topics in the Philosophy of Natural Science*, Cambridge: Cambridge University Press.

Hamlin, C. (1998), *Public Health and Social Justice in the Age of Chadwick: Britain, 1800-1854*, Cambridge: Cambridge University Press.

Jackson, W. (2012). "'The Collector will Call': controlling philanthropy through the annual reports of the Royal Infirmary of Edinburgh, 1837-1856," *Accounting History Review*, 22(1): 47–72.

Jeacle, I. and C. Carter (2012). "Fashioning the popular masses: accounting as mediator between creativity and control," *Accounting, Auditing and Accountability Journal*, 25(4): 719–51.

Jordan, S., L. Jorgenson and H. Mitterhofer (2013). "Performing risk and the project: risk maps as mediating instruments," *Management Accounting Research*, 24(2): 156–74.

Killian, S. (2015). "'For Lack of Accountability': the logic of the price in Ireland's Magdalen Laundries," *Accounting, Organizations and Society*, 43: 17–32.

Kurunmäki, L. and P. Miller (2011). "Regulatory hybrids: partnerships, budgeting and modernising government," *Management Accounting Research*, 22(4), 220–41.

Kurunmäki, L. and Miller, P. (2013). "Calculating failure: the making of a calculative infrastructure for forgiving and forecasting failure," *Business History*, 55(7): 1100–1118.

Kurunmäki, L., A. Mennicken and P. Miller (2016). "Quantifying, economising, and marketising: democratising the social sphere?" *Sociologie du Travail*, 58(4): 390–402.

Latour, B. (1986). "Visualization and cognition," *Knowledge and Society*, 6(1): 1–40.

Latour, B. (1987). *Science in Action: How to Follow Scientists and Engineers Through Society*, Boston, MA: Harvard University Press.

Law, J. (1984). "On the methods of long distance control: vessels, navigation, and the Portuguese route to India," *Sociological Review* 32(S1): 234–63.

Law, J. (1987). "Technology and heterogeneous engineering: the case of Portuguese expansion," in W. E. Bijker, T. P. Hughes and T. J. Pinch (eds): *The Social Construction of Technological Systems: New Directions in the Sociology and History of Technology*, Cambridge, MA: MIT Press.

Macgill, H. (1850). *The Life of Hugh Heugh DD*, Edinburgh: Fullarton.

McKinlay, A. and A. Mutch (2015). "'Accountable Creatures'; Scottish Presbyterianism, accountability and managerial capitalism," *Business History* 57(2): 241–56.

McKinlay, A. and E. Pezet (2017a). "Governmentality: the career of a concept," in A. McKinlay and E. Pezet (eds): *Foucault, Governmentality and Management: Rethinking the Management of Populations, Organizations and Individuals*, London: Routledge.

McKinlay, A. and E. Pezet (2017b). "Foucault, governmentality, strategy: from the ear of the sovereign to the ear of the multitude," *Critical Perspectives on Accounting* (forthcoming).

McKinlay, A., C. Carter, E. Pezet and S. Clegg (2010). "Using Foucault to make strategy," *Accounting, Auditing and Accountability Journal*, 23(8): 1012–31.

Marsh, C. (1985). "Informants, respondents and citizens," in M. Bulmer (ed.): *Essays on the History of British Sociological Research*, Cambridge: Cambridge University Press.

Miller, P. and T. O'Leary (2007). "Mediating instruments and making markets: capital budgeting, science and the economy," *Accounting, Organizations and Society*, 32(7–8): 701–34.

Miller, P., L. Kurunmäki and T. O'Leary (2008). "Accounting, hybrids and the management of risk," *Accounting, Organizations and Society*, 33(7–8): 942–67.

Morgan, M. S., and M. Morrison (eds) (1999). *Models as Mediators: Perspectives on Natural and Social Science*, Cambridge: Cambridge University Press.

Mutch, A. (2015). *Religion and National Identity: Governing Scottish Presbyterianism in the Eighteenth Century*, Edinburgh: Edinburgh University Press.

Poovey, M. (1995). *Making a Social Body: British Social Formation, 1830-1864*, Chicago, IL: University of Chicago Press.

Porter, M. (1985). "The mathematics of society: variation and error in Quetelet's statistics," *British Journal of the History of Science*, 18(1): 51–69.

Qu, S. and D. Cooper (2011). "The role of inscriptions in producing a balanced scorecard," *Accounting, Organizations and Society*, 36(6): 344–62.

Roberts, J. (1991). "The possibilities of accountability," *Accounting Organizations and Society*, 16(4): 355–68.

Roberts, J. (2001). "Trust and control in Anglo–American systems of corporate governance: the individualizing and socializing effects of processes of accountability," *Human Relations*, 54(12): 1547–72.

Rose, N. (1999). *Powers of Freedom: Reframing Political Thought*, Cambridge: Cambridge University Press.

Sage, D. (1827). *Memorabilia Domestica*, Edinburgh: Smith.

Schaffer, S. (1988). "Astronomers mark time: discipline and the personal equation," *Science in Context*, 2(1): 115–45.

Schinkel, W. and F. van Houdt (2010). "The double helix of cultural assimilationism and neo-liberalism: citizenship in contemporary governmentality," *British Journal of Sociology*, 61(4): 696–715.

Sennett, R. (2006). *The Culture of the New Capitalism*, New Haven, CT: Yale University Press.

Skaerbek, P. and Tryggestad (2010). "The role of accounting devices in performing corporate strategy," *Accounting, Organizations and Society*, 35(1): 108–24.

Tait, W. (1840). *Magdalenism: An Inquiry into the Extent, Causes and Consequences of Prostitution in Edinburgh*, Edinburgh: P. Richard.

Walker, S. (2006). "Philanthropic women and accounting: Octavia Hill and the exercise of 'Quiet Power and Sympathy'," *Accounting, Business & Financial History*, 16(2): 163–94.

Walker, S. (2008). "Accounting, paper shadows and the stigmatised poor," *Accounting, Organizations and Society*, 33(4–5): 453–87.

Webb, S. (2007). "The comfort of strangers: social work, modernity and late Victorian England – Part 1," *European Journal of Social Work*, 10(1): 39–54.

23

FINANCE

Skip McGoun

Now slip me snug about your ears,
I've never yet been wrong,
I'll have a look inside your mind
And tell where you belong!

(Rowling, 2000: 177)

1 Introduction

As institutions for professional education, schools of business must consider practice. Students and businesses alike expect them to prepare students to *do* business. What does it mean, though, to *do* accounting or to *do* finance? One might mean auditing and the other trading activities that appear to have little or nothing in common. Then again, one might mean managerial accounting and the other financial analysis, activities that one would be hard pressed to distinguish between. This is why the disciplines of accounting and finance are administratively housed within the same academic department at many universities. In terms of program content, the two have a common core from which they eventually diverge via increasing specialisation. And the later they diverge, the stronger the justification from a pedagogical standpoint for lodging them within the same academic unit.

As institutions for the advancement of knowledge as well as for its transmission, schools of business must also engage in scholarship. Unfortunately, the relationship between their pedagogical and scholarly roles can be problematic. It is relatively uncontroversial for scholarship to *support* practice. At least in theory, engagement in scholarship keeps accounting and finance professors current with disciplinary knowledge, to the benefit of students, and it creates disciplinary knowledge, to the benefit of businesses. But it can be highly controversial for scholarship to be *critical* of practice, and in more dimensions than just content that might discomfort students and peeve practitioners. Other aspects of accounting and finance scholarship are its methodologies (philosophies) and its methods (techniques), both of which can be sources of especially contentious academic disputes. In simple – and perhaps overly simple – terms, research can be positive (what and why practice *is*) or normative (what and why practice *ought to be*), and it can be undertaken with quantitative methods (through numbers) or qualitative methods (through words). Nowadays, supportive research tends to be positive and quantitative (why what is *is*) and definitive of the academic discipline (hence the use of the familiar term *mainstream* to describe it); critical research to be normative and qualitative (what what is *ought to be*) and interdisciplinary.[1] Although there is nothing to preclude normative quantitative or positive qualitative research, such research is relatively uncommon compared to the other two alternatives, an issue which this chapter will address. Because it is less controversial (supposedly more objective) to be addressing what *is* than what *ought to be* and it is more prestigious (supposedly more intellectually demanding) to be working with numbers than with words, supportive research more closely fits the common sense of the highly desirable adjective 'scientific'.[2]

Despite having a common pedagogical core, what accounting and finance do not have in common is a tradition of critical scholarship. It is not unusual to find offices of critical accounting professors next door to those doing more traditional research supportive of accounting and for both to be teaching familiar courses in the accounting curriculum in adjacent classrooms. However, one will never find critical finance professors anywhere, whether in offices or in classrooms. Unlike critical accounting, which *belongs* in some sense to accounting, critical finance belongs to no one discipline in particular and certainly not to finance. There is indeed a finance equivalent of critical accounting but it is scattered elsewhere in the academy under other names. It is most often found in the social sciences in international political economy and economic sociology (where it is known as SSF – Social Studies of Finance [Vollmer, Mennicken and Preda, 2009]), but it also turns up in unexpected places in the humanities in cultural studies, media studies, literature, rhetoric and even art. Accounting draws on other disciplines to create critical accounting; other disciplines draw on finance to create critical finance.

The fundamental questions addressed in this chapter, which has the working title "Beneath the sorting hat: critical accounting and critical finance," might have been historic (how critical accounting *has* impacted finance), speculative (how critical accounting *could* impact finance), and/or prescriptive (how critical accounting *should* impact finance). However, the puzzle that accounting and finance are institutionally connected, while critical accounting and critical finance are not, raises other issues that are more basic. What are the similarities between accounting and finance that have placed them together within the same academic department? What are the differences between accounting and finance that have led to a fecund critical tradition in one and no critical tradition in the other? And what are the consequences of the differential roles played by other disciplines in this commonly interdisciplinary scholarship – making contributions to accounting in critical accounting and receiving contributions from finance in critical finance?

An insightful approach to addressing these and any related questions is to explore the parallels that exist between accounting and finance departments in academia and the organisation of the Hogwarts School of Witchcraft and Wizardry in J. K. Rowling's Harry Potter series. In that particular school, the Sorting Hat assigns new Hogwarts students to one of four houses: Gryffindor ("Where dwell the brave at heart"); Hufflepuff ("Where they are just and loyal"); Ravenclaw ("Where those of wit and learning, Will always find their kind"); or Slytherin ("Those cunning folk use any means To achieve their ends") (Rowling, 1997: 118). Had the students been permitted to make their own choices, would they have been the same as those made by the Sorting Hat? Perhaps the Sorting Hat had no more power than to read the students' pre-existing characters and preferences: "I'll have a look inside your mind" for bravery, loyalty, learning, or cunning. Harry Potter for one was assigned to the house (Gryffindor) he would have selected on his own. Although universities do not have sorting hats to assign students to disciplinary PhD programs, we might assume that students sort themselves out without sorting hats, as they might well have done at Hogwarts had there been no sorting hat there. Students having certain backgrounds, preferences and values select accounting, while students otherwise endowed select finance. By this reasoning, the differences between accounting and finance are a consequence of the agency of the members of the academy.

There are, however, characters in the Harry Potter series whose assignments by the Sorting Hat appear to fit neither their characters nor their likely preferences. Although assigned to Gryffindor, Ravenclaw would have been a more appropriate fit for the studious Hermione Granger, and for lack of a better alternative, Neville Longbottom should have been placed in Hufflepuff. One might certainly argue that the Sorting Hat anticipated the bravery both would subsequently demonstrate, its antecedents being inside their minds without their knowing it. One might alternatively argue, however, that through their residence in Gryffindor, both of these students grew into its culture. Once in a PhD program, institutional demands and professional opportunities have a familiarly powerful effect on students' selections of research methodologies and methods, which are really only nominally left up to them.[3] Even after graduation and employment, scholars are restricted in the same ways, with additional constraints imposed by the need to exploit painfully acquired human capital. Thus there might be fundamental structural differences between the disciplines of accounting and finance that explain their divergent scholarly activities.

The following section reviews the compelling evidence that from the standpoint of practice, and hence from that of preparatory pedagogy, the contents of the accounting and finance disciplines are very similar. Yet there have been marked scholarly differences. Section 3 proffers a structural explanation for these differences. Accounting developed more deliberately as a 'soft-applied' science, in contrast to finance, which swiftly transitioned from that to a 'hard-pure' science. Consequently, accounting scholarship has been able to accommodate a critical tradition, while finance has not. Equally, the differences might also be a consequence of agency, and in Section 4 attention turns to the possible differences in backgrounds, preferences and values between accounting and finance students and professors. Section 5 then assesses the implications of the differing directions from which critical accounting and critical finance come – from inside of the former and from outside of the latter. The paper concludes with some brief speculation on the implications of the ongoing convergence of accounting and finance scholarship in the direction of finance.

2 To serve and protect

The Financial Accounting Standards Board (FASB)'s Statement of Financial Accounting Concepts Number 8 (FASB, 2010) leaves no doubt whom it is that financial reporting now is meant to serve and protect:[4]

> The objective of general purpose financial reporting is to provide financial information about the reporting entity that is useful to existing and potential investors, lenders, and other creditors in making decisions about providing resources to the entity. Those decisions involve buying, selling, or holding equity and debt instruments and providing or settling loans and other forms of credit.
>
> *(FASB, 2010, para. OB2)*

It goes on to explain what such decisions require:

> [D]ecisions by existing and potential lenders and other creditors about providing or settling loans and other forms of credit depend on the principal and interest payments or other returns that they expect. Investors', lenders', and other creditors' expectations about returns depend on their assessment of the amount, timing, and uncertainty of

(the prospects for) future net cash inflows to the entity. Consequently, existing and potential investors, lenders, and other creditors need information to help them assess the prospects for future net cash inflows to an entity.

(FASB, 2010, para. OB3)

Furthermore:

To assess an entity's prospects for future net cash inflows, existing and potential investors, lenders, and other creditors need information about the resources of the entity, claims against the entity, and how efficiently and effectively the entity's management and governing board have discharged their responsibilities to use the entity's resources.

(FASB, 2010, para. OB4)

In short:

General purpose financial reports are not designed to show the value of a reporting entity; but they provide information to help existing and potential investors, lenders, and other creditors to estimate the value of the reporting entity.

(FASB, 2010, para. OB7)[5]

Lest there be any remaining misunderstanding over who really matters, the statement makes it clear who does not matter:

Other parties such as regulators and members of the public other than investors, lenders, and other creditors, also may find general purpose financial reports useful. However, those reports are not primarily directed to these other groups.

(FASB, 2010, para. OB10)

The recurring phrase "investors, lenders, and other creditors" is redundant; all of them 'finance' – provide financial resources to – an entity. Therefore, according to this conceptual framework, financial accountants serve those who finance and no one else. Likewise, one might similarly say that managerial accountants serve those who manage. Because managers make decisions about allocating (in effect, providing) resources within the entity as agents of investors, there is in effect no economic difference between financial and managerial accounting: Both sorts of accounting serve finance. It goes without saying, then, that accounting must understand what finance does in order to serve the needs of finance and that finance must understand what accounting does in order to make sense of how its needs are being served. Clearly, there must be considerable commonality in the knowledge required for the practices of accounting and finance and consequently in educational programs in accounting and finance. Thus, one would not be remiss to also expect – and even to encourage (Pope, 2010) – considerable overlap in the scholarship of accounting and finance, both scholarship supportive of practice and scholarship critical of it. After 1950, however, there is considerable evidence that academic accounting and academic finance radically diverged.

3 The path to power

Becher and Trowler (2001) classify the cognitive aspects of academic disciplines along two dimensions – hard/soft and pure/applied – that generate the four quadrants. Although the terms in this classification are meant to be neutral and not imply any value judgments, their connota-

411

tions clearly do. In the hard/soft dichotomy reflecting the independence of knowledge from the knower, knowledge that is believed to be wholly 'out there' (hard) is superior to knowledge that is partially or wholly 'in here' (soft).[6] And in the pure/applied dichotomy reflecting the instrumentality of the knowledge, knowledge believed to have intrinsic value (pure) is superior to knowledge having contingent value (applied).[7]

Prior to 1950, academic accounting and academic finance were highly instrumental, engaged in the study and improvement of the practices of accounting and finance, as a consequence of which they fell within Becher and Trowler's soft-applied category. When PhD programs in business disciplines were in their relative infancy, this was an unquestioned characterisation:

> [T]he prime objective of doctoral programs [in business] is to make sure that holders of the doctorate have the necessary equipment to analyze significant problems in managerial decision making in a scientific manner … There is no denying that many aspects of the decision-making process defy precise scientific analysis. Doctoral programs in business must be addressed to a diverse range of activities in which the element of unpredictable human behavior bulks large.
>
> *(Pierson et al., 1959: 300)*

The phrases "significant problems in managerial decision making" and "the element of unpredictable human behavior" connote applied and soft. Although not alone among academic disciplines in this classification, accounting and finance scholarship shared the lowest academic status and poor reputation of the soft-applied category.

> Judging from the campus interviews, business dissertations are not held in high regard; often the comment was made that they chiefly involved description of business practice and required little use of sophisticated methods of analysis… [D]octoral candidates in business often do not have the preparation necessary to carry through a piece of research. In many instances the students have had the barest kind of exposure to the methods used in scientific investigations or to the tools needed in such undertakings.
>
> *(Pierson et al., 1959: 308)*

Thus, they were powerfully motivated to move up the academic ladder.

Accounting and finance have always been concerned with quantification; measurements of inputs and outputs, benefits and costs, revenues and expenditures, prices and values are their raw material – a fundamental attitude/approach embodied in Graham and Dodd's classic investment text *Security Analysis* (Graham and Dodd, 1934 [reprinted 1996]). Such methods did not demand competence in higher mathematics, however. Quantification for the analysis of the performance of activities (how they were done) and not just for their outcomes (what they did) was not widespread until around the time that Frederick Winslow Taylor published *The Principles of Scientific Management* (Taylor, 1914), which explicitly identified the scientific with the numeric in a managerial context. Quantification subsequently received a very significant boost 30 years later from the achievements of operations research – otherwise known as 'management science' – employing more sophisticated mathematics to improve military decision making during World War II. One might have expected that both accounting and finance would have been equally positioned in the late 1940s and early 1950s to exploit this wartime experience and the skills and interests it engendered, and to have employed more quantitative – and thus more scientific – methods to understand and improve the practices of accounting and finance and not just to document them. But finance followed a much faster track in that direction and left accounting behind.[8]

The metamorphosis of finance benefitted from the relatively large databases of securities markets' prices it had been generating and the development of electronic computers with which to make use of these databases to address theoretical problems posed by scholars in disciplines other than finance. One such scholar was Harry Markowitz, whose dissertation at the University of Chicago on the optimisation of investment portfolios was *about* linear programming, financial markets being a convenient source of the data with which to illustrate his method.[9] According to Markowitz in his 1990 Nobel lecture:

> Milton Friedman argued that portfolio theory was not Economics, and that they could not award me a PhD Degree in Economics for a dissertation which was not in Economics … [A]t this point I am quite willing to concede: at the time I defended my dissertation, portfolio theory was not part of Economics. But now it is.
>
> *(Markowitz, 1990)*

At that time it was not part of finance either, although now it is. Nor would it usually be designated as an interdisciplinary topic.[10] Among other scholars working with financial data were the authors of papers subsequently collected in a 1964 volume edited by Cootner *about* the behaviour of prices and their theoretical predictability (Cootner, 1964). These scholars included both mathematicians (Louis Bachelier, Clive Granger, Maurice Kendall, Benoit Mandelbrot, Matthew Osborne) and economists (Alfred Cowles, Oskar Morgenstern, Holbrook Working), the distinction between which was being erased as economists turned to mathematics as a source of status (McGoun, 1995a) and mathematicians turned to economics as a source of employment (McGoun, 1995b).[11]

Through their opportunistic infiltration into economics for the employment of their skills (and themselves), mathematicians, firmly hard-pure academics, upgraded the status of economics. In turn, through their use of financial data (securities markets' prices), mathematicians and economists initiated the same upgrade to finance:

> In summary, business finance became transformed into financial economics when university business schools recruited relatively large numbers of economists and applied mathematicians as part of their attempts at developing more analytical and "scientific" approaches to management studies.
>
> *(Whitley, 1986: 179–80)[12]*

However, this transformation of academic finance could not have occurred without the support of finance practitioners. As Whitley (1986) describes it:

> The apparent acquiescence of employers and financial elites in the colonization of business by economists and their intellectual goals has been crucial to its quick achievement since a rejection of the new skills and analytical approach would have affected student enrolments and thus the position of finance academics in business schools.
>
> *(Whitley, 1986: 179)*

One might argue, as does Whitley, that the expansion of the finance industry in the 1960s and 1970s, through the deregulation of old markets and the creation of new ones, led to a burgeoning demand for students trained in these new skills and analytical approach(es). One might otherwise argue that it largely worked the other way around, that students trained in the new skills and analytical approach drove the deregulation of old markets and the creation of new ones:

In finance, in particular, we have seen how research not only models the financial world, helping us to understand its inner dynamics and processes, but also changes the functioning of finance in operation. Finance in practice is now different from what it used to be as a result of finance research. The resultant knowledge has played a significant role in the creation of new markets in options, the emergence of new financial instruments, and very different approaches to the management of financial risk. Indeed finance research has been constitutive of finance itself.

(Hopwood, 2007: 1367)

Did expanding markets demand more sophisticated skills, or did more sophisticated skills expand markets? Regardless, each subsequently served to feed the other. It didn't matter whether or not any of this new science improved finance practice along with changing it; like the placebo effect in medicine it was sufficient that it could be made to appear (or it felt) as if it did. Use does not imply functional utility, and Whitley hints at this phenomenon:

Because of the novelty of many developments in the past twenty or so years and *the need to justify investment decisions and changes*, academics have become viewed as legitimating agents for many analysts and managers.

(Whitley, 1986: 186, italics added)

What held accounting back, miring it in the academic soft-applied slough while finance marched boldly onwards over firm ground in the direction of hard-pure? There were several material forces at work. First, finance data was in greater demand by other disciplines, specifically mathematics and economics, than was accounting data. Accounting data was not so standardised and manipulable – not so easily aggregated and/or assembled into time series – and not so obviously useful for empirical tests of the theories of current interest to mathematicians and economists.[13] The pioneer finance machine-readable database was subsequently produced by the Center for Research in Security Prices, founded in 1960 by two finance professors, Lorie and Fisher at the University of Chicago, and it soon became the identifying feature of real finance research. Second, the accounting certification process leading to designation as a Certified Public Accountant (CPA) in the US and Chartered Accountant (CA) in the UK has bound accounting much more tightly to practice than is the case with finance. This certification process has also meant that changes in accounting education and practice could not occur as quickly as they could and did in finance. Third, regarding differences between the UK and the US, where finance changed much more rapidly, the financial services industry in the UK was more conservative than in the US and, as a consequence, less open to changes in its structures and operations. Therefore, there was markedly less demand in the UK for the "new skills and analytical approach."

Finance was more likely to be organisationally independent of accounting at universities in the US than in the UK, leaving academic finance less freedom to change in the UK than in the US (Whitley, 1986). The commonalities discussed in the introduction to this chapter notwithstanding, business education in general and finance in particular were more popular and served more students in the US than in the UK, which justified separate departments.

A final condition that influenced the field of finance was the great post-war influx of students .... Not only did finance share the increased business school enrollment, but the recent return of the field to popularity as a subject of study has kept its instructors exceptionally busy on the courses offered. In a number of schools finance now ranks first from the point of view of total enrollment and of majors, surpassing the traditionally popular subjects of accounting, marketing and administration.

(Pierson et al., 1959: 395)

Across the Atlantic, accounting scholars were able to hinder changes in finance scholarship in the UK, where the former's greater influence enabled them to do so. Accounting did so because its emphasis upon professional certification retarded its own development as a science. Since then, professional certification as a Certified Financial Analyst (CFA) has taken hold in finance, but because this occurred after the transformation of finance, the CFA test reflects the new orientation of the profession.

Baker (2011) suggests other reasons why critical accounting topics, methodologies and methods might have held on longer in the UK than in the US. Most important is that the UK had developed a cadre of such scholars, who founded and supported a prestigious sympathetic journal *Accounting, Organizations and Society*,[14] while the apprentice-style system of doctoral education in the UK greatly facilitated passing the orientation on from one scholarly generation to another. One might also argue that UK scholars in general benefitted from a broader intellectual formation than those in the US, one that included current trends in philosophical thought, much of which originated in France and Germany and provided the underpinnings for critical analysis. Furthermore, the more extreme opposition between the Conservative and Labour parties in the UK, compared with relatively slight differences between Republicans and Democrats in the US, resulted in greater interest from both scholars and the educated public in political issues that had significant accounting components (Sikka and Willmott, 1997).

These different historical trajectories of accounting and finance have obvious consequences for critical research. A soft-applied science, such as accounting remained, is likely to be more methodologically and methodically diverse than a hard-pure science, such as finance became. In accounting, the normative, qualitative and interdisciplinary research characteristic of a critical standpoint remained academically legitimate, especially considering that the positive and quantitative research of a supportive standpoint was developing at a relatively slow pace and not wholly dominating and defining the discipline. In finance, normative and qualitative research, whether interdisciplinary and critical or not, was drowned in a tidal wave of positive and quantitative research that made finance 'finance' and relegated alternative research to the depths of academic respectability. In addition, one cannot ignore the fact that finance practitioners were avid paying customers of the 'hard-pure' research that finance was producing. The financial services industry could profit from it whether or not people understood it, or even whether or not it worked (Milo and MacKenzie, 2009). More conservative accounting practitioners were more content with accounting's soft-applied research, which had to meet higher standards of comprehensibility and utility.

In effect, this section has presented an essentially structural story; in Rowling's terms, Harry Potter became Gryffindor-ish after entering Hogwarts and then being assigned to that house by the Sorting Hat. Accounting and finance scholars are shaped by the institutional standards (and resident personalities) of the academic departments in which they study and work.[15] (Lee, 1995; Panozzo, 1997; Fogarty and Jonas, 2010). These standards are a consequence of a broader milieu that has included the research interests of other academic disciplines and the demands for research outputs and student skills from the practitioner communities, and perhaps even from the broader public. A powerful agency story should not be overlooked, however. Harry Potter was Gryffindor-ish before he entered Hogwarts and was identified as such by the Sorting Hat. Accounting and finance scholars, as individuals, are different. They shape accounting and finance at the same time as accounting and finance shape them.

4 Staring at the other person's shoes

There is an old joke: "Question: how do you tell the difference between an accountant and an actuary? Answer: the accountant is the one staring at the other person's shoes."[16] Finance scholars are not actuaries but their tools of the trade are sufficiently similar to make this a relevant contrast to accounting scholars. As described in the preceding section, while the discipline of finance moved in the direction of a physical science, becoming increasingly focused on 'things', accounting clearly remained a social science with a predominant emphasis on people. Accounting has had to remain in touch with the real world while finance can inhabit a theoretical world of perfect markets. Accounting has had to take into account the organisations that are the sources of its data along with the words and actions of the managers of those organisations. Finance has just had to look at the anonymous prices of market transactions detached from who bought and who sold and why they decided to do so. Accounting has had to pay attention to "the other person's shoes" while finance could be satisfied with the ones it was wearing itself. It is therefore little wonder that finance today is populated by people proud to identify themselves as 'rocket scientists' and with 'quants'.

Unfortunately, the agency story must be largely speculative. Information regarding the backgrounds and personalities of accounting and finance scholars – and specifically the differences between the two – remains scarce. Casual observation suggests that accounting scholars are inclined to have been undergraduate accounting majors and earned CPA or CA certifications prior to their PhD studies and/or have worked outside the academy as practicing accountants. According to Boyce (2004: 579):

> Most [accounting academics] are themselves the product of conventional accounting education programs, into which they self-selected, with pre-existing stereotypes about accounting, and they have been socialized into the existing system through their own education.

Boyce provides no firm evidence in support of this, however. Brown, Jones and Steele (2007) did find that the fraction of staff in accounting and finance departments in the UK with professional certification was substantial, despite falling from 74.1 per cent in 1982 to 50.1 per cent in 2004. Since these numbers include finance along with accounting, since the CFA (Certified Financial Analyst) professional qualification for finance academics is still in its infancy and since the amount of finance staff has grown more rapidly than that of accounting staff (in AACSB accredited programs) during this period,[17] these statistics are likely to significantly understate the professional qualifications of accounting academics.

In contrast, finance scholars appear more likely to have undergraduate degrees in more technical disciplines such as economics, mathematics or physics, and to have proceeded more quickly to PhD studies in finance without having experience with finance outside the academy. If this is accurate, we might hypothesise that accounting is less inclined than is finance to build theoretical models upon radically simplified assumptions and more inclined to acknowledge the importance of the idiosyncratic behaviour of individuals. Accountants might be more appreciative of the social and political influences upon accounting and the social and political consequences of accounting and in the course of their experiences to have formed personal opinions regarding such issues.

Suggestive differences in the intellectual breadth of accounting and finance PhD students were apparent as early as 1959. Regarding accounting:

> Interdisciplinary topics of research are highly desirable in the doctorate program in accounting. In the first place, accounting principles and procedures deal with business transactions and reports which arise from different segments of the firm. Secondly, the

contributions which can be made toward improved understanding of the functional areas of business through accounting analysis are unlimited.

(Pierson et al., 1959: 389)

Baker (2011) states that this approach to accounting doctoral education in the US, with its tolerance of different methodologies and methods, continued through the mid-1970s, based upon the personal experience of the author. By contrast, in the case of finance:

The most serious weakness in integration occurs between finance and nonbusiness subjects .... [S]tudents and often instructors oriented toward business lack interest in and awareness of the supporting and enriching value of work in nonbusiness subjects ....When interdisciplinary influences are rare in current doctoral research, it seems reasonable to think that integration with other fields is one of the weak points of the finance curriculum.

(Pierson et al., 1959: 407–8)

[C]urrent titles of doctoral theses in preparation and abstracts of accepted theses show little influence of an interdisciplinary nature. On the contrary, the thesis subjects show a sort of inward turning to technical or historical financial problems rather than a moving into interdisciplinary areas which in the history of many fields of thought have proved so fertile.

(Pierson et al., 1959: 418)

In short, accounting scholars have been more exposed to the experiences and events from which one might develop a critical perspective. Finance scholars might never have had to confront anything that would challenge their foundational metaphor of markets as (efficient) machines.[18] There is a substantial literature regarding the personalities of accounting students and accounting practitioners, although very, very little written about personalities in finance.[19] The reason is likely to be the powerful and pervasive stereotype of the accounting profession (about which jokes are told) and an obvious desire to test its veracity. Finance has only begun to acquire an equivalently strong image, for which extant studies are relatively rare. It would be too much of a stretch, however, to assume that having likely been undergraduate accounting students and accountants themselves and having undergone the corresponding socialisation (Clikeman and Henning, 2000), accounting scholars share their personalities. Simply having exited the profession to earn a PhD is telling evidence that at least some values differ. And "[d]octoral students may be the least studied group of individuals in the universe of the accounting discipline" (Fogarty and Jonas, 2010: 303).

5 Stranger in a strange land

Through some combination of structure and agency, critical accounting developed within accounting and critical finance elsewhere within the academy. Important consequences of these different origins are attributable to the interdisciplinary nature of critical research. One problem with interdisciplinary scholarship is that those who practice it have to have come from somewhere, that is, they have to have been formally trained within a discipline. In short, "in order to be interdisciplinary, one first has to have a discipline" (Fogarty, 2014: 1267). During that training, they might have taken courses outside that discipline or have undertaken independent studies outside of that discipline, and their dissertation might have addressed issues on the fringe of that discipline. As Harry Markowitz's experience has shown, the organisational structures of universities still necessitate their having a disciplinary home. The obvious effect of this is that there is one discipline within those making up their interdisciplinary scholarship that they know more about. A less obvious effect is as discussed in the two preceding sections. In terms of structure, they had to have been influenced by the values, preferences and biases inherent in the home discipline. In terms of agency, their pre-existing values, preferences and biases led to their original choice of that home discipline. As the Headmaster of Hogwarts, Albus Dumbledore would have to have treated all four houses equally – but one cannot believe that his having been a member of Gryffindor himself was without its effects on his behaviour.[20]

The rhetoric of schools of business is increasingly encouraging interdisciplinarity; in fact, it was the theme of the 2014 American Accounting Association (AAA) Doctoral Consortium. At that event, however, interdisciplinarity referred to transcending whatever barriers segregate financial accounting, managerial accounting, auditing and taxation (Fogarty, 2014). Apparently, even connections to finance and economics would have been bridges too far! Clearly, Frodeman's (2010) caution is being ignored: "'Interdisciplinarity' should not be treated as a shibboleth or a sign of one's advanced thinking. Neither is it an incantation that will magically solve our problems" (Frodeman, 2010: xxxii).[21] Meaningful interdisciplinarity for accounting means reaching out much farther – to the other social sciences, the humanities, and the arts.[22] Of course the farther one has to reach, the greater the commitment required to do so. Ties to familiar accounting content (or that of another home discipline) are strained in exchange for ties to an unfamiliar target discipline, the value – or credibility – of which connections might not be professionally acknowledged. Is one reaching out to a target discipline for a theory or research method to apply to a recognised home discipline problem, or are there reciprocal connections between the disciplines that are more comprehensive and more complex? (O'Dwyer and Unerman, 2014). Achieving the latter is more difficult – and professionally riskier – than the former.

The fundamental question here, however, is who benefits from interdisciplinarity? For a number of reasons, it is more likely that the audience for interdisciplinary scholarship will come from the home discipline. First, as indicated earlier, the simplest sort of interdisciplinarity is to borrow a theory or research method to address a home discipline problem of interest to a home discipline audience. Second, the scholar undertaking the research understands the home discipline audience best, knowing where and how to communicate to it, and the scholar might already have an acknowledged standing with it. And third, and most importantly, the interdisciplinary scholarship is likely to be intellectually weightier with respect to the home discipline than to the target discipline. Of course this applies most strongly to single-authored work, which Pfirman and Martin (2010) term "intrapersonal."[23] Multiple-authored works[24] will share these biases to some extent. The upshot is that critical, interdisciplinary accounting research that originates within accounting is likely to matter to accounting and hopefully to be read by the accounting community. Conversely, critical, interdisciplinary finance research, that at present originates outside finance, will not be read by the finance community no matter how relevant, or indeed how good, it might be.

6 And the winner is …

Most observers of current research in accounting and finance conclude that with a time lag, accounting has followed the path of finance, at least in the US. Roslender and Dillard (2003: 326–7) comment that

> Financial economics dominates mainstream accounting research in the U.S. Few, if any, alternatives are recognized as legitimate. Financial economics based research is seen as more rigorous and scientific, thus deserving privileged treatment.

Rather than finance following the lead of accounting and maintaining a tradition of qualitative research (if not critical, interdisciplinary research reaching out to other than the physical sciences), however small, accounting's following finance has threatened the health of its own critical tradition. Moreover there are indications that the tradition of behavioural accounting research has been seriously threatened as well (Williams, Jenkins and Ingraham, 2006).[25]

On the other hand, some authors are more sanguine about the trajectory of qualitative accounting research, at least in the UK and other parts of Europe. Panozzo (1997) contrasts "the dominance of a mainstream within the North American disciplinary matrix" with "an emergent European perspective whose vague identity is essentially to be found in the variety of methodological approaches" (Panozzo, 1997: 447). Lee and Humphrey (2006) suggest that the potential exists for this to influence finance. Unfortunately, their evidence for optimism at the time was thin. They reference Holland and Stoner (1996), Holland and Doran (1998), Stoner and Holland (2004), Dowd (2004) and Willman, Fenton-O'Creery, Nicholson and Sloane (2002). The third and fourth items were published in an edited volume entitled: *The Real Life Guide to Accounting Research*; the first item appears in the journal *Accounting and Business Research*, while the fifth is in the journal *Accounting, Organizations and Society*. Only the second appears in a finance publication, the *European Journal of Finance*. (And of course there is significant authorial overlap in this list.) Subsequently, a new journal *Qualitative Research in Financial Markets* has begun publication. Unfortunately, these nascent efforts have as yet had little impact, and little of the extant qualitative finance produced within finance could be considered *critical* finance. In 2009, Forslund and Bay (2009) celebrated the inauguration of a series of critical finance conferences in their paper "The eve of critical finances," but as successful as these annual conferences have been in attracting scholars from other disciplines in the social sciences and the humanities, they have failed to draw significant numbers of finance scholars let alone have an impact on finance itself. The dawn Forslund and Bay anticipated has not yet broken.

On the whole, accounting has very little influence on finance. Using citational analysis, Bricker, Borokhovich and Simkins (2003) found that in 1990 and 1991, only 232 citations (140 individual articles) out of 13,651 total citations in seven prominent finance journals (1.70 per cent) referred to accounting documents. Arnold, Butler, Crack and Altintig (2003) similarly found that of the 2,000 most-cited papers in a selection of six prominent finance journals for the period 1990–99, 35 (1.75 per cent) were from the *Journal of Accounting and Economics* and 16 (0.80 per cent) from the *Journal of Accounting Research*. Of these, only 11 of the 35 and 2 of the 16 were published during that same decade. In Biehl, Kim and Wade's (2006) principle component analysis of top business journals, finance showed considerable overlap with economics but was distinct from accounting. There appears to have been no studies of finance's influence on accounting, the powerful effect seemingly being taken for granted.[26]

Qualitative, critical, interdisciplinary research in finance and accounting would clearly appear to be an endangered species, at least under the purview of accounting and finance departments. It began to disappear in finance very shortly after World War II in the US and later in the UK. Although there were a number of forces resisting the move in the UK, the globalisation of finance and hence the globalisation of finance research inevitably meant that the UK was bound to fall in line behind the US. With yet another lag, one attributable largely to the official professionalisation of accounting, accounting in both the US and the UK eventually followed finance on the path to greater academic respectability (Ravenscroft and Williams, 2009). A sizable residue of qualitative research in accounting has managed to hang on in the UK, where a cadre of accounting academics so oriented has managed to reproduce itself. Critical research, as a subset of qualitative research, never had a chance to develop in finance.

As qualitative accounting research has begun to disappear in the US, so has critical accounting research. For how long the UK can continue to resist this process remains an open, not to mention, an interesting question.

This chapter was submitted by the author with the following title: "Beneath the sorting hat: critical accounting and critical finance."

Notes

1 One might also say that supportive research and critical research are looking at the same things but in different ways, from different perspectives, through different lenses, and with different ends.

2 Worth noting here is the peculiarly *performative* power that finance has been asserted to have. (MacKenzie, 2006). Positive research into what is becomes a self-fulfilling prophesy, that is, a theory of behaviour alters behaviour and becomes true from having been convincingly proposed.

3 In an ideal academic world, one chooses a research question and then the appropriate means of addressing it. (Nails suggest the use of hammers.) In the real world, the means come first. (Hammers seek out nails.)

4 It has not always been the same as this in the past, and some convincingly argue that the change has not been to the advantage of the economy (Ravenscroft and Williams, 2009; Murphy, O'Connell and Ó hÓgartaigh, 2013).

5 Interestingly, while accounting is concerned with enabling "investors, lenders, and other creditors" to estimate the (in some sense *absolute*) value of a reporting entity, finance is concerned with *relative* values.

6 In a Kuhnian sense, theories that are thought to concern that which is hard are likely to be more resistant to change than those concerning the soft, as would objects that are literally hard and soft.

7 One might argue that there is no such thing as knowledge independent of a knower (all knowledge is 'in here'), and that there is no such thing as "knowledge *of*" independent of "knowledge *for*," since all knowledge has a purpose. Such philosophical matters are not at stake here, and discussed elsewhere in this volume.

8 The canonical work by a sociologist of academia on the transition of finance from "soft/applied" to at least a simulacrum of "hard-pure" remains Whitley's paper "The transformation of business finance into financial economics" (Whitley, 1986), which has provided valuable background information for the following history.

9 It was, however, subsequently published as a paper in the *Journal of Finance* (Markowitz, 1952).

10 Interestingly, though, in 2007 it was still possible to describe similar research undertaken in 1965 as interdisciplinary. "The new accounting research was also strongly interdisciplinary in orientation. New fields of inquiry often are in both the sciences and the social sciences. Fama's research on efficient markets emerged at the interface of finance, economics, and statistics" (Hopwood, 2007: 1366).

11 More charitably, the mathematicians might have been looking for interesting problems in a new domain. Then again, the mathematics of economics is not that sophisticated or challenging.

12 It might be more accurate to emphasise that business schools were capitalising on a trend that was already well underway.

13 It has become much more so now, however.

14 The founding editor of the journal, Anthony Hopwood, had been trained at the University of Chicago, thereby earning the journal at least the respect, although not necessarily the agreement, of the mainstream.

15 Over 85% of accounting doctoral students report having been mentored during their doctoral programme, and such mentoring is positively correlated with their satisfaction with their doctoral education (Burkette and Pointer, 1998). The specifics of such "mentoring" have not yet been studied, however.

16 This joke is not cited in Miley and Read's paper "Jokes in popular culture: the characterization of the accountant" (Miley and Read, 2012). It is certainly consistent with their thesis that accountant jokes concern the stereotypical accountant personality, here damning their social skills with faint praise. It is perhaps telling that while accountant and actuary jokes are abundant on the Internet, finance jokes are comparatively scarce, and much less personal.

17 Between 1990 and 2004, the number of accounting faculty fell 2.8% (5,029 to 4,887), while the number of finance faculty increased 23.3% (3,274 to 4,036) (Fogarty and Markarian, 2007).

18 They are apparently able to ignore, or rationalise, examples of what appear to be quite inefficient market behaviours.

19 Andon, Chong and Roebuck (2010) is a recent example of a study regarding accounting, which provides a useful literature review and summary of prior studies. Worthington and Higgs (2003) is a rare example of a similar study regarding finance, which, ironically, was published in an accounting journal.

20 Excluded from this section are more personal problems with interdisciplinary research—"Less recognition by established scholars, fewer sustained funding opportunities, fewer journals, fewer peer reviewers, career trajectory not known, and long start-up time" (Pfirman and Martin, 2010: 391).

21 One could argue that the Consortium's heart is in the right place, however. A driving force for interdisciplinarity is societal relevance (which is how some interpret the related term "transdisciplinarity"), and this appears to be the AAA's motivation.

22 In light of the foregoing, it goes without saying that finance and, increasingly, accounting do not have to be encouraged to reach out to the physical sciences.

23 This is described as the formation of "Cognitive Connections," further elaborated as "Cross-fertilization – adapting and using ideas, approaches and information from different fields and/or disciplines" (Pfirman and Martin, 2010: 389).

24 This next level is "Intrapersonal: Collegial Connections; Team-collaboration – collaboration in teams or networks that span different fields and/or disciplines" (Pfirman and Martin, 2010: 389).

25 In Kinney's (2003) survey of the courses taken by students attending a 2002 doctoral consortium, 90% of the students took a (clearly quantitative) course in capital markets methods. Of the other research methods courses taken by students – behavioural (53%), analytic (33%), and general (33%) – none were clearly described as qualitative and might or might not have had qualitative components.

26 Beattie and Goodacre (2004) reported that 45.6% of the papers published by accounting *and* finance faculty in the UK and Ireland in 1998 and 1999 appear in other than accounting and finance journals, but the authors themselves are uncertain whether this is as large an outflow of influence from both disciplines combined as it appears to be.

References

Andon, P., K. M. Chong and Roebuck (2010). "Personality preferences of accounting and non-accounting graduates seeking to enter the accounting profession," *Critical Perspectives on Accounting*, 21(4): 253–65.

Arnold, T., A. W. Butler, T. F. Crack and A. Altintig (2003). "What influences finance research?" *The Journal of Business*, 76(2): 343–61.

Baker, R. C. (2011). "A genealogical history of positivist and critical accounting research," *Accounting History*, 16(2): 207–21.

Beattie, V. and A. Goodacre (2004). "Publishing patterns within the UK accounting and finance academic community," *British Accounting Review*, 36(1): 7–44.

Becher, T. and P. R. Trowler (2001). *Academic Tribes and Territories*, 2e, Philadelphia, PA: The Society for Research into Higher Education and Open University Press.

Biehl, M., H. Kim, and M. Wade (2006) "Relationships among the academic business disciplines: a multi-method citation analysis," *Omega*, 34(4): 359–71.

Boyce, G. (2004). "Critical accounting education: teaching and learning outside the circle," *Critical Perspectives on Accounting*, 15(4–5): 565–86.

Bricker, R., K. Borokhovich and B. Simkins. (2003). "The impact of accounting research on finance," *Critical Perspectives on Accounting*, 14(4): 417–38.

Brown, R., M. Jones and T. Steele (2007). "Still flickering at the margins of existence? publishing patterns and themes in accounting and finance research over the last two decades," *British Accounting Review*, 39(2): 125–51.

Burkette, G. D. and M. M. Pointer (1998). "The nature and occurrence of mentoring in accounting doctoral programs," *Accounting Educators' Journal*, 10(1): 47–60.

Clikeman, P. M. and S. L. Henning (2000). "The socialization of undergraduate accounting students," *Issues in Accounting Education*, 15(1): 1–17.

Cootner, P. H. (ed.), (1964). *The Random Character of Stock Market Prices*, Cambridge, MA: The MIT Press.

Dowd, K. (2004). "Qualitative dimensions in finance and risk management research," in C. Humphrey and B. Lee (eds): *The Real Life Guide to Accounting Research: A Behind the Scenes View of Using Qualitative Research Methods*, Oxford: Elsevier.

FASB (2010). "Statement of Financial Accounting Concepts Number 8: Conceptual Framework for Financial Reporting," Norwalk, CT: Financial Accounting Standards Board.

Fogarty, T. J. (2014). "A dream deferred: interdisciplinary accounting in the US," *Accounting, Auditing and Accountability Journal*, 27(8): 1265–70.

Fogarty, T. J., and G. Markarian (2007). "An empirical assessment of the rise and fall of accounting as an academic discipline," *Issues in Accounting Education*, 22(2): 137–61.

Fogarty, T. J., and G. A. Jonas (2010). "The hand that rocks the cradle: disciplinary socialization at the American Accounting Association's Doctoral Consortium," *Critical Perspectives on Accounting*, 21(4) 303–17.

Forslund, D. and T. Bay (2009). "The eve of critical finance studies," *Ephemera*, 9(4): 285–99.

Frodeman, R. (2010). "Introduction," in R. Frodeman (ed.): *The Oxford Handbook of Interdisciplinarity*, Oxford: Oxford University Press.

Graham, B. and D. Dodd (1996). *Security Analysis: The Classic 1934 Edition*, New York: McGraw-Hill.

Holland, J. and G. Stoner (1996). "Dissemination of price sensitive information and management of voluntary corporate disclosure," *Accounting and Business Research*, 26(4): 295–313.

Holland, J. and P. Doran (1998). "Financial institutions, private acquisition of corporate information and fund management," *European Journal of Finance*, 4(2): 129–55.

Hopwood, A. G. (2007). "Whither accounting research?" *The Accounting Review*, 82(5): 1365–74.

Kinney, W. R. (2003). "New accounting scholars – does it matter what we teach them?" *Issues in Accounting Education*, 18(1): 37–47.

Lee, B. and C. Humphrey (2006). "More than a numbers game: qualitative research in accounting," *Management Decision*, 44(2): 180–97.

Lee, T. (1995). "Shaping the US Academic Accounting Research Profession: The American Accounting Association and the Social Construction of a Professional Elite," *Critical Perspectives on Accounting*, 6: 241–61.

McGoun, E. G. (1995a) "Machomatics in egonomics," *International Review of Financial Analysis*, 4(2): 185–99.

McGoun, G. (1995b). "The history of risk "measurement," *Critical Perspectives on Accounting*, 6(6): 511–32.

MacKenzie, D. A. (2006). *An Engine Not a Camera*, Cambridge, MA: MIT Press.

Markowitz, H. M. (1952). "Portfolio selection," *Journal of Finance*, 7(1): 77–91.

Markowitz, H. M. (1990). "Nobel Prize Lecture: Foundations of Portfolio Theory".

Miley, F. and A. Read (2012). "Jokes in popular culture: the characterization of the accountant," *Accounting, Auditing and Accountability Journal*, 25(4): 703–18.

Milo, Y. and D. A. MacKenzie (2009). "The usefulness of inaccurate models: towards an understanding of the emergence of financial risk management," *Accounting, Organizations and Society*, 34(5): 638–53.

Murphy, T., V. O'Connell and C. Ó hÓgartaigh (2013). "Discourses surrounding the evolution of the IASB/FASB Conceptual Framework: what they reveal about the "Living Law" of accounting," *Accounting Organizations and Society*, 38(1): 72–91.

O'Dwyer, B. and J. Unerman (2014). "Realizing the potential of interdisciplinarity in accounting research," *Accounting, Auditing and Accountability Journal*, 27(8): 1227–32.

Panozzo, F. (1997). "The making of the good academic accountant," *Accounting, Organizations and Society*, 22(5): 447–80.

Pfirman, S. and P. J. S. Marti (2010). "Facilitating interdisciplinary scholars," in R. Frodeman (ed.): *The Oxford Handbook of Interdisciplinarity*, Oxford: Oxford University Press.

Pierson, F. C. et al. (1959). *The Education of American Businessmen: A Study of University-College Programs in Business Administration*, New York: McGraw-Hill.

Pope, P. F. (2010). "Bridging the gap between accounting and finance," *British Accounting Review*, 42(2): 88–102.

Ravenscroft, S. and P. F. Williams (2009). "Making imaginary worlds real: the case of expensing employee stock options," *Accounting, Organizations and Society*, 34(6–7): 770–86.

Roslender, R. and J. F. Dillard (2003). "Reflections on the interdisciplinary perspectives on accounting project," *Critical Perspectives on Accounting*, 14(3): 325–51,

Rowling, J. K. (1997). *Harry Potter and the Philosopher's Stone*, New York: Scholastic Inc.

Rowling, J. K. (2000). *Harry Potter and the Goblet of Fire*, New York: Scholastic Inc.

Sikka, P. and H. Willmott (1997). "Practising critical accounting," *Critical Perspectives on Accounting*, 8(1–2): 149–165.

Stoner, G. and J. Holland (2004). "Using case studies in finance research," in C. Humphrey and B. Lee (eds): *The Real Life Guide to Accounting Research: A Behind the Scenes View of Using Qualitative Research Methods*, Oxford: Elsevier.

Taylor, F. W. (1914). *The Principles of Scientific Management*, New York NY: Harper & Brothers Publishers.

Vollmer, H., A. Mennicken and A. Preda (2009). "Tracking the numbers: across accounting and finance, organizations and markets," *Accounting Organizations and Society*, 34(5): 619–37.

Whitley, R. (1986). "The transformation of business finance into financial economics: the roles of academic expansion and changes in U.S. capital markets," *Accounting, Organizations and Society*, 11(2): 171–92.

Williams, P. F., J. G. Jenkin, and L. Ingraham (2006). "The winnowing away of behavioral accounting research in the U.S.: the process for anointing academic elites," *Accounting, Organizations and Society*, 31(8): 783–818.

Willman, P., M. Fenton-O'Creevy, N. Nicholson and E. Soane (2002). "Traders, managers and loss aversion in investment banking: a field study," *Accounting, Organizations and Society*, 27(1–2): 85–98.

Worthington, A. C. and H. Higgs (2003). "Factors explaining the choice of a finance major: the role of student characteristics, personality and perceptions of the profession," *Accounting Education*, 12(3): 261–81.

SECTION VI

24

SUSTAINABILITY IS THE NEW CRITICAL?

Judy Brown and Jesse Dillard

So it has come to this. The global biodiversity crisis is so severe that brilliant scientists, political leaders, eco-warriors, and religious gurus can no longer save us from ourselves. The military are powerless. But there may be one last hope for life on earth: accountants.

(Jonathan Watts, Guardian, *28 October, 2010)*

1 Introduction

The objective of the critical accounting project[1] is to facilitate the formulation, implementation and evaluation of a progressive social agenda dedicated to improving the human condition though researching, teaching, studying, practising and applying accounting and accountability systems. Social justice represents the core principle by which accounting and accountability systems are assessed, both in terms of capabilities and possibilities as well as impediments and limitations. As is becoming palpably apparent, social justice cannot be separated from what has come to be articulated as 'sustainability' or 'sustainable development'.[2] Economic systems cannot survive outside of sustainable social systems and sustainable social systems cannot survive in the absence of sustainable natural systems. However, all indications are that the default schema within global market capitalism has inverted this hierarchy whereby the economic is paramount and the social and natural systems exist only to serve its bidding (Bateson, 1972, 1979). As is becoming more obvious daily, we ignore this distortion at our peril.

The critical accounting project appears to have migrated, some might argue mutated or transmogrified,[3] from a critical accounting project to an interdisciplinary accounting project to an interdisciplinary and critical accounting project (Roslender and Dillard, 2003; Broadbent and Laughlin, 2013). From its inception in the later 1970s, critical accounting has been a place where serious accounting scholars could challenge the neo-liberal hegemony and the associated ascendancy of neo-classical (financial) economics. Initially energised by historical materialism and political economy, the project attracted both emerging scholars and those a bit deeper into their careers, by providing an opportunity to engage the issues surrounding accounting in action at a more fundamental, holistic and reflexive level. Shareholders were recognised as only one of many segments of society to which accounting, as a discipline and a practice, has a responsibility and upon which accounting has an effect. The central aim was not to maximise shareholder value but to enhance social justice by facilitating a more democratic and egalitarian society.[4]

A wide range of social science theories and methodologies have been accepted, or tolerated, in studying accounting, organisations and society.[5] The project provided the preferred space for the academic accounting alternative by advocating a radical and critical intent directly questioning the status quo.

The question that arises is how does the critical accounting project maintain its focus and energy in light of the pluralistic evolution of this academic research genre. In the future, can the critical accounting project continue to serve as the primary site for the more politically and critically inclined who are searching for a broader, more relevant and effective platform from which to consider accounting and accountability systems as influencing, and being influenced by, their social, political, historical and economic contexts? How does, and can, the practice and craft of accounting facilitate, or inhibit, the long-term viability of a democratically governed society grounded in values such as justice, equality and trust and supported by sustainable economic, social and natural systems? In this chapter we consider the possibilities for the sustainable development of the critical accounting project in light of the emergence of sustainability as a critical research area (Dillard and Vinnari, 2017).[6]

Sustainability, or sustainable development, is emerging as a significant issue that is being seriously engaged by members of the critical accounting community. Our objective is to facilitate dialogue and debate regarding the possibilities associated with what we refer to as 'critical sustainability accounting', an emerging research genre in critical accounting. We explore this genre of research in accounting, considering its relationship to the critical accounting project. Have or will accounting scholars working in the area succumb to a trendy area that denudes the critical accounting project of its radical intent? Has or will the arena become colonised by steering media such as power and material resources so as to render it a lackey for its capitalist masters, as has been the case for the dominant accounting scholarship? Or does sustainability provide a fertile platform for critical perspectives on accounting? The destiny of critical sustainability accounting probably lies somewhere in between, depending on how its proponents choose to integrate, or not, the two.

We take the position that sustainability, as it relates to the flourishing of both social and natural systems, is an important, nay critical, area of study that encompasses a substantial component of a progressive social agenda dedicated to improving the human condition. In our opinion, critical accounting has a responsibility to address sustainability and sustainable development, especially as they relate to work organisations and corporate social responsibility (CSR). Though given the new public management initiatives and the growing importance of social movements, accounting is becoming much more influential in the public and not-for-profit sectors (NFP) as well.

In the following pages we initially consider sustainability and how we see it as potentially a significant dimension of the critical accounting project. Section three discusses the related social and environmental accounting perspectives that must be considered in developing what we refer to as the 'critical sustainability accounting project', potentially a significant and energising component of the critical accounting project. We then consider critical research that matters and suggest agonistics as a way of moving this project into the future.

2 What is sustainability?

At its most fundamental level, sustainability refers to the ability (of an individual, entity, institution, society, humanity) to use a resource (social, natural) so as not to deplete or permanently damage the resource. The level of resource utilisation does not go beyond the system's adaptive capacity (ability to replenish the resource) or its absorptive capacity (ability to absorb or neutralise the consequences/output). The most popular definition of sustainability (or sustainable development) comes from the World Commission on Environment and Development, also known as The Brundtland Report (United Nations, 1987, see Appendix). The commission states that the goals of economic and social development must be defined in terms of sustainability so that the needs of the present generation can be realised, especially the world's poor, but that these needs should not be met by compromising the ability to meet the needs of future generations. Meeting these standards requires attention to physical resources as well as the progressive transformation of both economic and social systems that are attentive to inequalities regarding access to resources as well as fair distribution in both the associated benefits and the costs. The associated strategic imperatives recognise the inseparability of the economic, social and ecological systems and are articulated as follows: reviving growth; changing the quality of growth; meeting essential needs for jobs, food, energy, water and sanitation; ensuring a sustainable level of population; conserving and enhancing the resource base; reorienting technology and managing risk; and merging environment and economics in decision making.

The Commission's report makes clear that sustainability and sustainable development not only encompass environmental issues but also include the sociopolitical domain as well. Inter-generational and intra-generational equity raises issues related to social issues such as population growth, production and consumption, distribution patterns and wealth (re)distribution. The commission concludes that the current modes of production, consumption and governance are not sustainable and that current policies do not adequately address the problem. What is needed is a serious and critical assessment of the current state with a view towards substantial change.

Sustainability in accounting has emerged as part of what has come to be called 'social accounting'.[7] The evolution of the titles of the seminal texts in this area is illustrative. One of the first texts in the field was Gray, Owen and Maunders' (1987) *Corporate Social Reporting: Accounting and Accountability*. Close to a decade later, Gray, Owens and Adams (1996) significantly revised the text and entitled it *Accounting and Accountability: Changes and Challenges in Corporate Social and Environmental Reporting*. The 2014 edition of this text is entitled *Accountability, Social Responsibility and Sustainability: Accounting for Society and the Environment*. The focus shifts from a rather narrow one on corporate social reporting to recognising the centrality of social and environmental sustainability as a, or the, focal point. There is also a discernible shift from complicity (working within the current regime) to opposition and confrontation (recognising the need to change the current regime). As the authors explain, accountability is integral in promoting social responsibility. One of, if not the, primary components of social responsibility is fostering sustainable social and natural systems. Accounting is a necessary, though not sufficient, component of accountability. Accountability is a prerequisite for social responsibility, and sustainability becomes a, or the, primary component of social responsibility.

As the perspective of social accounting has broadened, the focus of analysis and action has become more pluralistic. Not only are shareholders' information needs important, so are the needs of other interested parties such as the community, employees, the biosphere, gender and sexuality, ethnic minorities, indigenous peoples, civil society, non-governmental organisations (NGOs), government and regulatory agencies and so on. Accountings emerge from the accountability criteria set forth by the interested party, and the outputs are directed towards their particular needs (Brown and Dillard, 2015). As noted in the previous paragraph, the scope of accounting and accountability has broadened from corporate social and environmental reporting to accountings for society and the environment, and these accountings are directed towards facilitating sustainable economic, social and natural systems.

Gray *et al.* (2014) point out that there are many different opinions regarding the extent of the problems, what changes are needed and how best to bring about the desired changes. Further, any changes made, especially in developed countries, regarding population, production and consumption, and wealth distribution would have a significant effect on, and would be significantly affected by, the organisations and institutions therein. The primary focus in the accounting literature has been to work with organisations, mainly large, publicly held entities and to some lesser, though not insignificant, extent NFP/NGOs and government organizations. Much of the work relates to issues related to corporate social responsibility.[8]

2.1 Sustainability and corporate social responsibility

In accounting, sustainability and corporate responsibility are, at times, used synonymously, the reason being that traditionally accounting has been very closely associated with an individual entity, and one of, if not the, primary responsibilities of the entity is sustainability. The two terms are not synonymous, however. For example, Gray and Milne (2004) argue that sustainability is a systemic concept and the corporation is a component within this socio-eco system. In fact, a component of the system can be unsustainable and the system itself can be sustainable. Dillard and Murray (2013) explain how CSR is concerned with corporate influence regarding not only sustainability but also business ethics, philanthropy, community investment, legal compliance, animal rights, corruption, workers' rights and welfare, and human rights.[9] Each of these areas includes issues not associated with the responsibilities of an entity, and thus, cannot be considered totally within the corporation's sphere of influence. Sustainability might be concerned with many, but not necessarily all, of these issues as well as additional ones such as wild life migration and preserves. The overlap of sustainability and CSR is a primary purview of concern.

Drawing on various sources, Dillard and Murray (2013: 4) consider CSR within an ethic of accountability.[10] As a component of CSR, sustainability issues can be considered within this context. Corporations are conceptualised as social systems that facilitate goal-directed social integration. That is, they bring together resources (financial, natural, human and technical) and coordinate activities to attain specified outcomes. The corporation is an identifiable legal entity created by, and within, the legal jurisdiction of society. The responsibilities of the corporation to society arise from, and are associated with, rights granted by society and accepted by corporate management. As such, the entity participates as a member of an ongoing community, with a history of past actions that provide a basis for projecting the consequences of future actions as well as the expectation to be held accountable for the outcomes of those actions.[11]

Essentially, CSR means acting in the public interest. Acting in the public interest denotes acting so as to enhance the well-being of society, not just a segment thereof. Sustainability posits that the well-being of society implies a sustainable engagement with natural, social and economic systems. One way to conceptualise the well-being of society is to consider by what criteria institutions are justified in, and by, society. What legitimates their existence? It might be argued that a, if not *the*, legitimating criteria for any societal institution is to provide for the long-term viability of a democratically governed society grounded in such values as justice, equality and trust, supported by sustainable economic, social and natural systems. The legitimacy and utility of corporations, as societal institutions, should be evaluated in terms of these criteria, but such a general statement, in some respects, begs the question: Any institution can be held accountable to these criteria but each might contribute in different ways – what is the unique contribution of business to society? How is it different from other societal institutions such as education, defense/security, religion or government? One might argue that the economic sector's primary contribution is to provide goods and services, employment opportunities and investment opportunities for the citizens of a society. As a prominent component of the economic sector, corporations are evaluated by their ability to do so relative to alternative institutions, for example the state.

Acting in the public interest provides a moral context within which rights and responsibilities can be contemplated and action evaluated. Normatively, and somewhat simplistically, these rights and responsibilities can be described as follows. Corporations and their management are granted the right by society to employ its economic assets (financial, natural, human and technological) so as to provide goods and services, employment opportunities and investment opportunities. The right to use these assets is based on the presumption that corporate managers can more effectively and efficiently employ these assets than another group. Given that they are granted the right to use society's assets, corporate management accepts a fiduciary responsibility regarding the use of these assets. Part of fulfilling this fiduciary responsibility is to be held accountable for the use of these assets. Part of this responsibility includes providing relevant and timely information so as to render their actions transparent and understandable. Much traditional and critical accounting research and criticism is directed at the means by which corporate management can and should provide such information.

Generally, less attention is paid to the rights and responsibilities of the citizens and the state as the administrative authority within a democratic society. In such a society, power is (theoretically) conferred by the sovereign will of the people. The state is granted the administrative authority for articulating, implementing and regulating the means by which the will of the people is carried out. Given that corporate management is seen as the group most capable of carrying out the task of providing goods and services, the state grants them the right to use those assets through various means. In light of the expectations imposed on management, the state accepts the responsibility to provide the necessary infrastructure to facilitate the provision of goods and services. These might include education, security, viable legal and regulatory systems, transportation systems and reasonable governance systems. Given that corporate management recognises its fiduciary responsibility to society, society has the responsibility of specifying the criteria by which corporations are held accountable. It is imperative for all members of society to ensure that these criteria emerge from a process whereby all have a voice and the outcome reflects the norms and values of society, not those of powerful special interest groups. This might result in multiple criteria set and, thus, multiple accountings.

For example, if society concludes that corporations should be held accountable for the extent to which their activities (products and processes) are sustainable, then there is an obligation to enact pluralistic democratic processes whereby the requisite criteria are specified. In return, corporate management has an obligation to provide the necessary information, and the state has an obligation to monitor, evaluate and regulate corporate actions. Such negotiations and determinations are decidedly political and need to be carried out within and through democratic processes.

2.2 CSR perspectives on sustainability

Brown and Fraser (2006, also, Gray *et al.*, 2014) identify three general perspectives, or conceptualisations, of sustainability: the business case; those of stakeholders; and a critical perspective.[12] Generally, the business case presumes that any actions undertaken by a business should be supportable from the perspective of maximising shareholder value, defined in economic terms. A stakeholder perspective sees the corporation as being responsible to stakeholders beyond just owners/shareholders, but the current structures and institutions are sufficient to bring about the necessary change. The critical perspective, as defined by Brown and Fraser, sees fundamental changes in the status quo being required before the necessary reforms can be realised. Under various assumptions and conditions, each of the positions presents a rational approach. The debates (Brown and Dillard, 2013a) as to how sustainability should be implemented and what are the appropriate evaluation criteria should be undertaken through democratic processes. The irresolvable conflicts and ideologies should be recognised and the differences confronted. As Mouffe (2013) argues, such is the essence of democracy. Without difference and contestation, there is not democracy. As a result of difference and contradiction, space is created for new understandings to emerge.

Consider the business case. When queried as to the purpose of a corporation, one of the most recognisable responses is to maximise long-term shareholder wealth. Shareholder wealth is accepted as the evaluation criteria by which the performance of organisation management is to be judged. The neo-classical economic axioms upon which the rationality of this response depends privileges markets and market valuations. Commodification is required to create a market wherein value is determined. If there is no market, that is if there is no value, there is no recognition of attributes and detriments. The market is presumed to impound any relevant information and thus make the appropriate trade-offs regarding scarce resources, or at least the best that can be made in the situation. Corporate management acquires society's economic resources through a system of property rights, contracts and market transactions. Management's fiduciary responsibility is best achieved by making decisions that provide the greatest net economic return, based on cost–benefit analysis, valued using (anticipated) market valuations.[13] The goods and services are those demanded by the market. Competition motivates the efficient utilisation of society's resources. Regulation and the control of markets stifle the ability of markets to regulate and signal the appropriate actions. Economic valuations impound all relevant trade-offs. The information required to evaluate performance is economic/financial information, currently primarily provided though the traditional, shareholder-oriented accounting systems.

Within the business case scenario, sustainability is seen to be best pursued through market activity and controlled through market discipline. Market valuation reflects the value of scarce resources. If there is no market valuation, then it is inappropriate to consider the item. Externalities are insignificant. Exchange value recognises all knowable contingencies and anticipated future needs, and accurately reflects use value. Maximising economic value is the criteria by which organisation management is to be evaluated regarding its fiduciary responsibilities. For example, as non-renewable fuel becomes more expensive due to the reduction in supply, corporate management will find ways to decrease the use of these fuels through substitutes or more efficient operations. Sustainability issues are addressed, and resolved, by managers pursuing courses of action that maximise economic value. The appropriate response to sustainability is therefore to behave so as to maximise shareholder value. If one accepts this proposition, then maximizing shareholder value must be shown to be the best vehicle for facilitating a democratically governed society grounded in such values as justice, equality and trust, supported by sustainable economic, social and natural systems. Here, the presumption is that the market for economic goods and services provides the best mechanism for making the necessary valuations and trade-offs regarding scarce resources, especially those used in providing goods and services. Sustainability needs are addressed through self-interested responses to market valuations, and any necessary steps towards sustainability will be motivated through the market. Beyond that, no better solutions can be derived.

A stakeholder perspective takes a more pluralistic view in proposing that the interests of parties that are not direct market participants should also be included in the deliberations regarding sustainability. This necessitates that the market be supplemented or regulated in some circumstances. Generally, this perspective holds that solutions can be found within the current modes of production, consumption and governance. There is a recognition that, given the expanded set of participants, there is the need for more political processes to address market failures, distribution inequities and externalities. The accountability criteria associated with the broader constituency groups enlarges the domain of management's fiduciary responsibilities and requires that management provides a wider range of information. Responsiveness to the multiplicity of groups impacted by corporate performance requires a more multidimensional approach to accountability, and more participatory forms of governance. Stakeholder rights to information and participation are necessary to both safeguard against potential abuses of power and to enable renegotiation of the rules of the game over time.

A critical perspective takes a more negative view of the possibilities of addressing the problems of sustainability within the current market-based system. Proponents of this approach generally take a more adversarial position relative to current social institutions such as corporations, stemming from their skepticism about the potential for 'real' accountability in the absence of radical change. They highlight the merging of corporate and state power under neo-liberalism, noting that while concepts like stakeholder dialogue sound promising in theory, structural inequalities are such that reformist efforts will more likely reinforce rather than change the status quo. Voluntarist social responsibility and reporting initiatives, along with modest legislative reforms, are seen to obscure harmful corporate agendas. By emphasising moderation and centrist politics, stakeholder perspectives are also viewed as inhibiting far-reaching change. Externally prepared counter-accounts are seen as having more potential to expose the basic contradictions and exploitative aspects of neo-liberal hegemony and thereby challenge the status quo. There is also an emphasis on the importance of linking such accounts with collective political action.

Sustainability is an issue (problem) and a process. Critical analysis, with its keen awareness of power and politics, provides a means for analysing, evaluating and actualising sustainability as a problem and as a process. Recognising the complexity and plurality of sustainability, how might we imagine a critical accounting project that includes sustainability as a major element? We now consider how we might carry out critical accounting research that matters in addressing sustainability. Since the business case seems to prevail (Brown and Fraser, 2006), we will feature it in the following discussion of critical accounting research.

3 Sustainability as critical accounting research that matters

Members of the academy have a responsibility to serve as the conscience, critic and counselor of society.[14] As noted in the last section, critical accounting researchers are primarily concerned if, and how, accountants, accounting and accountability encourage and enhance progressive social programs that improve the human condition, especially as it relates to the democratic enabling of traditionally underrepresented constituencies.[15] Democratic enabling is fostered by democratic institutions and processes. A critical perspective concerns the critique of accounting practice and technique in organisations and society so as to increase the understanding of, and involvement in, the political processes regarding issues that affect their well-being. As noted in the introduction, the critical accounting project, while successful, has not been without its conflicts and antagonisms. The question becomes how can, and should, we envision the critical accounting project into the future so as to be informed but not inhibited by predispositions and past practices or without compromising the commitment to radical political action.

One strategy for undertaking critical research that matters is to explicitly embrace sustainability as a fundamental element in need of study that is central to enhancing the human condition. We have previously proposed agonistic pluralism (agonistics) as providing useful insights into how we might sustain and enhance a pluralistic ethos within social and environmental accounting as well as critical accounting.[16] Here, we propose that agonistics represents a context for the meaningful treatment of sustainability from a critical perspective, providing a theoretical platform for putting forth a critical sustainability accounting project. Agonistics is not proposed as a solution but as a means by which space can be created wherein new imaginings can emerge. Below we address the mingling of the critical accounting project with sustainability. We argue that if the critical accounting project can sustain and enhance a pluralistic ethos, it is more likely to maintain and enhance its energising critical perspective. Sustainability, as an urgent and encompassing problem, can be constructively addressed from a critical accounting perspective, and the critical accounting project can usefully mobilise sustainability as a central, organising principle that reflects the systemic nature of the problems relating to social and environmental justice. Next, we provide a brief outline of agonistics as it has been applied in, and to, accounting.

Dillard and Brown (2015) discuss taking an agonistic attitude toward accounting. The approach is characterised as agonistic dialogic accounting and was initially introduced into the accounting literature by Brown (2009). Agonistics has been developed primarily by Mouffe (1995, 1999, 2000, 2005, 2013; Laclau and Mouffe, 1985/2001) and provides the theoretical basis for Brown's work. Mouffe's approach reflects a post-structuralist approach that recognises the centrality of the construction and reconstruction of identity in conjunction with Gramscian notions of hegemony and power.

Agonistics fosters a pluralistic ethos by recognising the significant role difference, conflict and contestation at play in political encounters. Diversity and irresolvable differences are a requisite for democracy, and disagreements among adversaries are addressed through dialogue and debate. The emphasis is not on consensus, however, as the irresolvable differences, and ineradicable antagonisms such as those noted among the various perspectives of sustainability, are recognised as are the irreducible asymmetrical power relationships among the adversaries. Differences are recognised and enhanced, not assumed away or ignored.[17] Instead of consensus, the aim is to develop democratic processes that recognise discursive practices as the primary means for establishing, and destabilising, hegemonic regimes (e.g. neo-liberalism and the related business case for sustainability). By engaging in these discursive interactions and practices, participants (individuals and groups) possess, construct and reconstruct, social and political identities. Through the construction and reconstruction of social and political identities, coalitions (chains of equivalence) form around core issues, and political power can shift, leading to change.

According to Mouffe (2013), agonistics facilitates struggles against dominant hegemonic regimes by providing a more realistic theorising of the context wherein political confrontations take place. There is no final reconciliation of divergent views or the equalization of power asymmetries. Mouffe (1999) argues that what deliberative democrats propose as consensus is always temporary and incomplete, because underlying ideological differences (antagonisms) still exist. Agreement reflects political compromise influenced by inequalities (power, knowledge, influence, etc.) among the participants. Ultimate closure is not possible. Coerced closure in effect silences the voices of the less powerful. As a consequence, democratic processes are necessary to ensure ongoing dissent and contestation.

4 Critical sustainability accounting

The field of sustainability is decidedly intertwined with the critical accounting project (Gray *et al.*, 2014). The concerns of a significant portion of those working in the field seem to coincide with the critical accounting project. In fact, one might argue that the critical accounting project has always, and foremost, been concerned with social sustainability, and there is currently the realisation that social sustainability is directly tied to environmental sustainability. The primary tension seems to arise from the relative importance of the issues and the strategies employed to address them.[18] Ours is not to engage in this debate at this point. What we do propose is that any endeavour, devoid of politics, is in danger of becoming vacuous and impotent (Broadbent and Laughlin, 2013; Dillard and Brown, 2012; Roslender and Dillard, 2003). If politics and power are given due consideration, it seems to us, sustainability and the critical accounting project have much in common and much to commend each other of. Ultimately, our hope would be that components of each project merge into what might be termed the 'critical sustainability accounting project', intent on addressing social justice in a holistic and realistic way. We see agonistics as a conceptual framework that can prove useful in pursuing this transformation from both a process (how the transformation takes place) and content (the form the outcomes take) perspective related to both design and application.

Critically pluralistic engagements directed by agonistic encounters recognise that the outcomes of a political process reflect "the constitution of an ensemble of practices that make possible the creation of democratic citizens" dependent upon the "*availability* of democratic forms of individuality and subjectivity" (Mouffe, 2000: 95, emphasis in original). Consensus is neither required nor expected. Passion, emotion and collective identification are recognised as present, divisive and important. Democratic values are fostered through multiple democratic institutions, discourses and life encounters. The presence of power and antagonisms inherent in social systems leads to difference and conflicts. According to Mouffe (2000), power and antagonisms are necessary as the means through which political identities are formed, evaluated and changed.

A critical sustainability accounting project facilitates, and emerges from, pluralistic and democratic debate among the various interested parties. While coalitions are formed around particular issues, a decided effort is made to maintain the sociopolitical identity of the parties so that some group is not coercively absorbed into another, reducing the diversity in the field. For example, concerning sustainable accounting and reporting practices, there may be significant agreement that the current voluntary reporting regime does not provide much relevant information regarding the activities of a corporation; however, there may be significant differences over what constitutes improvements and how to facilitate the requisite changes. Those advocating the business case for sustainability would advocate decidedly different approaches from those taking a more radical (critical) perspective.

An agonistic conceptualisation of the critical sustainability accounting project explicitly recognises the presence and influence of power, practices and discourse present in addressing sustainability issues. Given a pluralistic world, consensus without exclusion is not a realistic possibility. The political nature of social systems arises from power being a significant constitutive element in social relations and social identities. The constitution of social relations and identities is an ongoing, iterative process. Instead of attempting to neutralise or eliminate it, agonistics embraces the inevitable presence of power and attempts to (re)constitute forms of power consistent with democratic objectives. Further, agonistics theorises the fluidity of a social context that arises from unstable and evolving positions, identities and alliances.

Applying the ideas of agonistics to the critical sustainability accounting project highlights the political nature of sustainability, focusing attention on sociopolitical action. In doing so, the historical dialectical tensions associated with these issues become more obvious and accessible. The interconnectedness of the social and natural systems is evident as is the source(s) and influence of power. Disagreements are explicitly identified and seen as legitimate outgrowths of the unresolvable conflicts and the extant asymmetrical power relationships. We see little within such an approach to sustainability that is inconsistent with the tradition of the critical accounting project.

As the contested and pluralistic context is more clearly articulated and understood, we anticipate alternative (new) accountings to emerge at this intersection of critique and sustainability. Central to any justification of critical sustainability accounting is the energy and diversity that has been characteristic of the critical accounting project over the years. Political positions must be identified, articulated, adopted and defended. Alternative perspectives are entertained and seriously engaged. Agonistics ensures that each, often ideologically opposing, alternative is given due consideration, and choices are evaluated within the context of democratic processes that recognise the reality of irreconcilable differences and asymmetrical power relationships. It is also recognised that action is likely to be the result of power, at times disguised as consensus, which obscures an indeterminate condition. Explicitly recognising the political and contestable nature of problems associated with sustainability provides a space wherein alternative positions can be articulated and debated.

Critical sustainability accounting explicitly acknowledges the existence and relevance of alternative sociopolitical positions and seriously entertains the alternative futures that might ensue. Deciding requires serious articulation of the pros and cons of the anticipated outcomes as the various alternatives are considered within appropriate democratic processes that are based on, and attempt to address, the realistic presumption of coercion, distortion and exclusion. The democratic processes that recognise the conflict and debate ensure that all voices have the right to be heard and considered, though not necessarily accepted nor agreed with. The participants do agree that each has the right to their views and each is guaranteed a voice in the debate. From the debate and conflict emerge an awareness of new or hitherto unrecognised alternatives and newly gained understandings of alternative positions.

A critical sustainability accounting project considers how to advance a pluralistic ethos through the application of critical dialogue and debate resulting in the fashioning of more democratic structures. We propose that agonistics would be helpful in initiating and sustaining relationships within critical sustainability accounting as well as among those within the larger community of practitioners and academics as well as civil society. The outcome would be more extensive information and action sets leading to the recognition of a variety of positions and alternatives related to a wide range of different perspectives providing a comprehensive context for pluralistic engagement and decision making. For example, local unions may be more interested in addressing hazardous working conditions while other factions of the labour movement might be concerned with workplace grievances at the national or international levels. Environmentalists may be concerned with the hazardous materials not primarily because they create dangerous working conditions but because of their effect on the local environment. Other environmentalists concerned with the same toxic discharges might focus on species extinction and the larger eco-system associated with global resource extraction and consumption. Alternatively, some concerned with the current capitalist hegemony might address it by focusing on the exploitation of human, social and cultural capital whereas others might feel that the problems are related to wealth creation and distribution. Some may seek radical change while others may believe that reformist change initiatives are more likely to be successful. Possibilities exist for each of these disparate positions to recognise common interests and to join together in political action without each losing their unique differences. Parties may be partners on some issues and adversaries on others.

A critical sustainability project, based on agonistics, expects and attempts to maintain differences within and across various constituencies and academic disciplines. Unlike traditional accounting research, the political, emotional and subjective are acknowledged and encouraged. Developing process is seen as at least as important as specifying content, especially as the processes sustain pluralistic, democratic dialogue and debate yielding alternative engagement media, contested negotiation, expanded decision processes and inclusive evaluation mechanisms that move beyond the foundations in the various academic communities as well as in the dominant neo-liberal framing at the societal level. This pluralistic ethos facilitated by the project encourages and engages various areas of expertise that assist in identifying, explaining and justifying different ways of knowing, doing and being. The challenge in taking pluralism seriously in an attempt to bring about a viable and vibrant critical sustainability project is to maintain the decidedly critical attitude that has provided the direction and energy of the critical accounting project. In Mouffe's (2000) phrasing, how do we (re)claim the political, where the political refers to the inherent conflict and antagonism that is ever present arising out the construction and reconstruction of self and group identities emerging from the processes of social integration.[19]

5 The future envisioned

Taking sustainability seriously by the critical accounting project recognises the inherent tension and antagonisms among the various participants partially as the result of the economic, social and environmental aspects of sustainability. Because of these philosophical, ideological and practical differences, the potential exists for constructing different framings and more comprehensive decision processes. A pluralistic ethos ensures that what emerges meaningfully and legitimately incorporates the varied perspectives, values and discourses where both commonalities and differences are anticipated. To this end, Vinnari and Dillard (2016) develop an (ANT)agonistic framework by integrating actor–network theory (Latour, 2004) and agonistics (Brown, 2009) in an attempt to theorise the processes associated with critical sustainability accounting.

Alternative perspectives may range from structural Marxism to neo-classical economics with one favoring a revamping of capitalistic systems and the other advocating the commodification of externalities so as to directly incorporate them into regimes of market discipline. Critical sustainability accounting contestations "could be structured around documented typologies of competing ideological discourses" (Brown, 2009: 332). Admitting inherent conflicts reveals the underlying value judgments, assumptions, uncertainties and techniques associated with the different groups and ideologies. As differences in values and assumptions are revealed, the possibility arises for all participants to better understand and defend their own positions as well as those taken and defended by their antagonists. Such clarity enhances the chances for more authentic and constructive dialogue that differentiates between primary and secondary disagreements, differentiates between imagined and actual conflicts, and more clearly and seriously articulates the core differences and contestations. While the differences and conflicts are not eliminated, the possibilities for more informed understandings and actions are enhanced.

As those involved in the critical sustainability project become more accountable to each other, power becomes more defused and opportunities for coercion and imposition are reduced. Articulating and communicating competing positions facilitates more realistic comparisons that reveal obscured assumptions, values and interests. The partiality and inadequacy of alleged universal positions are exposed, and asymmetrical power relationships become more visible. The desired outcomes are to enhance democratic consciousness and greater mutual agonistic respect, making it more difficult for one collective or discourse to lay claim to an uncontestable resolution.

We propose critical sustainability accounting as a means for taking pluralism seriously so as to construct a more comprehensive platform for the critical accounting project to explicitly engage with multiple sociopolitical perspectives as they relate to social and environmental sustainability. A pluralistic ethos recognises that no one position covers the entire terrain. Entertaining alternative representations facilitates comparisons and evaluation criteria whereby one position can be judged as preferable from another from a particular perspective, but no one perspective can be recognised as complete. Agonistic contestation supports a more explicit expression of the different ideologies, values, assumptions, worldviews and power relationships that underpin the alternative positions as well as those that are privileged and those that are disadvantaged. Overlaps and discontinuities can also be identified and clarified. In doing so, the formation of political alliances can be facilitated.

We see a pressing need for a vibrant critical accounting project as critical accounting moves into the future as facilitating, and being facilitated by, broader sustainability movements and disciplines that bring together the social and environmental needs for people and planet. Critical sustainability acknowledges the constructive and liberating conflictual pluralism envisioned by an agonistic theorising. A pluralistic ethos is created allowing the past to inform, but not inhibit or predetermine the future, and our actions emerge from the appropriated critical energy and insights that come from genuine political and social critique.

Notes

1 The "critical accounting project" is not presumed to be a homogenous amalgam but is comprised of a diverse set of ideologies, methodologies, methods, etc., something that is very evident throughout this collection.

2 For this discussion, we will use the terms sustainability and sustainable development interchangeably. While recognising that they have been used to designate somewhat differing concepts, the differences are not particularly critical to this discussion.

3 See for example, Grey, 1994; Hoskins, 1994; Lehman, 1999, 2001; Neimark, 1990, 1994; Tinker, Lehman and Neimark, 1991.

4 As evidenced by the variety of perspectives represented in this volume, there is much diversity in what these ideals mean and how they should be implemented.

5 Critical, Marxist, post-Marxist, pragmatist, structuralist, post-structuralist, postmodernist, etc.

6 We would argue that the critical accounting project has, since its inception, been concerned with the sustainability of economic, social and natural systems in the way traditional social critics have been with regards to the human condition. What seems to vary are the ways the problem is framed and the theories and methods applied.

7 We, along with Gray (2002), see social accounting as representing the universe of all accountings, of which traditional financial accounting happens to be one. Our use of the term is presumed to include both social and environmental components. We also presume that economic dimensions are included within the social.

8 Corporate social responsibility and corporate responsibility are used interchangeably and are seen to include economic, social and environmental dimensions.

9 See Blowfield and Murray (2008) for elaboration.

10 See Dillard (2007, 2008, 2011) and Dillard and Brown (2012, 2014).

11 See Dillard and Yuthas (2001) based on Niebuhr (1963).

12 We recognise that these do not represent homogenous groups and there may be overlaps and commonalities among them.

13 Market valuations require exclusivity in use and rivalry in consumption and are properly discounted using the appropriate interest rate.

14 This does not imply that academics can remove themselves from the social context wherein they reside, but carry out these responsibilities fully engaged in that society and in full knowledge of the limitations thus imposed.

15 These groups include both human and nonhuman beings.

16 Brown (2009); Brown and Dillard (2013a, b, 2014); Brown, Dillard and Hopper (2015); Dillard and Brown (2012); Dillard and Roslender (2011); Dillard and Yuthas (2013); Vinnari and Dillard (2016). Dillard and Brown (2015) provides a review of this work.

17 This relates to the debates between the deliberative democrats (Habermas) and agonistic democrats (Mouffe). See Gaffikin and Morrissey (2011); Hillier and Healey (2010); and Kapoor (2008) for reviews. Also see Brown and Dillard (2013b).

18 See, for example, Everett (2004, 2007); Everett and Neu (2000); Lehman (1999, 2001, 2010); Spence (2009); Spence, Hussilos and Correa-Ruiz (2010); Tinker et al. (1991); Tinker and Gray (2003).

19 Mouffe (2000: 101) contrasts the political with politics – the aggregate "of practices, discourses, and institutions which seek to establish a certain order and organize human coexistence in conditions that are always potentially conflictual."

References

Bateson, G. (1972). *Steps to an Ecology of Mind*, Chicago, IL: University of Chicago Press.

Bateson, G. (1979). *Mind and Nature*. New York: Bantam Books.

Blowfield, M. and A. Murray (2008). *Corporate Responsibility: A Critical Introduction*, Oxford: Oxford University Press.

Broadbent, J. and R. Laughlin (2013). *Accounting Control and Controlling Accounting*, Bingley: Emerald Publishers.

Brown, J. (2009). "Democracy, sustainability and dialogic accounting technologies: taking pluralism seriously," *Critical Perspectives on Accounting*, 20(3): 313–42.

Brown, J. and Fraser, M. (2006). "Approaches and perspectives in social and environmental accounting: an overview of the conceptual landscape," *Business Strategy and the Environment*, 15(2): 103–17.

Brown, J. and J. Dillard (2013a). "Agonizing over engagement: SEA and the "death of environmentalism" debates," *Critical Perspectives on Accounting*, 24(1): 1–18.

Brown, J. and J. Dillard (2013b). "Critical accounting and communicative action: on the limits of consensual deliberation," *Critical Perspectives on Accounting*, 24(3): 176–90.

Brown, J. and J. Dillard (2014). "Integrated Reporting: On the need for broadening out and opening up," *Accounting, Auditing and Accountability Journal*, 27(7): 1120–1156.

Brown, J. and J. Dillard (2015). "Dialogical accountings for stakeholders: on opening up and closing down participatory governance," *Journal of Management Studies*, 52(7): 961–85.

Brown, J., J. Dillard and T. Hopper (2015). "Accounting, accountants, and accountability regimes in pluralistic societies: taking multiple perspectives seriously," *Accounting, Auditing and Accountability Journal*, 28(5): 626–50.

Dillard, J. (2007). "Legitimating the social accounting project: an ethic of accountability," in J. Unerman, B. O'Dwyer and J. Bebbington (eds): *Sustainability Accounting and Accountability*, London: Routledge Press.

Dillard, J. (2008). "An ethic of accountability," *Research on Professional Responsibility and Ethics in Accounting*, 13: 1–18.

Dillard, J. (2011). "Framing sustainability within an ethic of accountability," in S. McNall, J. Hershauser and G. Basile (eds): *Sustainable Business Practices: Challenges, Opportunities, and Practices*, Vol. 1, Santa Barbara, CA: Praeger.

Dillard, J. and K. Yuthas (2001). "A responsibility ethic of audit expert systems," *Journal of Business Ethics*, 30(4): 337–59.

Dillard, J. and R. Roslender (2011). "Taking pluralism seriously: embedded moralities in management accounting and control systems," *Critical Perspectives on Accounting*, 22(2): 135–47.

Dillard, J. and J. Brown (2012). "Agonistic pluralism and imagining CSEAR into the future," *Social and Environmental Accountability Journal*, 32(1): 3–16.

Dillard, J. and A. Murray (2013). "Introduction: Corporate Social Responsibility – a research agenda," in K. Haynes, A. Murray and J. Dillard (eds): *Corporate Social Responsibility: A Research Handbook*, London: Routledge.

Dillard, J. and K. Yuthas (2013). "Critical dialogics, agonistic pluralism, and accounting information systems," *International Journal of Accounting Information Systems*, 14(2): 113–19.

Dillard, J. and J. Brown (2014). "Taking pluralism seriously within an ethic of accountability," in S. Mintz (ed.): *Accounting for the Public Interest: Perspectives on Accountability, Professionalism and Role in Society*. New York: Springer.

Dillard, J. and J. Brown (2015). "Broadening out and opening up: an agonistic attitude toward progressive social accounting," *Sustainability, Accounting, Management and Policy Journal*, 6(2): 243–66.

Dillard, J. and E. Vinnari (2016). "A case study of critique: critical perspectives on critical accounting," *Critical Perspectives on Accounting*, 43: 88–109.

Everett, J. (2004). "Exploring (false) dualisms for environmental accounting praxis," *Critical Perspectives on Accounting*, 15(8): 1061–84.

Everett J. (2007). "Fear, desire, and lack in Deegan and Soltys's social accounting research: an Australasian perspective," *Accounting Forum* 31(1): 91–7.

Everett, J and D. Neu (2000). "Ecological modernization and the limits of environmental accounting?" *Accounting Forum* 24(1): 5–29.

Gaffikin, F. and M. Morrissey (2011). *Planning in Divided Cities: Collaborative Shaping of Contested Space*, West Susssex: Wiley-Blackwell.

Gray, R. (2002). "The social accounting project and *Accounting Organizations and Society*: privileging engagement, imaginings, new accountings and pragmatism over critique?" *Accounting, Organizations and Society*, 27(7): 687–708.

Gray, R. and M. Milne (2004). "Towards reporting on the triple bottom line: Marages, methods and myths," in: A. Henriques and J. Richardson (eds): *The Triple Bottom Line: Does it all add up?* London: Earthscan.

Gray, R., D. Owen and K. Maunders (1987). *Corporate Social Reporting: Accounting and Accountability*, Hemel Hempstead: Prentice-Hall.

Gray, R., D. Owen and C. Adams (1996). *Accounting and Accountability: Changes and Challenges in Corporate Social and Environmental Reporting*, London: Prentice-Hall.

Gray, R., C. Adams and D. Owen (2014). *Accountability, Social Responsibility and Sustainability: Accounting for Society and the Environment*, Harlow, UK: Pearson.

Grey, C. (1994). "Debating Foucault: a critical reply to Neimark," *Critical Perspectives on Accounting*, 5(1): 5–24.

Hillier, J and P. Healey (2010). *The Ashgate Research Companion to Planning Theory*, Surrey: Ashgate.

Hoskin, K. (1994). "Boxing clever: For, against and beyond Foucault in the battle for accounting theory," *Critical Perspectives on Accounting*, 5(1): 57–85.

Kapoor I. (2008). *The Postcolonial Politics of Development*. New York: Routledge.

Laclau, E. and C. Mouffe (1985/2001). *Hegemony and Socialist Strategy: Towards a Radical Democratic Politics*, 2e, London: Verso.

Latour, B. (2004). *Politics of Nature*. Cambridge, MA: Harvard University Press.

Lehman, G. (1999). "Disclosing new worlds: a role for social and environmental accounting and auditing," *Accounting, Organizations and Society*, 24(3): 217–41.

Lehman, G. (2001). "Reclaiming the public sphere: problems and prospects for corporate social and environmental accounting," *Critical Perspectives on Accounting*, 12(6): 713–33.

Lehman, G. (2010). "Perspectives on accounting, commonalities and the public sphere," *Critical Perspectives on Accounting*, 21(8): 724–38.

Mouffe, C. (1995). "Democracy, pluralism: a critique of the rationalist approach," *Cardozo Law Review*, 16(5): 1533–45.

Mouffe C. (1999). "Deliberative democracy or agonistic pluralism?" *Social Research*, 66(3): 74–58.

Mouffe, C. (2000). *The Democratic Paradox*, London/New York: Verso Books.

Mouffe, C. (2005). *On the Political*, London/New York: Routledge

Mouffe, C. (2013). *Agonistics: Thinking the World Politically*, London: Verso Books.

Neimark, M. (1990). "The king is dead: Long live the king," *Critical Perspectives on Accounting*, 1(1): 103–14.

Neimark, M. (1994). "Regicide revisited: Marx, Foucault and accounting," *Critical Perspectives on Accounting*, 5(1): 87–108.

Niebuhr, R. (1963). *The Responsible Self*. San Francisco, CA: Harper Press.

Roslender, R. and J. Dillard (2003). "Reflections on the interdisciplinary perspectives on accounting project," *Critical Perspectives on Accounting*, 14(3): 325–52.

Spence C. (2009). "Social accounting's emancipatory potential: a Gramscian critique," *Critical Perspectives on Accounting*, 20(2): 205–27.

Spence, C., J. Husillos and C. Correa-Ruiz (2010). "Cargo cult science and the death of politics: a critical review of social and environmental accounting research," *Critical Perspectives on Accounting*, 21(1): 76–89

Tinker, T. and R. Gray (2003). "Beyond a critique of pure reason: from policy to politics to praxis in environmental and social research," *Accounting, Auditing and Accountability Journal*, 16(5): 727–61.

Tinker, T, C. Lehman and M. Neimark (1991). "Falling down the hole in the middle of the road: political quietism in corporate social reporting," *Accounting, Auditing and Accountability Journal*, 4(2): 28–54.

United Nations World Commission on Environment and Development (1987). *Our Common Future (The Brundtland Report)*. Oxford: Oxford University Press.

Vinnari, E. and J. Dillard (2016): "(ANT)agonistic democratic processes: pluralistic politicization through social and environmental accounting," *Critical Perspectives on Accounting*, 39: 25–44.

Watts, J. (2010). "Are accountants the last hope for the world's ecosystems?" *The Guardian*. https://www.theguardian.com/environment/2010/oct/28/accountants-hope-ecosystems.

Appendix

A/42/427. Our Common Future: Report of the World Commission on Environment and Development

Our Common Future, Chapter 2: Towards Sustainable Development

1   Sustainable development is development that meets the needs of the present without com-
    promising the ability of future generations to meet their own needs. It contains within it
    two key concepts:

*   the concept of 'needs', in particular the essential needs of the world's poor, to which
    overriding priority should be given; and
*   the idea of limitations imposed by the state of technology and social organization on
    the environment's ability to meet present and future needs.

2   Thus the goals of economic and social development must be defined in terms of sustain-
    ability in all countries – developed or developing, market-oriented or centrally planned.
    Interpretations will vary, but must share certain general features and must flow from a con-
    sensus on the basic concept of sustainable development and on a broad strategic framework
    for achieving it.
3   Development involves a progressive transformation of economy and society. A development
    path that is sustainable in a physical sense could theoretically be pursued even in a rigid
    social and political setting. But physical sustainability cannot be secured unless development
    policies pay attention to such considerations as changes in access to resources and in the
    distribution of costs and benefits. Even the narrow notion of physical sustainability implies
    a concern for social equity between generations, a concern that must logically be extended
    to equity within each generation.

III. Strategic Imperatives

27   The world must quickly design strategies that will allow nations to move from their pre-
     sent, often destructive, processes of growth and development onto sustainable develop-
     ment paths. This will require policy changes in all countries, with respect both to their
     own development and to their impacts on other nations' development possibilities. (This
     chapter concerns itself with national strategies. The required reorientation in international
     economic relations is dealt with in *Chapter 3*.)
28   Critical objectives for environment and development policies that follow from the concept
     of sustainable development include:

*   reviving growth;
*   changing the quality of growth;
*   meeting essential needs for jobs, food, energy, water, and sanitation;
*   ensuring a sustainable level of population;
*   conserving and enhancing the resource base:
*   reorienting technology and managing risk; and merging environment and economics
    in decision making.

25

ACTOR–NETWORK THEORY AND CRITICAL ACCOUNTING RESEARCH

Jane Baxter and Wai Fong Chua

1 Introduction

In this chapter we explore the critical possibilities of actor–network theory (ANT).[1] ANT has informed accounting studies published in high-profile journals, such as *Accounting, Accountability and Auditing, Accounting, Organizations and Society, Critical Perspectives on Accounting* and *Management Accounting Research*. These journals share a common genesis: a desire to give voice to methodologies and methods that challenge mainstream approaches to research and problematise our understandings of the *status quo* – or how we have normalised the functioning of society, organisations and individuals (Roslender and Dillard, 2003). As such, ANT has been positioned as a critical counterpoint to mainstream theorisations of accounting practice.

Nonetheless, commentators from sociology, management and accounting have asserted that ANT does not fulfil a critical role (Bloor, 1999; Hopper and Bui, 2016; Whittle and Spicer, 2008). Correspondingly, accounting researchers who have adopted ANT (for example, Briers and Chua, 2001; Chua, 1995; Dambrin and Robson, 2011; Jeacle, 2003; Preston, Cooper and Coombs, 1992) may find it useful to review the capabilities and limitations of ANT in constituting critical narratives. Considered against this background, it is pertinent to ask if the critical aspirations of ANT are misplaced. We argue this is *not* the case. The overall conclusion of this chapter is that ANT enables a critical accounting research trajectory. Moreover, critical research is an organic concept. There are multiple possibilities for critique and ANT is helping to reframe critique in contemporarily relevant ways.

In Section 2 we provide an overview of ANT and its application to critical accounting research, with criticisms of ANT being discussed in Section 3. Section 4 considers how ANT is reframing critique. Opportunities for future critical accounting research, reflecting the rejuvenating potential of ANT, are outlined in Section 5. A brief conclusion follows in Section 6.

2 The critical project, ANT and accounting research

The relationship between academia and accounting practice is complex, generating much debate without any definitive conclusions (see, for example, Ahrens *et al.*, 2008; Baxter Boedker and Chua, 2008). Nonetheless, there is a lingering belief that we *should* have an impact on practice – be it through traditional modes of teaching and the dissemination of research, or more active forms of engagement with professional and public spheres (Sikka and Willmott, 1997). It is in this context that critical accounting assumes importance, aiming to facilitate changed worldviews and renewed forms of practice.

To this end, critical accounting scholars have mobilised a variety of theoretical perspectives (Baxter and Chua, 2003), highlighting the interests embedded in accounting and the possibilities of change. These theoretical perspectives have included Marxism (Hopper and Armstrong, 1991; Shaoul, 1998; Tinker, Merino and Neimark, 1982), Habermas' theory of communicative rationality (Broadbent, Laughlin and Read, 1991), and various forms of postmodernism, represented by the work of Judith Butler (Messner, 2009; Roberts, 2009), Michel Foucault (Burchell 1985; Knights and Collinson, 1987; Miller and O'Leary, 1987) and Nigel Thrift (Boedker and Chua, 2013), for example.

Concern has been expressed that critical research risks becoming "obsessed with epistemological and ontological dilemmas" (Alcadipani and Hassard, 2010: 4), however. The accounting literature is not immune to such criticism. There has been healthy debate distinguishing the non-positivist philosophical underpinnings of critical accounting research (Chua, 1986; Morgan, 1988; Johnson, 1995; Lowe, 2004). Notwithstanding, in the main, critical accounting has great potential to contribute to the social sciences because it is manifested primarily in studies incorporating rich empirical research, highlighting how practices are "less obvious, natural, rational and well-ordered" (Alvesson and Deetz, 2006: 275). More recently, ANT has become prominent in its adoption by critical accounting researchers (Justesen and Mouritsen, 2011; Hopper and Bui, 2016).

ANT has offered a different pathway for critical accounting research. ANT is based on the sociology of translation, propelled by the writings of Latour (1987, 2005), Callon (1986), Law (1992) and others, for example Moll (2002). Central to ANT is the notion of a heterogeneous network. Law (1992: 380) states, "This lies at the heart of ANT, and is a way of suggesting that society, organizations, agents, and machines are all *effects* generated in patterned networks of diverse (not simply human) materials." Accordingly, accounting practices are not afforded any essential quality. Accounting is the result of situated practices, shaped by diverse, fluid and partial networks of enmeshed human and non-human actors.

Chapman, Chua and Mahama (2015) outline what they consider to be the three basic principles of ANT. These are generalised symmetry, recursivity and radical indeterminancy. Generalised symmetry signifies a shift from prevailing modernist views wherein scientific knowledge has been privileged over everyday ways of knowing. According to ANT, we must heed the effects of nature and society in research-based explanations (Latour, 1987). This has found expression in a very particular mandate, namely, researchers must take human actors *and* non-human actors or 'things' seriously. Both have agency or socio-material effects on other actors in a network. We cannot understand practice if our accounts are asymmetrical, privileging either social or natural accounts. Correspondingly, ANT encourages researchers to follow networks of people and non-human artefacts that shape accounting work. Qu and Cooper's (2011) research on the balanced scorecard highlights networks of human actors, such as consultants, managers and staff from a number of regions of a healthcare organisation, as well as non-human actors, including flip-charts, reports and emails. Accordingly, they incorporated the heterogeneity of actors engaged in the production of an accounting practice.

Recursivity emphasises that networks are constituted by, and constitutive of, heterogeneous assemblages of practices. Recursivity points to the flux and fragility of networks of association. ANT encourages us to problematise the seeming stability of some networks, as well as examining the instability of others (Law, 1992). How do some networks achieve stability, overcoming resistance, whilst others remain unsettled and contested? The balanced scorecard project of Qu and Cooper (2011), for example, did not become a stable and fact-like aspect of organisational functioning, despite the intentions of a number of actors. In comparison, Dambrin and Robson (2011) characterise a performance measurement system in the French pharmaceutical industry, which, notwithstanding its glaring incompleteness, operated with little resistance from sales personnel whose bonuses and promotional prospects were mediated by its opaque calculative practices.

Finally, 'radical indeterminancy' refers to a more nuanced construction of actors' interests. ANT displays an aversion to metanarratives that assume society or social structures are the result of invariant macro-interests. In contrast, ANT does not assume actors have simple, stable and unitary interests. In keeping with the notion of heterogeneity, actors have multiple, shifting and diverse interests. The mobilisation of actors' interests is central to processes of association. Actors form associations because of a convergence of their interests. This creates ties of varying strength and length, moderated by practices of *interessement*, understood as the co-option of others into projects (Callon, 1986). Ongoing differences in actors' interests lead to local resistance, assuming the form of contra strategies. To illustrate: Briers and Chua (2001) consider how a standard costing system began to lose support, becoming a matter of concern, as the interests of consultants, managers, engineers and business analysts shifted with the changing strategy of the organisation. Successive experiments to produce more robust product costs, which incorporated combinations of standard costing, activity-based costing, just-in-time control, revised business models and business process improvement, failed to enrol and stabilise the interests of actors. Eventually, activity-based costing emerged as the costing system championed by top management. This was facilitated by a global boundary object, "world best practice," which enabled heterogeneous local actors to become aligned with this new accounting technology (Briers and Chua, 2001: 265).

In addition to the three principles of ANT outlined by Chapman *et al.* (2015), we also include a principle of performativity (Callon, 2006). Performativity encapsulates the ontological conundrum posed by Callon, whereby ANT seeks to understand how a particular practice is "outside of the reality that it describes and simultaneously participate[s] in the construction of that reality as an object acting on it" (2006: 7). In so doing, ANT eschews an ostensive view of the world seeking essentialist representations of practice. In comparison, performativity highlights how particular practices, embedded in shifting networks of local actors and their associated discourses and artefacts, fabricate our world in multiple and contingent ways. As Mouritsen states in relation to his performative analysis of intellectual capital statements, an accounting technology "does not have a character one time and for all" (2006: 828). In this vein, Boedker (2010) elaborates how performativity highlights the futility of making firm statements regarding the fit of various strategic archetypes and management accounting practices.

ANT's emphasis on performativity has focused the attention of critical accounting research on the constitutive and multiple possibilities of accounting calculations (Justesen and Mouritsen, 2011). More generally, Miller and O'Leary (2007:701) highlight the important role that accounting calculations assume as "mediating instruments" between ideas and workable practices, in this instance, outlining the mediating role of capital budgeting practices in the coordination of the high technology microprocessor industry. The subsequent field studies of Mouritsen, Hansen and Hansen (2009) and Revillino and Mouritsen (2015) have typified how accounting calculations augment and regenerate innovation by providing new insights, mobilising action that is sometimes surprising. Even within a firm, accounting may be performed in varied ways. Mouritsen (1999) provides an account of how the calculation of a firm's indirect cost pool was constructed both as an object requiring control and an object promoting flexibility and customer service in different departments of the same organisation. As such, ANT has helped us to appreciate that the performativity and effects of accounting are differential and multiple, dependent importantly on the networks of human and non-human agents in which accounting calculations are constituted and also constitutive.

3 Criticisms of ANT

Despite its popularity, ANT is not immune to criticism, even from other critical researchers. In a nutshell, some critical researchers have stated that whilst ANT is "a valuable framework for the empirical analysis of the organising process, it cannot provide a critical account of organization" (Whittle and Spicer, 2008: 611). Tinker associates ANT with political conservativism. Bloor (1999) describes Latour's ideas as "a step backwards" (2005: 82), with Roslender arguing that postmodern theories, such as ANT, are 'regressive' because they are "devoid of any wider significance" (1996: 541) as a result of being seduced by local forms of knowledge, discourse and resistance. Whilst some of this crossfire is an inevitable outcome of different ways of seeing the world, researchers mobilising ANT need to be aware of arguments that may be raised against their endeavours, as well as emergent rejoinders from like-minded scholars. Such awareness may inform a more reflexive application of ANT and developments in critical accounting research, a theme considered later in this chapter.

The tenor of the claims just outlined is developed in commentaries outlining ANT's perceived critical deficiencies. For the purposes of this chapter, we will consider the recent comments of Hopper and Bui (2016). They listed five main criticisms of ANT: first, its treatment of non-human actors; second, the immorality of treating all actors as theoretically equal; third, a lack of normative criteria; fourth, a focus on micro-accounts of practice, ignoring important institutions; and, fifth, a failure to explain how and why networks have come into being (see Hopper and Bui, 2016: 14). We consider each of these points in turn.

First, there are genuine concerns about the status of non-human actors and their ability to "mobilise changes" (Hopper and Bui, 2016: 14). These are expressed as criticisms of the so-called agency imputed to non-human actors, a feature of Callon's account of the scallops of St. Brieuc Bay (Callon, 1986). This criticism is misdirected, however: ANT does not claim that non-human actors have intentions like human agents. Rather ANT supports the idea that non-human actors, when seen as part of a heterogeneous network, have *effects* on other actors (Law, 1992). Even Bloor, who is highly critical of Latour's work, argues that this "agency of things," an ability to stimulate our senses and inform decision-making processes, is recognised in the social sciences and is not particular to ANT (1999: 91). Nonetheless, questions have been raised regarding the characterisation of commonly accepted affordances of non-human actors (Whittle and Spicer, 2008). For example, incomplete performance measures are imagined to drive dysfunctional behaviour. However, this is more correctly directed at the unreflexive practices of some researchers, as ANT encourages an unpacking of such facts and their naturalisation, eschewing essentialist explanations of practice. Perhaps a more valid criticism than the one posed by Hopper and Bui (2016) is the failure of extant studies employing ANT to recognise the role of *sentient* actors who are non-human, such as animals. We will address this in a following section.

The second point canvassed by Hopper and Bui (2016) relates to the asserted immorality of ANT, stemming from a potentially equal characterisation of actors (Hopper and Bui, 2016). This criticism is not directed at the equal or symmetrical treatment of human and non-human agents. It is directed at an undifferentiated understanding of human actors in heterogeneous, flat networks. Despite an objective to follow actors connected to a network, the outcomes of ANT are argued to be perverse. There is concerted criticism that ANT is skewed towards "the victors" (Whittle and Spicer, 2008: 622), with the capacity to shape translation being unequally dispersed in actor-networks. There is an argued managerial bias in ANT, wherein managers, consultants and other key actors have dominated accounts of practice (Alcadipani and Hassard, 2010). Accounting research is no exception (Briers and Chua, 2001; Qu and Cooper, 2011). Whilst some would argue that this is the way of the world, Clarke (2002) makes the salient point that

ANT pays scant attention to actors operating at the margins of a network, or those silenced by their exclusion.

It could be countered, however, that there is no instrinsic predisposition to focus on victors and, indeed, it is not obvious that fishermen interested in scallops and buyers and sellers at strawberry markets could be seen as such. At the very least, ANT highlights how the agency of victors is fragile and that life could be otherwise. Similar to earlier critical research, ANT encourages analysis of 'the taken for granted' and the effort needed on the part of both humans and nonhumans for networks of interest to hold. Most particularly, ANT has enabled a re-examination of the power of science, its methods and the role of calculation in networks of influence (Latour, 1987; Latour and Woolgar, 1986).

The third limitation concerns ANT's lack of normative criteria. Traditional critical theory has a clear mandate, being the satisfaction and development of human needs (Alvesson and Deetz, 2006). Ideology critique provides normative criteria to facilitate this, mobilising evaluative benchmarks such as liberty, rights, emancipation, freedom from domination, equal opportunity and so on (Arrington and Watkins, 2002; Alvesson and Deetz, 2006). This enables extant practices to be critiqued in terms of their failings in relation to the unequal allocation of resources across classes, the domination of particular races by others, and the different life chances attributed to gender, for instance. In comparison, ANT is claimed to provide detailed descriptions of practice, which "ignore relations of oppression and sidestep any normative assessment of existing organizational forms" (Whittle and Spicer, 2008: 263).

It is certainly the case that writers like Latour have strong concerns about metanarratives that blackbox 'the social' into classes with predetermined interests. And indeed, ANT explicitly seeks to offer an alternative mode of theorising. The desire for a reinstatement of such normative criteria does not address the criticisms raised by Latour and his colleagues. Neither does it engage with other writings that argue that ideals thought to be enlightening or emancipatory or truthful at a particular socio-historical juncture, may also enslave and be productive of power. Foucault points out that "we are subjected to the production of truth through power and we cannot exercise power except through the production of truth" (1980: 93). He continues:

> I believe that anything can be deduced from the general phenomenon of the domination of the bourgeois class. What needs to be done is something quite different. One needs to investigate historically, and beginning from the lowest level, how mechanisms of power have been able to function.
>
> *(1980: 100)*

We are not claiming that ANT is motivated by the same concerns that drove Foucault's analysis of power-knowledges. Instead, it is to point out that the use of explicit normative criteria could oppress and may not perform an emancipatory function and hence question the imperative for this to be the benchmark of valid critique. Further, this criticism appears to be grounded in a discredited distinction between amoral description and normative analysis.

In addition, it may be argued that the detailed descriptions proffered by ANT allow us to understand how forms of resistance emerge, and how organisational participants engaging in acts of bricolage may achieve their interests with available resources. For example, Andon Baxter and Chua (2007) describe the resistance of call-centre staff to forms of performance measurement that shifted the emphasis towards efficiency rather than the quality of customer service. This resulted in a review by, and revision of, the performance measures by management. Likewise, McNamara, Baxter and Chua (2004) discuss the bricolage undertaken at an organisational periphery, with local action informing practices at the organisational core. Consequently, we contend that ideals of resistance and change do have a home in ANT.

ANT's emphasis on practices informs the fourth misgiving voiced by Hopper and Bui, namely ANT's seeming lack of attention to "powerful institutions such as corporations and the state" (2016: 14). This assertion is misplaced because governments and corporations are commonly recognised as actors involved in chains of association and translation (Andon *et al.*, 2007; Miller, 1991; Dambrin and Robson, 2011). Yet this avoids the substance of Hopper and Bui's assertion, wherein ANT is criticised because of a lack of acknowledgement of social structures. However, their contrary position is a recipe for never-ending disappointment according to Latour:

> [S]o much work has been dedicated to notions such as society, norms, values, culture, structure, social context, all terms that aim at designating what gives shape to micro interaction. But then, once this new level has been reached, a second type of dissatisfaction begins. Social scientists now feel that something is missing, that the abstraction … seems too great, and that one needs to reconnect, through an opposite move, back to the flesh-and-blood locational situations from which they started.… And so on *ad infinitum*.
>
> *(1999: 17)*

Latour proposed instead the notion of a "circulating entity." A circulating entity is a "*summing* up of interactions" in inscriptions and other artefacts (1999: 17). Circulating entities lead to local and contingent materialisations of our world (Latour, 1996, 1999). Yet ardent critics of Latour maintain that studying compressed, flat, circulating entities fails to recognise the hierarchical distribution of opportunities in actor-networks (Whittle and Spicer, 2008). Even those who are sympathetic to ANT, such as Clarke (2002), argue that the social world unfolds in well-worn patterns. And, in some ways, it is difficult to argue with this, given our lived experiences. However, ANT questions naturalised ways of acting. Why are some forms of interaction stabilised, overcoming resistance and controversy, appearing to be "macro-social" (Law, 1992: 380)? And we agree that future research could focus more on understanding not only the fragility and fluidity of entities but also on how and why some networks and chains remain relatively stable. The concept of 'institution' is not one that ANT engages with, except to deconstruct (see Latour, 2013). Nonetheless, it is instructive to bear in mind that even stabilised practices and august institutions such as 'Science' are fragile and fluid constructions. An understanding of durability and flux is central to ANT.

The final criticism raised by Hopper and Bui (2016) relates to their declaration that ANT does not explain the formation of networks. The validity of this claim depends on how you choose to interpret its intent, however. To an extent, we agree with Hopper and Bui because ANT does not encourage the types of histories that have distinguished Marxist-influenced accounting research (Tinker *et al.*, 1982), or even postmodern narratives detailing the conditions of possibility enabling the emergence of particular programmatic discourses and their emblematic practices (Burchell *et al.*, 1985; Loft, 1986; Miller and O'Leary, 1987). Consequently, some researchers have adopted a "pick and mix" approach (Whittle and Spicer, 2008: 624), combining ANT and Foucault's historiography. This has led to bristling criticism that is beyond the scope of the chapter (Tinker, 2005).

Nonetheless, Hopper and Bui's (2016) point is difficult to sustain when the principles of ANT are given due consideration. ANT does not study ready-made facts (Latour, 1987). ANT studies facts-in-the-making or the problematisation of taken-for-granted facts. This enables us to understand how and why networks were formed. For example, Jeacle's (2003) study of the adoption of standard sizing for ready-made clothing in the early twentieth century narrates why networks of association were formed, that is, to manage increasing overhead costs associated with alterations, and how actors were enrolled in this problematisation, that is, to achieve cost control, to improve buying performance and to improve the quality and consistency of the supply of ready-made garments.

4 ANT and the reframing of critique

Whilst these criticisms are acknowledged, it is our contention that ANT offers a vital and alternative form of critical social science. Indeed, Latour maintains that ANT continues, "a prestigious critical tradition … not letting it die away, or 'dropping into quiescence' like a piano no longer struck" (2004: 248). In brief, ANT epitomises critical social science because it highlights the possibility of change. Detailed accounts of taken-for-granted local associations and translations have a capacity to disrupt our conceptions of how practice operates, leading to new sets of practices being elevated and subjected to subsequent analysis and disruption (Doolin and Lowe, 2002). As such, ANT embodies a reflexive and recursive cycle of problematisation, highlighting the possibility that things can be otherwise (Alcadipani and Hassard, 2010). By attending to local contingent practices, ANT does not reify preordained orderings of society. ANT also liberates critical theory with respect to interests. Attending to the heterogeneity of local, contingent practices means that the interests of actors are not concealed by "modes of domination" (Doolin and Lowe, 2002: 73) but materialised in particular inscriptions, artefacts and translations. ANT replaces the presumed universalism, predetermination and permanence of interests with contingent, local and fragile translations.

As such, ANT reframes critical theory. This is because critique, as it is conventionally understood, has "run out of steam" (Latour, 2004: 225, 2010). The world has changed. Marxism is no longer as potent a global force after the dissolution of the USSR. Similarly, democracies built on Habermas' communicative rationality have not come to fruition. Considered against this backdrop, extant critical traditions are argued to be "fighting enemies long gone" and "conquering territories that no longer exist" (Latour, 2004: 225). Similarly, the analytical manoeuvres of ideology critique have become hackneyed. Working from a "deep dark" place, that is, an arena of privilege accessible only to those trained in debunking the beliefs of others, critical theorists make a series of startling but predictable revelations (Latour, 2004: 229). Our fetishes – the beliefs of the "great unwashed" – are the inexorable outcome of forces of power, domination, class, institutional structures, gender and race, to name the likely suspects (Latour, 2004: 239). Only those working from a well-rehearsed critical script are capable of seeing the hidden structures imprinted on our beliefs and practices. Where does this leave us?

ANT maintains a "critical spirit" (Latour, 2004: 225) but in a different way. It is the purpose of ANT to emancipate – but to emancipate society from "prematurely naturalized objectified facts" (2004: 227). Objectified facts are treated as black boxes and thereby taken for granted and no longer questioned or subject to resistance. Indeed, it has become the ongoing project of critical accounting researchers invoking ANT to engage with the problematisation of accounting 'facts'. As Peter Miller, who has been prominent in leading this vanguard, states:

> This problematizing of existing practices is itself an accomplishment. 'Problems' have to be made recognizable, a particular perception had to form, people have to be convinced that problems are intrinsic to a particular device rather than contingent, a measure of agreement has to be reached as to the nature of the problems identified, a consensus has to form that something needs to be done, and another way of calculating that fits the problem identified has to be made available. Then, and only then, do things change.
> *(Miller, 1998: 606)*

Briers and Chua (2001) illustrate this process of problematisation in action, outlining how the cost of a particular aluminium product had not been scrutinised for years, becoming fact-like as a result. But facts are fragile and tentative stabilisations held together by networks of associations, translating and mediating the interests of different actors. Facts can be destabilised, contested and re-negotiated as a result of a weakening of the ties in a network. In Briers and Chua's (2001) field study, this is associated with the introduction of new human actors (consultants and a top manager), a non-human actor offering an alternative but appealing way of calculating (activity-based costing) and the successful mobilisation of the interests of these actors. In another field study, Skaerbaek and Tryggestad (2010) narrate how a group of Danish mariners concerned about their livelihood contested the calculations of managers and consultants embedded in corporate strategy. Their research highlights pertinently that actors who are not part of "the governing strategic centre" may problematise seemingly objective facts also (Skaerbaek and Tryggestad, 2010: 111), reminding us of the potential power of actors on the periphery of networks.

Correspondingly, the critical spirit invoked by ANT replaces matters of fact with situated "matters of concern" (Latour, 2004: 242), while matters of concern embody politics – described as the politics of "misfires" by Callon (2010: 163), invoking shifting possibilities of inclusion and exclusion in relation to the framing of practices. Even seemingly settled naturalisations of practice are sites of ongoing political activity, being "constantly tested, criticized, debated, reconstructed and consequently subjected to endless redefinitions and reconfigurations" (Callon, 2010: 165). This is exemplified by Robson's critical mobilisation of ANT, questioning *why* accounting practices have adopted "numerical metaphors" (1992: 703) – in his case, explained by a need for stable, mobile and combinable accounting inscriptions enabling power effects from a distance. It is in this vein that Quattrone (2004a) encourages an ongoing critical accounting project problematising the networks of interests and power relations that cause some matters to be considered problematic and thereby requiring change, with others becoming invisible and inhabiting the *status quo*. Framed by ANT, critique emphasises the contingent and partisan interests informing extant networks, including the latent possibility that these associations may be mediated and translated otherwise.

5   ANT and future accounting research

ANT offers fecund possibilities to develop critical accounting in ways that are relevant, novel, refreshing and invoking of criticality. Starting at the heartland of ANT, Latour argues that there are "fetishes" that we hold dear in everyday life, such as "gods, fashion, poetry, sport, desire, you name it – to which naïve believers cling with so much intensity" (2004: 238–9). Rather than debunking fetishes, ANT makes them matters of concern by aiming to understand how they are assembled, maintained and/or changed. Latour's list of postmodern idols provides a good place for thinking about prospective ANT-based critical accounting research. This has begun already, with Quattrone's examination of God and accounting (2004b) and Jeacle's study of fashion and accounting (2003) as early examples. In contrast, the fetish of sport has received very little attention within critical accounting (although see, e.g., Andon and Free, 2012; Cooper and Johnston, 2012; Cooper and Joyce, 2013) – despite the fact most people are very passionate about sport. Sport is now big business too.

Sport is a field warranting the attention of critical accounting researchers. There are a variety of sporting codes that can be studied, for example, soccer, tennis, golf and athletics and a range of situations in which these are accomplished, such as amateur, professional, international and local. What makes sport so interesting is that it mobilises unique networks corralling government actors providing financial and infrastructural support, wealthy owners, shareholders, patrons, corporate sponsors, individual players and/or teams, coaches, administrators and emotional fans. Documenting these associations and the *interessement* of their interests may shed light on hitherto unstudied dynamics of organising, artefacts and calculation. Moreover, how are planning and control constituted in entanglements of human and non-human objects comprising a sport? Given the resources flowing into this space, in terms of "value in kind" (Burfitt, Baxter and Chua, 2009) and fiscal exchanges (Cooper and Johnston, 2012), many innovative, critical accounting projects would seem possible.

Further, Law (1992) draws our attention to the fact that networks are comprised not only of humans and inanimate objects. Animals are corralled into networks of association too. Animals are interesting actors because they are sentient yet we treat them (often quite horridly and) as lesser beings, although there is growing debate about the "personhood" of animals (Bryant, 2007). To date, animals have not attracted the attention of critical accounting researchers. It is difficult to understand why animals are invisible in accounting research when there are many controversies characterising primary production, animal-based sports and the burgeoning pet market. Where are the critical accounting studies investigating the economically significant live cattle export industry, including the conditions under which cattle are transported and slaughtered for food production? Why are the rights and interests of animals not made visible through studies of horse racing, wherein the commodification of thoroughbred horses results in over-breeding and training regimes that lead to the slaughter and euthanasia of thousands of horses each year? Moreover, how do emotion and calculation enmesh in decisions made regarding our pets' interests with respect to purchases of insurance, veterinary care and various accoutrements? Why is critical accounting research mute on these issues? A meticulous approach to following actors – all actors – provides a methodology and critical position to represent the interests of animals, a gap that must be redressed in future critical accounting research.

Finally, we suggest that ANT is ideally positioned to study the emergence of post-social relations in contemporary society. Knorr Cetina argues that we no longer experience social relations – there is a "collapse" in identity mediated by community, tradition and interpersonal relationships (1997: 4). Post-social relations in the knowledge era, in comparison, are an entanglement of humans and knowledge objects, often technologically mediated (Lowe, 2004). It is Knorr Cetina's position that our identities are shaped by relations to objects – such as accounting systems, tablets, smart phones, software applications and so on. ANT is very well positioned to study this changing nature of associations and identity formations, given an emphasis on the effects of networks of human *and* non-human objects. Correspondingly, there are opportunities to understand the changing nature of professionalism and expertise in object-mediated professional relations. What does it mean to be a tax professional, for example, when expertise is mediated by taxation authorities' electronic portals; clients' records maintained in spreadsheets and various software packages; and electronic forms of communication and knowledge repositories? It is also of great interest to understand how so-called 'lay people' interact with knowledge objects, making calculations and decisions in the context of post-social relationships. For example, how do parents engage with the My School website hosted by the Australian government, which enables comparative calculations of school performance that influence decisions about school enrolments and places of residence?

6 Conclusion

In this chapter we have argued that the distinguishing feature of critical accounting research is an ability to change how we understand practice and engage with it. ANT has an increasing role to play within this agenda, providing nuanced characterisations of the heterogeneous networks of association constituting local practices. ANT does this in an agnostic way, recognising entanglements of sentient actors, inscriptions and artefacts. ANT also facilitates recognition of the multiple, shifting and diverse interests that are enrolled in networks, sustaining local forms of resistance and controversy unsettling fact-building networks. Although ANT has been criticised by some critical accounting scholars, ANT remains committed to a critical tradition – rewritten as a concern for questioning the naturalisation of 'facts'. This has led to many interesting accounting research studies. However, ANT offers much greater prospect than extant research indicates. Studying our fetishes and recognising animals as sentient actors has great potential to reshape and develop the critical research agenda. ANT is also ideally positioned to problematise post-social relations and their consequences for the construction of expertise, identity and calculation. In short, it is our basic conclusion that ANT forms a vital part of any revitalisation of critical accounting research.

Note

1   Latour (1999) has expressed reservations about the term 'actor-network theory', arguing 'actor-network' may misdirect concern to the structure/agency debate and that 'theory' may shift attention from the language and practices of actors.

References

Ahrens, T., A. Becker, J. Burns, C. S. Chapman, M. Granlund, M. Habersam, A. Hansen, R. Khalifa, T. Malmi, A. Mennicken, A. Mikes, F. Panozzo, M. Piber, P. Quattrone and T. Scheytt, (2008). "The future of interpretive accounting research – a polyphonic debate," *Critical Perspectives on Accounting*, 19(6): 840–66.

Alcadipani, R. and J. Hassard (2010). "Actor-Network Theory, organizations and critique: towards a politics of organizing," *Organization*, 17(4): 419–35.

Alvesson, M. and S. Deetz (2006). "Critical theory and postmodernism approaches to organizational studies," *The Sage Handbook of Organization Studies*, London: Sage Publications.

Andon, P. and C. Free (2012). "Auditing and crisis management: the 2010 Melbourne Storm salary cap scandal," *Accounting, Organizations and Society*, 37(3): 131–154.

Andon, P., J. Baxter and W. F. Chua (2007). "Accounting change as relational drifting: a field study of experiments with performance measurement," *Management Accounting Research*, 18(2): 273–308.

Arrington, C. E. and A. L. Watkins (2002). "Maintaining 'critical intent' within a postmodern theoretical perspective on accounting research," *Critical Perspectives on Accounting*, 13(2): 139–57.

Baxter, J., C. Boedker and W. F. Chua (2008). "The future(s) of interpretive accounting research—a polyphonic response from beyond the metropolis," *Critical Perspectives on Accounting*, 19(6): 880–86.

Baxter, J., and W. F. Chua (2003). "Alternative management accounting research—whence and whither," *Accounting, Organizations and Society*, 28(2): 97–126.

Bloor, D. (1999). "Anti-Latour," *Studies in History and Philosophy of Science*, 30(1): 81–112.

Boedker, C. (2010). "Ostensive versus performative approaches for theorising accounting-strategy research," *Accounting, Auditing and Accountability Journal*, 23(5): 595–625.

Boedker, C. and W. F. Chua. (2013). "Accounting as an affective technology: a study of circulation, agency and entrancement," *Accounting, Organizations and Society*, 38(4): 245–67.

Briers, M. and W. F. Chua (2001). "The role of actor-networks and boundary objects in management accounting change: a field study of an implementation of activity-based costing," *Accounting, Organizations and Society*," 26(3): 237–69.

Broadbent, J., R. Laughlin and S. Read (1991). "Recent financial and administrative changes in the NHS: a critical theory analysis," *Critical Perspectives on Accounting*, 2(1): 1–29.

Bryant, T. L. (2007). "Sacrificing the sacrifice of animals: legal personhood for animals, the status of animals as property, and the presumed primacy of humans," *Rutgers Law Journal*, 39: 247–330.

Burchell, S., C. Clubb and A. G. Hopwood (1985). "Accounting in its social context: towards a history of value added in the United Kingdom," *Accounting, Organizations and Society*, 10(4): 381–413.

Burfitt, B. A., J. Baxter and W. F. Chua (2009). "Inter organisational alliances and the importance of accounting for value in kind transactions: exploring the role of formal management accounting controls," *Australian Accounting Review*, 19(2): 67–79.

Callon, M. (1986). "Some elements of a sociology of translation: domestication of the scallops and the fishermen of St. Brieuc Bay," in J. Law (ed.): *Power, Action, and Belief: A New Sociology of Knowledge*, London: Routledge.

Callon, M. (2006). "What does it mean to say that economics is performative?" *CSI Working Paper Series 005*. https://halshs.archives-ouvertes.fr/halshs-00091596/document, accessed 10 November, 2015.

Callon, M. (2010). "Performativity, misfires and politics," *Journal of Cultural Economy*, 3(2): 163–69.

Chapman, C. S., W. F. Chua and H. Mahama (2015). "Actor–network theory and strategy as practice," in D. Golsorkji, L. Rouleau, D. Seidl and E. Vaara (eds) *Cambridge Handbook of Strategy as Practice (Second edition)*, Cambridge: Cambridge University Press.

Chua, W. F. (1986). "Radical developments in accounting thought," *Accounting Review*, 61(4): 601–32.

Chua, W. F. (1995). "Experts, networks and inscriptions in the fabrication of accounting images: a story of the representation of three public hospitals," *Accounting, Organizations and Society*, 20(2): 111–45.

Clarke, J. (2002). "A new kind of symmetry: actor–network theories and the new literacy studies," *Studies in the Education of Adults*, 34(2): 107–22.

Cooper, C. and J. Johnston (2012). "Vulgate accountability: insights from the field of football," Accounting, *Auditing and Accountability Journal*, 25(4): 602–34.

Cooper, C. and Y. Joyce (2013). "Insolvency practice in the field of football," *Accounting, Organizations and Society*, 38(2): 108–29.

Dambrin, C. and K. Robson (2011). "Tracing performance in the pharmaceutical industry: ambivalence, opacity and the performativity of flawed measures," *Accounting, Organizations and Society*, 36(7): 428–55.

Doolin, B. and A. Lowe (2002). "To reveal is to critique: actor–network theory and critical information systems research," *Journal of Information Technology*, 17(2): 69–78.

Foucault, M. (1980). *Power/Knowledge: Selected Interviews and Other Writings 1972-1977*, edited by C. Gordon, Hemel Hempstead: The Harvester Press.

Hopper, T. and P. Armstrong. (1991). "Cost accounting, controlling labour and the rise of conglomerates," *Accounting, Organizations and Society*, 16(5): 405–38.

Hopper, T. and B. Bui (2016). "Has management accounting research been critical?" *Management Accounting Research*, 31:10–30.

Jeacle, I. (2003). "Accounting and the construction of the standard body," *Accounting, Organizations and Society*, 28(4): 357–77.

Johnson, P. (1995). "Towards an epistemology for radical accounting: beyond objectivism and relativism," *Critical Perspectives on Accounting*, 6(6): 485–509.

Justesen, L. and J. Mouritsen (2011). "Effects of actor–network theory in accounting research," *Accounting, Auditing and Accountability Journal*, 24(2): 161–93.

Knights, D. and D. Collinson (1987). "Disciplining the shopfloor: a comparison of the disciplinary effects of managerial psychology and financial accounting," *Accounting, Organizations and Society*, 12(5): 457–77.

Knorr Cetina, K. (1997). "Sociality with objects: social relations in postsocial knowledge societies," *Theory, Culture & Society*, 14(4): 1–30.

Latour, B. (1987). *Science in Action: How to Follow Scientists and Engineers Through Society*, Cambridge, MA: Harvard University Press.

Latour, B. (1996). "On actor–network theory: a few clarifications plus more than a few complications," *Soziale Welt*, 47: 369–81.

Latour, B. (1999). "On recalling ANT," *Sociological Review*, 47(S1): 15–25.

Latour, B. (2004). "Why has critique run out of steam? from matters of fact to matters of concern," *Critical Inquiry*, 30(2): 225–48.

Latour, B. (2005). *Reassembling the Social*, Oxford: Oxford University Press.

Latour, B. (2010). "An attempt at a 'compositionist manifesto'," *New Literary History*, 41(3): 471–90.

Latour, B. (2013). *An Inquiry into Modes of Existence. An Anthropology of the Moderns*, Cambridge, MA: Harvard University Press.

Latour, B. and S. Woolgar (1986). *Laboratory Life: The Construction of Scientific Facts*, Princeton, NJ: Princeton University Press.

Law, J. (1992). "Notes on the theory of the actor-network: ordering, strategy, and heterogeneity," *Systems Practice*, 5(4): 379–93.

Loft, A. (1986). "Towards a critical understanding of accounting: the case of cost accounting in the UK, 1914–1925," *Accounting, Organizations and Society*, 11(2): 137–69.

Lowe, A. (2004). "Postsocial relations: toward a performative view of accounting knowledge," *Accounting, Auditing and Accountability Journal*, 17(4): 604–28.

McNamara, C., J. Baxter and W. F. Chua (2004). "Making and managing organisational knowledge(s)," *Management Accounting Research*, 15(1): 53–76.

Messner, M. (2009). "The limits of accountability," *Accounting, Organizations and Society*, 34(8): 918–38.

Miller, P. (1991). "Accounting innovation beyond the enterprise: problematizing investment decisions and programming economic growth in the UK in the 1960s," *Accounting, Organizations and Society*, 16(8): 733–62.

Miller, P. (1998). "The margins of accounting," *European Accounting Review*, 7(4): 605–21.

Miller, P. and T. O'Leary (1987). "Accounting and the construction of the governable person," *Accounting, Organizations and Society*, 12(3): 235–65.

Miller, P. and T. O'Leary (2007). "Mediating instruments and making markets: capital budgeting, science and the economy," *Accounting, Organizations and Society*, 32(7): 701–34.

Moll, A. (2002). *The Body Multiple*, Durham, NC: Duke University Press.

Morgan, G. (1988). "Accounting as reality construction: towards a new epistemology for accounting practice," *Accounting, Organizations and Society*, 13(5): 477–85.

Mouritsen, J. (1999). "The flexible firm: strategies for a subcontractor's management control," *Accounting, Organizations and Society*, 24(1): 31–55.

Mouritsen, J. (2006). "Problematising intellectual capital research: ostensive versus performative IC," *Accounting, Auditing and Accountability Journal*, 19(6): 820–41.

Mouritsen, J., A. Hansen and C. O. Hansen (2009). "Short and long translations; management accounting calculations and innovation management," *Accounting, Organizations and Society*, 34(6): 738–54.

Preston, A. M., D. J. Cooper and R. W. Coombs (1992). "Fabricating budgets: a study of the production of management budgeting in the National Health Service," *Accounting, Organizations and Society*, 17(6): 561–93.

Qu, S. Q., and D. J. Cooper (2011). "The role of inscriptions in producing a balanced scorecard," *Accounting, Organizations and Society*, 36(6): 344–62.

Quattrone, P. (2004a). "Commenting on a commentary?: making methodological choices in accounting," *Critical Perspectives on Accounting*, 15(2): 232–47.

Quattrone, P. (2004b). "Accounting for God: accounting and accountability practices in the Society of Jesus (Italy, XVI–XVII centuries)," *Accounting, Organizations and Society*, 29(7): 647–83.

Revellino, S. and J. Mouritsen (2015). "Accounting as an engine: the performativity of calculative practices and the dynamics of innovation," *Management Accounting Research*, 28: 31–49.

Roberts, J. (2009). "No one is perfect: the limits of transparency and an ethic for 'intelligent' accountability," *Accounting, Organizations and Society*, 34(8): 957–70.

Robson, K. (1992). "Accounting numbers as "inscription": action at a distance and the development of accounting," *Accounting, Organizations and Society*, 17(7): 685–708.

Roslender, R. (1996). "Relevance lost and found: critical perspectives on the promise of management accounting," *Critical Perspectives on Accounting*, 7(5): 533–61.

Roslender, R. and J. F. Dillard (2003) "Reflections on the interdisciplinary perspectives on accounting project," *Critical Perspectives on Accounting*, 14(3): 325–51.

Shaoul, J. (1998). "Critical financial analysis and accounting for stakeholders," *Critical Perspectives on Accounting*, 9(2): 235–49.

Sikka, P. and H. Willmott (1997). "Practising critical accounting," *Critical Perspectives on Accounting*, 8(1): 149–65.

Skærbæk, P. and K. Tryggestad (2010). "The role of accounting devices in performing corporate strategy," *Accounting, Organizations and Society*, 35(1): 108–24.

Tinker, T. (2005). "The withering of criticism: a review of professional, Foucauldian, ethnographic, and epistemic studies in accounting," *Accounting, Auditing and Accountability Journal*, 18(1): 100–35.

Tinker, A. M., B. D. Merino and M. D. Neimark (1982). "The normative origins of positive theories: ideology and accounting thought," *Accounting, Organizations and Society*, 7(2): 167–200.

Whittle, A. and A. Spicer (2008). "Is actor network theory critique?" *Organization Studies*, 29(4): 611–29.

26

CRITICAL REALISM[1]

Sven Modell

1 Introduction

Critical accounting research constitutes a very diverse body of scholarship which is under-pinned by a broad range of philosophical schools of thought. One of the most recent streams of research to emerge and attract increasing attention is that informed by critical realism. Even though a pronounced element of realism has long prevailed in many bodies of critical accounting research, especially those informed by various strands of Marxist thought, critical realism offers a distinct alternative to more conventional forms of empirical realism characterised by a view of the world as independent of perceiving subjects. Originating in the pioneering works of Roy Bhaskar (1975, 1979), critical realism has increasingly come to be seen as a means of transcending the divide between such empirical realism and more extreme variants of postmodernist thought, underpinned by a strongly social constructivist position. As a philosophical school of thought, it has exercised significant influence on such disciplines as sociology (e.g. Archer, 1995; Sayer, 2000), economics (e.g. Lawson, 1997; Downward and Mearman, 2007), political science (e.g. Joseph, 2002a) and organisation studies (e.g. Fleetwood and Ackroyd, 2004; Reed, 2009), from which accounting scholars tend to draw inspiration. Its influence on the accounting literature has hitherto been relatively marginal, however, and it is only recently that it has begun to gather momentum as a philosophical foundation for critical accounting scholarship with a clearly articulated emancipatory intent (see Modell, 2015a, 2017).

This chapter introduces the foundations of critical realism and charts its development in the accounting literature. The chapter begins with an outline of the key philosophical premises of critical realism and a discussion of recent developments in critical realist thought which are relevant to my line of argument. These recent developments offer an opportunity to combine a distinctly realist ontology, grounded in a view of the world as an objective entity, with a strong sense of the subjectivity that has long been of central concern to postmodern thinkers. The general outline of critical realism is followed by a review of how this school of thought has begun to influence accounting research and an assessment of how an emerging body of research has contributed to furthering the emancipatory agenda that lies at the heart of the critical accounting project. Extending this line of argument, a research strategy through which the emancipatory potential of critical realism may be further developed is identified, and a discussion of how this research strategy differs from both Marxist and postmodernist accounting research then follows.

The chapter concludes with some brief remarks as to what I see as the distinct contributions of critical realism to critical accounting research and how it may be further developed as a basis for critical accounting scholarship.

2 The philosophical foundations of critical realism

As a philosophical point of departure for the social sciences, the most distinctive features of critical realism arguably reside in its ontology (Fleetwood, 2005; Elder-Vass, 2010). Whilst originally emerging as a critique of the propensity of the social sciences to emulate the empirical realism associated with the natural sciences (Bhaskar, 1979), critical realism has increasingly come to be conceived of as a position that combines a moderate version of realism with a moderate version of social constructivism (Elder-Vass, 2012). Similar to other forms of realism, critical realists recognise the existence of the social world as an objective, or rather objectified, entity and insist that the intransient properties of the world should not be confused with the more transient, socially constructed conceptions of what the world is like. In other words, certain properties of the world, which are typically manifest in durable social structures, are beyond the immediate grasp of individual human beings and are therefore relatively independent of human cognition and agency. This does not mean that socially constructed meanings and the agency that such meanings give rise to are inconsequential. Rather, through their interactions with social structures, human beings seek to make sense of the world and engage in individual and collective agency that either leads to the reproduction or transformation of such structures over time. However, social structures typically possess a multitude of properties and are generally not reproduced or transformed in a wholesale manner, but leave residues and have effects that are at least partly beyond the complete grasp and immediate influence of human beings. Hence, at any given time, human beings will only be able to perceive and make sense of a subset of the properties and workings of the social structures which shape their life conditions.

To explain how this incomplete knowledge of the world is related to the social processes that buttress stability and change, critical realists subscribe to a multilayered, or "stratified," ontology which typically portrays the world as divided into the domains of the *real*, the *actual* and the *empirical* (Bhaskar, 1975, 1986). The domain of the real is generally seen as constituted by objective social structures that are imbued with the *causal power*, or potential, to generate the events that, collectively, make up processes of structural reproduction and transformation. The occurrence of such events does not follow a deterministic, or law-like pattern, however but is dependent on an element of human agency which contributes to activate particular causal powers. Moreover, social structures are often imbued with a multitude of causal powers, which can amplify as well as counteract each other and give rise to what Bhaskar (1975) calls the multiple determination of events. This reduces the predictability of the process of structural reproduction and transformation and implies a need to distinguish the domain of the real from that of the actual. Processes of structural reproduction and transformation are said to occur in the domain of the actual, which is distinct from the domain of the real since the mere existence of certain structures and causal powers does not automatically generate particular events. Furthermore, the full effects of such processes are rarely, if ever, known or knowable to individual human beings. Certain events may occur without all human beings being able to empirically experience them through their subjective senses and act on them in such a way that particular sequences of events are reinforced or negated. Hence, it is necessary to distinguish the actual occurrence of events from the ability of human beings to experience them and separate the domain of the actual from that of the empirical. The tripartite division between the domains of the real, the actual and the empirical thus affirms the social constructivist emphasis on people's subjective, empirical experiences as an important precursor of human agency, without jettisoning the realist notion that the events which are being experienced are conditioned by objective structures.

Of central importance to this view of social development and, indeed, the possibilities of human emancipation, is the conception of human beings as reflexive agents (Bhaskar, 1986; Archer, 1995). Extending the general ontological framework developed by Bhaskar (1975, 1986), Archer (1995) elaborates how reflexive agency is implicated in a constant interplay with extant and emergent structures. Reflexivity is here defined as the mental capacity of human beings to consider themselves and their practices in relation to their social context, and vice versa, and enables human beings to envisage which causal powers would need to be activated for them to alter their structurally embedded life conditions. Without a capacity for reflexivity human beings would have few opportunities to engage in projects of radical social change and would be bound to reproduce social structures in a relatively routine manner. Unless social structures are inherently benign and conducive to human emancipation, such routine reproduction is unlikely to improve people's life conditions. Through extensive empirical work, Archer (2003, 2007, 2012) has sought to unpack how social structures interact with reflexivity in shaping individual strategies of social mobility and change and has developed a typology of how the, in her view, ubiquitous capacity for reflexivity among human beings manifests itself. In doing so, she conceives of reflexivity as a relatively autonomous phenomenon in relation to pre-existing social structures. However, her advances have increasingly been criticised for underplaying the extent to which social structures shape subjective identities and how such identities exercise a more direct influence on individuals' relative capacity for reflexivity (e.g. Mutch, 2004; Joseph, 2014; Vandenberghe, 2014). Similar concerns have led various writers to reconcile Archer's view of the possibilities of agency with those of other social theorists, such as Giddens (Stones, 2001, 2005) and Bourdieu (Elder-Vass, 2007, 2010), who place greater emphasis on the structural conditioning of individual identities and the routine reproduction of social structures. This allows for a more fine-grained conception of the possibilities of emancipation as conditioned by the co-existence of routine forms of agency alongside the development of reflexive action repertoires in relation to the objective life conditions that face individual human beings.

Synthesising these recent attempts to reconcile a critical realist ontology with those of other social theorists, Modell (2017) develops a framework which sees the possibilities of emancipation as an outcome of the context-specific interplay between *exogenous* and *endogenous* structures. Exogenous structures are the social structures which underpin the objective life conditions of individual human beings and are imbued with causal powers which both constrain and enable human emancipation. Exogenous structures, such as formal hierarchical positions in organisations and society, will constrain the possibilities of emancipation insofar as they exercise oppressive effects and prevent people from improving their life conditions. Such structures can also enable emancipation provided that they are imbued with the causal power to negate oppressive effects and offer opportunities for people to alter their life conditions. This view of the possibilities of emancipation is consistent with the traditional, critical realist conception of events as multiply determined by the interplay between the causal powers embedded in objective social structures. According to Modell (2017), however, it is also necessary to extend this view and pay greater attention to the endogenous structures, which shape the subjective propensity for reflexivity, to enhance our understanding of how individual human beings conceive of and act on their objective life conditions.

Endogenous structures represent the values, beliefs and norms which have been internalised by individual human beings and thus exercise a deep-seated influence on their subjective identities and relative propensity for either routine actions or reflexive agency. This necessitates a slight revision of the critical realist conception of social structures as primarily objective in nature and a recognition of subjectivity as having a real existence which goes beyond individual consciousness and empirical experiences. Endogenous structures imbue human beings with a propensity, or disposition, to act in particular ways that is prior to, rather than conjoined with, the actual occurrence of human agency and the events that follow from such agency. Whilst some human beings tend to act in a highly routine manner when faced with particular life conditions, others have internalised values, beliefs and norms that enhance their propensity for reflexivity. Individual human beings also possess a simultaneous capacity for routine actions and reflexive agency and one or the other may dominate depending on the specific tasks at hand. Similar to exogenous structures, endogenous structures are thus imbued with causal powers which both constrain and enable the possibilities of emancipation. As noted earlier, a certain propensity for human reflexivity is a necessary pre-condition for emancipation since it allows people to consciously consider and alter their actions in relation to their objective life conditions. Reflexivity also enables human beings to question routine actions and thus provides a basis for altering the endogenous structures that underpin such actions. Insofar as people have primarily internalised values, beliefs and norms that make them act in a highly routine, or even subconscious, manner in relation to oppressive life conditions, the possibilities of emancipation may be expected to be much more restricted

The discussion as outlined so far suggests that human emancipation will be constrained and enabled by an intricate interplay between the causal powers embedded in endogenous and exogenous structures. Figure 26.1 summarises the possibilities of emancipation emerging from this interplay. The possibilities of emancipation will be limited where endogenous structures mainly exercise constraining effects on individuals' propensity for reflexivity and exogenous structures offer few opportunities to alter their life conditions (lower left quadrant). Under such circumstances, human beings will be disposed to act in a highly routine manner whilst the wider social context in which they are embedded is likely to reinforce the routine reproduction of oppressive structures. By contrast, the possibilities of emancipation will be most extensive where endogenous structures make individuals highly reflexive and exogenous structures provide ample opportunities to take advantage of such reflexivity (upper right quadrant). This does not mean that the possibilities of emancipation are unconstrained by social structures, however. Even where the causal powers embedded in both endogenous and exogenous structures are mainly of an enabling nature, there will always be some constraining powers that hamper the

		Mainly constraining	Mainly enabling
Exogenous structures	**Mainly enabling**	Moderate possibilities of emancipation.	Extensive possibilities of emancipation.
	Mainly constraining	Limited possibilities of emancipation.	Moderate possibilities of emancipation.
		Mainly constraining	**Mainly enabling**
		Endogenous structures	

Figure 26.1 Ontological possibilities of emancipation (adapted from Modell, 2017: 24).

capacity for reflexivity and the ability of human beings to act. The possibilities of emancipation will be more moderate where only one of the two types of structures is imbued with strongly enabling powers. Some individuals may have a high endogenous disposition to act out their reflexivity and challenge exogenous structures even though the latter are relatively constraining (lower right quadrant). The emancipatory actions resulting from this are perhaps most notable where agents seek to overturn oppressive, but rather resilient, social orders through revolutionary means. Conversely, even though endogenous structures constrain the capacity for reflexivity, exogenous structures may be imbued with enabling powers that engender a degree of emancipation (upper left quadrant). Examples of this may be found where improvements in people's life conditions are due to external factors, such as changes in legislative or regulatory systems, but where the individuals who benefit from such changes are not reflexive enough to take an active part in bringing them about.

Consistent with the ontological foundations of critical realism, the outcomes of the interplay between endogenous and exogenous structures follow a non-deterministic pattern that is rarely within the full grasp of the people who are implicated in processes of structural reproduction and transformation. As noted earlier, exogenous, or objective, structures have an intransient existence that is removed from people's empirical experiences, which tend to be of a more transient nature. Similarly, the workings of endogenous structures are not necessarily well known to individual human beings. This is especially the case where such structures are imbued with causal powers that make human beings act in a highly routine or subconscious manner, since this limits people's ability to empirically experience and account for the rationales behind their actions. This imperfect ability of people to comprehend the structural conditioning of agency and, by implication, the possibilities of emancipation has important epistemological implications for researchers who seek to understand the workings of social structures and translate such understandings into critical research interventions. Most importantly, it strongly cautions against any tendencies to equate research subjects' empirical accounts of how particular events unfold with attempts to explain how social structures condition the possibilities of human emancipation. Equating people's empirical experiences of events with exhaustive explanations of what generates those events would be tantamount to committing what Bhaskar (1975) calls the epistemic fallacy of conflating epistemological statements about our knowledge of the world with ontological assumptions about what the world is like. Instead, critical realists emphasise that research observations based on people's empirical experiences are inherently fallible and under-determined by the complex interplay between the causal powers embedded in social structures (Bhaskar, 1975; Kaidesoja, 2007). Furthermore, any attempts on the part of researchers to explain the potential effects of this interplay are conditioned by a range of epistemic premises, such as the values, interests and authority structures that guide scholarly work at any given time. This renders critical-realist knowledge claims inherently relativist (Bhaskar, 1986; Lawson, 1997; Elder-Vass, 2012). It also implies that the ability of researchers to pursue critical interventions, aimed at furthering radical social change, is not only dependent on the ontological possibilities of emancipation but also on the issue of which knowledge claims are being sanctioned by the epistemic premises surrounding particular communities of scholars (Bhaskar, 1986; Collier, 1994).

The combination of a realist ontology and a relativist epistemology sets critical realism apart from conventional forms of empirical realism as well as stronger variants of social constructivism. In contrast to empirical realism, critical realists do not see scientific knowledge claims as direct, unmediated, reflections of how social events evolve. Empirical realism is typically associated with knowledge claims based on a Humean notion of causality, according to which the occurrence of observable events follows predictable, law-like patterns. However, in open social systems such notions of causality, which are typically manifest in co-variations between empirical observations, are, at best, only partial reflections of how events actually occur due to the complex interplay between a multitude of underlying, but only partially observable, causal powers (Bhaskar, 1975, 1979). Hence researchers need to go considerably beyond empirical observations if they wish to develop a deeper understanding of what causes particular events, whilst recognising that such understandings are profoundly influenced by the epistemic premises that condition scientific knowledge claims. For similar reasons, critical realists reject strongly social constructivist notions of scientific knowledge as reducible to how people make sense of their subjective experiences through their use of language. Whilst such an approach to knowledge formation can be found in many variants of postmodernist thought, critical realists object to it due to its understanding of social realities as primarily residing in the minds of perceiving subjects (Elder-Vass, 2012). As explicated earlier, however, it is possible to reconcile more moderate variants of social constructivism, which recognise that social structures can be of both endogenous and exogenous origin from the perspective of individual human beings, with a critical realist ontology. Yet, as demonstrated in the next section, it is only recently that more concerted efforts to explore the interplay between endogenous and exogenous structures have begun to feature in critical realist accounting research.

3 The emergence of critical realist accounting research

Although the first scattered references to critical realism in the accounting literature can be traced back to the late 1980s, it is only during the past decade that this perspective has begun to gather momentum and generate what may be described as a nascent research programme. The earliest serious engagement with critical realism can be found in Whitley (1988), who mobilises Bhaskar's work to critique the empirical realism underpinning economics-based, positivist accounting research. Similarly, Manicas (1993) and Armstrong (1994) make brief references to Bhaskar in their attempts to advance a realist alternative to emerging, postmodernist accounting research. These early works point towards a view of critical realism as a philosophical 'middle ground' between accounting research informed by empirical realism and stronger forms of social constructivism. Starting in the 2000s, this strand of thought has been further developed in a series of papers which mobilise critical realism as a basis for debating various methodological issues in accounting research straddling the ontological positions of realism and social constructivism (Brown and Brignall, 2007; Llewellyn, 2007; Modell, 2009, 2013, 2015b) A particular concern in these papers is the issue of how research methods and theories originating in such distinct ontological positions can be combined in a single empirical study and what implications this has for key methodological issues, such as the validity of research findings. In exploring these issues, they mainly follow the philosophical position set out in Bhaskar's founding works. With the exception of Llewellyn (2007), however, these contributions pay scant attention to the interplay between agency and structure that has exercised other critical realists such as Archer. Moreover, they are largely devoid of concerns with issues of key interest to critical accounting scholars, such as the question of how this interplay is implicated in processes of human emancipation.

Deeper engagements with Archer's work can be found in a series of papers by Ashraf and Uddin (2013, 2015a, 2015b, 2016). Drawing on Archer's (1995) early conceptual treatise, these papers mainly explore how exogenous, or objective, structures constrain and enable human agency and how the subsequent interplay between agency and extant and emerging structures fosters change and stability in management accounting practices. Nevertheless, they pay little attention to Archer's (2003, 2007, 2012) more recent works to explain how individual variations in reflexivity affect the agency exercised by various actors. In their longitudinal field study in the Pakistani Civil Aviation Authority, Ashraf and Uddin (2013, 2015b, 2016) examine how changes in external governance systems compelled various actors to mobilise and resist change in management accounting practices. However, even though the authors recognise that different actors may harbour different subjective interpretations of reforms, the underlying causes of change and resistance are nearly exclusively attributed to how exogenous structures, such as the formal, hierarchical positions held by various actors, enabled and constrained human agency. Similarly, in a field study of management accounting change in a Greek family-owned firm, Stergiou, Ashraf and Uddin. (2013) primarily examine how formal organisational positions enabled and constrained the implementation of new accounting practices. As the authors recognise, this led them to bracket the more subjective aspects of agency highlighted by Archer (2003, 2007, 2012). Hence individual variations in reflexivity, let alone the endogenous structures that shape such variations and the relative balance between reflexive and routine agency, have received little empirical attention in accounting research following Archer's variant of critical realism.

A similar lack of attention to endogenous structures can be found in accounting research following other strands of critical realist thought. As part of his continued critique of postmodern accounting research, Armstrong (2004, 2006) invokes Bhaskar's work to argue that such research promotes essentially naïve, idealist (rather than realist) interpretations of events whilst ignoring how objective realities, such as market competition and other economic mechanisms, reinforce the propensity of accounting practices to buttress oppressive social orders. Similar engagements with Bhaskar as the key source of inspiration for explaining the workings of exogenous structures can be found in empirical inquiries that primarily attribute changes in accounting practices to reforms in external governance structures and regulatory environments (Burrowes, Kastantin and Novicevic, 2004; Mutiganda, 2013). Whilst providing valuable insights into how such reforms may buttress and hamper change in accounting practices, these studies shed little light on the subjective deliberations of the agents who enact or resist reforms and thus ignore the role that reflexivity might play in furthering human emancipation. Similarly, in an empirical study of contested governance reforms in the UK social housing sector, Smyth (2012, 2016) combines Bhaskar's work with a dialogical analysis of the language that various actors mobilised to interpret such reforms, although pays little attention to how the subjective dispositions, which are manifest in individuals' interpretations, affect their relative propensity for reflexivity and ability to resist reforms.

The relatively one-sided emphasis on exogenous structures in much accounting research informed by critical realism is somewhat unfortunate, since it limits our insights into the processes through which individual human beings deliberate on the world and how their ability to do so is conditioned by their relative propensity for reflexivity. This arguably detracts from a more holistic understanding of how social structures condition the possibilities for human emancipation. Several of the studies reviewed in this section reveal profound concerns with how certain properties of exogenous structures, such as the power embedded in external governance structures and formal organisational positions, can affect the possibilities of emancipation (see especially Smyth, 2012, 2016; Ashraf and Uddin, 2015b, 2016). Little attention has been paid to how the causal powers of exogenous structures interact with those embedded in endogenous structures and how this interplay conditions the possibilities of emancipation. Moreover, none of the studies reviewed have nurtured explicit epistemological and methodological concerns with how critical realist accounting research can entail critical research interventions aimed at furthering human emancipation. This lack of clearly articulated emancipatory intent mirrors the longstanding criticisms of critical realism for sacrificing much of its critical edge in its efforts to establish itself as a general, explanatory philosophy of science. Such criticisms have been advanced by researchers with Marxist (Gunn, 1989; Roberts, 1999, 2002; Brown, Slater and Spencer, 2002) as well as postmodernist sympathies (Willmott, 2005), and need to be taken seriously if critical realism is to have a more profound impact on critical accounting research. In what follows, I sketch the contours of a research strategy which may address such criticisms and explain how this strategy differs from traditional Marxist and postmodern accounting research.

4 Realising the emancipatory potential of critical realist accounting research

In two recent papers, Modell (2015a, 2017) has begun to elaborate how the emancipatory potential of critical realist accounting research can be further developed through deeper engagement with contemporary advances in critical realist thought. The first of these papers advances a contingent conception of emancipation as dependent on the context-specific interplay between the causal powers embedded in endogenous and exogenous structures and contains some preliminary reflections on how researchers might advance critical research interventions that exploit the possibilities of emancipation emerging from this interplay (Modell, 2015a). This was used as a basis for contemplating how accounting research based on institutional theory, which has increasingly been criticised for its lack of critical insights, might be imbued with more innate concerns with emancipation. Extending this work, Modell (2017) develops a more general discussion of how the ontological possibilities of emancipation, summarised in Figure 26.1, may be translated into critical research interventions. Particular attention was paid to the epistemological and methodological ramifications of adopting a critical realist ontology and advancing research interventions entailing a pronounced element of *explanatory critique*. The notion of explanatory critique originates in Bhaskar's (1986) work and has come to be seen as a key, distinctive feature of the emancipatory impulse that is arguably inherent in critical realism (see Joseph, 2002b; Lacey, 2002). Such critiques entail systematic attempts to make theoretical sense of how the causal powers embedded in social structures might and actually do affect the possibilities of human emancipation, whilst recognising that the knowledge claims that emerge from such attempts are always fallible and conditioned by the epistemic premises that surround particular communities of scholars.

Modell (2017) extends the discussion of how explanatory critiques may be advanced by linking such critiques to the twin concepts of *retroduction* and *retrodiction* (see also Lawson, 1997; Elder-Vass, 2010, 2015). Retroduction denotes the process of working 'backwards' from empirical observations to develop theoretically informed conjectures about which individual causal powers are *potentially* responsible for the occurrence of particular events. Retrodiction, by contrast, is the empirically grounded process of assessing how multiple causal powers interact and *actually* give rise to particular events in specific contexts. Retroduction is a necessary, first step for such analyses in that it provides the analytical building blocks for retrodiction and facilitates the task of identifying which causal powers may be at work in particular social contexts. However, it is only by retrodicting how such powers interact that researchers may arrive at deeper, albeit partial and fallible, empirical insights into how particular events actually unfold (Elder-Vass, 2010, 2015).

By confronting research subjects with repeated sequences of retroduction and retrodiction, researchers may probe into which causal powers may be responsible for the events that serve to reproduce oppressive social orders and how such events may be mitigated or reversed. Modell (2016) argues that this analytical task can be facilitated by combining the process of retroduction and retrodiction with counterfactual thought experiments, whereby a set of 'what-if' questions are posed regarding which causal powers would need to be activated for oppressive effects to occur and how such effects might be mitigated if other causal powers were in place. Such thought experiments can help researchers develop theoretical models explaining how emancipation may be brought about and can thus enhance the process of retroduction. As researchers extend empirical analyses to include an element of retrodiction, they may also use counterfactual thought experiments to solicit the reactions of research subjects to theoretical explanations that favour dominant social actors and interests, asking them to reflect on how prevailing social orders are maintained and how they might be counteracted. This may provoke responses highlighting alternative, but previously unrecognised, explanations which may, in turn, stimulate further reflections on how the oppressive effects of particular causal powers might be mitigated or reversed (Lacey, 1997). This may expand the vistas of researchers and enlighten research subjects of which paths of emancipation may be available to them.

Whilst critical research interventions based on explanatory critiques may open up unforeseen opportunities for emancipation, researchers need to tailor their use of retroduction and retrodiction to help research subjects realise the ontological possibilities of emancipation outlined in Figure 26.1. This is likely to be particularly challenging in situations where both endogenous and exogenous structures mainly exercise constraining effects on the possibilities of emancipation (lower left quadrant in Figure 26.1). In such circumstances, the social structures which buttress oppressive accounting practices are likely to be very resilient, and individuals are unlikely to reflexively engage with such structures and envisage ways in which accounting can be turned into a vehicle for emancipation. This is, in turn, likely to reduce the possibilities for researchers to engage research subjects in counterfactual thought experiments aimed at identifying alternative ways of mobilising accounting. Even though it may be possible to retroduct which causal powers might counteract oppressive states of affairs, research subjects might struggle to articulate how these powers may be activated and thus leave researchers with little empirical data for the retrodictive part of the analysis.

A largely reverse situation is likely to emerge where both endogenous and exogenous structures mainly exercise enabling effects on the possibilities of emancipation (upper right quadrant in Figure 26.1). In such circumstances, researchers are likely to face the challenge of adjudicating between a myriad of causal powers that enable individual human beings to mobilise accounting in the pursuit of emancipation and then advancing empirically grounded explanations of how these powers actually interact and facilitate emancipatory processes. Retroductive analyses may still be valuable as a means of identifying relevant causal powers, but need to be combined with a very open-ended theoretical approach which allows for a broad range of potential explanations to emerge and shed light on the possibilities of emancipation. This poses the challenge of drawing appropriate boundaries around what are considered relevant theoretical conjectures and determining what might be the most likely and effective paths towards emancipation (see Modell, 2015b). Whilst counterfactual thought experiments may be of some help in this regard, researchers also need to embark on extended empirical engagements to retrodict how the interplay between multiple causal powers actually affects the possibilities of emancipation. This may require researchers to undertake multiple iterations between retroductive and retrodictive analyses to first develop potential theoretical explanations of particular events and then explore these conjectures empirically whilst remaining alert to the need to revise the initial explanations based on their empirical findings.

Other challenges emerge where the causal powers which enable emancipation mainly reside in either endogenous or exogenous structures. Under such circumstances, researchers need to hone their use of retroduction and retrodiction to probe into the types of structures which are most likely to facilitate emancipatory processes. This will have major implications for the focus of explanatory critiques. Where the possibilities of emancipation mainly emerge from endogenous structures (lower right quadrant in Figure 26.1), researchers need to concentrate on developing explanatory critiques that explore the issue of how such structures shape subjective identities and the propensity for reflexivity. Through such critiques, researchers can identify the causal powers which enable individual human beings to reflect on the possibilities of emancipation whilst asking counterfactual questions as to which powers might counteract reflexivity and how those powers might be reversed. This may, in turn, initiate a process whereby individuals and groups of agents come to question the exogenous structures that buttress oppressive accounting practices and gradually work out strategies for changing such structures (and thus fuelling a movement towards the upper right quadrant in Figure 26.1). By contrast, where enabling causal powers mainly reside in exogenous structures (upper left quadrant in Figure 26.1), researchers are better off honing explanatory critiques to explore the objective life conditions of human beings. This directs the process of retroduction and retrodiction towards the exogenous structures which facilitate emancipation whilst considering how individual human beings, who only possess a limited propensity for reflexivity, might benefit from the workings of such structures.

The pursuit of explanatory critiques, such as those outlined in the previous paragraphs, necessitates a highly contingent and open-ended view as to which substantive theories and research methods may be helpful for engendering human emancipation. Depending on whether researchers primarily concentrate such critiques on the workings of endogenous or exogenous structures, or choose to pay more equal attention to such structures, different theories and methods may be required to facilitate the process of retroduction and retrodiction. For instance, a focus on endogenous structures requires a profound engagement with people's subjective understandings of their identities, in combination with theories and methods that help researchers identify the causal powers behind the shaping of identities. By contrast, exogenous structures may be more readily identifiable through objective signifiers, such as different class structures and hierarchical positions in organisations and society, although the theories and methods that are mobilised to explain the workings of such structures need to recognise that they do not exercise a deterministic, or law-bound, influence on social events. This contingent tailoring of the choice of theories and methods to the research task at hand is underpinned by Bhaskar's (1975, 1986) view of critical realism as a universally applicable, philosophical "under-labourer," which is capable of supporting a broad range of substantive theories and research methods. Critical realists have also sought to maintain the open-endedness of research by avoiding ideological orthodoxies, whilst recognising that the scope of explanatory critiques is always conditioned by the epistemic premises that surround particular communities of scholars (see Lovering, 1990; Joseph, 1998). As explicated in the following paragraphs, these features set critical realism apart from Marxist as well as postmodernist accounting research.

Insofar as traditional Marxist accounting research is concerned, critical realism offers a less restricted view as to what constrains and enables human emancipation and how researchers can facilitate the process of emancipation. Even though critical realism has clear affinities with Marxism through its concerns with objective life conditions, which are *inter alia* manifest in social class structures, its stratified ontology may help overcome deterministic readings of Marx and the concomitant fallacy of viewing the possibilities of emancipation as primarily, or even exclusively, conditioned by changes in objective structures and other material conditions (Joseph, 2002b). As demonstrated in this chapter, the possibilities of emancipation are by no means given by changes in objective life conditions but emerge as a result of an indeterminate interplay between social structures and human agency. The approach to explanatory critique outlined earlier in this section extends this indeterminate view of the possibilities of emancipation by locating them in a somewhat broader understanding of social structures than the one typically found in Marxist accounting research. Even though the charge of determinism has been challenged by many accounting scholars with Marxist sympathies (e.g. Neimark, 1990; Bryer, 2000a, 2000b; Tinker, 2005), the main emphasis of such scholars has tended to be on the workings of exogenous structures rather than on the subtle processes through which human beings develop subjective identities and devise personal strategies of emancipation (see Roslender and Dillard, 2003; Cooper and Hopper, 2007). Hence Marxist accounting research can hardly be said to be conducive to a deeper understanding of the causal powers embedded in endogenous structures, which recent advances in critical realist thought have brought to the fore. Moreover, through its scepticism of ideological orthodoxies, critical realism aspires to maintaining and nurturing the theoretical and methodological pluralism which Marxist accounting scholars, such as Tinker (2005), have seen as a potential distraction for the critical accounting project. Whilst the refusal to subscribe to any particular ideological position as a basis for social critique has led to charges that critical realism is politically naïve (Roberts, 1999, 2002), a critical realist mode of explanatory critique can arguably sensitise researchers to a wider range of potential, but perhaps unanticipated, possibilities of emancipation. This may, in turn, open up novel ways for researchers to engage with accounting practices and can further a more expansive dialogue with research subjects about what might constitute alternative paths towards emancipation (Modell, 2017). At the same time, however, researchers need to be vigilant against any attempts by conservative forces to exploit the tolerance and open-endedness of critical realism and thereby neutralise its potential as a basis for critical research interventions (Collier, 1994).

The potential contributions of critical realism to postmodernist accounting research are, by and large, the reverse of what it offers to Marxist research. Postmodernist accounting researchers have repeatedly been criticised for underplaying the extent to which objective life conditions affect the possibilities of emancipation due to their preoccupation with the subjectifying effects of discourse and language (e.g. Neimark, 1990, 1994; Armstrong, 1994, 2015; Cooper, 1997; Arnold, 1998; Tinker, 2005). Critical realist writers who are more sympathetic to postmodernism have demonstrated how selected strands of postmodernist thought, grounded in weaker forms of social constructivism, can be reconciled with a realist ontology and how this may enhance our understanding of the possibilities of emancipation (Al-Amoudi, 2007; Joseph, 2004; O'Mahoney, 2011). O'Mahoney (2011), for instance, argues that postmodernists are wrong in mainly, or exclusively, ascribing the possibilities to resist oppressive social orders to the socially constructed discourses and counter-discourses that permeate social life, and that they need to recognise that individual human beings have real causal powers which interact with those embedded in objective structures. This resonates with the distinction between endogenous and exogenous structures advanced in this chapter and opens up the issues of how the causal powers, which make human beings resist or submit to subjectifying discourses, interact with the powers that shape their objective life conditions and engender emancipation. However, to enhance our understanding of how endogenous structures can be implicated in engendering emancipatory actions, postmodernist accounting researchers would need to abandon their allegedly uncritical engagement with managerial discourses (Armstrong, 2004, 2006) and delve more deeply into the subjective, lived experiences of those who are subjected to oppressive accounting practices (Armstrong, 1994, 2015). Failing to do so may lead postmodernist accounting researchers to reproduce managerial discourses in an un-reflexive manner and naturalise the ideology which is manifest in such discourses. The scepticism of ideological orthodoxies associated with critical realism may form a powerful antidote to such reproduction of managerial and kindred elite discourses and ideologies. As noted earlier, however, this scepticism is only likely to be maintained as long as researchers can keep the conservative forces, which may encroach on research interventions, at bay.

5 Concluding remarks

This chapter has introduced the foundations of critical realism and has sought to outline how recent developments in this philosophical school of thought might contribute to critical accounting research. Even though critical realism has attracted increasing interest among accounting scholars over the past decade, it is only recently that it has started to give rise to a more critical research programme underpinned by an explicit emancipatory intent. The key challenges ahead for critical realist accounting research thus pertain to how this emancipatory intent can be furthered and translated into concrete, critical research interventions. Whilst the challenge of upholding an explicit emancipatory intent is not unique to critical realist accounting research (see e.g. Arrington and Watkins, 2002; Roslender and Dillard, 2003; Roslender, 2015), I have offered some specific suggestions as to how critical realism can make a distinct contribution to critical accounting research by elaborating the notion of explanatory critique. The development of such critiques builds on the foundations of critical realism as a general, explanatory philosophy of science, but can sharpen its critical edge. In this chapter, I have extended the discussion of how such critiques may be advanced by linking them to the twin concepts of retroduction and retrodiction, and explaining how research interventions based on these analytical techniques need to be tailored to the ontological possibilities of emancipation which emerge in particular social contexts. It is hoped that this discussion will provide a starting point for empirical research which seeks to realise the emancipatory potential of critical realism. However, much work remains to be done to turn critical realist accounting research into a genuinely critical, empirically engaged, research programme.

Note

1   This chapter is significantly inspired by an earlier paper (Modell, 2017), which explores the emancipatory potential of critical realist accounting research. Selected parts of that paper have been reproduced with the permission of Elsevier Publishing Ltd.

References

Al-Amoudi, I. (2007). "Redrawing Foucault's ontology," *Organization*, 14(4): 543–63.

Archer, M. S. (1995). *Realist Social Theory: The Morphogenetic Approach*, Cambridge: Cambridge University Press.

Archer, M. S. (2003). *Structure, Agency, and the Internal Conversation*, Cambridge: Cambridge University Press.

Archer, M. S. (2007). *Making Our Way through the World: Human Reflexivity and Social Mobility*, Cambridge: Cambridge University Press.

Archer, M. S. (2012). *The Reflexive Imperative in Late Modernity*, Cambridge: Cambridge University Press.

Armstrong, P. (1994). "The influence of Michel Foucault on accounting research," *Critical Perspectives on Accounting*, 5(1): 25–55.

Armstrong, P. (2004). "Idealism and ideology: the Caterpillar controversy in critical accounting research," in Fleetwood, S. and S. Ackroyd (eds): *Critical Realist Applications in Organisation and Management Studies*, London: Routledge.

Armstrong, P. (2006). "Ideology and the grammar of idealism: the Caterpillar controversy revisited," *Critical Perspectives on Accounting*, 17(5): 529–48.

Armstrong, P. (2015). "The discourse of Michel Foucault," *Critical Perspectives on Accounting*, 27: 29–42.

Arnold, P. (1998). "The limits of postmodernism in accounting history: the Decatur experience," *Accounting, Organizations and Society*, 23(7): 665–87.

Arrington, C. E. and A. L. Watkins (2002). "Maintaining "critical intent" within a postmodern theoretical perspective on accounting research," *Critical Perspectives on Accounting*, 13(2): 139–57.

Ashraf, M.J. and S. Uddin (2013). "A consulting giant; a disgruntled customer: a 'failed' attempt to change management controls in a public sector organisation," *Financial Accountability and Management*, 29(2): 186–203.

Ashraf, M. J. and S. Uddin (2015a). "Management accounting research and structuration theory: a critical realist critique," *Journal of Critical Realism*, 14(5): 485–507.

Ashraf, M. J. and S. Uddin (2015b). "Military, 'managers' and hegemonies of management accounting controls: a critical realist interpretation," *Management Accounting Research*, 29: 13–26.

Ashraf, M. J. and S. Uddin (2016). "New Public Management, cost savings and regressive effects: a case from a less developed country," *Critical Perspectives on Accounting*, 41: 18–33.

Bhaskar, R. (1975). *A Realist Theory of Science*, Leeds: Leeds Books.

Bhaskar, R. (1979). *The Possibilities of Naturalism. A Philosophical Critique of the Contemporary Human Sciences*, Brighton: The Harvester Press.

Bhaskar, R. (1986). *Scientific Realism and Human Emancipation*, London: Verso Books.

Brown, R. and S. Brignall (2007). "Reflections on the use of a dual-methodology research design to evaluate accounting and management practice in UK university central administrative services," *Management Accounting Research*, 18(1): 32–48.

Brown, A., G. Slater and D. A. Spencer (2002). "Driven to abstraction? critical realism and the search for the 'inner connection' of social phenomena," *Cambridge Journal of Economics*, 26(6): 773–88.

Bryer, R. A. (2000a). "The history of accounting and the transition to capitalism in England: part one: theory," *Accounting, Organizations and* Society, 25(2): 131–62.

Bryer, R. A. (2000b). "The history of accounting and the transition to capitalism in England: part two: evidence," *Accounting, Organizations and Society*, 25(4–5): 327–81.

Burrowes, A. W., J. Kastantin and M. M. Novicevic (2004). "The Sarbanes-Oxley Act as a hologram of post-Enron disclosure: a critical realist commentary," *Critical Perspectives on Accounting*, 15(6-7): 797–811.

Collier, A. (1994). *Critical Realism*, London: Verso Books.

Cooper, C. (1997). "Against postmodernism: class oriented questions for critical accounting," *Critical Perspectives on Accounting*, 8(1): 15–41.

Cooper, D. J. and T. Hopper. (2007). "Critical theorising in management accounting research," in C.S., Chapman, A.G. Hopwood and M.D. Shields (eds): *Handbook of Management Accounting Research*, Oxford: Elsevier.

Downward, P. and A. Mearman (2007), "Retroduction as mixed-methods triangulation in economic research: reorienting economics into social science," *Cambridge Journal of Economics*, 31(1): 77–99.

Elder-Vass, D. (2007). "Reconciling Archer and Bourdieu in an emergent theory of action," *Sociological Theory*, 25(4): 325–46.

Elder-Vass, D. (2010). *The Causal Power of Social Structures*, Cambridge: Cambridge University Press.

Elder-Vass, D. (2012) *The Reality of Social Construction*, Cambridge: Cambridge University Press.

Elder-Vass, D. (2015). "Developing social theory using critical realism," *Journal of Critical Realism*, 14(1): 80–92.

Fleetwood, S. (2005). "Ontology in organization and management studies: a critical realist perspective," *Organization*, 12(2): 197–222.

Fleetwood, S. and S. Ackroyd (eds) (2004). *Critical Realist Applications in Organisation and Management Studies*. London: Routledge.

Gunn, R. (1989). "Marxism and philosophy: a critique of critical realism," *Capital and Class*, 37(1): 86–116.

Joseph, J. (1998). "In defence of critical realism," *Capital and Class*, 22(1): 73–106.

Joseph, J. (2002a). *Hegemony. A Realist Analysis*. New York: Routledge.

Joseph, J. (2002b). "Five ways in which critical realism can help Marxism," in A. Brown, S. Fleetwood and M.J. Roberts (eds): *Critical Realism and Marxism*, London: Routledge.

Joseph, J. (2004). "Foucault and reality," *Capital and Class* 28(1): 143–65.

Joseph, J. (2014). "Book review: *The Reflexive Imperative in Late Modernity*," *Journal of Critical Realism*, 13(1): 98–102.

Kaidesoja, T. (2007). "Exploring the concept of causal power in a critical realist tradition," *Journal for the Theory of Social Behaviour*, 37(1): 63–87.

Lacey, H. (1997). "Neutrality in the social sciences: on Bhaskar's argument for an essential emancipatory impulse in social science," *Journal for the Theory of Social Behaviour*, 27(2–3): 213–41.

Lacey, H. (2002). "Explanatory critique and emancipatory movements," *Journal of Critical Realism*, 1(1): 7–31.

Lawson, T. (1997). *Economics and Reality*, London: Routledge.

Llewellyn, S. (2007). "Case studies and differentiated realities," *Qualitative Research in Accounting and Management*, 4(1): 53–68.

Lovering, J. (1990). "Neither fundamentalism nor 'new realism': a critical realist perspective on current divisions in socialist theory," *Capital and Class*, 14(1): 30–54.

Manicas, P. (1993). "Accounting as human science", *Accounting, Organizations and Society*, 18(2–3): 147–61.

Modell, S. (2009). "In defence of triangulation: a critical realist approach to mixed methods research in management accounting," *Management Accounting Research*, 20(3): 208–21.

Modell, S. (2013). "Making sense of social practice: theoretical pluralism in public sector accounting research: a comment," *Financial Accountability and Management*, 29(2): 99–110.

Modell, S. (2015a). "Making institutional accounting research critical: dead end or new beginning?" *Accounting, Auditing and Accountability Journal*, 28(5): 773–808.

Modell, S. (2015b). "Theoretical triangulation and pluralism in accounting research: a critical realist critique," *Accounting, Auditing and Accountability Journal*, 28(7): 1138–50.

Modell, S. (2017). "Critical realist accounting research: in search of its emancipatory potential," *Critical Perspectives on Accounting*, 42: 20–35.

Mutch, A. (2004). "Constraints on the internal conversation: Margaret Archer and the structural shaping of thought," *Journal for the Theory of Social Behaviour*, 34(4): 429–45.

Mutiganda, J. C. (2013). "Budgetary governance and accountability in public sector organisations: an institutional and critical realism approach," *Critical Perspectives on Accounting*, 24(7–8): 518–31.

Neimark, M. K. (1990) "The king is dead. Long live the king," *Critical Perspectives on Accounting*, 1(1): 103–14.

Neimark, M. K. (1994). "Regicide revisited: Marx, Foucault and accounting," *Critical Perspectives on Accounting*, 5(1): 87–108.

O'Mahoney, J. (2011). "Embracing essentialism: a realist critique of resistance to discursive power," *Organization*, 19(6): 723–41.

Reed, M. I. (2009). "Critical realism in critical management studies," in M. T. Alvesson, T. Bridgman and H. Willmott (eds): *The Oxford Handbook of Critical Management Studies*, Oxford: Oxford University Press.

Roberts, J. M. (1999). "Marxism and critical realism: the same, similar, or just plain different?" *Capital and Class*, 23(2): 21–49.

Roberts, J. M. (2002). "Abstracting emancipation: two dialectics on the trail of freedom," in A. Brown, S. Fleetwood and M. J. Roberts (eds): *Critical Realism and Marxism*, London: Routledge.

Roslender, R. (2015). "Accountancy," in M. Bevir and R. A. W. Rhodes (eds): *The Routledge Handbook of Interpretive Political Science*, London: Routledge.

Roslender, R. and J. F. Dillard. (2003). "Reflections on the interdisciplinary perspectives on accounting project," *Critical Perspectives on Accounting*, 14(3): 325–51.

Sayer, A. (2000). *Realism and Social Science*, Thousand Oaks, FL: Sage Publishing

Smyth, S. (2012). "Contesting public accountability: a dialogical exploration of accountability and social housing," *Critical Perspectives on Accounting*, 23(3): 230–43.

Smyth, S. (2016). "Public accountability: reforms and resistance in social housing," *Public Management Review*, in press.

Stergiou, K., J. Ashraf and S. Uddin (2013). "The role of structure and agency in management accounting control change of a family owned firm: a Greek case study," *Critical Perspectives on Accounting*, 24(1): 62–74.

Stones, R. (2001). "Refusing the realism-structuration divide," *European Journal of Social Theory*, 4(2): 177–97.

Stones, R. (2005). *Structuration Theory*. London: Palgrave.

Tinker, T. (2005) "The withering of criticism: a review of professional, Foucauldian, ethnographic, and epistemic studies in accounting," *Accounting, Auditing and Accountability Journal*, 18(1): 100–35.

Vandenberghe, F. (2014). *What's Critical about Critical Realism? Essays in Reconstructive Social Theory*, London: Routledge.

Whitley, R. D. (1988). "The possibility and usefulness of positive accounting theory," *Accounting, Organizations and Society*, 13(6): 631–45.

Willmott, H. (2005). "Theorizing contemporary control: some post-structuralist responses to some critical realist questions," *Organization*, 12(5): 747–80.

INDEX

469